THE CONCISE
GARDENING
ENCYCLOPEDIA

❖

DAVID SQUIRE

The Concise
GARDENING
Encyclopedia

—————— ❖ ——————

DAVID SQUIRE

Illustrated by Vana Haggerty

LEOPARD

CONTENTS

INTRODUCTION

Gardening is one of the most popular leisure pursuits. It involves the satisfaction of encouraging plants to grow and, perhaps, to bear flowers or fruit. Additionally, it produces an attractive home environment that enhances the quality of life. And it is performed in the fresh air and involves exercise for the body and mind in surroundings that are restful and free from the stresses of normal life.

There are aspects of gardening that, at first sight, appear to demand the muscles of Hercules, but successful gardening is mainly a combination of inspiration, dedication and knowledge. We cannot provide the dedication but we hope that this comprehensive gardening encyclopedia will engender inspiration and provide the knowledge that helps to create a beautiful garden.

The book is formed of fifteen chapters, covering topics ranging from annuals and biennials, herbaceous perennials, and shrubs and small trees to vegetables and herbs.

There are chapters about more unusual aspects of gardening, such as making water gardens, growing plants in windowboxes, hanging baskets, pots, tubs and urns, and gardening in greenhouses, and practical sections on increasing plants, pruning and tackling garden projects such as constructing patios, paths and trellises.

At the back of the book are descriptions and illustrations of fifty-four pests and diseases, together with detailed advice on eradicating or preventing them, followed by a comprehensive list of useful gardening terms.

With this book at your elbow, successful gardening is only a few pages away.

ANNUALS AND BIENNIALS

These are some of the brightest and most rapid-growing of all garden plants. Annuals are raised each year from seeds to create a kaleidoscope of colour throughout summer, while biennials – although taking two seasons in which to produce their display – reveal unforgettable feasts of colour mainly in spring and early summer.

Annuals and biennials can be grown in flower borders totally devoted to them, or mixed with other plants such as shrubs, herbaceous perennials and bulbs, while some are ideal for growing in containers on patios. This chapter shows the wide range of annuals and biennials, as well as giving details of how to grow them. Preparing the site, potting-up, planting and looking after annuals are featured, as well as caring for biennials.

Other, more general advice is given separately, later in the book. Sowing hardy annuals is described on page 273, half-hardy annuals on page 272, and biennials on page 274. Pricking off seedlings, such as those of half-hardy annuals, is featured on page 263.

WHAT ARE ANNUALS AND BIENNIALS?

THESE are popular garden flowers, used to create colourful displays. They are easily raised from seeds.

• <u>Hardy annuals</u>: These complete their life-cycle in one season. They are sown outdoors in the positions in which they will grow and produce their flowers. With the onset of frosts in autumn, they soon die. They are mostly sown in spring, but some varieties can also be sown in late summer.

• <u>Half-hardy annuals</u>: Like hardy annuals, these also complete their life-cycle within one season. However, they are slightly tender and therefore are raised in gentle warmth in a greenhouse or conservatory in late winter or early spring, and planted outside as soon as all risk of frost has passed. Raising plants in this way gives them a long growing season.

• <u>Biennials</u>: Unlike annuals, these need two seasons in which to complete their growing cycle. In the first year, seeds are sown in early summer. The seedlings are either thinned to give the remaining plants more room, or moved to a nurserybed. In late summer or autumn (or the following spring in cold climates), plants are transferred to their flowering positions, where they bloom and die during the following year.

VARIABLE NATURE

Some plants can be grown in several ways. This is usually influenced by the climate, but can be solely for the convenience of gardeners and their desire to produce fresh plants each year.

BIENNIALS

ALCEA ROSEA *(Hollyhock), earlier known as Althaea rosea, is a perennial but is usually grown as a biennial. Seeds are sown outdoors in early summer and young plants put into flowering position in late summer or early autumn. The flowers appear during the following summer.*

CAMPANULA MEDIUM *(Canterbury Bell) develops masses of bell-shaped flowers in white, pink, blue or violet during early and into mid-summer. Sow seeds in late spring or early summer and transplant young plants into their flowering positions in autumn, spacing them 25–30cm/10–12in apart.*

ERYSIMUM x ALLIONII *(Siberian Wallflower), earlier known as Cheiranthus x allionii, produces sweetly scented flowers during late spring and into the latter part of early summer. Sow seeds in early summer and transfer plants to their flowering positions in late summer.*

HALF-HARDY ANNUALS

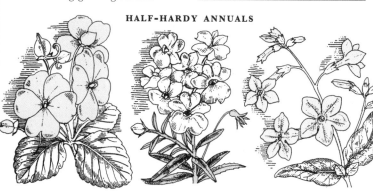

IMPATIENS HYBRIDS *(Busy Lizzie) produce masses of colourful flowers throughout summer. Sow seeds in gentle warmth in late winter or early spring, later planting them in borders. Plants are soon killed by frost in autumn.*

NEMESIA STRUMOSA *develops funnel-shaped flowers in compact flower heads during early and mid-summer. Flower colours include yellow, blue, scarlet, orange and bright red. Sow seeds in gentle warmth in late winter or early spring.*

NICOTIANA x SANDERAE *creates sweetly scented flowers in many colours throughout summer. Other Tobacco Plants include N. alata (N. affinis). Like all other half-hardy annuals, seeds are sown in gentle warmth.*

HARDY ANNUALS

AMARANTHUS CAUDATUS *(Love-lies-bleeding) is a hardy annual that develops long, drooping tassels packed with crimson flowers from mid-summer to the frosts of autumn. Seeds are sown during spring, in their flowering positions.*

CALENDULA OFFICINALIS *(Pot Marigold) is well known for its large, daisy-like flowers in bright yellow or orange that appear from late spring to the frosts of autumn. In spring, sow seeds where the plants are to flower.*

IBERIS UMBELLATA *(Candytuft or Globe Candytuft) is a hardy annual that has clusters of white, red or purple flowers from early to late summer. Sow seeds in spring in the position where the plants are to grow and thin out as necessary.*

PREPARING THE SITE

SINGLE and double digging are the traditional ways in which gardeners cultivate soil in winter. Most soils need only single digging, which entails systematically turning the top 25–27cm/10–11in of soil upside down, at the same time removing perennial weeds and mixing in well-decayed manure or compost.

Double digging is usually only necessary when new gardens are being created. It involves digging soil to the depth of two spade blades, but keeping soil from each level separate. This breaks up the lower depths and enables excess water to drain freely. When dug initially, the surface may appear uneven, especially if the soil has a high clay content, but by spring large clods will have broken down.

Digging in early winter provides a long period for frost, snow, ice and wind to break down the surface, thereby creating a friable tilth for sowing and planting.

Digging is often believed to be tiresome, but if small but increasing amounts are dug at one time, it can become a pleasant exercise. Also, it tidies up the garden.

Bindweed

Horsetail/ Scouring Rush

Dock/ Sorrel

Thistle

WHEN *digging soil, always remove perennial weeds. If pieces are left, they re-grow during the following summer and make cultivation difficult. They also rob soil of food and moisture.*

1. DOUBLE *digging is when soil is dug two spits (two spade blades) deep, and the two layers are kept separate. First, take out a trench the depth of a spade's blade and 45–60cm/18–24in wide. Place the soil at one end of the plot, ready for filling the last trench.*

2. USE *a garden fork to dig the lower spit, at the same time mixing in well-decayed manure or compost. This method of cultivating soil breaks up the lower depths, improving drainage and aeration. Roots are also more able to penetrate deeply into the lower soil.*

3. THEN *use a spade to dig out a further 45–60cm/ 18–24in-wide trench, placing the soil on top of the previously forked strip. Continue down the plot in the same way, at the end using soil that was removed from the first trench to fill the last one.*

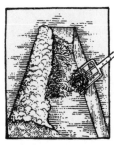  

1. SINGLE *digging is when soil is dug one spit deep (the depth of one spade blade). First, dig out a trench one spit deep and 30–38cm/ 12–15in wide across one end of the plot. Then, systematically dig sections of soil and place them upside-down in the trench's base.*

2. EACH *time a new trench is formed, place well-decayed manure or compost evenly along its base. While digging, remove perennial weeds (such as those illustrated left), as well as grubs of soil pests, such as cockchafers, leather-jackets and wireworms.*

3. USE *a spade to form another trench, placing the soil on top of the manure and compost. Continue in this way until the border has been dug. Do not break down large lumps of soil, as frost, snow, rain and wind will accomplish this during late autumn and winter.*

RIDGING SOIL

Although little used today, a form of soil cultivation known as ridging was performed, in past years, when digging clay soil during early winter. It exposed a larger area of soil to frost, winds and snow than normal digging, thereby encouraging a deeper tilth in spring when seeds were sown outdoors. Vegetable beds were the main recipients of this technique, but there is no reason why wide annual borders could not be treated in the same way.

A trench is taken out in the same way as when single digging, but instead of forming a level surface, ridges are formed. After taking out the initial trench, mark the soil into strips three spade blades wide. In each of these strips, dig out and place the first spadeful towards the middle, the second spadeful also towards the middle, and the third one on top. If this is repeated as the border is dug, ridges are formed. In spring use a garden fork or large rake to level the surface.

SOIL CULTIVATION

The need to prepare and cultivate soil has been known for thousands of years. At first, foot ploughs were widely used, while in India and Sri Lanka (Ceylon) buffaloes or bullocks waded through the water in paddy fields to churn up soil earlier softened by flooding.

An inventive but dangerous way to break up hard, impervious subsoil in the tropics and subtropics has been to explode 50g/2oz dynamite charges in holes 75–90cm/ 2½–3ft deep.

Several forms of hand-pushed cultivators have been popular in many countries; a range of fittings to plough, scarify and hoe could be quickly fitted to the framework.

POTTING UP
HALF-HARDY ANNUALS

❖

MOST half-hardy annuals are planted into gardens and containers on patios, directly from the seed-trays into which they were pricked out earlier (see page 263). However, those that are to be used to brighten homes are moved into small pots (see page 264). A few of these may also need to be repotted subsequently into larger pots.

EXTRA LARGE
BEDDING PLANTS

As well as potting up plants for home decoration, various summer-flowering bedding plants such as the Wax Plant (*Begonia semperflorens*) are frequently put into pots to produce extra large plants for garden and container decoration. To create bushy plants, it is essential to grow them in pots: the ends of their shoots are pinched off several times to encourage the development of sideshoots. If these plants were just left in seed-trays,

SINGLE DAHLIAS

Botanically, dahlias are tuberous-rooted perennials from Mexico. In temperate countries they are grown as half-hardy plants: they are unable to survive freezing conditions. As well as being raised by cuttings and division of tubers, there are many brightly coloured, single-flowered forms that can be raised by sowing seeds in gentle warmth in late winter and early spring. Plant them in gardens as soon as the risk of frost has passed.

their foliage would soon become congested. In pots, they can be increasingly spaced further apart.

ANNUALS AS HOUSEPLANTS

Many plants that are grown as annuals can be displayed indoors as well as in greenhouses and conservatories. These include primulas, Cineraria (Senecio cruentus), Persian Violet (Exacum affine) and Butterfly Flower (Schizanthus pinnatus), also known as Poor Man's Orchid. Some of these grow as perennials in their native countries, but in temperate regions, and as houseplants, are grown as annuals. The Slipper Flower (Calceolaria x herbeohybrida) grows as a biennial: it is sown one year and flowers the next. Other plants to grow in pots are featured on pages 266 to 268.

Plants to be used singly, as 'dot' plants, are also usually potted up, as they are large and dominant.

MAKING MORE SPACE

During spring, in greenhouses, when seeds are being sown, seedlings pricked out and young plants potted up, there is often insufficient space.

However, the normal benching can be supplemented by proprietary roof-shelves in aluminium greenhouses, or by suspending wooden planks, about 15–20cm/6–8in wide and 12–18mm/$^1/_2$–

$^3/_4$ in thick from wooden glazing bars. Metal coat-hangers can be bent to form trapezes, with their tops hooked over nails or screws.

Double-decker staging is easy to construct by standing planks of wood on large, inverted pots or traditional wooden seed-boxes stood on their sides. If seed-boxes are used, the plank can be nailed to them for extra security.

With all these forms of additional support for seedlings and plants, take care when watering them that excess water does not drip on those below.

1. WHEN *the leaves on seedlings which were earlier pricked out (see page 263), touch each other, the young plants should either be planted or moved into small pots. This is known as potting up. If left in trays plants compete for space.*

2. WATER *the plants the day before moving them into small pots. Tap the sides of the seed-tray to loosen the compost, making it easier to remove the plants. Use a small fork to lift a few plants out of the seed-tray. Place them on damp paper.*

3. FILL *the base of a clean pot (about 7.5cm/3in wide) with potting compost and gently firm it. If loam-based compost is used, place a small crock (broken piece of clay pot) in the base. If peat-based compost is used, there is no need to crock the pot.*

4. POSITION *a young plant on compost in the pot's base. The old soil-level mark (indicated by a dark stain on the plant's stem) should be about 12mm/$^1/_2$in below the pot's rim. Take care not to squeeze or damage the stem, as it may not recover.*

5. FIRM *compost to within 12mm/$^1/_2$in of the rim. It is essential that a space is left at the top of the pot, so that the plant can be watered. If the space is too small, not enough water is given; if too large, there is a risk of over watering.*

6. GENTLY *water the compost by using a fine-rosed watering-can. Allow the excess to drain, then stand the pots close together. As their foliage spreads and grows, space the pots further apart. Keep the compost evenly but not totally moist.*

PLANTING HALF-HARDY ANNUALS

❖

THESE tender plants are raised in gentle warmth in greenhouses in late winter and early spring. After germination, the seedlings are pricked out and given wider spacings (see page 263) and later slowly acclimatized to outdoor conditions.

HALF-HARDY annuals were traditionally hardened off in English pit lights.

HARDENING OFF PLANTS

If the plants were raised in a greenhouse, the easiest way to harden them off is initially to lower the temperature slowly and later to leave the ventilators and door fully open, first during the day and then at night.

Traditionally, half-hardy annuals have been hardened off in a garden frame – and this still is an excellent method. Alternatively, place plants on a sunny, sheltered patio during the day and put them in a greenhouse or indoors at night. Later, and if only a light frost is forecast, place several layers of newspaper over the plants. Remove them the following morning, after frost has disappeared.

When seeds have been sown indoors and the plants raised on window sills, increasingly ventilate the area and put the plants outside during the day.

PLANTING HALF-HARDY ANNUALS

These plants are quickly damaged by frost and therefore must not be planted until all frosts are over. They can bring colour to many places (see right). When planting them, always take out a hole large enough to accommodate the roots. Put the plant in position, spread out its roots and cover with soil or compost, ensuring it is well firmed. Then, lightly water it.

WINDOW SILLS can be used when acclimatizing half-hardy annuals to outdoor conditions in spring. At night, place them on cool window sills, while during the day put them outside on a warm, sheltered patio.

GREENHOUSES are the natural places in which to begin to harden off half-hardy annuals. Slowly increase ventilation during the day. Then, put plants outside during the day but back in the greenhouse at night.

SHELTERED corners outdoors are ideal when there is little risk of frost, but take care to move the plants inside at night, or to cover with sheets of newspaper if only a light frost is forecast. Remove these when the frost is over.

ANNUAL CLIMBERS are superb for bringing vibrant colour to trellises, pergolas and rustic poles during summer. They are especially useful in a new garden, where they soon create colour (see page 23).

SUMMER-FLOWERING bedding plants are widely planted in late spring and early summer. The range of colours is wide, while some are grown for their colourful foliage (see page 21).

WINDOWBOXES are alight in summer with half-hardy annuals. Most of these plants grow upright, but those in hanging baskets need trailing habits (see page 164).

TUBS, urns and troughs on patios create distinctive features when planted in spring with summer-flowering bedding plants. In tubs and urns use a large, dominant, central plant, with trailing types around it so that the container's sides are covered with colour.

ROCK GARDENS are mainly planted with alpine plants, but if large – or when newly constructed and not fully planted – small annuals are ideal for introducing 'instant' summer colour (see pages 104 to 105 for suitable plants).

WHEELBARROWS and other unusual containers can be transformed in summer. Use upright plants to create height, and trailers to clothe the sides. Ensure that the compost is kept moist throughout summer, as plants soon wilt and die if watering is neglected – even once.

LOOKING AFTER HARDY ANNUALS

HARDY annuals are easily grown and soon repay the cost of a few packets of seeds, creating a wealth of flowers from early to late summer and sometimes into early autumn. After sowing seeds (see page 273), regularly remove weeds from between the rows and the plants. If left, they suffocate the seedlings.

Thinning, supporting and watering seedlings are important tasks, and these are detailed below and on page 273. A number of hardy annuals develop into larger plants if sown in late summer the preceding year. They include clarkia, godetia and iberis.

IN AUTUMN

By the onset of autumn, most annuals are past their best and will not be displaying the bright spectacle they did a month or so earlier. Indeed, it is the beginning of autumn frosts that terminate the display; once this has happened, pull up all plants and place them on a compost heap. If they are seriously infested with pests or diseases, burn them. Rake leaves and debris off borders, as they are unsightly and may encourage pests and diseases.

DEAD-HEADING PLANTS

Regularly pinching off dead flowers from plants encourages the formation of further blooms. It prolongs the flowering period and reduces the risk of diseases attacking dead flowers and causing healthy ones to become diseased and unsightly.

Some plants, when ageing, cast their petals over the ground, becoming untidy. An example of this is Pot Marigold (Calendula officinalis), *which has large, bright, daisy-like flowers. Cutting off these dead flowers prevents the area becoming an eyesore.*

LOOKING AFTER BIENNIALS

BIENNIALS are easily grown and create a wealth of colour during their second year. After sowing them in drills in a seed-bed during late spring and early summer of the first year, remove weeds from the seed-bed, water the soil and either thin out the seedlings or transplant them to a nurserybed as soon as they are large enough to be handled.

In late summer or autumn of the same year, established plants can be moved to their flowering positions in gardens. Sometimes, however, when the weather is exceptionally cold or the soil is very wet, they are not moved until spring of the following year.

RE-FIRMING PLANTS

During winter, severe frosts often loosen soil around plants. Therefore, in spring, check each plant and use the heel of a shoe to ensure the soil around it is firm. At the same time, hoe around each plant to break up the crusty surface. This enables air and water to penetrate the soil.

HISTORIC HOLLYHOCKS

Although still widely known as Althaea rosea, *the Hollyhock is properly known as* Alcea rosea. *By nature it is a hardy perennial, but in more temperate climates it is usually grown as a biennial.*

It is thought to be a native of Asia Minor and India and was probably introduced into Europe about the time of the Crusades, during the eleventh to the thirteenth centuries, when it was known as the Holy-hoc. Hoc was the Anglo-Saxon word for mallow. Later, names such as Outlandish Rose and Rosa Ultramarina were accorded it by the Huguenots, the French Protestants who fled their native country during the seventeenth century, many to England.

THIN *out hardy annual seedlings as soon as they are large enough to handle. The spaces between them depend on the spread and height of plants (see page 16 for details, and pages 17 to 18 for individual spacings).*

MANY *hardy annuals need to be supported. Insert twiggy sticks between young plants, so that stems grow up and through them, eventually forming a canopy of leaves and flowers. If the sticks are too high, trim with secateurs.*

WATER *seedlings and young plants to ensure their roots do not become dry. Use a fine spray to avoid disturbing the soil. Oscillating sprinklers are useful for covering large areas, and can often be controlled by timers.*

PULL *up weeds from between rows of biennial seedlings. If left, they compete with the biennials for light and rob them of moisture and food. They may also harbour pests and diseases. Then, hoe between the rows.*

SOMETIMES, *seedlings are thinned to leave the strongest seedlings. Alternatively, when they are large enough to handle, gently fork up the young plants and replant them into nursery beds as shown above.*

IN LATE *summer or autumn, transplant young plants into their flowering positions. The distances between plants varies: many biennials are described on page 19, with recommendations on spacings.*

HALF-HARDY ANNUALS
Amaranthus – Gazania
❖

BECAUSE all seed-raised plants when growing in their native countries are hardy, the classification 'half-hardy annual' is solely a gardener's term to define plants that when grown in cooler climates need to be raised in gentle warmth. It also enables these plants to be given a longer growing period, which is especially important in cool climates.

RANGE OF
HALF-HARDY ANNUALS
Many plants can be classified in several ways. For example, the Snapdragon (*Antirrhinum majus*) is native to warm Mediterranean countries, where it persists as a hardy perennial. In temperate regions, however, it is usually grown as a half-hardy annual. It can also be raised as a hardy annual, but in many regions the growing season is so short that it is sown in shallow drills outside in mid to late summer and overwintered outdoors. In mid-spring, plants are transferred to their growing positions.

A further example is the South African Blue Marguerite (*Felicia amelloides*), a perennial in its native land but grown as a half-hardy annual in temperate regions.

Another advantage of growing plants as half-hardy annuals is that fresh, young, uniform plants are raised at the same time. This enables bedding displays in gardens, as well as in containers on patios, to be planned in detail.

CALLISTEPHUS CHINENSIS (*China Aster*) grows 38–45cm/15–18in high, although there are dwarf forms. They develop petal-packed flowers. Sow seeds 6mm/¹/4in deep in 16°C/61°F in early spring. Plant them 23–30cm/9–12in apart.

CLEOME SPINOSA (*Spider Flower/Spider Plant*) grows 90cm–1.2m/3–4ft high and develops large clusters of pinkish, spider-like flowers throughout summer. Sow seeds 3mm/¹/8in deep in 18°C/64°F in early spring. Plant them 38–45cm/15–18in apart.

COSMOS BIPINNATUS (*Cosmea/Mexican Aster*) grows 90cm/3ft high and displays white, crimson, pink or rose flowers during mid- and late summer. Sow seeds 6mm/¹/4in deep in 16°C/61°F in late winter or early spring. Plant them 50–60cm/20–24in apart.

AMARANTHUS HYPOCHONDRIACUS (*Prince's Feather*) grows 1.2–1.5m/4–5ft high and develops deep crimson flower spikes during mid- and late summer. Sow seeds 3mm/¹/8in deep in 15–16°C/59–61°F in early spring. Plant them 75–90cm/2¹/2–3ft apart.

ANTIRRHINUM MAJUS (*Snapdragon*) grows 23cm–1.2m/9–48in high, depending on the variety, and creates flowers from mid-summer to the frosts of autumn. Sow seeds 3mm/¹/8in deep in 15–20°C/59–68°F in late winter or early spring. Plant them 23–45cm/9–18in apart.

ARCTOTIS HYBRIDA (*African Daisy*) grows 30–60cm/1–2ft high and produces large, brilliantly coloured, daisy-like flowers throughout summer and until the frosts of autumn. Sow seeds 3–6mm/¹/8–¹/4in deep in 16–18°C/61–64°F in early spring. Plant them 23–38cm/9–15cm apart.

DIDISCUS CAERULEUS (*Blue Lace Flower/Queen Anne's Lace*) is 45–60cm/18–24in high and develops dainty clusters of lavender-blue flowers during mid- and late summer. Sow seeds 3mm/¹/8in deep in 15°C/59°F during early spring. When planting, space them 23cm/9in apart.

FELICIA AMELLOIDES (*Blue Daisy/Blue Marguerite*) grows about 45cm/18in high and develops sky blue flowers with central yellow discs from early to late summer. Sow seeds 3mm/¹/8in deep in 16°C/61°F in late winter or early spring. Plant them 23cm/9in apart.

GAZANIA x HYBRIDA (*Treasure Flower*) grows about 23cm/9in high, with richly coloured, large, daisy-like flowers in shades of orange, yellow, red, pink and ruby from mid-summer to the frosts of autumn. Sow seeds 6mm/¹/4in deep in 16°C/61°F in late winter. Plant them 30cm/12in apart.

HALF-HARDY ANNUALS
Heliotropium – Verbena
❖

HELIOTROPIUM x HYBRIDUM *(Cherry Pie/ Heliotrope) grows 30–45cm/12–18in high and produces dark violet, lavender or white flowers throughout summer. Sow seeds 6mm/ 1/4in deep in 16–18°C/ 61–64°F during late winter. Plant them 30–38cm/ 12–15in apart.*

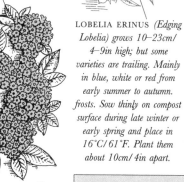

LOBELIA ERINUS *(Edging Lobelia) grows 10–23cm/ 4–9in high; but some varieties are trailing. Mainly in blue, white or red from early summer to autumn. frosts. Sow thinly on compost surface during late winter or early spring and place in 16°C/61°F. Plant them about 10cm/4in apart.*

IMPATIENS WALLERIANA *(Busy Lizzie) grows 45–60cm/1 1/2–2ft high and flowers profusely all summer. Sow seeds 3mm/1/8in deep in 16°C/61°F in early spring. Plant them 23–30cm/9–12in apart.*

FURTHER HALF-HARDY ANNUALS
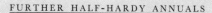

- Ageratum houstonianum *(Floss Flower/ Pussy-foot) – page 20.*
- Alonsoa warscewiczii *(Mask Flower).*
- Alyssum maritimum/Lobularia maritima *(Sweet Alyssum) – page 24.*
- Begonia semperflorens *(Wax Plant) – page 20.*
- Cotula barbata *(Pincushion Flower).*
- Emilia flammea *(Tassel Flower).*
- Felicia bergeriana *(Kingfisher Daisy) – page 104.*
- Gaillardia pulchella *(Blanket Flower) – page 25.*
- Mimulus *(Monkey Flower).*
- Nemesia strumosa – *page 22.*
- Salpiglossis sinuata *(Painted Tongue).*
- Tagetes erecta *(African Marigold).*
- Ursinia anethoides – *page 105.*

NICOTIANA ALATA *(Flowering Tobacco Plant) grows 60–90cm/2–3ft high and with clusters of tubular, fragrant flowers in a range of colours from early to late summer. Sow seeds 3mm/ 1/8in deep in 16°C/61°F during late winter and early spring. Plant them 23–30cm/9–12in apart.*

PETUNIA x HYBRIDA *grows 15–38cm/6–15in high, with trumpet-shaped flowers in many colours throughout summer. Lightly press seeds on the surface of compost in late winter or early spring and place in 16°C/61°F. Plant 15–30cm/6–12in apart.*

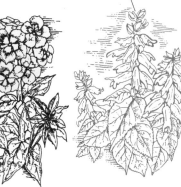

PHLOX DRUMMONDII *(Annual Phlox) grows about 38cm/15in high and develops dense heads of pink, purple, red, lavender and white flowers from mid- to late summer. Sow seeds 6mm/1/4in deep in late winter or early spring and place in 15°C/59°F. Plant them 23cm/9in apart. Also dwarf forms, 15–23cm/ 6–9in high.*

VERBENA x HYBRIDA *(Vervain) grows 15–38cm/ 6–15in high and from early summer to the frosts of autumn produces bright, dome-shaped heads of scarlet, carmine, blue and white flowers, set against dark serrated leaves. Sow seeds 3mm/1/8in deep in 16°C/61°F in late winter or early spring. Plant them 15–25cm/6–10in apart.*

TEXAS BEAUTY

Seeds of the Annual Phlox (Phlox drummondii) *were first sent from North America to England in 1835 by Thomas Drummond. The plant met with immediate success and by 1840 was said to be 'the pride and ornament of gardens'.*

SALVIA SPLENDENS *(Scarlet Salvia) grows 30–38cm/12–15in high and creates a mass of scarlet flowers from mid-summer to the frosts of autumn. There are also white, purple and salmon varieties. Sow seeds 6mm/1/4in deep in 16°C/ 61°F in late winter or early summer. Plant 23–38cm/ 9–15in apart.*

TAGETES PATULA *(French Marigold) grows 15–30cm/6–12in high and develops yellow or mahogany-red, daisy-like flowers throughout summer. There are both single and double-flowered forms. Sow seeds 6mm/1/4in deep in 16°C/ 61°F during late winter or early spring. Plant them 15–30cm/6–12in apart.*

HARDY ANNUALS
Anchusa – Clarkia

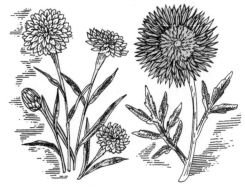

THESE are plants that can be sown outside in the positions in which they will flower. Sometimes, seeds are scattered on the soil's surface and lightly raked in. But it is much better to form drills about 23cm/9in apart.

Sowing seeds in drills enables weeds between the rows to be identified and removed while still small. Sow seeds thinly and evenly, and after germination thin the seedlings to the distances indicated on this and other pages.

Hardy annuals are ideal plants for children to sow, as they soon create a vibrant display which usually continues throughout summer. Most hardy annuals germinate within two to four weeks, although much depends on the moisture in the soil and its temperature: cold, wet soil delays the germination of seeds. The local climate also has a strong influence on germination.

HARDY VARIATIONS

As with half-hardy annuals, many hardy types have a different nature in their native countries. *Anchusa capensis*, for example, is a biennial in its native South Africa, but in temperate regions is better grown as a hardy annual. The well-known Black-eyed Susan (*Rudbeckia hirta*) is a short-lived perennial from North America and usually grown as a hardy annual. It can also be raised as a half-hardy annual, especially where the growing season is short.

CENTAUREA CYANUS *(Cornflower) grows 23–90cm/9–36in high and develops masses of pink, red, purple, blue or white, button-like flowers throughout summer. Sow seeds 12mm/ 1/2in deep in drills 23–30cm/9–12in apart during spring. Thin the seedlings 23–38cm/9–15in apart.*

CENTAUREA MOSCHATA *(Sweet Sultan) grows 50–60cm/20–24in high and produces white, yellow, pink or purple, cornflower-like flowers from early to late summer. Sow seeds 6mm/ 1/4in deep in drills 23cm/ 9in apart in spring. Subsequently, thin the seedlings 23cm/9in apart.*

CHRYSANTHEMUM CARINATUM *(Tricolor Chrysanthemum and often known as C. tricolor) grows 50–60cm/20–24in high with flowers about 6cm/2 1/2in wide in summer. Sow seeds in spring 6mm/ 1/4in deep in drills 23cm/9in apart. Thin to 15–23cm/6–9in apart.*

BORAGO OFFICINALIS *(Borage/Tailwort) is a well-known herb with blue, star-shaped, pendent flowers throughout summer. It grows 45–75cm/1 1/2–2 1/2ft high. Sow seeds 6–12mm/ 1/4–1/2in deep in drills 23cm/9in apart during mid-spring. Thin the seedlings 30cm/12in apart.*

CLARKIA PULCHELLA *grows about 45cm/18in high and develops dainty sprays of white, rose or violet flowers from mid to late summer. Native to North America, it has a branching and delicate nature with mid-green leaves. Sow seeds 6mm/1/4in deep in drills 23cm/9in apart during spring and early summer. Thin the seedlings 25–30cm/10–12in apart.*

ANCHUSA CAPENSIS *grows about 45cm/18in high and develops blue, saucer-shaped flowers in dense terminal clusters from mid- to late summer. Sow seeds 6–12mm/1/4–1/2in deep in drills 23cm/9in apart during spring. Later, thin the seedlings 15–23mm/6–9in apart.*

CALENDULA OFFICINALIS *(Pot Marigold) grows 30–60cm/ 1–2ft high, and from late spring to autumn produces large, bright yellow or orange flowers. Sow seeds 12mm/ 1/2in deep in drills 23cm/9in apart during spring. Thin the seedlings 30cm/ 12in apart.*

CLARKIA ELEGANS *grows 60cm/2ft high and from early to late summer develops white, lavender, salmon-pink, orange, purple or scarlet flowers. Sow seeds 6mm/ 1/4in deep in drills 23cm/ 9in apart during spring and early summer. Subsequently, thin seedlings 25–30cm/10–12in apart.*

A WEED IN CORNFIELDS

The pretty, blue Cornflower (Centaurea cyanus) used to be a troublesome weed in crops, but better threshing and improved seed technology has almost eliminated it. In years gone by, it was used in garlands, while in Saxony the flowers were boiled and added to beer to cure jaundice.

BEAUTIFUL · BIENNIALS

THESE are plants that are sown during one year, germinate and establish themselves as plants, and then develop flowers during the following season. They are hardy and able to survive outdoors during winter. Most of them flower in late spring and early summer, while a few continue in bloom throughout the summer.

Many, such as Hollyhocks *(Alcea rosea)*, Daisies *(Bellis perennis)* and Wallflowers *(Cheiranthus* and *Erysimum)* are hardy perennials that are normally grown as biennials. This enables a large number of plants to be raised at one time, so that a concentrated display can be created in gardens. Some are grown in flower beds in association with bulbs.

Foxgloves *(Digitalis purpurea)* and Forget-me-nots *(Myosotis alpestris)* are both natural biennials.

FURTHER BIENNIALS

- *Aquilegia vulgaris* (Granny's Bonnet/Columbine) – p. 40.
- *Erysimum alpinum* (Alpine Wallflower/Fairy Wallflower) – p. 104.
- *Lunaria annua* (Honesty, and earlier known by the name of *Lunaria biennis).*
- *Lunaria annua* 'Variegata' (Variegated Honesty) – p. 21.

Sowing and raising biennials is detailed on page 274, and looking after them on page 13. These pages include the depths at which seeds are sown.

After being thinned out, they are put into their flowering positions mainly in late summer or autumn, and sometimes in spring.

ERYSIMUM x ALLIONII *(Siberian Wallflower), also known as* Cheiranthus *x* allionii, *grows 38cm/15in high. In late spring and early summer it displays orange flowers. Sow seeds 6mm/ 1/4in deep in a seed-bed in early summer. Put plants into their flowering positions in late summer, setting them 25–30cm/10–12in apart.*

CHEIRANTHUS CHEIRI *(Wallflower) grows 20– 60cm/8–24in high and develops mainly red, yellow or orange flowers during late spring and early summer. Sow seeds 6mm/1/4in deep in a seed-bed in early summer; in late summer, plant dwarf varieties 25cm/ 10in apart, tall ones 30–38cm/12–15in.*

DIANTHUS BARBATUS *(Sweet William) grows 30–60cm/12–24in high and develops dense heads of flowers during early and mid-summer. Sow seeds 6mm/1/4in deep in a seed- bed in early summer. Move plants to their flowering positions in late summer, setting them 20–25cm/ 8–10in apart.*

ALCEA ROSEA *(Hollyhock) grows about 1.8m/6ft high. Sow seeds 12mm/1/2in deep in rows 23cm/9in apart in a seed- bed in early or mid-summer. In late summer, move young plants to their flowering positions, setting them 60cm/2ft apart.*

BELLIS PERENNIS *(Daisy) grows 10–15cm/ 4–6in high, and from spring to late summer produces white, pink or red flowers. Sow seeds 6mm/1/4in deep in early summer. In late summer, move them to their flowering positions, about 13cm/5in apart.*

CAMPANULA MEDIUM *(Canterbury Bell) grows 38–90cm/15–36in high, with white, pink, blue or violet flowers during early and mid-summer. Sow seeds 6mm/1/4in deep in a seed- bed in early summer. In autumn, plant them 25– 30cm/10–12in apart.*

DIGITALIS PURPUREA *(Foxglove) grows 90cm– 1.5m/3–5ft high. Spires of bell-shaped flowers develop in early and mid-summer. Sow seeds shallowly in late spring, then set plants 15cm/6in apart in a nurserybed. In late summer plant out 45–60cm/1 1/2–2ft apart.*

MYOSOTIS ALPESTRIS *(Forget-me-not) grows 10–20cm/4–8in high, and during late spring and early summer creates masses of blue flowers. Sow seeds 6mm/1/4in deep in a seed- bed during early summer. In late summer, plant them 15cm/6in apart.*

VIOLA x WITTROCKIANA *(Pansy) grows 15–23cm/ 6–9in high, normally flowers in late spring and early summer (also summer and winter types). Sow seeds 6mm/ 1/4in deep in early summer. In late summer, plant them out, about 23cm/9in apart.*

ANNUALS AND BIENNIALS
FOR PARTIAL SHADE

❖

N O PLANT will thrive in deep shade, but there are a few annuals and biennials that will survive partial or light shade. They are more tolerant of these positions if the soil is slightly moist: dry soil is a strain on plants and can soon cause their deaths when combined with deep shade.

Plants in these positions will not be as large or as floriferous as those in ideal conditions where light and moisture are readily available. Therefore, in shady areas plant them slightly closer together or thin the seedlings to smaller spacings.

If the area is moist as well as shady, slugs and snails will be more of a problem. Therefore remember to check all the plants regularly, especially in early summer when nights become warmer.

CANTERBURY OR COVENTRY BELLS?

During the sixteenth and seventeenth centuries, Campanula medium *(now widely known as Canterbury Bells) was called Coventry Bells. The name Canterbury Bells was then being used for* Campanula trachelium, *now known as Throatwort (from its use as a gargle) or Bats-in-the-Belfry. The flowers of Throatwort resembled the metal St. Thomas bells which were sold as badges to pilgrims visiting the shrine of St. Thomas à Becket in Canterbury Cathedral. The bells were often used by pilgrims to adorn their horses.*

BIENNIALS FOR LIGHT SHADE

- Aquilegia vulgaris *(Granny's Bonnet/Columbine)* – page 40.
- Bellis perennis *(Daisy)* – page 19.
- Campanula medium *(Canterbury Bell)*.
- Digitalis purpurea *(Foxglove)* – page 19.
- Myosotis *(Forget-me-not)* – page 19.

LINUM GRANDIFLORUM *(Flax) is a hardy annual 38–45cm/15–18in high and with rose-coloured flowers from early to mid-summer. Sow seeds 6mm/ 1/4in deep in drills 23cm/ 9in apart during spring, in their flowering positions. Thin the seedlings 13cm/5in apart.*

COLLINSIA HETEROPHYLLA *(Chinese Houses) is a hardy annual, 60cm/2ft high, with bright flowers from early to late summer. Sow seeds 6mm/ 1/4in deep in drills 23cm/ 9in apart during late spring, where the plants are to flower. Thin the seedlings 15cm/6in apart.*

ASPERULA ORIENTALIS *(Annual Woodruff) is a hardy annual, growing 30cm/12in high, with pale blue flowers during mid-summer. Sow seeds in spring or early summer, 6mm/1/4in deep in drills 23cm/9in apart. Thin the seedlings 10cm/4in apart.*

AGERATUM HOUSTONIANUM *(Floss Flower) is a half-hardy annual, 13–30cm/5–12in high and with bluish-mauve flowers throughout summer. Sow seeds 3mm/1/8in deep in late winter and place in 16–18°C/61–64°F. Later, plant them 15–25cm/ 6–10in apart.*

BEGONIA SEMPERFLORENS *(Wax plant) is a half-hardy annual, 15–23cm/6–9in high, with flowers throughout summer. Sow seeds thinly on the compost surface in late winter, place in 18°C/64°F and prick out the seedlings in small clusters. Later, plant 15–23cm/6–9in apart.*

COREOPSIS TINCTORIA *(Calliopsis and also known as C. bicolor) is a hardy annual, 23–75cm/9–30in high and with golden yellow, maroon or crimson flowers from mid- to late summer. Sow seeds 6mm/1/4in deep in drills 23cm/9in apart in spring, where they are to flower. Subsequently, thin the seedlings 15–30cm/ 6–12in apart.*

HESPERIS MATRONALIS *(Damask Violet/Sweet Rocket) is a short-lived perennial usually grown as a biennial, flowering in early summer. Sow seeds 6mm/ 1/4in deep in a seed-bed in early summer. Move young plants into a nurserybed and plant into a border in late summer or autumn. Set the plants 38–45cm/ 15–18in apart.*

NEMOPHILA MENZIESII *(Baby Blue Eyes and also known as N. insignis) is a hardy annual growing 23cm/9in high and with sky blue, saucer-shaped flowers from early to mid-summer. Sow seeds 6mm/1/4in deep in drills 23cm/9in apart in spring, where the plants are to flower. Thin the seedlings 15cm/6in apart.*

COLOURED AND VARIEGATED FOLIAGE

❖

COLOURFUL leaves of foliage plants introduce brightness and permanency throughout summer. Some of these plants can be sown where they are to flower, others in gentle warmth in spring, while a few are biennials.

Many of these plants have bright and strong colours, so use them carefully to ensure they do not dominate other plants. Some, such as *Atriplex hortensis cupreata*, can be used to create attractive backgrounds for other plants. *Kochia scoparia* 'Trichophylla', however, is ideal for creating height variations in borders. Ornamental cabbages form unusual banks of colour and are available in a wide range of shades. Some are 38cm/ 15in or more across, with attractively frilled edges to their leaves.

EUPHORBIA MARGINATA *'Summer Icicle' is a hardy annual about 45cm/18in high. The white leaves have green centres. It can also be raised as a half-hardy annual.*

PERILLA FRUTESCENS *'Nankinensis' is a half-hardy annual with bronze-purple, finely cut leaves. It grows about 60cm/2ft high.*

KOCHIA SCOPARIA *'Trichophylla' (Summer Cypress/Burning Bush) is grown as a half-hardy annual, 60–90cm/2–3ft high.*

AMARANTHUS TRICOLOR *(Joseph's Coat) is a half-hardy annual that grows 60–90cm/2–3ft high and has a mass of green leaves that are variegated with crimson or scarlet, and are beautifully overlaid with yellow and bronze.*

BRASSICA 'ROSE BOUQUET' *(Ornamental Cabbage) is best grown as a half-hardy annual. This variety has reddish-pink leaves, but there is a variety of others. Their colours are enhanced by autumn frosts.*

RICINUS COMMUNIS *'Carmencita' (Castor Oil Plant) is a half-hardy annual with large, deep-brown leaves, bright red flower buds and spiny seed pods. It grows 1.5–1.8m/ 5–6ft high.*

ZEA MAYS *(Sweet Corn) is well known as a vegetable, but there are also ornamental varieties with variegated leaves. They range in height from 90cm/3ft to 1.5m/ 5ft, and are raised as half-hardy annuals.*

ATRIPLEX HORTENSIS CUPREATA *(Red Mountain Spinach/Red Orach) is a hardy annual, about 1.2m/4ft high with beetroot-red foliage throughout summer. It is ideal as a dominantly coloured background for other plants.*

COLEUS BLUMEI *(Flame Nettle) is a tender greenhouse plant which, during summer, is ideal for planting in containers on a patio. Some varieties are superb in hanging baskets. The nettle-like leaves are vibrantly coloured with a range of bright, eye-catching shades.*

LUNARIA ANNUA *'Variegata', a biennial, grows about 75cm/2¹/2ft high and has variegated leaves and crimson flowers. The variety 'Stella' has creamy white leaves, blotched and splashed with green, and white starry flowers.*

TRANSPARENTLY HONEST

Lunaria annua *has many names, such as Two-pennies-in-a-purse, Shillings, and Money-in-both-pockets. These all refer to its unusual triple-skinned seed-pods. However, it gained the name Honesty not through their shape, but because the innermost skin is transparent.*

ANNUALS AND BIENNIALS FOR CHALKY SOILS

❖

MOST plants grow best in slightly acid soil. The acidity or alkalinity of soil is measured on the pH scale, ranging from 0 to 14. A pH below 7.0 is acid; above, alkaline or chalky.

Acid soils can be improved by adding lime in the form of hydrated lime or ground limestone. Chalky soils, however, are more difficult to change. Using acid fertilizers, such as sulphate of ammonia, and digging in some well-decomposed manure and compost helps to reduce alkalinity, but if the underlying ground has thick layers of chalk the problem is difficult to resolve. In these conditions, it is best to grow plants that like alkaline soil. Many annuals and biennials grow successfully in limy or chalky soils.

TESTING FOR LIME

Discovering if soil is alkaline or acid is easy. At one time, the only way for an amateur to judge the soil's pH was to use a soil-testing kit that involved mixing a soil sample with water, adding chemicals and comparing its colour against a chart which indicated the pH.

Nowadays, a meter with a probe and dial enables readings to be taken quickly and easily. The meter comes with directions, as well as instructions on how to adjust the soil pH. Digital soil pH testers are also available.

These are ideal tools for people who are slightly colour-blind.

LYCHNIS VISCARIA *(German Catchfly), a hardy annual, has a wealth of carmine flowers during early and mid-summer on plants 30cm/12in high. Sow seeds in spring, 6mm/¹/4in deep in drills 23cm/9in apart, where they are to flower. Later, thin the seedlings 7.5cm/3in apart.*

NEMESIA STRUMOSA *is a half-hardy annual with flowers in many colours during early summer and into the early part of late summer. Plants range in height from 20cm/8in to 45cm/18in. Sow seeds 3mm/¹/8in deep in 16°C/61°F in late winter or spring. Plant 10–15cm/4–6in apart.*

ZINNIA ELEGANS *(Youth-and-old-age) is a half-hardy annual 60–75cm/2–2¹/2ft high, although dwarf strains are only 15–30cm/6–12in. Wide colour range. Sow seeds 6mm/¹/4in deep in 16°C/61°F during early and mid-spring. Set plants 15–30cm/6–12in apart, depending on their height.*

COSMOS BIPINNATUS *(Cosmea) is a half-hardy annual, 90cm/3ft high and with white, crimson, pink or rose flowers during mid- and late summer. Sow seeds 6mm/¹/4in deep in 16°C/61°F in late winter or early spring. Plant them 50–60cm/20–24in apart.*

GODETIA GRANDIFLORA *is a hardy annual that flowers during summer. Many varieties, most 30–38cm/12–15in high, both double and single flowered. Sow in late spring, 6mm/¹/4in deep in drills 23cm/9in apart, where they are to flower.*

LAVATERA TRIMESTRIS *(Mallow) is a hardy annual, 60–90cm/2–3ft high and with rosy pink flowers from mid- to late summer. Sow seeds in spring, 12mm/¹/2in deep in drills 23cm/9in apart, where they are to flower. Thin the seedlings 45–50cm/18–20in apart.*

FURTHER PLANTS FOR CHALKY SOILS

- Alcea rosea (Althea rosea) *(Hollyhock)* – biennial, page 19.
- Arctotis x hybrida *(African Daisy)* – half-hardy annual, page 14.
- Centaurea cyanus *(Cornflower)* – hardy annual, page 16.
- Clarkia elegans – *hardy annual, page 16.*
- Coreopsis tinctoria – *hardy annual, page 20.*
- Delphinium consolida *(Larkspur)* – hardy annual, page 25.
- Echium lycopsis *(Purple Viper's Bugloss)* – hardy annual, page 17.
- Gypsophila elegans *(Baby's Breath)* – hardy annual, page 25.
- Iberis umbellata *(Candytuft)* – hardy annual, page 17.
- Lathyrus odoratus *(Sweet Pea)* – hardy annual, page 24.
- Linaria maroccana *(Toadflax)* – hardy annual, page 17.
- Linum grandiflorum *'Rubrum' (Scarlet Flax)* – hardy annual, page 18.
- Lobelia erinus – *half-hardy annual, page 15.*
- Lunaria annua *(Honesty)* – biennial, page 21.
- Malcolmia maritima *(Virginian Stock)* – hardy annual, page 18.
- Nigella damascena *(Love-in-a-mist)* – hardy annual, page 18.
- Petunia x hybrida – *half-hardy annual, page 15.*
- Phlox drummondii *(Annual Phlox)* – half-hardy annual, page 15.
- Rudbeckia hirta *(Black-eyed-Susan)* – hardy annual, page 18.
- Salvia splendens *(Scarlet Salvia)* – half-hardy annual, page 15.
- Scabiosa atropurpurea *(Sweet Scabious)* – hardy annual, page 18.
- Verbena x hybrida *(Vervain)* – half-hardy annual, page 15.

ANNUAL CLIMBERS

❖

MANY climbers can be easily raised from seeds. Some are hardy enough to be sown outdoors in the positions in which they will flower, others need the comfort of gentle warmth in late winter or spring to give them a start in life. Subsequently, they are planted out into their growing and flowering positions.

A few of these plants, such as the Cup-and-saucer Plant *(Cobaea scandens)*, grow as perennials and can also be grown in greenhouses and conservatories, where they attain slightly larger proportions than when outdoors.

All of the climbers listed here are ideal for bringing colour to walls and fences, but provide a supporting framework when growing them against walls. The soil at the base of a wall dries out rapidly, so water plants regularly.

FURTHER CLIMBERS

• Lathyrus chlorantha *'Lemonade' grows 1.5–2.4m/ 5–8ft high and develops sweet pea-like, green coloured flowers from mid- to late summer.*
• Lathyrus odoratus *(Sweet Pea)* – page 24.
• Mina lobata *(Quamoclit lobata) grows 1.2–1.8m/4–6ft high and produces several hundred stems bearing rich red flowers that mature through orange to yellow and finally white. Grow it as a half-hardy annual.*
• Rhodochiton atrosanguineum *(Purple Bell Vine) creates a mass of parasol-shaped, blackish-purple to crimson flowers during summer and into autumn.*

CONVOLVULUS MAJOR
(Ipomoea purpurea/ Pharbitis purpurea) *is a vigorous climber with funnel-shaped, purple flowers from mid- to late summer. Sow seeds in spring, where plants will flower, 12mm/ 1/2 in deep, 30cm/12in apart. Plants grow to 2.4–3m/8–10ft and soon cover supports.*

IPOMOEA TRICOLOR
'Heavenly Blue' (I. rubro-caerulea/I. violacea/ Pharbitis tricolor) *is the well-known Morning Glory and dislays red-purple to blue flowers from mid- to late summer. Sow seeds in gentle warmth in mid-spring and set young plants 30cm/12in apart. Plants grow about 2.4m/8ft high.*

TROPAEOLUM MAJUS
'Climbing Mixed' (Nasturtium) creates a wealth of cerise, scarlet, orange, yellow or cream flowers from early to late summer. Sow seeds in spring, where they are to flower and thin the seedlings 25–38cm/10–15in apart. Plants grow 1.8–2.4m/ 6–8ft high.

ASARINA SCANDENS
'Jewel Mixed' (Climbing Snapdragon) develops violet, white, pink and deep blue flowers about four months after sowing. Sow seeds in gentle warmth in mid-spring and set the plants 10cm/4in apart. It grows 1.2–2.4m/ 4–8ft high.

CAJOPHORA (CAIOPHORA) LATERITA
'Frothy' has 5cm/2in-wide flowers that change from coppery-orange to white. Sow seeds in gentle warmth in mid-spring and set the plants 10cm/4in apart in groups of four or five. It grows 1.2–1.8m/4–6ft high.

COBAEA SCANDENS
(Cup-and-saucer Plant/Cathedral Bells) develops purple, bell-shaped flowers about 6.5cm/2 1/2 in long during summer. Sow seeds in gentle warmth in early or mid-spring and plant 45cm/18in apart. It grows 3–6m/10–20ft high.

ECCREMOCARPUS SCABER *'Anglia Hybrids Mixed' (Chilean Glory Flower). Sow seeds in gentle warmth in early spring and put the plants outside as soon as all risk of frost has passed, setting them 45cm/ 18in apart. Plants grow 1.8–3m/6–10ft high.*

LATHYRUS LATIFOLIUS *has a perennial nature (but often raised from seeds) with flowers from early to late summer. Sow seeds 12mm/ 1/2 in deep in spring, where they are to flower. Thin the seedlings 38–45cm/ 15–18in apart. Plants grow 2.4–3m/8–10ft high.*

TROPAEOLUM PEREGRINUM *(Canary Creeper) produces irregularly shaped, yellow flowers from mid-summer to autumn. Sow seeds in gentle warmth in spring and set plants 75cm/ 2 1/2 ft apart, or sow in position in late spring. Plants grow 1.8–3m/6–10ft high.*

FRAGRANT
ANNUALS AND BIENNIALS
❖

FRAGRANCE is often considered to be an indication of a civilized garden. Dramatic splashes of colour are always attractive, but when combined with a pleasurable scent they are even more desirable. This combination is easily achieved by sowing or planting annuals and biennials.

There are many plants to choose from and some, such as *Matthiola bicornis*, introduce scent to evenings and nights. A superb and fragrant combination is the Night–scented Stock (*Matthiola bicornis*) and the Virginian Stock (*Malcolmia maritima*). Plant these together under a window: the straggly and sprawling nature of the Night–scented Stock is tempered by the shorter and tidier Virginian Stock.

OTHER
SCENTED PLANTS

• Centaurea moschata *(Sweet Sultan) – hardy annual.*
• Heliotropium x hybridum *(Heliotrope Cherry Pie) – half-hardy annual.*
• Hesperis matronalis *(Sweet Rocket) – biennial.*
• Limnanthes douglasii *(Poached Egg Plant) – hardy annual.*
• Matthiola bicornis *(Night-scented Stock/Perfume Plant/Evening Stock) – hardy annual.*
• Mirabilis jalapa *(Four o'Clock Plant/Marvel of Peru) – half-hardy annual.*
• Nicotiana alata *(Tobacco Plant) – half-hardy annual.*

LATHYRUS ODORATUS
(Sweet Pea) is a sweetly scented, hardy annual climber. Some grow 3m/ 10ft high, others only 45cm/ 1¹/2 ft. They flower from early to late summer.

MALCOLMIA MARITIMA
(Virginian Stock), a sweetly scented hardy annual, flowers for about eight weeks, four weeks after being sown.

NICOTIANA x SANDERAE *(Flowering Tobacco Plant) is well known for its sweetly scented flowers, which appear from early to late summer. It is a half-hardy annual.*

RESEDA ODORATA *(Mignonette) is a hardy annual, sweetly scented and attractive to bees. Sow seeds in spring, where they are to flower. Flowers appear from early summer to autumn.*

VERBENA x HYBRIDA *(Vervain) is a half-hardy annual with primrose-like, fragrant flowers borne in clustered heads from early summer to autumn. Verbena rigida also has fragrant flowers.*

ALYSSUM MARITIMUM *(Sweet Alyssum), now known as Lobularia maritima, develops flowers with a bouquet resembling new-mown hay. There are several flower colours, including white, shades of purple, pink and rose. It is a hardy annual usually grown as a half-hardy annual.*

WALLFLOWERS (Cheiranthus *and* Erysimum *species) are mostly sweetly scented. By nature they are perennial but invariably grown as biennials. Growing them in combination with tulips helps to extend the period of colour. Heights range from 15cm/6in to 45cm/18in.*

DIANTHUS BARBATUS *(Sweet William) is a cottage-garden flower with a sweet fragrance. Although a perennial plant, it is always grown as a biennial, when it flowers during early and mid-summer. Plants are 20–60cm/8–24in high, and are best planted 20–25cm/8–10in apart.*

MATTHIOLA INCANA *'Apple Blossom' (Stock) can be grown as a half-hardy annual. It has clove-scented flowers and grows 30cm/ 12in high. 'Legacy', 30– 38cm/12–15in high, is another superbly scented stock.*

THE GOOD PLANT

The name Verbena is thought to be derived from Herbena, meaning the good plant. This is because Vervain (Verbena officinalis) was widely used by early man, and featured in pagan religious practices.

ANNUALS FOR CUT FLOWERS

GROWING bright, attractive flowers that can be cut and displayed indoors in vases is a bonus with many hardy and half-hardy annuals.

To ensure that the flowers last a long time indoors, cut them in the morning while their leaves and stems are full of moisture. When severing the stems, use a sharp knife or scissors and cut at a 45-degree angle. Then remove the lower leaves and place the stems in buckets of deep, clean water in a cool, shaded room. During the morning, carefully arrange the flowers in vases.

Once arranged, check them every day, removing faded flowers and topping up with fresh water. Proprietary additives can be mixed with the water to extend the flowers' lives.

OTHER PLANTS

- Amaranthus caudatus (Love-lies-bleeding) – hardy annual.
- Antirrhinum majus (Snapdragon) – half-hardy annual.
- Coreopsis tinctoria (Tickseed) – hardy annual.
- Cosmos bipinnatus (Cosmea) – half-hardy annual.
- Lathyrus odoratus (Sweet Pea) – hardy annual.
- Reseda odorata (Mignonette) – hardy annual.
- Schizanthus pannatus (Butterfly Flower/Poor Man's Orchid) – half-hardy annual.
- Verbena x hybrida (Vervain) – half-hardy annual.

GAILLARDIA PULCHELLA (Blanket Flower) is a half-hardy annual, about 30–45cm/12–18in high, with large, daisy-like flowers from mid-summer to the frosts of autumn. Sow seeds 6mm/^{1}/$_4$in deep in 15°C/59°F during spring. Set the plants 25cm/10in apart.

BLANKET FLOWER

Gaillardia pulchella probably gained its common name from its colourful flowers that resemble the bright, zigzag-patterned blankets of the North American Indians.

GYPSOPHILA ELEGANS (Baby's Breath) is a hardy annual, 50–60cm/20–24in high, with clouds of white, pink or rose-coloured flowers throughout summer. Sow seeds where they are to flower, 6mm/^{1}/$_4$in deep and in drills 23cm/9in apart during spring. Thin the seedlings 25–30cm/10–12in apart.

IBERIS UMBELLATA (Candytuft/Globe Candytuft) is a hardy annual, 15–38cm/6–15in high, with domed heads of red, purple or white flowers from early to late summer. Sow seeds where they are to flower, 6mm/^{1}/$_4$in deep in drills 23cm/9in apart during early and mid-spring. Thin the seedlings 23cm/9in apart.

CALLISTEPHUS CHINENSIS (China Aster) is a half-hardy annual, 20–60cm/8–24in high and with large, daisy-like flowers throughout summer. There are also dwarf forms. Sow seeds 6mm/^{1}/$_4$in deep in 16°C/61° in early spring. Plant them 23–30cm/9–12in apart.

CALENDULA OFFICINALIS (Pot Marigold) is a hardy annual, 30–60cm/1–2ft high and with yellow or orange flowers throughout summer. Sow seeds 12mm/^{1}/$_2$in deep in drills 23cm/9in apart in spring, in position. Thin seedlings 30cm/12in apart.

DELPHINIUM CONSOLIDA (Larkspur) is a hardy annual, 90cm–1.2m/3–4ft high, with spires of pink, red, purple or white flowers from early to mid-summer. In spring, sow seeds 6mm/^{1}/$_4$in deep, where they are to flower. Later, thin the seedlings 23cm/9in apart.

GODETIA GRANDIFLORA, a hardy annual, grows 30–38cm/12–15in high and bears single, double or semi-double flowers in pink, white, cherry-red or salmon during mid- and late summer. Sow seeds where the plants are to flower, 6mm/^{1}/$_4$in deep and in drills 23cm/9in apart, in late spring. Thin the seedlings 15cm/6in apart.

NIGELLA DAMASCENA (Love-in-a-mist), a hardy annual and 45–60cm/1^1/$_2$–2ft high, has finely cut leaves and blue or white flowers from early to mid-summer. Sow seeds where the plants are to flower, 6mm/^{1}/$_4$in deep and in drills 23cm/9in apart during spring. Subsequently, thin the seedlings 15–23cm/6–9in apart.

HERBACEOUS PERENNIALS

❖

Herbaceous perennials are often featured in flower borders, either exclusively or mixed with shrubs, trees, annuals and summer-flowering bulbous plants. By nature, herbaceous perennials die down to ground-level in late summer or autumn and develop fresh shoots in spring or early summer. This style of growth enables them to live in areas where the temperature drops to freezing in winter. The roots, which are dormant during winter, enable survival from one season to another.

The range of herbaceous perennials is broad and there are varieties and species to suit many types of soil and position, from soils predominantly formed of clay to light and sandy types, and from salt-blown coastal sites to dry and sunny borders.

Planning, planting and looking after herbaceous perennials is covered in this chapter, while preparing the ground by single- and double-digging is featured on page 10. Raising new herbaceous perennials from seeds is discussed on page 274, and propagating by division on page 285.

WHAT ARE HERBACEOUS PERENNIALS?

❖

HERBACEOUS perennials are plants that each spring develop fresh shoots which grow and bear flowers before the onset of cold weather in late autumn. Their leaves and stems then die down, leaving the root part dormant during winter. However, most herbaceous borders are not so 'pure of spirit' and invariably become homes for other types of plants, perhaps bulbous-based or with a slightly woody nature. Even small bamboos are frequently included. This *pot-pourri* approach to herbaceous borders may not create one with a thoroughbred nature, but does produce a varied range of flowers, leaves and seed-pods. And it is this mixed nature that often enables borders to remain attractive over a long period and to create such a spectacular display right through to the frosts of autumn – or later.

HERBAL NATURE

Many of the plants now grown in herbaceous borders were once considered to have medicinal or domestic uses. Balm (Melissa officinalis) was used as a strewing herb to repel fleas and lice and to create a pleasing aroma, as well as being employed for its culinary qualities. The Oxe-eye Chamomile (Anthemis tinctoria), also known as Dyer's Chamomile, was used to produce a yellow dye, while the blue flowers of Borage (Borago officinalis) were added to ales to produce a 'cooling' taste. Tansy (Tanacetum vulgare), now often grown in the form 'Crispum', was earlier used to make pudding and cakes.

ACANTHUS MOLLIS *(Bear's Breeches) is an herbaceous plant well known for its dominant spires of flowers and large, deeply cut leaves that are said to have inspired motifs in early architecture.*

CENTRANTHUS RUBER *is a European native earlier known as* Kentranthus ruber. *It was introduced into Britain and soon become naturalized. Commonly, it is known as Red Valerian and valued for its red or deep pink flowers.*

AGAPANTHUS, *mainly from South Africa, has fleshy roots and a slightly tender nature. Plants are soon damaged by frost and normally need a sheltered position. However, the 'Headbourne Hybrids' are slightly hardier.*

CLEMATIS HERACLEIFOLIA *is an herbaceous species of clematis originally from China. It displays clusters of tubular, purple-blue flowers during mid- and late summer on plants up to 90cm/3ft high. Sometimes it is grown on supports formed of twiggy pea sticks.*

KNIPHOFIAS *are widely known as Torch Lilies and Red Hot Pokers. Like many herbaceous plants, the garden hybrids now far exceed the species in general cultivation. However, all Torch Lilies have similar flowers, resembling pokers.*

TROLLIUS x HYBRIDUS, *one of the Globe Flowers, is a cross between two species and the parent of many superb varieties which have globe-shaped flowers and a wide colour range. The British and European native* T. europeaus *was the first Globe Flower known in European Gardens.*

SMILACINIA RACEMOSA *is, like many herbaceous perennials, native to North America. Known as the False Spikenard, it develops terminal sprays of scented, creamy-white flowers on arching stems. It is an ideal plant for planting in moist soil and light shade.*

ZANTEDESCHIA AETHIOPICA, *the Arum Lily, is a relatively tender plant that in temperate and exposed climates needs protection during winter. Like many other plants with hardier forms, this too has one in the variety 'Crowborough'. This has encouraged its much wider use in flower beds.*

PLANTS THAT TEST THE RULE

Proper herbaceous plants die down to soil level in late autumn or early winter, but what of Lamb's Tongue and bergenias, both well-known residents of herbaceous borders? The Lamb's Tongue *(Stachys byzantina)* has large, tongue-shaped leaves densely covered with white, silvery hairs throughout winter. Bergenias, descriptively known as Elephant's Ears, have persistent, leathery leaves that look superb when covered in frost.

It must be remembered that the term herbaceous may, in some cases, be just a gardener's classification for a plant that when grown in a temperate climate is not sufficiently hardy to survive with all its leaves still in place. For example, Mediterranean plants often assume an herbaceous nature in cold climates, whereas in their native land they maintain leaves throughout the year.

Dahlias are popular in herbaceous borders, but the tubers are not able to withstand winters in temperate climates, even when insulated by several inches of soil. The tubers are therefore lifted immediately frost blackens the foliage, and placed in a frost-proof, dry shed. In spring or early summer they are divided and replanted into flower borders.

It is clear that to encompass the widest possible range of so-called herbaceous plants, gardeners need a pragmatic rather than a purist attitude. It is with this view in mind that the plants in this chapter have been selected.

USING
HERBACEOUS PERENNIALS

HERBACEOUS perennials are very adaptable and although usually used in borders backed by a hedge they can also be planted in other parts of gardens.

TRADITIONAL BORDERS

These are borders 1.8m/6ft or more wide and usually backed by an evergreen hedge such as Yew. The hedge protects plants from cold winds, as well as creating a pleasing background throughout the year. A variation on this is double-sided borders formed of two flower beds on either side of a broad grass path. An alternative to grass is a wide paved area formed of well-weathered flag stones. Unfortunately, borders such as these, totally dedicated to herbaceous perennials, are now a rarity.

MIXED BORDERS

These are formed mainly of herbaceous perennials, but also annuals, biennials and shrubs. Hedges can be used as a background, but cordon as well as bush fruit trees are a possibility and introduce a relaxed and informal cottage-garden atmosphere. However, when using fruit trees, ensure that plants are not deprived of light and circulating air around them.

> ### PROTECTING LAWN EDGES
>
> *Many herbaceous plants have a low, cascading nature that makes them ideal for the edges of borders. Unfortunately, when plants are positioned close to a lawn's edge the grass is invariably killed, leaving bare patches that are especially evident during winter. This can be avoided by placing a row of paving slabs along the edge. Plants can then be positioned right up to the border's edge. Also, the slabs make it easier to dig or fork over a border without tipping soil on the grass.*

LOW-GROWING PLANTS *smother the ground, creating a carpet of attractive leaves and, in some cases, flowers. Some of these plants have leaves that persist throughout winter, others just during the summer months.*

WOODLAND GARDENS, *where plants grow under a light canopy of tall, deciduous trees, provide homes for many shade-loving herbaceous plants. Some of these plants are described on page 38.*

SINGLE-SIDED BORDERS, *where plants are grown, arranged by colour, shape and height, with a wall, fence or hedge along the back, are a traditional way to grow herbaceous plants.*

WATERSIDE PLANTS

The edges of ponds are frequently paved to form firm standing areas from where fish and aquatic plants can be admired. However, it is also possible to plant moist areas around natural or man-made ponds with moisture-loving herbaceous plants as well as some border primulas. Bog gardens help to integrate a pond with its surroundings and together they form a dominant feature with a wide range of plants. Some have attractive flowers, while others display colourful or large leaves.

WOODLAND AND GROUND COVER

Many herbaceous plants happily grow in shade. They can be successfully grown with bulbous plants between shrubs and under a light, leafy canopy, preferably created by deciduous trees. This allows soil to receive rain during winter and sunshine in spring and early summer. A total canopy of evergreen trees keeps the soil too dry and the area excessively dark. Many ground-covering plants thrive in these conditions; a range is suggested on page 35.

TRADITIONALLY, *herbaceous borders were planted solely with herbaceous perennials. This meant that during winter the entire border was bare; the plants persisted through their dormant roots.*

MIXED BORDERS *are increasingly popular and are formed of a range of herbaceous perennials, annuals and biennials, bulbs, shrubs and even small trees. This system creates colour throughout the year.*

HERBACEOUS PLANTS *are ideal for planting alongside streams and ponds. Many plants survive or even thrive in these persistently moist positions, and a selection of these is suggested on page 39.*

> ### BORDER SHAPE
>
> **ISLAND BEDS,** *usually kidney shaped and set within a lawn, are mainly planted with herbaceous plants that do not need to be supported by twiggy sticks. A range of them is detailed on page 34.*
>
> **SINGLE ISLAND BEDS** *can be integrated even into small lawns. They are usually positioned towards a corner so that a focal point is created and the lawn is not fragmented into several small pieces.*
>
>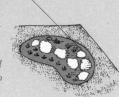
>
> **ISLAND BEDS** *should be between 1.8m/6ft and 2.4m/8ft at their widest points. This enables the soil to be hoed without having to walk all over it.*

PLANNING AND PLANTING

❖

PLANT herbaceous borders in early to mid-autumn, or during mid-spring. However, in mild areas, planting could continue from autumn until early winter, or start in early spring. Where new borders have been dug in winter, spring is the better time as the soil will have settled and the surface be broken down to a fine tilth. However, early flowering plants are best planted in autumn (see page 285 for the best times to divide established plants).

PREPARING THE BORDER

Do not try to plant herbaceous plants too early in spring as, if the soil is excessively wet, their soft crowns will decay. Also, cold soil prevents rapid establishment.

As soon as the surface soil is dry, systematically shuffle sideways across the bed, firming strips 25–30cm/10–12in wide at a time. This is time consuming, but better than using a garden roller. After firming, rake the surface level. The 'plan' (see right) can then be transferred to it.

PLANTING

Setting plants in the soil is a critical task; if positioned too deeply in cold, wet clay soil they may decay. Conversely, if planted shallowly in light soil that settles, their exposed crowns may become hard and the entire plant will be rocked, or topple over. Always put plants with long tap roots slightly deeper (about 2.5cm/1in) than before: these include acanthus, anchusas, Oriental Poppies and verbascums. The previous soil level is usually indicated by a dirty mark on each plant's crown.

Plants with fibrous roots, such as *Achillea ptarmica*, Michaelmas Daisies, phloxes and pyrethrums, must not be planted deeply, and this especially applies to surface-rooting plants such as London Pride, monardas and Lamb's Tongue *(Stachys byzantina)*.

Whatever the depth, firm planting is essential. Use the heel of your shoe to firm in large plants, and your hands for smaller ones. Afterwards, ensure that the soil is watered thoroughly.

MAKING YOUR PLAN

Detailed planning is essential if an herbaceous border, when in flower, is to look natural and in harmony with itself. Height variations, colour harmonies and contrast need consideration, as well as the planting practicalities of 'how many plants will I need?'

For this reason, both the heights of the mature plants and their planting distances are indicated for each of the plants illustrated from pages 31 to 45.

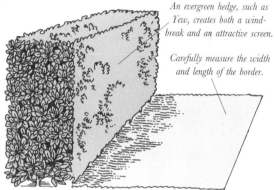

1. FIRST, *measure the width and length of the border. If you do not have a long tape-measure, tie knots every metre or yard in a long piece of string. Do not walk on the border too much, as this soon consolidates the soil unevenly.*

An evergreen hedge, such as Yew, creates both a windbreak and an attractive screen.

Carefully measure the width and length of the border.

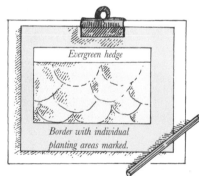

Evergreen hedge

Border with individual planting areas marked.

2. TRANSFER *the measurements onto scaled paper. Then, draw in the planting areas. The size of these depends on the planting distances: borders look best when plants are grouped in threes and planted in triangles. As an approximation, the space needed for each group is about twice the planting width indicated (in the following pages) for each plant.*

1. PLAN *the border carefully (see right), preferably setting plants in groups of three. Before planting, lay the plants on the soil to ensure that each group is in proportion with itself and neighbouring plants.*

2. USE *a trowel to form a deep hole so that roots are allowed to spread out and not become congested towards one side. Bury the crown slightly deeper than before: this allows for the soil to settle slightly after planting.*

3. FIRM SOIL *around the plants with fingers or feet. If the soil is too heavily compressed, air is excluded and plants suffer. Conversely, if the soil is not in close contact with the roots, establishment is delayed.*

3. TRANSFER *the design to the border, using a pointed stick to define the areas. Alternatively, use a thin trickle of sharp sand. Do not use lime, as this may make the area too alkaline. The planting areas invariably increase in size towards the back – or centre, if an island border – to accommodate larger and more dominant herbaceous perennials.*

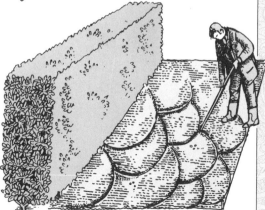

LOOKING AFTER HERBACEOUS PLANTS

BECAUSE herbaceous perennials develop fresh stems, leaves and flowers each year, it is vital that ample food and water are available to enable plants to grow healthily and vigorously throughout summer.

The first task in spring is to shallowly fork the soil between established plants, removing weeds and opening up the surface so that air and water can enter. Then, sprinkle a general fertilizer around plants and thoroughly water the soil. At this stage, in late spring or early summer, form a 5–7.5cm/2–3in-thick mulch of well-decayed compost between plants. There are many other mulches that can be used, including chopped bark. Peat has been used in the past, but its removal from peat beds is environmentally unfriendly. Also, birds usually scattered it over lawns and paths. Before applying any mulch, ensure the soil is moist.

AUTUMN OR SPRING?

Most gardeners cut down their herbaceous perennials in autumn, after their display is completely finished. This tidies up a border and ensures that pests and diseases on old stems and leaves can be destroyed by burning. Twiggy sticks, canes and proprietary supports can be removed and stored under cover during winter, but first remove soil from them and, if necessary, wash in disinfectant so that plants during the following year are not contaminated with problems carried over from the previous season.

Occasionally, however, plants are left as they are during winter. The idea is that frost on the old stems creates an interesting feature during the cold weather. If plants are treated in this way, cut them back in late winter, then remove their supports and rake off and burn all debris from the surface. This means that late winter can become a very busy time.

STAKING

Many herbaceous perennials do not need staking (see page 34). However, some, such as paeonies, dahlias and delphiniums, benefit from supports that eventually become covered by stems, leaves and flowers.

Three stout stakes, encircled by strong garden string at several heights. This is an excellent to way to support border dahlias.

Twiggy pea-sticks are ideal for most plants: insert them early in the season, so that shoots grow up and completely cloak them.

Curved, metal supports are ideal for supporting paeonies, as the stems can rest on the circular metal sides.

DEAD-HEADING PLANTS

Removing dead flower heads is time consuming, but certainly prolongs the display. In a large border this may not be important, but in small town gardens it is a useful activity.

Instead of just dropping spent flowers on the soil, put them on a compost heap.

FEEDING

Start the yearly cycle of feeding in spring (see left), then add a mulch to the soil's surface.

If the border has not been mulched, general fertilizers applied in a granular form are ideal, lightly pricked into the surface and then thoroughly watered. Apply these every three weeks until the latter part of mid-summer. If a mulch is present, use a liquid feed.

Take care not to over-feed lupins, eryngiums, artemisias, echinops and anaphalis as they may then produce rank and leafy growth, which is unattractive and susceptible to pests and disease attack. Many plants with silver or grey leaves are soon spoiled when fed too often. They are better when they are 'hungry'.

IN EARLY *spring, re-firm herbaceous perennials planted in autumn. The soil may have been loosened by frost. It is essential that roots and soil are in close contact if the plants are to grow quickly.*

DURING *spring and early summer, shallowly fork between plants, breaking up crusty surface soil to enable air and rain to penetrate. At the same time, pull up and remove all weeds.*

IN LATE *spring or early summer, sprinkle a general fertilizer between the plants. Then, lightly hoe it into the topsoil. Take care not to damage roots. Thoroughly water the bed.*

FORM *a 5–7.5cm/ 2–3in-thick layer of well-decomposed compost between plants in late spring or early summer, but first apply a general fertilizer and thoroughly water the soil.*

THROUGHOUT *summer, water the plants. Oscillating sprays make this task easier and do a superb job. Always apply water thoroughly, not just superficially dampening the surface.*

IN AUTUMN, *cut down plants to ground level and rake debris from the surface. This is woody and needs to be burned. Sometimes cutting down plants is left until late winter.*

TALL PLANTS

❖

 EXTRA-tall plants are ideal for creating both focal points and height variations in borders. Some, such as the more vigorous asters, produce a spectacle of massed flowers 60cm/2ft high, while the Globe Artichoke *(Cynara scolymus)* has fewer but more unusually shaped flower heads. Alternatively, the Ornamental Rhubarb *(Rheum palmatum)* has dominant foliage.

Where a garden is exposed to strong and constant winds, ensure tall plants are either staked or protected by screens or hedges. Tall hedges that filter wind are the long-term answer to the problem. Indeed, traditional double-sided herbaceous borders were often backed by Yew hedges. As well as giving protection, they provided an attractive backdrop.

OTHER TALL PLANTS

- Acanthus mollis
- Acanthus spinosus
- Achillea filipendulina
- Aster novae-angliae
- Aruncus dioicus
- Campanula lactiflora
- Crambe cordifolia
- Delphinium elatum
- Echinacea purpurea
- Eremurus robustus
- Eremurus *'Shelford Hybrids'*
- Ligularia dentata
- Macleaya cordata
- Onopordum acanthium
- Rudbeckia laciniata
- Verbascum bombyciferum (V. *'Broussa'*)

EREMURUS ELWESII *(Foxtail Lily/Desert Candle/King's Spear)* grows 1.8–2.7m/6–9ft high and develops fragrant, soft pink flowers in thick, poker-like heads during early and into mid-summer. There is also *'Albus'*, a white-flowered variety. Space plants 60–90cm/2–3ft apart.

GALEGA OFFICINALIS *(Goat's Rue)* grows up to 1.5m/5ft high and during early and mid-summer develops white or pale lilac flowers amid light green leaves formed of many small leaflets. *'Alba'* is a pure white variety. Space plants 60–75cm/2–2¹⁄₂ft apart. Ideal for backs of borders.

HELENIUM AUTUMNALE *(Sneezeweed)* reaches 1.2–1.8m/4–6ft high and develops large, daisy-like flowers from mid-summer to autumn. Some varieties are 60–75cm/2–2¹⁄₂ft high. Flower colours range from yellow, through orange to mahogany red. Space plants 30–45cm/1–1¹⁄₂ft apart.

ASTER NOVI-BELGII *(Michaelmas Daisy)* normally grows 90cm–1.2m/3–4ft high, but there are dwarf forms 23–38cm/9–15in tall. They bloom during late summer and into autumn, with large, daisy-like flowers. Colours include blue, red, pink, purple and white. Plant 23–38cm/9–15in apart.

ACONITUM NAPELLUS *(Monkshood/Helmet Flower)* grows 90cm–1.2m/3–4ft high, with deeply cut leaves and spires of hooded flowers during mid- and late summer. Colours include many tones of blue and violet, as well as ivory-white. They are distinctive and create a superb display. Plant them 30–38cm/12–15in apart.

CYNARA SCOLYMUS *(Globe Artichoke)* grows about 1.5m/5ft high. It is mainly grown for its edible flower heads, but is sufficiently decorative to be planted in a border. The purplish blue flowers appear during mid to late summer. Space plants 90cm/3ft apart. Protect the bases of plants in winter.

HELIANTHUS DECAPETALUS *(Thin-leaf Sunflower)* has rough, green leaves and 5–7.5cm/2–3in-wide yellow flowers from mid- to late summer. The best known varieties include *'Capenoch Star'* (lemon yellow) and *'Loddon Gold'* (golden yellow). Space these handsome plants 45–60cm/1¹⁄₂–2ft apart.

RHEUM PALMATUM *(Ornamental Rhubarb)* is 1.5–2.4m/5–8ft tall, with large, deeply cut, purple-red leaves that slowly lose their dominant colour. Tall, deep pink or red flowers appear in early and mid-summer. *'Atropurpureum'* has purple-tinged leaves and creamy white flowers. Space plants 90cm/3ft apart.

THALICTRUM DIPTEROCARPUM *(Meadow Rue)* grows 1.2–1.5m/4–5ft high, with small mauve flowers and dominant yellow anthers from early to mid-summer. It is sometimes sold as T. delavayi. Varieties include *'Hewitt's Double'* (double flowers). Space plants 45cm/18in apart.

LOW-GROWING PLANTS

❖

LARGE, distinctively-shaped, dominant plants always attract attention, but in small gardens are often overpowering, especially when seen *en masse* and close up. There are, however, many small plants to choose from and a few are illustrated and listed here.

Many of them act as ground cover and smother soil in leaves and flowers (ground covering plants are discussed on page 35). Others have a more upright nature, some combining attractive leaves with flowers. Lamb's Tongue (now called *Stachys byzantina* but earlier and more popularly known as *S. lanata* and *S. olympica*) is a superb example of a foliage plant for borders, whatever their size.

Any list of low-growing plants raises the question 'what exactly is low?' The low-growing plants featured here, all have a maximum height of about 60cm/2ft. These heights include flowers and therefore many plants appear less dominant when not in bloom. All are perfect for smaller borders, and ideal for varying the height in traditional borders.

POLYGONUM AFFINE *(Knotweed) forms mats of lance-shaped leaves. 'Darjeeling Red' has deep pink flowers from mid- to late summer; 'Donald Lowndes' has red flowers and copper-coloured leaves in autumn. Both grow 15–25cm/ 6–10in high. Set the plants 30–18cm/12–15in apart.*

POTENTILLA ATROSANGUINEA *(Cinquefoil) is a parent of many superb herbaceous perennials, most growing 38–60cm/15–24in high. These include 'Gibson's Scarlet' (brilliant scarlet) and 'Wm Rollison' (rich orange). Set plants 38–45cm/ 15–18in apart.*

PRUNELLA GRANDIFLORA *(Self-heal) grows 15cm/6in high, with purple-violet flowers from early summer to autumn. P. x* webbiana *is slightly larger; several varieties, including 'Loveliness' (pale violet) and 'Loveliness Pink' (clear pink). Space plants 38cm/15in apart.*

CYNOGLOSSUM NERVOSUM *(Hound's Tongue/Beggar's Lice) grows 45–60cm/1¹/₂–2ft high, with rough, grey-green, tongue-like leaves. Vivid blue, tubular, Forget-me-not-like flowers are borne on branching stems during early and mid-summer. Position the plants 30cm/12in apart.*

LYCHNIS x ARKWRIGHTII *grows about 30cm/12in high and produces lance-shaped, mahogany-shaded leaves. Brilliant scarlet-vermilion flowers, about 36mm/1¹/₂in wide, appear from early to mid-summer — sometimes slightly later. Set the plants 23–30cm/9–12in apart.*

EUPHORBIA POLYCHROMA (Æ. epithymoides) *is a bushy, shrubby, evergreen perennial about 45cm/18in high. The fresh green foliage is attractive, with wide clusters of sulphur yellow bracts during late spring and early summer. Space plants 45cm/1¹/₂ft apart.*

FURTHER PLANTS

- Ajuga reptans *(10–30cm/4–12in)*
- Alchemilla mollis *(30–45cm/12–18in)*
- Armeria maritima *(15–25cm/6–10in)*
- Aster novi-belgii *(dwarf varieties – 23–45cm/9–18in)*
- Bergenia cordifolia *(30cm/12in)*
- Brunnera macrophylla *30–45cm/ 12–18in)*
- Corydalis lutea *(15–25cm/6–10in)*
- Dicentra eximia *(30–45cm/12–18in)*
- Epimedium *species (23–30cm/9–12in)*
- Geranium endressii *(30–45cm/12–18in)*
- Geum x borisii *(30cm/12in high)*
- Heuchera sanguineum *(30–45cm/ 12–18in)*
- Hosta albo-marginata *(38–45cm/ 15–18in)*
- Limonium latifolium *(45–60cm/ 18–24in)*
- Saxifraga umbrosa *(30cm/12in)*
- Stachys byzantina *(30–45cm/12–18in)*

(Note: The measurements indicate their heights)

SEDUM SPECTABILE *(Ice Plant) is 30–45cm/ 12–18in high, with fleshy, whitish-green leaves. Pink flowers appear in clustered heads during late summer and into autumn. 'Autumn Joy' has large, bright rose-salmon flowers that assume bronze tinges. Set the plants 45cm/18in apart.*

DAHLIAS AND CHRYSANTHEMUMS

❖

DAHLIAS are richly coloured, tender, tuberous-rooted plants that are soon damaged by frosts. Therefore, in late spring or early summer of each year (as soon as all risk of frost has passed) newly raised plants are put into borders. Alternatively, the previous year's tubers can be divided and replanted.

DIVIDING TUBERS is an easy way to increase dahlias. Lift the tubers in autumn, cut down and store in a frost-proof shed or greenhouse, then divide in spring, ensuring that each part has at least one healthy eye (bud). Dust cut surfaces with a fungicide.

Growing dahlias is easy and their needs are quite simple; plenty of sun, moisture and food. In part, these are necessary because dahlias come from sunny Mexico, but mainly because within the span of a few months they grow from cuttings to plants often 1.5m/5ft high.

RANGE OF DAHLIAS

There are several types and they are classified according to their vigour as well as the shape and size of their flowers. The basic classifications for them are Bedding Dahlias and Border Dahlias.

• Bedding Dahlias are used to create a carpet of colour at or below knee height, and are normally raised from seeds sown in late winter or early spring.

• Border Dahlias form the larger group and include several types, all raised from cuttings or by division.

They include Single-flowered, Anemone-flowered, Collerette and Paeony-flowered types, as well as Decoratives which range from 75cm/2½ft to 1.5m/5ft tall and with varying flower sizes. Pompon types at about 90cm/3ft high are superb, while Cactus-like types include plants from 90cm–1.5m/3–5ft high with a range of various flower sizes.

To the purist who would grow only herbaceous perennials in a border, dahlias are taboo. But for bringing additional colour to borders, the dahlia has few peers.

CHRYSANTHEMUMS FOR HERBACEOUS BORDERS

The chrysanthemum family is formed of several types: annuals, those with an alpine nature, hardy perennials, and a wide group of half-hardy types which have become known as florists' chrysanthemums. These can be grown outdoors in herbaceous borders, where they are planted in late spring or early summer each year, when risk of frost has passed.

They are best planted in bold groups, in spaces specially left for them in borders. Fresh plants are raised each year from cuttings which have been developed from the previous year's plants.

In late autumn, pack cut-down chrysanthemum plants (stools) into boxes of compost. Place in a cold frame or light, cool shed and in late winter water and place in gentle warmth. Shoots will appear and these can also be used to form cuttings.

1. IN LATE winter, chrysanthemum roots (stools) that were cut down and boxed up in late autumn and placed in a cold frame or cool shed can be encouraged to develop shoots.

2. CUT OFF healthy shoots and trim below a leaf joint to 5–6cm/2–2½in long. Remove the lower leaves and dip their bases in hormone rooting-powder.

3. FILL and firm compost in a small pot and insert three or four cuttings about 18–25mm/¾–1in deep and 12mm/½in from the pot's side. Firm compost, water lightly and place in gentle warmth.

1. AS SOON *as frost blackens the leaves of dahlias, shorten back the stems and use a garden fork to dig under the tubers to lift them out of the soil. Take care not to spike the tubers with the fork.*

2. CUT *the stems to about 15cm/6in long, remove soil from around the tubers and leave them upside down in a shed or under a bench in a cool greenhouse for a couple of weeks. Ensure the area is vermin proof.*

3. PUT *the tubers into 10–13cm/4–5in-deep boxes. Pack slightly damp peat around and lightly over them, but do not cover their crowns. Place the boxes in an airy shed, at 5°C/41°F during winter.*

4. IN LATE *winter, re-pack the tubers into boxes of compost; water and place them in 15–18°C/59–64°. Sever shoots when 7.5cm/3in long; cut off the lower leaves and trim them beneath a leaf joint.*

5. INSERT *cuttings 2.5cm/1in deep in pots of equal parts moist peat and sharp sand. Several cuttings can be put in a 7.5cm/3in-wide pot, at least 12mm/½in from the side. Place in 15–18°C/59–64°.*

6. WHEN *rooted, pot them into individual pots filled with a general potting compost. Take care not to damage the roots. Water the compost well and when established reduce the temperature slightly.*

PLANTS THAT DO NOT NEED STAKING

A T ONE time it was assumed that all herbaceous plants had to be supported, and they were automatically planted in long borders backed by a hedge. Since the 1950s, however, self-supporting herbaceous plants have been increasingly used in borders that form islands in lawns (see page 28). This meant that the frontal lengths of borders increased dramatically and more low, self-supporting plants were needed. This does not mean that all tall plants – staked or self-supporting – should be omitted from borders, as they create variations in height.

Self-supporting herbaceous plants are a boon in small gardens, especially where space is limited for the storage of stakes throughout winter. Also, in town gardens it is often difficult to obtain twiggy supports.

(see page 28)

ANEMONE x HYBRIDA *(Japanese Anemone) grows 60–90cm/2–3ft high and develops flowers up to 7.5cm/3in wide from late summer to the frosts of autumn. There are several varieties, mainly in white or pink. Space plants 30–38cm/12–15in apart.*

CURTONUS PANICULATUS *(Aunt Eliza/Pleated Leaves) develops from corms and eventually creates a large clump. It grows 90cm–1.2m/3–4ft high and bears deep orange-red flowers in mid- and late summer. Space plants 23cm/9in apart.*

MERTENSIA VIRGINICA *(Virginian Cowslip/Roanoke-bells) grows 30–60cm/1–2ft high and has purple-blue flowers during late spring and early summer. From mid-summer onwards, plants die down completely. Space plants 25–30cm/10–12in apart.*

PHYTOLACCA AMERICANA *(Poke Weed/Red-ink Plant) grows 90cm–1.8m/3–6ft high and develops spikes of white flowers from early summer to early autumn, followed by dark purple berries containing a dark red juice. Space plants 90cm/3ft apart.*

CAMASSIA QUAMASH *(Common Camosh/Quamash), also known as C. esculenta, grows 60–75cm/2–2½ft high and bears white, purple or blue flowers in early and mid-summer. C. leichtlinii is slightly taller. Space plants about 15cm/6in apart.*

INULA HELENIUM *(Elecampane) grows 90cm–1.2m/3–4ft high and produces large, bright yellow, daisy-like flowers during mid- and late summer. Other species include I. royleana and I. hookeri. Set these plants about 38–45cm/15–18in apart.*

PHALARIS ARUNDINACEA 'Picta' *(Gardener's Garters) is a perennial ornamental grass with narrow, tapering leaves variegated cream and bright green. It grows 30–45cm/12–18in high and initially is planted 38–45cm/15–18in apart. But it soon forms a large clump. Replant it every two or three years.*

POLYGONATUM x HYBRIDUM *(Solomon's Seal/David's Harp) grows 60–75cm/2–2½ft high and develops white flowers up to 2.5cm/1in long in clusters of two or three during early summer. Space plants 30–38cm/12–15in apart. It is ideal for planting in light shade, although it grows practically anywhere.*

OTHER PLANTS

- *Acanthus*
- *Achillea*
- *Aconitum*
- *Agapanthus*
- *Alchemilla*
- *Anaphalis*
- *Armeria*
- *Astilbe*
- *Astrantia*
- *Bergenia*
- *Catananche*
- *Centaurea*
- *Crocosmia*
- *Dicentra*
- *Dictamnus*
- *Doronicum*
- *Echinacea*
- *Echinops*
- *Eremurus*
- *Eupatorum*
- *Euphorbia*
- *Helenium*
- *Helleborus*
- *Hemerocallis*
- *Heuchera*
- *Hosta*
- *Iris*
- *Kniphofia*
- *Limonium*
- *Lupinus*
- *Lychnis*
- *Lysimachia*
- *Lythrum*
- *Monarda*
- *Oenothera*
- *Onopordum*
- *Phlomis*
- *Pulmonaria*
- *Rudbeckia*
- *Scabiosa*
- *Sedum*
- *Sisyrinchium*
- *Stachys*
- *Trillium*
- *Trollius*
- *Verbascum*
- *Zantedeschia*

GROUND COVER PLANTS

❖

SMOTHERING soil with leaves is an ideal way to prevent the growth of weeds and to create a handsome backdrop for other plants. Many low-growing plants can be used and a few of them are suggested here.

Some plants flourish in shade and these are especially useful, but do not expect them to develop to their full size when light is scarce and there is a dearth of moisture.

Establishing herbaceous ground-covering plants in shade is sometimes difficult, but planting them in spring and ensuring their roots remain moist throughout the first season assists them. Unfortunately, the added moisture attracts slugs and snails. Regularly inspect leaves and check under plants.

OTHER PLANTS

- Ajuga reptans 'Atropurpurea'
- Bergenia cordifolia
- Brunnera macrophylla
- Epimedium perralderianum
- Epimedium pinnatum
- Geranium endressii
- Geranium grandiflorum
- Heuchera sanguinea
- Heucherella tiarelloides
- Lysimachia nummularia
- Nepeta x faassenii
- Polygonum affine
- Pulmonaria officinalis
- Stachys byzantina
- Tellima grandiflora

PULMONARIA SACCHARATA (Bethlehem Sage/ Lungwort) grows 30cm/ 12in high and has leaves spotted silvery-white. Pink flowers that slowly change to sky blue appear during spring. Space the plants 30cm/ 12in apart.

TOLMIEA MENZIESII (Pig-a-Back/ Youth on Age) grows about 15cm/ 6in high and covers the ground with Maple-like leaves. Greenish white flowers appear during early summer. It is ideal in partial shade. Space plants 30–38cm/ 12–15in apart.

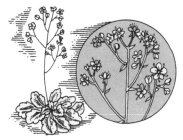

SAXIFRAGA UMBROSA (London Pride) forms masses of rosettes that carpet soil. Tiny pink, star-shaped flowers appear in clusters on stems about 20cm/ 8in high during late spring and early summer. Space plants 30cm/ 12in apart.

VERONICA GENTIANOIDES grows 23–38cm/ 9–15in high and smothers borders with leafy rosettes. Blue flowers borne in terminal clusters up to 15cm/ 6in long appear in early summer. The form 'Variegata' has creamy white leaves.

DRYAS OCTOPETALA (Mountain Avens) grows 7.5–10cm/ 3–4in high and creates a mat of deep green leaves. White, saucer-shaped flowers appear during early and mid-summer. Space plants 45cm/ 18in apart.

HOSTA FORTUNEI 'Albopicta' (Plantain Lily) grows about 45cm/ 18in high and displays pale green leaves variegated buff yellow. Space these ground-smothering plants 45cm/ 18in apart.

LAMIUM GALEOBDOLON 'Variegatum' (Variegated Yellow Archangel) grows 15–38cm/ 6–15in high, with silver flushed leaves and yellow flowers in early and mid-summer. Space plants 38cm/ 15in apart.

TIARELLA WHERRYI (False Mitrewort) grows 15–30cm/ 6–12in high, with ivy-shaped, pale green leaves. Creamy white flowers appear throughout summer. T. cordifolia (Foam Flower) is another superb ground-covering species.

GOD'S IMPRINT

Many early herbalists believed that 'God hath imprinted upon the Plants, Herbs and Flowers, as it were Hieroglyphicks, the signature of their Vertues'. For this reason, Pulmonaria officinalis, with its white-spotted leaves, was thought to cure diseased lungs. It is also known as Blue Lungwort, Jerusalem Cowslip and, amusingly, as Spotted Dog.

WINDY AND EXPOSED SITES

❖

STRONG winds make it very difficult to establish plants: they are either blown about or desiccated by drying winds. Temporary screens help to encourage young plants to become established, while watering and mulching the soil, as well as re-firming loose soil around plants in spring, encourages their development. The plants suggested here will thrive once established, but even they will not grow on a bleak, windswept mountain.

When establishing an exposed garden, first plant windbreaks and hedges to filter wind to reduce its strength. Brick walls create plant-damaging swirling winds on their lee sides and therefore stout hedges are better. Alternatively, temporary screens of hessian provide shelter.

OTHER PLANTS

- Alchemilla mollis
- Anaphalis triplinervis
- Anemone x hybrida
- *Asters (short types)*
- Centaurea dealbata
- Coreopsis grandiflora
- Dictamnus albus
- Eryngium maritimum
- Geranium endressii
- Geranium grandiflorum
- Gysophila paniculata
- Polygonum affine
- Potentilla – *hybrids of* P. atrosanguinea
- Rudbeckia hirta – *low-growing varieties*
- Scabiosa caucasica
- Sedum spectabile
- Veronica spicata

PROTECTING PLANTS

The importance of preventing extremely cold winds damaging newly planted herbaceous plants, trees and shrubs has been known for centuries. Screens have been created from two layers of wire-netting with straw between them. In the early 1800s the garden writer John Loudon recommended straw tied in rolls and strung together.

LYCHNIS CORONARIA (*Rose Campion/Mullein Pink*) grows about 45cm/ 18in high and displays a wealth of bright, crimson-magenta flowers from mid- to late summer. It is a short-lived perennial. Space plants 23–30cm/ 9–12in apart.

PLATYCODON GRANDI-FLORUM (*Balloon Flower*) grows 30–60cm/1–2ft high and develops balloon-shaped flower buds. These open throughout summer and reveal light blue, saucer-shaped flowers. The form 'Album' has white flowers. Space plants about 38cm/15in apart.

SCABIOSA CAUCASICA (*Caucasian Scabious/ Sweet Scabious*) grows 45–60cm/1½–2ft high, with low clusters of leaves and lavender-blue flowers about 7.5cm/3in wide on long stems from early to late summer. There are several varieties, in white, blue and purple. Space plants 38cm/15in apart.

CHELONE OBLIQUA (*Turtlehead/Snakehead*) grows 45–60cm/1½–2ft high and during mid- and late summer develops terminal clusters of deep rose, snapdragon-like flowers on stiff, upright stems. Space the plants 30–45cm/12–18in apart.

LIATRIS SPICATA (*Blazing Star/Gay Feather*) grows 60–75cm/ 2–2½ft high and during late summer develops wand-like spires of pink-purple flowers. Space plants 38cm/15in apart.

OENOTHERA MISSOURIENSIS (*Evening Primrose*) grows 10–15cm/ 4–6in high and creates a mass of yellow flowers up to 7.5cm/3in wide during summer. They open in the evening and each flower lasts for several days. Space plants 38cm/15in apart.

HEUCHERA SANGUINEA (*Coral Flower/Coral Bells*) grows 30–45cm/ 12–18in high and produces masses of slender stems bearing wispy, bright red, bell-shaped flowers throughout summer. The round or heart-shaped leaves carpet the ground. Space plants 38cm/15in apart.

STOKESIA LAEVIS (*Stokes' Aster*) grows 30–45cm/12–18in high and bears white, lilac, blue or purple flowers up to 7.5cm/ 3in wide during mid- and late summer and into autumn. Space the plants about 38cm/ 15in apart.

DRY AND SUNNY POSITIONS

Hot, dry, sunny borders make growing herbaceous plants difficult. But there are some plants that tolerate these conditions and, once established, thrive. Some of them are described here.

Do not leave the establishment of these plants to chance as, even though they survive in dry borders, plenty of well-decayed compost mixed with the soil assists them during their early years. Additionally, covering the soil with a mulch reduces moisture loss from the surface. Until the plants are established, cover the ground with leaves and stems. Before applying a mulch, always thoroughly water the soil.

Many Mediterranean plants survive in dry places, especially those with silver or white leaves.

KING'S SPEAR

Asphodelus is, undeservedly, less popular today than a century or so ago. The species Asphodelus luteus *was known to William Turner, the father of English botany, during the early 1500s, but is now properly called* Asphodeline lutea, *the King's Spear. It grows about 1.2m/4ft high and develops stiff spikes of sulphur yellow flowers.*

The Greeks ate roots of asphodelus and during the Middle Ages it was known as Cibo Regia, *food for a king. The Greeks often planted asphodelus around tombs to provide nourishment for spirits.*

BUPHTHALMUM SALICIFOLIUM *(Willow-leaf Ox-eye) grows up to 75cm/2¹/2ft high when left to form a tumbling bush. Bright, golden yellow, daisy-like flowers appear from early summer to autumn. The leaves are slightly hairy. Space the plants about 45cm/18in apart.*

MACLEAYA CORDATA *(Plume Poppy/Tree Celandine) grows up to 2.4m/8ft high and creates 90cm/3ft-long spires packed with small, pearly white flowers during summer. The lower leaves are large and deeply lobed. It is ideal for the back of a border. Position the plants 90cm/3ft apart.*

SOLIDAGO *'Goldenmosa' (Golden Rod) is a garden hybrid that grows 75–90cm/2¹/2–3ft high and develops 15–23cm/6–9in-long sprays of fluffy yellow flowers during mid- and into late summer. Space plants 38cm/15in apart. There are many other hybrids to choose from.*

ACHILLEA MILLEFOLIUM *(Yarrow/Sanguinary/Nose-bleed) grows about 60cm/2ft high and develops white to cerise flowers in large, flattened heads from early to late summer. Space the plants 30–38cm/12–15in apart. Varieties include 'Cerise Queen' with cherry red flowers.*

ARTEMISIA LUDOVICIANA *(White Sage/Cudweed) is a North American native and grows 60cm–1.2m/2–4ft high. It is mainly grown for its white, woolly leaves. Plant it about 38cm/15in apart. Other herbaceous types include A. lactiflora (White Mugwort), with deeply cut and lobed, mid-green leaves.*

BAPTISIA AUSTRALIS *(False Indigo/Blue False Indigo) grows 60cm–1.2m/2–4ft high and develops masses of blue, sweet-pea-like flowers during early summer. This North American plant sometimes takes a couple of seasons to become fully established. Space these magnificent plants 45–60cm/¹/2–2ft apart.*

HELIOPSIS SCABRA *(Orange Sunflower/Ox-eye), also known as H. helianthoides scabra, grows 90cm–1.2m/3–4ft high and develops single, daisy-like yellow flowers in mid- and late summer. Varieties include 'Golden Plume'. Space plants 45–60cm/1¹/2–2ft apart.*

NEPETA x FAASSENII *(Catmint) is a hybrid that grows 30–45cm/12–18in high and develops whorls of lavender blue flowers throughout summer. When planted in a group it is ideal for covering large areas. Space the plants about 30cm/12in apart. Cats are fascinated by it.*

OTHER PLANTS

- Anaphalis triplinervis
- Anthemis *spp.*
- Asphodeline lutea
- Catananche caerulea
- Centaurea dealbata
- Centaurea macrocephala
- Echinops ritro
- Eryngium *spp.*
- Gypsophila paniculata
- Limonium latifolium
- Sedum *spp.*
- Stachys byzantina

SHADY POSITIONS

EW gardens are not partially shaded during some part of the day and most plants, whatever their nature, tolerate this. Occasionally, however, neighbouring trees or buildings cast shade throughout the day. This is when shade-loving plants are needed.

ADAPTABLE PLANTS

All plants need sunlight to activate growth and to keep them healthy, but some have evolved to live under trees and therefore happily survive in shade. Although trees deprive plants growing underneath them of total light, they do provide shelter from cold winds, frosts and strong sunlight. Shade from evergreen trees and shrubs may be too dense and continuous for many plants, but deciduous trees allow more light to reach plants in winter, as well as sheltering them from late spring frosts. Most herbaceous plants, of course, are not able to benefit from extra light in winter, but deciduous trees enable more rain to reach plants than would evergreens.

PLANTS FOR DRY SHADE

- Anaphalus margaritacea
- Anaphalus triplinervis
- Crambe cordifolia
- Epimedium *x* rubrum
- Geranium ibericum
- Polygonum affine

LYTHRUM SALICARIA *(Purple Loosestrife/ Spiked Loosestrife) grows 60cm–1.2m/ 2–4ft high and from early to late summer reveals small, reddish purple flowers in spires up to 25cm/ 10in long. Space plants 38–45cm/ 15–18in apart.*

PELTIPHYLLUM PELTATUM *(Umbrella Plant) grows about 1m/ 3¹/₂ft high and displays pink flowers in parasol-like heads during late spring and early summer. Large leaves appear later. Space plants 90cm/ 3ft apart.*

PULMONARIA OFFICINALIS *(Jerusalem Cowslip/ Spotted Dog) grows 30cm/ 12in high and develops narrow oval green leaves with white spots. It flowers in late spring and early summer. Space plants 30cm/ 12in apart.*

AJUGA REPTANS *(Bugle/ Carpet Bugleweed) grows 10–30cm/ 4–12in high. Blue flowers in early and mid-summer. Space plants 38cm/ 15in apart.*

DICENTRA SPECTABILIS *(Bleeding Heart) grows 45–75cm/ 1¹/₂–2¹/₂ft high. Rosy red, heart-shaped flowers in early summer. Space plants 38cm/ 15in apart.*

HEMEROCALLIS HYBRIDS *(Day Lilies) are 60–90cm/ 2–3ft high and develop flowers in yellow, pink, red or ruby-purple in early and mid-summer. Space plants 45cm/ 18in apart.*

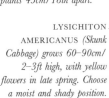

LYSICHITON AMERICANUS *(Skunk Cabbage) grows 60–90cm/ 2–3ft high, with yellow flowers in late spring. Choose a moist and shady position.*

SMILACINIA RACEMOSA *(False Spikenard/ Treacleberry) grows 75–90cm/ 2¹/₂–3ft high. During late spring and early summer it bears creamy white, scented flowers. It is ideal for shady, moist areas. Space plants 38cm/ 15in apart. The Star-flowered Lily-of-the-Valley (S. stellata) has star-shaped white flowers.*

PLANTS FOR DEEP SHADE AND MOISTURE-RETENTIVE SOIL

- Aruncus dioicus *(Goat's Beard)*
- Astilbe *x* arendsii *(Perennial Spiraea)*
- Cimicifuga racemosa *(Black Snake Root)*
- Epimedium perralderianum *(Bishop's Hat/ Barren Wort)*
- Helleborus foetidus *(Stinking Hellebore)*
- Helleborus niger *(Christmas Rose)*
- Helleborus orientalis *(Lenten Rose)*
- Polygonatum commutatum *(Giant Solomon's Seal)*
- Polygonatum *x* hybridum *(Solomon's Seal/ David's Harp)*
- Tiarella cordifolia *(Foam Flower)*
- Trillium grandiflorum *(Wake Robin)*
- Trillium undulatum *(Painted Wood-lily)*

Wake Robin (Trillium grandiflorum) has flowers that are at first white, then later flushed with rose-pink.

MOIST POSITIONS

MANY herbaceous plants thrive in moist soils, especially those that are fertile and therefore able to encourage rapid growth. This is essential with plants that each year grow from a dormant rootstock.

In addition to the plants featured here, many primulas are ideal for planting in soil that does not dry out in summer, perhaps in a bed alongside a garden pond. These include *Primula beesiana* (lilac-purple), *P. bulleyana* (light orange), *P. denticulata* (Drumstick Primrose – pale lilac, deep purple, rose, deep carmine or white), *P. florindae* (Giant Cowslip – light orange to blood red) and *P. japonica* (Japanese Primrose – magenta-red, but also white and pink).

OTHER PLANTS

- Astilbe *x* arendsii
- Gunnera manicata
- Hemerocallis *hybrids*
- Hostas
- Iris laevigata
- Iris pseudacorus
- Iris sibirica
- Cardiocrinum giganteum
- Ligularia dentata (Senecio clivorum)
- Lysichiton americanus
- Lysichiton camtschatcensis
- Lysimachia punctata
- Peltiphyllum peltatum
- Rodgersia pinnata
- Scrophularia aquatica
- Trollius *x* hybridus

EUPATORIUM
PURPUREUM *(Joe-pye Weed/Hemp Agrimony) grows 1.2–1.8m/4–6ft high and develops slender, dark stems and terminal clusters, about 10cm/4in wide, of rose-purple flowers during mid- and late summer. The variety 'Atropurpureum' has purple leaves and rosy-lilac flowers. Space plants 75–90cm/2¹/2–3ft apart. Plant in sun or partial shade.*

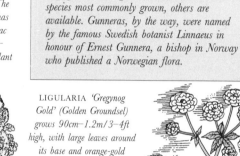

GIANT LEAVES

Few herbaceous plants are as eye-catching as Gunnera manicata, with its large, rhubarb-like leaves up to 3m/10ft across. It is ideal for planting right at the edge of a lake or a very large pond. Although G. manicata is the species most commonly grown, others are available. Gunneras, by the way, were named by the famous Swedish botanist Linnaeus in honour of Ernest Gunnera, a bishop in Norway who published a Norwegian flora.

LIGULARIA *'Gregynog Gold' (Golden Groundsel) grows 90cm–1.2m/3–4ft high, with large leaves around its base and orange-gold flowers from late summer into early autumn. Space plants 45cm/18in apart.*

CALTHA PALUSTRIS
(Marsh Marigold/Kingcup) grows 30–38cm/12–15in high and creates a mass of cup-shaped, bright yellow flowers during late spring and early summer. Space plants 23–30cm/9–12in apart. As well as being grown in moist soil at a pond's edge, it can be planted in water up to 10cm/4in deep.

FILIPENDULA
PURPUREA *(Dropwort, and also known as* Filipendula palmata *and* Spiraea palmata*) grows 60cm–1.2m/2–4ft high with tiny, carmine-rose flowers during mid-summer. Space plants 38–45cm/15–18in apart.*

RANUNCULUS
ACONIFIFOLIUS *'Flore-pleno' (Fair Maids of France) grows about 60cm/2ft high and has shining, pure white, button-like flowers during early summer. Ensure that the soil does not dry out. Space the plants 30–38cm/12–15in apart.*

ARUNCUS DIOICUS
(Goat's Beard) grows 1.2–1.8m/4–6ft high and reveals large, lax plumes of creamy white flowers during early and mid-summer. Position plants 45–60cm/1¹/2–2ft apart. It is especially attractive when planted near a pond. Moist, partial shade suits it best. It is often also called A. sylvester.

RHEUM ALEXANDRAE
(Ornamental Rhubarb) grows 75–90cm/2¹/2–3ft high and during early summer produces erect flower spikes, up to 45cm/18in long, packed with paper-like, creamy bracts. In many ways they resemble drooping tongues. Space plants 50–60cm/20–24in apart. It grows best in fertile, continuously moist soil.

THALICTRUM
SPECIOSISSIMUM *(Dusty Meadow Rue) grows 90cm–1.5m/3–5ft high and develops huge heads of fluffy yellow flowers during mid and late summer. The leaves are also attractive, deeply divided and blue-grey. Space plants 50–60cm/20–24in apart. Fertile, moisture-retentive soil is essenti*

CHALKY SOILS

CHALKY soils are difficult to make less alkaline, especially if the underlying layers are rich in chalk. Raised beds, perhaps 30cm/12in above the general level, can be created, but on an entire garden scale this is not practical and could be prohibitively expensive. Digging in well-decayed compost, peat or manure reduces alkalinity, but the effect is soon lost if water in the soil is extremely chalky. The long-term solution is to select plants that survive in chalky conditions. Some of the many excellent plants to choose from are suggested here.

Many gardeners spray chemicals on certain trees or shrubs to compensate for the soil type, but this is not really practical with herbaceous plants.

OTHER PLANTS

- Acanthus mollis
- Achillea ptarmica
- Anchusa azurea
- Asphodeline lutea
- Crambe cordifolia
- Echinops ritro
- Eremurus robusta
- Erigeron speciosum
- Gypsophila paniculata
- Helenium autumnale
- Hemerocallis *hybrids*
- Kniphofia – *range of species and varieties*
- Limonium latifolium
- Lychnis chalcedonica
- Rudbeckia hirta
- Verbascum *x* hybridum
- Veronica spicata

CORYDALIS LUTEA *(Yellow Fumitory) grows 15–25cm/6–10in high, with masses of yellow flowers from spring to late autumn. Space plants 25–30cm/10–12in apart. It often grows in old walls, where its colour is most welcome. It has the tendency, however, to seed itself and to produce copious seedlings.*

GAILLARDIA ARISTATA *(Blanket Flower) grows 60–75cm/2–2¹/₂ft high and reveals masses of large, daisy-like, yellow and red flowers about 7.5cm/3in wide from early to late summer. Space the plants 38cm/15in apart. Varieties include 'Dazzler'(orange-yellow and maroon-red) and 'Mandarin' (orange and red).*

HELLEBORUS ORIENTALIS *(Lenten Rose) grows about 45cm/18in high and develops saucer-shaped, cream flowers flecked with crimson during late winter and early spring. This plant has a promiscuous nature and has yielded flowers from white to pink. Ideally, plant it close to the edge of a path.*

AQUILEGIA VULGARIS *(Columbine/Granny's Bonnet) grows about 45cm/18in high and develops blue, pink, yellow, crimson or white flowers during early summer. Space plants 25–30cm/10–12in apart. The McKana hybrids are especially popular and widely grown, with beautiful long spurs on their flowers.*

CAMPANULA LACTIFLORA *grows 90cm–1.5m/3–5ft high and develops light lavender blue, bell-shaped flowers during early and mid-summer. Space the plants 38cm/15in apart. There are several superb varieties, including 'Loddon Anna' (flesh pink) and 'Pritchard's Variety' (deep blue).*

CENTRANTHUS RUBER *(Red Valerian) grows 45–90cm/1¹/₂–3ft high and develops red or deep pink, star-shaped flowers from early to late summer. Space plants 30cm/12in apart. Varieties include 'Coccineus' (deep red flowers) and 'Albus'(white): In previous years, centranthus was known as kentranthus.*

DORONICUM PLANTAGINEUM *(Leopard's Bane) grows 45–50cm/18–20in high and develops golden-yellow flowers about 6cm/2¹/₂in wide during late spring and early summer. Space plants 30–38cm/12–15in apart. Varieties include 'Miss Mason' (yellow).*

GEUM CHILOENSE *(Avens) grows 45–60cm/1¹/₂–2ft high and develops bowl-shaped flowers from early to late summer. Space plants 30–38cm/12–15in apart. Varieties include 'Lady Stratheden' (double, yellow) and 'Mrs. Bradshaw' (semi-double and scarlet). Popular and widely grown.*

IRIS GERMANICA *(London Flag/Purple Flag) grows 60–75cm/2–2¹/₂ft tall and develops rich blue flowers during early summer. There are short types (25–45cm/10–18in high) and tall ones (45–75cm/1¹/₂–2¹/₂ft). 'Golden Fair' (above) is short, with beautiful deep yellow flowers.*

SANDY SOILS

THESE soils are light, easy to dig and prepare, but invariably lack plant foods and especially bulky organic material such as manure and compost that would help retain both moisture and nutrients. Also, because such soils are well aerated, organic material soon decays.

IMPROVING SANDY SOIL

When preparing a border, dig in well-decayed compost or manure to enable moisture to be retained. Also, in spring, water the soil thoroughly and form a 5–7.5cm/ 2–3in-thick mulch of well-decayed compost over bare soil between plants. This prevents moisture evaporating from the surface and returns nutrients to the soil. It also helps to keep the soil cool.

OTHER PLANTS

- Achillea filipendulina
- Achillea clypeolata
- Achillea taygetea
- Alstroemeria 'Ligtu-hybrids'
- Anaphalis triplinervis
- Anthemis tinctoria
- Bergenia cordifolia
- Catananche caerulea
- Centaurea dealbata
- Centranthus ruber
- Crambe cordifolia
- Dictamnus albus
- Echinops ritro
- Eryngium maritimum
- Gypsophila paniculata
- Polygonum affine
- Stachys byzantina
- Verbascum x hybridum

ASPHODELINE LUTEA
(King's Spear) grows about 1.2m/4ft high and develops stiff spikes of fragrant, sulphur yellow flowers during early and mid-summer. Space plants 45cm/1½ft apart. Earlier, this plant was known as Asphodelus luteus and is known as Asphodel and, in North America, as Jacob's Rod. It is very distinctive plant and should not be hidden behind other plants.

LIMONIUM LATIFOLIUM
(Statice/Sea Lavender) has a woody root-stock and grows 45–60cm/1½–2ft high. During mid- and late summer it develops lavender blue flowers in heads up to 23cm/9in wide. Space plants 45cm/ 18in apart. The variety 'Violetta' has violet flowers. Flowers can be easily dried.

CYNARA CARDUNCULUS
(Cardoon) grows 1.5–2.1m/ 5–7ft high and develops large, blue or purple flower heads during mid- and late summer. Space plants 90cm/3ft apart. Large, prickly leaves, white beneath.

ERIGERON SPECIOSUS *(Fleabane) grows about 45cm/18in high and develops clusters of daisy-like purple flowers from early to late summer. Space plants 30cm/12in apart. Varieties include 'Darkest of All' (violet-blue), 'Felicity' (pink), 'Foerster's Liebling' (deep pink), 'Gaiety' (bright pink) and 'Quakeress' (mauve-pink).*

ANCHUSA AZUREA
(Bugloss/Alkanet) grows 90cm–1.5m/3–5ft high. Bright blue, salver-shaped flowers appear during early and mid-summer. Space plants 30–38cm/12–15in apart. Varieties include 'Loddon Royalist' (gentian blue), 'Dropmore' and 'Morning Glory' (both deep blue).

ANAPHALUS YEDOENSIS
(Pearl Everlasting) grows about 60cm/2ft high, with grey-green leaves and bunched heads of small, white flowers from mid- to late summer. Space plants 30–38cm/ 12–15in apart. It is ideal for planting in dry, sandy soil, and can be used in flower arrangements.

ANTHEMIS CUPANIANA
grows 60–30cm/8–12in high and develops daisy-like white flowers with yellow centres during early and mid-summer. These are borne above finely dissected, aromatic, grey leaves. Space plants 25cm/10in apart. It creates good displays in containers as well as beds.

BURNING BUSH

Fragrant, white flowers

Variously known as Bastard Dittany, Dittany, Fraxinella and Gas Plant, the Burning Bush (Dictamnus albus) was introduced into Britain from Europe during the reign of Queen Elizabeth I, in the sixteenth century. The plant owes part of its fame to the flower spikes which have minute reddish-brown glands that secrete an etheric oil which is strongest when the flower is fading. If a lighted match is set against the flower it responds with a reddish, crackling flame.

CLAY SOILS

❖

CLAY soils are notoriously heavy and difficult to cultivate, as well as being wet and cold. However, they are usually richer in plant foods than sandy soils, where nutrients are rapidly leached out of the topsoil.

Many herbaceous perennials grow in clay soil, but ensure it is well drained so that it is not continually wet during winter, which encourages roots to decay and prevents rapid warming in spring. For this reason, clay soils are frequently described as 'late'.

Before planting herbaceous plants, dig the soil thoroughly and deeply, breaking up the subsoil but ensuring soil from different levels is not mixed. When digging, mix plenty of manure and compost into the soil. This will aid drainage and improve fertility.

OTHER PLANTS

- Achillea filipendulina
- Alchemilla mollis
- Centaurea dealbata
- Centaurea montana
- Coreopsis verticillata
- Epimedium pinnatum
- Epimedium x rubrum
- Hostas – *range of species and varieties*
- Ligularia dentata (Senecio clivorum)
- Macleaya cordata
- Phlomis fruticosa
- Polemonium caeruleum
- Potentilla – *Garden Hybrids*
- Rheum palmatum
- Sidalcea malviflora
- Stachys byzantina (S. olympica/S. lanata)

PLATYCODON GRANDIFLORUM *(Balloon Flower) grows 30–60cm/ 1–2ft high, with blue flowers in summer. Plant about 38cm/15in apart.*

SIDALCEA MALVIFLORA *grows 75cm–1.2m/ 2¹⁄2–4ft high, with flowers throughout summer. Space 45cm/18in apart.*

HEMEROCALLIS HYBRIDS *(Day Lilies) grow 60–90cm/2–3ft high and bear a wealth of flowers up to 18cm/7in wide. Space plants 45cm/18in apart. There are many varieties.*

LYSIMACHIA PUNCTATA *(Yellow Loosestrife) grows 60–75cm/2–2¹⁄2ft high and develops spires of bright yellow, cup-shaped flowers from early to late summer. Space plants 38–45cm/ 15–18in apart.*

RUDBECKIA FULGIDA *(Coneflower) grows 60– 90cm/2–3ft high and develops large, daisy-like, yellow to orange flowers from mid- to late summer. Space plants 45–50cm/ 18–20in apart.*

ASTER x FRIKARTII *grows 60–75cm/2–2¹⁄2ft high and has dark green leaves and orange-centred, 5cm/2in-wide, blue flowers from mid-summer to autumn. It is a hybrid between A. amellus and A. thomsonii. Most other asters will also survive in clay soil, but ensure it is not at all waterlogged.*

ASTRANTIA MAJOR *(Masterwort) grows 50– 60cm/20–24in high and develops star-like, greenish pink flowers during early and mid-summer. Space plants 30–38cm/12–15in apart. Other astrantias include A. carniolica, with white, star-like flowers tinged pink during mid- and late summer.*

CRAMBE CORDIFOLIA *(Colewort) grows 1.5– 1.8m/5–6ft high and develops broad, heart-shaped leaves and widely branching stems that bear countless white flowers during early summer. Space plants 90cm–1.2m/3–4ft apart. It is ideal for planting at the backs of borders, where it creates a dramatic display.*

GERANIUM PRATENSE *'Johnson's Blue' (Meadow Crane's-bill) grows 38cm/ 15in high and develops light blue flowers from mid-summer to autumn. Space plants 38cm/15in apart. There are several other superb species and varieties, some with double flowers.*

ICELANDIC DYE

The flowers of Meadow Crane's-bill, native to much of the Northern Hemisphere, are said to have been used in Iceland to create a blue-grey dye for the clothing of the heroes of the sagas. Early names include Odin's Grace and Odin's Favour, as well as Gratia Dei, *a translation of the German word* Gottesgnade.

COASTAL AREAS

❖

SALT-LADEN wind and strong and violent gusts are the problems affecting gardening in coastal areas. Many plants can survive these conditions, but they need a good start in life and this includes creating a screen to protect them from strong winds. Hedges and, on a large scale, screens of pine trees can be used, but these take some time to become established.

On a shorter time scale, temporary wattle-hurdles and canvas screens enable roots of small plants to become established. Other ways to assist plants include improving soil to speed up root establishment, staking plants and mulching in spring. Also, it is beneficial to put plants in small groups, so that each is able to offer protection to its neighbour.

OTHER PLANTS

- Anemone x hybrida
- Armeria plantaginea (A. pseudarmeria)
- Catananche caerulea
- Cynara scolymus
- Cynoglossum nervosum
- Crambe cordifolia
- Echinops ritro
- Eryngium giganteum
- Eryngium maritimum
- Eryngium planum
- Euphorbia wulfenii
- Limonium latifolium
- Lychnis coronaria
- Myosotidium hortensia
- Salvia superba
- Scrophularia aquatica
- Sedum spectabile
- Stachys byzantina

EUPHORBIA GRIFFITHII *is 60–75cm/2–2½ft high and develops flame-like bracts in clusters up to 10cm/4in across during early summer. Space plants 50–60cm/ 20–24in apart. Varieties include 'Fireglow' (brilliant flame orange) and 'Dixter' (orange-red). After flowering, the bracts fade to green.*

OLD-AGE ELIXIR

Eryngiums were grown in Elizabethan gardens, but the European native Sea Holly (Eryngium maritimum) was used medicinally. In the late sixteenth century it was said that the roots, when preserved with sugar, 'are exceeding good to be given to old and aged people that are consumed and withered with age, and which want natural moisture'.

PHLOMIS RUSSELIANA *grows 75cm-1.2m/ 2½-4ft high and reveals whorls of yellow flowers during early and mid-summer. Space plants about 38cm/15in apart. The Jerusalem Sage (P. fruticosa) also has similar whorls of brighter yellow flowers.*

ASTER AMELLUS *(Italian Aster) grows 45–60cm/1½–2ft high and creates a mass of 5cm/2in-wide, daisy-like flowers during late summer and into autumn. Space plants 38cm/15in apart. Varieties include 'King George' (violet-blue) and 'Sonia' (rose-pink).*

CENTAUREA MACROCEPHALA *grows 90cm-1.5m/3-5ft high and develops stout stems that produce yellow, thistle-like flowers about 7.5cm/3in wide during early and mid-summer. The leaves are rough and light green. Space plants 50–60cm/20–24in apart. Position it at the back of a border.*

ERYNGIUM ALPINUM *is 45–60cm/1½–2ft high and develops greenish blue leaves around its base. From mid-summer to early autumn it reveals steel blue flowers. Space plants 30–38cm/12–15in apart. The flowers are ideal for winter flower decorations.*

KNIPHOFIA HYBRIDS *(Torch Lily/Red Hot Poker) range in height from 45cm/ 1½ft to 1.5m/5ft high. They all create poker-like heads, in colours including yellow, orange and red. Plant them about two-thirds of their height apart.*

DIERAMA PULCHERRIMUM *(Wand Flower/Angel's Fishing Rod) grows 1.2–1.5m/4–5ft high and develops deep red flowers from mid-summer to autumn. Space plants about 38cm/ 15in apart. Varieties include shades of pink, purple and violet, as well as white.*

VERONICA SPICATA *grows 15–45cm/6–18in high and develops dense, terminal spires of blue flowers from early to the end of summer. Varieties include 'Barcarolle' (rose pink). 'Crater Lake Blue' (ultramarine blue), 'Pavane' (deep pink) and 'Heidekind' (beautiful, glowing deep pink).*

ATTRACTIVE FOLIAGE

❖

THESE plants have colourful or attractively shaped leaves – or both. Some, such as Lady's Mantle *(Alchemilla mollis)*, have a gentle and demure appearance, while others, like *Ophiopogon plansicapus* 'Nigrescens', are dominantly coloured and if used too frequently in a border can be overpowering to the eye. They also tend to dominate other plants and therefore must be used with great care if they are not to be obtrusive.

Several of these plants agreeably nestle alongside path and border edges; they include Lady's Mantle, *Bergenia cordifolia, Astilbe* x *arendsii* and *Festuca glauca*. Others grow higher and need more space. These include *Scrophularia aquatica* 'Variegata', *Euphorbia characias* and *Rodgersia podophyllum*.

OTHER PLANTS

- Acanthus mollis
- Aegopodium podagraria *'Variegata'*
- Anaphalis triplinervis
- Artemisia lactiflora
- Artemisia ludoviciana
- Cynara cardunculus
- Epimedium perralderianum
- Epimedium x rubrum
- Hosta – *wide range*
- Melissa officinalis *'Aurea'*
- Pulmonaria saccharata *'Leopard'*
- Pulmonaria saccharata *'Argentea'*
- Stachys byzantina
- Tiarella cordifolia

EUPHORBIA CHARACIAS *grows 90cm–1m/3–4ft high, with blue-grey, oblong leaves. During early summer the leaves are surmounted by sulphur yellow flowers and paper-like bracts. Space plants 75–90cm/2½–3ft apart.*

OPHIOPOGON PLANSICAPUS *'Nigrescens' grows about 20cm/8in high and develops narrow black leaves. White-tinged violet flowers appear during summer, followed by purple-black berries. Space plants 30cm/12in apart. Plant in well-drained, fertile soil.*

SCROPHULARIA AQUATICA *'Variegata' (Water Figwort), grows 90cm/3ft and displays green leaves attractively splashed and striped cream. Space these handsome plants 38–45cm/15–18in apart.*

RODGERSIA PODOPHYLLA *grows 90cm–1.2m/3–4ft high and displays mid-green, horse-chestnut-like leaves and pale buff flowers during early and mid-summer. Space plants 60cm/2ft apart. R. pinnata has deep green leaves.*

ALCHEMILLA MOLLIS *(Lady's Mantle) grows 30–45cm/12–18in high, with light green, hairy leaves surmounted from early to mid-summer by yellowish green, star-shaped flowers. Space these spectacular plants 30–38cm/12–15in apart. Ideal for edging paths.*

BERGENIA CORDIFOLIA *grows 30cm/12in high, with mid-green, glossy, rounded leaves with a heart-shaped base. During mid- and late spring it develops clusters of bell-shaped, lilac-rose flowers. Space plants 30–38cm/12–15in apart.*

ASTILBE x ARENDSII *grows 60–75cm/2–2½ft high, with fern-like, deep green leaves and lax, pyramidal spires of flowers during early and mid-summer. Space plants 38cm/15in apart. There are many colours including red, pink and white.*

FESTUCA GLAUCA *is an ornamental grass, about 23cm/9in high and with blue-grey leaves. During early and mid-summer, purple spikelets appear on stems about 30cm/12in long. Space plants 15–23cm/6–9in apart. It is superb when three or five plants are grown in a cluster near to a path's edge, especially at the junction of two paths.*

HANDSOME RUE

For centuries, Rue (Ruta graveolens) *was used as an antiseptic and antidote to poisons. During the seventeenth and eighteenth centuries it was strewn in law courts as protection against gaol fever. However, it also has very attractive leaves; the variety 'Jackson's Blue' forms a neat mound about 45cm/18in high of bright, blue-grey leaves. Although strictly an evergreen shrub, it is frequently grown in herbaceous borders.*

CUT FLOWERS FOR HOME DECORATION

❖

Herbaceous plants are ideal for providing flowers to fill vases indoors in summer. Most flowers are cut from plants growing in borders, but to prevent them being spoiled – and if space allows – grow a few in an out-of-the-way corner.

Never cut flowers for home decoration from wilting plants. In fact, the ideal way is to water the plants thoroughly and to cut the flowers early the following morning, before the full force of the sun reaches them. Cut the stems at a 45-degree angle and remove the lower leaves. Then, place the stems in a bucket of deep, cool water for twenty-four hours before arranging them. Special additives can be put in the water to encourage the flowers to last longer.

OTHER PLANTS

- Achillea ptarmica
- Acontinum napellus
- Aster amellus
- Aster novi-belgii
- Centaurea dealbata
- Doronicum plantagineum
- Echinops ritro
- Gaillardia aristata
- Gypsophila paniculata
- Liatris spicata
- Limonium latifolium
- Lychnis chalcedonica
- Phlox paniculata
- Physostegia virginiana
- Pyrethrum – *hybrid varieties*
- Rudbeckia laciniata
- Scabiosa caucasica
- Solidago – *Garden Hybrids*

CATANANCHE CAERULEA *(Cupid's Dart) grows 45–60cm/1½–2ft high and has blue flowers during early and mid-summer. Varieties include 'Major' (deep lavender blue) and 'Alba' (white). Space plants 30–38cm/12–15in apart. The flowers can be displayed fresh or dried.*

CHRYSANTHEMUM MAXIMUM *(Shasta Daisy) grows 75–90cm/2½–3ft high and develops white flowers up to 7.5cm/3in wide from early to late summer. Space plants 38cm/15in apart. Varieties include 'Horace Read' (creamy white), 'Wirral Pride' (semi-double/white).*

COREOPSIS VERTICILLATA *grows 45–60cm/1½–2ft high, with finely divided, somewhat fern-like, bright green leaves. Throughout summer it bears yellow flowers. Space plants 30–38cm/12–15in apart. Varieties include 'Grandiflora' (rich yellow) and 'Zagreb' (golden yellow).*

LUPINS *'Russell Strain' grow about 90cm/3ft high and create long spires of pea-like flowers during early and mid-summer. Space plants 60–75cm/2–2½ft apart. The wide range of varieties includes white, blue, red, pink and yellow.*

LYSIMACHIA PUNCTATA *(Yellow Loosestrife) grows 60–75/2–2½ft high and develops bright yellow flowers in large clusters, up to 38cm/15in long from early to late summer. Space plants 38–45cm/15–18in apart.*

ZANTEDESCHIA AETHIOPICA *'Crowborough' (Arum Lily) grows 45–75cm/1½–2½ft high and produces white flowers during mid- to late summer. Space plants 38–45cm/15–18in apart.*

ACHILLEA FILIPENDULINA *(Fern-leaf Yarrow) grows 90cm–1.2m/3–4ft high and develops 10–15cm/4–6in-wide heads of lemon yellow flowers from mid- to late summer. Space plants 75–90cm/2½–3ft apart. 'Coronation Gold' has deep yellow flowers from early to late summer.*

AGAPANTHUS *'Headbourne Hybrids' (African Lily) grow 60–75cm/2–2½ft high and develop violet-blue to pale blue flowers in umbrella-like heads from mid- to late summer. These hybrids are slightly hardier than the species types. Space these distinctive plants 38–45cm/15–18in apart.*

ALSTROEMERIA *'Ligtu Hybrids' (Peruvian Lily) grow 60–75cm/2–2½ft high and develop masses of trumpet-shaped flowers in pink, scarlet, flame, orange, yellow and white from early to late summer. Space plants 30cm/12in apart. They are ideal for room decoration, as well as creating bright displays in borders.*

SHRUBS AND SMALL TREES

Shrubs and trees form the permanent framework of most gardens. Some trees and shrubs are deciduous (shedding their leaves in autumn and producing fresh ones in spring), while others are evergreen and throughout the year are clothed in attractive leaves. A few of these are semi-evergreen in cold winters.

Shrubs and trees have many decorative qualities and apart from magnificent displays of flowers in winter, spring or summer, several of them are grown for their coloured or variegated leaves, richly shaded bark and shoots, or decorative berries in autumn and into early winter. Others are known for richly coloured leaves in autumn.

While buying and planting shrubs and trees is covered in this chapter, pruning them is discussed on pages 304 to 309. Hedges are also featured in this chapter and a wide range of flowering as well as foliage types are described. Planting a hedge is detailed within this chapter, while pruning and clipping hedges is covered on page 300.

BUYING SHRUBS AND TREES

◆

As MUCH care and thought is needed when buying garden plants as for any item in the home. Indeed, as shrubs and trees often outlive many household items – as well as perhaps dominating gardens for several decades – their selection needs much more careful thought.

Always buy shrubs and trees from reputable sources, as you not only want to be assured the plant is healthy, but that it is the variety you want. Send away for catalogues from well-known nurseries, as well as visiting local garden centres. And do not be unduly influenced by prices: high prices do not invariably mean better plants. Have a general look at the nursery or garden centre: if it is neglected and radiates little pride, this may be reflected in the quality of plants. And if in doubt about plants, talk to the manager to gain a further opinion. Inferior shrubs seldom recover to develop into satisfactory healthy plants.

WHAT TO LOOK FOR

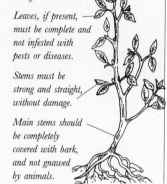

Always inspect plants before buying them: if they are bought through the mail, check them when received and advise the supplier soon after if you are not satisfied.

Leaves, if present, must be complete and not infested with pests or diseases.

Stems must be strong and straight, without damage.

Main stems should be completely covered with bark, and not gnawed by animals.

Bare-rooted plants should have roots well spaced out and not clustered at one side.

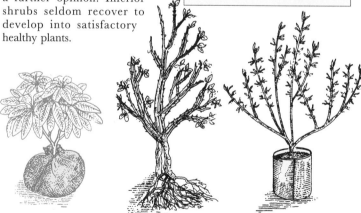

BALLED *plants are mainly conifers or small evergreen shrubs with hessian tightly wrapped around the root-ball. They are mainly sold during late summer and early autumn, or in spring.*

BARE-ROOTED *plants are deciduous shrubs and trees that have been dug up during their dormant period (late autumn to late winter), wrapped and despatched to customers for planting.*

CONTAINER-GROWN *shrubs and trees are either evergreen or deciduous, and can be planted throughout the year. These are sold mainly by garden centres, direct to gardeners.*

EARLY NURSERIES

Perhaps the first assurance that good, healthy plants would be offered for sale by nurserymen was in the seventeenth century, when in 1605 James I of England (James VI of Scotland) granted a charter to the Company of Gardeners which prevented the sale of 'dead and corrupt plants, seeds and stockes, and trees'.

Monastic gardens were probably the first source of seeds and plants in Europe. However, ornamental gardens in Persia certainly long pre-date the Christian era and their influence spread to Europe, possibly through Turkey, in about the middle of the fourteenth century. Earlier the Romans had been instrumental in spreading southern European plants throughout their empire.

AMERICAN NURSERIES

The earliest nurseries in North America were established by Robert Prince on Long Island in 1737, and slightly later by John Bartram in Philadelphia. Both were centres for the import of European plants, as well as the export of native ones. And both nurseries published extensive catalogues of trees, shrubs and herbaceous plants.

Incidentally, during the Revolutionary War (1793–1802), shipments of plants from Prince's Nursery to the Empress Joséphine in France were allowed to travel unharmed, in much the same way that the English nurseryman John Kennedy was allowed to travel regularly between London and France during the Napoleonic Wars (1805–1815) to advise Joséphine about her garden at Malmaison, just outside Paris. Joséphine also bought many plants from Kennedy's nursery, at a cost of £2,600 in 1802 alone.

WHERE TO BUY...

Shrubs and trees can be bought from several sources.
- Garden centres *mainly sell container-grown plants and therefore it is essential to visit them in a car, although some centres offer a delivery service within a limited area. From late autumn to late winter they may also sell bare-rooted shrubs, mainly roses.*
- Nurseries *offer bare-rooted as well as container-grown shrubs and trees. The container-grown ones – evergreen and deciduous – are available throughout the year, bare-rooted ones in winter and they are usually delivered by carriers. Balled evergreens are sent out in late summer and early autumn, as well as spring.*
- High street garden shops usually *offer a limited but popular range of container-grown plants, as well as bare-rooted shrubs, trees and roses from autumn to late winter.*
- Mail order nurseries *offer bare-rooted deciduous trees and shrubs, as well as balled evergreens. Specialist tree and shrub nurseries issue catalogues and it is wise to order the plants early. They are delivered by carriers.*

PREPARING AND PLANNING A SHRUB BORDER

◆

MANY trees and shrubs are selected for specific places, perhaps to create focal points or to hide unattractive features. But they can also be used to form borders, when they are planted on their own or perhaps with under-plantings of some small bulbs. Alternatively, they can be used in mixed plantings, where they jostle with herbaceous plants. Another choice is a floriferous winter garden or a scented border. But whatever the feature, it does need planning to ensure that colours do not clash, small shrubs are not hidden, and the balance between 'foliage' and 'flowering' shrubs is satisfactory.

Sketch out the garden's shape and size on graph paper, then draw in the borders and shrubs. When it looks right, try to visualize it on the ground by laying a hosepipe or thick rope to simulate the border's edge. View the area from all angles, as well as from upstairs rooms before finally deciding on the design.

HEIGHTS AND SPREADS

When planning a border, knowing the height and spread of each shrub or tree after a few years is essential. Therefore, throughout this book, heights and spreads of shrubs are given for a period of ten to fifteen years after being planted in good soil, an ideal position and a suitable climate.

Improve soil prior to planting by installing drainage, thorough cultivation and addition of decomposed organic material. Later, mulching and keeping the soil moist also helps. Unfortunately, it is more difficult to provide ideal positions when the area is windswept and exceptionally cold. In these areas, long-term planning includes planting windbreaks and hedges to reduce the wind's speed.

1. WHEN *shrubs and trees are planted into existing gardens, their selection is relatively easy. But for bare-site areas detailed planning is essential.*

2. SKETCH *the site's shape on graph paper, marking in fixed points such as fences and the house. Mark the paths and draw in borders. Then add shrubs and trees.*

3. TRANSFER *the plan to the garden. Slight modification may be necessary, so first outline the shape of the beds by using a long hose-pipe or rope.*

ASSESS *soil acidity by using a simple soil-testing kit: a sample is mixed with water, an indicator fluid added and the result compared with a colour chart to indicate the acidity. Alternatively, use a soil pH meter.*

MAKING SOIL LESS ACID

The amount of lime needed to reduce soil acidity (raising the pH) depends on the form in which it is applied and type of soil. As a guide, the following amounts of lime will decrease acidity by about 1 pH. First, however, check the soil with a pH soil-testing kit (left).

Soil	Hydrated lime	Ground limestone
Clay	610g/sq m (18oz/sq yd)	815g/sq m (24oz/sq yd)
Loam	405g/sq m (12oz/sq yd)	545g/sq m (16oz/sq yd)
Sand	205g/sq m (6oz/sq yd)	270g/sq m (8oz/sq yd)

SCENTED GARDENS

These are a special delight, and although climbers smothering arches with rich scents and colours are frequently thought to be the epitome of a scented garden, fragrant shrubs alongside a path are just as desirable.

It is possible to have scented shrubs in flower throughout the year, but winter is when they are especially appreciated. A few winter-flowering shrubs can be a bonus in all gardens. Ensure they are planted relatively close to a path, so that there is no temptation to tread on borders when trying to smell their fragrance. Incidentally, if elderly people are likely to use the path, make sure it is firm. For blind people ensure thorny roses are not nearby, and form paths with gravel edgings so that the sound, when walked on, indicates the edges. Create scented gardens in wind-sheltered positions and with a garden bench nearby, so that the fragrances can be appreciated at leisure.

CHLOROSIS

Acid-loving shrubs and trees in chalky soils often become chlorotic, causing leaves to whiten and bleach.

Chlorosis occurs when iron is 'locked up'. Adding ordinary iron to the soil does not help, because the high pH makes it unavailable to plants. To overcome this, apply chelated iron (sold as Sequestrene). Two or three applications a year should keep plants healthy.

Magnesium may also be deficient and is sometimes included in chelated products. Alternatively, apply Epsom salts (magnesium sulphate) as a foliar feed. Dissolve 3g in 1 litre (½oz in 1 gal) of water. First, test this on a few plants.

PLANTING A CONTAINER-GROWN SHRUB

REMOVING from one house to another is invariably traumatic and fraught with problems, even for the most resilient person: being transferred from its nursery position to a place in a garden can be just as traumatic for a shrub, tree or conifer.

In earlier times, the only choice between the types of plants to plant was 'bare-rooted' or 'balled'. Deciduous trees and shrubs were invariably sold as bare-rooted plants for planting during their dormant seasons (late autumn to late winter). Evergreens – and especially conifers – were sold as balled plants. These plants had been dug up and their roots (and soil) tightly wrapped in hessian. Planting time for these is during late summer and early autumn, or in spring when the soil has warmed up after winter.

Nowadays, a wide range of shrubs and trees is sold as container-grown plants. These are deciduous or evergreen trees and shrubs, as well as conifers, and can be planted at any time when the weather allows and the soil is not frozen or excessively wet.

CONTAINER-GROWN PLANTS
These have revolutionized gardening and enabled the modern fever for instant gardens to be satisfied.

Buy container-grown plants only from reputable nurseries: occasionally, plants in containers are offered for sale that until a few weeks earlier had been growing in nurserybeds, and therefore are not fully established in the container. When planting these, soil falls away from the roots and you are left with a plant which only pretends to be container grown. Ideally, the plant should have roots that fill – but not over-fill – the container, holding the compost in a firm ball.

1. UNTIL *the introduction of container-grown plants, most evergreen shrubs were sold 'balled': that is, the root-ball wrapped in hessian. They are still occasionally sold in this state. Take care not to knock the root-ball, as this dislodges its soil.*

2. THE *day before planting, thoroughly water the root-ball. Leave the hessian in place and dip the complete root-ball in a bucket of water until air bubbles cease to rise. Allow all water to drain away before planting the shrub or conifer.*

3. DIG *a hole large enough to accommodate the roots. Fork over its base, then firm to leave a slight mound. Place the roots on top and carefully remove the hessian. Tease out constricted roots and firm friable soil in layers around them.*

1. THE *first step when planting a container-grown shrub or tree is to ensure the compost is moist. The day before planting, water the compost. It may be necessary to do this twice if exceptionally dry. Do not plant it if the ground is frozen or excessively wet, or the weather very cold.*

2. DIG *out a hole, wide and deep enough to accommodate the root-ball. Fork over the base, then firm and leave a slight mound. Place the plant in the hole and remove the container. The top of the soil ball should be slightly lower than the surrounding soil; this allows for subsequent soil settlement.*

3. GENTLY *firm friable soil in layers around the root-ball, taking care not to disturb its position and to push it sideways. Use the heel of your shoe to firm it evenly. When complete, thoroughly but gently water the soil to enable small particles to settle closely around the roots.*

RAPID ESTABLISHMENT
After planting a shrub or tree, rapid establishment is essential, for several reasons:
• To anchor it in the soil and to prevent wind rocking it and loosening the roots. For this reason, use strong stakes to secure trees (see page 50).
• To enable roots to absorb quickly water and chemicals from the soil, thereby initiating growth processes. Water at this stage is especially important to replenish that lost by transpiration through the leaves. This is a continuous process that keeps leaves and stems cool. It also plays a role in the absorption of water from the soil, and its distribution throughout the plant.

Establishment is encouraged by watering the soil around trees and shrubs, then covering with a 7.5cm/3in mulch (layer of decomposed organic material). Additionally, preventing cold winds blowing on plants reduces transpiration (right).

WIND PROTECTION

Cold winter and spring winds damage newly planted conifers and evergreen shrubs. Form a temporary screen of hessian on the windward side. Straw or hay sandwiched between two layers of wire-netting is another method – it can be formed into a U-shape and secured to the ground with strong stakes. Do not completely enclose plants, as a circulation of air is needed around their leaves and stems. In summer, newly-planted container-grown plants may also need protection from hot winds.

PLANTING A BARE-ROOTED SHRUB OR TREE

THESE are deciduous and planted during their dormant period, from late autumn to late winter, when free from leaves. They are usually ordered from nurseries and delivered by carriers, sometime during winter. If poor weather prevents them being planted immediately, dig a trench in a sheltered part of your garden and cover their roots with soil (see opposite, top). However, if the soil is not frozen or excessively wet, and the delay is only for a few days, place them in a cool, dry shed or cellar. Loosen the wrappings to enable air to circulate around the stems.

PREPARATION FOR PLANTING

Remove all packing material and inspect the roots and branches. Cut off damaged roots and trim the ends off, particularly long ones. The roots should be relatively straight and spaced out around the trunk's base. Indeed, unless container-grown trees are in exceptionally large containers it is far better to buy them as bare-rooted types. A walk around many garden centres soon reveals large trees with their roots confined to containers often less than 30cm/12in wide. Trees with twisted roots never recover so that the plant is never securely anchored by the roots to the soil.

Also, check the branches and use sharp secateurs to cut off damaged ones, leaving the remaining ones spaced out. If the roots are dry, stand them in a tub of water overnight before planting.

PLANTING AND STAKING

Planting is described and illustrated below, and the range of stakes to the right. Whatever the method of staking, choose strong stakes – preferably of chestnut, oak, ash or spruce – long enough to allow at least 38cm/15in to be driven into the soil, with the stake's top just below the lowest branch.

Vertical stakes are inserted after the hole has been dug but before the tree is placed in position. If put in afterwards, the tree's roots may be damaged. Oblique stakes and H-types are put in afterwards, but because they extend out from the trunk may later impede grass cutting. The H-type is often used as a remedial support for standard trees if an earlier one has decayed. Also, if a tree is expected eventually to be self-supporting – such as large oaks and elms – it is easily removed later.

During the first few months after using a tree tie to secure a trunk to a stake, check it regularly to ensure the trunk's girth is not being restricted. Also, ensure that soil settlement has not caused the tree tie to strangle the trunk.

Because bare-rooted trees and shrubs are planted in winter, frost may later lift the soil. Therefore, in spring, re-firm the soil. At the same time, adjust the tree tie.

When a tree is planted in a lawn, do not replace turves close to the trunk as this will deprive the plant of both nitrogen and moisture. After a few years, the branches spread and bare soil is not so noticeable. If the tree is deciduous, plant some small spring-flowering bulbs underneath.

1. SOMETIMES, *bare-rooted shrubs and trees arrive when either the soil is frozen or too wet. Also, you may not have the time to plant them immediately. Dig a trench 30cm/12in deep.*

2. CREATE *a small slope at one edge of the trench. Place the roots in the base and stems on the slope. Space them evenly and take care not to put them in one congested heap.*

3. SPREAD *soil over them and gently firm. Plants can be left like this for several weeks, but at the first opportunity plant them. Keep the soil moist to prevent roots drying.*

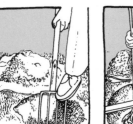

1. PLANT *bare-rooted deciduous shrubs and trees during their dormant period, from late autumn to late winter and whenever the soil is neither frozen nor too wet. Dig out a hole. Place the soil on a piece of sacking.*

2. FORK *over the hole's base and form a small mound. Position the plant, spread out its roots and use a straight board to check it is slightly deeper than before. The old level is indicated by a dark mark on the stem.*

3. WORK *friable soil over, between and around the roots. Lift the stem up and down several times to enable friable soil to run between the roots. Replace friable topsoil in thin layers and firm it with your heel.*

METHODS OF STAKING

Securing trunks of newly planted trees to stakes is essential to prevent roots being rocked. There are three basic methods:

- *Vertical stakes are inserted while trees are planted, and positioned on the windward side of the trunk. The top must be just below the lowest branch.*

wind

- *Oblique stakes are inserted after planting and best used for bushes or half-standards. The stake's top must face into the wind.*

wind

- *H-stakes are inserted after a tree has been planted and often used as a remedial measure.*

PLANTING A HEDGE

ONCE planted, a hedge might remain part of a garden for thirty or more years. Both its selection and planting therefore need care. A range of hedges primarily grown for their foliage is described and illustrated on page 60, and flowering ones on page 61. In addition, several of the trees and shrubs recommended on page 64 for use in coastal areas can also be used as shelter belts and hedges where salt-spray is a problem.

CHOICE OF PLANTS

Hedges are created from several types of plants, which influences the times they are planted:
• Balled plants: usually evergreen shrubs and conifers; planted in late summer and early autumn, or in spring when the soil is warm.
• Bare-rooted plants: planted from late autumn to late winter.
• Container-grown plants: planted at any time when the soil and weather allow. Fuller details on page 49.

PREPARING THE AREA

Prepare the planting position a few months before setting plants in the ground, using a spade to dig about 30cm/12in deep and a garden fork to break up the trench's base. If a single row of hedging plants is to be planted, prepare an area 30cm/12in wide. However, when planting a double, staggered row, prepare an area 15–18in/38–45cm wide.

Ensure all weeds are removed and fork in generous amounts of well-decayed compost. If the area is very wet, form a ridge and raise the soil level 15–30cm/6–12in, to a width of 60cm/2ft.

PLANTING THE HEDGE

When setting plants in a single row, use the spacings indicated on pages 60 to 61. However, for hedges formed of two rows (with individual plants staggered) space the plants about one-third of the suggested spacings further apart in the rows, with a similar distance between them.

1. THOROUGH *soil preparation is just as essential for hedges as when planting shrubs and trees. Dig out a deep, wide trench, forking over the base and adding compost.*

2. POSITION *each plant so that it is slightly deeper than before (to allow for soil settlement) and spread friable soil around and over its roots. Ensure the plants are upright.*

3. FIRM *the soil by treading along the row. Loose planting leaves air pockets around the roots and retards establishment. It also encourages soil to become dry very quickly.*

Firm planting is essential, as well as spreading out the plant's roots.

Young plants will need to be watered until they are fully established, especially if the weather is dry immediately after they are planted. In such circumstances, it is more difficult to establish large plants than small ones.

Regular dressings of general fertilizers are essential in spring during a hedge's early years, especially if growth is slow and the soil sandy and poor.

It is essential to prune all hedging plants – except conifers – soon after they are planted. This encourages the development of shoots low down on plants, creating bushy growth from the hedge's base to its top.

Where hedges are planted along a boundary, ensure the plants are positioned at least half the expected width of the hedge in from the edge of your property. If planted directly on the boundary line, the hedge will intrude on the neighbouring property. Some neighbours will not mind this, but there is a risk that others will cut off shoots and leaves protruding on their side and may return them to you.

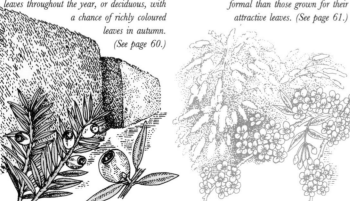

HEDGES *grown for their attractive foliage can be evergreen, with green or variegated leaves throughout the year, or deciduous, with a chance of richly coloured leaves in autumn. (See page 60.)*

HEDGES *primarily grown for their flowers create dominant features, less formal than those grown for their attractive leaves. (See page 61.)*

WALLS, FENCES AND HEDGES

If you live in a city, then the first choice of a barrier to separate your garden from a neighbour's is probably a brick wall or, at least, a high boarded fence. However, walls are expensive and time-consuming to construct and more likely than hedges to be blown over during high winds. Also, hedges are living parts of gardens and better able to harmonize with their surroundings.

Fences have a softer texture and outline than brick walls, but even these need clothing with climbers or wall-shrubs.

Hedges create less wind turbulence than walls and fences as they filter wind rather than creating a barrier that generates buffeting, plant-damaging currents.

WINTER-FLOWERING SHRUBS AND TREES

❖

D URING the cold, dull days of winter, flowering shrubs and trees are especially welcome. They range in size from ground-hugging types to those 1.8m/6ft or more high. Therefore, there are shrubs to fit all gardens, and several of them are featured here.

Because they bring colour to gardens when few other plants are flowering, position them where they can be seen easily; perhaps at the junctions of paths, sides of patios or as focal points a little way down a garden.

Winter-flowering shrubs need little pruning, other than removing dead, crossing or diseased shoots in spring, after the flowers fade.

Plant small bulbs under deciduous types to create extra colour and interest in spring.

OTHER SHRUBS AND TREES

- **Erica x darleyensis:** *Early winter to late spring; range of varieties – white, pink or purple.*
- **Erica lusitanica:** *early winter to late spring; white.*
- **Chimonanthus praecox:** *early to mid-winter; yellow; spicy scent.*
- **Hamamelis japonica:** *late winter to early spring; yellow.*
- **Lonicera fragrantissima:** *early winter to early spring; creamy-white; fragrant.*
- **Mahonia japonica:** *early winter to early spring, lemon-yellow; lily-of-the-valley fragrance.*

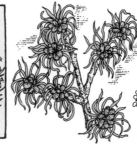

ERICA HERBACEA
(E. CARNEA)
HEATHER/ SNOW HEATHER/ SPRING HEATHER
Height: 20–30cm/8–12in
Spread: 38–60cm/15–24in
Mound-forming, spreading, evergreen shrub with light green leaves, flowering from late autumn to late spring, depending on the variety. Wide colour range.
<u>Easily grown</u>

HAMAMELIS MOLLIS
CHINESE WITCH HAZEL
Height: 1.8–2.4m/ 6–8ft
Spread: 1.8–2.4m/ 6–8ft
Deciduous shrub or small tree with golden-yellow, spider-like, sweetly scented flowers in early or mid-winter and continuing until early spring. Leaves turn yellow in autumn. Several forms: 'Pallida' has pale yellow flowers.
<u>Slow growing</u>

MAHONIA 'CHARITY'
HOLLY GRAPE
Height: 1.8–2.4m/ 6–8ft
Spread: 1.5–1.8m/ 5–6ft
Evergreen shrub with stiff, dark green, holly-like leaves and 23–30cm/ 9–12in-long spires of deep yellow flowers from late autumn to late winter. Ideal for planting in a wild garden, in moist soil and light, dappled shade.
<u>Winter colour and fragrance</u>

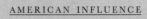

CORNUS MAS
CORNELIAN CHERRY/ SORBET
Height: 2.4–3m /8–10ft
Spread: 1.8–2.4m / 6–8ft
Twiggy, deciduous shrub with dark leaves and small, yellow flowers from mid-winter to mid-spring. Edible, cherry-like, red fruits follow the flowers. In autumn, leaves assume reddish-purple shades before falling.
<u>Slow-growing</u>

DAPHNE MEZEREUM
FEBRUARY DAPHNE/ MEZEREON/ MEZEREUM
Height: 1.2–1.5m/ 4–5ft
Spread: 75cm/1.2m/ 2¹/2–4ft
Bushy, deciduous, somewhat erect shrub with scented, purplish-red flowers from late winter to mid-spring. These are followed by red, poisonous berries. Also, a white-flowered form.
<u>Winter scent</u>

DAPHNE ODORA
WINTER DAPHNE
Height: 1.2–1.5m/ 4–5ft
Spread: 1.2–1.5m/ 4–5ft
Bushy, slightly tender, evergreen shrub with shiny, mid-green leaves. Pale purple flowers appear in clustered heads from mid-winter to mid-spring. The form D. o. 'Aureomarginata' is hardier, with narrow creamy-white edges to the leaves.
<u>Delicious fragrance</u>

VIBURNUM TINUS
(LAURUSTINUS)
Height: 1.8–2.4m/ 6–8ft
Spread: 1.8–2.1m/ 6–7ft
Bushy, rounded, evergreen shrub with mid- to deep green leaves and white, pink-budded flowers from late autumn to late spring. 'Eve Price' has a dense, compact habit and pink-tinged flowers that are carmine when in bud.
<u>Easily grown</u>

AMERICAN INFLUENCE

The Mahonia family was named in honour of the Irish-American horticulturist Bernard McMahon, who lived from 1775 to 1816. He left Ireland for political reasons, in 1796 settled in Philadelphia and in 1806 published The American Gardener's Calendar, *which was still being reprinted more than fifty years later. He established a nursery and seed shop, which became a meeting point for botanists and nurserymen. Indeed, many seeds collected by plant hunters in North America were passed to him for germination, including those gathered by the Captains Merriwether Lewis and William Clark during their journey across North America during the first few years of the nineteenth century. Two well-known genera of plants named after these two men include* Lewisia *(herbaceous and evergreen semi-succulent perennials now grown in rock gardens) and* Clarkia *(a genus of hardy annuals).*

SPRING-FLOWERING SHRUBS AND TREES

❖

TO MANY people, pink-flowered Japanese cherries are the epitome of spring, but there are other trees and shrubs to choose from. Dominant splashes of Gorse *(Ulex)* are eye-catching on commons in spring, but also try planting the double-flowered form in your garden. Forsythia has a shorter flowering period, but is just as dominant when in bloom. Magnolias are also attractive, with large and spectacular flowers.

Some spring-flowering shrubs need regular pruning – but not all. Forsythia, for instance, needs to be pruned immediately its flowers fade, cutting out flowered wood; whereas Gorse needs no regular treatment, although leggy plants can be cut back in spring.

OTHER SHRUBS AND TREES

- Forsythia x intermedia: *early to mid-spring; golden-yellow. Many other forsythias flower during this season.*
- Pieris japonica: *early to mid-spring; white.*
- Prunus 'Kanzan': *mid- to late spring; double, purple-pink.*
- Prunus x yedoensis: *early and mid-spring; almond scented and bluish-white.*
- Ulex europaeus 'Plenus': *mainly early to late spring; double and yellow.*
- Viburnum x burkwoodii: *early to late spring. Scented.*

CHAENOMELES X SUPERBA

CYDONIA/JAPONICA FLOWERING QUINCE/ JAPANESE QUINCE/
Height: 1.2–1.8m/4–6ft
Spread: 1.2–1.8m/4–6ft
A stiffly lax, deciduous shrub with clusters of flowers from early to late spring. Several varieties, in colours including red, crimson, vermilion, orange-scarlet and pink.
Hardy and slow growing

CYTISUS X PRAECOX

WARMINSTER BROOM
Height: 1.5–1.8m/5–6ft
Spread: 1.5–1.8m/5–6ft
Tumbling, cascading, deciduous shrub with arching stems bearing grey-green leaves. During mid- and late spring it bears fragrant, creamy-white flowers. 'Allgold' has rich, bright yellow flowers.
Easy to grow

KERRIA JAPONICA

JAPANESE ROSE/ JEW'S MALLOW
Height: 1.2–1.8m/4–6ft
Spread: 1.2–1.8m/4–6ft
Slender-stemmed, deciduous, rather lax shrub with bright green leaves and yellow-orange flowers during mid and late spring. 'Pleniflora' (widely known as Bachelor's Buttons) is popular and has double flowers.
Easy to grow

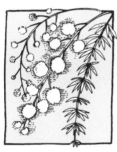

AMELANCHIER LARMARCKII

(A. CANADENSIS)
JUNE BERRY/ SERVICEBERRY/ SHADBUSH/SNOWY MESPILUS
Height: 2.4–3m/8–10ft
Spread: 2.4–3m/8–10ft
Large, rounded, deciduous, shrub with leaves turning soft red or yellow tints in autumn. Pure white flowers during mid-spring.
Ideal as a focal point

BERBERIS X STENOPHYLLA

Height: 1.5–1.8m/5–6ft
Spread: 1.8–2.4m/6–8ft
Widely grown, evergreen shrub with long, arching stems bearing small, dark green leaves and golden-yellow flowers during mid-spring. Round, purple berries appear in autumn, but they are rather sparse. It is often grown to form a wide, dense, arching hedge.
Easy to grow

CAMELLIA X WILLIAMSII

CAMELLIA
Height: 1.8–2.4m/6–8ft
Spread: 1.2–1.8m/4–6ft
Well-known, slightly tender evergreen shrub with glossy, dark green leaves. Flowers late winter to mid-spring, with many varieties in a range of colours, including white, pink and red, in single, semi-double and double forms.
Ideal in a wild garden

MAGNOLIA STELLATA

(M. KOBUS STELLATA)
STAR MAGNOLIA
Height: 2.4–3m/8–10ft
Spread: 2.4–3.6m/8–12ft
Spreading, deciduous tree or large shrub with white, star-shaped, fragrant flowers during early and mid-spring. 'Rosea' has pink-flushed flowers, while the variety 'Water Lily' has larger flowers with more petals.
Slow growing

KEEPING KISSING IN FASHION

Gorse – also known as Furze and Whin – flowers mainly in spring. In some areas it continues in bloom intermittently through to late winter of the following year. This nearly year-around blooming encouraged the old saying:

*'When Gorse is out of bloom,
Kissing is out of season'*

For this reason, a sprig of Gorse was often put into bridal bouquets.

Mistletoe, a parasitic shrub that lives upon trees such as apples, is used to encourage kissing at Christmas. It was originally a wholly English custom but has spread to most countries settled by the English: any person found standing under a bunch of mistletoe at Christmas must now expect to be kissed.

Part of this early enthusiasm for kissing is said to derive from an early English custom of men and women freely kissing when meeting and parting, which continued until the early seventeenth century.

EARLY SUMMER-FLOWERING SHRUBS AND TREES

❖

EARLY summer encourages even more shrubs to burst into flower, flooding gardens with colour. In large gardens, complete borders can be devoted to them, but they are just as attractive when planted close to paths, perhaps just around a corner where they create a surprise – especially when both colourful and scented. Mock Orange (*philadelphus*) is especially fragrant and always attracts attention.

A few of these shrubs, such as potentilla, flower from early to late summer, while others continue from late spring to early or mid-summer. The exact times of flowering are strongly influenced by the weather in your area; planting a shrub against a warm wall encourages early flowering.

OTHER SHRUBS

- Carpenteria californica: *early to mid-summer; white.*
- Deutzia *'Magician': early to mid-summer; mauve-pink edged in white. Also, 'Mont Rose' (pink).*
- Helianthemum nummularium: *early to mid-summer; range of varieties in colours including orange-yellow, yellow, copper, scarlet, pink and cream.*
- Philadelphus *Hybrids: early to mid-summer; mainly white.*
- Potentilla *Hybrids: early to late summer; range of colours.*
- Syringa vulgaris: *early summer; range of colours.*

KOLKWITZIA AMABILIS
BEAUTY BUSH
Height: 1.8–3m/3–10ft
Spread: 1.5–2.4m/5–8ft
Upright, but slightly drooping and spreading, deciduous shrub with stems covered in peeling, brown bark. During late spring and early summer it develops pink flowers with yellow throats. 'Pink Cloud' is popular, with clear pink flowers.
<u>Spectacular shrub</u>

PAEONIA SUFFRUTICOSA
(P. MOUTAN)
MOUTAN PAEONY/ TREE PAEONY
Height: 1.2–1.5m/4–5ft
Spread: 1.2–1.8m/4–6ft
Outstandingly attractive, slightly tender shrub with white, single flowers up to 15cm/5in across during early summer. Several forms, including 'Rock's Variety' (white with crimson blotches).
<u>Damaged by frost</u>

SENECIO 'SUNSHINE'
Height: 1.2–1.5m/4–5ft
Spread: 1.2–1.8m/4–6ft
Dome shaped, evergreen shrub bearing silvery-grey leaves with white, felted undersides. Yellow, daisy-like flowers appear in clustered heads during early and into mid-summer. The foliage is especially attractive when covered with frost or a light covering of snow.
<u>Easy to grow</u>

BUDDLEIA GLOBOSA
ORANGE-BALL TREE
Height: 2.4–3.6m/8–12ft
Spread: 2.1–3m/7–10ft
A slightly tender evergreen shrub that during cold winters can lose some of its leaves. During late spring and early summer it develops clusters of scented, rounded, orange-yellow flowers at the ends of long, slightly lax stems.
<u>Often damaged by frost</u>

CISTUS 'SILVER PINK'
ROCK ROSE
Height: 60–90cm/2–3ft
Spread: 60–90cm/2–3ft
Low-growing evergreen shrub with thick-textured, dark green leaves and 7.5cm/3in-wide, clear pink flowers with yellow centres during early and into mid-summer. There are other hybrids, including C. x lusitanicus.
<u>Ideal for small gardens</u>

HEBE 'MIDSUMMER BEAUTY'
Height: 1–1.2m/3½–4ft
Spread: 1.2–1.5m/4–5ft
Bushy, evergreen shrub bearing light green leaves with reddish undersides. From early to late summer – sometimes into autumn – it bears long tassels of lavender-coloured flowers. Other hebes include 'Great Orme' (bright pink).
<u>Easy to grow</u>

WEIGELA
HYBRIDS (DIERVILLA)
Height: 1.5–1.8m/5–6ft
Spread: 1.5–1.8m/5–6ft
Deciduous hybrids created by crossing Weigela florida with Asiatic species. Spectacular flowers during late spring and early summer. Varieties include 'Abel Carrière' (soft rose), 'Bristol Ruby' (rich ruby-red) and 'Avalanche' (vigorous and white).
<u>Easy to grow</u>

LONE-BUSHES IN IRELAND

Thorn trees have had historic significance as places of judicial assemblies in Britain since before the Romans arrived. They have also had important roles in Ireland, where solitary thorn trees were known as Lone Bushes. They were revered and believed to be trysting trees for 'the Little People'. It was said that these trees were ideal because of their appearance, often looking like 'miniature monarchs of the forest'. To cut down a Lone Bush was thought to bring ill luck and possibly death.

It was the custom for passing pilgrims to hang medals, crucifixes and rosary beads on these trees in acknowledgement of, and thanks for, cures obtained from them.

Thorn trees at crossroads had further significance because the partings of roads were considered meeting places of the spirits. It was also the custom for funeral processions to stop and place crosses on the branches before passing on to the cemetery.

LATE-SUMMER FLOWERING SHRUBS AND TREES

❖

BY MID-SUMMER, gardens frequently reveal a surfeit of flowers, but there are many more exciting shrubs waiting to burst into bloom. Some may have been in bloom since mid-summer, while others reveal their glories solely in late summer and through to the frosts of autumn.

A few of these shrubs have a dominant size, while others are better suited to small gardens. Many, such as *Yucca gloriosa* and *Ceanothus* 'Gloire de Versailles', can be merged into 'mixed' borders to live cheek-by-jowl with herbaceous perennials (plants that die down to soil level in autumn). *Hydrangea macrophylla* is a well-known late-flowering shrub and includes the Hortensia (Mophead) and Lacecap types.

OTHER SHRUBS AND TREES

- Ceanothus *'Gloire de Versailles': early summer to early autumn; soft powder-blue.*
- Fuchsia magellanica: *mid-summer to autumn; crimson and purple.*
- Hydrangea macrophylla *(Hortensia and Lacecaps): mid- to late summer; blue and pink.*
- Lavandula spica: *mid- to late summer; pale grey-blue. 'Hidcote' is deep purple-blue.*
- Romneya coulteri: *mid- to late summer; white.*
- Yucca gloriosa: *late summer to late autumn; creamy-white, tinged red.*

THE BAMBOO GARDEN

Bamboos are members of the grass family that bring many attractive qualities to gardens: they have attractive stems and leaves, create often near- impenetrable screens and, even in gentle breezes, produce a continuous rustling. They like moisture-retentive soil that does not dry out during summer, and shelter from cold winds. And they grow well in sun or partial shade.

Transplanting them is best left until the soil has warmed up in early summer, and do not be surprised if during the first season the stems die back slightly or make little growth. No pruning is needed. They create a new and unusual dimension to gardens and once established need no attention.

Their range is wide and includes:
- Arundinaria japonica *(3–4.5m/10–15ft high): large, dark, glossy green leaves.*
- Arundinaria murieliae *(1.8–2.4m/6–8ft high): beautiful arching stems with narrow, bright green leaves.*
- Arundinaria nitida *(2.4–3m/8–10ft high): purple stems with light green leaves.*
- Arundinaria viridistriata *(1–1.5m/3½–5ft high): dark green leaves striped rich yellow.*
- Phyllostachys nigra *(2.4–3m/8–10ft high): Young stems mature to black after several seasons.*
- Sasa veitchii *(60cm–1.2m/2–4ft high): shiny, green leaves with straw-coloured edges in autumn.*

CARYOPTERIS x CLANDONENSIS
BLUEBEARD
Height: 60cm–1.2m/2–4ft
Spread: 60cm–1.2m/2–4ft
Hardy, deciduous shrubs with narrow, aromatic, grey-green leaves and upright stems bearing clusters of blue flowers during mid- and late summer. Varieties include 'Arthur Simmonds' and 'Heavenly Blue'.
<u>Easy to grow</u>

ESCALLONIA – *VARIETIES*
Height: 1.5–2.1m/5–7ft
Spread: 1.5–2.1m/5–7ft
Rounded, bushy, evergreen shrub with flowers from early to late summer and even into early autumn. Varieties include 'Crimson Spire' (bright crimson), 'Donard Brilliance' (rose-red), 'Peach Blossom' (pink) and 'Pride of Donard' (bright rose).
<u>Easy to grow</u>

EUCRYPHIA x NYMANSENSIS
Height: 3–4.5m/10–15ft
Spread: 1.8–2.4m/6–8ft
Quick-growing evergreen tree with erect branches, shiny green leaves and cream flowers during mid- and late summer. Other eucryphias include E. glutinosa, which is slow growing and has white flowers with large, yellow centres.
<u>Plant in a wild garden</u>

HIBISCUS SYRIACUS
ALTHAEA
Height: 1.8–2.4m/6–8ft
Spread: 1.5–1.8m/5–6ft
Hardy, deciduous shrub with stiff stems and rich green leaves. From mid-summer to autumn it bears a succession of flowers in a wide colour range (depending on variety) including white, pink, red and purple.
<u>Slightly tender</u>

HYDRANGEA PANICULATA *'GRANDIFLORA'*
Height: 2.4–3.6m/8–12ft
Spread: 2.4–3.6m/8–12ft
Hardy, deciduous shrub with terminal clusters up to 30cm/12in long of white flowers, which age to pink, during mid- and late summer. Hydrangea arborescens is another late-flowering hydrangea, with large, dull white flowers.
<u>Vigorous growing</u>

HYPERICUM *'Hidcote'*
(H. patulum 'HIDCOTE')
Height: 90cm–1.2m/3–4ft
Spread: 1.2–1.5m/4–5ft
A deciduous or semi-evergreen shrub with deep green leaves and a profusion of golden-yellow, saucer-like flowers from mid-summer to autumn. The smaller H. olympicum is ideal for planting in sinks or large rock gardens.
<u>Easy to grow</u>

COLOURED LEAVES

LOWERS are attractive but invariably transient in their display. Coloured leaves, however, can be with you throughout the year if the plant is evergreen, or from spring to autumn when deciduous. And even the departure of deciduous leaves in autumn initiates bright colours. Trees and shrubs with bright autumn colours are detailed on page 58.

Some of these shrubs are small and ideal for planting in mixed borders. Others are tall and dominant and better as focal points towards the end of a garden. They can even be used to create colour contrasts, with perhaps the rich purple leaves of *Cotinus coggygria* 'Foliis Purpureis' set against the soft, rich yellow leaves of *Robinia pseudoacacia* 'Frisia'.

OTHER SHRUBS AND TREES

- Acer negundo *'Variegatum': deciduous; pale green leaves irregularly edged in white.*
- Artemisia arborescens: *deciduous or semi-evergreen; silver-white.*
- Calluna vulgaris *'Gold Haze': evergreen; bright gold leaves.*
- Gleditsia triacanthos *'Sunburst': deciduous and spineless; bright yellow young leaves.*
- Griselinia littoralis *'Dixon's Cream': evergreen; apple green leaves splashed creamy-white.*
- Ruta graveolens *'Jackman's Blue': evergreen; glaucous blue.*

CORYLUS MAXIMA
'PURPUREA'
PURPLE-LEAF
FILBERT/ HAZEL
Height: 2.4–3m/ 8–10ft
Spread: 2.4–3m/ 8–10ft
Deciduous shrub with large, rounded, rich-purple leaves. Other hazels include C. avellana 'Aurea' with soft-yellow leaves and yellow catkins up to 6cm/ 2¹/₂in long in late winter.
Very hardy

COTINUS
COGGYGRIA
'FOLIIS PURPUREIS'
Height: 3–3.6m/ 10–12ft
Spread: 2.4–3m/ 8–10ft
Also known as 'Notcutt's Variety', this hardy, deciduous shrub has foliage first crimson, later rich purple and with light red shades in autumn. Soft, wispy flowers cover the shrub in early and mid-summer.
Easy to grow

EUONYMUS
JAPONICA
'OVATUS AUREUS'
Height: 1.2–1.5m/ 4–5ft
Spread: 1–1.2m/ 3¹/₂–4ft
Hardy, evergreen shrub with mid-green leaves edged and suffused in creamy-yellow. It needs a sunny position for the leaves to retain their colour. There are many other variegated forms.
Slow growing and compact

ACER JAPONICUM
'AUREUM'
Height: 3–4.5m/ 10–15ft
Spread: 2.4–3.6m/ 8–12ft
Hardy, deciduous tree with beautiful soft-yellow leaves that turn rich crimson in autumn. Other forms include 'Aconitifolium' (deeply lobed leaves that assume ruby-crimson tints in autumn) and 'Vitifolium' (crimson tints in autumn).
Slow growing

ACER PALMATUM
'ATROPURUREUM'
Height: 3–4.5m/ 10–15ft
Spread: 2.4–3m/ 8–10ft
Hardy, deciduous tree with brilliant purple leaves in summer, assuming rich crimson-purple shades in autumn. Also A. p. 'Dissectum Atropurpureum' (finely divided bronze-purple leaves) and A. p. 'Dissectum' (soft green).
Shelter from cold winds

CATALPA
BIGNONIOIDES
'AUREA'
GOLDEN INDIAN BEAN TREE
Height: 3.6–4.5m/ 12–15ft
Spread: 3.6–4.5m/ 12–15ft
Hardy, deciduous tree with large, velvety, soft-yellow leaves. White, foxglove-like flowers, marked in yellow and purple, appear during mid-summer. These are followed by slender beans.
Slow growing

PHILADELPHUS
CORONARIUS
'AUREA'
GOLDEN-LEAVED
MOCK ORANGE
Height: 1.8–2.4m/ 6–8ft
Spread: 1.5–1.8m/ 5–6ft
Dense, deciduous shrub with bright yellow leaves, which, in summer, often become greenish-yellow. Creamy-white flowers during early and mid-summer.
Full or light shade

ROBINIA
PSEUDOACACIA
'FRISIA'
COMMON ACACIA/ BLACK
LOCUST/ FALSE ACACIA
Height: 6–7.5m/ 20–25ft
Spread: 3–4.5m/ 10–15ft
Hardy, deciduous tree with leaves first golden-yellow, later pale green. They are formed of small leaflets. Creamy-white fragrant flowers in early summer.
Plant as a focal point

SAMBUCUS
RACEMOSA
'PLUMOSA AUREA'
GOLDEN ELDER
Height: 1.8–2.4m/ 6–8ft
Spread: 1.8–2.4m/ 6–8ft
Hardy, deciduous, bushy shrub with deeply divided, golden-yellow leaves. Yellow flowers appear during mid and late spring followed by scarlet berries during mid-summer.
Slow growing

COLOURED BARKS AND SHOOTS

❖

TREES with coloured barks, as well as shrubs with attractive shoots, are especially welcome in winter and early spring, when often there is little colour about and leaves have not yet arrived on deciduous plants.

Some of these trees, such as the Paperbark Tree (*Acer griseum*) can be planted as specimens in lawns, while others look superb when grouped together and surrounded in spring by crocuses. Birches are especially attractive when used in this way; plant them so that low rays from the sun can glance on their trunks.

The Windmill Palm (*Trachycarpus fortunei*) needs a mild climate. Eventually it has a long, attractive trunk and it can be planted close to a path.

OTHER SHRUBS AND TREES

- Acer griseum: *buff-coloured bark flakes to reveal light orange-brown underbark. Leaves colour in autumn.*
- Arbutus x andrachnoides: *peeling, cinnamon-red bark.*
- Betula ermanii: *peeling bark, orange-brown changing to creamy-white.*
- Betula jacquemontii: *white, peeling bark.*
- Betula utilis: *outstandingly attractive peeling bark, orange to brown or coppery-brown.*
- Cornus alba: *red stems.*
- Cornus alba 'Sibirica': *bright crimson shoots.*

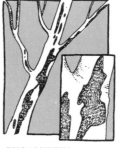

EUCALYPTUS NIPHOPHILA
ALPINE SNOW GUM/ SNOW GUM
Height: 6m/20ft
Spread: 4.5m/15ft
Hardy, wind-resistant, deciduous tree with outstandingly attractive bark. On young trees the bark is bluish-white. After four or five years, bark is shed annually, revealing pale cream underbark.
Fast growing

PRUNUS SERRULA
Height: 4.5–6m/15–20ft
Spread: 3.6–4.5m/12–15ft
Hardy, deciduous tree with spectacular bark peeling in strips to reveal polished, mahogany-like, reddish-brown underbark. During mid-spring it develops small, white flowers, although it is the bark that is the main attraction. Many gardeners who grow this tree regularly polish the bark.
Slow growing

TRACHYCARPUS FORTUNEI (CHAMAEROPS EXCELSA)
CHUSAN PALM/ FAN PALM/ WINDMILL PALM
Height: 1.8–3m/6–10ft
Spread: 1.8–2.4m/6–8ft
Beautiful palm, with large fans of mid-green, pleated leaves often 90cm/3ft across. The trunk becomes covered in dark fibres that create a wonderful feature.
Not fully hardy

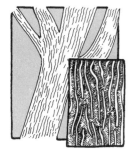
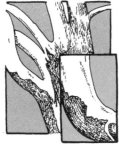
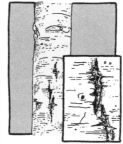

ACER DAVIDII
SNAKEBARK MAPLE
Height: 4.5–6m/15–20ft
Spread: 2.4–3m/8–10ft
Hardy, deciduous tree with grey bark lined in white. The form 'George Forrest' has spreading branches with dark green leaves that assume handsome tints in autumn. A. pensylvanicum also has bark that is attractively striped in white.
Plant in light shade

ARBUTUS ANDRACHNE
GRECIAN STRAWBERRY TREE
Height: 3–4.5m/10–15ft
Spread: 2.4–3m/8–10ft
Slightly tender, but becoming hardier, evergreen tree with peeling, cinnamon-red bark. White flowers in terminal clusters during early and mid-spring, followed by unusual orange-red, strawberry-like fruits.
Needs shelter

BETULA PAPYRIFERA
CANOE BIRCH/ PAPER BIRCH/ WHITE BIRCH
Height: 4.5–6m/15–20ft
Spread: 3–3.6m/10–12ft
Beautiful, hardy, deciduous tree with gleaming white bark that peels in strips, especially on old trees. In autumn, the triangular, mid-green leaves assume attractive yellow shades.
Ideal specimen tree

AUTUMN-COLOURED LEAVES

MANY deciduous shrubs and trees have leaves that assume rich tints of red and yellow in autumn before falling. In years when the weather is dry in autumn and a frost rapidly stops growth, the colours are richer than ever.

The Stag's Horn Sumach (*Rhus typhina*) is ideal in small gardens but many other autumn brighteners have a uniform, slightly clinical outline that makes them more suitable as focal points towards the bottom of a garden or perhaps framed in a lawn. These include the Swamp Cypress (*Taxodium distichum*) and the Sweet Gum (*Liquidambar styraciflua*). *Acer cappadocicum* has a more irregular shape and eventually creates a dominant feature. Position it towards the end of a garden.

OTHER SHRUBS AND TREES

- Cercidiphyllum japonicum: *red and yellow autumnal tints.*
- Enkianthus campanulatus: *brilliant red shades.*
- Ginkgo biloba: *bright gold in autumn. Deciduous conifer.*
- Hamamelis mollis: *yellow leaves in autumn.*
- Liriodendron tulipifera: *tulip-shaped leaves become butter-yellow in autumn.*
- Malus tschonoskii: *rich red and yellow autumnal foliage.*
- Quercus rubra: *dull crimson then deep reddish-brown.*
- Taxodium distichum: *leaves bright red in autumn.*

LIQUIDAMBAR STYRACIFLUA
BILSTED/ RED GUM/ SWEET GUM
Height: *5.4–6m/ 18–20ft*
Spread: *2.4–3.6m/ 8–12ft*
Hardy, pyramidal, deciduous tree with dark green, maple-like, lobed leaves that assume rich orange and scarlet shades in autumn. The form 'Lane Roberts' has black, crimson-red autumn colours.
Ideal on lawns

ACER CAPPADOCICUM
MAPLE
Height: *5.4–6m/ 18–20ft*
Spread: *3.6–4.5m/ 12–15ft*
Hardy, deciduous tree, spreading with age. The five- or seven-lobed dark green leaves become soft yellow in autumn. The form 'Aureum' has red foliage when young, becoming golden-yellow. 'Rubrum' turns gold.
Eventually large

KOELREUTERIA PANICULATA
CHINA TREE/ GOLDEN RAIN TREE/ PRIDE OF INDIA
Height: *3–4.5m/ 10–15ft*
Spread: *2.4–3m/ 8–10ft*
Handsome, hardy, deciduous tree with large, mid-green leaves up to 35cm/ 14in long and formed of several leaflets. In autumn they assume yellow tints. Yellow flowers appear in mid-summer.
Eventually large

PARROTIA PERSICA
Height: *3–4.5m/ 10–15ft*
Spread: *3–3.6m/ 10–12ft*
Hardy, deciduous shrub or tree with rounded, mid-green leaves that in autumn develop crimson, gold and amber tints. Sometimes, these also include yellow. Additionally, the bark on old trees flakes in patches. Plant this tree in either light shade or full sun.
Slow growing

RHUS TYPHINA
STAG'S HORN SUMACH/ VELVET SUMACH
Height: *2.4–3.6m/ 8–12ft*
Spread: *3–3.6m/ 10–12ft*
Spreading, deciduous shrub with brown-felted stems and mid-green leaves formed of many leaflets that assume rich orange-red, purple and yellow tints in autumn. The form 'Laciniata' has deeply divided leaves.
Ideal for small gardens

ON THE COFFEE TRAIL

'There's an awful lot of coffee in Brazil', goes the well-known song, but this world-famous drink originated many miles away, in Abyssinia, now Ethiopia. The date when the virtues of the coffee shrub (Coffea arabica) were discovered is uncertain: one story tells of a prior who, upon learning that his cattle sometimes browsed on this shrub and then bounded all night on the hills, became curious. He then tried the beans on his monks to prevent them sleeping at matins.

Constantinople coffee shop

The drink spread through Egypt and Syria, reaching Constantinople in 1511, where in 1554 a coffee-shop was opened. Coffee later became a popular drink in Vienna and Germany. The first coffee-houses in England opened in Oxford in 1650 and a few years later in St. Michael's Alley in the City of London. The passion for coffee spread rapidly among the wits and beaux, and especially among traders who used coffee-houses as places to discuss commerce. Merchants and brokers engaged in the Russian trade congregated in a subscription room at the Baltic coffee-house, while the Chapter in Paternoster Row was the resort of booksellers. There was also The Jamaica for the West Indian trade, while Lloyd's, Robin's and The Jerusalem were for general traders.

North American licence

The first licence to sell coffee in North America was granted in 1670. The Blue Anchor Tavern was opened in Philadelphia in about 1684. Ye Crown Coffee House was opened in 1711 on Boston Pier by Jonathan Belcher, and later Fraunce's in New York joined the ranks.

The French traveller Thevenot took coffee to France in 1662, but it was Soleiman Aga, the Turkish Ambassador, who made it fashionable in Paris.

BERRIES AND FRUITS

❖

THESE bring a further dimension to gardens and are especially welcome in autumn – many of them persist through to late winter. Botanically, berries are fleshy or succulent fruits and contain a number of seeds. To gardeners, the difference is usually of no matter, as both of them create attractive features. Birds, however, are usually more tempted by fruits than berries, which tend to be harder. Nevertheless, few berries escape the attention of birds, especially during long, cold winters.

Some plants do not produce berries until both male and female plants are present. Where this is necessary, one male plant will normally pollinate several females, so buy them in a ratio of three to five females to one male.

OTHER SHRUBS AND TREES

- Aucuba japonica: *bright scarlet berries on female plants.*
- Crataegus x prunifolia: *large, persistent, red fruits.*
- Daphne mezereum: *scarlet berries (but poisonous).*
- Hippophae rhamnoides: *masses of bright orange berries.*
- Mahonia japonica: *bunches of blue-black berries.*
- Malus: *'Golden Hornet': bright yellow berries.*
- Malus: *'Red Sentinel': persistent, deep red fruits.*
- Viburnum opulus: *translucent red berries.*
- Viburnum davidii: *bright turquoise berries.*

FOOD OF THE GODS

It was not without good reason that the Swedish botanist Carolus Linnaeus named the cocoa tree Theobrama cacao, *theobrama meaning 'food of the Gods'. Long before Christopher Columbus chanced upon the American continent, cocoa was prized as a drink in Peru and Mexico. Indeed, the name chocolate is derived from xocotlatl, a contraction of two Nahuatl words meaning fruit and water. Cocoa was introduced into Europe in 1502 when Christopher Columbus returned with the first beans. However, they failed to impress Queen Isabel la Catónica, who claimed that they could not compensate for his inability to find a route to the East Indies.*

The cocoa beans are borne in pods that resemble small rugby footballs. These ripen to orange, red and purple.

PERNETTYA MUCRONATA
Height: 75–90cm/ 2½–3ft
Spread: 1.2–1.5m/ 4–5ft
Hardy, evergreen shrub with glossy, dark green leaves. Small, white flowers in early summer; clusters of berries in autumn, in colours including white, pink, rose, purple and red. The presence of both male and female plants is essential to produce a crop of berries.
<u>Ideal for acid soils</u>

ARBUTUS UNEDO
CANE APPLES/ KILLARNEY STRAWBERRY TREE
Height: 3.6–5.4m/ 12–18ft
Spread: 3–4.5m/ 10–15ft
Evergreen shrub with white or pink, pitcher-shaped flowers from early autumn to early winter. These often appear at the same time as orange-red, strawberry-like fruits that resulted from the previous year's flowers.
<u>Slightly tender</u>

CALLICARPA BODINIERI GIRALDII
BEAUTY BERRY
Height: 1.2–1.5m/ 4–5ft
Spread: 1.5m/ 5ft
Deciduous, bushy shrub with pale green leaves that assume yellow and red tints in autumn. The lilac-coloured, late-summer flowers are followed by exceptionally attractive round, deep lilac to violet-blue berries.
<u>Not fully hardy</u>

COTONEASTER HORIZONTALIS
FISH-BONE COTONEASTER/ HERRINGBONE COTONEASTER
Height: 45–60cm/ 1½–2ft
Spread: 1.5–1.8m/ 5–6ft
Hardy, deciduous shrub; spreads or grows upwards. Branches like fish-bones bear dark green leaves. Small, pink, early-summer flowers are followed by red berries.
<u>Easy to grow</u>

PYRACANTHA
'WATERERI'
FIRETHORN
Height: 1.8–2.4m/ 6–8ft
Spread: 1.8–2.4m/ 6–8ft
Hardy, evergreen, dense and twiggy shrub with white flowers in early summer and bright red berries from autumn to late winter. Other species and varieties have orange-red, rich yellow and orange berries.
<u>Easy to grow</u>

SKIMMIA JAPONICA
Height: 90cm–1.2m/ 3–4ft
Spread: 1.2–1.5m/ 4–5ft
Hardy, evergreen, dense shrub with leathery, pale green leaves. Creamy-white, fragrant flowers in late spring and bright red berries in late summer on female plants. Male and female plants are needed to produce berries. There are several attractive forms.
<u>Slow growing</u>

SORBUS
'JOSEPH ROCK'
Height: 4.5–5.4m/ 15–18ft
Spread: 2.4–3m/ 8–10ft
Hardy, deciduous tree with a compact but upright habit and green leaflets that assume orange-red shades in autumn. Cream-coloured flowers in late spring and creamy-yellow berries, maturing to amber, in autumn.
<u>Easy to grow</u>

FOLIAGE HEDGES

Hedges are essential features in gardens, creating both privacy and beauty. Also, they are better than walls at providing shelter from cold, strong winds: solid screens create turbulence, while hedges gently filter strong gusts.

Hedges range in height from the diminutive Edging Box (*Buxus sempervirens* 'Suffruticosa') to the somewhat infamous hybrid conifer Leyland Cypress (X *Cupressocyparis leylandii*). Its growth rate is impressive: 3.6m/12ft in six years and 15m/50ft in fifteen. It is therefore better in large gardens, where it can be planted as a windbreak. The form 'Castewellan Gold' has golden-yellow foliage in summer.

Planting hedges is detailed on page 51.

OTHER SHRUBS AND TREES

- Buxus sempervirens 'Suffruticosa': *evergreen; plant 23cm/9in apart; low hedge.*
- Carpinus betulus: *deciduous; plant 45–60cm/ 1½–2ft apart; tall.*
- Chamaecyparis lawsoniana: *evergreen; conifer; plant 38–45cm/15–18in apart; tall.*
- X Cupressocyparis leylandii: *evergreen; conifer; plant 60–75cm/2–2½ft apart; fast-growing.*
- Ilex aquifolium: *evergreen; plant 45cm/1½ft apart, medium to tall.*

THE EFFECT OF HEDGES

The wind-reducing ability of hedges – and area affected – can quite easily be calculated. For instance, on the lee side and at a distance twice the height of the hedge, the wind's speed is reduced by 75%. Reductions continue, but decrease in proportion to the distance from the hedge. Even at a distance of thirty times the hedge's height, the wind's speed is reduced.

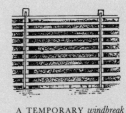

A TEMPORARY *windbreak can be effective while waiting for shelter-belt plants to become established. Form it of strips of wood nailed to posts. Double-thickness wire netting also reduces the wind's speed.*

THIS *simplified (and not to scale) diagram shows how the benefit of a hedge or windbreak can be felt at a distance up to thirty times its height.*

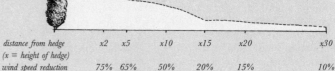

distance from hedge (x = height of hedge)	x2	x5	x10	x15	x20	x30
wind speed reduction	75%	65%	50%	20%	15%	10%

FAGUS SYLVATICA
COMMON BEECH/ EUROPEAN BEECH
Height: 3–3.6m/10–12ft
Width: 90cm–1.5m/3–5ft
Hardy deciduous tree that when planted 45–60cm/ 1½–2ft apart creates a formal hedge with bright green leaves, becoming dark and assuming rich yellow and russet tints in autumn. Eventually forms a tall hedge, about 5.4m/18ft.
Quick growing

LIGUSTRUM OVALIFOLIUM
CALIFORNIA PRIVET/PRIVET
Height: 1.2–1.8m/4–6ft
Width: 60–75cm/2–2½ft
Evergreen or semi-evergreen (depending on the severity of the climate) with glossy, mid-green leaves. Set the plants 30–38cm/12–15in apart. The yellow-leaved form (L. o. 'Aureomarginatum') is less vigorous but more colourful.
Widely grown

LONICERA NITIDA
CHINESE HONEYSUCKLE
Height: 90cm–1.5m/3–5ft
Width: 45–60cm/1½–2ft
Evergreen, dense hedge, ideal where little space is available. Set the plants 23–30cm/9–12in apart. Ensure the sides and top are clipped with a slight slope to encourage snow to slip off. Thick snow splays out the sides of this hedge and severely damages it.
Dense and small-leaved

LONICERA NITIDA
'BAGGESON'S GOLD'
Height: 90cm–1.5m/3–5ft
Width: 45–60cm/1½–2ft
Evergreen, dense hedge, formed of small, yellow leaves that turn golden-green in autumn. Set the plants 23–30cm/9–12in apart. This shrub can also be grown as a specimen in a border, or against a wall where it can grow up to 1.8m/6ft tall.
Plant in full sun

PRUNUS LAUROCERASUS
CHERRY LAUREL/ COMMON LAUREL
Height: 3–4.5m/10–15ft
Width: 1.2–1.5m/4–5ft
Hardy, evergreen shrub with leathery, shiny, mid-green leaves. In spring it bears white flowers in tassels. Set the plants 45–60cm/1½– 2ft apart. Some forms are smaller: 'Otto Luyken' forms a somewhat sprawling hedge.
Vigorous growth

TAXUS BACCATA
ENGLISH YEW/YEW
Height: 1.8–2.4m/6–8ft
Width: 75–90cm/2½–3ft
Dense, hardy evergreen conifer with dark green leaves. Set the plants about 45cm/1½ft apart. It is an ideal hedging shrub for forming arches – use a stiff wire frame initially to train and shape the arch. It creates a neat formal hedge, with square edges.
Slow growing

FLOWERING HEDGES

◆

WITH FLOWERING hedges, no boundary need be bare of colour. And there are many low-growing types that can be planted as attractive internal hedges to separate one part of a garden from another.

Individual plants are planted closer together than if used as specimens in a border, so that a hedge with an even height and thick base can be created quickly. Initially, plants need to be pruned more drastically than normal to encourage bushiness from ground level. If neglected, hedges soon lose their shape and cease to be attractive garden features.

Planting hedges is detailed on page 51.

OTHER SHRUBS

• Berberis darwinii: *evergreen; plant 30–38cm/12–15in apart; orange-yellow flowers during mid- to late spring; prune after flowering.*
• Berberis x stenophylla: *evergreen; plant 45–60cm/ 1½–2ft apart; yellow flowers during mid- to late spring; prune after flowering. Eventually it forms a wide, dense, dominant and arching hedge.*
• Escallonia: *evergreen; plant 60cm/2ft apart; range of flower colours, early to late summer; prune after flowering.*
• Rosmarinus officinalis 'Fastigiata' ('Miss Jessop's Upright'): *evergreen; plant 30–38cm/12–15in apart; mauve flowers, mid-spring to late summer; trim after flowering, or prune old ones more severely in spring, when growth begins.*

ROSE HEDGES

For rose devotees hedges formed of these deciduous shrubs are an essential element of gardens. There are many to choose from – most flowering during early and mid-summer – and these include:

• 'Ballerina': hybrid musk; plant 38–45cm/15–18in apart; 1.2m/4ft high; single, blossom-pink flowers.
• 'De Meaux': centifolia type; plant 38cm/15in apart; 90cm/3ft high; pure pink flowers.
• 'Little White Pet': modern shrub rose; plant 30–38cm/12–15in apart; 60cm/2ft high; small, white, pompon-like flowers.
• 'Nevada': modern shrub rose; plant 75–90cm/2½–3ft apart; 1.5–2.1m/5–7ft high; semi-double, cream-white flowers.
• 'Queen Elizabeth': floribunda; plant 60–75cm/2–2½ft apart; 1.5–1.8m/5–6ft high; clear pink, fragrant flowers.
• Rosa rugosa 'Frau Dagmar Hastrup': species type; plant 60–75cm/2–2½ft apart; 1.2–1.5m/4–5ft high; single, flesh-pink, delicate and very attractive.
• Rosa rugosa 'Roseraie de l'Hay': species type; plant 60– 75cm/ 2–2½ft apart; 1.5m/5ft high; rich, wine-purple, scented flowers. In autumn the round hips (sometimes called heps) become a rich orange-red.
• 'Windrush': single-flowered English rose; plant 45cm/ 1½ft apart; 1.2m/4ft high; lemon-yellow, fragrant flowers. Vigorous, branching growth.

FORSYTHIA x INTERMEDIA
'SPECTABILIS'
GOLDEN BELLS
Height: 1.8–2.1m/6–7ft
Width: 60–75cm/2–2½ft
Hardy, deciduous shrub with dark green leaves and masses of bright yellow flowers during spring. Set the plants 38–45cm/15–18in apart. Prune as soon as the flowers have faded.
Quick growing

FUCHSIA MAGELLANICA
'RICCARTONII'
Height: 1–1.2m/3½–4ft
Width: 60–90cm/2–3ft
Tender, deciduous shrub with red and purple flowers from mid-summer to autumn. Set the plants 30–38cm/ 12–15in apart. Plants are often cut down to ground level by frost. In spring, prune to soil level.
Ideal in coastal areas

GENISTA HISPANICA
SPANISH GORSE
Height: 90cm–1m/3–3½ft
Width: 1–1.2m/3½–4ft
Deciduous, spreading shrub with golden-yellow flowers during early and mid-summer. Set plants 45cm/ 1½ft apart. Tends to spread: clip back after flowering. Ideal for forming a hedge at the top of a bank, when it cascades.
Slightly tender

LAVANDULA SPICA (L. ANGUSTIFOLIA/ L. OFFICINALIS)
Height: 75–90cm/2½–3ft
Width: 45–60cm/1½–2ft
Hardy, evergreen shrub with pale, grey-blue flowers from mid- to late summer. Set the plants 38–45cm/15–18in apart. Clip off the dead flower heads after flowering. For a lower hedge use the well-known 'Hidcote'.
Easy to grow

POTENTILLA FRUTICOSA
SHRUBBY CINQUEFOIL
Height: 1.2–1.5m/4–5ft
Width: 60cm/2ft
Hardy, deciduous shrub with pale green leaves and buttercup-yellow flowers from late spring to late summer. Set the plants 25–30cm/10–12in apart. After flowering, clip off dead flowers.
Easy to grow

SPIRAEA x ARGUTA
BRIDAL WREATH/ FOAM OF MAY
Height: 1.5–1.8m/5–6ft
Width: 75–90cm/2½–3ft
Hardy, deciduous shrub with masses of white flowers during mid and late spring. Set the plants 38–45cm/ 15–18in apart. After the flowers fade, clip back the complete plant, lightly removing the flowers.
Easy to grow

SHRUBS AND TREES FOR ACID SOILS

ACID SOILS need not be a problem for gardeners. Instead, they offer the opportunity to grow a wide range of shrubs and trees denied to gardeners living in chalky areas. And many of these acid-loving plants brighten spring with flowers in a wide range of colours. They are especially suited to shaded or woodland gardens, where dappled light filters through to them. This deciduous canopy also gives some protection from spring frosts. Additionally, these shrubs need moisture-retentive soil thoroughly enriched with peat or very well-decomposed compost.

As well as creating a glorious display of flowers, many deciduous, acid-loving shrubs have leaves that in autumn assume attractive, colourful tints.

OTHER SHRUBS AND TREES

- Camellia japonica: *late winter to mid-spring; range of colours.*
- Daboecia cantabrica: *late spring to early winter; purple-pink; also forms in white and pink.*
- Eucryphia: *mid- to late summer; cream or white flowers with yellow centres.*
- Magnolia: *wide range of flowers (often fragrant), usually in spring, but* M. grandiflora *later in the year.*
- Nyssa sylvatica: *mainly grown for its richly coloured leaves in autumn.*

FOTHERGILLA MONTICOLA
Height: 1.5–2.1m/ 5–7ft
Spread: 1.5–1.8m/ 5–6ft
Hardy, deciduous shrub with glossy, dark green leaves that assume rich tints in autumn. Bottlebrush shaped, sweetly scented, creamy-white flowers appear in late spring. A related species, F. major, is not so spreading.
Slow growing

KALMIA LATIFOLIA
CALICO BUSH/ MOUNTAIN LAUREL/ SPOONWOOD
Height: 1.5–2.1m/ 5–7ft
Spread: 1.5–1.8m/ 5–6ft
Hardy, evergreen shrub with glossy, leathery, mid to dark green leaves and clusters of bright pink flowers during early summer. 'Clementine Churchill' is rich rose-red. Leaves poisonous to cattle.
Easy to grow

PIERIS 'FOREST FLAME'
Height: 1.5–1.8m/ 5–6ft
Spread: 1.5–1.8m/ 5–6ft
Hardy, evergreen shrub, noted for its brilliant red shoots in spring that slowly turn pink, cream, then green as summer arrives. Clusters of white, pitcher-like flowers during late spring and early summer. Plant in light shade. Vulnerable to frost.
Ideal in a wild garden

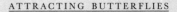

AZALEAS
EVERGREEN TYPES; RANGE OF VARIETIES
Height: 90cm–1m/ 3–3½ft
Spread: 1.2–1.5m/ 4–5ft
Large group of slightly tender shrubs: need shelter from cold winds and early morning sun. Funnel-shaped flowers in late spring. Some azaleas are deciduous, many having rich autumn-coloured leaves as well as flowers.
Slow growing

ENKIANTHUS CAMPANULATUS
Height: 1.8–2.4m/ 6–8ft
Spread: 1.2–1.5m/ 4–5ft
Hardy, rather upright, deciduous shrub with dull green leaves that assume rich shades in autumn. During late spring it bears creamy-white flowers with red veins in pendulous clusters. It is ideal in wild gardens, with an overhead canopy of leaves.
Slow growing

ERICA CINEREA
BELL HEATHER/ SCOTCH HEATHER/ TWISTED HEATHER
Height: 23–30cm/ 9–12in
Spread: 23–30cm/ 9–12in
Hardy, evergreen shrub with terminal flower clusters from early summer to early autumn. All ericas, callunas and daboecias grow well in acid soils, although some also tolerate lime.
Ground covering

RHODODENDRON
'PINK PEARL'
Height: 1.5–1.8m/ 5–6ft
Spread: 1.5–1.8m/ 5–6ft
Hardy, evergreen type with large trusses of flesh-pink flowers during spring and early summer. The wide range of other hybrids includes varieties 90cm–1.5m/ 3–5ft high. Plant in full sun or dappled sunlight, in well-drained soil.
Needs slight shade

ATTRACTING BUTTERFLIES

Scent and butterflies are a pleasing duo and several scented shrubs encourage butterflies. These include:
- *Butterfly Bush* (Buddleia davidii): *well known for its mid- to late summer flowers in several colours. Also, Buddleia alternifolia.*
- *Lavender* (Lavandula spica): *Grey-blue flowers from mid- to late summer.*
- *Lilac* (Syringa): *several species, from the large-flowered types to smaller ones such as Syringa microphylla.*
- *Privet* (Ligustrum ovalifolium): *cream, heavily scented flowers in mid-summer. Mostly, the flowers on hedging plants are clipped off and therefore are only seen on free-standing shrubs.*

CHALKY SOILS

❖

THERE are many shrubs, trees and conifers that thrive in alkaline soils. Although it is possible to treat localized areas within a garden with chemicals to help reduce soil alkalinity – as well as growing them in specially-prepared soil in raised beds – for long-term success it is better to choose plants that happily live in chalky soils.

When planting shrubs and trees in very chalky situations it is worth preparing the soil thoroughly. Take out a wide planting hole and dig down at least 50cm/20in to break up the subsoil. At the same time, dig in plenty of peat or well-decomposed compost. A sprinkling of bonemeal encourages rapid establishment.

OTHER SHRUBS AND TREES

- **Acers:** *range of species, many grown for their attractive leaves.*
- **Caryopteris x cladonensis:** *bright blue; mid to late summer.*
- **Chimonanthus praecox:** *yellow; early to mid-winter.*
- **Cistus:** *many species; early to mid-summer.*
- **Genista:** *several species, yellow and gold; late spring to mid-summer.*
- **Rhus typhina:** *grown for its coloured leaves in autumn.*
- **Sorbus:** *many species, grown for their berries.*

MOIST AND BOGGY AREAS

Some gardens have a natural high water-table, with surface soil awash in winter. Drainage is possible, but if surrounding gardens are also excessively wet there is a risk of encouraging their surplus water to pass into your garden. Do not despair as there are plants that tolerate moist and boggy soils, such as:

- *Dawn Redwood* (Metasequoia glyptostroboides): *deciduous conifer with flaking bark and mid-green leaflets that assume pink, red and brown shades before falling in autumn.*
- *Swamp Cypress* (Taxodium distichum): *also known as the Bald Cypress, this deciduous conifer has orange-brown, scaly shoots and leaves that turn russet in autumn.*
- *Willow* (Salix): *these are well known for their water-loving nature, but most are too large and invasive for small gardens. However, consider growing Salix alba 'Chermesina' and cutting its stems back to within a few inches of the ground annually in late winter to encourage the development of brilliant orange-scarlet shoots. The shoots of 'Vitellina' are yellow.*
- *Red-barked Dogwood* (Cornus alba): *like the previous shrub, grown for its coloured stems, which are red. Other forms are 'Sibirica' with bright crimson shoots. Cornus stolonifera 'Flaviramea' has yellow to olive-green stems. C. s. 'Kelseyi' has purple-brown shoots.*

BUDDLEIA ALTERNIFOLIA
Height: 2.1–3.6m/7–12ft
Spread: 2.4–3.6m/8–12ft
Hardy, deciduous shrub with a cascading nature – especially when grown as a small tree – with narrow, pale-green, willow-like leaves and sweetly scented lavender-blue flowers during early summer. 'Argentea' has hairy, silvery leaves.
Grown as a tree or shrub

CERATOSTIGMA WILLMOTTIANUM
HARDY PLUMBAGO
Height: 75–90cm/2½–3ft
Spread: 75–90cm/2½–3ft
Twiggy, low-growing shrub with small, dark green, diamond-shaped leaves that turn red in autumn. Small, rich blue flowers appear in terminal clusters during late summer. Becomes hardier with age. Can be grown in herbaceous borders.
Slightly tender

DEUTZIA x ROSEA
Height: 90cm/3ft
Spread: 90cm/3ft
Hardy, deciduous, low-growing and compact shrub with bell-shaped pink flowers on arching branches during early and mid-summer. There are several superb forms, including 'Campanulata' (white and purple) and 'Carminea' (rose-pink flowers).
Young growths in spring can be frost damaged

LABURNUM x VOSSII
GOLDEN CHAIN TREE
Height: 3–3.6m/10–12ft
Spread: 2.4–3m/8–10ft
Hardy, deciduous tree with green leaves and pendulous bunches of slightly fragrant, golden-yellow flowers in early summer. The seeds of all laburnums are poisonous, but this form does not produce seeds freely. Do not plant it near a pond.
Parts are poisonous

MALUS FLORIBUNDA
JAPANESE CRAB
Height: 3–3.6m/10–12ft
Spread: 3–3.6m/10–12ft
Hardy, deciduous tree with mid-green leaves and masses of bright carmine buds that open in late spring to reveal pale pink flowers. These are followed by yellow fruits. There are further types, with flowers and fruits in several other colours.
Forms a focal point

PAEONIA LUTEA LUDLOWII
TREE PAEONY/ TIBETAN PAEONY
Height: 1.2–1.8m/4–6ft
Spread: 1.2–1.8m/4–6ft
Shrubby, deciduous paeony with deeply segmented pale green leaves and large, golden-yellow, fragrant flowers during early summer. Slightly hardier than the normal type.
Shade from early-morning sun.

SHRUBS AND TREES FOR COASTAL AREAS

THE HAZARDS of living in coastal areas are strong winds and salt-laden sea spray, which can blow several miles inland. There are, however, many shrubs and trees that survive these conditions. Several conifers survive in front-line positions and include the Monterey Cypress (*Cupressus macrocarpa*), Corsican Pine (*Pinus maritima*) and the Austrian Pine (*Pinus nigra*). Second-line defence conifers include the fast-growing X *Cupressocyparis leylandii*, the Scot's Pine (*Pinus sylvestris*) and the Serbian Spruce (*Picea omorika*).

Once the wind's speed has been decreased, the range of possible plants increases markedly and many of them are described and illustrated here.

OTHER SHRUBS

- Elaeagnus x ebbingei: *hardy evergreen shrub; leathery, silvery-grey leaves.*
- Euonymus japonicus: *bushy evergreen shrub; glossy, dark green leaves; many attractively variegated forms.*
- Hebe brachysiphon: *slightly tender evergreen shrub; white flowers, early to mid-summer.*
- Olearia x haastii: *hardy evergreen; white flowers during mid-summer.*
- Pittosporum tenuifolium: *slightly tender evergreen; grown for its wavy edged leaves.*

SPARTIUM JUNCEUM
SPANISH BROOM/ WEAVERS' BROOM
Height: 1.8–2.4m/ 6–8ft
Spread: 1.8–2.4m/ 6–8ft
Hardy, deciduous shrub with rush-like green stems. The mid-green leaves soon fall off after maturing, while the pea-like, golden-yellow, fragrant flowers appear from early to mid-summer.
<u>Quick growing</u>

SYMPHORICARPOS ALBUS
(S. RACEMOSUS)
SNOWBERRY/ WAX-BERRY
Height: 1.5–1.8m/ 5–6ft
Spread: 1.8–2.1m/ 6–7ft
Hardy, deciduous, suckering, thicket-forming shrub with mid-green leaves and small flowers during mid-summer. These are followed by white berries from early autumn to late winter. Several varieties.
<u>Easy to grow</u>

TAMARIX TETRANDRA
TAMARISK
Height: 2.4–3.6m/ 8–12ft
Spread: 2.4–3.6m/ 8–12ft
Hardy, deciduous shrub with pale to mid-green leaves and bright pink flowers during late spring. The whole shrub has an attractive wispy appearance. Related shrubs include T. pentandra with rose-pink flowers.
<u>Survives windy areas</u>

GRISELINIA LITTORALIS
Height: 3–5.4m/ 10–18ft
Spread: 2.4–3.6m/ 8–12ft
Slightly tender evergreen shrub with leathery, thick, lustrous, apple green leaves. Ideal as a hedge or specimen shrub. There are two superb forms: 'Variegata' with leaves edged in white, and 'Dixon's Cream' with leaves splashed creamy-white. Can also be grown as a hedge.
<u>Slow growing</u>

HIPPOPHAE RHAMNOIDES
SALLOW THORN/ SEA BUCKTHORN
Height: 1.8–2.4m/ 6–8ft
Spread: 1.8–2.4m/ 6–8ft
Hardy, deciduous, bushy shrub – eventually 7.5m/ 25ft or more high – with narrow, silvery leaves. It is best known for its masses of bright orange berries from autumn through late winter. Berries shunned by birds.
<u>Ideal as a windbreak</u>

OLEARIA MACRODONTA
DAISY BUSH
Height: 1.8–2.4/ 6–8ft
Spread: 1.8–2.1/ 6–7ft
Superb, evergreen shrub, with a slight musky odour. It bears holly-like, mid-green leaves and small, daisy-like flowers in tight clusters up to 15cm/ 6in wide during mid-summer. It survives even in extremely windy, salt-blown and exposed areas.
<u>Slightly tender</u>

DYEING TROUBLE

Up to the latter part of the sixteenth century, woad was widely used to dye cloth blue. Indeed, the Saxon green, well-known during the Middle Ages, was produced by first dyeing in a weak woad solution and then with weld, a wild mignonette. And a deep purple shade could be produced if madder powder was added. Woad was therefore the universal dye of the time and woad growers had a rigid monopoly.

Indigo was used as a dye by the Egyptians and Greeks in antiquity. In the sixteenth century it was imported to Europe and Britain, deriving the name indigo as it was imported from India. This tropical shrub, Indigofera tinctoria, proved to create a dye superior to woad. The growers of woad quite correctly envisaged the loss of their monopoly in the dyeing trade and therefore labelled Indigo 'the devil's dye'. Despite this and other edicts, especially in Saxony, it eventually became the most popular dye in Europe. During the early years of the British occupation of India, trading in indigo was very important. It was eventually replaced by a synthetic dye.

Indigofera tinctoria (Indigo)

LOOKING AFTER TREES AND SHRUBS

 PART from pruning (see page 297 onwards) trees and shrubs need relatively little attention. However, there are a few tasks from which they benefit:

• Watering: Young, newly planted trees and shrubs must be regularly watered until well established. Thoroughly soak the soil, rather than just dampening the surface, which does very little good.

• Mulching: Young, newly planted shrubs and trees especially benefit from a 7.5cm/3in-thick layer of decomposed compost placed around them. First, remove all weeds and water the soil. Mulches are best applied in spring.

• Dead-heading: Immediately flowers fade, snap off the flower heads. This directs the plant's endeavours away from seed production.

• Water-shoots: Use a sharp saw to cut off thin, sappy shoots close to the trunk. Pare the surface smooth with a sharp knife.

• Transplanting: Young trees and shrubs are relatively easy to move and plant (see pages 49 to 50), but mature ones are difficult. Evergreen types are best moved in late summer or early autumn, or in spring but after the soil has become warm. Deciduous types are transplanted when dormant.

Moving excessively large trees is best tackled in stages: the first year digging a trench around half the root-ball and refilling with peat and topsoil to encourage the development of fibrous roots; the second year completing the trench; and during the next season, digging up and moving.

In home gardens, few large trees are transplanted; shrubs are more likely to be moved and these can usually be dug up and replanted during the same season.

 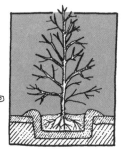 

1. MOVE *established trees by digging around and underneath the soil ball. Wrap in hessian. Sandwich rollers between boards, place the soil ball on top and pull out of the hole.*

2. PLACE *the soil ball gently in a hole and spread out the roots. Pack and firm a mixture of peat and friable soil in layers over them. The peat will help in the retention of water.*

3. FIRMLY *stake the tree from at least three positions. Use loops of hose-pipe around the trunk, then guy ropes. In spring, cut back some branches to reduce loss of water from the leaf area.*

COVERING *the soil around a shrub or tree with a 7.5cm/3in-thick layer of well-decayed compost reduces moisture loss from the soil, as well as preventing the growth of annual weeds. Thoroughly water the soil before adding the mulch.*

REMOVE *faded flowers from shrubs such as large-flowered rhododendrons to prevent the formation of seeds and to direct the plant's endeavours into growth. Do not leave the dead heads on the ground, as they can look very untidy.*

SOME *trees develop masses of water-shoots on their trunks. These must be removed by using a sharp saw to cut them back to the trunk. Then, use a sharp knife to smooth raised parts. This also prevents the formation of more shoots.*

MOVING ESTABLISHED TREES

DURING *medieval times, trees were frequently moved while in full leaf.*

Large, established trees and shrubs have been moved for several thousand years. The Egyptians carried trees in wicker baskets suspended from poles borne by slaves. The Greek philosopher Theophrastus, writer and botanist, in about 300 BC detailed the art of moving large trees; while the Romans knew the advantages of cutting back shoots and branches to reduce water loss.

In the 1600s, the English diarist and gardener, John Evelyn, suggested an ingenious way to transplant mature trees: dig a large trench around the subject, undermining the root-ball. In winter, fill the trench with water which, when the temperature fell, would freeze and enable the root-ball to be removed without breaking.

In the seventeenth century, André le Nôtre's skills, when transplanting established trees to create 'instant' gardens at Versailles, were an inspiration to other gardeners. In the 1700s the English landscape designer Lancelot 'Capability' Brown designed a tree-transplanting apparatus formed of a stout pole fixed to an axle and two large wheels.

During the 1800s, the British landscape gardener William Barron became famous for moving very large trees. In 1880 he moved a gigantic, thousand-year-old yew in a churchyard about 54m/60yds to prevent its branches damaging the church.

MOVING *a large magnolia from Bordeaux to Paris in 1857.*

ROSES FOR ALL GARDENS

Most gardens have at least one rose bush or a climbing rose clambering over a door, trellis or pergola. The range of roses is wide and includes Species and Old Roses as well as the popular and widely grown Hybrid Tea and Floribunda types. These roses, as well as Miniature and Patio Roses, together with Climbers, Ramblers and those that scale pillars or clamber into trees, are featured in this chapter.

Standard, half-standard and weeping standard roses, which create beacons of colour when used as focal points in lawns, or variations in height when planted among bush types, are also covered. Some roses can be used to form flowering hedges or to create ground-cover, while a few can be planted in hanging-baskets and displayed on a patio, and some of these, too, are described.

The ideal soil and site, buying and planting, feeding and looking after roses are outlined in this chapter, while advice on pruning a wide range of these distinctive plants is given on pages 310 to 313.

THE ROMANCE OF THE ROSE

❖

EW flowers are so highly prized as the rose. It is a flower steeped in history and finely woven within the fabric of Man's development. At one stage roses were prized for both their medicinal value and beauty.

Roses belong to the genus Rosa and are mainly native to the cooler parts of the Northern Hemisphere, in Asia (especially China), Europe (including Britain) and North America.

Botanists suggest that there are approaching three thousand species of roses, but the number of good ones is probably no more than one hundred and fifty. And of these, relatively few have contributed to the vast range of garden varieties grown today.

ROSES *featured in many early herbals. In 1597 the barber-surgeon and herbalist John Gerard published his* Herball.

VICTORIAN MAGIC

During the late Victorian era, novelty and magical tricks were popular, as reported in 1891 by the magazine Scientific Mysteries. *Changing white roses into red ones was achieved – usually to the amazement of a crowd – by sprinkling the petals with aniline crystals and then spraying them with eau-de-Cologne. The petals rapidly become a rich crimson-blush.*

SPECIES ROSES

The earliest cultivated roses were 'wild' species and the results of their natural and impromptu matings. Examples of species roses are the Dog Rose *(Rosa canina)* and the well-known Sweetbriar or Eglantine *(R. rubiginosa* but earlier called *R. eglanteria).* The natural crossing of the Dog Rose with the French or Provins Rose *(R. gallica)* produced the White Rose of York *(R. x alba).*

OLD ROSES

Closely associated with Species Roses are the so-called Old Roses (often known as Old Fashioned Roses). These are varieties that arose as sports or hybrids between Species Roses. Sports are mutations that occur naturally on plants: flowers often reveal a different colour or formation. These Old Roses are usually grouped according to their parentage and were the main ones grown before the introduction of Hybrid Teas.

CHINESE ROSES

Until the arrival in Europe of Chinese roses, between 1792 and 1824, the only cultivated roses were Species and Old Roses. The four Chinese roses that were introduced over a span of thirty-two years were hybrids and the result of rose breeding in China for many centuries. They introduced colours previously unknown in European roses. Many new types were created, such as Hybrid China Roses, Hybrid Perpetuals, Noisettes, Boursaults, Bourbon and Tea Roses. Many of these are still popular, and available from specialist nurseries.

The crossing of Hybrid Perpetuals and Tea Roses created the first Hybrid Tea rose in 1867, while, during the early 1920s, Floribundas were produced by the Danish rose breeder Svend Poulsen. Hybrid Tea (Large-flowered Bush Roses) and Floribundas (Cluster-flowered Bush Roses) have proved to be the most popular of all garden roses.

THIS *engraving of knights and ladies in a rose garden appeared in* Das Heldenbuch *(The Book of Heroes) printed in 1477, although known in manuscript form several years earlier. It is a collection of medieval German epics, some from the thirteenth century.*

THIS *illustration from* Das Heldenbuch *shows two knights receiving chaplets of roses – together with kisses – from their ladies before going into battle. Other woodcuts from the book are less romantic and reveal the brutality of battle. The book depicts the activities of Dietrich of Bern and the brothers Ortnit and Wolfdietrich, who feature widely in many Germanic legends.*

TYPES OF ROSES

ROSES are remarkable deciduous shrubs, and their success owes much to their hardiness and willingness to be domesticated. They pollinate freely between themselves and are also amenable to botanists tampering with their sex-life to create further hybrids and varieties. Additionally, gardeners are easily able to increase their plants by budding or, for some types, by taking cuttings or layering shoots. Indeed, by budding (uniting a desired variety with the root-stock of a variety of known vigour) the creation of plants with a predictable size is enabled. Some root-stocks make it possible to grow roses on ground which otherwise might not be fully satisfactory for them.

These practical qualities have combined to enable nurserymen to widen the colour spectrum, to encourage longer flowering seasons and to tailor a shrub's shape, so as to form bushes, to create standards of several different heights, and to produce beautiful weeping standards.

GRANDIFLORA

This is a term that frequently appears in rose catalogues and books. It is a North American term, and refers to vigorous Floribunda-type varieties of rose with large, shapely, Hybrid Tea-type flowers. 'Queen Elizabeth', introduced in 1954, is an excellent example of the Grandiflora type.

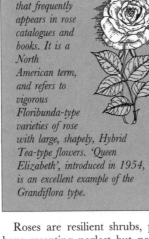

Roses are resilient shrubs, perhaps resenting neglect but nevertheless usually surviving it. However, when correctly planted and established, pruned and fed you will have a shrub with a life expectancy of fifteen or more years. The skills needed to grow roses successfully are detailed here, on pages 69 to 70 and on page 86.

SPECIES ROSES *are those that at one time could be found growing wild. They include R. rubrifolia (now R. glauca) which is native to Central and Southern Europe (page 79).*

OLD ROSES *include a wide range of old-fashioned types derived through hybridization or as sports from species types. The Bourbon 'La Reine Victoria' is a superb Old Rose (pages 80 to 82).*

MODERN SHRUB ROSES *are later introductions than the Old Roses, but still hybrids between Species and Old Roses. 'Frühlingsgold' is one of these attractive roses (page 83).*

SHAPE AND COLOUR

The size of flowers varies widely: some species have eight or less petals, while many Hybrid Tea and Floribunda types have forty or more in each flower. Colours range through most shades, from the brightest white to darkest red, but not a proper blue. This is because the rose family does not have the genetic ability to create blue in the same way as many other plants.

Bush-shaped plants are popular and range from Miniatures at only 23cm/9in high to Floribundas 1.8m/6ft or more tall. Some Species and Old Roses have a bush shape, while others are prostrate and ideal for forming ground cover. There are even roses that can be planted in hanging baskets. Climbers and Ramblers drench walls, arbours, arches and pergolas in colour, while some clamber into trees.

HYBRID TEA *(Large-flowered Bush Roses) types have long flower stems. Their flowers are initially high-pointed and graceful, later reflexed, and are borne singly or in small clusters (pages 72 to 74).*

FLORIBUNDAS *(Cluster-flowered Bush Roses) bear flowers in large clusters (trusses) and create masses of colour over a long period. They are superb in garden beds and borders (pages 75 to 77).*

MINIATURE ROSES *are increasingly popular. They have a diminutive nature, with scaled-down buds, flowers, petals, stems and leaves. Few Miniature roses grow more than 38cm/15in high (page 78).*

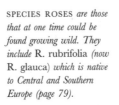  

PATIO ROSES *are a relatively new group and, correctly, are low-growing Floribundas. Most grow between 45cm/1½in and 60cm/2ft high; they have a more robust nature than the miniatures (page 78).*

CLIMBERS *have larger flowers than ramblers and more permanent growth. Also, they have the ability to repeat-flower after their first flowering. 'Golden Showers' is a well-known climber (page 84).*

RAMBLERS *are a group with varied origins. They have supple stems which develop mainly from the plant's base. 'Albertine' is ideal for growing over pergolas, arches and arbours (page 85).*

BUYING AND PLANTING

❖

THERE are three main forms in which roses can be bought: 'bare-rooted', 'pre-packed' and 'container-grown'. Each of these forms has both advantages and disadvantages.

• Bare-rooted roses are grown in the open ground in nurseries and dug up during their dormant period (late autumn to late winter) and sold either direct to customers or through mail-order. They usually arrive packed in large, multi-layer paper sacks which have been stitched closed. In earlier times they were wrapped in pyramidal straw bundles. Remove the wrapping and, if your soil is not frozen or waterlogged, plant them immediately. If planting cannot take place directly, but will happen within a week, leave the plants in their packages and place in a cool shed or garage. Where planting cannot be performed within a number of weeks, unpack the plants and bury their roots (known as heeling-in) in a sheltered, well-drained part of a garden.

• Pre-packed roses are grown in the same way as bare-rooted types and dug up during their dormant period. Their roots are then covered with moist peat and the entire plant wrapped in polythene. Unfortunately, this encourages premature growth if kept too warm. These are frequently sold through high street shops. As soon as you get them home, untie the packages and treat in the same way as bare-rooted types.

• Container-grown roses, as the name suggests, have been grown in containers from when they were small plants. Sold throughout the year, they can be planted whenever the soil is neither frozen nor waterlogged. Before planting, check the compost is evenly moist.

PREPARING FOR PLANTING

Bare-rooted and pre-packaged roses need to be checked over before they are planted. Cut back damaged shoots to sound wood. Also, prune off shoots with leaves or heps (fruits) on them, as well as thin and twiggy growths. Cut off dead, damaged and excessively long roots, so that they are not more than 30cm/12in long.

To ensure that the roots and stems are plump and full of moisture, immerse them in water for at least twenty-four hours (right).

TRANSPLANTING ESTABLISHED ROSES

If you move to an established garden it is possible a bush rose may need to be moved. If old and neglected it is best dug up and discarded and replaced with a young bush. However, first dig out a hole and fill with fresh soil. Move the bush during its dormant period – late autumn to late winter.

ENSURING ROOTS ARE MOIST

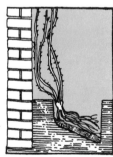

Never plant bare-rooted roses when their roots are dry. Place them in a large bucket deeply filled with clean water for at least twenty-four hours. This ensures that they are plump and full of moisture when planted and able to establish themselves quickly.

If the weather is dry and roses are planted with shrivelled roots, they may die. But if roots are plump and moist they will have a better chance of survival.

WHEN *planting a bare-rooted bush rose, dig a hole 50–60cm/20–24in wide and 20–25cm/8–10in deep. Fork the base and add moist peat. Form a slight mound and spread roots over it. Use a straight stick to check that the union between the variety and roots (just below the lowest stem) is 2.5cm/1in below the surface.*

HOLD *the bush upright and dribble friable soil around and between the roots. Slightly lifting and lowering the stem several times enables soil to fall between the roots, filling the spaces. Replace soil over the roots, in layers only 5cm/2in thick at one time, and ensure it is well firmed between them. Ensure the bush is upright.*

CONTINUE *to firm soil in layers around and over the roots until the surface is level. Use the heel of a shoe to ensure it is firm and then use a fork or rake to level the surface. If foot marks are left, water will rest in them. Never fill the hole and cover the roots in one operation, as pockets of air may then be trapped around the roots.*

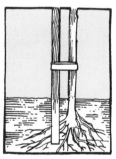

PLANTING *container-grown roses needs the same soil preparation as for bare-rooted types. Form a hole, place moist peat in the base and position the plant, still in its container. Its top should be 12mm/½in below the surface. Carefully remove the container and pack and firm good soil around it. Water the soil thoroughly.*

WHEN *planting a standard rose, dig a hole, form a mound and place moist peat over it. Insert a stake on the windward side, about 7.5cm/3in off-centre. Position the plant and check it is slightly deeper than before. Spread out the roots and firm soil over them. Tie the stem firmly to the stake in three places.*

TO PLANT *a climber against a wall, position the roots not less than 38cm/15in from it. Dig a hole and fill it with moist peat. Position the roots in the hole and check that they are slightly deeper than before. Spread and firm good soil over and between the roots. Thoroughly water the soil several times.*

FEEDING

 BUSH roses must be regularly fed to encourage the yearly development of fresh shoots that later bear flowers. Feed them three times a year, once in spring, then in early summer and, lastly, in mid-summer. Do not feed them after this time as soft shoots will be produced that will be damaged by winter frosts. Always combine the application of a mulch with the feeding programme; first hoe shallowly and remove weeds, apply the fertilizer and water in (if granular or powder). Only then should a mulch be applied. Once a mulch is in position, use a proprietary liquid feed at the recommended strength – never experiment.

DUSTING *the soil around roses with a granular or powder fertilizer in spring and summer is the traditional way to feed them. Shallowly hoe the fertilizer into the surface, then lightly but thoroughly water the soil.*

APPLYING *a liquid rose fertilizer diluted in water around plants provides readily-available food for roses. Make several applications, during spring and summer. Always keep to the recommended strength.*

FOLIAR *feeding is relatively new and provides an 'instant' tonic for plants as it rapidly gets into a plant's sap-stream. It is an ideal method of feeding for improving exhibition plants at the very last moment.*

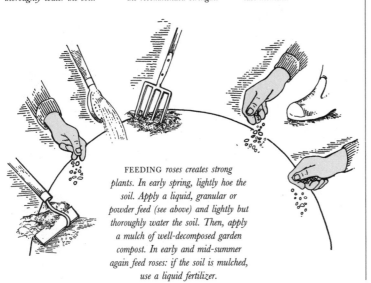

FEEDING *roses creates strong plants. In early spring, lightly hoe the soil. Apply a liquid, granular or powder feed (see above) and lightly but thoroughly water the soil. Then, apply a mulch of well-decomposed garden compost. In early and mid-summer again feed roses: if the soil is mulched, use a liquid fertilizer.*

EXHIBITING ROSES

 WHEN growing roses becomes a passionate hobby, exhibiting a few blooms is a logical trend. The season before exhibiting your own roses, inspect those displayed by experts. There is much to learn and listening to the judges more than pays off when exhibiting your own. Carefully read the rules of the show and do not be tempted to enter too many blooms during the first season of exhibiting your own roses.

TYING *soft, thick, white wool around a half-open, dry bloom two or three days before the show helps to lengthen the petals and to create an attractive outline. Each morning, slightly loosen and re-secure the tie.*

A CONICAL *bloom-protector secured to a stake about two weeks before the show helps to give protection during a wet season. Water spotting is then prevented. Ensure the cone does not drip rain water on other blooms.*

WIRING *roses with weak necks gives them support (but check that the rules allow this). There are two methods: either encircle the stem with a loop or coiled wire, or pierce the bud with a wire, then tie it to the stem.*

DISPLAYING EXHIBITION ROSES

TRADITIONALLY, *roses were displayed in specimen boxes holding six or twelve blooms. Fresh green moss was packed in the box and glass tubes positioned so that when the blooms were added they did not touch. Graduate the flower sizes.*

DISPLAYS *in bowls are very attractive. Avoid colour clashes where mixed varieties are displayed; position pastel shades between those with strong colours and form an even outline. Ensure that the bowl's size, colour and shape are suitable.*

VASES HOLDING *three or six blooms are popular in some shows. The vases are usually provided: pack with short rushes and remove lower thorns and leaves from the stems. Ensure the blooms do not touch. Fill the vase with clean water.*

FRAGRANCE

RICH fragrances wafting through a garden create a feeling of well-being and homeliness. This is also another facet to gardening and one which is easily achievable with a little planning. And of all garden plants, roses reveal some of the most varied scents.

SHRUB ROSES

These, like the climbers and ramblers featured in the box opposite, are frequently rich in unusual fragrances.
• Banana: *Rosa soulieana* (Species) reveals white flowers in sprays.
• Clove: *Rosa* x *paulii* has white flowers with golden stamens. Also, *R.* x *paulii rosea*, with single, pink flowers.
• Clover: 'Fritz Nobis' (Modern Shrub Rose) reveals fresh pink flowers with darker shading.
• Musk: 'Day Break' (Hybrid Musk) with rich yellow buds opening to yellow flowers with golden stamens. 'Penelope' (Hybrid Musk) bearing large clusters of creamy pink flowers.
• Myrrh: 'Magenta' (listed as a Modern Shrub Rose or Hybrid Musk) with rosy magenta to pale mauve flowers, and said to have the soft colouring of Old Roses.
• Orange: 'Callisto' (Hybrid Musk) with rich creamy yellow flowers.
• Raspberry: 'Adam Masserich' (Bourbon Rose) with large, semi-double, rich pink flowers. 'Cerise Bouquet' (Modern Shrub Rose) with cerise-pink, semi-double flowers. 'Great Western' (Bourbon Rose) with rich crimson-purple flowers with maroon shading. 'Kathleen Harrop' (Bourbon Rose) with clear pink flowers, showing light crimson on the reverse.

• Raspberry-drop: *Rosa canina* 'Andersonii' (Species type) with large, intense deep pink flowers.
• Sweet and apple-like: 'Nymphenburg' (Modern Shrub Rose) with fully-double, warm salmon-pink flowers shaded with cerise and orange-yellow.
• Sweet and lemony: 'Mme. Hardy' (Damask Rose). White flowers, copper at first.
• Sweet Pea: 'Vanity' (Hybrid Musk) with single, deep pink flowers borne in large, lax trusses.

'DUTCH GOLD', (Hybrid Tea) has a vigorous and upright nature, with large golden flowers.

SHELTERED POSITIONS

Choose a warm, wind-sheltered position close to a path, so that fragrances can be easily appreciated. Take care that thorn-covered stems cannot cause harm to faces, and especially to eyes.

HYBRID TEAS

Many of these bush-type roses have a sweet fragrance and some, such as 'Alec's Red', are ideal for cutting to decorate rooms.
• White and cream: 'Evening Star' and 'Polar Star'.
• Lilac and mauve: 'Blue Parfum'.
• Pink: 'Double Delight', 'Mary Donaldson', 'My Choice', 'Ophelia', 'Paul Shirville' and 'Royal Highness'.
• Red: 'Alec's Red', 'Barkarole', 'Deep Secret', 'Ena Harkness', 'Ernest H. Morse', 'Fragrant Cloud', 'Royal William' and 'Wendy Cussons'.
• Yellow: 'Champion', 'Dutch Gold' and 'Pot o' Gold'.
• Orange and blends: 'Just Joey' and 'Whisky Mac'.

FLORIBUNDA ROSES

Like Hybrid Teas, these are also rich in fragrance and are ideal for drenching beds and borders in scent as well as colour.
• White and cream: 'Iceberg' and 'Margaret Merril'.
• Pink: 'Champion Cocktail', 'Dearest', 'Harry Edland', 'Radox Bouquet', 'Scented Air', 'The Fisherman's Cottage' and 'Valentine Heart'.
• Red: 'Dusky Maiden' and 'Geranium Red'.
• Yellow: 'Arthur Bell', 'Korresia' and 'Mountbatten'.
• Orange and blends: 'Daylight', 'Elizabeth of Glamis', 'Fragrant Delight' and 'Iced Ginger'.

DWARF POLYANTHAS

These are one of the parents of Floribundas, with small Rambler-type flowers in closely-packed clusters. They flower over a long period and some are richly scented.
• 'Katharina Zeimet': white.
• 'Nathalie Nypels': rose pink.
• 'Yvonne Rabier': white.

'ALEC'S RED' (Hybrid Tea) develops large, cherry-red flowers and strong shoots bearing dark green and glossy leaves.

RAMBLERS AND CLIMBERS

Some Ramblers and Climbers have unusual fragrances, such as:
• Apple: 'François Juranville' (R: coral-pink); 'Paul Transon' (R: coppery orange) and 'René André' (R: soft apricot-yellow).
• Cloves: 'Blush Noisette' (C: semi-double and lilac-pink).
• Fruity: 'Leander' (S/C: a warm, deep apricot).
• Musk: 'Paul's Himalayan Musk' (R: blush-pink).
• Myrrh: 'Constance Spry' (S/C: clear pink) and 'Cressida' (S/C: apricot-pink).
• Orange: 'The Garland' (R: creamy salmon) and 'Veilchenblau' (R: magenta, fading to lilac).
• Paeony: 'Gerbe Rose' (R: soft pink-tinted cream).
• Primrose: 'Adelaïde d'Orléans' (R: creamy white) and 'Félicité et Perpétué' (R: creamy white).
• Sweet Pea: 'Mme Gregoire Staechelin' (C: glowing pink).
[Note: R = Rambler; C = Climber; S/C = Shrub/climber]

HYBRID TEAS
White, Ivory and Cream
❖

HYBRID Tea roses are often considered to be the aristocrats of the rose world. They have long stems and flowers, initially with a high-pointed and graceful outline. Later they open and the petals bend backwards.

In some books, Hybrid Tea roses are referred to by their new name, Large-flowered Bush Roses (sometimes shortened to LF Bush), but mostly they are still known as Hybrid Teas or HTs.

Their colour range is wide and from here until page 74 they are grouped according to their shade, from white to blends of orange.

WHITE HYBRID TEAS
These are not dramatic. Instead, they introduce a cool, restful aura to both gardens and flower arrangements indoors. There are many excellent varieties to choose from, including:

• 'Elizabeth Harkness': Scented, ivory flowers with a touch of pink and gold. Bushes grow about 82cm/32in high and 60cm/2ft wide. It is free-flowering and equally good in beds or for cutting to decorate rooms indoors.

• 'Evening Star': Large, lightly scented, white flowers borne singly or in clusters on bushes about 90cm/3ft high and 60cm/2ft wide. Attractive leaves. Each flower has about twenty-five petals.

• 'Message': Large, lightly scented white blooms with a greenish cast. Growth is upright, about 90cm/3ft high and spreading to 60cm/2ft.

• 'Pascali': Long-lasting, large, white blooms which are resistant to damage from rain. Growth is upright, about 75cm/2½ft high and about 50cm/20in wide.

• 'Peaudouce': Also known as 'Elina', it has moderately scented, ivory flowers with a lemon centre. Bushes grow 1m/2½ft high and about 75cm/2½ft wide.

• 'Polar Star': Large, white flowers borne on strong, upright stems. Bushes grow about 1m/3½ft high and 72cm/28in wide. An ideal white variety for cutting.

• 'Silver Wedding': Lightly scented, creamy white blooms borne on bushy plants about 50cm/20in high and wide.

'POLAR STAR'
has white flowers and richly dark-green foliage.

ROSE HIP JAM
Boil washed rose hips (fruit) in an equal amount of water for 15 minutes. Strain, add sugar and boil until thickened.

HYBRID TEAS
Yellow and Gold
❖

YELLOW Hybrid Teas have an impressive richness and in mid-summer help to recall the brightness and vitality of spring.

Yellow is a colour that remains visible for a long time in the increasing darkness of evenings, long after red and scarlet have been lost in the twilight. They are therefore superb for planting around or near to the edges of terraces and patios.

YELLOW HYBRID TEAS
Yellow is an all-embracing term and ranges from light yellow, with flushes of pink, to those totally saturated in yellow. Varieties to choose from include:

• 'Dutch Gold': Strongly scented, large, golden-yellow blooms which do not fade with age. Bushes are vigorous, growing to about 1m/3½ft high and about 75cm/2½ft wide.

• 'Freedom': Lightly scented, rich, bright yellow flowers on bushes with an upright stance, 75cm/2½ft high and 60cm/2ft wide.

• 'Grandpa Dickson': Lightly scented, pale-yellow blooms which, in hot weather, assume pink flushes. Resistant to rain damage, it grows 75cm/2½ft high and 50cm/20in wide.

• 'Miss Harp': Moderately scented, deep bronze-yellow flowers that are resistant to damage from wet weather. Bushes are about 82cm/32in high and 60cm/2ft wide.

• 'Peace': Perhaps the best known of all roses, with lightly scented, large, light yellow flowers flushed pink. Bushes grow 1.2m/4ft high and 90cm/3ft wide.

• 'Peer Gynt': Bright yellow flowers with pink tints on their edges. Bushes have a compact nature, about 82cm/32in high and 60cm/2ft wide.

• 'Simba': Lightly scented, clear yellow flowers which appear in flushes. The blooms, which are resistant to weather damage, are borne on bushes 60cm/2ft high and 50cm/20in wide.

• 'Sunblest': Light scent and bright yellow flowers borne prolifically on bushes 90cm/3ft high and 60cm/2ft wide. An excellent variety for cutting to decorate rooms.

• 'Valencia': Moderately scented, large, light amber-yellow blooms borne on bushes about 90cm/3ft high and 60cm/2ft wide.

'SIMBA' is clear yellow, with foliage that is resistant to damage from wet weather. Plants are compact and full of leaves.

HYBRID TEAS
Pink and Blush

❖

PINK and blush covers a wide spectrum of colours, from pinkish-white to light red, and between these is the classic pink with a demure but warm nature. Pink roses – like red ones – have romantic associations and for this reason alone are well worth growing.

There are many varieties to consider and they include:

• 'Abbeyfield Rose': Deep rosy-pink flowers on bushes 60cm/2ft high and wide. It is an ideal variety for growing in small areas.

• 'Admiral Rodney': Large, moderately scented, pale rose-pink petals with pink reverses. Bushes are moderately vigorous, about 60cm/2ft high and wide.

• 'Blessings': Large, moderately scented, rosy salmon-pink blooms on vigorous, upright bushes, sometimes 1.2m/4ft high and 75cm/2½ft wide.

• 'Mary Donaldson': Scented, classically high-centred, salmon-pink flowers borne singly or in wide sprays. It is ideal in beds in gardens and grows about 90cm/3ft high and 60cm/2ft wide.

• 'Paul Shirville': Fragrant, large, soft salmon-pink flowers that are ideal in gardens and for cutting to decorate homes. Bushes grow 75cm/2½ft high and wide.

• 'Pink Favorite': Popular in North America, with large, deep pink flowers with high centres. Bushes grow to 75cm/2½ft high and 60cm/2ft wide.

• 'Pink Peace': Well-scented, large, deep-pink flowers on upright growth. Bushes grow 1m/3½ft high and about 75cm/3ft wide.

• 'Prima Ballerina': Scented, large, deep rose-pink flowers – often said to be cherry-pink. Superb in beds in gardens, growing to about 1m/3½ft high and 60cm/2ft wide.

• 'Royal Highness': Well-known in North America, with large, classically shaped, moderately fragrant, pearly-pink flowers on bushes about 1m/3½ft high and 72cm/28in wide.

• 'Savoy Hotel': Lightly scented, large, light pink flowers with deep tones. The bushes are 90cm/3ft high and 60cm/2ft wide.

• 'Silver Jubilee': Lightly scented, large and shapely peach-pink flowers on bushes 1m/3½ft high and 60cm/2ft wide.

• 'Wendy Cussons': Large, very fragrant, cherry-red to deep pink flowers on bushes 90cm/3ft high and 60cm/2ft wide.

'PAUL SHIRVILLE' has beautiful pink flowers on shrubby plants with shiny, dark foliage.

HYBRID TEAS
Crimson, Scarlet and Vermilion

❖

THESE are dramatic colours and can soon outmatch white, yellow and pink varieties if used in large and dominant groups. It is often better to have a complete bed of these colours than to run the risk of overwhelming lighter colours planted nearby.

These colours are so saturated that in twilight they soon appear black, but in bright sunlight they are dominant and eye-catching.

There are many varieties to choose from:

• 'Alexander': Slightly fragrant, vermilion red flowers, ideal in beds in gardens as well as for cutting and displaying indoors. Bushes grow up to 1.5m/5ft high and 75cm/2½ft wide.

• 'Big Chief': Exceptionally large, deep crimson flowers on vigorous, upright growth. Bushes grow about 1m/3½ft high and about 60cm/2ft wide.

• 'Deep Secret': Fragrant, deep crimson flowers. It is said to be the darkest of all red roses. Bushes are vigorous, up to 90cm/3ft high and 75cm/2½ft wide.

• 'Ernest H. Morse': Fragrant, large, crimson flowers borne prolifically through summer. It is ideal in flower beds and for cutting to decorate homes. Bushes grow about 75cm/2½ft high and 60cm/2ft wide.

• 'Fragrant Cloud': Popular variety, with fragrant, dusky-scarlet flowers on vigorous bushes about 75cm/2½ft high and 60cm/2ft wide.

• 'Papa Meilland': Large, blackish-crimson and velvet-like flowers on plants growing to 90cm/3ft high and 60cm/2ft wide.

'VELVET FRAGRANCE' forms a dominant bush, with dark green leaves and a vigorous stance.

• 'Red Devil': Large, exhibition-type, fragrant blooms on bushes which grow to about 1m/3½ft high and 75cm/2½ft wide.

• 'Royal William': Fragrant, deep red blooms on vigorous bushes which reach 1m/3½ft high and 75cm/2½ft wide.

• 'Ruby Wedding': Slightly fragrant, ruby-crimson flowers borne on branching bushes, about 75cm/2½ft high and 60cm/2ft wide.

• 'Super Star': Moderately scented, large, vermilion flowers on bushes about 90cm/3ft high and 75cm/2½ft wide.

• 'Velvet Fragrance': Large, fragrant, dark velvet-crimson flowers on bushes 1m/3½ft high and 72cm/28in wide.

HYBRID TEAS
Apricot, Orange and Copper

THESE are warm colours; they do not have the brightness and vitality of yellow, neither do they have the fiery nature of red. Instead, they have a near indefinable quality that has led to some varieties being classified variously as orange or soft red. For example, 'Cheshire Life' is usually put among the oranges, but occasionally with the reds.

There are many varieties with these colours to choose from, and these include:

• 'Apricot Silk': Lightly scented, large, orange-red blooms with a silky sheen. It is ideal for cutting and displaying indoors, as it has long stems and the blooms last for a long time when cut. Bushes grow about 90cm/3ft high and 60cm/2ft wide.

• 'Beauté': Moderately scented, large, apricot-orange blooms on vigorous, branching bushes up to 75cm/2½ft high and 60cm/2ft wide.

• 'Bettina': Medium-size, orange blooms with reddish veining. It is ideal in flower arrangements. Bushes grow 75cm/2½ft high and 60cm/2ft wide.

• 'Cheshire Life': Moderately scented, large blooms usually described as orange, but occasionally as orange-red and vermilion-orange. Bushes grow 75cm/2½ft high and 60cm/2ft wide.

• 'Dawn Chorus': Develops masses of slightly scented, glowing-orange flowers with a yellow base. Bushes grow to 90cm/3ft high and 75cm/2½ft wide.

• 'Diorama': Moderately scented, large, yellowish-orange flowers, flushed red. Bushes are branching and about 75cm/2½ft high and 60cm/2ft wide.

• 'Doris Tysterman': Lightly scented, orange-red flowers often described as tangerine. Bushes grow up to 1.2m/4ft high and 75cm/2½ft wide.

• 'Fulton Mackay': Moderately scented, golden apricot blooms on upright growth, on bushes 75cm/2½ft high and 60cm/2ft wide.

• 'Johnnie Walker': Large, apricot-coloured blooms on upright and branching bushes, 1m/3½ft high and 75cm/2½ft wide.

• 'Just Joey': Fragrant, large, coppery orange flowers that pale towards their edges. It is ideal in flower beds as well as a cut flower for home decoration. Bushes grow 75cm/2½ft high and 60cm/2ft wide.

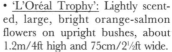

'JUST JOEY', *with coppery-orange flowers, is ideal for planting in beds in gardens as well as for cutting to display indoors.*

• 'L'Oréal Trophy': Lightly scented, large, bright orange-salmon flowers on upright bushes, about 1.2m/4ft high and 75cm/2½ft wide.

• 'Lover's Meeting': Lightly scented, reddish-orange blooms on vigorous, branching stems. Bushes grow 60cm/2ft high and wide.

• 'Princess Royal': Spicily scented, golden apricot flowers with a hint of bronze. The blooms have a classical shade, with high centres, and are borne on bushes 82cm/32in high and 60cm/2ft wide.

• 'Remember Me': Fragrant, large, rich coppery orange blooms borne in sprays on bushes 90cm/3ft high and 60cm/2ft wide.

• 'Rosemary Harkness': Sweetly fragrant, medium-sized, orange-yellow blooms blended with salmon. It is ideal when grown in beds. The bushes have a branching habit, 75cm/2½ft high and about the same in width.

• 'Royal Romance': Classically shaped, with moderately scented, large, salmon-pink and peach flowers borne amid bushy growth. Bushes grow 75cm/2½ft high and 60cm/2ft wide. 'Whisky Mac' is one of its parents.

• 'The Lady': Fragrant, large, honey-yellow blooms edged in salmon and borne in wide sprays. Bushes have an upright nature, growing to about 90cm/3ft high and 60cm/2ft wide.

• 'Troika': Moderately scented, large, reddish-orange flowers with yellow and pink flushes. It is ideal for planting in flower beds, as well as for cutting for home decoration – the flowers are shapely, do not fade and have long stems. Bushes grow about 90cm/3ft high and 75cm/2½ft wide.

• 'Whisky Mac': Strongly scented, large, golden apricot flowers on bushes 75cm/2½ft high and 60cm/2ft wide. The young foliage is reddish and very attractive.

'TROIKA' *has reddish-orange flowers with yellow and pink flushes; it is ideal as a cut flower.*

'BLUE' ROSES

It is probable that no true-blue rose will ever be created, as the blue pigment, delphinidin, is not present in the rose family. Nevertheless, two varieties come quite close to achieving the 'impossible'.

• *'Blue Parfum': Strongly scented, large, mauve-pink flowers on bushes about 75cm/2½ft high and 60cm/2ft wide.*

• *'Blue Moon': This is considered to be the best 'blue', with lemon-scented, lilac-mauve blooms borne on upright and branching stems. Bushes grow about 90cm/3ft high and 60cm/2ft wide. It is prized by flower arrangers.*

FLORIBUNDAS
White and Cream

FLORIBUNDAS have a more relaxed and informal nature than Hybrid Teas and are superb in beds in gardens, either on their own or mixed with shrubs and other plants. Floribundas are now properly known as Cluster-flowered Bush Roses (sometimes shortened to CF Bush), but invariably in rose catalogues they are still listed as Floribunda (occasionally shortened to Flor).

These floriferous roses flower during the latter part of early summer and into mid-summer, with repeat-flowering later. Their range of colours is wide, and they are described between this page and page 77.

'MARGARET MERRIL' *has large, high-centred, blush-white flowers with a satin sheen. The dark green foliage is resistant to diseases.*

WHITE FLORIBUNDAS
There is a surprisingly small range of white floribundas.
• 'Grace Abounding': Moderately scented, with showy clusters of creamy, buff-white flowers borne amid shrubby growth up to 90cm/3ft high and 75cm/2½ft wide.
• 'Iceberg': Lightly scented with large, showy clusters of white flowers borne freely on bushes about 82cm/32in high and 60cm/2ft wide. Unfortunately, during hot weather the flowers become slightly pink. Often it continues to flower into late autumn and occasionally well into winter.
• 'Ivory Fashion': Lightly fragrant, ivory-white, semi-double and large flowers that open flat. Sometimes, they shade to pale buff in the centre and during wet seasons are susceptible to black spot. Bushes are vigorous, up to 90cm/3ft high and 75cm/2½ft wide.
• 'Margaret Merril': Strongly and richly scented, large but dainty, high-centred, blush-white blooms. They are prized for their satin sheen. Bushes are upright, to about 82cm/32in and about 60cm/2ft wide. The dark green foliage tends to be resistant to damage from disease.
• 'Yvonne Rabier': Although introduced in 1910, before Floribundas were created, it has a similar nature and therefore is included here. It is a cross between *Rosa wichuraiana* and a Polyantha. It bears clusters of fragrant, milky white, small blooms on bushy yet compact plants about 45cm/1½ft high and wide. It needs only light pruning.
This bushy but low-growing rose is listed in some rose catalogues as a Dwarf Polyantha.

FLORIBUNDAS
Yellow and Gold

'MOUNTBATTEN'
has large, mimosa-yellow flowers on bushes with a shrub-like stance.

THESE, like yellow Hybrid Teas, have a dramatic impact on a garden, especially when seen en masse. And because they have more flowers their influence is even more apparent. There are many varieties to choose from, some bold and strong, others demure.
• 'Allgold': Lightly scented, with large clusters of small, buttercup-yellow flowers on branching bushes 60cm/2ft high and 50cm/20in wide. It is often thought to be one of the best yellow-flowered floribundas.
• 'Amber Queen': Well-scented, amber-yellow flowers borne in large clusters. Bushes grow about 50cm/20in high and 60cm/24in wide. When young, the leaves are reddish, but slowly become dark green. Upright growth.
• 'Arthur Bell': Well-scented, golden yellow flowers borne singly and in clusters on vigorous, upright bushes about 82cm/32in high and 60cm/2ft wide.
• 'Bright Smile': Moderately scented, bright yellow flowers borne in clusters on plants about 45cm/1½ft high and wide.
• 'Burma Star': Scented, large, light amber flowers borne on upright bushes, about 1.2m/4ft high and 60cm/2ft wide.
• 'Golden Years': Lightly scented, large, richly golden yellow flowers borne in clusters on bushes 72cm/28in high and 60cm/24in wide. Plenty of foliage.
• 'Honeymoon': Moderately scented, medium-sized and rosette-shaped canary-yellow flowers on vigorous growth. Growing to about 90cm/3ft high and 60cm/2ft wide, this bush has handsome foliage.

• 'Korresia': Scented, bright yellow flowers with wavy petals. It is superb when planted in flower beds and for cutting to decorate rooms indoors. Bushes grow about 75cm/2½ft high and 60cm/2ft wide.
• 'Mountbatten': Moderately scented, large, mimosa-yellow flowers borne in small clusters. It is shrub-like and grows 1.2m/4ft high and 82cm/32in wide. A strong, tall and bushy variety.
• 'Princess Alice': Lightly scented, medium-sized, bright yellow flowers borne in large clusters on bushes 1m/3½ft high and 60cm/2ft high.
• 'Sunsilk': Lightly scented, large, lemon-yellow flowers borne on upright growth on bushes 82cm/32in high and 60cm/24in wide.

FLORIBUNDAS
Pink and Blush
❖

THESE are reserved and demure colours, neither clinical and pure, like white, nor saturated with colour as are the dominant reds. Indeed, pink is a desaturated red and contains only a small proportion of red pigments. The range of pink varieties varies widely, from those with only a small amount of pink to those only a few shades less than red.

• 'Chanelle': Moderately scented, creamy pink flowers, although sometimes described as shell-pink and amber-pink. The growth is bushy and plants grow about 75cm/2½ft high and 60cm/2ft wide.

• 'City of Leeds': Slightly fragrant, medium-sized, blush salmon-pink flowers borne on bushy, vigorous and upright plants. Bushes grow 75cm/2½ft high and 60cm/2ft wide.

• 'Dearest': Spicily fragrant, with salmon-pink or light rosy pink, camellia-like flowers. They are ideal for cutting to decorate rooms indoors, as well as growing in beds in gardens. Bushes grow 60cm/2ft high and wide.

• 'Escapade': Sweetly musk rose-scented, rosy violet flowers, but verging towards pink. They have

'CITY OF LEEDS' *reveals blush, salmon-pink flowers on vigorous, upright bushes.*

---

a single, almost wild rose nature. The 82cm/32in high and 60cm/2ft wide bushes are ideal for planting in a mixed border.

• 'Pink Parfait': A North American variety, either light pink or pink with a creamy base. Bushes grow 75cm/2½ft high and 60cm/2ft wide.

• 'Queen Elizabeth': Lightly scented, large, cyclamen-pink flowers borne in big, open trusses on vigorous bushes, 1.5m/5ft or more high and up to 90cm/3ft wide. Often used to form a hedge.

• 'Radox Bouquet': Well-scented, rose-pink flowers, often quartered and with a cottage-garden look. They are much prized by flower arrangers. Bushes grow 90cm/3ft high and 60cm/2ft wide.

RED AND ROMANTIC

In the language of flowers, red roses have several meanings:
• *Red rose bud means* You are young and beautiful.
• *Fully-open red rose implies* Beauty.
• *Deep red rose tells of* Bashful shame.

FLORIBUNDAS
Red and Vermilion
❖

THESE are dominant, dramatic colours that need to be used carefully if they are not to subdue nearby and less strong ones. There are many varieties to choose from.

• 'Anne Cocker': Large clusters of neatly-spaced, bright vermilion flowers borne on vigorous, upright bushes, 90cm/3ft high and 60cm/2ft wide.

• 'Beautiful Britain': Lightly scented, medium-sized clusters of tomato-red flowers on vigorous, bushy plants, about 75cm/2½ft high and 60cm/2ft wide.

• 'Chorus': Slightly scented, large, bright red flowers borne in big trusses on vigorous and bushy plants up to 75cm/2½ft high and 60cm/2ft wide.

• 'City of Belfast': Medium-sized flowers, variously described as red, velvety orange-scarlet or just

'BEAUTIFUL BRITAIN' *has dominant, tomato-red flowers on bushy plants.*

---

scarlet. It is ideal for growing in small gardens as the bushes grow 60cm/2ft high and wide.

• 'Dusky Maiden': Fragrant, almost single, crimson flowers with deeper shading. Grows to 75cm/2½ft high and 60cm/2ft wide.

• 'Europeana': Lightly scented, large, showy, dark red flowers borne in large trusses. Bushes grow to a height of 72cm/28in, and 60cm/2ft wide.

• 'Evelyn Fison': Lightly scented, with large trusses of bright red flowers. Bushes grow 75cm/2½ft high and 60cm/2ft wide.

• 'Frensham': Medium-sized, deep crimson flowers borne in large clusters on vigorous, branching bushes up to 1.2m/4ft high and 75cm/2½ft wide.

• 'Lilli Marlene': Lightly scented, velvety, deep crimson flowers and coppery foliage. Bushes will grow to a height of 72cm/28in and 60cm/2ft wide.

• 'Memento': Slightly scented, salmon-red to cherry-pink flowers borne on bushy, vigorous and upright bushes, 75cm/2½ft high and 60cm/2ft wide. The flowers are resistant to rain.

• 'Rob Roy': Lightly scented, large, crimson-scarlet blooms borne in lax clusters on bushes growing to 90cm/3ft high and 60cm/2ft wide.

• 'Trumpeter': Lightly scented, large, showy trusses of medium-sized, bright vermilion flowers. Sometimes they are considered to be orange-red. Bushes are 50cm/20in high and 45cm/18in wide.

• 'The Times Rose': Slightly scented, large, dark red flowers borne in large trusses on vigorous, spreading bushes about 60cm/2ft high and 75cm/2½ft wide.

FLORIBUNDAS
Apricot, Copper and Orange
❖

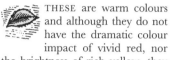

THESE are warm colours and although they do not have the dramatic colour impact of vivid red, nor the brightness of rich yellow, they are most welcome as they create a soothing ambience. They neither brighten dramatically when in strong sunlight, nor dull too much when light starts to diminish in the evening. There are many varieties to choose from, such as:

• 'Apricot Nectar': Moderately scented, large, pale apricot petals which shade to gold at their base. They appear singly or in clusters, on plants 60cm/2ft high and wide.

• 'Anne Harkness': Lightly scented, apricot-yellow or just apricot flowers borne in large clusters on vigorous, strong, upright bushes, up to 1.2m/4ft high and about 60cm/2ft wide.

• 'Fellowship': Scented blooms borne in widely spaced clusters. Their colour is said to be a fusion of Spanish orange and glowing embers. It is ideal for planting in beds, as well as creating hedges, and grows up to 90cm/3ft high and 60cm/2ft wide.

• 'Geraldine': Lightly scented, rich orange flowers borne in clusters amid spreading growth. It is ideal

'ORANGE SENSATION' *develops orange-vermilion flowers in large clusters.*

for planting in beds, as well as cutting to decorate rooms indoors. Bushes grow 75cm/2½ft high and 60cm/2ft wide.

• 'Iced Ginger': Lightly scented, buff to coppery pink blooms borne in clusters on branching bushes 90cm/3ft high and 60cm/2ft high.

• 'Golden Slippers': Full, Hybrid Tea-shaped flowers with orange-flame petals with pale gold reverse. Bushes are 50cm/20in high and 45cm/18in wide.

• 'Julie Cussons': Moderately scented, brilliant orange-salmon flowers borne on bushes about 90cm/3ft high and 60cm/2ft wide.

• 'Orange Sensation': Lightly scented, orange-vermilion flowers borne in big clusters on bushy plants 72cm/28in high and 60cm/2ft wide.

• 'Southampton': Clusters of slightly ruffled, apricot-orange flowers occasionally flushed pink. It is ideal both in borders and as a cut flower for the decoration of rooms indoors. Bushes grow to about 1.2m/4ft high and 75cm/2½ft wide.

• 'Woburn Abbey': Golden orange flowers borne in large clusters on upright bushes, 90cm/3ft high and 60cm/2ft wide. Its brightness is probably derived from 'Masquerade', one of its parents.

UNUSUAL SHADES

Pink, yellow, red and orange are always popular colours, but rose enthusiasts are always searching for unusual shades or mixtures of colour. Many rose catalogues offer a medley of unusual colours.

• 'Brownie': Introduced in 1969, this rose has slightly fragrant blooms in shades of tan, edged in pink and with an attractive yellow reverse. It grows about 60cm/2ft high.

• 'Café': The sweetly fragrant, flat, fully-double flowers are a combination of unusual colours – coffee and cream. The plants are bushy and stocky, with attractive olive-green leaves that, with the flowers, create a memorable display.

• 'Edith Holden': Also known as 'The Edwardian lady', it was introduced in 1988 and reveals russet-brown blooms with gold tints. It grows 1m/3½ft high.

• 'Jocelyn': Double, flat, dull mahogany flowers that slowly become purplish-brown. They are borne in small clusters. It grows to about 60cm/2ft high.

'ICED GINGER' *reveals buff to coppery pink blooms in clusters on branching stems.*

• 'Victoriana': Introduced in 1976, the sweetly scented, full and rounded flowers of this Floribunda are an attractive mixture of vermilion and silver. The sturdy bushes grow to about 75cm/2½ft.

LAVENDER, PURPLE AND MAUVE

These are unusual colours in Floribundas and therefore introduce a welcome change from reds, yellows and shades of orange. They do need careful positioning to prevent them being dominated by nearby plants. Here are a few to consider:

• *'Lavender Pinocchio': Large, brownish-lavender flowers which open flat. Some experts suggest that the colour is lavender blue-grey. Bushes grow 75cm/2½ft high and 60cm/2ft wide.*

• *'Lilac Charm': Well-scented, large, lavender flowers with golden stamens on red filaments. It is free-flowering and the flowers are borne in small trusses on branching stems. Bushes grow 60cm/2ft high and wide.*

• *'Old Master': Large, deep carmine-pink flowers, edged with silvery white, borne on bushes 82cm/32in high and 60cm/18in wide.*

• *'Purple Splendour': Large, clear, glowing purple flowers borne on erect stems on bushes up to 90cm/3ft high and 60cm/2ft wide.*

• *'Shocking Blue': Scented, large, lilac-mauve flowers borne on bushy plants up to 75cm/2½ft high and 60cm/2ft wide.*

MINIATURE ROSES

THESE have a miniature stature. Few of them are taller than 38cm/15in, some only 23cm/9in, so when planting, space them about 30cm/12in apart, and only 20cm/8in for smaller varieties.

WIDE RANGE OF USES

They are ideal for planting along the edges of borders, in pots on patios and in window-boxes. Those growing in pots can be taken indoors while in bloom, but they are not pot plants and must soon be returned outside, as prolonged stays in too warm positions encourages soft growth.

When grown in pots, ensure that the compost does not dry out as the roots are then soon damaged. Similarly, when grown in window-boxes, check the compost frequently during summer. Also, regularly remove dead flowers to encourage further blooms.

In winter, move Miniature roses in pots and window-boxes to sheltered positions, away from strong winds. No pruning is needed at the time Miniatures roses are planted. Later, the only pruning established ones need is to trim diseased and weak shoots with scissors in late winter.

MINIATURE roses are ideal in window-boxes. They can also be grown in troughs and placed on patios and balconies.

MINIATURE VARIETIES

- '**Baby Masquerade**': Slightly fragrant, yellow to pink and red flowers; 45cm/1½ft high.
- '**Cinderella**': White flowers tinged pink; 30cm/12in high.
- '**Darling Flame**': Orange-red flowers with yellow anthers; 38cm/15in high.
- '**Easter Morning**': Large, ivory-white flowers; 25cm/10in high.
- '**Green Diamond**': Lime-green flowers; 30cm/12in high.
- '**New Penny**': Orange-red to copper-pink; 25cm/10in high.
- '**Pour Toi**': Creamy white; 30cm/12in high.

THE EDGES *of paths and patios can soon be filled with colour during summer.*

WHEN *planted in pots, Miniature roses can be grown on patios and balconies.*

THEY *can be taken indoors for short periods, but avoid high temperatures.*

PATIO ROSES

THIS is a relatively new group of roses and, in size, falls somewhere between miniatures and small Floribundas. Indeed, they are really small Floribundas and for this reason they are sometimes called Dwarf Cluster-flowered Bush Roses, or DCF (Patio) Bush. Most of them are between 45cm/1½ft and 60cm/2ft high, although a few of them only reach 38cm/15in. Their nature is more robust than that of miniature roses, with a bushy and repeat-flowering habit.

In some catalogues and books, Patio Roses have become a distinct group, while in others they are added to the Floribundas or just put with the Miniature types. Patio roses are pruned in the same way as are Floribundas, but lightly. The range of varieties is wide and includes:

- '**Anna Ford**': Vivid, orange-red; 45cm/1½ft high.
- '**Bianco**': White; 45cm/1½ft high.
- '**Cider Cup**': Deep apricot-pink; 45cm/1½ft high.
- '**Claire Rayner**': Striped orange and yellow; 38cm/15in high.
- '**Conservation**': Apricot-pink; 45cm/1½ft high.
- '**Drummer Boy**': Deep, bright crimson; 38cm/15in high.
- '**International Herald Tribune**': Violet-purple; 45cm/1½ft high.
- '**Mandarin**': Deep pink, with orange-yellow centre; 38cm/15in high.
- '**Peek-a-Boo**': Apricot; 45cm/1½ft high.
- '**Petit Four**': Pink and white; 38cm/15in high.

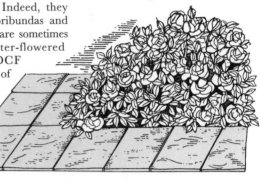

- '**Ray of Sunshine**': Yellow; 38cm/15in high.
- '**Red Rascal**': Bright crimson; 38cm/15in high.

- '**Robin Redbreast**': Red, with a pale centre; 45cm/1½ft high.
- '**Saint Boniface**': Scarlet; 60cm/2ft high.
- '**Sweet Dream**': Apricot-peach; 45cm/1½ft high.
- '**Wee Jock**': Deep crimson; 38cm/15in high.
- '**Top Marks**': Bright, vivid orange-vermilion; 38cm/15in high. Double and lightly scented.

HANGING BASKET

For an unusual display in a hanging basket, the ground-covering 'Hertfordshire' can be used. It is a member of the County Series of ground-cover shrubs and has compact growth, with masses of single, delicately coloured, carmine-pink flowers. It spreads to about 90cm/3ft wide. Ensure that compost in the basket does not become dry.

SPECIES ROSES

❖

THESE encompass roses which at one time could be found growing wild, alongside their natural hybrids and sports (mutations). Many of them are grown for their beautiful flowers, while some have fruits (heps or hips) with attractive shapes and colours. The flowers mostly have only five petals, but double-flowered forms have occurred as sports in the wild, while both double and semi-double forms have been selected to grow in gardens. There are many of these species (and their forms) available from garden centres and specialist nurseries, and some of them are included here:

• *Rosa californica* 'Plena': Sweetly scented, semi-double, deep pink flowers which cascade during the latter part of early summer and into mid-summer. These are followed by red heps. Height: 1.8m/6ft. Spread:1.2–1.8m/4–6ft.

• *R. canina* 'Andersonii': Rich, brilliant pink flowers with a raspberry-drop fragrance during early summer. These are followed by red heps. Height: 1.8–2.1m/6–7ft. Spread: 1.2–1.8m/4–6ft.

ROSA GLAUCA, *but earlier known as* R. rubrifolia, *has grey-purple leaves and cerise-pink flowers during early summer.*

• *R. ecae:* Prickly stems with fern-like leaves and bright, golden yellow flowers about 2.5cm/1in across during late spring and early summer. Height: 1.5m/5ft. Spread: 1.5m/5ft.

• *R. foetida* 'Bicolor': Known as the Austrian Copper, the shrub has a suckering nature and single flowers which are copper-red on the upperside and yellow on the reverse during late spring and early summer. Height: 1.5m/5ft. Spread: 1.2m/4ft.

• *R. glauca (R. rubrifolia):* Well-known for its grey-purple leaves and glaucous purple stems. During early summer it produces single, cerise-pink flowers about 36mm/1½in wide, in small clusters. However, it is mainly grown for its attractive foliage.

• *R. hugonis:* Arching stems with fern-like leaves and creamy yellow, 5cm/2in-wide, saucer-shaped flowers during late spring and early summer. Height: 2.1m/7ft. Spread: 1.8m/6ft.

ROSA CALIFORNICA *'Plena' has sweetly-scented, deep pink flowers during the latter part of early summer and into mid-summer.*

• *R. moyesii* 'Geranium': Arched branches bearing brilliant red flowers about 6.5cm/2½in wide during early summer. In autumn these are followed by flask-shaped, glossy red heps. Height: 2.4m/8ft. Spread: 2.1m/7ft.

• *R. x paulii* 'Rosea': A vigorous, low-growing and trailing shrub with large, fragrant, fresh pink flowers with a white centre throughout summer. It is ideal for covering banks and old tree stumps. Height: 60–90cm/2–3ft. Spread: 1.8m/6ft.

• *R. spinosissima (R. pimpinellifolia):* This is the Scotch, Scottish or Burnet Rose, a low, thicket-forming shrub with pretty white flowers during late spring and early summer. Height: 60–90cm/2–3ft. Spread: up to 1.2m/4ft. This is the parent of the many so-called Scottish Roses.

• *R. rubiginosa (earlier known as R. eglanteria):* This is the well known Sweetbriar or Eglantine. The leaves are strongly fragrant, especially during warm, moist, summer evenings. The single, bright pink flowers appear during early summer. These are followed by orange-scarlet heps. Height and spread: 1.8–2.4m/6–8ft.

• *R. sericea pteracantha:* Small, fern-like foliage on stems noted for their extremely large, flat, red, translucent thorns. They are mahogany-red on young stems; their growth is encouraged by pruning the plant back severely in late winter. The creamy white, single flowers, up to 5cm/2in

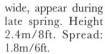

ROSA FOETIDA *'Bicolor' has flowers that are copper-red on the upperside and yellow on the reverse.*

wide, appear during late spring. Height 2.4m/8ft. Spread: 1.8m/6ft.

• *R. xanthina* 'Canary Bird': Prickly stems with graceful, fern-like leaves and bright, canary-yellow flowers about 42mm/1¾in wide during late spring and early summer. Height and spread: 2.1m/7ft.

• *R. willmottiae:* Arching stems bearing dainty, fern-like leaves and small, rosy purple flowers up to 36mm/1½in across during late spring and early summer. Small, orange-red heps. Native of North-west China, its seeds were introduced into Britain in 1904. The plant is named after the gardener and rosarian Miss Ellen Willmott.

ROSA XANTHINA *'Canary Bird' is very popular, with fern-like leaves and bright, canary-yellow flowers during late spring and into early summer.*

OLD ROSES
Alba, Bourbon, Centifolia and China Roses
❖

 SOMETIMES known as Old-fashioned Roses, these are the types that developed from Species Roses through natural or selective hybridization, or as sports. They were especially popular during the nineteenth century and form hardy shrubs, many with unsurpassed fragrance. The flowers are mainly double, some with a carnation or camellia form, and appear during early and mid-summer, some later. A few flowers are 'quartered', and this means that the petals are in four densely crowded groups. The centre is flat and sometimes forms an eye.

Old Roses can be grouped according to the wild species from which they developed. Occasionally, some have their origination in several groups. These roses are featured between here and page 82.

'FÉLICITÉ PARMENTIER' *(Alba) has rosette-like, fresh-pink flowers that reflex almost to a ball.*

'LOUISE ODIER' *(Bourbon) reveals warm pink flowers, softly shaded with lilac.*

ALBAS
Hardy, vigorous, upright shrubs with strong stems, a few large prickles and grey-green leaves. Flower colour ranges from white to pink and they flower during the latter part of early summer and into mid-summer.
• 'Alba Maxima' (Jacobite Rose): Fragrant, double flowers, first blush-tinted but later turning creamy white. Height: 1.8m/6ft. Spread: 1.5m/5ft.
• 'Celestial': Sweetly scented, semi-double flowers that have golden stamens and shell-pink petals. Height: 1.8m/6ft. Spread: 1.2m/4ft.
• 'Félicité Parmentier': Fully double, rosette-like, fresh pink flowers fading to cream at their edges. Height and spread: 1.2m/4ft.
• 'Maiden's Blush': Double, blush-pink flowers that are shaped like rosettes. Height: 1.5m/5ft. Spread: 1.2m/4ft.

'FANTIN-LATOUR' *(Centifolia) has a delicate scent and blush-pink flowers that deepen to shell-pink.*

BOURBONS
These have China and Portland roses, as well as others, in their parentage. Most are strongly fragrant, with globular or cup-shaped flowers, about 7.5cm/3in wide, from early summer to autumn.
• 'Adam Messerich': Raspberry-like fragrance; semi-double, rich pink flowers. Height: 1.8m/6ft. Spread: 1.5m/5ft.
• 'Louise Odier': Scented, cup-shaped, warm pink flowers softly shaded with lilac. Height: 1.5m/5ft. Spread: 1.2m/4ft.
• 'Mme. Isaac Pereire': Fragrant, tightly-packed, cup-shaped and quartered, deep madder-pink flowers. Height: 1.5–1.8m/5–6ft. Spread: 1.2–1.5m/4–5ft.
• 'Souvenir de la Malmaison': Strongly-fragrant soft pink flowers, cupped at first but later flat and quartered. Height and spread: 90cm–1.2m/3–4ft.

CENTIFOLIAS
Provence or Cabbage Roses are descended from *R. centifolia*. The flowers, which appear in clusters during early and mid-summer, are invariably scented.

• 'Centifolia' (Cabbage Rose): Richly fragrant, globular, clear pink flowers. Height 1.5m/5ft. Spread: 1.2m/4ft.
• 'Fantin-Latour': Delicate scent, with blush-pink flowers deepening to shell-pink. Height: 1.8m/6ft. Spread: 1.5m/5ft.
• 'Robert le Diable': Mixture of colours; parma violet, dark purple and vivid cerise, fading to grey. Height and spread: 90cm/3ft.
• 'Tour de Malakoff': Fragrant; mainly purple-magenta, fading to grey and lavender. Height: 1.8m/6ft. Spread: 1.5m/5ft.

CHINAS
These form pretty, somewhat twiggy bushes. Most are slightly tender and must not be planted in frosty positions.
• 'Hermosa': Fragrant, globular, pink flowers. Quite hardy. Height: 90cm/3ft. Spread: 60cm/2ft.
• 'Mutabilis': Flame-coloured buds open to coppery yellow, single flowers. Needs shelter. Height: 2.4m/8ft. Spread: 1.8m/6ft.
• 'Old Blush China' (Monthly Rose): Pale pink flowers over a long period. Height: 1.2m/4ft. Spread: 90cm/3ft.

'HERMOSA' *(China) produces fragrant, pink flowers that are almost globular.*

OLD ROSES
Damask, Gallica, Hybrid Musk and Hybrid Perpetual Roses
❖

THE range of these roses is wide; many are ideal in shrub borders as well as for planting with herbaceous plants in mixed borders. They introduce height and focal points to large borders. Some, such as the Damasks, have an old heritage, while others, like Hybrid Musks, are much more recent.

'MME. HARDY' *(Damask) has cupped, white flowers with a lemon-like redolence.*

DAMASKS
Most of these have fragrant, double flowers, 7.5cm/3in wide, during early and mid-summer.
• 'La Ville de Bruxelles': Very fragrant, large, fully-double, rich pink flowers. Height: 1.5m/5ft. Spread: 1.2m/4ft.
• 'Mme. Hardy': Lemon-like fragrance, with cupped, white flowers. Height: 1.8m/6ft. Spread: 1.5m/5ft.
• 'Marie Louise': Large, intensely pink flowers that open flat, later becoming soft mauve. Height and spread: 1.2m/4ft.

GALLICAS
A large group of long-established roses. They form hardy, compact shrubs with few thorns. The flowers are richly scented, 5–7.5cm/2–3in wide, and borne during the latter part of early summer and into mid-summer.
• 'Belle de Crécy': Richly fragrant, cerise-pink buds opening to reveal a soft parma violet. Strong, arching stems. Height: 1.2m/4ft. Spread: 90cm/3ft.
• 'Empress Joséphine': Little scent, but superb, loosely-double flowers; clear, rich pink. Height and spread: 90cm/3ft.
• 'Officinalis' (Apothecary's Rose and Red Rose of Lancaster): Large, semi-double, light crimson flowers. Golden stamens. Height and spread: 1.2m/4ft.
• 'Tuscany Superb': Fragrant, large, deep crimson flowers, fading to purple. Height: 1.5m/5ft. Spread: 90cm/3ft.

'TUSCANY SUPERB' *(Gallica) is famed for its superb, deep crimson flowers.*

'BUFF BEAUTY' *(Hybrid Musk) has warm apricot-yellow flowers borne in large trusses.*

HYBRID MUSKS
These are derived from *Rosa moschata* (Autumn Musk Rose), but are now only distantly related.

They were mostly – but not all – bred by The Revd J. Pemberton in the early twentieth century. Flowering is mainly in early and mid-summer, and intermittently until the frosts of autumn.
• 'Ballerina': Masses of hydrangea-like heads that reveal small, single, pale pink, slightly scented flowers. Height and spread: 1.2m/4ft.
• 'Buff Beauty': Tea-scented, with almost Hybrid Tea-like, warm apricot-yellow flowers borne in large trusses. Height and spread: 1.5m/5ft.
• 'Felicia': Aromatically fragrant, silvery salmon-pink flowers with a Hybrid Tea shape. Height and spread: 1.5m/5ft.
• 'Penelope': Musk-scented, semi-double, rich creamy pink flowers that reveal yellow stamens. Later it develops coral-pink heps. Height and spread: 1.8m/6ft.
• 'Prosperity': Sweetly scented, ivory-white, semi-double flowers. Height: 1.8m/6ft. Spread: 1.2m/4ft.

HYBRID PERPETUALS
These were popular in Victorian and Edwardian times and have Portland, Bourbon and China roses in their ancestry. They form vigorous shrubs, with 'cabbage-like', rounded and double flowers in clusters from early to late summer. Each flower can be up to 10cm/4in wide; most are fragrant.
• 'Baroness Rothschild': Fragrant, large and flat flowers with dark rose petals shading to shell-pink at their edge. Height: 1.5m/5ft. Spread: 90cm/3ft.
• 'Baron Girod de l'Ain': Richly scented, large, crimson flowers with a thin, white edging. Height: 1.5m/5ft. Spread: 1.2m/4ft.
• 'Ferdinand Pichard': Richly fragrant, with a repeat-flowering nature. The globular, pinkish-white flowers are striped purple and crimson. Height: 1.2m/4ft. Spread: 30cm/3ft.
• 'Gloire de Ducher': Fragrant, full, deep crimson flowers that slowly turn purple. Height: 1.8m/6ft. Spread: 1.2m/4ft.
• 'Reine des Violettes': Scented, quartered flowers in shades of lilac and purple. Height: 1.8m/6ft. Spread: 1.5m/5ft.

'BARONESS ROTHSCHILD' *(Hybrid Perpetual) has large, flat flowers, dark rose and shading to shell-pink.*

OLD ROSES
Hybrid Sweetbriars, Moss, Portland, Scotch and Tea Roses
❖

THESE are further roses that are ideal in gardens. Some have a long heritage, such as the Moss types which are forms of Centifolia roses, while others, such as the Hybrid Sweetbriars, are newer and introduced mainly during the last few years of the nineteenth century.

HYBRID SWEETBRIARS
These are also known as Penzance Briars and are the products of crosses using *Rosa rubiginosa* (*R. eglanteria* and commonly known as Sweetbriar and Eglantine) and *R. foetida* (Austrian Briar). The varieties are richly scented and borne in small clusters during early and mid-summer.
• 'Amy Robsart': Richly fragrant, large, semi-double, deep rose-pink flowers and scarlet heps. Height and spread: 1.8–2.4m/6–8ft.
• 'Janet's Pride': Fragrant, single, bright cherry-pink flowers with a pale centre. Height: 1.8m/6ft high and 1.5m/5ft wide.
• 'Lady Penzance': Fragrant, single with coppery yellow tints. Height and spread: 1.8m/6ft.

'LADY PENZANCE' *(Hybrid Sweetbriar) has fragrant, coppery yellow flowers.*

'WILLIAM LOBB' *(Moss Rose) is also known as the Old Velvet Rose and develops dark crimson flowers that fade to a demure violet-grey.*

MOSS ROSES
These are sports (natural mutations) derived from *Rosa centifolia* 'Muscosa', or hybrids originated from these sports. However, the mossy glands are less noticeable on the hybrids. The flowers, fragrant and up to 7.5cm/3in across, appear in early and mid-summer.
• 'Comtesse de Murinais': Fragrant, blush-pink flowers that fade to white. Height: 1.8m/6ft. Spread: 1.2m/4ft.
• 'Louis Gimard': Fragrant, large, globular flowers with light crimson petals with lilac tones. Height: 1.5m/5ft. Spread: 90cm/3ft.
• 'Maréchal Davoust': Fragrant, large, intense carmine-pink flowers that slowly become lilac and purple. Height and spread: 1.2m/4ft.
• 'William Lobb' (Old Velvet Rose): Richly scented, dark crimson flowers that fade to a demure violet-grey. Height and spread: 1.8m/6ft.

PORTLAND ROSES
These are hardy and compact bushes, often with a suckering nature and developing Damask-type flowers up to 7.5cm/3in wide. The flowers appear mainly during the latter part of early summer and into mid-summer and frequently continue to late summer and autumn. They are borne singly or in small clusters.
• 'Comte de Chambord': Heavily fragrant, warm pink flowers with lilac tones that become flat and quartered. Height: 1.2m/4ft. Spread: 90cm/3ft.
• 'Jacques Cartier': Strongly scented, rich pink and rosette-shaped flowers; each is full and quartered. Height 1.2m/4ft. Spread: 90cm/3ft.
• 'Rose de Rescht': Very fragrant, purple-crimson flowers. Height: 90cm/3ft. Spread: 75cm/2½ft.

SCOTCH ROSES
These suckering, hardy and vigorous roses owe their parentage to *R. spinosissima*, widely known as the Scotch Rose, or Burnet Rose. These roses have fragrant, saucer-shaped flowers, borne singly or in small clusters during early and mid-summer.

'STANWELL PERPETUAL' *(Scotch Rose) has pale blush-pink flowers that open flat and reveal quartering.*

'COMTE DE CHAMBORD' *(Portland Rose) with warm pink flowers and lilac tones. The flowers open flat and become quartered.*

• 'Falkland': Fragrant, semi-double, pale pink flowers with their bases tinted yellow. Height and spread: 1.2m/4ft.
• 'Stanwell Perpetual': Sweetly scented, pale blush-pink flowers that open flat to reveal quartering. They mainly appear during mid-summer but often continue throughout the rose season. Height and spread: 1.2m/4ft.
• 'William III': Fragrant, semi-double, purplish-crimson flowers fading to lilac-pink. Height and spread: 60cm/2ft.

TEA ROSES
These are not usually put with Old Roses, but as many have a long heritage they are worth including here. In 1824 a sulphur-yellow rose was introduced from China and became known as a Tea Rose. This is the originator of many superb varieties. Most are 75–90cm/2½–3ft high.
• 'Lady Hillingdon': Strongly tea-scented, with apricot-coloured flowers.
• 'Marie van Houtte': Fragrant, delicate and pretty, cream-tinged, carmine-pink flowers.

MODERN SHRUB ROSES

❖

THESE are hardy shrubs, created from a wide range of parents, chiefly during the twentieth century. They are mainly crosses between modern bush roses and strong climbers and ramblers. The shape of their flowers is invariably modern, rather than old-fashioned and is unlike those of Old Roses. But they have the blessing of being strong, robust and free-flowering, often intermittently throughout summer. There are many varieties and some are suggested here.

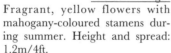

'FRÜHLINGSMORGEN' reveals rose-pink flowers with yellow centres and purplish-maroon stamens during early summer.

• 'Autumn Fire': Deep blood-red flowers, with darker shading, during early and mid-summer, followed by a further display in early autumn. It develops large, orange-red heps. Height and spread: 1.8m/6ft.
• 'Bloomfield Abundance': It is quite similar to 'Cécile Brunner' and bears open sprays of blush-pink flowers. Height: 1.8m/6ft. Spread: 1.5m/5ft.
• 'Cerise Bouquet': Arching stems bearing semi-double, cerise-pink, early and mid-summer flowers with the tantalizing fragrance of raspberries. Height: 2.7m/9ft. Spread: 2.4m/8ft.
• 'Fritz Nobis': Clove-scented, small, Hybrid Tea-like, fresh pink flowers, especially in early summer. Attractive heps in autumn. Height and spread: 1.8m/6ft.

• 'Frühlingsanfang': Fragrant, large, single, ivory-white flowers during early and mid-summer, which are followed in autumn by maroon-red heps. Height and spread: 2.7m/9ft.
• 'Frühlingsgold': Richly fragrant, single, large, pale yellow flowers with deeper-coloured stamens during early and mid-summer. Height and spread: 2.1m/7ft.
• 'Frühlingsmorgen': Rose-pink flowers with yellow centres and purplish-maroon stamens during early summer. Sometimes a small crop appears in late summer, with large maroon-red heps in autumn. Height: 1.8m/6ft. Spread: 1.5m/5ft.
• 'Golden Wings': Fragrant, yellow flowers with mahogany-coloured stamens during summer. Height and spread: 1.2m/4ft.
• 'Jacqueline Dupré': Semi-double, blush-white flowers often 10cm/4in across almost continuously throughout summer. Height and spread: 1.8m/6ft.
• 'Magenta': Richly scented, rosy-magenta to pale mauve flowers borne in branching sprays and spreading bushes. Height: 1.5m/5ft. Spread: 1.2m/4ft.
• 'Nevada': Semi-double, creamy white flowers with a blush tint during early and mid-summer. Further flowers appear intermittently throughout the summer. Height and spread: 2.1m/7ft.

'NEVADA' has semi-double, creamy white flowers with a blush tint. It is one of the best-known Modern Shrub Roses.

• 'Nymphenburg': Apple-scented double, warm salmon-pink flowers shaded cerise-pink and orange, with a yellow base to the petals. As a bonus it has large, turban-like orange-red heps in autumn. Height: 2.4m/8ft. Spread: 1.8m/6ft. Strong, arching growth.
• 'Sally Holmes': Masses of creamy white flowers in large bunches almost continuously throughout the rose season. Height and spread: 1.2m/4ft.
• 'Scarlet Fire': Single, bright scarlet flowers with golden stamens during early and mid-summer. Long-lasting, pear-shaped red heps in late summer and autumn. Height: 2.1m/7ft. Spread: 2.1–2.9m/7–9ft.
• 'Zigeunerknabe': Dark, violet-purple flowers on a prickly shrub during early summer. Height: 1.5m/5ft. Spread: 1.2m/4ft.

ENGLISH ROSES

These are roses which have been bred and introduced by David Austin Roses. They have a shrub-like habit and combine a recurrent flowering habit with a wide colour range, yet they retain the charm and fascination revealed by Old Roses. Additionally, nearly all of them have a pleasing fragrance. There are many varieties of English Rose to choose from and each year more are added.
• 'Abraham Darby': Large, deeply cupped flowers in shades of apricot and yellow. It has the bonus of a rich, fruit-like fragrance. Flowering begins in early summer and continues for the rest of the season. Height and spread: 1.5m/5ft.
• 'Constance Spry': Clear pink flowers with myrrh-like fragrance during summer. Height and spread: 1.8–2.1m/6–7ft.
• 'Graham Thomas': Rich, pure yellow flowers with a cupped formation and a refreshing Tea Rose fragrance. Flowering is almost continual throughout summer. Height and spread: 1.2m/4ft.
• 'Heritage': Soft pink flowers with a lemon-like fragrance; repeat-flowering throughout summer. Height and spread: 1.2m/4ft.
• 'The Countryman': Clear pink flowers with an Old Rose fragrance. It flowers twice during summer, each with a good crop. Height: 90cm/3ft. Spread: 1m/3½ft.
• 'Red Coat': Large, single, crimson-scarlet flowers continuously through the rose season. Height: 1.5m/5ft. Spread: 1.2m/4ft.
• 'Shropshire Lass': Delicate flesh-pink, fading to white, but only once during the season. Height: 2.4m/8ft. Spread: 1.8m/6ft.
• 'Winchester Cathedral': White flowers at intervals throughout summer. Height and spread: 1.2m/4ft. Bushy growth.

CLIMBERS

❧

THESE have a more permanent framework than ramblers, and their flowers, when compared with those of ramblers, are larger and borne singly or in small clusters. And they generally have the ability of repeat flowering after their first flush of flowers.

Climbers can be arranged into four main groups, according to their parentage, although there are some that do not neatly fit into any of these groups. And, of course, there are also Modern Climbers (see opposite).

CLIMBING BOURBONS

Hardy, with flowers that reveal a beautiful Old Rose appearance. They also often have a repeat-flowering nature.
• 'Blairi No. 2': Not an exciting name but a beautiful rose, deep pink at the centre and paling at its edge. Only one good flush of flowers a year. Height 4.5m/15ft.
• 'Kathleen Harrop': Fragrant and soft-pink; almost perpetual flowers in season. This rose is a sport of 'Zéphirine Drouhin', but slightly less vigorous and with a more attractive colour. Height: 3.6m/12ft.

CLIMBERS are superb for clothing walls, but first secure a trellis to the wall to support them. The trellis should be positioned slightly away from the wall, to allow stems to pass behind it.

'ÉTOILE DE HOLLANDE, CLIMBING', *has strongly fragrant, deep crimson flowers.*

CLIMBING HYBRID TEAS

These are usually sports of bush varieties, with flowers that reveal a Hybrid Tea nature.
• 'Allen Chandler': Fragrant, large, semi-double, bright crimson flowers with golden yellow stamens. Height: 4.5m/15ft.
• 'Étoile de Hollande, Climbing': Strongly fragrant and deep crimson. Height: 5.4m/18ft.
• 'Guinée': Strongly fragrant and deep, velvety crimson. Golden stamens. Height: 4.5m/15ft.
• 'Mrs. Sam McGredy, Climbing': Coppery orange flowers flushed with scarlet. Height: 4.5m/15ft.
• 'Ophelia, Climbing': Richly-fragrant, with pale blush-pink buds. Height: 3.6m/12ft.
• 'Shot Silk, Climbing': Scented and in shades of cerise-pink with orange-scarlet and yellow. Height: 5.4m/18ft.
• 'Souvenir de Claudius Denoyel': Richly-fragrant and bright crimson. Height: 5.4m/18ft.
• 'Sutter's Gold, Climbing': Fragrant with buds flushed gold and peach. Height 3.6m/12ft.

CLIMBING TEA ROSES

These have flowers slightly resembling those of Hybrid Tea types, but perhaps slightly nearer to Noisettes (see below). A warm position is essential.
• 'Lady Hillingdon, Climbing': Richly Tea Rose-scented, apricot-yellow flowers. Height: 4.5m/15ft.
• 'Mrs Herbert Stevens, Climbing': Tea Rose-scented, white flowers tinged green. Height: 6m/20ft.
• 'Paul Lede': Tea Rose-fragrant, yellow-buff flowers flushed carmine at the centre. Height: 3.6m/12ft. Very free-flowerng.
• 'Sombreuil, Climbing': Superbly Tea Rose-scented, creamy white flowers. Height: 3.6m/12ft.

'MERMAID' *has large, single, yellow flowers with a delicate fragrance. It grows up to 9m/30ft high.*

NOISETTE CLIMBERS

Small and rosette-shaped blooms, on plants that have a repeat-flowering nature. A warm, sunny wall is essential.
• 'Aimée Vibert': Musk-fragrant, small, double, pure white flowers. Height: 4.5m/15ft.
• 'Alister Stella Gray': Double, rosette-shaped, yellow flowers, with a repeat-flowering nature. Height: 4.5m/15ft.

'NEW DAWN' *is a Modern Climber with silvery blush-pink flowers.*

• 'Blush Noisette': Richly clove-scented, semi-double and cup-shaped, lilac-pink flowers. Height: 4.5m/15ft.
• 'Céline Forestier': Tea Rose-scented, pale yellow flowers. Height, 2.4m/8ft.
• 'Gloire de Dijon' (Old Glory Rose): Richly fragrant, large, buff-yellow flowers often tinted gold and pink. Height 4.5m/15ft.

MODERN CLIMBERS

Relatively new; flowers resemble those of Hybrid Teas.
• *'Breath of Life': Fragrant and apricot-pink. Height: 2.4m/8ft.*
• *'Danse du Feu': Semi-double and orange-scarlet. Height: 3m/10ft.*
• *'Golden Showers': Scented, semi-double, golden yellow flowers fading to cream. Height: 3m/10ft.*
• *'New Dawn': Fruity fragrance and silvery blush-pink. Height: 3m/10ft.*
• *'Pink Perpétué': Bright rose-pink. Height 4.5m/15ft.*

RAMBLERS

❖

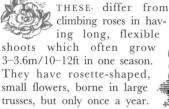

THESE differ from climbing roses in having long, flexible shoots which often grow 3–3.6m/10–12ft in one season. They have rosette-shaped, small flowers, borne in large trusses, but only once a year. Their growth is vigorous but graceful. They are ideal for clothing arches and pergolas, or rambling through bushes and into trees.

Ramblers can be grouped according to their parentage, but there are some with various origins and a few of these are described in the box opposite (other ramblers).

MULTIFLORA HYBRIDS

These have small flowers borne in large trusses and on stiff growths.
• 'Bleu Magenta': Violet-crimson flowers fading to parma violet and grey. Height 4.5m/15ft.
• 'Bobbie James': Fragrant, semi-double, creamy white flowers borne in large trusses. Height: 9m/30ft.
• 'Goldfinch': Well-scented, yolk-yellow flowers fading to soft, milky white. Height 3m/10ft.
• 'Rambling Rector': Superbly fragrant, semi-double, small, creamy white flowers. Dense, twiggy growth. Height: 6m/20ft.
• 'Veilchenblau': Orange-scented, dark magenta flowers fading to lilac. Height: 4.5m/15ft.
• 'Violette': Crimson-purple flowers fading to maroon. It has the bonus of golden stamens. Height: 4.5m/15ft.

SEMPERVIRENS HYBRIDS

These hybrid roses are graceful, with long, slender but strong stems. The small flowers are borne in sprays.

'ALBERTINE'
is one of the most popular ramblers, with fragrant flowers that open to reveal coppery pink petals.

• 'Adelaïde d'Orléans': Primrose-scented, semi-double, creamy white flowers. Height: 4.5m/15ft.
• 'Félicité et Perpétué': Primrose-scented, pompon-like, creamy white flowers. The buds are tinted pink. Height 6m/20ft.
• 'Princess Louise': Slightly fragrant, soft pink buds which open to reveal creamy blush flowers. Height: 3.6m/12ft.

WICHURAIANA HYBRIDS

This group includes the majority of ramblers; they are graceful with large flowers in elegant sprays.
• 'Albéric Barbier': Fruitily fragrant, fully double, creamy white flowers about 7.5cm/3in wide. Height: 7.5m/25ft.
• 'Albertine': Richly fragrant, with reddish-salmon buds which open to reveal coppery pink flowers. Height: 6m/20ft.

• 'American Pillar': Well-known rambler, with single, bright pink flowers. Height 4.5m/15ft.
• 'Crimson Shower': Superb rambler, with bright crimson flowers from mid-summer to early autumn. Height 4.5m/15ft.
• 'François Juranville': Apple-like fragrance and double, coral-pink flowers. They open flat and reveal yellow bases to the petals. Height 7.5m/25ft.
• 'Léontine Gervais': Graceful climber with pink flowers tinged with orange and copper. Height: 7.5m/25ft.
• 'Paul Transon': Apple-like fragrance to the medium-sized, coppery orange flowers borne in small clusters. Usually, there is repeat flowering in early autumn. Height: 4.5m/15ft.
• 'René André': Apple-like fragrance to the small, cupped, soft apricot-yellow flowers which are flushed in pink and borne on trailing stems. Height: 6m/20ft.
• 'Sander's White': Fragrant, small, semi-double, pure white flowers borne on trailing stems. Height: 5.4m/18ft.

'AMERICAN PILLAR'
is vigorous, with single, bright pink flowers. It is well-known and popular.

'VEICHENBLAU'
produces bunches of dark magenta flowers that fade to lilac. The stems do not have thorns.

OTHER RAMBLERS

In addition to ramblers which derive from Multiflora, Sempervirens and Wichuraiana sources, there are several others. Included in them are:
• *'Kew Rambler': Derived from Rosa soulieana, it has strongly fragrant, single, rose-pink flowers with a white eye. Height: 5.4m/18ft.*
• *'Mme. Sancy de Parabère': A slightly fragrant Boursault type, with 13cm/5in wide, soft pink flowers. Height: 4.5m/15ft.*
• *'Paul's Himalayan Musk': A popular rambler, with sprays of small, blush-pink flowers. It is vigorous and ideal for climbing into trees. Height: 9m/30ft.*
• *'The Garland': A richly orange-scented cross between* Rosa moschata *and* R. multiflora. *It develops small, creamy salmon flowers. Height: 4.5m/15ft.*
• *'Weetwood': Pendulous sprays of pink flowers, each about 6.5cm/2½in wide. Height: 7.5m/25ft.*

PILLARS, TREES AND SCREENS

THERE are many roses that vigorously clamber into trees. Some are more than 9m/30ft high, while others have a shorter stature and are suitable for creating feasts of colour 2.4–3m/8–10ft high.

Establishing a new rose around the base of a tree is neither easy nor rapid. This is because soil around a tree is invariably impoverished and dry; the roots of trees absorb all nutrients and the canopy of leaves prevents soil close to the trunk becoming moist. Therefore, dig a large hole about 45cm/18in deep and 1m/3½ft from the tree and fill it with a mixture of decomposed compost and good soil. Plant the rose's roots in it and keep them moist, especially during the first season. Additionally, feed it two or three times every year, as the tree will be in competition with the rose.

'GOLDEN SHOWERS' *(Modern Climber) is ideal as a pillar rose, about 3m/10ft high and with blush-pink flowers.*

COVERING TREES

Old trees can be transformed by training climbers to wander through their branches. No regular pruning is needed and once established there is little to do but to feed them a couple of times a year, during early and mid-spring. The range of suitable roses is wide and they do not have to be exceptionally vigorous. Indeed, many of them are only 3m/10ft high but well able to clothe a small tree with colour. Roses to consider include:

• 'Awakening': Blush; 3–3.6m/10–12ft; climber.
• 'Bobby James': Creamy white; 9m/30ft; rambler.
• 'Blush Rambler': Apple blossom-pink; 2.7m/9ft; rambler.
• 'Cécile Brunner, Climbing': Light pink; 3.6m/12ft; climber.
• 'Dr. W. Van Fleet': Soft pink; 6m/20ft; rambler.
• 'Emily Gray': Butter-yellow; 4.5m/15ft; rambler.
• 'Félicité et Perpétué': Creamy white; 6m/20ft; rambler.
• 'Francis E. Lester': White, tinted blush; 4.5m/15ft; rambler.
• 'Leverkusen': Lemon-yellow; 3m/10ft; climber.
• 'Meg': Pink with an apricot centre; 3–3.6m/10–12ft, climber.
• 'Mme. Grégoire Staechelin': Rosy carmine-pink; 6m/20ft; climber.
• 'Paul's Himalayan Musk': Blush-pink; 9m/30ft; rambler.
• 'Scharlachglut': Bright red; 3m/10ft; shrub rose.
• 'Sympathie': Rich, blood-red; 4.5m/15ft; climber.
• 'Veilchenblau': Dark magenta and fading to lilac; 4.5m/15ft; rambler.
• 'Wedding Day': Creamy-white to blush; 7.5m/25ft; rambler.

'WHITE COCKADE' *(Modern Climber) is a pillar rose, about 2.1m/7ft high with pure white, Hybrid Tea-like flowers.*

PILLAR ROSES

These are less vigorous than the varieties mainly used to clamber into trees: they are usually 2.4–3m/8–10ft high, occasionally slightly higher. They have a repeat-flowering nature.

The range of varieties is wide:
• 'Aloha' (Modern Shrub Rose): Clear pink and repeat-flowering.
• 'Bantry Bay' (Climber): Deep pink and semi-double.
• 'Compassion' (Modern Climber): Salmon-pink, petals tinted apricot-orange.
• 'Dreaming Spires' (Climber): Yellow and scented.
• 'Handel' (Modern Climber): Creamy blush, edged pink.
• 'Phyllis Bide' (Rambler): Yellow, flushed salmon-pink.
• 'Pink Perpétué' (Modern Climber): Bright rose-pink.
• 'La Reine Victoria' (Bourbon Shrub): Shell-pink.

IMPENETRABLE BARRIERS

Some roses create dense barriers that are ideal for keeping out stray animals and to provide privacy. Suitable roses include:
• 'Blanc Double de Coubert' (Rugosa): Large, semi-double, pure-white flowers throughout most of summer. Height: 1.8m/6ft. Spread: 1.5m/5ft.
• 'Constance Spry' (English Rose): Strongly myrrh-fragrant, clear pink flowers. Height and spread: 1.8–2.1m/6–7ft.
• 'Frühlingsgold' (Modern Shrub Rose): Fragrant and pale yellow. Height and spread: 2.1m/7ft.
• 'Nevada' (Modern Shrub Rose): Semi-double and creamy white. Height and spread: 2.1m/7ft.
• *Rosa x cantabrigiensis* (Hybrid): Pale yellow flowers. Height and spread: 3m/10ft.
• 'Roseraie de l'Hay' (Rugosa): Scented and rich, wine-red. Height and spread: 2.1m/7ft.

CLIMBERS FOR COLD WALLS

Roses are never fully happy when planted against a north-facing wall. Apart from low temperatures and freezing winds (which they can usually tolerate when in their dormant state), in summer they tend to be drawn towards the light. However, there are a few climbers and ramblers that tolerate such conditions.
• *'Albéric Barbier' (rambler).*
• *'Félicité et Perpétué' (rambler).*
• *'Mme. Grégoire Staechelin' (climber).*
• *'Mme. Plantier' (Alba climber).*
• *'Morning Jewel' (climber).*
• *'New Dawn' (Modern climber).*
• *'Zéphirine Drouhin' (Bourbon climber).*

STANDARDS AND WEEPING STANDARDS

❖

THESE are superb for creating 'height' in rose beds and as centre-pieces in lawns. There are several types of Standard roses, from low and small ones in pots to those 1.5–1.8m/5–6ft tall.

STANDARD ROSES

These are budded by nurserymen on established root-stocks, 1m/39in above the ground, where they form heads 1.5m–1.8m/5–6ft high. Strong stakes are essential. Both Hybrid Tea and Floribunda varieties are used.

• Hybrid Tea varieties to choose include: 'Just Joey' (copper-orange), 'Ruby Wedding' (ruby-red), 'Silver Wedding' (creamy white), 'Simba' (yellow), 'Tequila Sunrise' (yellow, edged scarlet).

• Floribunda varieties include 'Amber Queen' (amber-yellow), 'Golden Wedding' (yellow), 'Iceberg' (white) and 'Intrigue' (dark red).

'TEQUILA SUNRISE' (Hybrid Tea) is often used to create standard roses. It has yellow blooms edged in scarlet.

HALF-STANDARD ROSES

These have a lower stature than full standards; varieties are budded onto root-stocks 75cm/2½ft above the ground, where they form heads 1.3–1.6m/4½–5½ft high.

• Hybrid Tea varieties include: 'Paul Shirville' (soft salmon-pink), 'Royal William' (deep red) and 'Savoy Hotel' (light pink).

• Floribunda types include: 'Amber Queen' (amber-yellow), 'Golden Years' (golden), and 'Margaret Merril' (blush-white).

PATIO STANDARDS

The varietal parts are budded on root-stocks 75cm/2½ft above ground level, and form dense, rounded heads. They become packed with flowers through much of summer and into autumn and create dominant features. They are ideal when close to patios and for growing in large pots.

• Varieties to consider include: 'Cider Cup' (peach), 'Muriel' (pink), 'Red Rascal' (red) and 'Sweet Magic' (orange).

MINIATURE STANDARDS

These are even smaller than patio roses, and are budded onto root-stocks 50cm/20in above the ground. When the head matures, its top is about 90cm/3ft tall. These are ideal for growing in large pots on patios. Avoid positions in strong draughts.

• Varieties include: 'Baby Masquerade' (bicolor), 'Colibri '79' (apricot and orange), 'Orange Sunblaze' (scarlet) and 'Pink Sunblaze' (pink).

WEEPING STANDARDS

These are well-known for their beautiful outline, often with stems cascading and reaching nearly to the ground. To be fully appreciated, a weeping standard is best planted as a feature on a lawn.

Weeping standards are created by budding the varietal part onto a root-stock about 130cm/51in above the ground. When mature, the head is then 1.5–1.8m/5–6ft high, with stems trailing evenly from around the top.

• Mainly rambler varieties are used to create a cascading outline: 'Albéric Barbier' (cream), 'Crimson Showers' (red), 'Débutante' (clear rose-pink), 'François Juranville' (salmon-pink), 'Goldfinch' (yellow, fading to white), 'Princess Louise' (creamy blush) and 'Sander's White' (white).

• Climbing roses with arching stems are also used and these include: 'Félicité et Perpétué' (white) and 'New Dawn' (silvery blush-pink; a Modern Climber).

'AMBER QUEEN' (Floribunda) creates spectacular standard roses. It bears large clusters of amber-yellow blooms.

SHRUBBY STANDARDS

These involve the budding of Shrub Roses on to root-stocks, 1m/39in above ground level.

• Varieties include: 'Ballerina' (light pink), 'Canary Bird' (golden yellow) and 'Bonica' (pink).

GROUND-COVER STANDARDS

Ground-cover roses are budded on root-stocks, 1m/39in high.

• Suitable varieties include: 'Gwent' (yellow), 'Hertfordshire' (carmine), 'Kent' (white) and 'Surrey' (pink).

SMALL TRAILING STANDARDS

These require less room than full standards and are budded on root-stocks 1m/39in high. They mature to 1.3m/4½ft.

• Varieties include 'Nozomi' (blush) and 'Suma' (red).

HEDGES

ROSES create superb hedges, whether along a perimeter or within a garden. However, unlike traditional hedging plants, such as Yew and Privet, roses are deciduous and therefore during winter have bare, leafless stems. For this reason, if privacy is desired throughout the year they are not suitable. Do not expect to be able to form a rigid outline, with a uniform height and width. Rather, they have a lax and informal nature.

'LITTLE WHITE PET' forms a low hedge packed with white flowers.

PLANTING A ROSE HEDGE

Plant bare-rooted rose bushes during their dormant period, from late autumn to late winter. Dig out a trench and add garden compost or manure: use the spacings suggested for each group. Plant firmly and keep the soil moist. In spring, cut back the plants hard to encourage bushiness.

LOW HEDGES

These are up to 75cm/2½ft high and formed of Miniature, Patio, Dwarf Polyantha and short-growing Floribundas. They are planted in a single row, with 30–38cm/12–15in between the plants. Ensure the foliage overlaps. Varieties include: 'Little White Pet' (white), 'Marlena' (scarlet-crimson) and 'The Fairy' (rose-pink).

MEDIUM-HEIGHT HEDGES

These range from 75cm/2½ft to 1.5m/5ft high and are planted 45cm/1½ft apart. To create a dense, thick hedge, plant them in two rows, staggered and about 45cm/1½ft apart.

Varieties to consider include: 'Celestial' (shell-pink), 'Iceberg' (white) and 'Masquerade' (yellow, red and pink).

TALL HEDGES

These grow 1.5m/5ft to 2.1m/7ft high and are best reserved for boundaries. Plant them 75–90cm/2½–3ft apart. Varieties include 'Felicia' (silvery pink), 'Penelope' (pink, flushed apricot) and 'Queen Elizabeth' (pink).

'CELESTIAL', an Alba type, forms a medium-height hedge, with sweetly scented, shell-pink flowers.

GROUND COVER

GROWING roses to form an attractive covering of the soil is increasing in popularity. However, do not expect them to form a weed-smothering blanket of stems, leaves and flowers in the same way as many other ground-cover plants. Instead, they produce a magnificent blanket of colour. For this reason, never plant them in soil plagued with perennial weeds, as these will continue to grow and be difficult to eradicate. Always dig out perennial weeds before planting roses.

These roses are superb for covering steep banks (where it would be difficult to mow grass), masking manhole covers, and creating colourful edges to rose beds.

'SURREY', one of the County Series of ground-cover plants, has rich, reddish-pink, single flowers.

MODERN SHRUB ROSES

These are a relatively recent introduction and usually develop large trusses of flowers. They are easily grown and many have a repeat-flowering nature; others flower once but over a long period.

Varieties include: 'Max Graf' (apple-scented and pink), 'Nozomi' (pearly pink to white), 'Partridge' (white), 'Rosy Cushion' (pink), 'Snow Carpet' (white).

'PARTRIDGE', a Modern Shrub Rose, has low, prostrate growth and forms a wide carpet, often 2.4m/8ft across, of single, white flowers.

Further Modern Shrub Roses that cover the ground include: 'Raubritter' (pink), 'Running Maid' (deep pink) and 'Scintillation' (semi-double, bluish-pink).

COUNTY SERIES

These are popular and create a mass of flowers from the latter part of early summer to the middle of autumn. Most of them grow between 30cm/12in and 45cm/18in high, and with a 60cm/2ft to 1.2m/4ft spread. Varieties to consider include:
• 'Avon': Pearly white.
• 'Essex': Rich reddish-pink.
• 'Gwent': Bright lemon-yellow.
• 'Hampshire': Glowing scarlet.
• 'Hertfordshire': Carmine-pink.
• 'Norfolk': Bright yellow.
• 'Suffolk': Bright scarlet.
• 'Warwickshire': Deep rosy red.
• 'Wiltshire': Deep rosy pink.

LOOKING AFTER ROSES

PART of the pleasure of roses is looking after them. Regular attention is essential, from spring to autumn as well as protecting them during winter, especially when they are growing in cold and exposed positions.

Feeding (page 70) and pruning (pages 310 to 313) are important, and here are some other jobs that need attention. If bush roses such as Hybrid Teas and Floribundas are neglected their life-span is dramatically reduced.

The mulch should not touch the stem.

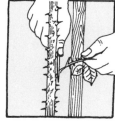

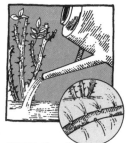

DURING *summer, remove sucker shoots growing from below soil level. Remove some soil and trace the sucker to its base. Wear a stout glove and pull off the sucker, close to its base. Replace and firm soil around the root: loose soil encourages suckers.*

SUCKERS *sometimes grow from the stem of a standard rose. Do not pull them off (in the same way as those at ground level). Instead, use a sharp knife to cut the sucker flush with the stem. Avoid unnecessary cutting, as this may damage the stem.*

WATER *the soil around roses regularly in summer, especially during droughts. Thoroughly soak the soil; just dampening the surface does more harm than good. Perforated hose laid on the soil makes this job easier and spreads water evenly.*

LARGE *Hybrid Tea flowers (often for exhibiting) can be produced by disbudding the blooms. As soon as the small buds growing from the leaf-joints just below the main flower are large enough to handle, bend them sideways so that they snap off cleanly. Make sure you do not tear the stem.*

MULCH *roses to prevent the growth of weeds, conserve soil moisture, keep soil cool and provide some nutrients. In spring, shallowly hoe the soil, remove any weeds, apply a feed and water the soil. Then, apply a 10cm/4in-thick layer of well-decayed garden compost or manure over the soil.*

WHEN *cutting fresh roses for home decoration, use sharp scissors or a knife. Cut stems just above a leaf-joint and do not take too many from one plant, or from the same position. Preferably, cut the stems early in the morning, when they are full of moisture. Place them in deep, cool water.*

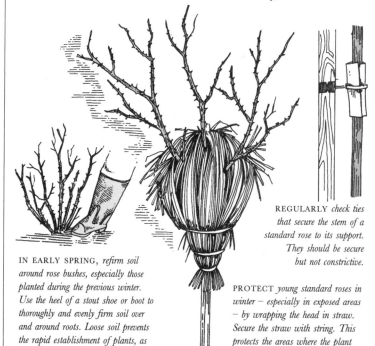

FROM *spring to autumn, remove weeds by shallow hoeing. This also breaks up crusty surface soil and enables air and moisture to penetrate. But hoeing too deeply damages roots and encourages suckers.*

REMOVE *dead flowers from bush roses. Cut the stem back to slightly above the second or third leaf below the dead flowers, removing the complete truss. Do not dead-head Shrub Roses grown for their heps (fruits).*

APPLY *chemical weed-killers through a dribble-bar attached to a watering-can solely used for that purpose. Only apply weed-killers when the weather is dry and there is little or no wind to disturb the spray.*

IN EARLY SPRING, *refirm soil around rose bushes, especially those planted during the previous winter. Use the heel of a stout shoe or boot to thoroughly and evenly firm soil over and around roots. Loose soil prevents the rapid establishment of plants, as well as encouraging the development of suckers from the roots.*

REGULARLY *check ties that secure the stem of a standard rose to its support. They should be secure but not constrictive.*

PROTECT *young standard roses in winter – especially in exposed areas – by wrapping the head in straw. Secure the straw with string. This protects the areas where the plant was budded. In spring, carefully remove the string and straw.*

ROCK GARDENS

❖

Rock gardens are increasingly popular and create superb settings in which a wide range of small plants can be grown. These are a medley of true alpines, small perennials, miniature conifers, dwarf shrubs and trees, and miniature bulbs. Additionally, annuals and biennials can be used as temporary fillers to create colour while longer-lived plants become established. Within this chapter a wide range of suitable plants is featured.

The selection and preparation of the site is detailed, together with the choice of rocks. A rock garden can be built on a slope, but raised beds, dry-stone walls, scree beds, peat beds and stone sinks also create places in which rock garden plants can be grown.

Looking after rock gardens is important and this includes inspecting plants before buying them, preparing the soil, planting, weeding, feeding, dividing congested plants and mulching the soil with gravel chippings. All of this is detailed within this chapter.

ROCK-GARDEN FEATURES

 APART from natural slopes, there are many other places where rock-garden plants can be cultivated. Dry-stone walls create terraces on sloping land, while raised beds, with sides formed like dry-stone walls, enable plants to be grown at about waist height. They also introduce general height to gardens.

On patios, sink gardens make attractive features. Old stone sinks are traditional for this purpose, but white, glazed sinks can be modified and made equally attractive (see page 96).

Blocks of tufa can also make attractive features on patios and terraces, and are even sometimes used on balconies.

NATURAL STONE PAVING, *with gaps left between the stones, creates an ideal home for many rock-garden plants (see page 96).*

LOOSE STONES *often occur naturally at the base of a rocky outcrop. These screes can be recreated (see page 95).*

BLOCKS *of compressed peat form homes for acid-loving plants. These are ideal woodland features (see page 95). Peat beds are best formed on slight slopes so that the plants can be clearly seen.*

OLD STONE SINKS *can be filled with free-draining compost, then planted with small plants, miniature bulbs and dwarf conifers (see page 96). They are ideal features on patios or in small areas.*

TUFA, *a form of magnesium limestone, creates ideal homes for many rock-garden plants. Position it on a patio, in a scree bed or in a rock garden (see page 95).*

NATURAL *slopes create ideal situations for rock gardens. Rocks can be positioned to create naturalistic strata (see page 93). Careful construction is essential, as once built this will be a major, permanent feature.*

FREE-STANDING *rock gardens make it possible to grow plants on flat sites. A pond adds further interest, and a small waterfall feature can also be added.*

DRY-STONE WALLS *are ideal homes for rock garden plants. Additionally, the walls can be used to create terraces (see page 94).*

RAISED BEDS *formed of attractive stones create features that make rock gardening possible in flat areas (see page 94). They also help to give height and variation to flat areas, as well as separating one part of a garden from another.*

SITE, ASPECT AND ROCKS

TO ENSURE the long-term success of a rock garden, it must be constructed with care and in a suitable position:

• Choose a site that faces the sun, although slight shade for part of the day is acceptable. Indeed, it is better to have light shade than to risk plants becoming over-heated, but it is most important to avoid constantly shaded positions.

• Do not position rock gardens under trees. They drip water on plants long after rain has stopped. Also, in autumn, leaves fall from deciduous trees and create constant dampness around plants, encouraging the presence of pests and onset of diseases.

• The soil must be well drained to prevent water remaining at the bases of stems and around roots during winter.

• A windbreak formed of evergreen conifers, on the side most exposed to cold winds, helps to protect plants during winter.

• Ensure that the area is free from pernicious perennial weeds such as Horsetail and Couch Grass. If these weeds become established, it may be necessary to dismantle the whole rock garden and to sift all the soil.

• Check that soil pests such as wireworms and cockchafers are not present in great numbers. Newly dug pasture land is usually plagued with these pests.

EVERGREEN *conifers planted on the cold, windswept side will protect plants during winter. They help to filter strong wind and cause less turbulence than walls.*

CHOOSE *a bright, sunny position that is preferably lightly shaded during part of the day.*

CHOOSE *a place away from deciduous trees, which shade the plants and shed leaves in autumn.*

PREFERABLY, *the site should have a gentle slope which faces the sun.*

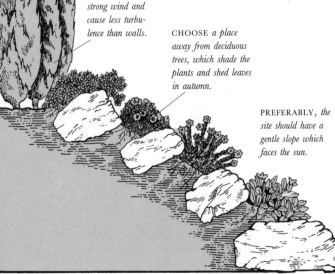

RANGE OF ROCKS

A wide range of stones can be used in rock gardens. Preferably use local materials, as they blend best with the surroundings. There are five main types of stone: sandstone, limestone, granite, slate and tufa (mentioned on page 95).

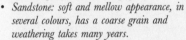 Granite

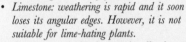 Westmorland

 York Stone (sandstone)

 Slate

 Tufa

• *Sandstone: soft and mellow appearance, in several colours, has a coarse grain and weathering takes many years.*
• *Limestone: weathering is rapid and it soon loses its angular edges. However, it is not suitable for lime-hating plants.*
• *Granite: weathering is exceptionally slow; the stone is fine-grained and hard.*
• *Slate: weathering is not fast, but quicker than granite; available in shades of green, grey or purple. Initially, it has sharp edges.*

BUYING ROCKS

Choose the type of rock you want (see above), then contact a local supplier to enquire about its cost and the charge for haulage. The cost of carriage can be a major consideration, so telephone a few suppliers before making a decision.

Local stone will be cheaper and more likely to harmonize with its surroundings than stone quarried several hundred miles away. Do not mix different types and ensure it will be in a range of sizes.

Find out when the stone will be delivered and inspect it before it is unloaded. It should not be tipped from the delivery lorry, as this damages the surface of the stone.

MOVING *large stones can be a problem; large rollers and long crow-bars are one solution, or use a sack-trolley or wheelbarrow.*

There is always the temptation to pick up natural stones from the countryside and to take them home, but this is not only theft, it is also detrimental to the environment. In addition, it is never worth economizing by using broken pieces of concrete: these will be a permanent eye-sore, as the broken pieces do not have strata or a natural apearance. They will remain a heap of concrete, rather than a rock garden that will please.

AMOUNT OF STONE?

Estimates of the amount of stone required vary and, clearly, depend on the type of construction. A rock garden with only a slight slope needs fewer pieces of stone than a steep slope, or one where many layers (strata) are needed to keep the soil in place.

As an estimate of the amount of stone needed, a rock garden 3m/10ft square requires about 2 tonnes/4410lbs of stone, in a range of sizes.

ROCK GARDENS ON NATURAL SLOPES

 SLIGHTLY sloping area that faces the sun – but is lightly shaded for part of the day – provides the most easily constructed home for rock-garden plants. Unlike raised beds or free-standing rock gardens, little soil moving is needed, other than to ensure good drainage.

GOOD DRAINAGE

If the surface is slightly sandy and the top 30cm/12in of soil is exceptionally well drained, rocks can be laid directly on the surface. Usually, however, it is necessary to remove the top 25cm/10in of soil and to prepare the ground thoroughly. In the base, form a 10cm/4in-thick layer of clean bricks or stones. Ensure it is not contaminated with building rubbish. Firm this base and form a 5cm/2in layer of sharp sand on top. Rake this level and add about 10cm/4in of topsoil.

FORMING *a sloping terrace, with rocks appearing in natural-looking strata, is the normal way to construct a rock garden.*

SLOPING *outcrops, as they occur in nature, look good towards the base of rock gardens.*

LAYING THE STONES

Spread out the stones, so that their size, shape and strata can be seen. Start putting the stones in place from the base upwards. The two main formations for them are sloping, with the stones terraced and forming a natural stratum, or producing outcrops where the length of each stratum is limited and more at random.

Of these two, the terraced type is the easier to create as the position of each stone is clearly dictated by that of its neighbour.

EARLY ROCK-GARDEN WRITERS

As nurseries started to grow, rock-garden plants, gardening magazines and books featured them. Rock gardens were constructed at the Royal Botanic Gardens, Kew, in 1867 and four years later at the Royal Botanic Garden, Edinburgh. In 1870, the garden writer, William Robinson, published Alpine Flowers for English Gardens. *It was much acclaimed and an inspiration to rock-garden enthusiasts. Eight years later he included hardy-alpine and rock-garden plants in* Hardy Flowers, *while in* Gardening Illustrated *there were repeated suggestions to get rid of shells and other ornamentation and to focus on growing plants.*

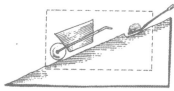

START *digging from the top of the slope, rather than the base. It is then easier to remove the soil.*

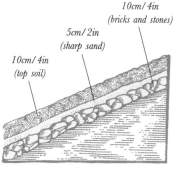

10cm/4in (bricks and stones)

5cm/2in (sharp sand)

10cm/4in (top soil)

UNLESS *the soil is light and sandy, dig out the area to a depth of 25cm/10in and prepare as shown.*

EACH STONE *must tilt backwards slightly, with one-third to one-half of it buried. This ensures it is firmly in the soil and appears natural. Never just spread the stones at random on the soil's surface; it disturbs the eye and does not look natural.*

PLANNING LARGE ROCK GARDENS

If the rock garden is large, it is possible to combine the 'sloping terrace' design with the 'outcrops'. At the base, use outcrops to give the impression that under the soil there are large rocks just peeping out. If space allows, form a pier of several rocks to create the impression of a continuous outcrop.

DESIGNING AND PLANNING

With large rock gardens the area must be planned on paper before setting rocks in position. Strings pegged on the soil's surface make it easy to judge how it will look and, if possible, arranging the stones on the ground in their approximate positions gives a fuller idea of the finished rock garden.

Getting extra large stones into position and manoeuvring them is a three-person job: two to move the stone and the other to view it from several paces away to gain an overall impression. A team is also necessary to reduce the risk of injury to backs and arms. As well, choose a day when the surface soil is dry: accidents are more likely to occur when both soil and rocks are wet; and the soil is soon turned to mud by repeatedly walking on it when wet.

LEAVE *small areas at the base of rocks so that plants can be put in them. Moisture runs off rocks and keeps roots moist and cool.*

RAISED BEDS

❖

RAISED beds are ideal for introducing 'height' to flat gardens. They also create excellent homes for rock-garden plants. Because they are raised, they make it easier for gardeners in wheelchairs, as well as those who cannot readily bend, to look after the plants. By restricting the bed's width to about 1.5m/5ft it is possible to reach most of the plants from a sitting position.

ECONOMIC CONSTRUCTION

Raised beds are cheaper to construct than rock gardens on slopes as the stones are cheaper; the sides can even be made from rail sleepers or re-constituted stone.

To ensure long life and safety, raised beds must be strongly constructed on sound foundations, especially if the walls are more than 30cm/12in high. Dig out a trench around the perimeter, fill with 5cm/2in of clean rubble, compact it and form 10cm/4in-thick concrete foundations. The lowest layer of bricks can then be cemented to the foundations, but leave weep-holes every 1.2m/4ft to enable surplus water to drain from the compost. The rest of the wall is formed by overlapping the bricks, and without the benefit of mortar. Do not construct the sides more than 90cm/3ft high.

FILLING THE CENTRE

When the walls are complete, fill the base one-third deep with clean rubble, then top up with friable, weed-free topsoil to within 2.5cm/1in of the top. Allow the soil to settle for a couple of weeks, then set the plants in position. After planting, form a layer of 2.5–3.6cm/1–1½in-thick stone chippings or 6mm/¼in shingle over the surface of the soil.

DRY-STONE WALLS

❖

AS WELL as providing homes for rock-garden plants, dry-stone walls enable attractive terraces to be created. The height should be limited to 1.2m/4ft and weep-holes must be included every 1.2m/4ft along the base to enable surplus water to drain from the soil. If this is omitted, the pressure of water during wet winters will push over the wall. Battering the wall (leaning it backwards) and filling behind it with rubble also aids its long-term survival.

CREATING A STRONG BASE

Foundations are needed, similar to those necessary for raised beds. Cement the lowest two layers of stones together (allowing for seep-holes) and then continue upwards, fitting the stones together but not using mortar between them. Tilt each stone slightly backwards and set plants between them as each level is put in place. Pack soil firmly between the stones and around the plants. At the top, use slightly wider stones to form a capping. When it is complete, gently spray the wall with water until the plants are established.

When building a dry-stone wall, rather than just picking pieces of stone off a heap at random and trying to make them fit, it is easier to spread them out on the ground and to select those that naturally fit together.

> ### SHINGLE EDGING
>
> *Along the wall's base, dig out a strip 5–7.5cm/2–3in deep and 20–25cm/8–10in wide. Fill it with 6mm/¼in shingle. This has several functions: it prevents grass growing close to the wall's base, enables trailing plants to bush out and trail to the wall's base without being damaged, and creates a distinct edging line for lawn mowers. In addition, it enables the lawn's edge to be cut with long-handled edging shears.*

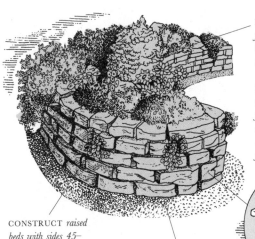

FILL *with well-drained friable topsoil to within 2.5cm/1in of the top of the wall.*

IF THE *wall is more than 30cm/12in high, form a strong base of compact rubble and 10cm/4in-thick concrete foundations.*

CONSTRUCT *raised beds with sides 45–90cm/1½–3ft high. If the sides are higher than 90cm/3ft, they may become unstable. The pressure of water tends to push out the sides.*

DIG OUT *an area 20–25cm/8–10in wide and 5–7.5cm/2–3in deep around the wall and fill with a 6mm/¼in layer of shingle.*

SLOPE *the wall backwards and fill behind it with clean rubble to aid drainage of the soil behind the wall.*

DO NOT *construct the wall higher than 1.2m/4ft. If too high, the wall becomes unstable.*

FORM *foundations of compacted clean rubble and a 10cm/4in-thick strip of concrete. Never skimp on foundations, as if you do the wall may soon collapse.*

SCREE BEDS

SCREES naturally occur at the bases of cliffs or gullies and are formed of small, loose stones scattered on the surface. In gardens, it is possible to construct a scree bed at the lower end of a rock garden, creating further opportunities to grow rock garden plants. Screes are less expensive – and easier – to construct than rock gardens, and create large areas for plants.

Even if you do not have space for a rock garden, it is still possible to form a scree at the base of a wall, surrounded by a path to prevent surface stones being scattered.

CONSTRUCTING A SCREE

Mark out an area at the base of the rock garden; in nature, the area of a scree slowly widens, until from above it appears like a giant splash of water that has spread. Therefore, rather than tapering the scree to a point, gradually widen it to a mushroom-shape.

Dig out the area to 38cm/15in deep and fill the base with

ALPINE OR ROCK-GARDEN PLANTS?

The two terms are often used very loosely and have come to mean any plant which is suitable for growing in a rock garden. However, an alpine plant is one that lives on a mountain, above the upper limit of the tree line but below the area where snow lies throughout the year.

15cm/6in of clean, compacted rubble. Form a 5cm/2in-thick layer of coarse sand or gravel over the rubble, then a mixture of one part topsoil, one of moist peat and three of grit. After plants have been put in place, form a 2.5cm/1in-thick layer of 6mm/¼in shingle over the surface. This coating ensures that the surface is well drained and that leaves do not rest on damp soil. It also prevents heavy drops of rain falling on soil and then splashing plants with dirty water.

It is not necessary to pack the area with plants, as the surface shingle looks attractive and forms a frame for the flowers and leaves.

———

TO CREATE an impression that the scree bed is a natural feature, position a few large rocks to form a natural outcrop.

DIG SOIL *to 38cm/15in deep; form a compacted 15cm/6in-thick layer of clean rubble.*

FORM *a 5cm/2in layer of coarse sand or gravel over the rubble, then 15cm/6in of scree compost (see above).*

AFTER *planting, form a 2.5cm/1in-thick layer of 6mm/¼in shingle.*

PEAT BEDS

THESE are ideal places for growing acid-loving plants. They are not formed of stones and their similarity to rock gardens is the stratified layers of peat blocks which form and often enclose them. Occasionally, they are surrounded by logs or railway sleepers, especially when formed on a steep slope and where soil retention is vital.

Peat beds are best positioned in light shade, as most of the plants grown in them are native to woodland areas.

CONSTRUCTING PEAT BEDS

Before deciding to create a peat bed, check that the underlying soil is not chalky. If it is, there is no point in forming the feature as even though the peat is initially acid, its continual absorption of chalky water will make it unsuitable for acid-loving plants. Use either a chemical-reaction pH kit, or one with a probe and a dial.

When on a flat surface or slight slope, the edging can be formed of peat blocks which have been soaked in water and allowed to drain slightly.

Use peat blocks to form levels in the same way as rocks in rock gardens. Fill with a mixture of equal parts peat and topsoil around and between the blocks of peat. After positioning the peat blocks and adding compost, allow them to settle for a couple of weeks before setting the plants in place. Last, cover the surface with moist peat or bark chippings.

TUFA GARDENS

Tufa is a type of magnesium limestone in which lime-hating plants can be grown. It is porous and absorbs and retains masses of water. Pieces of tufa are ideal for placing in rock gardens and scree beds, but it can also be featured on its own on patios: holes for plants can be chipped out with a hammer and chisel. When planting, wash most of the soil off the roots, push them into the hole and pack well-drained compost around them.

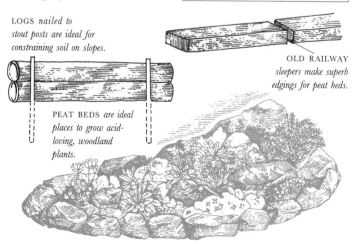

LOGS *nailed to stout posts are ideal for constraining soil on slopes.*

OLD RAILWAY *sleepers make superb edgings for peat beds.*

PEAT BEDS *are ideal places to grow acid-loving, woodland plants.*

SINK GARDENS

OLD stone sinks, with sides about 15cm/6in high, are ideal homes for small rock-garden plants. Miniature bulbs and dwarf conifers can be mixed with them, with trailing plants at the sides.

Old stone sinks are expensive, but an alternative is to modify a glazed sink (detailed on the opposite side of the page). They are deeper than the earlier stone type and need more trailing plants to make the sides less bland.

PLANTING A STONE SINK

Thoroughly scrub the sink and position it on four strong house bricks. Do not place the sink directly on the ground as it is then too easy for slugs and snails to attack the plants. Make sure it does not tilt, but make it slope slightly towards the drainage hole.

Place a piece of perforated gauze over the plug hole and then put a layer of broken clay pots or pebbles over the base. Form a thin layer of sharp sand over this and half fill it with compost, made firm; use a mixture of equal parts topsoil (or potting compost), moist peat and grit. If lime-hating plants are being planted, ensure that the potting compost does not contain any chalk.

Place a couple of large rocks on the compost and adjust their height so that the stones are half buried. Add more compost, at the same time put in the plants. When planting is complete, the compost's surface should be about 2.5cm/1in below the rim. This allows for a 12mm/½in layer of

Position on four strong bricks to prevent tilting.

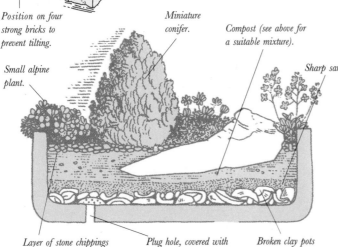

Small alpine plant.

Miniature conifer.

Compost (see above for a suitable mixture).

Sharp sand.

Layer of stone chippings on the surface.

Plug hole, covered with perforated gauze.

Broken clay pots or clean pebbles.

CONVERTING AN OLD GLAZED SINK

Thoroughly wash and remove grease from the inside and outside of the sink. Scratch the outside to roughen it, then coat with a PVA bonding glue. Mix equal parts of cement powder, sharp sand and peat, add water and coat the sides, top and about 5cm/2in down into the inside. Allow to dry for several weeks.

rock chippings or pea-shingle, and a 12mm/½in space between the rim and the shingle. This space at the top of the sink is essential to allow plants to be adequately watered and to prevent stone chippings falling out.

PLANTS TO CHOOSE

There are many small rock-garden plants to choose from and a wide range is featured throughout this book. But ones especially to look for include:
• *Androsace primuloides (A. sarmentosa):* Deep rose flowers during spring and early summer.
• *Antennaria dioica* 'Rosea': Deep pink flowers during late spring and early summer.
• *Campanula cochleariifolia:* Blue bells from mid-summer to autumn.
• *Edraianthus pumilio:* Lavender-blue flowers from late spring to mid-summer. Grey-green leaves.
• *Erinus alpinus:* Bright pink, starry flowers from early spring to late summer. Evergreen and tufted.
• *Hebe buchananii* 'Minor': White flowers during early summer.
• *Lewisia cotyledon:* Pink flowers with white veins during late spring and early summer.
• *Saxifraga burseriana:* Pure white flowers during late winter and early spring.
• Miniature bulbs such as *Narcissus cyclamineus, N. bulbocodium, Crocus chrysanthus, Iris danfordiae, I. reticulata, Eranthis hyemalis* and *Cyclamen coum.*

BETWEEN PAVING

Many small, low-growing rock-garden plants can be successfully grown in cracks between pieces of natural stone paving. These include species of thyme, arenaria, armeria, acaena, saxifraga and sedum. If the area is large, position the plants mainly at the edges, so that a clear path can be left where people mostly walk.

Plants growing in paving are especially at risk in winter.
• *Do not sprinkle salt over ice or snow to melt it, as it makes the soil toxic to plants. Also, do not scatter sand over the area as this damages the leaves.*

ROCK-GARDEN PLANTS

THE RANGE of plants grown in rock gardens is exceptionally wide, from true alpines to bulbs, dwarf conifers and shrubs. But the majority are perennials and popularly represented by Gold Dust (*Alyssum saxatile*), aubrieta, Rock Cress (*arabis*), saponaria and saxifragas.

Rock-garden purists might blanch at the thought of such a medley of plants, but there are no set rules and the imagination and enthusiasm of gardeners is the only limiting factor.

SIZE LIMITATION

Although there is certainly an 'anything goes' philosophy about selecting plants, the size of the rock garden imparts its own limitations. The deciduous, purplish-red leaved and dome-shaped Japanese Maple *Acer palmatum* 'Dissectum Purpureum' and its green-leaved brother 'Dissectum', both grow up to 1.2m/4ft high and 1.8m/6ft wide. In a large rock garden they are superb, but for small areas they are too dominant. But there are many suitable dwarf shrubs – often prostrate and not more than 30cm/12in high – and these are ideal in even the smallest area.

MINIATURE BULBS

Few eyes are not captured by the flowers of bulbous plants in late winter and early spring. They are harbingers of a new season and once planted are easily grown. The initial cost of buying a few bulbs is more than repaid by their ability to produce flowers each year – and with no attention. They do, however, attract mice and often a layer of fine-mesh wire-netting, laid on the soil's surface, is needed to protect them in winter, when other food is scarce.

HERBACEOUS *perennials are popular and usually very hardy occupants of rock gardens. The hybrid Geranium 'Ballerina' grows 15–23cm/6–9in high and develops pink, heavily veined flowers from early to late summer or early autumn.*

ANNUALS, *which are raised each year from seed, are superb 'fillers' for rock gardens. They are inexpensive and ideal for carpeting rock gardens in colour. Sweet Alyssum (Lobularia maritima/Alyssum maritimum) is an example.*

DWARF *shrubs create permanence in rock gardens and although some are large, others, such as the North American Sand Myrtle (Leiophyllum buxifolium) which forms an evergreen shrub about 30cm/12in high, are ideal.*

TEMPORARY COLOUR

During their early years, clothing the whole rock garden with permanent plants might be a financial problem and this is where annuals can help. Additionally, there are always bound to be gaps that need remedial attention in early summer.

Some annuals are hardy and can be sown where they are to flower; others need the comfort of gentle warmth in late winter or early spring to start them off. Annuals to consider include Sweet Alyssum (now properly called *Lobularia maritima* but more popularly and widely known by its early name *Alyssum maritimum*). Although hardy, it is usually raised as a half-hardy annual in gentle warmth. The Poached Egg Flower (*Limnanthes douglasii*) and Baby Blue Eyes (*Nemophila menziesii*), however, can be sown where they are to flower.

There are also biennials to consider and these include Daisies (*Bellis perennis*) and the Alpine Wallflower (*Erysimum alpinum*).

HARDY PERENNIALS *are the most widely grown occupants of rock gardens. These include* Arabis ferdinandi-coburgii *with white flowers and brightly variegated leaves. The form 'Variegata' has white-edged leaves.*

SUB-SHRUB

Some shrubs are small in nature, with a woody base and upper stems dying back each winter. In their own country they are usually woody and permanent, but in cooler regions produce growth that does not survive during winter.

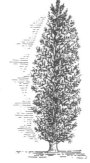

TRUE *alpine plants include Edelweiss* (Leontopodium alpinum) *and grow between the permanent snow line and the uppermost limit of trees. Edelweiss comes from the European Alps, while others originate in other mountainous areas.*

MINIATURE *bulbs, such as the Hoop Petticoat Daffodil* (Narcissus bulbocodium), *bring colour to rock gardens in late winter and early spring. Other bulbous or cormous types include crocuses, irises, scillas, tulips and cyclamen.*

MINIATURE *and slow-growing conifers provide interest throughout the year. An example is* Juniperus communis 'Compressa', *with greyish-green leaves and column-like stance. Other conifers are spreading, bun- or dome-shaped.*

CORMS AND MINIATURE BULBS
Chionodoxa – Ipheion
❖

MOST corms and bulbs plant-ed in rock gardens flower during late winter and spring. Some, such as *Cyclamen coum*, flower in mid-winter, while *C. hederifolium* (*C. neapolitanum*) appear from late summer to early winter. Most have a miniature stance, about 15cm/6in or shorter, but a few are taller.

Spring-flowering bulbs and corms are planted in late summer or early autumn, as soon as they are available. Autumn and early winter-flowering types are planted in spring or early summer.

IN GROUPS

These are diminutive and gregari-ous plants which look best when planted in small groups, where their colour impact is reinforced. When planting them, either take out a small, flat-based hole and spread out the bulbs to a few inches apart, and then return soil over them, or use a small trowel to plant them individually.

CORM OR BULB?

At first sight these appear quite similar and, indeed, they are both underground food storage organs that enable survival during periods when they are dormant.
- *Bulb: Formed of fleshy, modified leaves and with a bud-like structure. Within the centre of each bulb there is a dormant shoot.*
- *Corm: Formed of a swollen and thickened stem-base and covered with a papery skin. At the corm's top is a bud which produces a shoot and roots.*

Early spring bulbs such as crocus-es, chionodoxas and irises benefit from being planted in the shelter of a large rock, whereas autumn- and early winter-flowering types are better in large displays.

With all of these bulbs, avoid spreading them too thinly and over a large area, as their impact will be lost. Always mark the area they occupy to avoid other plants being inadver-tently planted on top, or too close to them.

Never plant bulbs in soil that is badly drained, as they will decay. Preferably, choose well-drained but moisture-retentive soil. Add peat if the soil is light and sandy, but mix in sharp sand where slight drainage is needed. If the area is boggy, installation of drains is essential.

CHIONODOXA LUCILIAE *(Glory of the Snow) grows 15cm/6in high and during late winter and early spring creates a wealth of light blue, white-centred flowers. Plant them 7.5cm/3in apart.*

CROCUS CHRYSANTHUS, *7.5–10cm/3–4in high, has golden-yellow flowers during late winter and early spring. There are also white, blue and purple types. Plant them 7.5cm/3in apart.*

CYCLAMEN COUM *grows about 7.5cm/3in high and develops 18mm/¾in-long flowers in shades of pink and carmine from mid-winter to early spring. These appear above kidney-shaped, mid-green, marbled leaves. Plant them 10cm/4in apart.*

CYCLAMEN HEDERIFOLIUM, *the Baby Cyclamen, earlier called* Cyclamen neapolitanum, *grows 10cm/4in high and develops mauve to pink flowers from late summer to early winter. Plant them 13cm/5in apart.*

ERANTHIS HYEMALIS *(Winter Aconite) has lemon-yellow, cup-shaped flowers, 2.5cm/1in wide and backed by a light-green ruff, during late winter and spring. These are 10cm/4in high and borne amid deeply cut leaves. Plant the bulbs about 7.5cm/3in apart.*

FRITILLARIA MELEAGRIS *(Snake's Head Fritillaria/Checkered Lily), 30–38cm/12–15in high, bears bell-shaped, 36mm/1½in long, white and purple checkered flowers during mid- and late spring. The flowers seldom fail to attract atten-tion. Plant them about 13cm/5in apart.*

FRITILLARIA PALLIDIFLORA *is up to 30cm/12in high and therefore is best suited to large rock gardens. During mid-spring, clusters of yellow, bell-shaped flowers appear with grey-green leaves. Plant 15cm/6in apart.*

IPHEION UNIFLORUM *(Spring Starflower) forms clumps with white to violet-blue flowers, about 15–20cm/6–8in high, during mid- and late spring. The flowers are slightly scented. Plant the bulbs about 7.5cm/3in apart.*

NATURAL DIE-DOWN

After the flowers fade, allow them to die down naturally. Also, do not disturb the leaves while they wilt, shrivel and die. If they are tied up, the food value in them does not return to the bulb; pulling off leaves is even worse. When all signs of life have left them, the remnants of loose leaves can be gently pulled up, but with-out disturbing the bulbs or corms.

CORMS AND MINIATURE BULBS
Iris – Tulipa

ROCK-GARDEN corms and bulbs are superb on their own but can be further enhanced by combining them with other plants. Here are a few combinations to consider:

• *Chionodoxa luciliae* (Glory of the Snow) has blue flowers during late winter and early spring. Plant Gold Dust *(Alyssum saxatile)* so that its golden-yellow flowers highlight those of the bulb.

• *Cyclamen coum* and the Winter Aconite *(Eranthis hyemalis)* form a pleasing partnership, flowering in mid-winter and early spring.

• The Winter Aconite is also a superb partner for clumps of Snowdrops, such as *Galanthus nivalis* 'Flore-pleno'.

• For a medley of shape and colour use the yellow-flowered *Narcissus cyclamineus* 'February Gold' with the blue-headed *Chionodoxa luciliae*. This combination of plants flowers in late winter and early spring.

• *Scilla tubergeniana* and the Winter Aconite form a pleasing colour and shape combination.

ANGEL'S TEARS

The Spanish native Narcissus triandrus *'Albus' has dropping, creamy-white flowers during early and mid-spring. It is known as Angel's Tears and several stories exist about the way this name was gained. They differ slightly but all revolve around the distress or euphoria of a Spanish guide called Angelo or Angel. One story tells of him making an exhausting climb and breaking into tears when finding this plant.*

• *Tulipa tarda*, with its early and mid-spring flowers, can be combined with the Pasque Flower *(Pulsatilla vulgaris)*.

• Form a spring-flowering combination of *Tulipa kaufmanniana* 'The First' and the perennial-type potentilla, *tabernaemontani*, also known as *P. verna* and the Spring Cinquefoil. It has bright yellow flowers about 12mm/¹⁄₂in wide from mid- to late spring.

• For an unusual combination try *Iris reticulata* and wild thyme.

IRIS RETICULATA *is popular, 15cm/6in high and widely grown. During late winter and early spring it develops deep bluish-purple flowers with orange blazes. Plant the bulbs 7.5–10cm/3–4in apart.*

NARCISSUS BULBOCODIUM *(Hoop Petticoat Daffodil) is 7.5–13cm/3–5in high and bears yellow, hoop-like trumpets during late winter and early spring. Plant them about 7.5cm/3in apart.*

NARCISSUS CYCLAMINEUS *has petals that sweep back, away from the trumpet. They grow 15–20cm/6–8in high and flower in late winter and early spring. Plant them 7.5cm/3in apart.*

IRIS DANFORDIAE *has a diminutive stance, only 10cm/4in high. During mid- and late winter it produces sweet and honey-scented, vivid lemon flowers about 7.5cm/3in across. Plant the individual bulbs 7.5–10cm/3–4in apart.*

IRIS DOUGLASIANA *is a tall, Californian species, 30–45cm/12–18in high. Each stem bears up to five 7.5cm/3in-wide flowers in shades of lavender and bluish-purple in early summer. Plant the bulbs 38–45cm/15–18in apart.*

IRIS INNOMINATA *is another North American iris, about 15cm/6in high and bearing buff, cream, yellow or orange flowers about 6.5cm/2¹⁄₂in wide during early summer. It is ideal for planting in peat beds. Plant it 23cm/9in apart.*

SCILLA TUBERGENIANA, *one of the squills, grows 7.5–10cm/3–4in high and has pale blue flowers in late winter and early spring. Plant it with the Common Snowdrop (Galanthus nivalis). Plant the bulbs 7.5–10cm/3–4in apart.*

TULIPA KAUFMANNIANA *(Waterlily Tulip) grows 15–25cm/6–10in high, with star-like flowers during early and mid-spring. The normal species is white with red and yellow flushes. Plant the bulbs about 13–15cm/5–6in apart.*

TULIPA TARDA *is popular, 15cm/6in high and several flowers are borne in terminal clusters on each stem during early and into mid-spring. They are white, with a large, bright centre. Plant the bulbs 3.5–10cm/3–4in apart.*

MINIATURE AND SLOW-GROWING CONIFERS
Chamaecyparis – Juniperus

CONIFERS introduce permanency to rock gardens. They also create features around which other plants can be clustered for protection. Miniature conifers usually remain relatively small, but slow-growing types are planted while small and although they grow slowly there comes a time when they are too large. At this stage, dig them up in spring and plant into a large tub or in the garden.

Renew the soil where the conifer was growing and replant another, preferably in spring. After planting – and especially if the weather is warm – keep the soil moist and lightly mist-spray the foliage several times a day.

JUNIPERUS COMMUNIS
'Compressa' is widely grown and ideal for rock gardens as, even after ten years, it is usually less than 45cm/18in high. The needle-like, dark green foliage is closely set, compact and upright.

JUNIPERUS COMMUNIS
'Depressa Aurea' is prostrate, with golden-yellow foliage in spring, turning bronze in winter. After ten years it is about 30cm/12in high and 1.2m/4ft wide.

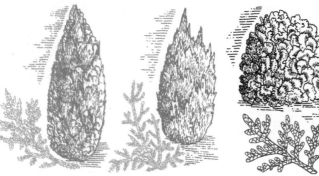

CHAMAECYPARIS LAWSONIANA *'Aurea Densa'* is compact and slow growing, with densely packed, flattened sprays of golden-yellow leaves. Initially it is bun-shaped; about 50cm/20in high after ten years.

CHAMAECYPARIS LAWSONIANA *'Ellwood's Pillar'* has a miniature habit, reaching only 50–60cm/20–24in after ten years. The beautiful foliage is compact, bluish-grey and feathery. It is especially attractive in winter.

CHAMAECYPARIS LAWSONIANA *'Pygmaea Argentea'* is slow growing and rounded, with bluish-green foliage tipped creamy-white. Even after ten years it is seldom more than 45cm/18in high.

JUNIPERUS COMMUNIS *'Golden Showers'* reveals yellowish-bronze foliage in winter and bright yellow in spring as growth commences. After ten years it reaches 1.2–1.5m/4–5ft high. Reserve it for large areas.

JUNIPERUS X MEDIA *'Gold Sovereign'* is a superb conifer with a low, spreading nature, and bright yellow foliage throughout the year. After ten years it is about 50cm/20in high and 75cm/2½ft wide.

JUNIPERUS SQUAMATA *'Blue Star'* has a bushy, somewhat sprawling nature with steel-blue, needle-like foliage. After ten years it is about 38cm/15in high and 45cm/18in wide, and creates a superb feature.

CHAMAECYPARIS PISIFERA *'Squarrosa Sulphurea'* has a rounded shape and its juvenile foliage is a bright sulphur colour. After ten years it is about 75cm/2½ft high.

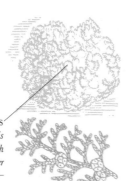

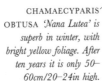

CHAMAECYPARIS OBTUSA *'Nana Lutea'* is superb in winter, with bright yellow foliage. After ten years it is only 50–60cm/20–24in high.

PLANTING INTO A GARDEN

Large conifers removed from rock gardens are more difficult to move and establish than small ones. This is because the roots have a larger area of foliage to supply with moisture. If, after moving a conifer in spring, the weather becomes cold and windy, either insert a stake as a temporary support, or use guy-ropes. Also, by reducing the flow of cold air over the foliage the strain on the roots to absorb moisture is reduced.

Either form a screen of hessian supported by stakes, or put a layer of straw or hay between two layers of wire-netting and support it on the windward side of the conifer. If the weather is dry, water the soil regularly and also mist-spray the foliage.

When transferring a miniature conifer – especially a tall one – from a rock garden into a pot, place it initially in a wind-sheltered corner until it is established and self-supporting.

MINIATURE AND SLOW-GROWING CONIFERS
Juniperus – Thuya
❖

ALL conifers in rock gardens need especially careful positioning, as they form a permanent framework. Some conifers are tall, others bun-shaped or even prostrate, and their shape and size need careful consideration before selecting their positions. When too large they can, of course, be moved to a container or part of a garden (see page 100), but this should not be done regularly.

LARGE ROCK GARDENS
In a large rock garden there is more opportunity to use tall and dominating conifers, perhaps with a few narrowly columnar types such as *Taxus baccata* 'Standishii' or the pencil-thin *Juniperus virginiana* 'Skyrocket'. If there is a path that meanders through a large rock garden, these conifers can be positioned on either side of it. However, do not plant narrow

and tall conifers at the very top, as they will look like chimney pots. Instead, put them at the base, or half to three-quarters of the height up the mound so that from a distance they fuse and harmonize the rock garden with the background and sky.

BUN-SHAPED
Small, bun-shaped miniature conifers are easier to position, but more attention needs to be given to their colour. Bright yellow, grey, as well as steel-blue ones are available; the yellow and golden ones immediately capture the eye and can be too dominant at the front of a rock garden. Steel-blue and blue-grey conifers are especially attractive in winter when surrounded by snow. Therefore plant them on flat areas and where they can be readily seen in winter weather.

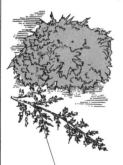

JUNIPERUS SQUAMATA *'Holger' has a spreading habit and eventually is suitable only for large rock gardens when, after ten years, it is about 50cm/20in high and 75cm/2½ft wide. In spring it is creamy yellow, but is bluish-green in winter.*

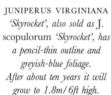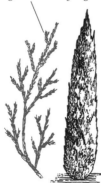

JUNIPERUS VIRGINIANA *'Skyrocket', also sold as J. scopulorum 'Skyrocket', has a pencil-thin outline and greyish-blue foliage. After about ten years it will grow to 1.8m/6ft high.*

PINUS SYLVESTRIS *'Beauwronensis' is a dwarf form of the Scots Pine, reaching only 60cm/2ft high and 3m/3½ft wide in ten years. The foliage is grey-green and forms a beautiful feature, especially in spring with its new growth.*

TAXUS BACCATA *'Standishii' is slow growing and creates a narrow column of gold leaves. In ten years it is about 1m/3½ft high and may need to be moved. Nevertheless, it is well worth planting at the base of a rock garden.*

THUJA ORIENTALIS *'Aurea Nana' forms a rounded cone-shape, packed with vertical fans of yellow-green foliage. In winter it becomes tarnished gold. After about ten years this conifer is often still only 60cm/2ft high.*

THUYA PLICATA *'Stoneham Gold' has bright, rich golden-yellow foliage during summer as well as in winter. After ten years it is usually between 60cm/2ft and 90cm/3ft high. If a beacon of colour is needed, choose this conifer.*

FURTHER DWARF CONIFERS

All measurements given here are after ten years of growth.
- Chamaecyparis lawsoniana *'Ellwood's Gold': Soft, feathery, gold-tinged foliage in summer (1.2m/4ft high).*
- Chamaecyparis lawsoniana *'Gnome': Miniature stature, with deep green foliage (20–30cm/10–12in high).*
- Chamaecyparis lawsoniana *'Minima Aurea': Yellow leaves (50cm/20in high).*
- Chamaecyparis lawsoniana *'Minima Glauca': Globular (60cm/2ft high).*
- Chamaecyparis obtusa *'Nana Gracilis': Sprays of dark green foliage (60cm/2ft high).*
- Chamaecyparis pisifera *'Boulevard': Intense silver-blue foliage (90cm/3ft high).*
- Picea abies *'Little Gem': Dwarf, with bright new shoots in spring (30cm/12in high).*

Prostrate types need to be seen from above and from relatively close-by; therefore, use them by the sides of paths and towards the front of a rock garden.

SCREE BEDS
Although dwarf conifers are not traditionally part of scree beds, they nevertheless look handsome there and can be used instead of rocks to create height. Grey or steel-blue conifers look best. Choose three bun-shaped species and use them to indicate decreasing height. Always use odd-numbers of plants in this situation. They create height contrasts and form attractive backgrounds for small groups of miniature bulbs. And, by using conifers that are blue-leaved, white and yellow flowers are especially highlighted.

Towards the lower edge of a scree bed, perhaps where it meets a path or lawn, plant a prostrate miniature conifer so that its foliage cuts across both features. If possible, position it so that the foliage spreads downwards, not up.

DWARF SHRUBS AND TREES
Acer – Euryops

THERE is a surprisingly wide range of dwarf shrubs and trees suitable for planting in rock gardens. Some are best reserved for large areas, but there are many that grow only 15cm/6in high so they can be fitted into small places.

In addition to the shrubs and small trees illustrated and described on this and the following page, there are others to consider, including:

• *Cotoneaster congestus* 'Nanus' is dwarf and evergreen, less than 30cm/12in high and with bluish-green leaves and red berries.

• *Cotoneaster dammeri* is 5–7.5cm/2–3in high and with a wide spread, often to 1.8m/6ft. It is therefore only suitable for large rock gardens. The evergreen leaves are dark green and glossy, with white flowers in early summer and round, red berries in late summer and autumn.

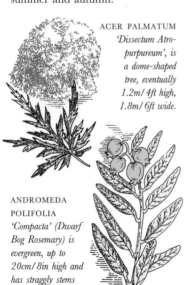

ACER PALMATUM 'Dissectum Atropurpureum', is a dome-shaped tree, eventually 1.2m/4ft high, 1.8m/6ft wide.

ANDROMEDA POLIFOLIA 'Compacta' (Dwarf Bog Rosemary) is evergreen, up to 20cm/8in high and has straggly stems 50cm/20in long.

CALLUNA VULGARIS (Heather/Ling) is a hardy evergreen with varieties in many colours and sizes, from 10cm/4in to 60cm/2ft. Select small varieties.

COTONEASTER MICROPHYLLUS THYMIFOLIUS, a mound-forming and prostrate evergreen shrub about 30cm/12in high and 50cm/20in wide, has white flowers and red berries.

• *Cytisus ardoini* is 20cm/8in high with an arching habit and golden-yellow flowers which appear during mid- and late spring.

• *Cytisus demissus* is seldom more than 10cm/4in high, with large yellow flowers during late spring.

• *Cytisus decumbens* is prostrate, about 15cm/6in high and with bright yellow flowers during late spring and early summer.

• *Erica herbacea* (earlier known as *E. carnea*) has several low-growing varieties, some 15cm/6in high.

• *Erica cinerea* 'Coccinea', a form of Bell Heather, is 15cm/6in high and bears deep carmine-red flowers from early summer to autumn. There are several other low-growing varieties.

• *Erica tetralix*, the Cross-leaved Heath, has grey foliage and pink flowers throughout summer.

• *Genista lydia* is only suitable for large rock gardens; its stems, up to 60cm/2ft high, are covered with golden-yellow flowers during late spring and early summer.

• *Genista sagittalis* has winged, prostrate stems and bright yellow flowers during early summer.

• *Thymus drucei* (Wild Thyme and earlier known as *T. serpyllum*) grows up to 7.5cm/3in high and 60cm/2ft wide, with flowers in a range of colours from white, through pink to red, from early to late summer. 'Annie Hall' is smaller, with pale pink flowers, while 'Coccineus' is rich crimson.

• *Vaccinium vitis-idaea* (Cowberry/Mountain Cranberry) is evergreen, semi-prostrate and up to 15cm/6in high with a 45cm/18in spread. It is ideal for planting in peat beds, where it develops white or pale flowers during late spring and early summer.

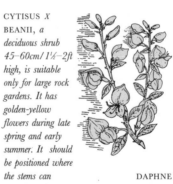

CYTISUS X BEANII, a deciduous shrub 45–60cm/1½–2ft high, is suitable only for large rock gardens. It has golden-yellow flowers during late spring and early summer. It should be positioned where the stems can cascade.

DAPHNE CNEORUM (Garland Flower), an evergreen, grows 15cm/6in high and 60cm/2ft or more wide. During late spring and early summer it has scented, rosy-pink flowers. There is also a white form, 'Pygmaea', which is prostrate.

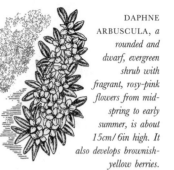

DAPHNE ARBUSCULA, a rounded and dwarf, evergreen shrub with fragrant, rosy-pink flowers from mid-spring to early summer, is about 15cm/6in high. It also develops brownish-yellow berries.

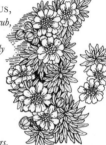

EURYOPS ACRAEUS, a dwarf evergreen shrub, grows about 30cm/12in high and slightly wider. During late spring and early summer, the silver-grey leaves are surrounded by bright yellow, 2.5cm/1in-wide daisy-like flowers.

DYERS' WEED

Genistas are superbly bright garden plants. Earlier, Genista tinctoria was known as the Dyer's Greenweed or Dyer's Broom. It yields a strong yellow dye and from early times was used to dye wool. When combined with Woad it created a green dye known as Kendal Green. Kendal Green was the name of the place where the process was first introduced by Flemish immigrants during the eighteenth century.

The plant is European, and grows up to 90cm/3ft high and 1.8m/6ft wide. From early to late summer it bears deep yellow flowers. The form 'Humifusa' is prostrate, up to 10cm/4in high and 60cm/2ft wide.

DWARF SHRUBS AND TREES
Genista – Zauschneria

SOME dwarf shrubs and trees are fully hardy and able to withstand the coldest of climates. Others, such as the Californian Fuchsia (*Zauschneria californica*), are not always able to survive the rigours of winter in temperate climates, except when planted in warm positions. Light, dry soil also helps them.

LOW-GROWING SHRUBS

Many of these plants are naturally low to enable survival in cold and exposed areas, where strong winds would batter and destroy tall, upright types. In addition, they are mainly deciduous, so that a fresh cloak of new, undamaged leaves appears each year. And being low, they are often covered by a protective layer of snow during winter. *Salix arbuscula*, for example, is native to Scandinavia, Northern Russia and Scotland, all areas where strong winds soon damage tall and exposed shrubs.

ACID-LOVING SHRUBS

Many shrubs must be given acid conditions, such as those present in peat beds. If planted into chalky soil they soon die. Suitable plants include some of those featured on these and the previous pages, such as:
• *Andromeda polifolia* 'Compacta'
• *Leiophyllum buxifolium*
• *Pimelea coarctica*
• *Polygala chamaebuxus*
• *Salix arbuscula*
• *Vaccinium vitis-idaea*
Other acid-loving shrubs include:
• *Gaultheria miqueliana*: Evergreen, up to 30cm/12in high and with dark green leaves. Bears small white flowers in early summer and white berries in autumn.
• *Galtheria procumbens* (Partridge Berry/Winter Green/Checkerberry): A North American evergreen up to 15cm/6in high and spreading to 90cm/3ft or more. Masses of shiny, dark green leaves and white or pink flowers in mid- and late summer. Red berries.

• *Vaccinium nummalaria:* Evergreen and compact, with arching shoots clothed in small, dark, glossy-green leaves. It grows about 25cm/10in high and during late spring and early summer bears rosy-red flowers, followed by black, round, edible berries.

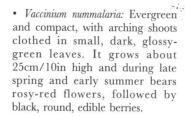

• *Vaccinium praestans:* A creeping deciduous shrub, up to 10cm/4in high, with bell-shaped, white to reddish flowers in early summer. These are followed by 12mm/½in-wide bright, glossy red berries. In North America it is known as Kamchatka Bilberry.

HYPERICUM OLYMPICUM 'Citrinum' *is evergreen, with large, lemon-yellow flowers during mid- and late summer. It grows about 25cm/10in high and 30cm/12in wide. The ordinary type has golden-yellow flowers.*

PIMELEA COARCTICA *(also sold as P. prostrata) is evergreen, with grey-green leaves, occasionally edged red, and white flowers in early summer. This plant has an attractive prostrate nature and spreads up to 60cm/2ft.*

LEIOPHYLLUM BUXIFOLIUM *forms an evergreen shrub that requires an acid soil, such as in a peat bed. It grows about 30cm/12in high and during early summer bears clusters of starry, white flowers which are at first pink.*

POLYGALA CHAMAEBUXUS *(Ground Box), is a dwarf, evergreen shrublet 10–15cm/4–6in high. From late spring to mid-summer it bears cream and yellow flowers tipped with purple. It must be planted in acid soil.*

SALIX ARBUSCULA *(Dwarf Willow) is a low-growing, deciduous shrub with creeping woody stems, up to 45cm/18in high and spreading to 60cm/2ft. The leaves are deep green, and slender, grey catkins appear in mid-spring.*

ZAUSCHNERIA CALIFORNICA *(Californian Fuchsia) is distinctive, with red, tubular, fuchsia-like flowers during late summer and autumn. It grows up to 45cm/18in high and is not fully hardy in cold, exposed and wet areas.*

GENISTA PILOSA *forms a neat shrub up to 45cm/18in high and spreading to 90cm/3ft. It drenches the ground with whip-like shoots and small, yellow flowers from late spring to mid-summer.*

HEBE BUCHANANII *'Minor' is only 5cm/2in high and 10–15cm/4–6in wide, and ideal for planting in a sink garden. Its dull green, evergreen leaves form an attractive foil for the small, white, stemless flowers in early summer.*

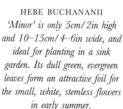

HEBE VERNICOSA *forms an evergreen shrub about 20cm/8in high. The reddish-brown stems bear thick, fleshy, mid-green leaves tipped pale yellow. White, 2.5cm/1in-wide flowers appear in mid-summer.*

ANNUALS AND BIENNIALS
For the rock garden
❖

THESE are popular and inexpensive flowers, easily raised from seeds and certain to brighten rock gardens from late spring to the frosts of autumn.

• Half-hardy annuals: These are sown in seed-trays in late winter or early spring in a greenhouse and given gentle warmth until they germinate. The temperature is then reduced slightly and when the seedlings are large enough to handle they are transferred to other seed-trays and spaced out, so that each plant has more space. Later they are progressively acclimatized to outdoor conditions and planted out when all risk of frost has passed.

• Hardy annuals: These are sown in mid- to late spring in the positions in which they are to flower. Sow seeds thinly and when the seedlings are large enough to handle, thin them out,

ADONIS AESTIVALIS
(Pheasant's Eye): Hardy annual; 30cm/12in high; thin to 30cm/12in apart. Deep crimson, cup-shaped flowers in summer. Light green leaves.

ALYSSUM MARITIMUM
(now correctly Lobularia maritima *and widely known as Sweet Alyssum): Half-hardy annual; 7.5–15cm/ 3–6in high; plant them 20cm/8in apart. Flowers throughout summer.*

ANAGALIS ARVENSIS
'Caerulea' (form of the Scarlet Pimpernel): Hardy annual; 5cm/ 2in high; thin to 15cm/6in apart. Dark blue, saucer-shaped flowers during summer.

ANTIRRHINUM MAJUS *(Snapdragon): Half-hardy annual; choose low-growing varieties; plant 20–25cm/8–10in apart. It acts as a perennial in mild areas and will grow again the following year.*

usually to between 15cm/6in and 30cm/12in apart, depending on the species. The seed packet will indicate the distance.

• Biennials: These are sown one year to produce flowers during the following one. Sow seeds in a seed-bed outdoors, in a sheltered position, during late spring and early summer. When the seedlings are large enough to handle, thin them to between 5cm/ 2in and 10cm/4in apart, depending on the species, but ensure they are not left congested throughout summer. Keep the seed-bed regularly watered and free from weeds. In early autumn, transfer plants to their flowering positions. In exceptionally cold areas, moving them can be delayed until early spring.

CALANDRINA UMBELLATUM *(Rock Purslane): Perennial usually grown as a half-hardy annual or biennial; 15cm/6in high; plant 23cm/ 9in apart. Magenta flowers, from mid-summer to autumn.*

ASPERULA ORIENTALIS *(Annual Woodruff): Hardy annual; 30cm/12in high; thin to 10cm/4in apart. Mid-green leaves and blue flowers.*

LOOKING AFTER ANNUALS
Once they are planted, half-hardy annuals need little attention, except to keep them free from weeds, and to water the soil regularly during dry periods. Once these plants suffer from dry soil, they mature rapidly and do not fully recover, whatever treatment then given.

Hardy annuals are better equipped to withstand dry periods, but even these suffer and may not recover. When the seedlings are 7.5–10cm/3–4in high, insert pea-sticks between and around them so that stems and leaves grow up and through them. If the pea-sticks later appear to be too high, use secateurs to cut them off so that only leaves and flowers can be seen.

Check the plants regularly to ensure pests are not present, and spray as necessary. Slugs and snails are the biggest problem when plants are young.

LOOKING AFTER BIENNIALS
These are hardy plants that are able to survive outdoors during winter. However, when young they are equally as susceptible to slug damage as other plants.

In spring, re-firm soil around the roots of biennials planted in autumn; frost often loosens the soil and if not firmed the plants do not grow rapidly. In autumn, when transplanting them, put a few plants to one side to act as spares for plants that do not survive the winter.

ERYSIMUM ALPINUM *(Alpine Wallflower/ Fairy Wallflower): Biennial; 20cm/8in high; plant them 10–15cm/4–6in apart. Bushy, with dark green leaves and scented, sulphur yellow flowers during late spring and early summer.*

ESCHSCHOLZIA CALIFORNICA *(Californian Poppy): Hardy annual; 30–38cm/12–15in high; thin them 23cm/9in apart. Blue-green leaves and bright-faced, poppy-like flowers.*

FELICIA BERGERIANA *(Kingfisher Daisy): Half-hardy annual; 15cm/6in high; plant 15cm/6in apart. Daisy-like, light-blue flowers from early summer to autumn. It creates a magnificent display.*

ANNUALS AND BIENNIALS
Anagalis – Verbena
❖

THE range of annuals and biennials that can be sown or planted in rock gardens is wide. In addition to the ones illustrated here and on page 104, there are others to consider, such as:
• *Anagalis linifolia* 'Gentian Blue' is grown as a half-hardy annual, reaches 15–23cm/6–9in high and bears blue flowers from early to late summer. Plant it 25–30cm/10–12in apart.
• *Eschscholzia caespitosa* (also known as *E. tenuifolia*) is a hardy annual, and grows 13cm/5in high. From early summer to autumn it has blue-green, finely divided leaves and 2.5cm/1in-wide yellow flowers. Thin the seedlings to 15cm/6in apart.
• *Felicia bergeriana* (Kingfisher Daisy) is a half-hardy annual, 15cm/6in high and bearing steel-blue flowers with yellow centres

from early to late summer. Space the plants about 15cm/6in apart.
• *Gazania* x *hybrida*, usually raised as a half-hardy annual, grows 23cm/9in high and from mid-summer to the frosts of autumn has a wealth of large, daisy-like flowers in many colours. Space 25–30cm/10–12in apart.
• *Gilea lutea* (Stardust and earlier known as *Leptosiphon hybridus*), a hardy annual, grows 10–15cm/4–6in high and from early summer to autumn has a feast of brightly coloured, star-shaped flowers. Mixed-coloured varieties include flowers in yellow, orange, red and pink. Thin the seedlings to 10cm/4in apart.
• *Linaria maroccana* (Toadflax) is a hardy annual that grows 20–30cm/8–12in high and during early and mid-summer creates a wealth of snapdragon-like flowers in colours including violet, blue,

NEMESIA STRUMOSA: *Half-hardy annual; 20-45cm/8-18in high; plant them 10-15cm/4-6in apart. Yellow, orange, pink, scarlet, cherry-red and blue flowers from early to late summer.*

NEMOPHILA MENZIESII (Baby Blue Eyes): *Hardy annual; 23cm/9in high; thin them 15cm/6in apart. White-centred, sky-blue, saucer-shaped flowers from early to late summer.*

NIEREMBERGIA 'Mont Blanc': *Half-hardy annual; 15cm/6in high; plant 15cm/6in apart. Compact and spreading, with masses of 2.5cm/1in-wide white flowers throughout summer.*

red, yellow and pink. They are borne amid narrow, light green leaves. Thin the seedlings to 15cm/6in apart.
• *Mesembryanthemum criniflorum* (Livingstone Daisy), grown as a half-hardy annual, is 10–15cm/4–6in high and displays daisy-like, pink, crimson, orange, rose and apricot flowers from early to late

summer. Space these succulent plants about 30cm/12in apart.
• *Phacelia campanularia* is a hardy annual with grey leaves and blue, bell-shaped flowers about 2.5cm/1in wide from early summer to the frosts of autumn. Thin the seedlings to 15cm/6in apart.
• *Platystemon californicus* (Cream Cups) is a hardy annual, about 30cm/12in high and superb when grown in drifts in large rock gardens. During mid-summer it has masses of saucer-shaped, 2.5cm/1in-wide, pale yellow or cream flowers. Thin the seedlings to 10cm/4in apart.
• *Ursinia anethoides* is a half-hardy annual, growing 23cm/9in high and bearing orange, daisy-like flowers with purple centres from early to late summer. Space the plants 25cm/10in apart.
• *Verbena* x *hybrida* is grown as a half-hardy annual and creates a wealth of colourful flower heads in a range of colours from early summer to autumn. For growing in rock gardens, choose dwarf varieties, about 23cm/9in high, and plant them 15–23cm/6–9in apart.

IONOPSIDIUM ACAULE (Violet Cress): *Hardy annual; 7.5cm/3in high; not necessary to thin them. Small, four-petalled, pale mauve or white flowers tinged with purple from early summer to autumn.*

LIMNANTHES DOUGLASII (Poached Egg Flower): *Hardy annual; 15cm/6in high; thin to 10cm/4in apart. Light green leaves and yellow, saucer-shaped flowers edged in white from early to late summer.*

LINUM GRANDIFLORUM 'RUBRUM' (Scarlet Flax): *Hardy annual; 30cm/12in high; thin to 13cm/5in apart. Easily grown annual, well known for its saucer-shaped, bright crimson flowers and pale green leaves.*

PORTULACA GRANDIFLORA (Sun Plant): *Half-hardy annual; 15-23cm/6-9in high; plant them 15cm/6in apart. Bright-green leaves and saucer-shaped, red, purple or yellow flowers with bright yellow centres from early summer to autumn.*

ROCK-GARDEN PERENNIALS
Acaena – Arabis

THESE are plants that, once planted, continue for several years before having to be lifted, divided and young pieces from around the outside replanted.

The range of perennials is wide and they are featured from this page to page 114. They are always popular and form the main range of plants grown in rock gardens, filling them with both beautiful, colourful flowers and attractive leaves.

• *Acaena buchananii* (New Zealand Burr), grows 2.5–5cm/1–2in high and spreads to 60cm/2ft, has grey-green leaves and amber-brown burrs.

• *Achillea tomentosa*, growing 15–20cm/6–8in high and spreading to 30cm/12in, develops downy, grey-green leaves. Bright yellow flowers, in heads up to 7.5cm/3in across, appear from mid-summer to autumn.

• *Aethionema* 'Warley Rose', 10–15cm/4–6in high and spreading to 38cm/15in, is ideal for rock gardens and dry-stone walls. Its leaves are grey-green, with rosy-red flowers in dense heads during spring and early summer.

LIVE-FOR-EVER

During the late sixteenth century, the herbalist and barber-surgeon John Gerard wrote that Antennaria dioica *was widely known as Live-long and Live-for-ever. He referred to brown-yellow thrumme (thread-like material) collected from the centre of flowers and which could be kept for a long time. For this reason, the plant was also known as both Life Everlasting and Mountain Everlasting.*

• *Alchemilla alpina* (Alpine Lady's Mantle), 15cm/6in high and about 25cm/10in wide, has silvery-edged green leaves and star-shaped, yellowish-green flowers from early to late summer. Often used in flower arrangements.

ANACYCLUS DEPRESSUS *(Mount Atlas Daisy) grows about 5cm/2in high and spreads to 30cm/12in. The finely divided, grey-green leaves are smothered with 5cm/2in-wide, white flowers from early to late summer. Remove dead ones regularly.*

ANDROSACE PRIMULOIDES *'Chumbyi' (Rock Jasmine and sometimes sold as A. sarmentosa 'Chumbyi') is 10cm/4in high and spreads to about 45cm/1½ft. From mid-spring to early summer it bears heads of rose-pink flowers.*

• *Androsace lanuginosa* (Rock Jasmine), 36mm/1½in high and spreading to 38cm/15in, forms trailing mats of silver-green leaves, with pink flowers from early summer to autumn. 'Leichtlinii' has white flowers with a red centre.

ANDROSACE SARMENTOSA *(Rock Jasmine) grows 10–13cm/4–5in high and spreads to 60cm/2ft. From mid-spring to early summer it displays dome-shaped heads of rose-pink flowers on 5–10cm/2–4in-long stems.*

ACAENA MICROPHYLLA *(New Zealand Burr) grows up to 5cm/2in high and spreads 45cm/18in or more. When young the leaves are silvery, later bronze-green. The characteristic crimson burrs appear from mid-summer onwards and form an attractive display.*

AETHIONEMA PULCHELLUM *grows 15–23cm/6–9in high and about 38cm/15in wide. It forms mats of leaves and from late spring to mid-summer bears heads of pale pink, cross-shaped flowers. It needs well-drained soil.*

ALYSSUM SAXATILE *(Gold Dust) grows 15–30cm/6–12in high and spreads to 45cm/18in, with an evergreen, shrubby nature. From mid-spring to early summer it bears golden-yellow flowers. There are several varieties.*

ANTENNARIA DIOICA *'Rosea' (Cat's Ear/Rosy Pussy Paws) is 10–15cm/4–6in high and spreads to 45cm/1½ft, with deep pink flowers borne amid a creeping mat of stems during late spring and early summer. Well-drained soil is essential.*

AQUILEGIA FLABELLATA PUMILA *(Alpine Columbine) grows 10–15cm/4–6in high and wide, with nodding, cap-like, pinkish-mauve flowers from late spring to mid-summer. The flowers appear above beautiful bluish-green leaves.*

ARABIS CAUCASICA *(Rock Cress and earlier known as A. albida) is 23cm/9in high and spreads to 50cm/20in or more. From early spring to early summer it displays white flowers above grey-green and hoary leaves. Cut it back as soon as the flowers fade.*

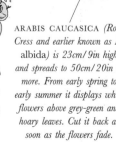

ROCK-GARDEN PERENNIALS
Arabis ❖ *Aubrieta*

IN addition to the rock garden perennials illustrated here, there are other superb plants to choose from.

• *Arenaria grandiflora* grows 5–7.5cm/2–3in high and spreads to 25cm/10in. It has bright green leaves and displays white, funnel-shaped flowers from late spring to late summer.

• *Arenaria montana*, 10–15cm/ 4–6in high and spreading to 45cm/18in, forms a mat of mid-green leaves. During late spring and early summer the leaves are smothered in bright white, saucer-shaped flowers.

• *Arenaria purpurascens*, 7.5cm/3in high and spreading to 30cm/12in, develops purple, star-shaped flowers during mid- and late summer.

• *Armeria maritima* (Common Thrift), 15–23cm/6–9in high and spreading to 30cm/12in, is more vigorous than *A. caespitosa* (illustrated). In large rock gardens, however, it grows in dominant grey-

LADIES' CUSHION

This is another of the many common names given to Thrift (Armeria maritima), together with Sea Pink and Gilly Flower. At one time, it was botanically known as Statice maritima *and* S. armeria, *and was introduced into Tudor gardens when knot gardens became fashionable. The English gardener and herbalist, John Parkinson, in the early seventeenth century wrote of Thrift being one of the first plants used for forming knot gardens. It was clipped into shape. The Romans knew of this plant's ability to reduce sand erosion, while medicinally it was credited with 'stopping the Humours'.*

ARTEMISIA SCHMIDTIANA *'Nana' is dwarf, only 7.5cm/3in high and 30cm/12in wide. In autumn, the finely divided silvery-grey leaves form an attractive mound.*

ASPERULA SUBEROSA, *an alpine species, is only 7.5cm/3in high and spreads to 15cm/6in. It develops shell-pink flowers in early and mid-summer. In winter, protect it from rain.*

ASTER ALPINUS *is only 15cm/6in high and clump forming. During mid-summer it has purple-blue, 25–36mm/ 1–1½in-wide, daisy-like flowers with orange-yellow centres.*

green hummocks peppered from late spring to mid-summer with pink flower heads up to 2.5cm/1in wide. There is also a white-flowered form.

• *Artemisia nitida* (also known as *A. lanata*), up to 5cm/2in high and spreading to 23cm/9in, forms grey-green, evergreen cushions. The leaves are finely dissected and yellow flowers appear from mid-summer to early autumn.

• *Asperula lilaciflora caespitosa*, up to 7.5cm/3in high and spreading to 15cm/6in, has bright green leaves and lilac-pink, tubular flowers during early and mid-summer.

• *Astilbe glaberrima saxatalis*, 10–15cm/4–6in high and wide, has finely dissected leaves and pale pink and cream flowers from early to late summer. Position astilbes towards the base of a rock garden, where the soil is moist.

ARABIS FERDINANDI-COBURGII *'Variegata', 10–13cm/4–5in high and about 25cm/10in wide, is well known for its variegated leaves. In spring and early summer it has white flowers.*

ARENARIA BALEARICA *(Sandwort) is only 2.5cm/1in high. It forms a carpet 45cm/1½ft wide of mid-green leaves. From spring to mid-summer it has small, white flowers.*

ARMERIA CAESPITOSA *(Thrift), 5–7.5cm/2–3in high, forms a 15–23cm/ 6–9in-wide, evergreen mound of grey-green leaves. During late spring it develops pink flowers.*

ASTILBE CHINENSIS *'Pumila' is a diminutive rock-garden astilbe, about 23cm/9in high and 30cm/12in wide. From mid-summer to autumn it has rose-purple flower spires.*

AUBRIETA DELTOIDEA, *7.5–10cm/3–4in high and spreading to 60cm/2ft, is smothered in purple to rose-lilac flowers during spring and early summer. There are many varieties.*

AUBRIETA DELTOIDEA *'Aureovariegata' is about 7.5cm/3in high and spreads to 45cm/1½ft. The leaves are handsomely variegated in green and gold, and it has lavender flowers.*

ROCK-GARDEN PERENNIALS
Campanula – Edraianthus
❖

CAMPANULAS are popular and easily grown rock garden perennials and in addition to the two illustrated here there are others that are well worth growing.

• *Campanula carpatica*, 23cm/9in high and spreading to 38cm/15in, is best in large rock gardens. During mid and late summer it bears cup-shaped flowers in colours ranging from blue to purple. There is also a pretty white-flowered variety.

• *Campanula portenschlagiana* (also known as *C. murialis*), 15cm/6in high and spreading to 45cm/18in or more, is long-lived and with heart-shaped, mid-green leaves. From early summer to late autumn it bears purple, bell-like flowers. It can be rampant, so be prepared to cut it back when the flowers fade.

• *Campanula zoysii*, 7.5cm/3in high and spreading to 15cm/6in, is sufficiently diminutive for most rock gardens, although it tends to be short-lived. Preferably, it needs the comfort of an alpine house, but will survive outdoors when given protection from excessive moisture during winter. Its light blue flowers appear during mid-summer.

DIANTHUS
Pinks offer an amazing range of plants for rock gardens. The Cheddar Pink (*Dianthus gratianopolitanus*) is illustrated here, but there are others worth considering, many of which are superbly scented.

CAMPANULA GARGANICA, *at 13–15cm/5–6in high and spreading to 30cm/12in, has mid-green, kidney-shaped leaves and massed blue flowers from late spring to autumn.*

CAMPANULA COCHLEARIIFOLIA (*C. pusilla and widely known as Fairy Thimbles) is 10–15cm/4–6in high and spreads to 30cm/12in. Blue, bell-shaped flowers.*

CERASTIUM TOMENTOSUM (*Snow-in-Summer) is 10–15cm/4–6in high and spreads to 45cm/1½ft. The leaves are woolly and oblong and from late spring to mid-summer covered with white flowers.*

CASSIOPE LYCOPODIOIDES *is mat-forming and often classified as a shrub. It is 5–7.5cm/2–3in high and spreads to 38cm/15in. White flowers appear in mid and late spring.*

CORYDALIS CASHMERIANA *grows 15cm/6in high and spreads to 23cm/9in. From late spring to late summer the finely dissected, blue-green leaves are smothered by blue flowers. It grows best in peaty, well-drained soil.*

DIANTHUS GRATIANOPOLITANUS (*Cheddar Pink and earlier known as D. caesius) grows about 20cm/8in high and spreads to 30cm/12in or more. The fragrant, fringed, pink flowers appear from late spring to mid-summer.*

DIASCIA *'Ruby Field', about 23cm/9in high and with the same spread, develops ruby-coloured flowers from late spring to mid-summer. Pinch out the tips of shoots to encourage it to become bushy.*

DODECATHEON MEADIA (*Shooting Star), 30–45cm/12–18in high and 25cm/10in wide, is best reserved for large rock gardens. Rose-purple flowers appear during late spring and into the early part of summer.*

• *Dianthus alpinus* (Alpine Pink), 10cm/4in high and about 15cm/6in wide, forms mats of deep green leaves. From late spring to late summer it develops pale pink to purple flowers, each with a white eye. There is also a white-flowered form. Unfortunately, it is rather short-lived and new plants need to be raised every couple of years.

• *Dianthus deltoides* (Maiden Pink) is an old and well-established favourite, about 20cm/8in high and with a similar spread. The leaves are narrow, and mid- to dark green, while the early summer to early autumn flowers range in colour from red to white. It is an ideal plant for positioning in crevices between rocks and for planting between paving stones.

• *Dianthus neglectus* (also known as *D. pavonius*), 10–20cm/4–8in high and about 15cm/6in across, forms tufts of grey-green leaves. It is a variable species and creates masses of flowers during mid- and late summer. These range from pale pink to deep crimson.

EDRAIANTHUS SERPYLLIFOLIUS *forms a mat of deep green leaves about 2.5cm/1in high and spreads to 23cm/9in. In early summer it develops purple flowers at the tips of stems.*

ROCK-GARDEN PERENNIALS
Erinus – Iberis
❖

GENTIANS are popular rock garden plants, often creating vast sheets of colour. In addition to those illustrated here, there are many others to consider.

• *Gentiana farreri*, 10cm/4in high and spreading to 25cm/10in, is one of the best for a rock garden. From late summer to mid-autumn, the narrow, lance-shaped, light green leaves become awash with blue, trumpet-like flowers with white throats.

• *Gentiana gracilipes*, 15–23cm/6–9in high and spreading to 38cm/15in, forms tufts of narrow mid-green leaves. During mid- and late summer, branching stems bear funnel-shaped purple flowers that are striped with green.

GENTIANA VERNA (*Spring Gentian*) *grows 7.5cm/3in high and spreads to 15cm/6in. During late spring and early summer it develops 2.5cm/1in-long, blue flowers. Well-drained, chalky soil is essential for this plant.*

GERANIUM 'Ballerina', *a hybrid about 20cm/8in high and spreading to 30cm/12in, has pink flowers up to 2.5cm/1in wide, from early to late summer. The flowers are heavily veined in deep pink and the leaves are lobed.*

GERANIUM SUBCAULESCENS, *10–15cm/4–6in high and spreading to 30cm/12in or more. From late spring to mid-autumn it bears 2.5cm/1in-wide, bright crimson-magenta flowers. There are several other forms.*

ERINUS ALPINUS (*Summer Starwort*), *7.5cm/3in high and spreading to 15cm/6in, forms evergreen tufts of mid-green leaves and starry, bright pink flowers from early spring to late summer. It is ideal for planting in a scree.*

FRANKENIA THYMAEFOLIA (*Sea Heath*), *about 7.5cm/3in high and quickly spreading to form a mat, is covered in clear pink flowers during mid-spring and late summer. Use well-drained soil and a position in full sun.*

GENTIANA ACAULIS (*Trumpet Gentian*) *grows 7.5cm/3in high and spreads to 38cm/15in. During late spring and early summer it produces deep blue flowers, up to 7.5cm/3in long. They stand clear above the mats of mid-green leaves.*

• *Gentiana septemfida*, 23cm/9in high and spreading to 30cm/12in, is easily grown but only suitable for large rock gardens. From mid- to late summer it produces clusters of 3.6cm/1½in-long, purple-blue trumpet-shaped flowers.

• *Gentiana sino-ornata* is a superb autumn-flowering species. It is about 15cm/6in high and spreads to 38cm/15in, with bright blue, trumpet-shaped flowers from early autumn to early winter. The 5cm/2in-long trumpets are striped in pale green.

• *Gentiana* 'Stevenagensis', 10cm/4in high and spreading to 30cm/12in, produces 5cm/2in-high, rich blue trumpets during late summer and early autumn.

UNGRATEFUL PLANT

The Yellow Gentian or Gentian Root (Gentiana lutea) was probably the first cultivated gentian to be introduced from Europe into England. It was then called Baldmoney, Bitterwort or Felwort, known for its medicinal qualities and used to flavour liqueurs. It grows about 1m/3½ft high and when grown by nineteenth-century gardeners proved so difficult that it was said to signify ingratitude. The gentian family was named in honour of Gentius, King of Illyria, an ancient region in the Balkans.

GEUM MONTANUM *grows 15–30cm/6–12in high and with a 23–30cm/9–12in spread. From late spring to mid-summer it produces yellow flowers.*

GYPSOPHILA REPENS (G. prostrata), *grows up to 15cm/6in high and spreads to 45cm/18in. From early to late summer it bears white to pink flowers.*

IBERIS SEMPERVIRENS 'Little Gem' (*Perennial Candytuft*), *10cm/4in high and spreading to 23cm/9in, has white flowers during late spring and early summer.*

ROCK-GARDEN PERENNIALS
Leontopodium - Omphalodes

LEWISIAS are popular rock-garden plants and native to the western states of North America. Most of them form an evergreen rosette of semi-succulent leaves; some have thick, starchy, edible roots. They all need well-drained soil, as water that remains at their centre during winter quickly causes decay. Plant them in crevices between rocks. When planted in other positions, surround them with a mulch of stone chippings. Covering them with small glass tents also helps to keep them dry during winter. There are many species to choose from and one of them, *Lewisia cotyledon*, is illustrated at right; others include:
• *Lewisia brachycalyx*, up to 7.5cm/3in high and spreading to 20cm/8in, has a rosette of fleshy leaves from which flower stems develop. The shiny white or pinkish flowers appear late in spring.

• *Lewisia tweedyi*, 15cm/6in high and spreading to 23cm/9in, is evergreen, with loose rosettes of mid-green leaves and 5cm/2in-wide, pale pink flowers during mid- and late spring.
• *Lewisia rediviva* (Bitter Root), 7.5cm/3in high and spreading to 15cm/6in, forms a rosette which dies during early summer when 5cm/2in-wide white or rose-pink flowers appear.

PERENNIAL FLAX
Choose from a wide range of Linums:
• *Linum perenne*, an herbaceous perennial with blue flowers, is illustrated opposite.
• *Linum narbonense* 'Heavenly Blue' has an herbaceous nature – sometimes evergreen in mild areas – growing to 38cm/15in high and spreading to 30cm/12in. Between early summer and early autumn it produces rich blue flowers with white centres.

LEONTOPODIUM ALPINUM *(Edelweiss), 20cm/8in high and spreading to 23cm/9in, reveals grey-green leaves and white flowers surrounded by woolly bracts in early and mid-summer.*

LINARIA ALPINA *(Alpine Toadflax), 7.5–15cm/ 3–6in high and spreading to 23cm/9in, has sprays of violet flowers from early to late summer.*

LITHOSPERMUM DIFFUSUM *(often sold as Lithodora diffusa), is 15cm/6in high and spreads to 60cm/2ft. It has blue flowers in summer. 'Heavenly Blue' and 'Grace Ward' are popular.*

LEWISIA COTYLEDON, *with a dense rosette of mid-green, fleshy, spoon-shaped leaves, develops clusters of star-like, pink flowers on 20cm/8in stems during late spring and early summer.*

LINUM PERENNE ALPINUM *(Alpine Flax), about 15cm/6in high and spreading to 20cm/8in, has blue flowers from early to late summer. They fade quickly, but are renewed.*

LYCHNIS ALPINA ROSEA *(Alpine Campion), grows about 10cm/4in high and with a similar spread. It has deep pink flowers from late spring to mid-summer. There is also a white form.*

OENOTHERA MISSOURIENSIS *(Ozark Sundrops) is 15cm/6in high and spreads to 45cm/1½ft. Yellow flowers up to 7.5cm/ 3in appear in summer.*

OMPHALODES VERNA *(Blue-eyed Mary), is 15cm/ 6in high and spreads to 30cm/12in. From early to late spring it has bright blue, white-throated flowers.*

MAZUS REPTANS, *up to 5cm/2in high and spreading to 30cm/12in, has lilac-coloured flowers from early to late summer.*

AGE-OLD PLANT

The flax now known as Linum usitatissimum *and widely called the Common Flax or Linseed is claimed to be one of the first plants to become associated with man. Indeed, its second name implies 'the most useful', while flax is derived from the Old English* fleaux, *meaning to braid or interweave. It was cultivated during early antiquity in Egypt for its fibre, later in India, Argentina and China for its seed that yields Linseed Oil.*

This flax, a graceful annual, with pale blue flowers in early and mid-summer, has many traditions: in the Middle Ages the flowers were thought to offer protection against sorcery.

ROCK-GARDEN PERENNIALS
Ourisia – Primula
❖

THE wealth of plants which can be grown in rock gardens is wide and in addition to those featured on previous pages here are others to consider.

• *Oxalis enneaphylla*, 7.5cm/3in high and spreading to 15cm/6in, creates hummocks of grey, partially folded leaves. During early and mid-summer these are covered with 2.5cm/1in-wide, funnel-shaped white flowers.

• *Oxalis magellanica*, 5cm/2in high and spreading to 30cm/12in, forms a mat of bronze leaves. The white, cup-shaped flowers appear during late spring and early summer.

• *Papaver alpinum*, a short-lived perennial, is about 20cm/8in high and spreads to 15cm/6in. It is ideal in a rock garden or scree bed where, from late spring to mid-summer, it displays flowers in a range of colours from white to yellow and red above mounds of deeply dissected grey-green leaves.

POPPY POWER

The poppy family includes many different types of plants, including annuals, biennials and herbaceous perennials. Papaver alpinum *is ideal for growing in rock gardens, together with* P. miyabeanum *(Japanese Alpine Poppy). But it is the Opium Poppy* (P. somniferum) *and Field Poppy* (P. rhoeas), *both annuals, that are first remembered when poppies are discussed. And it is the Field Poppy that is used as a symbol of Remembrance.*

• *Phlox subulata* (Moss Phlox) is 10–13cm/4–5in high and spreads to 38cm/15in. It has a sub-shrubby nature and forms a mat of narrow, mid-green leaves. During mid- and late spring it is smothered in pink or purple flowers.

PENSTEMON ROEZLII, *from the western states of North America, is 10–23cm/4–9in high and spreads to 30cm/12in. It is smothered in lavender to violet-blue flowers in clusters during mid-summer. It has narrow, lance-shaped, mid-green leaves.*

PHLOX DOUGLASII *(Alpine Phlox), 5–10cm/2–4in high and spreading to 45cm/18in, reveals masses of pale-lavender flowers during late spring and early summer. There are many varieties, in colours including pink and white.*

POLYGONUM AFFINE *'Donald Lowndes', 15–23cm/6–9in high and spreading to 45cm/18in, develops into a mat of spoon-shaped leaves (bright green when young but later brown), and rosy-red flowers during early summer.*

There are several varieties, including 'Scarlet Flame' (scarlet) and 'Temiscaming' (pale red).

• *Pleione bulbocodioides* (also known as *P. formosana*), 15cm/6in high and about the same width when in flower, creates 7.5–10cm/3–4in-wide trumpets in white to mauve-pink during mid- and late spring. Most pleiones are not suitable for growing outdoors in a rock garden, but this species is ideal if the soil is well drained and the situation sheltered.

OURISIA COCCINEA, *15–30cm/6–12in high and spreading to 45cm/18in or more, creates dense mats of mid-green leaves. From late spring to autumn it bears tubular, scarlet flowers on erect stems.*

OXALIS ADENOPHYLLA, *7.5cm/3in high and with a 15cm/6in spread, has crinkled, grey-green, pleated leaves and cup-shaped, 2.5cm/1in-wide, satin-pink flowers with veining from late spring to mid-summer.*

PARAHEBE LYALII, *about 20cm/8in high and spreading to 25cm/10in, has leathery, green leaves and white flowers with pink veins during mid- and late summer. It is easier to grow than most other plants in this genus.*

POTENTILLA AUREA *(Golden Cinquefoil), 10cm/4in high and spreading to 30cm/12in, forms a bright mound of shiny yellow flowers from early summer to the frosts of autumn. It is mat-forming and ideal when creeping over rocks.*

PRIMULA 'Wanda' *is a superb hybrid alpine primula, 10–15cm/4–6in high and with the same spread. It flowers during mid- and late spring, revealing purple-red flowers in clusters above large, spoon-shaped, shiny mid-green leaves.*

PRIMULA VIALII, *which grows up to 30cm/12in high and with a 23–30cm/10–12in spread, creates poker-like heads of lavender-blue flowers during early and mid-summer. These are borne above large, pale green, spoon-shaped leaves.*

ROCK-GARDEN PERENNIALS
Pulsatilla – Sedum

❖

THE range of rock-garden perennials continues, with some that have a delicate nature in wet, temperate climates and therefore need cosseting. Examples of these plants include:

• *Raoulia hookeri* (also known as *R. australis*) forms mats of silvery leaves no more than 12mm/½in high and spreading to 30cm/12in. During late spring it reveals rather insignificant yellow flowers.

• *Raoulia eximia* (Vegetable Sheep), up to 7.5cm/3in high and spreading to 30cm/12in, forms silvery-white hummocks. It is only suitable outdoors in a sunny position and well-drained soil.

• *Raoulia lutescens*, about 12mm/½in high and spreading to 45cm/18in, forms mats of grey-green leaves. During mid- and late spring these are peppered with minute, lemon-yellow flowers.

PULSATILLA VULGARIS (Pasque Flower), 25cm/10in high and spreading to about the same width, has mid-green, finely cut leaves and purple, cup-shaped flowers during mid- and late spring. It is a variable species and some forms have pale pink or red flowers.

RANUNCULUS GRAMINEUS, 25–30cm/10–12in high and with a similar spread, has narrow, grey-green leaves and loose sprays of bright, golden-yellow flowers from late spring to mid-summer.

SAPONARIA OCYMOIDES, *7.5cm/ 3in high and spreading to 30cm/12in, is ground-hugging. From mid-summer to autumn it bears rose-pink flowers. 'Rubra Compacta' has reddish-pink flowers and is compact.*

SANGUINARIA CANADENSIS *'Flore Pleno' (Bloodroot), 15cm/6in high and spreading to 30cm/12in, has pale-green, lobed leaves and petal-packed white flowers during mid- and late spring. It is ideal in peat beds.*

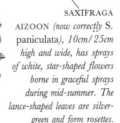

SAXIFRAGA AIZOON *(now correctly S. paniculata), 10cm/25cm high and wide, has sprays of white, star-shaped flowers borne in graceful sprays during mid-summer. The lance-shaped leaves are silvergreen and form rosettes.*

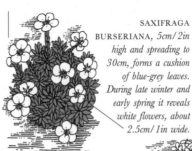

SAXIFRAGA BURSERIANA, 5cm/2in high and spreading to 30cm, forms a cushion of blue-grey leaves. During late winter and early spring it reveals white flowers, about 2.5cm/1in wide.

SAXIFRAGA COCHLEARIS *'Minor', 10cm/4in high and spreading to 20cm/8in, forms compact, silver hummocks and sprays of white flowers during early summer. It is ideal for planting in rock crevices.*

PASQUE FLOWER

For many years this hardy European plant with finely cut, fern-like leaves was known as Anemone pulsatilla. *It is claimed to have gained the name Pasque Flower from the Old French* pasques, *meaning Easter and referring to its flowering period; while* pulsatilla *derives from* pulsare, *meaning to shake or beat, and dates from classical times as the flowers appear to be shaken by the wind. Earlier, this plant was praised for its medicinal value, being considered a cure for arthritis. But it is poisonous and at one time was known as Laughing Parsley because it was said that people eating it would die of laughter!*

• *Ramonda myconi* (also known as *R. pyrenaica*), 10–15cm/4–6in high and about 23cm/9in wide, forms a rosette of evergreen, deep green and hairy leaves. During mid- and late spring stems about 10cm/4in long bear flat-faced, lavender-blue flowers, each with a central cone of yellow stamens. There are many forms, such as 'Alba' (white), 'Rosea' (pink) and 'Coerulea' (blue).

• *Rhodohypoxis baurii*, about 7.5cm/3in high and spreading to 15cm/ 6in, is a South African perennial. The narrow, hairy, pale green leaves become smothered with rosy-red flowers from mid-spring to early autumn. There are several varieties, extending the flower colour to white, pink and purple. Well-drained but moisture-retentive soil is essential, together with protection in winter.

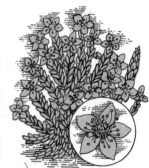

SAXIFRAGA COTYLEDON *'Southside Seedling', about 25cm/10in high and 20cm/ 8in wide, forms a basal rosette of strap-like leaves. During early and mid-summer it develops arching sprays of white flowers, heavily spotted red. It is ideal for planting in crevices.*

SEDUM ACRE *'Aureum' (Biting Stonecrop), up to 5cm/2in high and spreading to 30cm/12in or more, forms a mat of yellowish-green leaves. During early and mid-summer it develops flattened heads of yellow flowers. It spreads attractively over the bases of rocks.*

ROCK-GARDEN PERENNIALS
Sedum – Thymus
❖

MANY sedums are bright-faced, reliable and easily grown plants for rock gardens.
- *Sedum acre* (Biting Stonecrop), 2.5–5cm/1–2in high and spreading to 38cm/15in, is evergreen and forms a mat of mid-green succulent leaves. During early and mid-summer these are smothered in flat heads of yellow flowers.
- *Sedum ewersii*, 10–15cm/4–6in high, spreading to 45cm/18in and with a trailing nature, has grey-green leaves and pink or red flowers during late summer.
- *Sedum kamtschaticum* 'Variegatum', about 15cm/6in high and spreading to 30cm/12in, has distinctive dark green, succulent leaves edged cream and red. The flowers are golden yellow.

HOUSELEEKS

These are sempervivums and one of the species that is suitable for a rock garden is featured and illustrated below. Others include:
- *Sempervivum montanum*, about 2.5cm/1in high and spreading to 23cm/9in, forms dull green rosettes up to 5cm/2in across. From early to late summer it develops reddish-purple flowers on stems about 13cm/5in high.
- *Sempervivum soboliferum* (also known as *Jovibarba sobolifera* and commonly as Hen and Chicken Houseleek) is about 2.5cm/1in high and spreads to 25cm/10in or more. The rosettes are formed of bright green leaves, flushed red, and surmounted during mid-summer by yellow, bell-like flowers.

SILENE SCHAFTA, 10–15cm/4–6in high and spreading to 30cm/12in, forms tufts of lance-shaped, mid-green leaves. From mid-summer to early autumn it develops sprays of bright, magenta-pink flowers on 10–15cm/4–6in-long stems. It is an easily grown species and forms spreading mats and tufts.

SISYRINCHIUM BERMUDIANUM (Blue-eye Grass), 15–23cm/6–9in high and about the same wide, forms clumps of erect, stiff, grass-like leaves. During late spring and early summer it develops star-shaped, light blue flowers with yellow bases. It is native to North America and the western part of Ireland.

THYMUS X CITRIODORUS (Lemon-scented Thyme), about 23cm/9in high and spreading to 38cm/15in, forms a mat of mid-green, lemon-scented leaves. Pale lilac flowers appear during summer. Varieties include 'Silver Queen' with silver-green, variegated leaves, illustrated above.

SEDUM SPATHUIFOLIUM 'Cappa Blanca', 5–10cm/2–4in high, spreading to 23cm/9in. Yellow flowers appear in early summer.

SEDUM SPURIUM, about 10cm/4in high and spreading to 30cm/12in, has rich pink flowers during mid- and late summer.

SEMPERVIVUM ARACHNOIDEUM (Cobweb Plant/Houseleek), about 2.5cm/1in high and spreading to 25cm/10in. Rosy-red flowers appear in early and mid-summer.

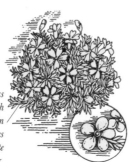

SILENE ACAULIS (Moss Campion), 5cm/2in high and spreading to 30cm/12in or more, has mid-green leaves and pink flowers in late spring and early summer.

THYMUS SERPYLLUM (Wild Thyme), up to 7.5cm/3in high and spreading to 45cm/18in or more, with narrow, grey-green and sometimes hairy leaves. Flowers appear from early to late summer, in a range of colours. There are several superb varieties, including 'Annie Hall' (pale pink), 'Coccineus' (rich crimson) and 'Albus' (white).

WALL SITTERS

The Latin sedum, *meaning plant that sits, gives a clue to the nature of most of the plants in this genus. There are a few species, such as the Ice Plant (*Sedum spectabilis*) and Orpine (*S. telephium*), that are best in an herbaceous border, but most prefer to sit on natural stone walls or to live in a rock garden. The yellow-flowered Biting Stonecrop (*S. acre*) is a scrambler and known to the herbalist and barber-surgeon, John Gerard, in the late sixteenth century as Wall-pepper, Jacke-of-the-Butterie and Pricket.*

*The Stone Orpine (*S. reflexum*) was eaten in Holland in salads, the leaves having a pleasant taste, while the seventeenth-century French botanist, Joseph Tournefort, considered it good for 'hartburne'.*

ROCK-GARDEN PERENNIALS
Verbascum – Waldsteinia

❖

FEW rock garden plants have the simplicity yet the extra-ordinary fascination revealed by violas. Apart from the dramatic appeal of Garden Pansies (*Viola* x *wittrockiana*), with their large faces and wide colour range, there are many others.

• *Viola bifolia*, 5–7.5cm/2–3in high and spreading to 30cm/12in, has bright green, kidney-shaped leaves and yellow, violet-like flowers during mid- and late spring.

• *Viola gracilis*, 10cm/4in high and spreading to 25cm/10in or more, has deep purple flowers about 2.5cm/1in in width from mid-spring to early summer. These flowers have a pansy-like outline, with various varieties increasing the colour range to purple-black and yellow.

• *Viola labradorica* 'Purpurea', about 10cm/4in high and spreading to 30cm/12in or more, has mid-green leaves that assume a purple tinge. During mid- and late spring it develops mauve-coloured, violet-like flowers.

GARDEN PANSIES

These are hybrids and varieties of *Viola* x *wittrockiana*. To the rock-garden purist they may be too brazen and rich in colour to be considered as partners for demure alpines, but in a new rock garden they offer nearly instant colour. And these seed-raised plants can be removed later if they have offended too many eyes.

There are both summer- and winter-flowering varieties. The summer ones bloom from late spring to early autumn, while winter ones flower from early winter to late spring. Each year new varieties are introduced: choose low-growing types as they harmonize with other plants.

VERBASCUM DUMULOSUM, 20–30cm/ 8–12in high and about the same in width, has a shrubby nature with grey-green and slightly woolly leaves. During early and mid-summer it produces clusters of clear yellow flowers.

VERBASCUM 'Letitia', 15–20cm/6–8in high and spreading to 30cm/12in or more, forms a diminutive shrublet with lance-shaped, grey-green leaves and spikes of clear, bright yellow flowers from early to late summer.

VERONICA PECTINATA, 7.5cm/3in high and spreading to 30cm/12in or more, has a prostrate nature with toothed, grey-green leaves. During late spring and early summer it has deep blue flowers with a white eye. 'Rosea' has pink flowers.

VERONICA PROSTRATA (also sold as V. rupestris and V. teucrium prostrata), grows 10–15cm/4–6in high and with a spread of 30cm/12in or more. From late spring to mid-summer the mid-green leaves are smothered with deep blue flowers in spires.

VIOLA LUTEA, 15–20cm/6–8in high and spreading to about 23cm/9in, forms mats of mid-green leaves. During early and mid-summer it produces bright-faced, yellow flowers which seldom fail to attract attention. It is one of the most easily grown violas.

GREAT MULLEIN

Few plants have collected as many common names as the Great Mullein (Verbascum thapsus). These include Yellow Mullein, Clown's Lungwort, Candlewick Plant and Hag's Taper. It is found wild in Europe and temperate Asia, as well as North America, although it is doubtful if it is a true native of that area.

Its uses are wide; the poor were said to have put the thick, woolly leaves in their shoes to create extra warmth; the Romans dipped the stems in tallow and used them as torches; witches used them in sorcery; while the juice of the leaves and flowers when put on warts eased their removal. As well, the seeds, when put in ponds, are said to stupefy fish so that they can be removed by hand. Earlier, it was used to treat cattle, and was therefore called Bullock's Lungwort.

VIOLA CORNUTA (Horned Pansy/Horned Viola), 15–23cm/6–9in high and spreading to 38cm/45in, has mid-green leaves and deep lavender flowers about 2.5cm/1in wide during early and mid-summer. Several varieties include 'Alba' (white).

WALDSTEINIA FRAGARIOIDES (Barren Strawberry) has strawberry-like, dark green and three-lobed leaves. Plants grow about 15cm/6in high and spread to 25cm/10in. During early summer it has golden-yellow flowers on stems 10–13cm/4–5in high. If it becomes invasive and likely to swamp other plants, clip it back in spring.

BUYING AND CARE OF PLANTS

 THOROUGHLY inspect all plants before buying them and do not be tempted to buy a plant because it is cheap. If it dies soon after, it will have been an expensive mistake.

Most rock-garden plants are sold in spring. Inspect each one thoroughly: apart from the points detailed at the bottom of this part of the page, check that the size of the plant is in balance with the pot. If the plant is much larger than the root area it indicates that it has been kept in the same pot for too long and that the roots are constricted. Conversely, if the soil-ball is much larger than the foliage it indicates that the plant has been re-potted recently and the roots may not be properly established.

LOOKING AFTER PLANTS
Rock-garden plants are usually quite tough and hardy. Indeed, they readily withstand low temperatures, but these can be lethal when combined with rain. For this reason, a mulch of pea-shingle is used to keep the leaves and stems dry.

WINTER PROTECTION

Plants with tender leaves may need protection from heavy rains during winter. Tents formed of small panes of glass can be propped up on bricks, but secure the glass so that it cannot be blown about and cause harm. The ends must be left open for ventilation. Small, tent-like cloches can also be used, but must be pegged into the soil to prevent them being blown about. Also, ensure they cannot harm children, cats and dogs.

Weeding, feeding, watering and mulching with shingle are the main jobs when looking after rock-garden plants. Every three or four years it may be necessary to lift plants in spring and to replant young pieces from around the outside of each clump.

THOROUGHLY INSPECT *plants before buying them: look at the plant as well as the compost and pot.*

LEAVES *and flowers must not be damaged by pests and diseases.*

ENSURE *the plant is clearly labelled.*

DO NOT *buy plants with roots coming out of the drainage hole.*

BRIGHT *young shoots indicate active growth.*

COMPOST *should be moist but not waterlogged.*

DO NOT *buy plants which have slime or moss on the pot.*

WEEDING *is a continual task, especially during spring and summer. Unfortunately, there is no alternative to removing weeds by hand; pull them up early, while they are still small.*

LIFT *and re-plant congested plants in spring. Carefully divide them and replant young pieces from around the outside of the clump. Discard the old, tough and woody parts at the centre.*

IN AUTUMN, *remove leaves that have blown on plants from nearby trees. If left, they cause dampness around plants and encourage decay and the presence of slugs and snails.*

FEED *plants in spring, if possible before topping up the mulch of stones around them. Choose a balanced feed, not one rich in nitrogen that subsequently causes too much lush growth.*

NEWLY PLANTED *young plants need frequent watering in spring and early summer until they are established. Watering is also necessary during prolonged dry periods, but it must be thorough and not just dampen the soil's surface, which will do more harm than good. Do not moisten leaves or stems, as this causes decay.*

MULCHING *plants with an 18–25mm/¾–1in-thick layer of gravel chippings ensures leaves do not rest on soil. In addition, it prevents heavy splashes of rain falling on bare soil and then on plants. The chippings also act as a deterrent to snails and slugs. Instead of stone chippings, use bark chippings on peat beds.*

REMOVING *dead flower heads is not a major task on rock garden plants, but it does tidy them up.*

BY AUTUMN, *some plants may appear straggly and unkempt. This is the time to tidy them up and to remove long stems. If left, they encourage the presence of pests and the onset of decay. Do not leave this task until late winter or early spring, as newly emerging bulbs may be damaged, especially if you have to tread on the rock garden to reach some of the other plants.*

WATER GARDENING

Ponds are fascinating garden features and create an opportunity to grow a wide range of plants and to provide homes for fish and other water creatures. The range of materials used to make a pond is wide and includes concrete, flexible liners and rigid, pre-moulded shells.

Additionally, it is possible to construct a pond so that the water's surface is level with the surrounding ground, or raised. Mini-ponds in large wooden barrels or stone sinks are attractive and are particularly suitable for patios.

Fountains are further elements that can be introduced to garden ponds, while waterfalls help to integrate them with other garden features, such as rock gardens.

The many and varied water plants include waterlilies, oxygenating plants that are planted in containers, freely floating types and moisture-loving plants that can be planted in moist soil around pond edges.

Keeping the water clean and fish and water plants healthy are also featured in this chapter.

WATER GARDENING
❖

DURING the last fifty years, water gardening has become a popular hobby, with water features constructed in gardens of all shapes and sizes. Even ponds in tubs on small patios are a possibility.

Many different constructional materials are available, each with its advantages. Waterfall units have enabled rock and water gardens to be integrated, with pumps activating waterfalls and fountains. Few other aspects of gardening create as much attention and continued interest as a garden pond.

MATERIALS

Early pools were always concrete, and usually square or rectangular. Now informal shapes are also possible (page 121).

Flexible liners allow ponds of many shapes (page 119).

Moulded shells are available in various sizes, shapes and materials (page 120).

MOST *ponds are set into the ground and can be viewed from all sides.*

FULLY *or partially raised ponds make construction easier. See page 122 for building methods.*

SOME *ponds are raised above ground level on one side, with the other side set into a bank. This helps to blend one level with another (page 122).*

EVEN *the smallest patio can accommodate a pond in a large tub. Choose miniature plants (page 123).*

CASCADING *water bubbling over a series of waterfalls enlivens the entire garden. When made from flexible liners or rigid waterfall units they are easily installed (page 125).*

FOUNTAINS *can be purely functional, with water directly spouting out of a pond's surface. Alternatively, formal bowls, or statues issuing forth water create eye-catching features in gardens. Pumps and a water source are essential (page 126).*

WILDLIFE *ponds create havens for aquatic creatures, from fish to frogs and newts. Bird life is also encouraged, as are insects and small mammals (page 124).*

SELECTING AND PREPARING THE SITE

❖

THE approximate position of a new garden pond is usually known: you have probably spent at least a year looking out of a window and visualizing the pleasures it will bring. But there are a few constructional as well as positional factors to consider.

The siting of a pond within an existing garden is often a conflict between the desired position and existing features. Selecting a suitable site is detailed below and at right.

POSITIONING THE POND

It is relatively easy to imagine a pond when installed in an existing garden, but also think of the future and the growth of nearby trees. Your present friendly and considerate neighbours might move and their successors not be so pleased with a wildlife pond immediately on their boundary.

Here are a few considerations regarding position:
• Avoid shaded positions. A pond needs at least seven hours of sunshine a day.
• Do not site it under trees; they not only cast shade but, if deciduous, shed their leaves in autumn. If these are not prevented from falling into a pond, they drop to the bottom, decay and create gases toxic to fish.
• When calculating the shade created by existing trees, try to think what their size might be in ten or more years' time.
• Do not position ponds near trees with poisonous berries or fruits, such as laburnum.
• Large trees nearby may have roots that will puncture liners, or crack concrete or rigid shells.
• Some trees, such as plum and Blackthorn, harbour Waterlily Aphids and cause infestations repeatedly throughout summer.

EARTH REMOVAL

Perhaps the most daunting task when constructing a pond is digging out the desired area and removing the soil. Landscape gardeners often use skips, but nevertheless barrowing large quantities of soil is a formidable task. Soil naturally bulks up when dug out: topsoil increases in volume by about one-quarter, subsoil by up to one-third. There is a temptation to convert excavated soil into a rock garden, but subsoil should always be removed entirely. Friable topsoil can be scattered thinly on borders, or later used in the construction of a rock garden after the area has been drained.

• Avoid positions exposed to cold winds; they singe the foliage of tender plants and may blow over tall, marginal ones. Also, in winter they cause temperatures to fall dramatically. Coniferous hedges 3–4.5m/10–15ft high and positioned 2.4–3m/8–10ft on the northerly side of the pond will reduce the wind's speed but will not cast shade.
• If the land slopes, do not dismiss its suitability for a pond: one side could be level with the surface, with the other raised.

• If waterfalls and fountains are desired, ensure water pipes and electricity cables can be installed without having to burrow under existing patios, walls or paths.
• Ensure the pond is not sited above land drains, power or telephone cables, or mains drainage pipes.
• If an informal pond with a bog garden is being constructed, it is best positioned at the lowest part of a garden. And, if possible, always put wildlife ponds towards the end of a garden.

THERE *are ponds of many shapes and for all gardens. Rectangular or square ponds, earlier made of concrete but now often formed from a rigid shell, are ideal in formal gardens and settings.*

LOBE-SHAPED *ponds introduce an unusual form to patios, or other informal settings. Another possibility is to position a three-lobed pond at the junction of three broad, gravel paths.*

KIDNEY-SHAPED *ponds create an informal effect and are ideal for siting in a lawn, perhaps towards one corner where a focal point can be created. Position the lobed side towards the house.*

OCTAGONAL *ponds have a distinctly formal nature and are ideal in the centres of patios. Nevertheless, their regular outlines can be softened by using tall, spiky-leaved marginal plants.*

TRIANGULAR *ponds are unusual, formal and ideal in a corner of a patio. Use tall, iris-like marginal plants to soften the sharp corners, and softer, lax, sprawling plants between them.*

RAISED *ponds create unusual features and are ideal where the disposal of excavated soil is difficult. They can be round or irregular and used in both formal and informal settings.*

INSTALLING A FLEXIBLE LINER

❖

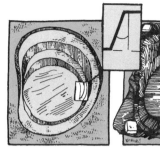

LSO known as a pool liner, a flexible liner enables ponds of all shapes and sizes to be constructed. Sheeting sizes up to 9m/30ft x 6m/20ft are readily available, while ones above this size can be ordered. Although these liners are flexible, it is more difficult to persuade them to assume the shape of a small corner, so this must be considered when designing the pond. Thin liners are more flexible but not as durable as thick ones.

MATERIALS

Basically, there are three types of materials for flexible liners. Always buy the best quality you can afford: after thoroughly preparing the site it is false economy to buy the cheapest liner, as it will soon need replacing.

All liners have either price or durability advantages:
• Polyethylene (more widely known as polythene) sheeting creates low-cost, relatively short-

ESTIMATING THE SIZE OF THE LINER

This is not difficult and is best carried out after the area has been excavated. Measure the total width and length, then add twice the total depth to each measurement. Add a further 30cm/12in to both the length and width to allow for the flaps that will have paving stones put on them. Examples of these measurements are:
• *Pond A: 2.4m/8ft long, 1.8m/6ft wide and 60cm/2ft deep. The sheet needed would be 3.7m/13ft x 3.3m/11ft.*
• *Pond B: 3.6m/12ft long, 1.8m/6ft wide and 90cm/3ft deep. The sheet needed would be 5.7m/19ft x 3.7m/13ft.*
If possible, buy a slightly larger sheet than necessary, so that there is no worry about it fitting and there is plenty of width for the flaps.

4. WHEN *the pegs are level, the pencil marks will indicate the levels. Make adjustments as necessary. Remove sharp stones and form a 3.6cm/1¹/2in-thick layer of sand in the base. Fill holes in the sides.*

5. CONTINUE *to pad the sides with soft sand, forming a 20-degree angle. Put a layer of sand on the shelf. Slightly dampen the sand and smooth its surface. If not level, irregularities will show up later.*

6. PLACE *the flexible liner in the hole, taking care not to disturb the sand. As necessary, form pleats to reduce excess liner around the sides and in the base. When in position, place bricks along the edges.*

lived ponds. Ultra-violet rays soon degrade it, especially if there is always a gap between the top of the pond and the water's surface. For this reason, it is unsuitable for small ponds in a series of waterfalls. Better-quality types are guaranteed for ten or so years.
• PVC liners are strong and about half the price of butyl sheeting. Some PVC liners are reinforced with netting. Whatever the grade,

look for a guarantee and buy the best quality you can afford.
• Butyl sheeting is the best of all lining materials and has the longest life expectancy. It is unaffected by ultra-violet rays and will last twenty years or more – even fifty. Look for a guarantee and indication of its life-expectancy. Because it is unaffected by sunlight, it can be used to form pools in waterfalls.

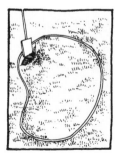

1. LAY *a hose-pipe or thick rope on the surface to form the size and shape of the pool and use a spade to cut the outline on the turf or soil. Then, mark an area about 25cm/10in larger all round the pool.*

2. IN THE *outer strip, remove soil to 7.5cm/3in deep. Then, dig out the central area to about 75cm/2¹/2ft deep, at the same time forming a shelf about 23cm/9in wide and 23cm/9in deep.*

3. CUT *pegs 15cm/6in long and mark each one 5cm/2in from its top. Knock these in, 7.5cm/3in deep and 90cm/3ft apart, around the top and on the shelf. Use a spirit-level to check their tops are level.*

7. PLACE *a hose-pipe in the hole and gently fill with clean water. As the water level rises, remove the bricks and, as necessary, readjust the liner. Creases can often be removed by manipulating the liner.*

8. USE SHARP *scissors to cut off surplus liner to leave a 15cm/6in flap. This is turned over, flat on top of the sand. It is essential that this flap is quite wide as otherwise it may fall back into the pond.*

9. USE THREE *parts soft sand and one of cement as a bedding mixture for the edging slabs. Each stone's top must be flush with the surface and overhang the pool's edge by 5cm/2in. Cement between them.*

INSTALLING A MOULDED POND

 SOMETIMES called rigid liners, pre-formed ponds and moulded shells, these 'ready-made' ponds enable water gardens to be established very rapidly. Sometimes, even the largest shells may be too small for a very large garden: however, several can be linked together by a series of waterfalls – but they do need the benefit of a sloping garden.

These shells can also be used fully or partially in the construction of raised ponds (page 122).

RANGE OF MATERIALS
Earlier, the life expectancy of a moulded pond was not great and many experts disapproved of them because of their lack of depth – sometimes less than 38cm/15in – and their garish, unnatural colours. Nowadays however, they are available in a wide range of colours and often have a life-span of twenty or more years. Also they are deeper.

During the 1950s, metal-shelled ponds were available, but these were only 25cm/10in deep and not practical as the water soon froze solid in winter. Today, there are three main materials:
• Plastic liners are the cheapest, only semi-rigid and usually created from vacuum-formed polythene in a range of colours, including green, brown, blue and grey. Careful installation is vital to ensure the surfaces are not stressed. With age, ridges and corners crack, while the surface deteriorates when exposed to strong sunlight. Therefore, it is essential that the edges are covered with paving slabs and the water-level is not allowed to drop so that the sides are exposed to direct light.
• Reinforced plastic liners are more rigid and resistant to damaging rays of

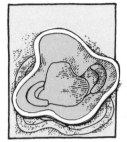

1. PLACE *the shell in position and mark on the ground the extremes of its outer edge, as well as those of the shelves. Also, mark an area 25cm/10in wide to accommodate a row of edging slabs.*

2. DIG OUT *the area to the total size of the shell, at the same time forming the shelves. The bottom should be about 5cm/2in deeper than the shell. Also, dig out the edging area, about 7.5cm/3in deep.*

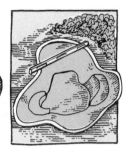

3. ENSURE *soil in the hole's base is firm and compact, then add a 5cm/2in-thick layer of soft sand. Put the shell in place and firm it on the sand. Use a builder's spirit-level to check that the rim is level.*

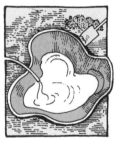

4. WHEN *level, pack soft sand or friable soil between the shell and ground. Firm it with the end of a stick. If gaps are left, they unduly stress the shell which may crack in the future. Fill the shell with clean water.*

5. CHECK *that the shell fits on top of the outer area. If necessary, pack soft sand beneath it. Then, form and firm a layer of sand level with the shell's top but about 5cm/2in below the surrounding lawn.*

6. CEMENT *edging stones around the pond, so that they overhang by 5cm/2in. Use slabs 30cm/12in wide; narrow ones may topple into the pond. Then, add the plants (page 127) and, later, the fish.*

ultra-violet. The best types are guaranteed for at least ten years, sometimes twenty, and provide a water depth of 45cm/1½ft or sometimes more.
• Glass-fibre shells are formed of glass fibres bonded with a resin, creating a material with a life expectancy of twenty or more years. These shells are not damaged by ultra-violet rays, nor do

they rot or allow water to seep through. However, like all shells they need careful installation to prevent them being stressed when placed on an uneven base. They are available in green, blue, black and grey.

Because glass-fibre shells are not damaged by ultra-violet light, they are often used as pools in a series of waterfalls.

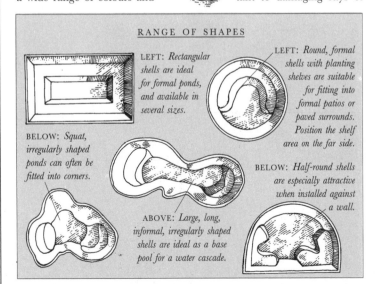

RANGE OF SHAPES

LEFT: *Rectangular shells are ideal for formal ponds, and available in several sizes.*

BELOW: *Squat, irregularly shaped ponds can often be fitted into corners.*

ABOVE: *Large, long, informal, irregularly shaped shells are ideal as a base pool for a water cascade.*

LEFT: *Round, formal shells with planting shelves are suitable for fitting into formal patios or paved surrounds. Position the shelf area on the far side.*

BELOW: *Half-round shells are especially attractive when installed against a wall.*

CONCRETE PONDS

❖

GARDEN ponds have traditionally been made of concrete and were usually square or rectangular. This involved vast preparations with timbers and shuttering that were only used for a week or so. However, it is also possible to make a pond without the use of this shuttering, but it has to be a simple, uncomplicated oval or round shape, although a kidney outline is possible.

CHOOSING THE RIGHT DAY

Late spring and early summer or late summer and early autumn are the best times for amateurs to lay concrete, when there is no risk of frost and the weather is not excessively hot. It is essential that concrete dries slowly and evenly. After being mixed, concrete takes about two hours (less on a warm day) to begin setting, three or four days before it gains any appreciable strength and a week before it reaches half its ultimate strength.

Many experts suggest it takes four or five weeks to reach full strength. During this time it is easily damaged, especially at the edges. If the weather gets too hot soon after concrete is laid, cover with planks and damp sacking, and keep it moist for about five days – slightly longer if very hot.

AFTER HARDENING

Tidy up the site, but do not tread on the edges. Paint the pond's surface with a proprietary sealant, allow to dry and fill with water. If a surface sealing material is not used, it is essential to fill and empty the pond several times to remove toxic chemicals from the concrete. Some experts also advise filling the pond a couple of times even when using a sealant. Kits to test the water to ensure it is not too alkaline are available (see page 139). Using a pump (see page 128) to empty the pond makes the task much easier. When the water is as required, introduce plants and fish.

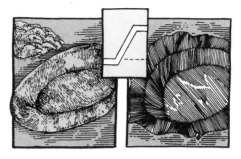

1. SELECT *a suitable site (see page 118) and dig out a hole, making it 15cm/6in deeper than desired and 30cm/12in wider to allow for the thickness of concrete.*

2. CREATE *sides with a 45-degree angle. Shuttering is not used and if the sides are steep the concrete will slip down before it sets. Line the hole with thick polythene sheeting.*

3. SPREAD *a 10cm/4in-thick layer of concrete over the base and up the sides. Making the mixture slightly stiffer than normal ensures it does not slip off the sides. Spread it evenly.*

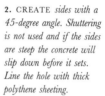

4. TO CREATE *added strength, press wire-netting reinforcement over the sides and 23cm/9in into the pond's centre. Cover the base with another piece of wire-netting, cut to shape.*

5. ENSURE *the wire-netting is bedded into the concrete. Then, lay a further layer of concrete, 5cm/2in thick, over it. Press it firmly into position using a trowel to smooth the surfaces.*

6. ALLOW *the concrete to dry thoroughly, but not too quickly as cracking may then occur. During hot weather, place planks across the pond and cover it with damp hessian to slow drying.*

THICK PLYWOOD *is ideal as it creates a smooth surface when removed. Alternatively, wide planks of wood can be used.*

WIRE-NETTING *reinforcement.*

ANGLED *bracing timbers are essential to ensure the shuttering remains firm when concrete is packed behind it.*

AFTER *the base has set, the sides are constructed.*

STRONG *timbers braced between the shuttering. Use narrow V-shaped wedges to tighten them.*

TRADITIONAL *concrete pools are square or rectangular, as this makes the erection of shuttering easy. Strong timbers for cross-bracing and planks or thick ply-wood for shuttering are essential.*

MIXTURES AND MIXING TIPS

• *Use a mixture of 1 part cement powder, 1^1/$_2$ sharp sand, and 2^1/$_2$ 20mm aggregates. Alternatively, use 1 part cement powder and 3^1/$_2$ of combined aggregates.*
• *Always buy fresh bags of cement.*
• *Ensure the sand and aggregates are not contaminated with rubbish such as wood, soil or plants.*

• *Do not try to tackle the job on your own. With two or three people helping the job is a pleasure; on your own it can be a nightmare.*
• *An electrically-operated mixer is well worth hiring and will certainly repay its cost.*
• *Keep children and domestic pets indoors while working.*

RAISED PONDS

❖

FEW water-garden features are as impressive as a raised pond with a fountain or cascade of water tumbling into a lower pool. The main problem with a raised pond is its exposure to low temperatures that damage brick-work. Also, there is a risk of ice pushing the sides outwards.

There is a greater risk of fish being killed, but a heater (see page 128) can reduce this.

It is often claimed that raised ponds are safer for toddlers than ground-level ones. However, as most children are inquisitive and would consider the sides of a pond as a challenge, the only way to make it safe is to form a strong wire-netting covering.

Ensure that an electricity supply is available during winter for water heaters, but first consider the cost of electricity during very cold weather.

MANY ADVANTAGES

Apart from the dangers from low temperatures and inquisitive, agile young children, raised ponds have many advantages:
• Wheelchair gardeners are able to admire the plants and fish without the risk of rolling in.
• Looking after the pool is often easier because it is not necessary to bend down continually.
• When the pond needs emptying, water is syphoned out cheaply and easily, rather than having to buy and power a pump.
• It also overcomes the major difficulty of disposing of subsoil that is necessary when constructing a ground-level pond. Topsoil can be spread over borders or eventually used to construct a rock garden, but thick, boot-loving clay is another matter and must invariably be removed, usually an expensive task.

RAISED *ponds can be made from concrete and bricks. A wall two bricks thick (about 23cm/9in) is essential to withstand the outward pressure of water. Then, render the inside. Strong foundations for the wall and base are vital if parts are not to settle within a few years. Then, cover the inside with a couple of coats of a sealant; allow each coat to dry thoroughly.*

STRONG, *rigid shells are ideal and if made of glass fibre last twenty or more years. Place the shell on a 5cm/2in-thick layer of soft sand over a strong, well-compacted or concrete base. Construct a surrounding wall of house bricks or strong, ornamental blocks, ensuring the shell's rim fits over the top course. Cement a row of coping stones over the liner's edge.*

FLEXIBLE, *strong liners — preferably butyl sheeting — are essential, as they will have to withstand low temperatures. Strong foundations and walls two bricks thick are vital. Additionally, an insulating layer of polystyrene between the liner and wall is advisable. Ensure the top edge of the liner is secured in a layer of mortar, under the coping stones.*

RAISED PONDS *need not be formed at one level, but can be a combination of several. In this way, waterfalls and ornamental fountains may be used in the design and a more interesting water feature created.*

PONDS ON SLOPES

Sloping gardens can make gardening difficult, but they also create opportunities to make your garden unique. A pond half-way down a slope, with a terrace of weather-worn flagstones on either side, always captures attention. It is vital to build *strong foundations for the pond's wall which must be two bricks thick. Also, if the pond is made from a rigid shell, a base of compacted hardcore with a thick layer of soft sand on top ensures the weight of the shell and water is spread out.*

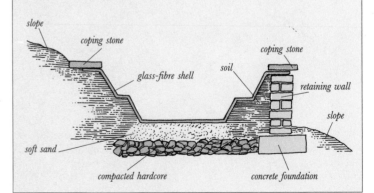

slope

coping stone

glass-fibre shell

soft sand

compacted hardcore

soil

coping stone

retaining wall

slope

concrete foundation

MINI-PONDS

❖

IN SMALL gardens, where a large, raised or ground-level pond cannot be accommodated, a miniature pond in a large tub or stone sink is an ideal way to continue water gardening.

Unfortunately, a tub of water on a patio immediately attracts children and it therefore needs to be covered with wire-netting. Even though it is just a tub of water, children can still come to harm and care is always needed.

LARGE *tubs and deep, stone sinks are ideal containers in which to form miniature ponds. When planted with small waterlilies and other aquatic plants they create fascinating features. Fish can also be added to them.*

WINTER CARE

The greatest danger to miniature ponds in tubs or stone sinks is cold weather and extremely hot sunshine. Hot sunshine mainly affects stone sinks; water in them becomes much warmer than a similar volume in a wooden container. However, it is in winter that the main problem arises as the water may freeze and kill the fish and plants. The best solution is to move the container into a cool greenhouse in early winter. Alternatively, pack plastic bags filled and sealed with straw or hay around the sides, but this can look unsightly and is not very effective. Sometimes, miniature ponds are let into the patio's surface, with slabs around them. The water temperature drops less quickly than in tubs, but it is still necessary to remove the fish and plants in winter.

SAFETY-FIRST POOL

Another small water feature is a 'mini-pool'. This is not deep enough to cause danger to children.

These mini-pools are often formed of small fountains which cascade water on pebbles. The water drains into a small, underground reservoir from which the fountain draws water. Water trickling over pebbles is both attractive and soothing.

It would be wishful thinking to believe that children would not be attracted by them, but as long as the only danger is wet knees they become an acceptable risk to many parents. But do not blend this feature with a children's sand-pit as it soon becomes clogged.

1. BEFORE *positioning and filling a tub with water, check that it is sound and that the base is not rotten. If decayed, discard and seek a better container. If the tub is in good condition it can be immediately filled with water and thoroughly washed. At the same time, check that it is waterproof: occasionally, the sides shrink but when filled to the brim with water for a few weeks the wood expands and seals the gaps. During this period, place the tub in a cool corner, away from strong sunlight.*

2. IF THE *tub continues to leak it is necessary to line it with thick, black flexible polythene. Form pleats inside so that it looks neat. Fill with water and when full cut off the polythene level with the tub's top (below).*

3. WHEN *full of water, it can be planted. This is done in late spring or early summer, the latter being the best if the weather is still very cold. Use the same technique of planting as for plants in ponds (page 127). Use plastic mesh baskets. Where the leaves of waterlilies would become submerged, initially place the basket on a few half-bricks. Remove the half-bricks progressively as the plant grows bigger, so that it is slowly lowered down into the water.*

PLANTS FOR MINI-PONDS

Waterlilies:
• Nymphaea *'Aurora': Colour first pinkish yellow, then orange and later red. It spreads about 45cm/1¹/₂ ft.*
• N. *'Candida': Cup-shaped, white flowers with golden stamens.*
• N. *'Graziella': Free flowering, with orange flowers that reveal orange-red stamens. It has the bonus of having leaves splashed in purple.*
• N. *pymaea alba: Small, white flowers with yellow stamens. The flowers, usually only 2.5cm/1in across, are borne freely. It grows in shallow water and therefore needs protection against falling temperatures and freezing water in winter.*

Marginals:
• Carex stricta *'Bowles Golden': About 45cm/1¹/₂ ft high, with narrow golden leaves. Plant it in water 5cm/2in deep.*
• Scirpus tabernaemontanii *'Zebrinus' (Zebra Rush/Porcupine Quill Rush): Quill-like stems banded in green and white. Plant in 15cm/6in of water. Grows to 90cm/3ft.*

Floaters:
• Hydrocharis morsus-ranae *(Frog Bit): Bright green leaves; but be prepared to cut it back regularly.*
• Pistia stratiotes *(Water Lettuce): Floating leaves die down in winter.*

BOG GARDENS
AND WILDLIFE PONDS
❖

BOG GARDENS, when planted with moisture-loving plants, help informal ponds to blend with their surroundings. The range of plants suitable for planting in them is wide and includes moisture-loving ferns, herbaceous perennials and many primulas which, when planted in large drifts, create spectacular features.

Some boggy areas are natural, but they can also be created. Do not make the area too wide as it is then difficult to put in the plants and to look after them.

KEEP MOIST

From spring to autumn, regularly check that the soil remains moist, but not waterlogged. When constructing the boggy area,

ensure that the surface of the compost is fractionally below the water surface in the pond. This often helps to keep it moist. Nevertheless, the compost must not become saturated as this quickly encourages the roots to rot and the plants to die. If soil drainage does become a little problematic, remove some soil and pierce the flexible liner several times with a garden fork. If at all possible, spread further grit directly over the liner.

The Skunk Cabbage (Lysichiton americanus).

1. UNLESS *there is a natural boggy area alongside your pond, it is necessary to create one – but it should not become waterlogged. Dig out a hole 38–45cm/15–18in deep, giving each side a gentle slope.*

2. SMOOTH *the sides and form a 5cm/2in layer of soft sand over the base and sides. Place a flexible liner in it. The pool-side edge should be large enough to tuck under the side of the pond's rigid shell (or flexible liner).*

3. TRIM OFF *the liner's edges (other than at the pond's edge), but leave an overhang of at least 15–23cm/6–9in. Place a few pebbles on top to ensure the liner remains in place along the edges and sides.*

4. PIERCE *12mm/½in holes every 90cm/3ft in the liner's base, then form a 5–6.5cm/2–2½in-thick layer of clean grit in the base. Fill the hole with fertile, moisture-retentive compost.*

5. COVER *the edges of the liner with pebbles to make them more attractive and to prevent deterioration in the material from sunlight. Thin liners are especially prone to damage in this way.*

6. START *planting from the centre of the bog garden outwards. If necessary, stand on planks to prevent the soil becoming consolidated which eventually can make it become waterlogged.*

BOG GARDEN

Soil that remains moist throughout the year is essential for the growth of bog garden plants. Many of these are illustrated and described on pages 137 to 138.

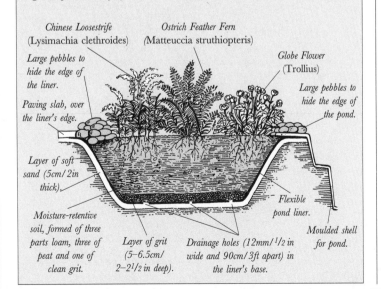

Chinese Loosestrife (Lysimachia clethroides)

Ostrich Feather Fern (Matteuccia struthiopteris)

Globe Flower (Trollius)

Large pebbles to hide the edge of the liner.

Large pebbles to hide the edge of the pond.

Paving slab, over the liner's edge.

Layer of soft sand (5cm/2in thick).

Flexible pond liner.

Moisture-retentive soil, formed of three parts loam, three of peat and one of clean grit.

Layer of grit (5–6.5cm/ 2–2½ in deep).

Drainage holes (12mm/½ in wide and 90cm/3ft apart) in the liner's base.

Moulded shell for pond.

WILDLIFE POND AND NATURAL ENEMIES

Bog gardens are essential parts of wildlife ponds, enabling plants to be grown that provide havens for insects, birds, amphibians and small mammals. Use a flexible liner to make an informal pond, with a bog garden alongside it. Within a couple of years, frogs and newts will be established in the pond. There may also be a few mosquitoes in summer, but these will be controlled when fish eat their eggs.

They are only a menace in stagnant water. Every inhabitant in your wildlife pond will have its own enemies, and that is part of nature. But garden chemicals are a different problem and, if used, they soon find their ways into wildlife food chains. Do not use chemicals to control insects or disease, nor herbicides to kill weeds in lawns alongside ponds.

CONSTRUCTING WATERFALLS

❖

WATERFALLS add sparkle to water gardens, but they only usually look right in informal settings – fountains are better in precise, formal ponds (see page126). Construction materials include concrete, pre-formed rigid shells, and flexible liners (butyl types, as they are resistant to ultra-violet rays).

SELECTING A PUMP

If the head – the difference between the water's surface in the main pond and that in the top waterfall – is less that 1.2m/4ft, the size of pump needed is much smaller than if the head of water is 1.8m/6ft or more. Also, if the width of each sill area is 15cm/6in or less this too reduces the volume of water that a pump needs to supply to the topmost pond. Keep all of the sills about the same width.

Do not select a small pump because it is cheap, as the resulting flow over the sills will be disappointing. Manufacturers of pumps will be able to advise about the size needed.

PRE-SHAPED SHELLS

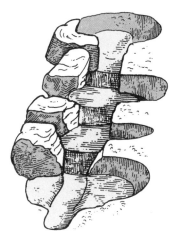

IN EARLIER years, watercourses and waterfalls were always made of concrete. It is a versatile material and forms waterfalls of many shapes and sizes. However, mixing and moving concrete is heavy work and it may need reinforcement with wire-netting if the pool is large (see page 121). Nevertheless, its ability to be moulded into shapes that personalize the waterfall to your garden often compensates for the added work. Paint all surfaces with a proprietary waterproofing sealant. Excavate each pool area deeper and wider than needed to allow for 10–15cm/4–6in-thick concrete. Do not economize on its thickness.

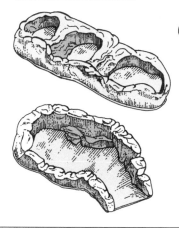

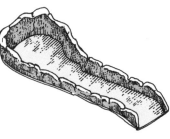

RIGID SHELLS, formed of either individual cascades, several together or just a watercourse, are available in a wide range of shapes and sizes. Preferably, use glass-fibre types, as they are long lasting and resistant to ultra-violet rays.

USING RIGID SHELLS

1. PUT *the shells into position, ensuring the mouth of each one overlaps the unit below. Mark an area slightly larger and dig out the soil. Use a spirit-level to check that the tops of the units will be level. Water must remain in them even when water is not being pumped. Install piping to carry water from the pump.*

2. INSTALL *the lower unit first, bedding it on an evenly thick, 5cm/2in layer of soft sand. Check that its top is level, then fill around it with sand or friable soil. Continue fitting the units, ensuring an overhang on each so that water tumbles into the lower one, at a position about one-third in from the side nearest the cascade.*

3. USE A *hose-pipe to fill the top pool to check if water splashes evenly, and that each unit retains water. If water cascades lopsidedly, adjust the levels. After checking them, repack and firm sand or friable soil around them. Install the pipe from the pump: camouflage its outlet with a large paving slab or rock.*

USING A FLEXIBLE LINER

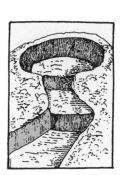 

1. WHEN *making a flight of waterfalls from several pieces of flexible liner it is possible to make each cascade exactly the shape you desire. It does not have the size constraints imposed by rigid shells (see above). Starting from the base, dig out each pool. Make the watercourse curve slightly so that it appears to be a natural feature.*

2. SLOPE *the base of each pond backwards, so that it always retains water. Then spread 2.5cm/1in of soft sand over the surface. Starting from the lowest pool, position the liner to extend to the top of the waterfall on the higher side, and the base of the lower one. Spread the liner up the sides and overlap the top by about 20cm/8in.*

3. WHEN *all the liners are in position, use an adhesive to keep the lower flap of each waterfall in place. Use a hose-pipe to fill the ponds, then place large stones or slabs over the edges to keep them firm. Install the water inlet pipe at the top and camouflage it with rocks and plants. Then introduce plants to the pools.*

PUMPS,
FOUNTAINS AND LIGHTS

❖

WATER pumps and lights transform water gardens, but unless installed correctly water and electricity are a dangerous combination. Installing electricity is not cheap and needs the services of a competent electrician. Transformers which reduce the power to 12 or 24 volts make the installation safer, but where large volumes of water for waterfalls are involved a mains-powered pump is essential.

The installation must include a residual current device (RCD) that will trip out the power supply should a fault occur. Also, heavy-duty cables and plastic conduit are essential to connect the pump to the power supply. Always make the installation capable of providing power for additional equipment, such as pool heaters.

WATER PUMPS

There are two types of pump used in water gardens: the most popular one is the submersible, the other the surface type.

• *Submersible pumps are designed to be totally submerged and to work silently. They are easily installed: after placing a pump in a pond, run the cable to the pool's side and use a waterproof connector to link it to a mains electricity supply or a transformer. There is a wide range of submersible pumps and the type required depends on the volume of water to be moved.*

• *Surface pumps are needed where large, or several, fountains are to operate and large volumes of water are needed.*

FOUNTAINS

Few garden features are as fascinating as a fountain. There are many shapes and sizes of jet and a few are shown here. As well, there are statues that spurt water, while pool-side ornaments such as gargoyles disgorge spouts immediately into pools. Where fountains are sited directly in ponds there are a few important considerations:

• The height of the spray should not rise to a distance of more than half the pond's total width.

• The spray should not fall on waterlilies or marginal plants, as they are quickly damaged by this, especially when flowering.

• Floating water plants are soon disturbed by spray and pushed around the pond.

• In windy areas, install fountains that produce large water droplets. Some fountains function like a geyser and produce a tumbling mass of water.

• Keep water-filters clean as fine-nozzled fountains soon become clogged.

• Consult a specialist before buying a fountain and pump. Explain the fountain's size, if it is a secondary feature (the other, perhaps, a waterfall) and the length and size of the piping.

• For safety, fountains with sprays of water up to 1.2m/4ft high can be powered by low-voltage submersible pumps. However, for water sprays 2.1m/7ft high a mains-powered submersible is needed, while for fountains over this height a surface pump is essential. Do not economize on the pump's size. It is always better to have a pump too large.

Waterproof connection, in a dry trap under a strong flag stone.

Submersible pump: position above the silt and on a wide, concrete plinth. Regularly clean the filter.

Waterproof, electrical cable.

Outlet pipe to fountains or waterfalls.

BELOW: *On some pumps, the jet part is integral with the pump, making installation simple.*

LEFT: *Ornamental fountains are easily operated by a small submersible pump.*

ABOVE: *A pump's power is measured by the volume of water it can pump in an hour.*

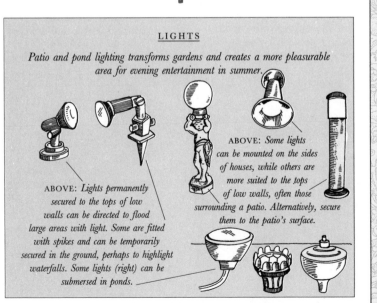

LIGHTS

Patio and pond lighting transforms gardens and creates a more pleasurable area for evening entertainment in summer.

ABOVE: *Lights permanently secured to the tops of low walls can be directed to flood large areas with light. Some are fitted with spikes and can be temporarily secured in the ground, perhaps to highlight waterfalls. Some lights (right) can be submersed in ponds.*

ABOVE: *Some lights can be mounted on the sides of houses, while others are more suited to the tops of low walls, often those surrounding a patio. Alternatively, secure them to the patio's surface.*

PLANTING

WATERLILIES are often available from water-plant nurseries throughout the summer, although it is certainly easier to plant them early in the year. They are best planted during late spring or early summer. Choose early summer in cold climates. Other aquatics are planted between late spring (or early summer in cold areas) and late summer, when actively growing.

In earlier times it was usual to put plants in soil in a pond's base: this is not now recommended. Always plant into a plastic mesh basket or similar container as this allows more control over the plant, such as adjusting the depth to which it is placed in the water. It also makes lifting, repotting and feeding easier.

As soon as plants arrive from suppliers, unwrap them and submerge the roots in a bucket of clean water. Plant them as soon as possible. If there is a delay, leave them in water and place the bucket in a cool, shaded, well-illuminated corner.

RANGE OF PLANTS

In addition to waterlilies, there is a wide range of other plants that can be planted in ponds. Some of these are solely decorative, others are essential to the lives of fish and other creatures in ponds (see pages 129 to 130).
- *Waterlilies are the most popular of water plants. Always choose varieties that suit the pond's depth (pages 131 to 132).*
- *Marginals are positioned on shelves within the pond (pages 135 to 136).*
- *Oxygenators, as their name suggests, are submerged and help to aerate and keep the water clean (page 133).*
- *Floaters live freely in the water (page 134).*
- *Bog plants live in moist soil around ponds (pages 137 to 138).*

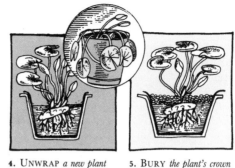
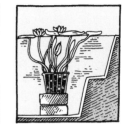

4. UNWRAP *a new plant and place in a bucket of water. Do not allow its roots to become dry. Form a hole in the loam and spread out the roots. Cover with loam and firm it over them.*

5. BURY *the plant's crown slightly deeper than before (see mark on stem), with the surface of the loam 3.6–5cm/ 1½–2in below the basket's top. Then add 2.5cm/ 1in of grit.*

6. WATER *the compost, then place in the pond. The leaves of waterlilies must float on the surface. Place the container on bricks. As plants grow, progressively remove the bricks (see below).*

PLANTING DEPTHS

Planting aquatic plants in plastic mesh or other proprietary containers creates the opportunity to position them at the right depth throughout their first year. The containers for waterlilies and marginal plants can be slowly lowered throughout the first season. Always select waterlilies that suit the depth of water as if too vigorous – even when the plant's container is on a pond's base – the leaves protrude out of the water, dominating the pond and smothering less demanding water plants. Ensure the baskets will not fall over.

PLACE *marginal plants on blocks to raise their leaves above the surface.*

NEWLY PLANTED *waterlilies need raising to prevent leaves being submerged.*

OXYGENATING *plants can be immediately placed on the pond's base.*

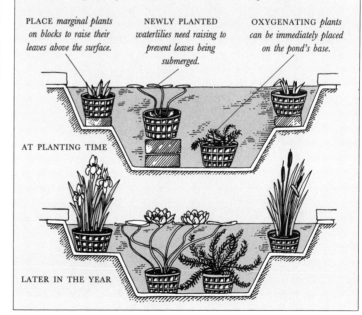

AT PLANTING TIME

LATER IN THE YEAR

1. PLASTIC MESH *planting baskets are widely available in several sizes, from 10cm/ 4in to 30cm/ 12in wide. Most are square, others round, some kidney-shaped and ideal for shelves in round ponds.*

2. TO PREVENT *compost falling through holes in a planting basket, line the inside with coarse hessian. Ensure it completely covers the inside of the basket. Louvred types of basket do not need lining.*

3. FILL *the basket two-thirds full with heavy loam enriched with a sprinkling of bonemeal to assist in the development of roots. Ensure the loam is free from decaying debris, such as old roots.*

LOOKING AFTER PONDS

LOOKING after fish and plants is not difficult and here are a few techniques and pieces of equipment that can make water gardening even more of a pleasure. Water heaters and filters are expensive initially, but some of the ideas here are inexpensive and just common sense.

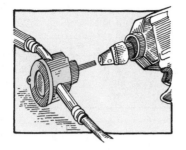

EMPTYING PONDS *at ground level is laborious when buckets are used. However, inexpensive pumps are available and some can be powered by electric drills. They pump about 750 litres/200 gallons an hour, but cannot be used continuously to operate fountains. Raised ponds can be emptied by syphoning the water through a length of hose pipe.*

FEEDING RINGS *prevent fish food floating all over the pond. Uneaten food can then be removed easily.*

FISH FEEDERS *that float and discharge food when rocked by fish help to prevent food wastage and water contamination.*

POND HEATERS *are essential in winter to create an open area of water amid ice. This allows an exchange of gases between the water and air – essential for the health of fish – and eases the pressure of ice on the pond's sides. Some heaters are operated by mains electricity, others through a transformer, and these are much safer to install and use. Most float and therefore need to be in position at the first sign of ice. To ensure that ice-free space is created, a heater is needed for every 2.3–4.6sq m/25–50sq ft of the pond's surface, but this is determined by the heater's power. Check with a specialist supplier.*

FEEDING WATER *plants is made easy when fertilizer is applied in sachets that can be inserted into compost in spring and mid-summer.*

NEVER *create ice-free areas by breaking ice. Instead, install a water heater (below left) or repeatedly place a metal kettle of boiling water on the ice. It is usually necessary to refill the kettle several times with more boiling water. Ensure it does not fall in – tie it to a rope!*

INITIAL *filling and topping up of ponds must be carried out with care. If empty, place a bucket on the pond's base and allow water to gently trickle over the rim. For topping up, tie a piece of canvas over the pipe's end. This prevents the water being unduly disturbed.*

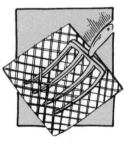

NETTING *attached to a wooden or metal framework is ideal for preventing children falling in, birds fishing and leaves blowing into ponds in autumn. Wire netting impaled on a garden fork is superb for removing leaves.*

FILTERS

Most ponds do not have filters, but if you keep Koi Carp *they are essential. There are two main types, mechanical and biological. The mechanical type uses a pump to draw water through filters that remove dirt floating in the water. It is usually installed in the pond and water passing through it is piped to fountains and waterfalls. Biological types need a pump that must run continuously. The unit operates outside the pond.*

FISH FOR GARDEN PONDS

UNLIKE any other garden feature, water gardening involves plants and living creatures. Most people – and especially children – are captivated by fish, while dragonflies and damselflies are enchanting as they hover over a pond in summer. Frogs and newts also have their charm, but are more esteemed by enthusiasts of wildlife ponds than owners of a small, ornamental pool on a patio.

RANGE OF FISH

Goldfish are the most popular fish for ponds, widely available and colourful. Shubunkins, which were

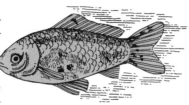

THE LONDON SHUBUNKIN has a similar shape to a goldfish. The blue form is seen most often, but there are others.

developed from goldfish, are also widely seen. Most are hardy, such as the Common Goldfish, London Shubunkin, Bristol Shubunkin, Comet and Sarasa Comet, and can be left outside throughout winter. In cold areas, the Bristol Shubunkin must be taken indoors in winter.

The fancy forms, such as Fantail and Moor, are even less hardy and must be taken indoors at the onset of cold weather in autumn; some experts recommend them only for aquariums indoors. Other fancy forms, such as Veiltail, Oranda, Ranchu, Celestial, Lionhead and Pompon, are kept only in aquariums indoors.

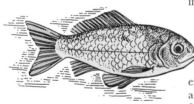

THE COMMON GOLDFISH is a popular fish for garden ponds. It is inexpensive to buy, reliable and never fails to create interest.

BUYING AND STOCKING

Introduce fish to ponds between late spring and late summer, when the pool's temperature is at least 10°C/50°F. Leave about five weeks between planting and adding fish. Large fish are usually expensive, while small ones are sometimes difficult to establish. Therefore, look for fish 7.5–13cm/3–5in long. Always buy from a reputable source. As fish are companionable, buy several.

They are usually sold in water in a polythene bag, plus a burst of oxygen. Fish can exist in this way for twenty-four hours if kept cool, but put them into the pond soon.

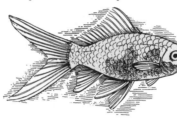

THE SARASA COMET is very ornamental, with a white and red body and flowing tail.

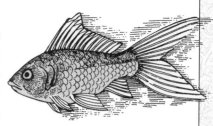

THE COMET GOLDFISH has large fins that enable rapid movement for short distances.

Place a clean plastic bucket in the pond – covered by water – and gently lower the unopened polythene bag into it. After three or four hours the temperatures in the bag and pool will be about equal. Carefully open the bag and allow the fish to swim out. Do *not* just tip them into the water.

Do not introduce too many fish: an approximation of the number is 2.5cm/1in of fish (including tail) to each 30 x 30cm/12 x 12in of pond surface. *Koi* carp need more space, about one fish to every 1.5 x 1.5m/5 x 5ft of surface area.

BASIC FISH ANATOMY

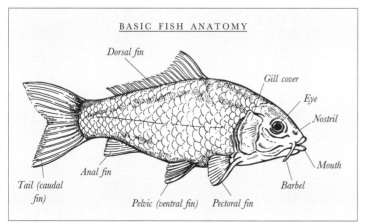

Dorsal fin

Gill cover

Eye

Nostril

Mouth

Barbel

Pectoral fin

Pelvic (ventral fin)

Anal fin

Tail (caudal fin)

KOI – FANCY CARP

These are increasingly popular fish for ponds, but only if large. Koi is the Japanese name for carp, with the ornamental forms correctly known as Nishikigoi but invariable just called koi. Occasionally they are called Fancy Carp.

Koi were recorded in Japan more than 1600 years ago and have been bred for a wide range of colours, from white, through gold and blue to black. Some are speckled in several colours, including silver, and may reach 75cm/2½ ft or more in length. They therefore need a large pond, at least 1.2m/4ft deep.

Koi stir up silt on the pond's base, clouding the water. This makes it necessary to cover the base with shingle or gravel and to install a filter. Keeping koi has become a cult and before putting them into a pool it is wise to study a specialist book.

OTHER
COLD-WATER POND FISH
❖

THE WIDE range of fish suitable for ponds includes, as well as goldfish and shubunkins, a choice of other cold-water fish. Most are best suited to life in large ponds and especially to those intended to attract wildlife.

There is often a temptation to put *any* fish into a garden pond, but don't: first check their suitability and certainly avoid introducing predatory types such as Pike, Perch and Catfish.

GOLDEN RUDD *eventually grows 15–20cm/6–8in long in a garden pond, although it has been known to reach 45cm/18in in lakes and rivers. It has an attractive silvery shade overlaid with a golden hue, but is best identified by its reddish fins.*

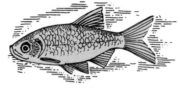

MINNOWS *are popular and widely found in ponds, streams and lakes. They grow about 7.5cm/3in long, are normally silvery but during the breeding season in spring the male changes to green, strongly flushed with red. They live in shoals.*

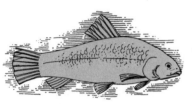

GOLDEN ORFE *has an attractive salmon or pale golden body. They are timid and best bought in pairs. Only put them in well-aerated ponds with a surface area of 3.75sq m/40sq ft or more.*

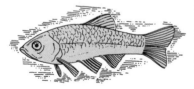

TENCH *live towards the bottom of a pond, clouding the water as they stir around in the silt. They are often known as 'doctor' fish, but there is little evidence to suggest they have curative powers. The Golden Tench (above) has a pale orange body, while the Green Tench (below) is much duller.*

OTHER FISH

• **Blue Orfe:** *Increasingly popular, with pale blue scales and a rather slower nature than the golden type.*
• **Gudgeon:** *A scavenger and prone to stirring up silt.*
• **Rosy Minnow:** *A North American fish with a salmon-orange body. It does not grow very large and is well able to survive the coldest winter.*
• **Three-spined Stickleback:** *It has an aggressive nature, grows 6–8cm/2$\frac{1}{2}$–3$\frac{1}{2}$in long and is best put in wildlife ponds. Male fish have a metallic blue hue and a red belly when spawning.*

OTHER
POND WILDLIFE
❖

WILDLIFE ponds are more likely than formal ponds – which are usually found on patios – to encourage animals such as common frogs, toads, newts, small mammals, dragonflies, pond skaters and damselflies.

Birds are also encouraged and if these are song birds there is no problem. Wildlife ponds, however, entice herons and they soon steal fish. If birds are a continual problem, the only solution is to cover the pond in netting.

THE COMMON FROG *is a frequent visitor to garden ponds.*

THE COMMON TOAD *has a voracious appetite for slugs and snails.*

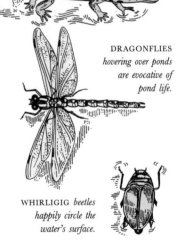

THE COMMON *or Smooth Newt visits ponds to breed during spring and summer.*

DRAGONFLIES *hovering over ponds are evocative of pond life.*

OTHER POND LIFE

• **Damselflies:** *Pretty and dainty, they flit over the pond in summer. They lay eggs in the water, some of which become food for fish. They are encouraged by plants that surround wildlife ponds.*
• **Ram's Horn Snail:** *Unlike the plant-damaging Great Pond Snail with its corkscrew-shaped shell, the Ram's Horn Snail has a Catherine-wheel outline. It feeds on debris and helps to keep the pond clean.*
• **Small mammals:** *Water Voles and Water Shrews are encouraged by food supplies near wildlife ponds, as well as by water. Grass snakes also frequent the same area.*

WHIRLIGIG *beetles happily circle the water's surface.*

POND SKATERS *skid to and fro across the surface.*

PYGMY WATERLILIES

YGMY, dwarf or miniature waterlilies have a diminutive nature and are ideal for planting in small ponds as well as in water gardens in tubs and stone sinks. They are excellent for planting in ponds where the water depth does not exceed 23cm/9in above the surface of the planting container. This means that if the container is 10cm/4in deep, the total depth of the pond should be no more than 32cm/13in. Even though classified as pygmies, there are many variations in their vigour. However, each plant covers $^1/_{10}$–$^1/_4$ sq m/1–3 sq ft of the water's surface. The flowers are smaller – 5–10cm/2–4in wide – but are no less attractive than their larger cousins. They are, however, more easily damaged in severe winters than waterlilies with a thicker insulation of water above their roots.

Whatever the sizes of the plants, when planting always ensure the leaves are not drowned (see page 127 for planting instructions).

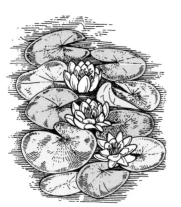

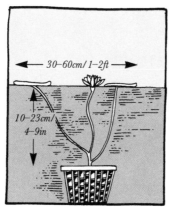

30–60cm/ 1–2ft

10–23cm/ 4–9in

PYGMY WATERLILIES

- Nymphaea 'Aurora': Changeable colours, first pinkish yellow, then orange and later red.
- N. 'Graziella': Free flowering, with orange flowers.
- N. laydekeri 'Lilacea': Scented; pale pink and darkening with age.
- N. odorata minor: Scented; white and star-shaped, with yellow stamens.
- N. odorata 'W. B. Shaw': Fragrant, with pink flowers.

- N. 'Paul Hariot': Changeable colours, first yellow, later orange and then red. The leaves are attractively marked in brown.
- N. pygmaea alba: A real miniature, with flowers only 2.5cm/1in wide. White with yellow stamens.
- N. pygmaea 'Helvola': The smallest yellow-flowered waterlily. Star-shaped, pale yellow flowers with golden stamens.

SMALL WATERLILIES

THESE are more vigorous than the pygmy types, although some authorities name some pygmy waterlilies as small ones; and conversely, a few small ones are classified as pygmies. For example, some experts classify the deep pink flowered *N. laydekeri* 'Purpurata' as a pygmy type, others as a small one. Clearly, plants are not as uniform as sausages and depending on their circumstances some may be more or less vigorous.

Small waterlilies are ideal for ponds with 15–45cm/6–18in of water above the container. Their spread is more dramatic than pygmy types, each plant occupying $^1/_4$–1$^1/_{10}$ sq m/3–12 sq ft of the water's surface.

As the vigour of waterlilies increases, so too does the range of plants from which to choose. Colours include white, pink, red, yellow and orange. The widths of their flowers are 10–15cm/4–6in and therefore they are more dominant than the pygmy types.

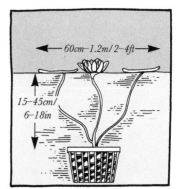

60cm–1.2m/ 2–4ft

15–45cm/ 6–18in

SMALL WATERLILIES

- Nymphaea 'Albatross': Large white flowers with golden centres. Attractive leaves, purple when young.
- N. 'Firecrest': Fragrant, bright pink flowers streaked orange and red. The stamens are tipped in red.
- N. 'Froebeli': Wine red flowers with orange stamens. Olive green leaves. Widely grown and very reliable flowering.
- N. 'James Brydon': Popular and prolific, with orange-red flowers and orange stamens. Purplish leaves. It grows well in light shade.

- N. laydekeri 'Fulgens': Bright red flowers, darkening with age, and orange-red stamens. It bears many flowers, but only a few leaves, which have purple undersides. The leaves have long stems.
- N. 'Sioux': Buff-yellow flowers that turn to peach then copper-orange. The green leaves are peppered deep brownish-red.
- N. 'William Falconer': Dark red cup-shaped flowers with yellow centres. Also has attractive, dark green leaves.

MEDIUM WATERLILIES

MEDIUM waterlilies need a position where their crowns are covered with 30–60cm/ 12–24in of water. Their spread is variable, often 1.2–1.5m/4–5ft and a single plant could cover 2 sq m/20 sq ft or more. The flowers are larger than the small types and up to 21cm/7in across.

Some waterlilies are classified in either medium or vigorous categories. For example, 'Mrs Richmond' is sometimes placed with vigorous types, other times with the medium ones. Clearly, although some vigorous types can be grown in relatively shallow water, they invariably spread further than the medium-vigorous ones, and some need deeper water to prevent their leaves for ever rising above the surface.

These are popular varieties and suit most ponds. However, always check the water's depth before introducing them. Ponds soon become a jungle of leaves if over-vigorous types are selected.

VIGOROUS WATERLILIES

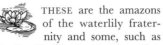

THESE are the amazons of the waterlily frater-nity and some, such as *N. alba*, *N.* 'Charles de Meurville', *N.* 'Gladstoniana' and *N. tuberosa* 'Richardsonii', are more suited to lakes than garden ponds. They lack the daintiness of the pygmy types, but in a large setting form dominant features.

They need 45–90cm/1½–3ft of water over their roots. The size of their flowers is up to 25cm/10in wide and each plant will easily spread 1.5–2.4m/5–8ft or more. Therefore, it could be disastrous to think big in a small pond! Some of the most vigorous lilies can easily cover 4.5 sq m/50 sq ft. And as such lilies obliterate the surface it is impossible to grow more choice plants if the pond is small. With the selection of all lilies, the maxim must be to choose varieties that suit the pond's size.

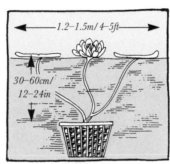

1.2–1.5m/4–5ft

30–60cm/ 12–24in

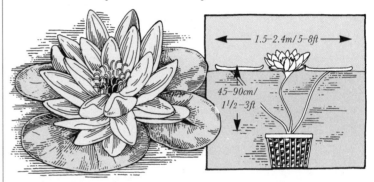

1.5–2.4m/5–8ft

45–90cm/ 1½–3ft

MEDIUM WATERLILIES

- Nymphaea 'Amabilis': *Fragrant, rose-pink flowers with a flat, star-shaped nature. The pink darkens with age.*
- N. 'Gloriosa': *Scented, rose-red flowers that are borne prolifically throughout summer.*
- N. 'Gonnère': *Also known as 'Snowball', it has semi-double white flowers with yellow stamens.*
- N. marliacea 'Albida': *Fragrant, white flowers with yellow stamens.*
- N. marliacea 'Rosea': *Fragrant, with pale pink flowers and golden stamens. The young leaves are an attractive purplish-green.*

- N. 'Mme. Wilfron Gonnère': *Cup-shaped, rich pink flowers flushed with white. Attractive deep rose centres.*
- N. 'Moorei': *Pale yellow flowers with yellow stamens.*
- N. 'René Gerard': *Large, star-shaped, red flowers with golden stamens. A very free-flowering variety.*
- N. 'Rose Arey': *Large, star-shaped rose-pink flowers with yellow stamens.*
- N. 'Sunrise': *Scented, bright yellow flowers with golden stamens. The underside of each leaf is an attractive red shade.*

VIGOROUS WATERLILIES

- Nymphaea alba: *Vigorous and only suited to very large ponds. Cup-shaped, white flowers with yellow stamens. It is often seen in lakes, and when seen en masse is very dramatic.*
- N. 'Attraction': *Free flowering with red flowers, flecked in white and displaying golden stamens.*
- N. 'Charles de Meurville': *Vigorous plant with large, rich red flowers which can grow to 25cm/10in across. Only suitable for a very large pond.*
- N. 'Colonel A. J. Welch': *Yellow flowers and lightly marbled leaves. It needs a very large pond with deep water.*

- N. 'Colossea': *Scented, blush pink flowers that fade to white. Golden stamens. Only for large ponds.*
- N. 'Gladstoniana': *Enormous white flowers with golden stamens. Only suitable for deep, large ponds.*
- N. marliacea 'Chromatella': *Bowl-shaped, yellow flowers. Very free flowering and reliable.*
- N. 'Mrs Richmond': *Globular pink flowers that turn red with age. Golden stamens. Vigorous and needs a deep pond.*
- N. tuberosa 'Richardsonii': *Very vigorous and perhaps best suited to lakes and deep water, about 90cm/3ft or more. Cup-shaped white flowers with yellow stamens.*

OXYGENATING PLANTS
❖
Ceratophyllum – Tillaea

ALSO known as submerged aquatics and water weeds, these oxygenating plants are essential for the well-being of fish and to keep water clean. They also provide shelter for spawning fish and their fry. Additionally, they release oxygen into the water and absorb mineral salts that, if not removed, would encourage the presence of algae. Ponds that do not have oxygenating plants become green and dirty, with fish that have to come to the surface repeatedly to gasp in air. This is especially likely to happen during warm weather in summer.

Most oxygenating plants grow completely below the surface, but a few, such as the Water Violet (*Hottonia palustris*), display attractive flowers. Some have a vigorous nature and unless regularly pruned will soon engulf a pond.

All these plants need to be planted in a meshed container placed on the pond's base. This enables easy removal should it become necessary, as well as aiding propagation by division of plants and taking of cuttings.

FONTINALIS ANIPYRETICA *(Willow Moss) is slow-growing, with evergreen, dark green leaves that spread out to form mossy patches. It is an ideal oxygenator to have when fish are spawning. Increase it by dividing large clumps in late spring or summer. It is superb in full sun or light shade. A related species, F. gracilis, is not so common and is smaller, with thread-like leaves.*

HOTTONIA PALUSTRIS *(Water Violet) is a British native plant and one of the few oxygenating plants that develop flowers. These are lilac coloured and borne in whorls on stiff, upright stems, about 20cm/8in above the water's surface in early summer. In autumn, stems die down and the plant overwinters as dormant buds. The beautiful leaves are feathery, finely divided and bright green.*

LAGAROSIPHON MAJOR *(Goldfish Weed), also known as Elodea crispa, is a superb oxygenating plant from South Africa that survives in all but the coldest climates. The small, narrow, curling leaves tightly clasp the stems and although it can be invasive in large ponds – where plants cannot be easily reached for pruning – is definitely worth growing. Take cuttings every three years, in spring or summer.*

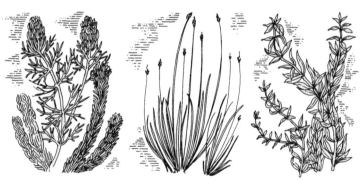

CERATOPHYLLUM DEMERSUM *(Hornwort) has bristle-like, dark green leaves arranged in whorls. In autumn, stems fall to the pond's base and the plant survives in a dormant form. It is hardy and grows well in cold water. It is increased in summer by division or cuttings.*

ELEOCHARIS ACICULARIS *(Hairgrass) is a dainty grass with green, hair-like stems and a tufted habit, 13–15cm/5–6in high. It forms runners and is easily increased by breaking off parts in late spring or summer and replanting them. It is not suitable for very cold regions.*

ELODEA CANADENSIS *(Canadian Pondweed) is a popular oxygenator, but very invasive and therefore needs regular trimming in summer. Stems are packed with dark green leaves, with the bouquet of thyme. When severed they can be used in spring or summer as cuttings, and soon develop roots.*

MYRIOPHYLLUM SPICATUM *(Water Milfoil) develops long, trailing stems clothed in finely cut, feathery whorls of light green leaves. It is ideal for a small pond and is increased easily by weighting small pieces into compost during summer. It develops red-petalled flowers, slightly above the surface.*

POTOMOGETON CRISPUS *(Curled Pondweed) has large, curly-edged, reddish, lance-like leaves attached to wiry stems. It is invasive and needs regular pruning. In early summer it develops small, pinkish-white flowers slightly above the water's surface. Take cuttings in summer.*

TILLAEA RECURVA, *now properly known as Crassula recurva and widely sold as Crassula helmsii, is native to Australia and known as the Swamp Stonecrop. It is vigorous, with evergreen, fleshy leaves. Divide congested plants in spring, or take cuttings during late spring or early summer.*

FLOATING PLANTS
❖
Azolla–Stratiotes

THESE are plants with no visible means of support: they float freely with leaves and stems on or just below the surface. Their roots trail beneath them. Some have flowers, most do not.

Some of these plants are native to warm countries and therefore, in order to survive in temperate climates, they must be put in a bucket of water and soil during winter and placed in a frost-proof greenhouse or light shed. In spring, after the risk of frost has passed, they can be reintroduced to a pond. Some other floaters just drop to the pond's base in autumn and survive as buds that re-grow in spring.

These plants can be bought from early to late summer and need only be carefully dropped into the water.

VITAL ROLE

In addition to being attractive and playing a minor role in aerating water, in large ponds they help to fill blank areas between waterlilies and marginal plants along a pond's edges. The main problem with vigorous floaters in large and deep ponds is that it is difficult to reach them to prune them if they become invasive. Fortunately, however, it is plants from warm countries that are most invasive and these are invariably reduced or killed by frosts.

Vigorous forms of floaters such as the Greater Duckweed (*Lemna polyrhiza* but now properly known as *Spirodela polyrhiza*) and Thick Duckweed (*L. gibba*) should not be introduced to ponds. For this reason, always buy plants from reputable nurseries.

LEMNA MINOR *(Common Duckweed/Lesser Duckweed) is an invasive floater that soon covers the surface with small, bright green leaves. Small roots dangle below the leaves. It grows rapidly and therefore needs repeated thinning. It is hardy and survives most winters.* Lemna trisulca *is the least invasive species.*

EICHHORNIA CRASSIPES *(Water Hyacinth) is notorious in warm countries for blocking waterways. Frost, however, soon kills it and therefore plants are overwintered in buckets of water and soil in greenhouses. In warm areas, blue, lavender and yellow flowers appear in summer.*

AZOLLA CAROLINIANA *(Fairy Moss/Mosquito Plant) is a popular floater, forming dense mats of pale green fronds that turn red in autumn. Winter frosts and ice cut back plants; in very cold areas, overwinter plants in containers filled with water and soil. In spring, replace in a pond.*

HYDROCHARIS MORSUS-RANAE *(Frog Bit) is ideal for small ponds and develops bright green, kidney-shaped leaves and small, white three-petalled flowers during mid-summer. It is hardy and survives outdoors in most winters. Congested plants can be divided in summer.*

PISTIA STRATIOTES *(Water Lettuce/Shell Flower) needs a warm climate and is soon killed by frost. Place in a bucket of water and soil and put in a greenhouse during winter. It develops floating rosettes formed of felted, lettuce-like leaves. It is ideal for the rarity enthusiast.*

TRAPA NUTANS *(Water Chestnut/Trapa Nut) is a tender, annual floater, soon killed by frost. The black, chestnut-like fruits fall to the pond's base in autumn, overwinter and produce new plants in spring. However, fruits are only produced in warm countries.*

STRATIOTES ALOIDES *(Water Soldier/Water Aloe) is hardy, with sword-like leaves borne in clusters that resemble the tops of pineapples. White flowers appear in mid-summer, then the plant sinks to the pond's base. In late spring, plants rise naturally until they are just below the surface.*

MARGINAL PLANTS
Acorus – Hypericum

HESE are adaptable plants, mainly living in shallow water at the edges of ponds. Some will also grow in boggy areas around ponds. The depth of water needed varies, and therefore this is indicated for each of the plants featured on this and the following page.

These plants have their roots submerged, but the major parts of their stems and leaves are above the surface.

UNIFYING THE POND
Growing water-loving plants at the edges of a pond helps to unify it with the surrounding garden, although this can also be achieved by planting bog plants in moist soil around a pond (see pages 137 to 138). Marginal plants also introduce informality to the edges of formal ponds.

To ensure marginal plants are in the correct depth of water (the distance between the top of their soil ball to the surface of the water) plant them in individual containers. Then, either place them on shelves within the pond or on bricks or upturned clay pots. Ensure that this added base will not tear lining materials. Never plant water-plants directly into soil in the pond's base, and do not put several different plants in the same container.

In dry, hot summers, ensure that the water level in the pond does not fall and expose the roots of these plants.

CALLA PALUSTRIS *(Bog Arum/Water Dragon) develops dark green, heart-shaped leaves and white flowers like Arum Lilies during summer. However, they are smaller than those of the Arum Lily. Plant it in 5–10cm/2–4in of water. Lift and divide congested plants in spring.*

CALTHA PALUSTRIS *'Plena' (Double Marsh Marigold/Double Kingcup) has round to heart-shaped, green leaves and large, double, yellow, buttercup-like flowers during late spring and early summer. It grows in water up to 5cm/2in deep. Divide clumps in late summer.*

CAREX STRICTA *'Bowles Golden' grows about 45cm/1¹/₂ ft high and develops narrow, golden leaves. Plant it in water up to 5cm/2in deep, and divide congested clumps in spring. Carex riparia 'Variegata' has leaves variegated green and white, and is 45–60cm/1¹/₂–2ft high.*

ACORUS CALAMUS *'Variegatus' (Variegated Sweet Flag) develops erect, green leaves with cream stripes along their edges. It grows 60–90cm/2–3ft high and forms a dominant feature. Bruised leaves have a tangerine-like bouquet. Plant in 7.5–15cm/3–5in of water. Divide congested plants in spring or summer.*

ALISMA PLANTAGO-AQUATICA *(Water Plantain/Mad Dog Weed) has flower heads that often reach 75cm/2¹/₂ ft high but has leaves only 15–30cm/6–12in tall. The small, pink flowers produce seeds that create self-sown plants. Plant in 5–15cm/2–6in of water. Divide clumps in late summer after the flowers fade.*

BUTOMUS UMBELLATUS *(Flowering Rush/Water Gladiolus) is a superb plant, with inverted, umbrella-like heads of rose-pink flowers on stems up to 1.2m/4ft high during mid-summer. The leaves are rush-like. Plant in 7.5–13cm/3–5in of water. To prevent plants becoming congested, divide in spring every two or three years.*

GLYCERIA SPECTABILIS *'Variegatus' (Manna Grass/Variegated Water Grass) is vigorous, up to 90cm/3ft high and with green leaves variegated white and yellow. Plant it in water up to 15cm/6in deep. Its invasive roots will penetrate plastic sheeting. Divide congested plants in spring every two or three years.*

HOUTTUYNIA CORDATA *'Plena' smothers the ground in bluish-green, heart-shaped leaves. Double white flowers appear in early summer. There is also a variegated form, with reddish-green leaves splashed cream and yellow. Plant in water 5–10cm/2–4in deep and lift and divide congested clumps in spring.*

HYPERICUM ELODES *(Marsh Hypericum/Marsh St. John's Wort) grows 23–30cm/9–12in high, spreads up to 45cm/1¹/₂ ft and has rounded, woolly leaves. During mid- to late summer it develops yellow, bowl-shaped flowers. Plant it in water up to 5cm/2in deep, and divide congested clumps in spring.*

MARGINAL PLANTS
Iris – Scirpus

IRIS LAEVIGATA
(Japanese Water Iris) grows 45–60cm/ 1¹/₂–2ft high and displays royal blue flowers during early summer. There are several superb varieties including I. laevigata 'Variegata' *with cream and green leaves. Plant these in water up to 15cm/ 6in deep and lift and divide congested clumps as soon as their flowers fade.*

IRIS PSEUDACORUS
(Yellow Flag Iris) grows 90cm–1.2m/ 3–4ft high and in early summer develops yellow flowers. Plant them in water up to 30cm/ 12in deep. The form 'Variegata' has green leaves striped in yellow. Lift and divide congested clumps as soon as their flowers fade. Plant the variegated form in water 15cm/ 6in deep.

MENYANTHES TRIFOLIATA *(Bog Bean/ Buck Bean/ Marsh Trefoil) grows about 25cm/ 10in high, with three-lobed, broad bean-like green leaves. White, starry flowers appear on stiff, upright stems during early summer. It can be invasive, so always plant it in a container. It is ideal for water up to 7.5cm/ 3in deep. Lift and divide in spring.*

OTHER MARGINAL PLANTS

- Cotula coronopifolia *(Golden Buttons/ Brass Buttons) is an annual with small, button-like yellow flowers throughout summer. Plant it in water up to 10cm/ 4in deep.*
- Lobelia cardinalis *(Cardinal Flower) is a short-lived perennial, about 60cm/ 2ft high and with scarlet flowers during mid- and late summer. Plant it in shallow water.*
- Mentha aquatica *(Water Mint) has a creeping nature, with small, lavender-coloured flowers. Plant it in water up to 7.5cm/ 3in deep.*
- Mimulus ringens *(Lavender Water Musk/ Allegheny Monkey Flower) grows about 75cm/ 2¹/₂ft high and reveals lavender-blue flowers during mid- and late summer. Plant it in water 5–10cm/ 2–4in deep. There are other related water-loving species.*
- Myosotis scorpioides *(Water Forget-me-not and also known as M. palustris) grows 23cm/ 9in high and develops pale blue, yellow-eyed flowers from late spring to mid-summer. It grows in water up to 7.5cm/ 3in deep.*

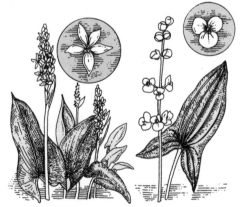

PONTEDERIA CORDATA *(Pickerel Weed) has heart-shaped, glossy green leaves up to about 60cm/ 2ft high and produces spikes of purple-blue flowers on upright stems during mid- and late summer. Each flower has a yellow eye. This marginal plant can be planted in water up to 23cm/ 9in deep. In late spring or early summer, lift and divide congested plants. It is ideal for all ponds, where it softens sharp edges. Its leaves will arch over edging slabs.*

SAGITTARIA SAGITTIFOLIA *(Arrowhead/ Swamp Potato/ Swan Potato) has light green, arrow-shaped leaves. From mid- to the early part of late summer it develops white flowers, clustered on upright, 60cm/ 2ft-high stems. Plant it in water up to 23cm/ 9in deep, and in early and mid-summer lift and divide congested plants. The Japanese Arrowhead (S. japonica leucopetala) is another water-loving and less invasive species.*

SCIRPUS TABERNAEMONTANII *'Zebrinus' (Zebra Rush/ Porcupine Quill Rush) grows up to 90cm/ 3ft high and forms quill-like stems banded in green and white. With age, they tend to become completely green. Plant it in water up to 15cm/ 6in deep and divide congested plants in late spring or early summer, every year. If plants are left to become congested, the stems are not so attractive. Cut down old stems in autumn.*

SACRED LOTUS

This superb water plant grows wild from Southern Asia to Australia. Earlier known as Nelumbium speciosum, *later* Nelumbo speciosum *and now* Nelumbo nucifera, *it has been widely grown in the Orient for its edible rhizomes and seeds, while the flowers are sacred to Buddhists. The leaves, which rise above water and shed all the moisture, encouraged an early Hindu proverb:*
'The good and virtuous man is not enslaved by passion nor polluted by vice; for though he may be immersed in the waters of temptation, yet like a lotus leaf he will arise uninjured by them.'

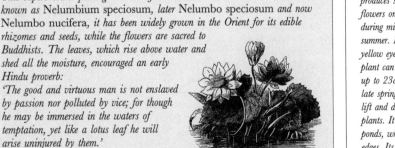

BOG-GARDEN PLANTS

Astilbe - Lythrum

LIKE marginal plants (pages 135 to 136), bog plants can be used to create interest around a pond. However, unlike marginal plants, bog plants are planted outside the pool, in soil that is continually moist, but not waterlogged and airless.

VARIOUS NAMES

Bog plants are also known as waterside plants, moisture-loving plants and poolside plants, and need soil that is always moist, not just when it rains. Although many plants survive in continually moist soil, not all are truly bog plants. Those that are amenable to life in wet soil, but that do equally well in damp soil in garden borders, are not true bog plants.

Boggy areas can be made by burying a flexible liner and filling it with moisture-retentive soil (see page 124).

These plants have their roots permanently in moist soil, but their stems, leaves and flowers are totally above the surface. There are many suitable plants, some low and ideal for fusing the pond with the edge of a bog garden. Others are tall and dominant and best positioned at the extreme edge of the area. Do not attempt to plant the area with plants that are too large, as the pond will then cease to be the dominant feature. The Prickly Rhubarb *(Gunnera manicata)*, for example, needs careful positioning if it is not to appear oppressive.

HOSTA FORTUNEI *'Albopicta' (Plantain Lily) grows about 45cm/1¹/₂ft high, with pale green leaves broadly variegated in light yellow. There are many other low-growing hostas with variegated leaves. Grow in full sun or light shade. Lift and divide congested plants in early spring.*

IRIS SIBIRICA *(Siberian Iris) grows 60–90cm/2–3ft high and develops blue flowers during early summer. There are several varieties. The mid-green, slender, sword-like leaves die down in autumn. It thrives in moist soil. Lift and divide congested clumps every four or five years in autumn, or during spring when growth has resumed.*

HEMEROCALLIS *(Day Lily) is superb at the side of a pond, in full sun or light shade. The garden hybrids are best, in colours including yellow, orange, red and pink from early summer to late mid-summer. Plant it in large groups. Cut stems to slightly above the ground after the flowers fade, and divide plants in autumn or spring.*

EUPATORIUM CANNABINUM *(Hemp Agrimony) grows 60cm– 1.2m/2–4ft high and develops slightly rounded heads of small, reddish-purple flowers from mid to late summer. The form 'Plenum', with double, purple-pink flowers, is more widely grown. Divide congested clumps in mid-spring.*

LYSICHITON AMERICANUS *(Skunk Cabbage) develops pointed, oval, grass-green leaves up to 90cm/3ft long and spectacular arum-like, yellow spathes on stems 23–45cm/ 9–18in high during spring and early summer. It thrives in moist soil. Raise new plants from seeds. L. camtschatcensis has pure white spathes.*

ASTILBE x ARENDSII *(Perennial Spiraea) grows 60–90cm/2–3ft high and develops lax spires of red, pink or white flowers amid deep green, fern-like leaves from early summer to late mid-summer. It thrives in moist soil and full sun or light shade. Divide large and congested plants in mid- to late spring.*

GUNNERA MANICATA *(Prickly Rhubarb/Giant Rhubarb) grows up to 3m/10ft high and is famed for its large, dark green, rhubarb-like leaves. It is only suitable for the largest garden, perhaps as a focal point towards the back of an informal pond. Remove crowns from the mother plant and replant in late spring.*

LYSIMACHIA CLETHROIDES *(Chinese Loosestrife/Gooseneck Loosestrife) grows 75– 90cm/2¹/₂–3ft high and reveals arching spires of star-shaped, small, white flowers from mid to late summer. It is ideal in moist soil and full sun or light shade. Divide large, congested clumps in autumn or early spring.*

LYTHRUM SALICARIA *(Purple Loosestrife/Spiked Loosestrife) grows 1.2– 1.5m/4–5ft high and develops long spires of small, reddish-purple flowers throughout summer. Varieties include 'The Beacon' (rose-crimson), 'Robert' (rose-red) and 'Lady Sackville' (rose-pink). Divide congested plants in autumn.*

BOG-GARDEN PLANTS
❖
Onoclea–Trollius

MOISTURE-LOVING FERNS

Many ferns grow happily in almost barren soil on the sides of mountains, while others cling to life in natural stone walls. However, there are several that grow well in moist soils.

The Sensitive Fern (Onoclea sensibilis) and the Royal Fern (Osmunda regalis) are featured below, but the Ostrich Feather Fern (Matteuccia struthiopteris) is also ideal for waterside planting or in bog gardens. It is also known as

the Shuttlecock Fern, and this aptly describes the elegant, arching fronds. It spreads by means of underground rhizomes and after a few years forms a large, imposing clump.

The Hart's-tongue Fern (Phyllitis scolopendrium) can also be grown in moist soil and is especially suited to shaded positions. There are several forms, some with attractively crinkled edges to the leaves.

Onoclea sensibilis

Osmunda regalis

FURTHER BOG-GARDEN PLANTS

• Aruncus dioicus *(Goat's Beard)*, also known as A. sylvestris, grows about 1.5m/5ft high and develops lax plumes of creamy white flowers in early and into mid-summer.
• Filipendula ulmaria *(Meadowsweet/ Queen of the Meadow)* grows about 75cm/ 2¹/₂ft high, with fragrant, creamy white flowers from early to the latter part of mid-summer. However, it is best grown in the form 'Aurea', which is smaller, with golden green leaves.
• Schizostylis coccinea *(Crimson Flag)* grows about 75cm/2¹/₂ft high and develops star-shaped, bright scarlet flowers during late summer and autumn – and often later. The variety 'Major' has deep red flowers and those of 'Mrs Hegarty' are clear pink.
• Zantedeschia aethiopica *(Arum Lily/Trumpet Lily/Calla Lily)* is well known for its large, white, somewhat trumpet-like flowers. It is best seen in bold clumps.

POLYGONUM BISTORTA *(Knotweed/Snakeweed/ Bistort)* is invasive and grows up to 90cm/3ft high. The form 'Superbum' has long spires of pink flowers, mainly in early summer although a further flush sometimes appears later. Divide congested plants in autumn or spring.

ONOCLEA SENSIBILIS *(Sensitive Fern)* is a hardy, vigorously spreading fern that grows up to 60cm/2ft high and develops pale green fronds. At the first frost in autumn, the fronds turn brown, but new ones appear again in spring, first coloured pink, then green. Lift and divide large and congested plants in spring.

OSMUNDA REGALIS *(Royal Fern/Flowering Fern)* is majestic; 1.2–1.8m/4–6ft high and with pea-green fronds. In autumn, these are cut down and fresh ones appear in spring. Protect the crowns with the old leaves during winter. In spring, lift and divide congested plants into large pieces, each with several crowns.

PELTIPHYLLUM PELTATUM *(Umbrella Plant)* grows 90cm–1.2m/ 3–4ft high; in spring it develops tall, upright stems that bear umbrella-like heads of pink flowers. Then, the very dominant, large-lobed leaves appear, initially green but slowly changing to bronze in autumn. Divide the roots in spring.

PRIMULA DENTICULATA *(Drumstick Primula)* grows 30cm/12in high; although a perennial, it is usually grown as an annual or biennial and creates deep purple flowers in spring and early summer. It looks good when planted in large drifts.

There is also a white-flowered form. Raise fresh plants from seeds.

RODGERSIA PINNATA is a hardy herbaceous perennial, 90cm–1.2m/ 3–4ft high with large, deep green, sometimes bronzed, leaves throughout summer. Choose a place in full sun and slightly sheltered from wind, and ensure that the soil does not become dry during summer. Divide congested plants in spring.

TROLLIUS x HYBRIDUS *(Globe Flower)*, an herbaceous plant, grows 45–60cm/1¹/₂–2ft high and during early summer reveals masses of large, buttercup-like flowers amid deeply divided mid-green leaves. Varieties include flowers in pale yellow, fiery-orange and yellow. Divide plants in autumn or spring.

REPAIRS TO PONDS

EAKING ponds are a disaster for fish and plants, as well as creating an unplanned boggy area around the pool. Throughout summer there is usually a normal water loss from ponds: when waterfall pumps start up they cause a sudden but temporary drop in the water's surface. Also, marginal plants and waterlilies transpire masses of water on a hot day, in addition to normal evaporation from the pond's surface.

If the loss of water occurs suddenly through a crack or tear, ensure the fish and other pond life are put in large containers, and the plants in buckets of water. If the damage to the pond is serious, consider putting a liner inside it. This is often the surest way to stop water leaking, although repairs are possible (see below).

REPAIRS TO RIGID SHELLS

Good quality materials are much less likely to become damaged than low-cost economy ones.
• Vacuum-formed polythene types are especially likely to be stressed and twisted. Also, ultra-violet rays degrade thin materials.
• Shells are stressed if not positioned on a firm bed of soft sand. Ensure the edges are well supported with compacted soil or soft sand.
• Dropping a shell causes cracks. Repair kits are readily available.
• Do not allow children to walk inside the shells when they are empty, and before being formed into a pond, as they will crack.

CRACKS IN CONCRETE: *These occur through old age, subsidence, inquisitive tree roots, frost or incorrect construction. If the surface is being worn away, rub with a wire brush to remove loose material, then use several coats of a sealant. For cracks, use a chisel to ensure the gap is wider an inch or so below the water surface than level with it. This ensures that waterproof mastic remains in the crack. For large and extensive cracks, it is necessary to use mortar.*

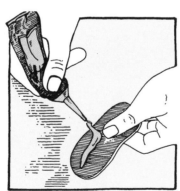

TEARS IN FLEXIBLE LINERS: *Inferior quality liners have a limited life-span: some last only a few years, whereas others have a life of twenty or more seasons. Damage occurs because the liner was laid on stony ground, through roots of invasive trees or marginal plants, or by standing in the pool while wearing spiky shoes. Proprietary repair kits are available – follow the instructions carefully, and do not economize on the size of the patch.*

PROBLEMS WITH WATER

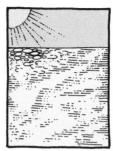  

GREEN *water is usually caused by excessive amounts of algae; fish love this soup, but it is unsightly. Excessive sunlight, insufficient surface space and a lack of submerged plants create the problem. Chemical controls are possible.*

THE *water's surface sometimes becomes polluted. Place a sheet of newspaper on it, then lift off. Surface pollutants stick to it. Pollution from dead leaves and drowned and decayed animals means that draining is essential.*

DIRTY *water is often caused by scavenging fish stirring up sediment or causing compost to seep from containers. Therefore, replant the containers, using hessian liners. Put gravel on top. Remove existing sediment with a pool vacuum.*

 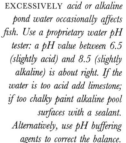 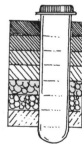

SOME *water weeds grow rapidly during hot summers and cause congestion, impeding fish and suffocating other plants. Whatever the type, cut them back carefully and slowly so that fish and their fry have time to escape the area. The weeds can be placed on a compost heap. Some marginal plants are also invasive, and need to be thinned out during summer. But take care not to spoil their shape.*

EXCESSIVELY *acid or alkaline pond water occasionally affects fish. Use a proprietary water pH tester: a pH value between 6.5 (slightly acid) and 8.5 (slightly alkaline) is about right. If the water is too acid add limestone; if too chalky paint alkaline pool surfaces with a sealant. Alternatively, use pH buffering agents to correct the balance.*

CLEANING OUT PONDS

To clean a pond, choose a warm day in early summer. First clear a path to the pool, if necessary removing a few marginal plants. Place them in buckets or fabricated ponds in a shaded position. Also, remove fish and other pond life to shaded holding pools. Pump out the water (see page 128), continually checking for fish. Scrub the pond's sides with clean water, remove the water and refill with tap water (see page 128). Replace plants and slowly reintroduce the fish (see page 128).

PROBLEMS WITH FISH

AFTER a glimpse of the problems with fish, illustrated here, it may be thought that fish are continually ill. In reality, most fish are never infected or attacked. Most problems are a result of inadequate feeding, dirty conditions and damage through bad handling. Buying fish from a reputable stockist prevents the introduction of many diseases, and they should be introduced carefully into a pond so that they are not unduly stressed (see page 129). Ensure that chemical sprays do not contaminate the pond, and that seeds from poisonous plants cannot fall in. Additionally, in winter, do not knock the ice: install a water heater so that part of the surface remains free of ice (see page 128).

FUNGUS *is a common problem; a growth looking like cotton wool develops on fish. Weak, underfed or stressed fish are especially likely to be infected. Avoid rapid temperature changes and immediately use a proprietary fungicide.*

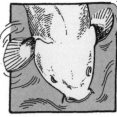

GILL FLUKE *is a microscopic worm that becomes fixed to gills and is first noticed when a fish moves violently and constantly. Proprietary remedies are available and it is invariably necessary to treat all of the fish in the same pond.*

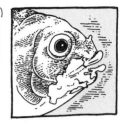

MOUTH FUNGUS *is seen as white growths on the jaws. It soon spreads and causes decay. Use a proprietary treatment immediately the fungus is seen. Pollution of the water contributes to the problem, and undernourished fish are vulnerable.*

ANCHOR WORMS *cause distress to fish, creating small lumps into which the head of the 12mm/¹/₂in-long worm is anchored. The worm's body hangs loose, causing the fish to swim in circles. Proprietary treatments are widely available.*

BIRDS *are a constant pest, especially if gulls or kingfishers are present. Herons even wade into ponds to take fish. Either construct a wire-netting cover or form a 45cm/1¹/₂ft-high wire fence to prevent them walking directly into the pond.*

DROPSY *is not common, but is very serious. Scales project from a bloated body. Also, the fish's eyes protrude. The kindest action is to kill the fish humanely. Remove it and hold it firmly, then sharply knock the back of its head several times.*

PROTOZOAN SKIN PARASITE *is microscopic. It is only discernable when fish rub themselves against the sides and have a slimey, bluish-grey covering on their bodies. Proprietary treatments are available, but seriously infected fish should be humanely killed.*

ULCERS *are caused by bacteria which gain entry through damaged scales, spreading and causing fish distress. Humanely kill badly infected fish, but if noticed early, treat the others with a proprietary remedy. For large fish, consult a veterinary surgeon as soon as possible.*

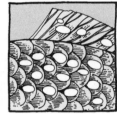

WHITE SPOT *is first noticed when fish zig-zag around the pond in a frenzy. They become peppered with white spots. It is essential to use a proprietary cure immediately. But it is kinder to humanely kill badly infected fish than to allow them to suffer.*

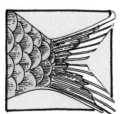

FIN ROT *is a bacterial disease that causes tissue between the two outer parts of the tail to decay. If neglected, fish die. Fish with long tails are likely to become infected. There are proprietary cures – but treat the fish early to prevent extensive damage.*

FISH LEECH *are about 2.5cm/1in long and attach themselves to the sides of fish, causing an injury that encourages the presence of diseases. Proprietary cures are available. Fortunately, it is not a common problem in garden ponds.*

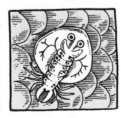

FISH LOUSE, *about 6mm/¹/₄in wide, has a sucker-like disc to attach itself to fish. The first sign is when a fish swims in circles and rubs itself against the pond. Initially, dab with paraffin to remove, then use an antiseptic.*

WATER PESTS

Many agile insects are predators in ponds, eating eggs and fry and even wrestling with small fish. There is little that can be done to control them, especially in large and wildlife ponds.

However, if these desperadoes of the pond world are seen,

Water Boatman

remove them. The water boatman, great diving beetle and dragonfly larvae are the main problems, but so is the water scorpion, which sucks dry the body of its victim.

Dragonfly Larva

Great Diving Beetle

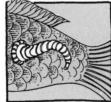

PROBLEMS WITH PLANTS

PREVENTING and controlling pests and diseases of water plants by the use of chemicals is not possible, as fish and other pond life would soon be killed. Therefore, vigilance is necessary to remove affected leaves and to use clean water to spray them, forcing insects into the water where fish can eat them. When washing leaves, do not use strong jets that would damage unaffected leaves. And take care not to spray flowers. Alternatively, weigh down leaves so that insects and their larvae are washed off.

WATERLILY LEAVES

Various insects and diseases (in addition to Waterlily Crown Rot described opposite) decimate waterlily leaves. Here are a few of them:

BROWN CHINA MARK MOTHS *lay eggs on leaves of waterlilies and other aquatic plants. They hatch and the cream-coloured larvae, about 2.5cm/1in long, chew oval to round areas out of leaves to make protective cases for themselves. Remove eaten leaves, together with the leaf cases. If left, they soon start to rot.*

LEAF-MINING MIDGES *eat narrow, serpentine lines all over lily pads, eventually skeletonizing them. Pull up and destroy leaves seriously affected. The fish in well-stocked ponds will soon eat the larvae.*

WATERLILY APHIDS *quickly spoil the appearance of waterlily pads. They suck sap from stems and leaves that are above the surface, as well as from flowers. Additionally, the aphids excrete honeydew on which a black mould grows. As soon as aphids are seen, wash them off plants by using a spray of clean water. The fish will then eat these common pests.*

WATERLILY BEETLES *are important pests: both the adult beetle and larvae chew holes in pads. Spraying with chemicals is not advisable; submerging them for a day washes them off. Also, spraying with clean water helps in their eradication. In autumn, cut down plants to reduce the beetles' chance of surviving during winter.*

WATERLILY LEAF SPOT *is caused by a fungus that first forms red patches near to the edges of pads, which later turn black. Damp, warm weather often initiates an infection. Eventually, these areas decay and form holes. Remove leaves as soon as the problem is seen.*

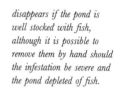

BLOODWORMS, *about 2.5cm/1in long, are the larvae of midges. They create unsightly raised areas on a pond's base, especially if it is liberally coated in silt. Occasionally, they chew roots of water plants such as lilies, but are never an intolerable nuisance as the larvae are invariably eaten by fish. The midge is a non-biting type and of no danger to humans.*

CADDIS FLIES *can be a problem, but if fish are present the larvae are soon eaten. The caddis flies visit ponds during evenings, laying eggs in or near the water. They hatch and the larvae, when making homes, first use pieces of dead plants, shells and sand. Sometimes, they tear away roots, leaves and flower buds of water plants. Usually, the problem* disappears if the pond is well stocked with fish, although it is possible to remove them by hand should the infestation be severe and the pond depleted of fish.

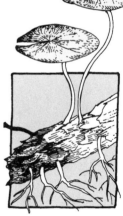

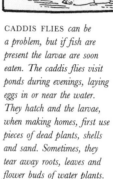

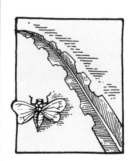

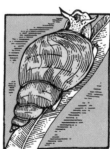

IRIS SAWFLY LARVAE, *about 18mm/³/4in long and dull, bluish-grey, chew the leaves of certain irises, especially the Japanese Water Iris (I. laevigata) and Yellow Flag Iris (I. pseudacorus). They tear leaves, leaving saw-like edges. Cut off seriously damaged leaves and pick off and destroy the grubs. Early control is essential to prevent further infestations.*

SNAILS *such as the Great Pond Snail, with a somewhat corkscrew shell, can wreak havoc with waterlilies and marginal plants. Usually their diet is dead leaves and stems, but if present in vast numbers, by necessity they resort to live plants. Pick them off, mainly from the undersides of leaves. Do not use chemical sprays or slug pellets in ponds, as they will cause pollution.*

WATERLILY CROWN ROT *is a fungus that causes crowns of waterlilies to rot, turn black and to develop appalling smells. The base decays, causing leaves to yellow and become detached from the crown. Once it is present, infected plants are best removed. Check all plants and watch for symptoms. Buy plants from reputable water-plant nurseries and inspect them before planting.*

WINDOWBOXES AND TROUGHS

Windowboxes and troughs packed with bright flowers traditionally create beacons of colour during summer. However, they can form attractive displays all year round, filled with colourful miniature conifers and dwarf and berried shrubs in winter, and bulbs and biennial plants in spring.

This chapter reveals how to use these plants to create attractive windowboxes throughout the year.

Positioning and securing windowboxes beneath windows, together with the philosophy of using them seasonally and selecting the right plants, are detailed and illustrated here, as are the important questions of choosing the right plants to suit variously coloured walls – such as white, grey, red or dark – and creating displays that drench the air under windows in rich scents.

Selecting suitable composts, setting plants in windowboxes or troughs, watering and keeping them tidy is also illustrated and described within this chapter. Raising half-hardy annuals is featured in sowing seeds in greenhouses on page 272, and sowing biennials is covered on page 274.

DESIGN FACTORS

A VARIETY of materials is used to construct windowboxes and troughs. Although some materials can be used for both purposes, others are best restricted to one. Whatever the materials, do not use windowboxes or troughs larger than 90cm/3ft long (and preferably only 75cm/2½ft) as longer boxes may break when full. On a wide window sill it is better to use two short windowboxes, as there is then less chance of breakages if they are moved when full of soil and plants.

RANGE OF MATERIALS

• <u>Wood</u> is ideal and windowboxes formed of it can be tailored to suit any width of window sill. Although soil is often put directly in it, it is better to place a plastic or galvanized metal trough inside. This both protects the wood from water and enables displays to be changed more easily from one season to another. It also helps to keep the compost cool in summer.

• <u>Plastic</u> creates durable windowboxes and troughs if thick and rigid. Although frequently used on its own, plastic is better employed as an inner box for wooden windowboxes.

• <u>Terracotta</u> has a texture and colour that harmonizes with all plants. Either position on strong sills, or use as troughs on patios or the tops of low walls.

• <u>Reconstituted stone</u> creates superb troughs for patios, but is too heavy for use in windowboxes except on large, concrete sills.

• <u>Concrete troughs</u> are another possibility, but can only be used on patios, as when large they are extremely heavy.

• <u>Glass fibre</u> is a popular, long-lived material, ideal in troughs and windowboxes.

• <u>Recycled cellulose</u> fibre troughs, although not aesthetically pleasing to all eyes, are ideal as low-cost, short-lived windowboxes or as troughs for putting at the edges of flat roofs to create cascading colour in summer.

———

TERRACOTTA *creates attractive, firmly based windowboxes and troughs. They are heavy, especially when filled with compost, and therefore when used as windowboxes are best positioned on stone or concrete sills, rather than being held on brackets.*

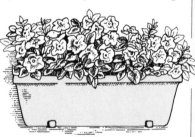

RIGID, *plastic troughs are sometimes used on their own as windowboxes. Although functional and relatively inexpensive, they do not look as attractive as those with inner and outer boxes.*

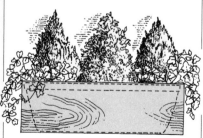

ATTRACTIVE *outer, wooden containers into which plastic inner troughs can be placed are the best way to display and grow plants in windowboxes. Seasonal displays can then be changed quickly.*

DOUBLE-LEVEL WINDOWBOXES

Extra colour is easily created by securing one windowbox above another. As well as positioning them under windows, attractive features can be created against long, bland walls. Paint the windowbox to contrast with the wall's colour, and select plants that harmonize with the box and surroundings.

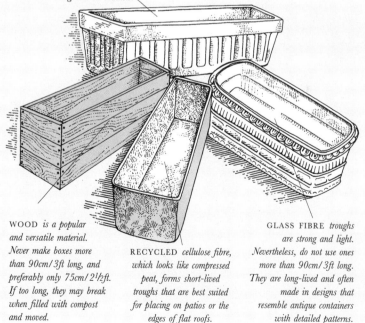

WOOD *is a popular and versatile material. Never make boxes more than 90cm/3ft long, and preferably only 75cm/2½ft. If too long, they may break when filled with compost and moved.*

RECYCLED *cellulose fibre, which looks like compressed peat, forms short-lived troughs that are best suited for placing on patios or the edges of flat roofs.*

GLASS FIBRE *troughs are strong and light. Nevertheless, do not use ones more than 90cm/3ft long. They are long-lived and often made in designs that resemble antique containers with detailed patterns.*

POSITIONING AND SECURING WINDOWBOXES

WINDOWBOXES are obviously associated with windows. But their trough-like design makes them ideal for displaying in other places too. Away from windows they can be used to brighten many places, which are described on page 145. When used to decorate windows, however, it is the type of window that influences their positions.

TYPES OF WINDOW

• Sash windows are formed of two areas of glass which can be raised and lowered. This arrangement leaves the sill area uncluttered and with space for windowboxes. Wooden windowboxes with inner plastic troughs are ideal. Alternatively, use terracotta types if the ledge is extremely strong and made of stone or concrete.

Rather than placing windowboxes directly on the sill, position them on 12–18mm/$^{1}/_{2}$–$^{3}/_{4}$in-square, 15–20cm/6–8in-long, pieces of wood. This ensures that air circulates under the container's base and is especially important when the box or sill is made of wood. Shallow drip-trays also can be used.

Usually, these boxes when filled with compost are quite steady, but in winter, if planted with conifers, they could be badly buffeted by wind. Therefore, secure the windowbox to the wooden framework of the window.

• Casement windows are those hinged at their outer edges and therefore when opened swing out over the sill. This prevents windowboxes being placed on the sill and makes it essential to position them on brackets secured 15–20cm/6–8in below the sill's edge. This distance is influenced by the heights of the plants.

Strong brackets and firm wall fixings are essential (see opposite). Ensure that the brackets have lips at their edges to prevent boxes falling off. This is especially important in windy positions

SASH *windows create ideal homes for window-boxes, enabling plants to be admired from both outside and within. This is especially important when scented plants are used.*

CASEMENT *windows hinge outwards. Therefore, windowboxes must be secured well below the sill, so that flowers and foliage are not damaged when the windows are opened.*

POSITIONING *window-boxes in narrow spaces between symmetrical windows produces an unusual feature. But ensure that the box can be easily watered and looked after.*

• Plastic-framed windows have many designs: some are like casements, while others hinge in a cantilever fashion and open out in a wide arch over the sill. Whatever the type, it usually means that the windowbox has to be supported on brackets slightly below the sill.

SECURING THE BRACKETS

Windowboxes secured to walls are usually supported by two brackets screwed into the brickwork and held by masonry fixings. Position the brackets 15–20cm/6–8in (about one-fifth of the box's length) in from each end.

To fix the brackets, measure 15–20cm/6–8in down from the sill, plus the depth of the box. Position one bracket vertically and mark the wall. Use a masonry drill to form holes, then insert wall fixings and use galvanized screws to hold the bracket to the wall. Then, approximately position the other bracket and place a piece of wood across them, with a spirit-level on top. When they are level, mark the wall, drill and plug it and screw the bracket into place.

PROPRIETARY *brackets to secure windowboxes are readily available Some brackets protrude underneath, others fit behind.*

HOME-MADE *brackets are easily constructed. Rivet the metal strips together and brace the bracket with a piece of metal at about 45 degrees.*

PARLOUR GARDENING

In Victorian times, indoor gardening became known as parlour gardening. People who were unable to garden outdoors were encouraged to grow potted plants in troughs.

The design and decorations on these troughs varied according to the rooms in which they were to be placed. Those used in parlours frequently had a rustic appearance, while those for dining rooms had ornate designs.

A plant box for a parlour

For use in a dining room

WINDOWBOXES AS TROUGHS

❖

TROUGHS are more versatile than windowboxes and can be displayed in many places. Some of these uses are illustrated here and include the bases of balconies, and on the tops and sides of walls. But there are others to consider.

RANGE OF USES

• <u>Patio edges</u> are soon brightened during summer by planting troughs with bright-faced flowers and positioning them either on low balustrades or directly on a patio's surface. If placing on low walls, use a combination of short, bushy plants and trailing types, so that the wall becomes clothed in colour. However, if the troughs are placed directly on the ground use upright plants.

Placing ground-based troughs on 2.5cm/1in-square strips of wood (or bricks) helps to reduce the risk of slugs and snails attacking plants during warm summer evenings and nights. Soft plants are soon devastated by slugs and snails, sometimes overnight.

WIND FACTOR

Balconies and the tops of walls are often buffeted by winds, so take care not to use too many tall plants. Unless the trough is secured to a wall, it is best just to create a display of frost-tender bedding plants throughout summer. Lysimachia nummularia 'Aurea', the yellow-leaved form of the trailing, herbaceous perennial Creeping Jenny, is ideal for softening the edges of balconies and troughs on walls.

• <u>Flat roofs</u> on garages and home extensions can be brightened in summer, but avoid blocking gutters. Place troughs planted with trailing plants along the edges. There are many trailing summer-flowering bedding plants to choose from, including forms of lobelia, petunias and impatiens. Place each trough on four or five 2.5cm/1in-square pieces of wood, and ensure the compost is kept

moist. During hot summer days, it may be necessary to water several times. Putting moisture-retentive materials such as Perlite and Vermiculite in the compost helps it to retain moisture.

Colour harmonize these plants with their backgrounds (see pages 148 to 149). Putting spring and winter displays in these positions is not practical, as they will be blown about and the compost becomes too wet.

• <u>Summer-houses</u> need brightening in summer. Windowboxes secured under windows are attractive, but also place troughs on verandahs or surrounding areas. Either put drip-trays under the troughs, or place them on bricks, to prevent wood underneath from rotting rapidly.

• <u>Edges of ponds</u> can be brightened by positioning troughs of bushy and trailing summer-flowering plants around them. Place these on 2.5cm/1in-thick pieces of wood: this enables water to pass underneath and reduces the risk of slugs and snails feasting on the plants. Do not completely encircle a pond in this way, or it may then look like a well! However, if the patio edge around a pond is at an uneven height above the water, trailing plants may help to camouflage this. Also, if the liner is tatty or the pond leaks around its edges and therefore exposes large amounts of lining material, the plants help to cloak it.

The edges of raised ponds can also be brightened with troughs of plants, but do not encircle them completely. Use trailing plants

TROUGHS *supported on bricks or on two upright logs inserted into the ground create eye-catching features, in winter as well as throughout summer. In late spring and summer, use slug and snail baits to protect the plants.*

———

that camouflage the trough's sides and merge with the pond's edges. Avoid having stems and flowers trailing into the pond, as they soon decay and contaminate the water. And remove troughs in late summer, before the flowers start to fall off in large numbers.

If your pond is plagued with cats sitting on the edges and looking for fish, these troughs help to make it more difficult for them, although not impossible.

CREEPING JENNY

For more than a hundred years, Creeping Jenny (Lysimachia nummularia) has been widely recommended for growing in pots and for positioning where it can trail. Also known as Creeping Charlie, Moneywort, Herb Twopence, Meadow Runagates and Twopenny Grass, it was widely used to heal wounds. Fresh leaves were bruised, then applied to cuts and abrasions. It was said that hurt or wounded serpents would seek out the plant, which was why it was also sometimes called Serpentaria.

Creeping Jenny (Lysimachia nummularia)

POSITION *troughs at the edges of balconies, so that trailing plants can cascade through the railings. Place drip-trays under the troughs to prevent water splashing on walls or people below.*

TROUGHS *are ideal for brightening the tops of walls, especially those up to about 75cm/2½ft high. With high walls there is a risk of troughs falling off and harming people.*

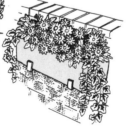

USE *brackets – similar to those employed to secure windowboxes under windows – to hold troughs against walls. These are ideal for brightening high walls. Use bushy and trailing plants.*

SEASONAL PHILOSOPHY

THE EASIEST way to create a display in a windowbox is just to plant it in spring with a variety of summer-flowering plants. However, apart from being unadventurous, this does not make the best use of a windowbox. Instead, have three inner plastic troughs and rotate them within the same outer windowbox.

• Spring displays: These are planted in late summer or early autumn with bulbs and spring-flowering plants such as wall-flowers and placed in a cool, out-of-the-way, rain-protected position until the bulbs start to flower in spring. Then, the winter display is removed from the outer window-box and replaced with the spring-flowering one.

As well as spring-flowering bulbs and biennial plants (which are sown in seed-beds outdoors in early summer, grown and planted into containers in autumn), minia-ture conifers and variegated small-leaved ivies can be used to create extra colour. Bulbs to choose include crocuses, Grape Hyacinths (*Muscari armeniacum*), hyacinths and short-stemmed tulips.

HYACINTH MANIA

In 1597 there were only four varieties of what came to be called the Dutch or Common Hyacinth (Hyacinthus orientalis). By 1725 this had increased to more than 2000, but by 1911 had shrunk to no more than 300.

Hyacinths were widely grown in Britain in the 1630s, but it was Holland that led their development with the raising of double-flowered forms. Their introduction was quite by chance: the Dutch bulb grower Pieter Voerhelm had for many years discarded double forms, but when illness interrupted his vigilance one of them remained which later gained his attention.

*Double
Hyacinth*

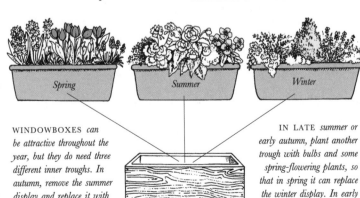

Spring   *Summer*   *Winter*

WINDOWBOXES *can be attractive throughout the year, but they do need three different inner troughs. In autumn, remove the summer display and replace it with a trough planted with a winter display.*

Outer windowbox

IN LATE *summer or early autumn, plant another trough with bulbs and some spring-flowering plants, so that in spring it can replace the winter display. In early summer, exchange the spring display for a summer one.*

LONDON'S FLOWER SELLERS

From the beginning of the Georgian period, in 1714, more interest was given to decorative gardening, including plants for homes as well as gardens. Town gardening emerged as a leisure activity and many enterprising gardeners started to travel around with barrows or horse-drawn carts offering plants growing in clay pots for sale. These included small conifers and shrubs. Additionally, artificial flowers made of silk, paper and wire were sold by specialists.

• Summer displays: These are mainly formed of frost-tender summer-bedding plants. Gera-niums, fuchsias and tuberous-root-ed begonias are among other plants that are used. Because these plants are susceptible to low tem-peratures, the trough cannot be planted until the risk of frost has passed. However, if a greenhouse, sunroom or conservatory is avail-able, these plants can be planted in the inner plastic trough slightly earlier and put into the window-box later, when all risk of frost has passed.

After removing the inner trough which held the spring display, dis-card the biennial plants but leave the bulbs in the trough until their leaves die down, then move them to borders, around shrubs. Some gardeners leave them in the inner trough for the following season, but to ensure a good display, always plant new bulbs.

• Winter displays: These are placed into the outer windowbox in autumn, after the summer display has finished. Plants such as miniature conifers, winter-flowering heathers and small-leaved variegated ivies are widely used in these displays.

In late winter or early spring, the winter display is removed and replaced with a spring one.

The box holding the winter dis-play is put in a cool, lightly-shad-ed position, where it can remain throughout summer. Keep the compost moist.

HERBS NEAR KITCHEN DOORS

Many low-growing and bushy herbs are ideal for windowboxes and troughs, especially as they can then be positioned near kitchen doors. Although individual herbs can be planted directly into a trough or window-box, it is better to leave them in separate pots. Chives, Thyme, Marjoram, Tarragon, Welsh Onions, Parsley and Mint are all possibilities for growing in this way.

CHOOSING THE RIGHT PLANTS

PART from selecting plants which form attractive combinations, it is essential that when bought they are sturdy, strong and healthy. It is false economy to buy cheap, inferior plants as they never recover to produce attractive displays. This is especially important with plants intended for planting in windowboxes and troughs – as well as tubs, pots, urns and hanging baskets – as the display is concentrated and a few inferior plants can spoil the design for several months.

SELECTING PLANTS

Apart from buying healthy, floriferous and vigorous plants (see opposite), there are a few general factors to consider.

• Avoid tall plants, especially when intended for winter displays. Buffeting autumn and winter winds soon devastate displays with tall conifers, especially in windowboxes secured to first-floor window sills. (However, tall plants can be used on wind-protected patios.)

MANY summer-flowering half-hardy bedding plants are sold in 'strips', each formed of several young plants. If more are needed, a complete seedtray of them can be bought. These plants are raised from seeds sown in late winter or early spring, and cannot be planted outside until all risk of frost has passed.

• To create the 'body' of the display, use compact plants, but avoid creating a flat, uninteresting surface. Some displays have randomly varying height, while others either peak in the middle or, if in a trough positioned with one of its ends towards a corner, have a slightly triangular outline. Most displays, however, have an irregular 'natural' shape.

SMALL conifers are usually bought in 6–7.5cm/ 2¹/₂–3in-wide pots. Check that their roots are not constricted through neglect. Also, ensure the compost is moist and the plants do not have areas bare of foliage.

EARLY summer-flowering pot plants, such as Cinerarias (Senecio cruentus), are sold in 7.5–13cm/3–5in-wide pots. Complete with their pots they are placed in windowboxes to create colour early in the year.

VARIEGATED ivies are also sold in small pots. Usually, there are three plants growing in the same pot, as this creates a bushy and more saleable plant more quickly than when only one plant is used.

DO NOT *buy inferior plants as they never recover and may leave bare gaps in windowboxes and troughs, spoiling the overall display. Do not buy thin, spindly plants, an indication that they have been grown too close together and neglected. Neither buy small plants in relatively large pots, nor large plants in small pots.*

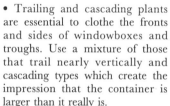

Small plants in large pots may not be properly rooted and established.

Do not buy thin, spindly plants.

WHEN *buying flowering plants in pots for placing in windowboxes to create temporary colour, avoid those that are in full bloom when bought. Such plants will not create a long display. Instead, buy those with masses of flower buds that are just showing colour. Check that the flower buds are evenly arranged around the plant, and not just on one of its sides.*

• Trailing and cascading plants are essential to clothe the fronts and sides of windowboxes and troughs. Use a mixture of those that trail nearly vertically and cascading types which create the impression that the container is larger than it really is.

• Use foliage plants that trail and cascade in addition to flowering types, as they tend to create a sense of permanency.

• Variegated trailing plants, such as small-leaved ivies and the Variegated Ground Ivy (*Glechoma hederacea* 'Variegata'), create colour in winter, spring and summer arrangements. Small-leaved ivies used indoors can be moved outdoors into containers, but do this in spring so that they have the entire summer in which to become accustomed to the somewhat cooler conditions. They are then better able to survive winters outdoors than if put directly outside in autumn.

CHECK *all plants to ensure they are free from pests and diseases. Small plants are easily checked, but with large ones look both above and under their leaves. Also, check around soft buds and shoot tips. Pests such as greenfly (aphids) breed prolifically if not noticed.*

Inspect the undersides of leaves, as well as their tops.

RED AND GREY BACKGROUNDS

CHOOSE plants to harmonize or contrast with their backgrounds. It takes only a few moments to plan, and is time well spent. Apart from getting the best from plants, it creates a more unified and attractive display.

The range of background colours can be put into four general groups: red-brick and grey backgrounds are discussed here, while white and dark backgrounds are covered on page 149.

RED-BRICK BACKGROUNDS

These form dominant backgrounds that can overwhelm plants unless used in large clusters. Plants with white, soft blue, silver and lemon flowers form attractive contrasts. Silver-leaved plants are also highlighted by red walls. There are many combinations of plants to suit these positions.

• Spring displays: For sunny positions use the following combinations: light blue Forget-me-nots (*Myosotis*) and white hyacinths; bronze and cream Wallflowers

RED-BRICK *backgrounds highlight summer displays of white Marguerites* (Chrysanthemum frutescens), *soft blue flowers (stocks and trailing lobelia), and silver foliage (Senecio bicolor/S. maritima). Paint the windowbox white.*

(*Cheiranthus cheiri*) and pink and white Daisies (*Bellis perennis*); Grape Hyacinths (*Muscari armeniacum*) and white tulips; variegated small-leaved ivies (*Hedera helix*), Grape Hyacinths and white tulips.

In shaded areas, use a combination of variegated, small-leaved ivies and yellow Polyanthus.

• Summer displays: For sunny positions use white Marguerites (*Chrysanthemum frutescens*), soft blue Stocks, (trailing lobelia) and the silver foliage of *Senecio bicolor* (also known as *S. maritima*); or trailing Sweet Alyssum (*Alyssum maritimum/Lobularia maritima*), soft blue stocks and *Senecio bicolor*.

In shaded positions use a combination of light-coloured fuchsias and violas.

GREY STONE BACKGROUNDS

These have a softer and less dominant effect than red-brick walls. Use pink, red, deep blue and deep purple flowers.

MANY *spring-flowering displays are enhanced by red-brick backgrounds, such as white tulips, small-leaved ivies with yellow variegations and the Grape Hyacinth* (Muscari armeniacum).

• Spring displays: For sunny positions use boxes entirely packed with Wallflowers (*Cheiranthus cheiri*); deep blue Forget-me-nots (*Myosotis*) and pink tulips; deep blue Forget-me-nots and pink or blue hyacinths; a complete display of blue hyacinths.

In shaded positions use Polyanthus, either in one colour to suit the background or a mixture.

• Summer displays: For displays in full sun use windowboxes entirely drenched with bushy and trailing pink Petunias; lobelia (*Lobelia erinus*) and scarlet geraniums (pelargoniums); blue-flowered Star of Bethlehem (*Campanula isophylla*) and stocks (*Matthiola incana*); Petunias, Star of Bethlehem (*Campanula isophylla*), pink-flowered Ivy-leaved geraniums and red geraniums (pelargoniums); dark blue Heliotrope (*Heliotropium* x *hybridum*), red Fuchsias and red and yellow varieties of the Basket Begonia (*Begonia* x *tuberhybrida* 'Pendula'). In shaded positions use red or pink Fuchsias, Heliotrope or Cherry Pie (*Heliotropium* x *hybridum*), begonias and Nasturtiums (*Tropaeolum majus*).

GREY-STONE *walls enhance and highlight reds, pinks, deep blues and purple. This summer-flowering display is formed of Petunias, Star of Bethlehem* (Campanula isophylla), *pink-flowered Ivy-leaved Geraniums and red geraniums (pelargoniums).*

COMBINATIONS *of red, blue and yellow create attractive features against grey walls. For example, dark blue Heliotrope* (Heliotropium x hybridum), *red Fuchsias and red and yellow varieties of the Basket Begonia* (Begonia x hybridum 'Pendula').

CHERRY PIE

Few plants have such an appetite-whetting name as Heliotrope. It is said to have gained its common name Cherry Pie through the scent its flowers emit. However, to many people the sweet, scent is more evocative of embroidery and old slippers. It also has a medicinal use when used to counteract 'clergyman's sore throat'.

The evocative nature of several Victorian varieties may have encouraged gardeners to grow them. Who could resist names such as 'Beauty of the Boudoir' and 'Miss Nightingdale'?

When first introduced from Peru, Heliotropes had washy blue flowers, but nowadays they range from lavender to dark purple.

The plant is said to have gained the name Turnsole because the flowers constantly turn to the sun.

WHITE AND DARK BACKGROUNDS

WHITE and dark backgrounds are clearly at opposite ends of the spectrum, but they have one element in common – they are both dominant. They therefore need strongly coloured plants in large clusters to create displays. Colours such as bright yellow and red are ideal for white backgrounds, and yellow and white for dark ones.

WHITE BACKGROUNDS

Many houses, especially those with pebble-dashed surfaces, are painted white, creating clinical backgrounds that especially benefit from bright flowers in windowboxes and troughs. Choose mainly yellow, gold, scarlet, red and dark blue flowers, as well as generous amounts of green foliage. There are many plants from which to choose, for both spring and summer displays. Here are a few combinations to consider.

• Spring displays: For sunny positions choose Forget-me-nots

AURICULAS

During the 1800s, Auriculas (Primula auricula) *were widely recommended for planting in windowboxes and for window gardening. They were introduced into England in the late 1600s and reached the peak of their popularity about 1850 when miners and silk weavers in northern counties took up their cultivation.*

(Myosotis) and golden Wallflowers *(Cheiranthus cheiri)*; Daisies *(Bellis perennis)* and red Wallflowers; blue and red hyacinths and crocuses.
• Summer displays: Golden-faced Marigolds, dark red geraniums (pelargoniums) and yellow Zinnias, complemented by Emerald Fern

DARK *walls create strong contrasts for bright, light colours. To create a semi-formal design in spring and early summer, place three or five Cinerarias in a windowbox (they look better in odd numbers). They are not hardy, so only use them when the risk of frost is low. They are often seen in city windowboxes, where the buildings give warmth and protection.*

(Asparagus densiflorus 'Sprengeri'); trailing, red-flowered nasturtiums *(Tropaeolum)*, Iceland Poppies *(Papaver nudicaule)* and yellow Slipper Flowers *(Calceolaria* x *herbeohybrida)*, together with the Emerald Fern; mixtures of geraniums (pelargoniums), Petunias, Zinnias, calceolarias and bright-faced Marigolds.

DARK BACKGROUNDS

There are probably two types of dark backgrounds, those which are naturally dingy and others that have been planned that way to create a distinctive feature, and could be called 'designer darkness'. Dramatically light colours are needed to brighten them.
• Spring displays: White or yellow hyacinths; hyacinths and yellow crocuses; yellow-variegated small-leaved ivies, hyacinths and crocuses; Cinerarias (in warm positions); bright-faced Polyanthus; white tulips; yellow daffodils (choose one of the low-growing types).

ALL-YELLOW *windowboxes are dramatic and create beacons of colour when seen against dark backgrounds. Here is a strongly coloured windowbox filled with Creeping Jenny (Lysimachia nummularia), yellow Slipper Flowers (Calceolaria x herbeohybrida) and tuberous-rooted begonias (Begonia x tuberhybrida). For extra colour, use the yellow-leaved Creeping Jenny.*

• Summer displays: Creeping Jenny *(Lysimachia nummularia)*, yellow Slipper Flowers *(Calceolaria* x *herbeohybrida)* and tuberous-rooted begonias *(Begonia* x *tuberhybrida)*. For extra colour throughout summer use the yellow-leaved form of Creeping Jenny *(Lysimachia nummularia* 'Aurea'); Basket Begonia *(Begonia* x *tuberhybrida* 'Pendula').

AFRICAN MARIGOLD

Although Tagetes erecta *is widely known as the African Marigold, it originated in Mexico. It was introduced into Spain in the early sixteenth century and became naturalized along the Algerian coast. In 1535, an expedition was mounted to free Tunis from the Moors. The corsairs believed the marigold to be native to Africa and it was reintroduced under the name* Flos Africanus.

WHITE *backgrounds are ideal for highlighting yellows, reds, scarlets and greens. Here is an arrangement of golden-faced Marigolds, dark red geraniums (pelargoniums) and yellow Zinnias. These are complemented by the Emerald Fern (Asparagus densiflorus 'Sprengeri'). Paint the windowbox light blue.*

YELLOW, RED AND BLUE *hyacinths look dramatic against white walls and can be accompanied by polyanthus in mixtures of gold, blue and scarlet. Many pansies flower in spring, with colours including yellow, violet and ruby. They contrast superbly with the upright and soldier-like hyacinths.*

WINTER DISPLAYS 1

WINDOWBOXES and troughs can be as interesting during winter as they are in summer. Although at that time of year they are not packed with colour, they can be rich in textures and shades of green, as well as attractively varied in shape.

WHEN TO PLANT THEM
To ensure that winter displays are established by the onset of winter, put the plants in the inner trough during mid- to late summer, if they are to be removed from their pots and planted directly into compost. But if the plants are left in their pots, planting can be left until late summer or early autumn (see page 146 for seasonal philosophy of planting).

Winter displays can be retained from one year to another and during spring and summer placed in a cool, lightly shaded position. Ensure the trough is slightly raised off the ground to prevent slugs feasting on plants during summer.

Hedera helix *'Glacier'*

Hebe *x* franciscana *'Variegata'*

Chamaecyparis lawsoniana *'Pygmaea Argentea'*

Euonymus fortunei

Erica herbacea

Gaultheria procumbens

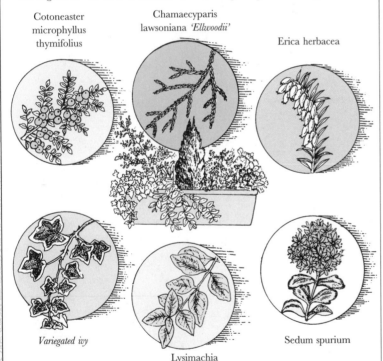

Cotoneaster microphyllus thymifolius

Chamaecyparis lawsoniana *'Ellwoodii'*

Erica herbacea

Variegated ivy

Lysimachia nummularia *'Aurea'*

Sedum spurium

BRIGHT, *packed window-boxes are especially welcome in winter. They introduce colourful flowers, attractively shaped and textured conifers and variegated trailing plants such as ivies.*

ALTHOUGH *winter windowboxes do not have the colour impact of summer-flowering types, there are many beautiful shades of green and shapes of conifers.*

IN ADDITION *to the colourfully flowered* Erica herbacea *(earlier and popularly known as E. carnea), there are some varieties with attractively coloured foliage.*

RANGE OF PLANTS
These range from dwarf and slow-growing conifers to variegated shrubs and trailing plants. Eventually, some may become too large for a windowbox or trough. Then, the conifers can be moved into rock gardens, or replanted into large tubs, with trailing plants around them.

The demarcation between late winter and early spring is often uncertain and invariably depends on the climate of your area. Therefore, small, early spring-flowering bulbs can be grown in small pots and put among the more permanent occupants such as conifers. Crocuses are ideal for this, but do not try and force them into producing early flowers.

A wide range of winter brightening plants is illustrated here, and others are featured on the next page (151).

HOUSELEEKS

Houseleeks were recommended during Victorian times for growing in window gardens. They are thought to have gained their name because the Romans grew them in pots in front of their houses. However, the word Leek is said to be derived from the Anglo-Saxon leac, *meaning a plant, and therefore a Houseleek is literally a house plant. Its evergreen nature is reflected by its many common names, such as Ayron, Ayegreen and Sengreen, which date back to the fourteenth century. Its other names include Hen-and-Chickens and Old-Man-and-Woman.*

WINTER DISPLAYS 2

IN ADDITION to the plants featured here and on page 150, there are others to consider:
• *Aucuba japonica* 'Variegata' (Spotted Laurel): Also known as 'Maculata', in gardens it forms a large, evergreen shrub. When young and in a small pot, however, it is ideal for displaying in windowboxes. The glossy, green leaves are splashed with bright yellow and are especially attractive when young. Avoid positions exposed to cold winds, as the leaves then become damaged.
• *Buxus sempervirens* 'Suffruticosa' (Edging Box): A small, hardy evergreen, often used to form miniature hedges around herb gardens. When small and growing in pots it can be used in windowboxes, where the small, dark green and glossy leaves create attractive foils for variegated trailing plants.
• *Euonymus japonicus* 'Microphyllus Variegatus': Dwarf, evergreen shrub with small leaves that reveal

---

PARTRIDGE-BERRY

The North American creeping, evergreen shrub Gaultheria procumbens *is frequently added to winter displays in windowboxes. It has many common names, including Partridge-berry, as the bright red berries it bears were used to feed partridges. It is also known as Winter-green, Checkerberry, Tea-berry and Mountain Tea, as it can be used as a substitute for tea or for flavouring real tea.*

---

white edges. When young and small it can be grown in pots and placed in winter windowboxes. *E. j.* 'Microphyllus Pulchellus' ('Microphyllus Aureus') has small leaves with golden variegations.
• *Hebe* x *andersonii* 'Variegata': A handsome, evergreen shrub with dull green variegated leaves edged

JUNIPERUS COMMUNIS *'Compressa':* Dwarf and compact conifer with dark green, needle-like, silver-backed leaves set tightly around the plants. It is ideal for windowboxes and troughs, as it reaches only 40cm/16in after ten years.

ERICA HERBACEA: Earlier known as Erica carnea *and commonly as the Spring or Snow Heather. From late autumn to late spring it creates a mass of colour. Varieties in colours including white, pink and rose-purple.*

EUONYMUS FORTUNEI: There are many colourfully variegated varieties of this trailing or climbing evergreen shrub. Choose small plants and when they become too large for a windowbox put them into a garden border or large tub.

in creamy white. Eventually it becomes too large for a windowbox and can be put into a tub or border.
• *Hedera helix:* This small-leaved ivy has many handsomely variegated forms. Select the brightest ones you can find for winter use, and position at the fronts or sides of the boxes.
• *Vinca minor* 'Variegata' (Variegated Lesser Periwinkle): This grows large, with a trailing and sprawling nature and green and creamy white variegated, evergreen leaves. Eventually it becomes too big for windowboxes and can then be planted into a border. However, when young it is ideal for softening the edges of a variety of containers.

Vincas have been popular camouflaging and ground-covering plants for several centuries, and because of their creeping nature were originally classified as varieties of clematis. Earlier they were known as Joy of the Ground.

CINERARIAS

Earlier known as Cineraria cruenta, *but now as* Senecio cruentus, *this widely grown houseplant is famed for flowers that appear in dome-shaped heads from early winter to early summer.*

The Victorians recommended it for window gardening and in many cities today it can be seen in windowboxes, especially those that are serviced by professional gardeners and florists. Few pot plants create such reliable displays as those produced by Cinerarias, especially at that time of the year.

Cineraria (Senecio cruentus)

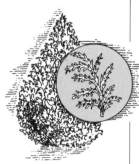

CHAMAECYPARIS LAWSONIANA *'Ellwoodii':* Slow-growing, eventually large conifer with a column-like outline formed of tightly packed, dark green foliage. For extra colour choose 'Ellwood's Pillar'.

CHAMAECYPARIS LAWSONIANA *'Pygmaea Argentea':* Small, bush-like conifer with bluish-green foliage tipped creamy white. Its shape contrasts with column-shaped conifers: position between them.

CHAMAECYPARIS PISIFERA *'Boulevard':* Popular, slow-growing, cone-shaped conifer with soft, intense silver-blue foliage. Do not allow the compost to become dry as the foliage will then become unsightly.

SPRING DISPLAYS 1

❖

AS SOON as winter recedes, a wealth of bulbs and biennial plants burst into flower. Exactly when this happens depends on the weather. Some areas seldom have severe frosts and therefore spring could be six or more weeks in advance of exposed areas three to five hundred miles away.

PLANTING A SPRING DISPLAY

These are created by planting bulbs, biennial plants, trailing ivies and small conifers into compost in an inner trough-like container in late summer or early autumn and putting this into a windowbox in early spring. Alternatively, plants can be grown in separate pots and just placed in the trough.

Bulbs such as *Crocus chrysanthus*, *Iris danfordiae*, *Iris reticulata*, daffodils, miniature narcissus, hyacinths and *Tulipa greigii* are all planted when their bulbs become available in late summer or early autumn. The depths to which they

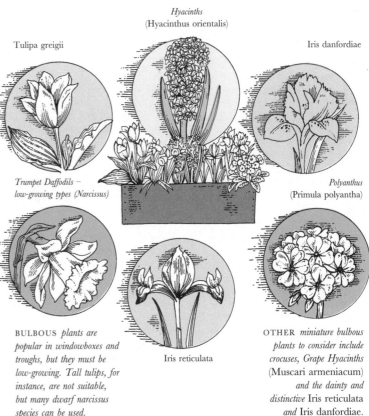

Hyacinths
(Hyacinthus orientalis)

Tulipa greigii

Iris danfordiae

*Trumpet Daffodils –
low-growing types (Narcissus)*

Polyanthus
(Primula polyantha)

BULBOUS *plants are popular in windowboxes and troughs, but they must be low-growing. Tall tulips, for instance, are not suitable, but many dwarf narcissus species can be used.*

Iris reticulata

OTHER *miniature bulbous plants to consider include crocuses, Grape Hyacinths* (Muscari armeniacum) *and the dainty and distinctive* Iris reticulata *and* Iris danfordiae.

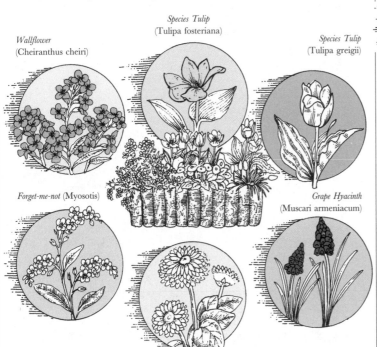

Wallflower
(Cheiranthus cheiri)

Species Tulip
(Tulipa fosteriana)

Species Tulip
(Tulipa greigii)

Forget-me-not (Myosotis)

Grape Hyacinth
(Muscari armeniacum)

Double Daisy
(Bellis perennis)

SPRING *displays in windowboxes and troughs can be a feast of colour, full of bulbous plants such as Grape Hyacinths and short-stemmed Species Tulips, and biennials like Forget-me-nots, Double Daisies and Wallflowers.*

THESE *displays need to be planned in mid-summer and planted in late summer or early autumn. They are then put in a cool corner.*

AS SOON *as the flowering plants burst into life and create an array of colour, remove the winter display from a windowbox and replace it with the spring one. Keep the compost moist, especially when plants are flowering.*

are buried vary, but a general indication is to cover them with compost to twice their own depth. For example, a bulb 5cm/2in deep is put in a hole 15cm/6in deep, so that 10cm/4in of compost covers the bulb's top. However, always check with the instruction on the bulb packet.

When planting directly in compost in a container, start by putting conifers at the back and positioning them equally apart. Form clusters of bulbs; tall ones towards the middle and miniature types at the ends and along the front. When using biennials, such as wallflowers, dot them between other plants but behind the bulbs.

Trailers are the last to be planted, at the front.

When planted, gently but thoroughly water the compost and place the container in a cool, sheltered position until the bulbs start to create a display.

POLYANTHUS

These belong to the primula family and are hybrids between Primroses (Primula vulgaris) *and Cowslips* (P. veris). *They are also thought to contain a dash of* P. juliae. *They have a perennial nature and each year create a wealth of colour.*

SPRING DISPLAYS 2

❖

N ADDITION to the plants featured here and on page 152, there are others to choose from for spring displays. These include many that are also featured in winter displays, such as miniature conifers, variegated evergreen shrubs and small trailing plants. To enable them to be swapped quickly between seasonal displays they must be planted in their own pots.

SINGLE-THEME DISPLAYS

Using just one type of plant in a windowbox can create an arresting display. Either use only one colour, or a mixture. For example:
• For a dominant display of yellow, saturate the windowbox with short-stemmed trumpet daffodils. Plant good quality bulbs in an inner trough in late summer or early autumn. Put them in two layers; position the bases of bulbs in the lower layer about 15cm/6in deep, then cover with a thin layer of compost. Position bulbs in the upper layer with their bases between the necks of the lower layer of bulbs.

Fill and firm the trough with compost until 12mm/½in below the rim. Water the compost and

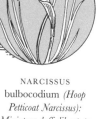

POLYANTHUS *develop large, dome-heads of cream, white, blue, yellow, pink, and scarlet flowers in spring. They grow about 20cm/8in. Plant them in late summer or early autumn. Only a few plants are needed to create a memorable display.*

NARCISSUS bulbocodium *(Hoop Petticoat Narcissus): Miniature daffodil, up to about 13cm/5in high and with hoop-like, yellow, 2.5cm/1in-long trumpets during late winter and early spring. Plant bulbs in clusters.*

NARCISSUS CYCLAMINEUS *is a miniature daffodil. In windowboxes it flowers in late winter and early spring. It grows 15–20cm/6–8in high, bearing bright yellow flowers with long trumpets and swept-back petals.*

place the trough in a cool position until early spring, when the flower buds reveal colour and the trough can be placed in a windowbox.
• The Common Hyacinth *(Hyacinthus orientalis)* develops stiffly upright, soldier-like spires of flowers that, unlike daffodils with their informal outlines, create rigidly-shaped outlines that are ideal where formality is desired. They are also available in a wide colour range – white, yellow, pink, red and blue – that enables more varied colour designs to be produced. Plant the bulbs in late summer or early autumn, with 7.5cm/3in spaces between them and their bases 13–15cm/5–6in deep.

Do not mix different varieties in the same container, as there is then risk that they will not flower at the same time. However, a way to ensure different types flower at the same time is to plant each bulb in an individual pot and at flowering time to select those at the same stage of development.

LARGE FAMILY

Large, trumpet-type daffodils are well known, but there are many others including miniature ones that are ideal for planting in windowboxes and troughs. The multiflowered Poet's Narcissus (Narcissus poeticus) *develops heads massed with flowers and grows about 38cm/15in high.*

CHEIRANTHUS CHEIRI *(Wallflower): Earlier known as* Erysimum cheiri *and includes dwarf varieties that flower from mid-spring to early summer. They are ideal for growing in windowboxes.*

TULIPA KAUFMANNIANA *(Water-lily Tulip): A distinctive species tulip, with 8cm/3½in-long white flowers, with red and yellow on the outside, during early and mid-spring. Flowers open to a width of about 10cm/4in wide.*

DAFFODILS *with trumpet-like heads create dramatic displays. However, choose short-stemmed types to reduce the risk of damage from strong winds. Plant them in bold groups and position the windowbox in a sheltered area.*

SCOTTISH ROMANCE

Wallflowers are thought to have been introduced into Britain at the time of the Norman Conquest in the eleventh century. Three centuries later they were found growing on the walls of a Scottish castle. Scott of Tushielaw, son of a border chieftain, fell in love with Elizabeth, daughter of the Earl of March and, disguised as a minstrel, courted her. Her father imprisoned her to deter him, but Elizabeth dropped a piece of wallflower as an encouragement. When trying to elope, she slipped and died, so distressing her suitor that he then wandered throughout Europe, singing and wearing a sprig of wallflower in his cap in memory of his lost love.

Wallflower

SUMMER DISPLAYS 1

S UMMER is the brightest time for windowboxes: they are drenched in colour from when spring displays fade to the onset of frosts in autumn.

The plants are susceptible to damage from low temperatures and therefore cannot be put outside until all risk of frost has passed. However, when plants are grown in an inner box, they can be planted slightly earlier and at night placed in a greenhouse or conservatory. During daytime, place them outdoors on a warm, wind-sheltered patio. This way, troughs packed with colour can be ready for putting into a windowbox as soon as the spring-flowering display fades.

PLANTS TO CONSIDER

In addition to the plants illustrated here and up to page 157 there are many others, including:
• *Anagallis linifolia* 'Gentian Blue': Growing 15–23cm/6–9in high with a sprawling nature, it develops masses of 12–18mm/

IVY-LEAVED GERANIUMS

These popular trailing plants, correctly called Pelargonium peltatum, *are equally useful in windowboxes and in hanging baskets. When introduced from South Africa to Britain in 1701 they were known as Shield-leaved Geraniums, on account of their leaf-stalks joining the leaves right at their centres.*

1/2–3/4in wide, rich blue flowers with bright centres from early to late summer. Plant it where the stems can spread and trail over the container's edges. It colour-contrasts with Sweet Alyssum (*Alyssum maritimum/Lobularia maritima*) along the fronts of windowboxes and creates an eye-catching display throughout summer.

THERE *are many plants that can be used in summer displays, in medleys of colours that are sure to attract attention. Plant them in an inner trough; as soon as the spring display is over, replace it with a summer one, but not until all risk of frost has passed.*

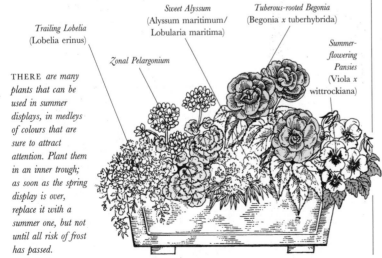

Trailing Lobelia (Lobelia erinus)

Zonal Pelargonium

Sweet Alyssum (Alyssum maritimum/ Lobularia maritima)

Tuberous-rooted Begonia (Begonia x tuberhybrida)

Summer-flowering Pansies (Viola x wittrockiana)

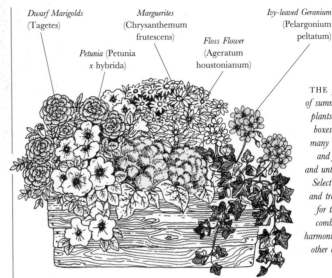

Dwarf Marigolds (Tagetes)

Petunia (Petunia x hybrida)

Marguerites (Chrysanthemum frutescens)

Floss Flower (Ageratum houstonianum)

Ivy-leaved Geranium (Pelargonium peltatum)

THE *permutations of summer-flowering plants in window-boxes is wide and many are described and featured here and until page 157. Select both upright and trailing plants, for the display in combinations that harmonize with each other or make good contrasts.*

• *Asparagus densiflorus* 'Sprengeri' (Emerald Fern): A superb cascading foliage plant that is ideal for creating backgrounds for smaller plants. It has long, arching, wiry stems packed with green, needle-like leaves.
• *Coleus blumei* (Flame Nettle): A tender foliage plant widely grown indoors during summer. In warm areas it is also ideal in windowboxes and troughs. Most varieties are upright and bushy, but some have a trailing nature and are ideal for planting at the fronts and sides of windowboxes. Trailing types include 'Scarlet Poncho' and 'Molten Lava'. Both of these can be raised from seeds which should be sown in gentle warmth in late winter or early spring.
• Conifers (miniature and slow-growing types): These are mainly used to create colour in winter and spring displays in windowboxes, but they can also be used in summer arrangements. They are especially useful in exposed and cold areas, as they help to give protection to annual plants.

ZONAL PELARGONIUMS

Although frequently known as bedding geraniums, these are pelargoniums and characterized by having horse-shoe markings on their rounded leaves. In 1710, the shrubby Pelargonium zonale *was introduced into Britain from South Africa and was soon known as* Geranium Africanum. *It became a favourite plant in summer-bedding displays in gardens, as well as for growing in greenhouses and conservatories. Later, they were known as Nosegay Geraniums, while in 1863 the first double-flowered form was raised in France. 'Paul Crampel' was introduced in 1903 and has remained popular ever since.*

SUMMER DISPLAYS 2

❖

FUCHSIAS are popular summer-flowering plants for windowboxes. Although some species are relatively hardy and can be planted in borders in temperate climates, the majority are soon damaged by low temperatures and therefore cannot be put outside until all frosts have ceased.

Some varieties have a cascading nature that soon drenches the sides of windowboxes with colour, while others are bushy. Both have a role to play: trailing types at the ends of windowboxes, bushy ones towards the centre. Avoid varieties with a stiffly upright stance; rather, select those with a lax nature such as 'Lena' (semi-double, pink and magenta) and 'Swingtime' (double, red and milky-white). Trailing types (also suitable for growing in hanging-baskets) include 'Cascade', 'Jack Acland', 'La Campanella' and 'Walsingham'.

PLANTING DISTANCES

Plants in windowboxes and troughs are planted much closer than in flower borders in gardens. This is because colour-drenched windowboxes are essential: if bare patches occur the whole display looks untidy and unappealing, even when the other plants are creating a good show. Therefore, when using these plants in borders, set them further apart than the distances recommended here.

It is possible to plant a windowbox entirely with fuchsias, but companionable plants include Zonal Geraniums (pelargoniums), marigolds, salvias and begonias.
• *Glechoma hederacea* 'Variegata' (Variegated Ground Ivy): Creates a mass of mid-green, kidney-

CALCEOLARIA *x* HERBEOHYBRIDA *(Slipper Flower): Height 20–30cm/8–12in; plant 20–25cm/8–10in apart. It is often grown as a house-plant; outdoors it flowers during early and mid-summer, bearing bright, pouch-like flowers.*

BRACHYCOMBE IBERIDIFOLIA *'Splendour' (Swan River Daisy): Height 23–30cm/9–12in; plant 15–20cm/6–8in apart. Each plant creates a mass of large, daisy-like flowers in blue to purple or white with ebony eyes.*

CAMPANULA CARPATICA *'Bellissimo': Height 15cm/6in, then, trailing plant 20–23cm/ 8–9in apart. Position at the sides and fronts of boxes, so that it covers edges with chalice-shaped, blue or white flowers throughout summer.*

CAMPANULA ISOPHYLLA *(Star of Bethlehem): Height 15cm/6in, then trailing; plant 20cm/8in apart. Superb trailing plant with masses of blue flowers from mid- to late summer. There is also an attractive white-flowered form that looks good against a red wall.*

CENTAUREA CYANUS *'Ultra Dwarf' (Cornflower): Height 20–30cm/8–12in; plant 15–23cm/6–9in apart. It creates neat mounds of flowers, in blue or mixed colours, from early to late summer. Do not use tall varieties.*

shaped leaves with white markings, in bushy clusters at the plant's top and then clustered around long, trailing stems. It is ideal at the fronts and sides of windowboxes, as it cloaks them in leaves without creating a high, dome-shaped top that obscures plants at the back.

As a bonus, it has lilac-blue flowers during late spring and early summer.
• *Hedera helix* (Ivy): There are many small-leaved, variegated varieties that can be used to trail from around the edges of all types of windowboxes.

Select the leaf colours to suit the colour vibrancy of the display. For example, if the windowbox is bursting with exceptionally bright colours, the ivies can be garish. But when the colours are demure and reserved, ensure that the ivies do not dominate the display. Indeed, these trailing plants should be secondary features, just clothing the sides of windowboxes and softening their outlines.

CONVOLVULUS TRICOLOR *'Rose Ensign': Height 10–15cm/4–6in, then trailing, plant 20–23cm/8–9in apart. It develops masses of rose, lemon, pink and white, trumpet-shaped flowers from mid to late summer. Plant at the fronts and sides.*

MORNING GLORY

When first introduced into cultivation in the early part of the 1600s, this tropical American plant was known as Convolvulus major, *then* Ipomoea purpurea *and latterly* Pharbitis purpurea. *Despite all these botanical name changes it has continued to be popular and grown as a half-hardy annual climber in temperate zones, where it drenches supports with clusters of 7.5cm/3in-wide purple flowers from mid- to late summer. Their colour fades with age.*

It became known as Morning Glory because its flowers appeared to open and to be at their best in the mornings.

SUMMER DISPLAYS 3

EGONIAS are a large and varied family, many ideal for growing in containers on patios, including windowboxes.

• The tuberous-rooted *Begonia* x *tuberhybrida* is dramatic and dominant in windowboxes, with single or double flowers often 13cm/5in or more wide, from early to late summer. Flower colours include yellow, pink, red and scarlet.

They are usually grown from dormant tubers planted in boxes of moist peat in early spring, and later transferred to separate pots when shoots appear. After all the frosts have gone they are planted into windowboxes and other containers outdoors. The Basket Begonia (*Begonia* x *tuberhybrida* 'Pendula') is a trailing form, widely used in hanging baskets and at the sides of windowboxes.

• The fibrous-rooted Wax Begonia *(Begonia semperflorens)* is as much at home in displays indoors as in flower borders outdoors. Also, it is supreme in windowboxes. It forms bushy plants, 15–23cm/6–9in high and wide, with masses of red, pink or white flowers from early to late summer.

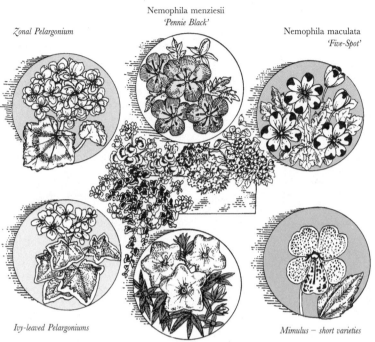

Zonal Pelargonium

Nemophila menziesii 'Pennie Black'

Nemophila maculata 'Five-Spot'

Ivy-leaved Pelargoniums

Nierembergia 'Mont Blanc'

Mimulus – short varieties

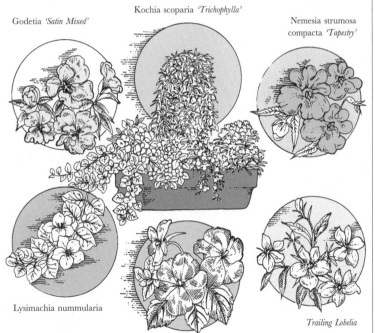

Godetia 'Satin Mixed'

Kochia scoparia 'Trichophylla'

Nemesia strumosa compacta 'Tapestry'

Lysimachia nummularia

Impatiens – Trailing and compact types

Trailing Lobelia

THE *range of plants suitable for growing in windowboxes in summer is much wider than those used for hanging baskets or even tubs on patios. Some are trailing, others bushy.*

Whatever their nature, they must create a colourful display throughout summer, or at least until the onset of late summer.

Miniature conifers and variegated, evergreen trailing plants are especially useful in exposed and cold areas: they give slight protection to annuals and provide permanent colour.

Wax Begonias are easily raised from seeds sown on the surface of compost in late winter or early spring in 16°C/61°F. Germination takes two to four weeks and when the seedlings are large enough to handle they are pricked out individually, or in small clusters, into seed-trays. Harden off the plants and put them outdoors when all risk of frost has passed.

Nip out the growing tips of plants several times to encourage them to be much bushier.

NORTH AMERICAN BEAUTIES

Throughout much of the Victorian era, Nemophila maculata *was popular in garden flower beds. It is an attrative, bushy, North American hardy annual. In North America it is commonly known as Five Spot, while in Britain the same name is used as a varietal name.*

The best known nemophila is Baby Blue Eyes (Nemophila menziesii), *with white-centred sky-blue flowers, saucer-shaped and about 30mm/1¼in across. Incidentally, the name Nemophila means grove-lover and was chosen on account of the habitats of many of these species.*

SUMMER DISPLAYS 4

THERE are many more flowering and attractively foliaged plants for planting in windowboxes to create a summer display.

• _Heliotropium_ x _hybridum_ (Heliotrope/Cherry Pie) produces a wealth of flowers, ranging from dark violet through lavender to white. Most plants grow 38–45cm/15–18in high, but in windowboxes lower-growing varieties such as 'Dwarf Marine' at 30–35cm/12–14in are better. It has royal purple, fragrant flowers.

Sow seeds 6mm/¼in deep in late winter or early spring and place them in 16°C/61°F. Germination takes two to four weeks. When the seedlings are large enough to handle, transfer them into seed-trays and slowly acclimatize to outdoor temperatures. Plant them into windowboxes when frosts have ceased, setting them 25cm/10in apart. A few plants will create a dominant feature.

• Yellow-leaved Creeping Jenny (_Lysimachia nummularia_ 'Aurea') creates colour through its yellow leaves and bright yellow, cup-shaped flowers that appear during early and mid-summer. It is hardy and increased by dividing established plants in autumn or spring and replanting young shoots from around the outside of the clump.

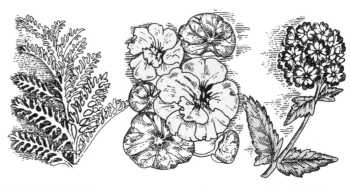

SENECIO bicolor 'Silver Dust' (also known as S. cineraria/S. maritimus): Height 20–25cm/8–10in; plant 20–25cm/8–10in apart. Forms low mounds of fern-like, silvery leaves. Ideal for creating unusual colour throughout summer.

TROPAEOLUM majus 'Double Gleam Mixed' (Nasturtiums): Height 20–30cm/8–12in, then trailing; plant 15–20cm/6–8in apart. Cascading and trailing, with semi-double flowers in orange, yellow and bright scarlet.

VERBENA x hybrida (Vervain): Height 20–25cm/8–10in, plant 15–; 25cm/6–10in apart. Several bushy and trailing varieties to choose from. Plant trailing types at the fronts and sides, with the bushy ones positioned in the centre.

• _Nicotiana alata_ (Tobacco Plant/Ornamental Tobacco Plant/Jasmine Tobacco Plant) has sweetly scented flowers from early to late summer. Some varieties are 90cm/3ft tall, but there are several lower-growing types and these are ideal for windowboxes. These include 'Domino F1 Hybrid Mixed' which grows 25–30cm/10–12in high with flowers in many colours, and 'Nicki Bright Pink', similarly sized with pink flowers. 'Breakthrough Mixed' is similarly sized, flowering early and with a compact habit. It is tolerant of the heat and therefore ideal in hot climates.

Sow seeds 3mm/⅛in deep from late spring to mid-spring, placing them in 16°C/61°F. Germination takes ten to fourteen days. When the seedlings are large enough to handle, transfer them to seed-trays and slowly acclimatize to outdoor conditions. Plant these low-growing varieties about 20cm/8in apart in windowboxes.

PANSIES (Violas): Height 10–15cm/4–6in; plant 10–15cm/4–6in apart. Many varieties to choose from, in mixed and single colours. Ideal for creating vibrant nests of colour, but ensure that they will not dominate other plants.

PETUNIA x hybrida (Garden Petunia): Height 10–15cm/4–5in – some cascading and ideal for the fronts of boxes; plant 20cm/8in apart. Single or mixed colours, in shades of white, blue, pink, blush, cerise, scarlet and violet.

SALVIA splendens (Scarlet Salvia): Height 20–30cm/8–12in – choose low-growing varieties; plant 20–25cm/8–10in apart. Range of varieties in scarlet, deep purple and mixtures. S. s. 'Splendissima' is superb in cool, wet areas.

SCENTED WINDOWBOXES

❖

WINDOWBOXES packed with scented flowers and fragrant foliage are a source of enjoyment throughout the year. Spring and summer are rich in scented flowering plants, while in autumn and winter many small conifers can be relied upon to provide other pleasant fragrances. Here are a few scented flowers that can be grown successfully in windowboxes.

- Common Hyacinth *(Hyacinthus orientalis):* Strongly sweet, especially when windowboxes are completely planted with them.
- *Crocus chrysanthus:* Strong and sweet fragrance.
- Flowering Tobacco Plants *(Nicotiana alata):* Use low-growing varieties. Richly sweet flowers.
- Heliotrope *(Heliotropium* x *hybridum):* Fragrance resembles the redolence of cherry pies.
- *Iris danfordiae:* Honey-scented small flowers.
- *Iris reticulata* (Reticulated Iris): Violet bouquet.

POSITIONING SCENTED WINDOWBOXES

Many of the fragrances given off by flowers are not strong, and therefore they need to be grown en masse. Sometimes this can be achieved by devoting a complete windowbox to them, such as to hyacinths in spring. But windowboxes are usually made up with many plants and individual fragrances become more difficult to detect. Scented windowboxes are best used on ground-floor windows, especially those in warm, sheltered positions.

'THE PERNICIOUS WEED'

Few plants have such a divisive reputation as Nicotiana tabacum, *the Tobacco Plant and a close relative of the Ornamental Tobacco Plant that is widely planted in gardens and windowboxes. It has generated vast profits for tobacco companies, created massive tax revenues for nations, and contributed to the deaths of many people.*

- Pansies *(Viola* x *wittrockiana):* The cool, sweet fragrance is not particularly noticeable unless they are grown *en masse.*
- Stocks 'Apple Blossom': Double pink and white flowers.
- Sweet Alyssum *(Alyssum maritimum/ Lobularia maritimum):* bouquet of new-mown hay, with a slight honey fragrance.

MINIATURE CONIFERS
The freshness of pine forests is well known, but other evergreen conifers offer surprisingly varied scents when their foliage is bruised. Many miniature conifers that are grown in windowboxes in winter and spring have unusual fragrances, including:
- *Chamaecyparis lawsoniana* 'Ellwoodii': resin and parsley.
- *Chamaecyparis lawsoniana* 'Pygmaea Argentea': resin and parsley.
- *Chamaecyparis pisifera* 'Boulevard': emits a resinous smell.
- *Juniperus communis* 'Compressa': bouquet of apples.

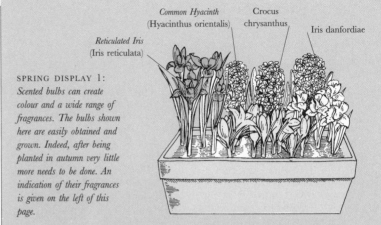

Common Hyacinth (Hyacinthus orientalis) Crocus chrysanthus Iris danfordiae
Reticulated Iris (Iris reticulata)

SPRING DISPLAY 1:
Scented bulbs can create colour and a wide range of fragrances. The bulbs shown here are easily obtained and grown. Indeed, after being planted in autumn very little more needs to be done. An indication of their fragrances is given on the left of this page.

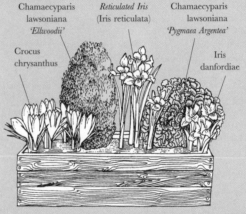

Chamaecyparis lawsoniana 'Ellwoodii' Reticulated Iris (Iris reticulata) Chamaecyparis lawsoniana 'Pygmaea Argentea'
Crocus chrysanthus Iris danfordiae

SPRING DISPLAY 2:
Miniature conifers create permanency in windowboxes and a colourful background for spring-flowering bulbs. Additionally, they offer protection for the bulbs grown in areas exposed to strong winds. Many conifers have unusually fragrant foliage and the bouquets for those conifers featured here are indicated on the left of this page.

Sweet Alyssum (Alyssum maritimum/ Lobularia maritima) Cherry Pie/ Heliotrope (Heliotropium x hybridum) Flowering Tobacco Plant (Nicotiana alata) Pansies (Viola x wittrockiana)

SUMMER DISPLAY
Rich medleys of colour and scent are easily created in summer. Here is a mixture of plants that can be increased from seeds each year. Alyssum maritimum/ Lobularia maritima *has the bouquet of new-mown hay,* Heliotropium x hybridum *is like cherry pie,* Nicotiana *is sweet, while* Viola x wittrockiana *is cool and sweet.*

COMPOST AND PLANTING

THE NATURE of the compost used in windowboxes is important, as there is relatively little of it and it has to support a large number of plants.

There are two basic types of compost: loam-based and peat-based. Increasingly, other composts are on sale as alternatives for peat-based types. The continual digging of peat from peat-beds destroys the environments of many plants, animals and insects. Several alternatives are available: some made from coir fibre, others from materials such as bark and wood fibre, paper and straw.

• Loam-based composts are traditional composts and formed of loam (good topsoil), peat and sharp sand. The loam must be partially sterilized to kill harmful organisms, and as this is a specialized treatment, the compost is best bought ready mixed. Within the potting mixture range there are several strengths of fertilizer: for plants in windowboxes choose John Innes potting compost No. 2.

Use loam-based compost for winter displays of miniature conifers, small shrubs and evergreen trailing plants. Also, this type is good for spring displays of bulbs and biennial plants.

• Peat-based composts are based on peat and are ideal in windowboxes in summer, where it is essential that the compost is able to retain plenty of moisture. They are lighter than loam-based composts but do not have such a reserve of plant foods, and therefore regular feeding is essential throughout summer. Also, once dry, peat-types are more difficult than loam-based types to moisten again. Wherever possible, use coir-based or other environmentally friendly composts for planting summer displays.

• Compost additives such as perlite and vermiculite can be used in summer to assist in the retention of moisture.

• Feed plants regularly in summer, using a balanced fertilizer about every two weeks from mid- to late summer. Do not use one with a high nitrogen content as this produces lush stems and leaves at the expense of flowers. Moreover, if plants are given too high concentrations of fertilizers there is a risk that they will be irreparably damaged.

PLANTING

Always firm compost around the roots of plants to prevent small air pockets occurring. Unless roots are in close contact with soil particles, their growth is retarded. However, do not pack soil around the plant's neck, so that young stems become bruised and damaged. This can encourage the onset of diseases.

PLANTING SEQUENCE

When putting plants directly into compost, start at the front of the box and at one end. First, plant low, trailing types. When these are in place, put the rear row into position, firming compost around them. Ensure the compost of the surface is about 12mm/1/2in below the rim, so that plants can be watered properly.

Begin planting at the front

WHEN planting directly into compost in an inner trough, ensure it is not in immediate contact with the wooden base. Place it on 12mm/1/2in pieces of wood. As an added precaution to prevent water dripping on people below, place a shallow drip-tray in the base.

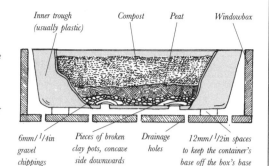

Inner trough (usually plastic)　Compost　Peat　Windowbox

6mm/1/4in gravel chippings　Pieces of broken clay pots, concave side downwards　Drainage holes　12mm/1/2in spaces to keep the container's base off the box's base

---

PLUNGING POTS

As an alternative to planting directly into compost, plants can be left in their pots and placed directly in a windowbox or, preferably, first into an inner trough. Ensure the rims of the pots are about 12mm/1/2in below the top edge of the windowbox. An option is to pack moist peat around the pots to help keep their compost cool and moist. However, never cover the compost in the pots, as the plants in them must be watered individually and the surface compost must be examined to see if water is needed. When the surface is light-coloured and crumbly, further moisture is needed; if dark and slightly shiny, the compost is sufficiently moist.

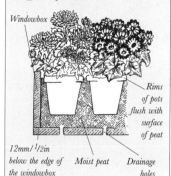

Windowbox

Rims of pots flush with surface of peat

12mm/1/2in below the edge of the windowbox　Moist peat　Drainage holes

---

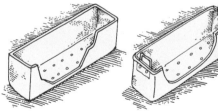

INSTEAD *of putting plants directly into a wooden windowbox, plant them or position their pots in a plastic outer one. This gives the wood a longer life and enables displays to be changed quickly.*

AN ALTERNATIVE *to plastic is galvanized metal. This can be home-made and tailored to fit inside a wooden windowbox. After cutting and folding the metal to shape, use rivets to hold the sides together.*

WHETHER *formed of plastic or metal, the inner trough should fit snugly inside a wooden windowbox, but with a slight space at either end so that fingers can be inserted for easy removal and replacement.*

WATERING

KEEPING the compost in windowboxes evenly moist is not easy and requires attention several times a day in summer if it is not to dry out and the plants to suffer. Compost that is free-draining as well as water retentive is essential. This is achieved by ensuring that water can escape from the compost through drainage holes, and using moisture-retentive compost. Additives such as perlite and vermiculite help to retain moisture.

APPLYING WATER

In summer, when windowboxes are packed with flowers, inspect the compost every morning. If the surface is lightly coloured and crumbly, it needs water. If dark, it is probably sufficiently wet. Never let the compost dry out between waterings as it contracts and allows water, when applied, to run out. If this happens, wait about an hour and apply further water.

Most windowboxes can be watered from outside, but those secured to upper-storey windows may have to be watered from inside the room. If this is impossible, special watering lances are available and, combined with a pair of step ladders, watering is usually possible from the outside. Ensure the ladder is stable.

When using a hosepipe, never turn it on full as the jet will damage the compost or blast young plants out of the box. Try not to splash water on flowers and leaves; persistent moistening of them encourages deterioration, and if they are covered with water droplets when the sun is fully out it may cause burning. Therefore, water the plants early in the morning and in the evening, but early enough in late summer so that moisture splashed on leaves is dry by nightfall.

FEEDING AND WATERING

If the plants are being fed, always water the compost first to ensure that the roots of plants will not be damaged by a too strong concentration of plant food. Watering the compost first also enables the fertilizer to spread evenly throughout the compost.

EARLY IRRIGATION

The Egyptians irrigated crops by use of a shaduf *(sometimes spelt* shadoof*) which basically was a bucket pivoted on a counter-balanced pole. A water receptacle was lowered into the river, filled and then swung up and around, and the water poured into an irrigation channel.*

Counterbalanced pole

WHERE *windowboxes have large clusters of tubs or pots in front of them use a hosepipe with a 1.2m/4ft-long cane tied to its end. Curve the end of the pipe downwards and apply water in a slow trickle, rather than a sudden jet.*

WINDOWBOXES *at ground-floor level are easily watered with an ordinary watering-can without the rose in place. Do not use an enormous can as it is difficult to lift when full and water then tends to splash everywhere.*

SPECIALLY *designed extensions to hoses are available to enable windowboxes at first-floor level to be watered from ground-level or while standing on a low, firmly secured step ladder. They are also ideal for watering hanging baskets.*

GREEN AT A PRICE

During the latter part of the 1800s watering-pots, as they were then called, were usually made of tinplate and sold in red or green. But as green paint was more expensive, most were red. Those made of zinc were more durable, unpainted and heavier. Later ones were made of galvanized iron, with brass screw roses. There are several designs: some with crescent-shaped, slightly domed tops which helped to prevent water splashing out when full and being carried. There were two types of handle: those positioned across the can, and others, known as 'Paxtons', running in the direction of the spout. This design enabled the water to be poured with greater ease and precision. The base of each watering-pot stood on three equally-spaced bosses.

Range of Victorian watering-pots

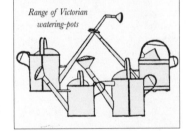

ELIZABETHAN IRRIGATION

The reign of Elizabeth I saw the publication of several gardening books. Thomas Hill wrote a book in 1558 which was enlarged in 1563 and 1577 and became The Gardener's Labyrinth. *He emphasized the importance of water and one illustration showed water being poured into irrigation channels between flower beds. A later book,* The Compleat Gardn'er *(1693), showed a type of stirrup pump.*

KEEPING PLANTS TIDY

◆

THE DIFFERENCE between a good and an exceptionally attractive display in a windowbox or trough is only a few minutes of careful attention each day. Within a few weeks of being planted, summer-flowering displays are established and creating a radiant array of flowers and leaves. As the summer progresses, flowers fade and stems and leaves often become bent or damaged.

• <u>Removing dead flowers</u>: As soon as flowers fade, pinch them off to encourage the development of others. If left, they can cause the onset of diseases. Where the flowers are borne in large clusters, completely remove the flower stems and always cut them just above a leaf-joint. Short spurs die back and may cause the onset of destructive diseases.

• <u>Creating bushiness</u>: Many plants in windowboxes can be left to create bushy shapes on their own. Others, such as the Wax Begonia (*Begonia semperflorens*), need to have their growing tips removed

several times to encourage the development of sideshoots. If this is necessary, always pinch them off immediately above a leaf-joint. Snapping shoots sideways is another way of removing them. Before doing this, water the plants as it is easier to snap stems when they are full of moisture.

REGULARLY *remove faded flowers. Cut off their stems close to a leaf joint. If dead flowers are left on plants, they encourage the development of seeds rather than the formation of further flowers heads.*

NIPPING *out the growing tips of plants encourages the development of sideshoots and creates a bushy plant. Always pinch out the shoot just above a leaf-joint, taking care not to leave short pieces of stem on the plant.*

THROUGHOUT *summer, leaves become damaged and unsightly. Smarten up windowboxes either by using a sharp knife or snapping them sideways. Damaged leaves become brown and can be infected with diseases.*

REPLACING OLD PLANTS

Towards the end of summer, some plants may not look at their best. If they are growing in separate pots they can be easily removed and replaced with fresh plants: pot-grown chrysanthemums are good replacements as they remain in flower for several months. If plants are growing directly in compost in the windowbox, they can still be removed and replaced by fresh ones. Take care not to disturb the other plants.

Do not leave shoot tips on the compost, as they encourage the presence of diseases. Instead, place them on a compost heap.

• <u>Damaged leaves and stems</u>: In a garden display, a few broken leaves or damaged shoots sometimes remain unnoticed, but in windowboxes they are easy to see. Remove dead or damaged leaves, either by using a knife or snapping them sideways. Scissors can also be used.

Check the leaves carefully every few days to discover the presence of pests and diseases before they attain epidemic proportions. Pages 340 to 343 provide an idea of the types of pests and diseases that can be expected.

• <u>Replacing damaged plants</u>: This is detailed above and, in preparation for this, each year grow a few spare plants in pots ready for transferring to a container. Alternatively, bright-faced pot plants can be bought throughout summer. And if they are still in flower in late summer, transfer them into conservatories.

Troughs packed with summer-flowering plants can also be given an extended lease of life in late summer by moving them into conservatories. Do this before the onset of autumn frosts.

FESTOONING WINDOWS

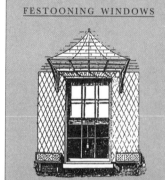

During the late nineteenth century in England, France, Italy and Spain it was common to festoon windows with climbing plants. Netting, strings and brackets were erected and soon clothed with fast-growing climbers such as Canary Creeper, Morning Glory and Sweet Peas.

HANGING BASKETS
AND WALL BASKETS

Hanging baskets at head height and wall baskets at waist level create superb displays throughout summer. Wall baskets can be secured under and between windows, and hanging baskets at the sides of windows and doors, at the edges of porches and verandahs, on roof gardens and from the edges of car ports. Baskets fitted with drip trays can be used in lobbies and porches. Mostly, these containers are planted with half-hardy annuals and tender perennials, but they also create homes for low and sprawling roses and even a few herbs and vegetables.

As well as suggestions for suitable plants the choice of basket – wire-framed or plastic and with a drip tray in its base – is explained in this chapter, together with the selection of composts and the addition of moisture-retentive materials. Securing a hanging basket, watering the compost and keeping plants healthy and tidy are also important and are illustrated and described in this chapter.

Raising half-hardy annuals from seed is featured in sowing seeds in greenhouses on page 272.

DESIGN FACTORS

❖

Hanging baskets are superb for providing splashes of colour against walls, as well as brightening car ports, porches, lobbies, verandahs, courtyards, terraces and roof gardens. They also introduce further summer colour and decoration when hanging from pergolas.

In warm climates it is possible to grow plants in baskets during winter, but in temperate regions the relatively small amount of compost in them is likely to freeze during wet and cold winters. Therefore, hanging baskets are best used in summer, from after the last frosts in spring to the onset of early ones in autumn. They can, however, be planted several weeks earlier and placed in a frost-proof greenhouse

FEW *garden features are as attractive as hanging baskets. They create strong bursts of colour and provide further opportunities to grow plants, especially in small gardens.*

or conservatory until it is safe for them to be put outdoors. Indeed, this is the best way to grow them, as from the moment they are put outside they create dominant displays.

Trailing plants can also be grown indoors in hanging baskets, either with their pots removed and planted into compost, or just placed in a plastic basket. Planting indoor hanging baskets is described and illustrated on page 167.

Unless a basket has a complete, non-drip base, it is essential that indoor types have drip-trays built into their bases to prevent carpets and furniture being damaged by water. Several designs of these baskets are available.

DESIGN POSSIBILITIES

No other plant container is as versatile as a hanging basket. They can be positioned to highlight garden features, or to cloak certain others, and can be located wherever a firm fixing is available. Here are a few ideas about how to use them:

• Position a couple of baskets either side of a front door, but take care to put them where they will not be knocked. When hanging them, allow for an expansion in their width by mid-summer. This can be up to double the basket's normal width.

• Secure baskets either side of a large window: ensure that each bracket is located so that cascading foliage appears to cut across the window's vertical edges. If the basket is positioned to leave space at the window's edges, the effect will be unplanned and fragmented in its appearance.

• When secured to a whitewashed courtyard wall, allow space around each basket, so that it appears to be framed by an

unending background. If hanging baskets are hung so that their foliage overlaps each other, the area's size appears to be dramatically diminished.

• Never position a basket close to the corner of a building, as it may be knocked. Also, if it is too near a corner it appears to be an afterthought and not associated with the overall design. It is also likely to be buffeted by wind.

• To prevent passers-by knocking their heads or shoulders on hanging baskets, put a planted tub underneath, but not where water from the basket will drip on plants.

• Car ports are quickly given a more exciting and colourful appearance by positioning a couple of hanging baskets on either side. Choose plants with either white flowers or silver leaves, so that they show up well at night. Avoid head-hitting positions.

• Camouflage unsightly drainpipes with hanging baskets at head height, and clusters of tubs at ground level.

• In summer, lobbies and porches are ideal places for relatively hardy houseplants (see pages 177 to 179 for suitable plants).

WINDOWS *frequently look dull and uninspiring. They can, however, be brightened throughout summer by positioning similarly sized hanging baskets on either side of them. Also, position wall baskets under windows.*

VERANDAHS *create slightly weather-sheltered places for hanging baskets. They introduce colour as well as rounded and cascading shapes to the often dominant vertical and horizontal frameworks.*

COURTYARDS *are enclosed by walls and buildings which can be easily brightened by a few hanging baskets. Take care not to position them where they could be knocked, and do not place them too near corners.*

CREATE *dominant features by placing troughs, large pots and hanging baskets in groups. These look especially attractive when highlighting windows. However, take care that hanging baskets do not drip water on plants in tubs or troughs below them.*

CHOOSING THE RIGHT PLANTS

❖

THE RANGE of plants that can be grown in hanging baskets is wide, and each year further ones are introduced by seed companies. However, they all have several things in common:

• They create a display of flowers or leaves from early to late summer. If plants are primarily grown for their flowers, new ones should appear regularly throughout summer. If plants are grown mainly for their leaves, these must remain attractive, even when old and at summer's end.

• They must be able to flourish in small amounts of compost and, preferably, not be invasive.

• They must respond to regular feeding from mid- to late summer, which encourages the regular development of flowers.

• Preferably, plants should be in flower when planted in late spring or early summer.

• Choose plants that are not susceptible to pests and diseases. For example, although some Nasturtiums are ideal for planting in

hanging baskets, they attract blackfly, especially when grown in country areas with nearby crops of beans. For this reason, they are better grown in town gardens.

SINGLE-COLOUR THEMES

As well as creating medleys of colours and plants, it is equally exciting to plant hanging baskets with just one type of plant and in a single colour. There are many plants to choose from, including:

• Balcon Geraniums: These continental geraniums create masses of flowers, often in mixed colours but also available separately in scarlet, salmon and lilac.

• *Calceolaria integrifolia (C. rugosa)* 'Sunshine': Superb in a hanging basket, creating a feast of pouch-like, bright yellow flowers throughout summer.

• *Campanula carpatica* 'Bellissimo': Available in white or blue and creating a distinctive display of shallow bell-shaped flowers. It is ideal for growing in porches and lobbies, as well as outdoors.

LOBBY BASKETS

Sheltered lobbies and porches create opportunities to protect baskets, normally hung outside, from buffeting wind and torrential rain. Additionally, trailing, relatively hardy indoor plants can be grown there during summer. A range of plants for lobbies and porches is recommended on pages 177 to 179, and plants that harmonize with each other are on page 180. Always ensure that these plants are in drip-proof containers and that they cannot be knocked.

Indeed, it is a perennial and after flowering can be planted into a flower border.

• *Impatiens:* Several single-coloured forms with pendulous habits to choose from, including white, pastel pink, wine red, salmon, scarlet and lavender.

• Ivy-leaved Geraniums (Pelargoniums) have a straggly, rural appearance: choose plants of the same variety and position against a colour-harmonizing wall. The various colours include white, pink and red.

• *Lobelia erinus:* Choose trailing varieties, in colours including white, crimson, lilac and blue.

• *Mimulus* 'Malibu Orange': Beautiful orange flowers during summer. For a colour contrast, place a basket of this mimulus between two planted with *Mimulus* 'Malibu Mixed'.

• *Nierembergia* 'Mont Blanc': Creates masses of 2.5cm/1in-wide, cup-shaped, white flowers throughout summer. Position in full sun and regularly remove dead flowers to encourage the development of others.

• Petunias: There are many single-coloured, cascading forms well-suited for hanging baskets. Their colours include blue, ruby, white, pink, rose and salmon.

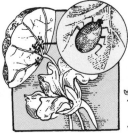

SINGLE-COLOUR *baskets create dominant displays (opposite), but ensure they harmonize with the background colour (page 181). Select plants that cascade and totally cloak their baskets.*

SOME *plants particularly attract pests: blackfly have a particular liking for Nasturtiums. In areas where these pests are a persistent problem, grow other plants. Greenfly is another major plant pest.*

IN MIXED *baskets combine foliage plants with flowers. Many foliage plants are better able to survive adverse conditions than flowering types, and therefore assure a long-lasting, bright display throughout summer.*

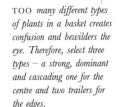

TOO *many different types of plants in a basket creates confusion and bewilders the eye. Therefore, select three types – a strong, dominant and cascading one for the centre and two trailers for the edges.*

TRY *colour variations within the same type of plant to reduce the risk of vigorous plants swamping their neighbours. This also creates a more evenly-shaped hanging basket than if different ones are used.*

DO NOT *pack too many plants into the same basket, as they will try to suffocate each other. Also, baskets that are too crowded tend to have a limited life, with the display becoming bare during mid-summer.*

BASKETS,
COMPOSTS AND LINERS

H ANGING baskets are unique containers and create unusual environments for plants. For that reason, care is essential when selecting the materials needed to create them.

• Baskets: There are three basic types: those with a plastic-coated wire framework; ones made of plastic with a drip-tray fitted into their bases; and large, bowl-shaped, plastic containers which have entire bases, without any provision for drainage or drip-trays underneath.

The wire type is ideal on patios, but where drips of water may spoil other plants or damage floors in lobbies and porches, the type with a drip-tray is best. Those without any drainage facility are used indoors, where plants are planted directly into them (see page 167).

It is easier to create a dominant display in a large basket than in a small one. And the large one, when filled with compost, has the advantage of not drying out as rapidly. But always select a size of basket that harmonizes with its intended surroundings.

• Liners: Their purpose is to prevent compost falling through gaps in wire-framed baskets and to assist in the retention of moisture. Many are formed from recycled materials, and are either moulded to the basket's shape or flat and pre-cut so that they fit snugly.

Black plastic is frequently used as a liner. Although not aesthetically pleasing, it is soon covered with trailing stems. Dustbin liners or old plastic bags are inexpensive alternatives to consider.

Sphagnum moss has been the traditional liner for baskets, but it is costly and gathering it is not environmentally friendly. It is useful, however, for placing over the compost after planting, creating an attractive appearance and reducing moisture loss.

• Metal brackets: These are essential to support hanging baskets. Choose strong ones.

COMPOSTS FOR HANGING BASKETS

Compost is crucially important when growing plants in hanging baskets, where a plant's root growth is restricted to frameworks 25–50cm/10–20in wide and about half as deep.

Proprietary composts are widely available and some have extra materials in them that assist in moisture-retention. Some varieties also include slow-acting fertilizers.

It is possible to make your own compost, but if only a few baskets are to be planted it is much easier to buy it in bags, ready prepared.

Peat-based composts are better than loam-based types for hanging baskets, as they retain more moisture. To assist this, add moisture-retaining additives such as perlite and vermiculite to the compost.

In past years, shredded cork was frequently used to retain moisture in hanging baskets, as well as in windowboxes.

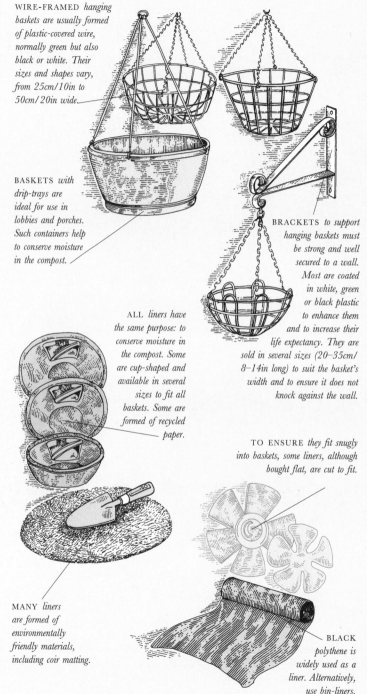

WIRE-FRAMED hanging baskets are usually formed of plastic-covered wire, normally green but also black or white. Their sizes and shapes vary, from 25cm/10in to 50cm/20in wide.

BASKETS with drip-trays are ideal for use in lobbies and porches. Such containers help to conserve moisture in the compost.

BRACKETS to support hanging baskets must be strong and well secured to a wall. Most are coated in white, green or black plastic to enhance them and to increase their life expectancy. They are sold in several sizes (20–35cm/ 8–14in long) to suit the basket's width and to ensure it does not knock against the wall.

ALL liners have the same purpose: to conserve moisture in the compost. Some are cup-shaped and available in several sizes to fit all baskets. Some are formed of recycled paper.

TO ENSURE they fit snugly into baskets, some liners, although bought flat, are cut to fit.

MANY liners are formed of environmentally friendly materials, including coir matting.

BLACK polythene is widely used as a liner. Alternatively, use bin-liners.

PLANTING A WIRE-FRAMED BASKET

❖

PLANT hanging baskets in spring, using half-hardy annuals as well as foliage plants like the Licorice Plant (*Helichrysum petiolatum*/*H. petiolare*) and tender perennials such as pelargoniums and cascading fuchsias.

INFLUENCE OF FROST

The precise time in spring when hanging baskets are planted depends on the weather. Some areas are frost free in early spring, while others still have frosts until early summer. However, it is possible to plant baskets before the risk of frost has passed, and instead of immediately placing them outdoors to put them temporarily in a frost-proof greenhouse or conservatory. This also gives plants a chance to become established and to create a display before being placed outdoors. However, while these baskets are waiting to be put outside, do not expose them to high temperatures. If possible, put the baskets outside during the day and move them back into a greenhouse at night. Alternatively, open the door and ventilators fully during the day.

After hanging baskets are placed outdoors, low temperatures are sometimes forecast at night. Plants can be given slight protection by placing a couple of layers of newspaper over them. Wedging the papers under the supporting chains is usually quite sufficient to hold them in position, as at that time of year the frost risk is from clear skies, rather than cold, searing winds.

CAREFUL WATERING

After initially watering the compost, take care during the following three or four weeks not to excessively moisten the compost, as this could keep it unnecessarily wet and cold, delaying establishment and encouraging roots to decay. However, once the plants are growing strongly and their roots are spread throughout the compost, more water is needed. Always apply water gently, as until roots fill the surface compost there is a risk of it being disturbed and washed about by forceful jets of water.

INITIAL STOPPING

A few young plants, such as fuchsias and foliage plants, need stopping (removal of shoot tips) to encourage them to develop sideshoots and become bushy. Pinch back the shoots to just above a pair of leaves. Place the removed shoot tips on a compost heap: do not leave them in the basket as this could encourage the onset of diseases. It is also unsightly. Removing the soft tips of shoots also makes plants less attractive to greenfly.

> ### EQUIPMENT NEEDED
>
> - *Bucket to hold the basket secure while being planted.*
> - *Clean, wire-framed basket.*
> - *Compost for hanging baskets – it must be able to retain moisture.*
> - *Black polythene.*
> - *Scalpel or sharp knife for slitting the polythene.*
> - *Range of trailing plants.*
> - *One central cascading plant.*
> - *Sphagnum moss.*
> - *Watering-can.*

HANGING IN A GREENHOUSE

Place newly planted hanging baskets in frost-proof greenhouses or conservatories to enable rapid establishment. Do not place them outside until all risk of severe frosts has passed, and keep the compost moist during this period.

Strong hook

1. PLACE *a wire-framed basket in the top of a bucket and line it with black polythene. Mould it to the basket's shape, then cut off 5cm/2in above the rim. The plastic may need further trimming later.*

2. PLACE *a handful of moist peat in the basket's base, then add and firm the compost to about half the container's depth. Take care not to push compost or your fingers through the plastic sheeting at the sides.*

3. MAKE *5cm/2in-long slits in the polythene, at about 10cm/4in apart and level with the surface of the compost. Push the roots of trailing plants through each hole, then cover and firm them with compost.*

4. ADD *more compost and plant a dominant, cascading plant in the centre. The surface of its soil-ball should be 12–18mm/¹/₂–³/₄in below the basket's rim. Add trailing plants around it, cover and firm with compost.*

5. WHEN *the planting is complete, the compost's surface should be 12mm/ ¹/₂in below the basket's rim. This enables the compost to be watered. Place a thick layer of sphagnum moss over the surface and rim.*

6. LEAVE *the basket in a bucket and gently water the compost twice so that it settles around the roots of plants. When excess water has drained, suspend the basket in a greenhouse until it is established.*

PLANTING
INDOOR HANGING BASKETS

❖

DISPLAYING houseplants in hanging baskets introduces a new dimension to indoor gardening. There are two basic ways to achieve this: taking the plants out of their pots and planting them into compost in a container, or leaving them in their pots and standing them in a flat-based, plastic hanging basket.

INDOOR hanging baskets introduce eye-height colour. When used in conjunction with troughs, they create attractive room dividers. Alternatively, suspend them over a coffee table, where they cannot be knocked.

Clearly, wire-framed, outdoor-type hanging baskets are not suitable for use indoors, as water would drip over carpets. Instead, plastic types with drip-trays built into them are used when plants are left in their pots. They can also be used where plants are removed from their containers, although if plants are watered carefully, containers with neither drainage holes nor drip-trays can be used.

The main advantage of leaving plants in their pots and just placing them in a basket, is that as plants cease flowering they can be replaced. Also, invasive types can be removed without radically affecting other plants. It is, however, slightly more difficult to water them, as each plant must be attended to separately, unlike the other method when all the plants are in the same compost. For either method, if the position is shaded, use foliage plants rather than flowering plants.

1. HOUSEPLANTS *can be left in their pots and displayed in a flat-based hanging basket fitted with a drip-tray. Pre-arrange the plants on a sheet of paper, then form a 2.5cm/1in-thick layer of pea-shingle in the basket's base.*

2. WATER *the plants a few hours before arranging them. Fill the container with plants, starting from the centre and working towards the outside. Position plants with their attractive 'face' sides pointing towards the basket's outside.*

3. TO REDUCE *the amount of watering needed, pack moist peat between the pots. This also helps to keep the compost cool. Do not cover the compost, as each pot must be watered individually, according to the dryness of the compost.*

1. ONE *way to grow plants in hanging baskets indoors is to remove their pots and plant them directly into a container. First, cut a piece of paper to the size and shape of the basket's base, and arrange the plants attractively on it.*

2. POSITION *a container in the top of a plastic bucket, to hold it firm. Fill the container's base with 18mm/³⁄4in of shingle, then a layer of peat-based potting compost, so that its surface is about 15cm/6in below the container's rim.*

3. SET *the plants in the container, using the same arrangement as shown in step one. Remove the pots, position the plants and pack compost around them. Ensure the surface of each root-ball is 12–18mm/ ¹⁄2–³⁄4in below the rim.*

FOLIAGE PLANTS FOR INDOOR HANGING BASKETS

• Devil's Ivy (*Epipremnum pinnatum/Scindapsus aureus):* Trailing stems bearing shiny green leaves blotched in yellow.

• Emerald Fern (*Asparagus densiflorus* 'Sprengeri'): Arching, wiry stems packed with long, needle-like leaves.

• Mother of Thousands (*Saxifraga stolonifera* 'Tricolor'): Roundish to heart-shaped, green leaves edged in white and pink, and long, wiry stems often 60cm/2ft or more long, bearing small plantlets.

• Spider Plant (*Chlorophytum comosum* 'Variegatum'): Long, tapering, cascading, green and white leaves. Eventually, it can form a plant more than 90cm/3ft across.

• Swedish Ivy (*Plectranthus coleoides* 'Marginatus'): Attractive light green leaves with scalloped edges about 5cm/2in wide that reveal broad, white edges.

• Swedish Ivy (*Plectranthus oertendahlii):* Trailing stems with 2.5cm/1in-wide, slightly heart-shaped, green leaves with prominent veins.

FLOWERING PLANTS FOR INDOOR HANGING BASKETS

• Basket Begonia (*Begonia* x *tuberhybrida* 'Pendula'): Wide colour range of pendulous flowers borne in clusters during summer. Single and double-flowered forms.

• Flame Flower (*Episcia cupreata):* Trailing stems bearing oval, 5–7.5cm/2–3in-long, dark green leaves with silver or pale green veins. During summer it develops tubular, orange-red flowers with yellow eyes.

• Goldfish Plant (*Columnea gloriosa):* Trailing stems up to 90cm/3ft long, packed with small leaves and tubular, 7.5cm/3in-long scarlet and yellow flowers from late autumn to spring. Requires high temperatures in winter.

• Italian Bellflower (*Campanula isophylla):* Easily grown, with blue, star-shaped flowers from mid-summer to early autumn. There also is a white-flowered form.

• Lady's Eardrops (*Fuchsias):* There are many slightly tender, trailing fuchsias that can be grown in indoor hanging baskets. Ensure the compost does not become dry.

SECURING A BASKET

Few gardening sights are more sobering and regrettable than a hanging basket that has fallen from a broken bracket and burst apart on the ground. And except for the devastation caused by freak summer storms, such catastrophes are usually avoidable.

DANGER POINTS

There are always weak and vulnerable points in the construction of anything, and here are a few to be aware of when securing hanging baskets:

• Always use proper masonry fixings when securing brackets to walls; never knock matchsticks into holes instead of sound fixings. And ensure the drill size is compatible with the fixing; builders' merchants and hardware shops will always advise on this.
• Do not reuse corroded brackets stored from several years earlier.
• Do not reuse partly corroded screws, as they may break and the bracket collapse. Also, if their heads snap off it is difficult to remove them from the wall.

SECURING TO BARGE-BOARDS

In bungalows where the eaves extend about 38cm/15in beyond the brickwork, it is possible to screw strong cup-hooks into the barge-board. However, this can only be done if the barge-board is made of wood, rather than plastic. Never underestimate the weight of a basket when watered: buy the strongest fixing possible.

• Always check chains used to secure hanging baskets to their brackets. Replacement chains are available to suit baskets from 25cm/10in wide to 50cm/20in wide. If chains that are too small are used, it puts unnecessary strain on both the basket and the chain, causing them to warp and break.

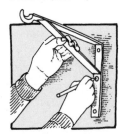

WHEN *fitting a wall-bracket, hold it upright and in position, then use a pencil to mark the wall with the positions of the securing holes. If the bracket is at an angle, the weight of the basket may eventually twist it off the wall.*

DRILL *the wall – ensuring it is sound and firm – and use masonry fixings to plug it. The size of the drill must enable the fixing to fit snugly; it usually needs a few light taps of a hammer to make it flush with the wall's surface.*

USE *galvanized screws that are long enough to pass through the holes in the bracket and to the depths of the holes. First, partly turn both screws into the wall, then tighten. Do not screw one in fully before attending to the other one.*

WATERING HANGING BASKETS

No other plant containers are as exposed to drying sun and winds as hanging baskets. It therefore is not surprising that they need special attention and watering several times a day during the height of summer. Apart from watering the baskets in the ways illustrated, there are a few other ways to consider, which can reduce the frequency of watering:

• Proprietary hose-pipe fittings and trigger mechanisms enable the baskets to be watered from ground level.
• On exceptionally hot days, dampen the wall and patio area around baskets. This is because hot walls reflect heat and speed up the drying process.
• Mix water-retentive additives, such as vermiculite and perlite, to composts (see page 165).
• If water runs out of the compost, leave it for half an hour and then water again. The first watering will expand the compost, the second one will saturate it.

• If the basket is large, put a plastic saucer in its base while planting it. This acts as a reservoir, full of moist compost.
• During very hot days, drop a few ice-cubes on top of the compost. These eventually melt and provide extra water.

IMMERSING IN A BOWL

Peat-based composts that become dry are difficult to re-moisten. If this happens, take down the basket and immerse the complete compost area in a bowl of water until bubbles cease to rise. Allow to drain before replacing on a bracket.

WATERING *hanging baskets is not easy: one way is to stand on a stool and use a watering-can. This is very difficult, as well as perilous. However, filling the can only half full makes the task easier. Remove the rose from the can.*

TYING *the end of a hose-pipe to a 1.2m/4ft-long cane makes watering easier. Raise the cane and gently trickle water on the compost until it spills over the edge. Bend the top of the hose over to prevent water running back down it and up your sleeves.*

HANGING *baskets suspended too high to be watered from step-ladders are best fitted with pulleys so that they can be lowered. Ensure the pulley mechanism is safe and the basket will not fall. Also, beware of water dripping on passers-by.*

FUCHSIAS

❖

EW plants capture such attention and admiration as fuchsias. They are native mainly to Southern and Central America and in general are tender in temperate countries and thereby vulnerable to frosts. A few, such as *Fuchsia magellanica*, are relatively hardy, but those grown in hanging baskets are tender.

SUITABLE PLANTS

Although it is possible to raise your own fuchsias from cuttings, if only a few plants are needed it is much easier to order established plants from specialist nurseries, or to buy them from garden centres. Whatever the source, they cannot be planted outdoors until all risk of frost has passed. However, if a frost-proof greenhouse or conservatory is available, hanging baskets can be planted earlier and placed in them until outdoor conditions improve. Ensure these plants have had their shoot tips removed to encourage the development of sideshoots. Not all varieties are suitable for hanging baskets, but the following are superb.

FUCHSIAS FOR HANGING BASKETS

• 'Cascade': Single; white sepals flushed carmine, and deep red petals. Attractive drooping habit.
• 'Falling Stars': Single; pale scarlet sepals and turkey-red petals with slight orange tints.

PARTS OF A FLOWER

Fuchsia flowers appear complex, but have the same basic parts as other flowers. Their intricate nature has made them widely known as Lady's Eardrops.

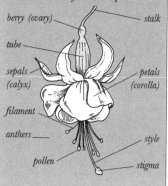

berry (ovary) — stalk
tube
sepals (calyx) — petals (corolla)
filament
anthers
pollen — style
— stigma

SINGLE FLOWERS *are distinguished by having only four petals. They reveal a simple elegance. These include old varieties, such as 'Achievement', 'Brutus', 'Coachman', 'Dr. Foster' and 'Display'.*

SEMI-DOUBLE FLOWERS *have five, six or seven petals. These include 'Alice Hoffman', 'Lena', 'Muriel', 'Papoose', 'Phyllis', 'Pink Pearl', 'Snowcap', 'Trase', 'Walsingham' and 'Westminster Chimes'.*

DOUBLE FLOWERS *have eight or more petals, and to many eyes appear too cluttered. Examples include 'Annabel', 'Constance', 'Dollar Princess', 'Harry Gray', 'Heidi Ann', 'Pink Galore' and 'Swingtime'.*

• 'Golden Marinka': similar to 'Marinka', but with golden foliage.
• 'Harry Gray': Double; white sepals, shading to rose-pink, and white petals shading to rose-pink.
• 'Jack Acland': Single; bright pink tube and sepals, and deep rose petals.
• 'La Campanella': Semi-double; white sepals flushed white, and imperial purple petals changing to a more suitable lavender.
• 'Lakeside': Single; vigorous and branching variety with bluish-violet petals veined in bright pink. As the flowers mature, this fades to a shade of lilac.
• 'Lena': Semi-double; very free-flowering, with rosy-magenta petals, flushed pink and paling at their bases. The flowers are medium sized.
• 'Marinka': Single; rich red sepals, and dark red petals.
• 'Swingtime': Double; rich, shiny red sepals and milky-white coloured petals.
• 'Walshingham': Semi-double; off-white and rose-pink sepals, and pale-lilac petals.

NAUTICAL INTRODUCTION

The introduction of fuchsias from Southern and Central America into England is uncertain, but one story tells how, in the 1790s, James Lee, the owner of the famous Vineyard Nursery in London, saw a fuchsia growing in the window of a cottage in Wapping. It was said to have been brought from South America by a sailor and given to his mother. Stories suggest that Lee paid eighty guineas for it. It is more likely that Lee got the plants from Kew Gardens, donated by Captain Firth on return from South America.

Fuchsia macrantha

WHEN *planting a basket totally with fuchsias, create a quick display by planting five or seven bushy and trailing plants of the same variety around the edges.*

WHEN *mixing fuchsias with other plants, plant a dominant, cascading variety in the centre. Put trailing plants around the edges to clothe the basket's sides.*

FUCHSIAS *are superb in hanging baskets, as their flowers can be readily seen at eye-height. It is essential, however, to choose cascading types (see above and right).*

PLANTS FOR HANGING BASKETS 1

THE range of summer-flowering, half-hardy plants that can be grown in hanging-baskets is wide. They are also ideal for planting in wall baskets, where they help to cloak the sides with flowers. However, not all plants that are recommended for wall baskets and mangers can be planted in hanging baskets, as they are either too large or without a trailing or pendulous habit.

RAISING PLANTS

• Floss Flower (*Ageratum houstonianum*): Sow seeds 3mm/⅛in deep in early spring in 10–16°F/50–61°F. Germination takes ten to fourteen days. When the seedlings are large enough to handle, transfer them to seed-trays and later acclimatize to outdoor conditions.

PLANTING DISTANCE

Plants in hanging baskets are planted much closer together than when in a border in a garden, or even in tubs. This is because hanging baskets are relatively small and a colour-packed display is essential. In wall baskets and mangers, plants at the edges can be left slightly further apart because those in the centre are usually relatively large and dominant. Although the spacings suggested in the plant listings from here and until page 174 may appear close, they create successful displays.

Regular attention is necessary to ensure pests and diseases do not manage to establish themselves in the display.

AGERATUM HOUSTONIANUM *(Floss Flower): Height 13–30cm/5–12in, plant 13–15cm/5–6in apart. Ideal when forming a collar in large hanging baskets or wall baskets. Clustered, powder-puff-like blue, pink or white flowers in summer.*

ALYSSUM MARITIMUM *(now Lobularia maritima): Height 7.5–15cm/3–6in, plant 15cm/6in apart. Carpeting and trailing, in white, rosy-red and deep purple throughout summer. Plant trailing types of this plant around the sides of baskets.*

ANAGALLIS LINIFOLIA *'Gentian Blue' (Pimpernel): Height 15–23cm/6–9in, plant 13–15cm/5–6in apart. Low growing and sprawling, with masses of 12–18mm/½–¾in-wide, rich blue flowers with bright coloured centres, from early to late summer.*

ASARINA PURPUSII *'Victoria Falls': Height 13–15cm/5–6in, plant 15–20cm/6–8in apart. It creates a tumbling fountain of cerise-purple, 5cm/2in-long trumpets from early summer to autumn. The stems often trail for 38cm/15in.*

BEGONIA SEMPERFLORENS *(Wax Plant): Height 15–23cm/6–9in, plant 15–20cm/6–8in apart. Bushy, floriferous plants, packed with flowers from early to late summer. Many attractive colours, including white, pink and scarlet.*

BEGONIA x TUBERHYBRIDA *'Pendula' (Basket Begonia): Height 15–20cm/5–8in, plant 25cm/10in apart. Slender, trailing stems that create a dominant feature in hanging baskets. Colours include red, yellow and pink, from early to late summer.*

• Sweet Alyssum (*Alyssum maritimum/Lobularia maritima*): Sow seeds 6mm/¼in deep during late winter and early spring in 10–13°C/50–55°F. Germination takes seven to ten days. Later, prick out the seedlings into small clusters and slowly acclimatize them to outdoor temperatures.

• Pimpernel (*Anagallis linifolia*): Sow seeds 3mm/⅛in deep in late winter or early spring and place in 16°C/61°F. Germination takes two to three weeks. When the seedlings are large enough to handle, transfer them to small pots or seed-trays and slowly acclimatize to outdoor conditions.

• *Asarina purpusii:* Sow seeds on the surface of compost during late winter and early spring in 21–24°C/70–75°F. Germination takes two to four weeks. When large enough to handle, transfer the seedlings into small pots or seed-trays and slowly acclimatize to outdoor conditions.

• Wax Plant (*Begonia semperflorens*): Sow seeds thinly on the surface of compost (do not cover) during late winter and early spring. Water lightly and place in 16–20°C/61–68°F. Germination takes two to four weeks. When large enough to handle, prick off the seedlings into small clusters and gradually acclimatize them to outdoor conditions and temperarures.

• Basket Begonia (*Begonia x tuberhybrida* 'Pendula'): Plant tubers in 7.5–10cm/3–4in-deep boxes filled with moist peat in early and mid-spring and place in 18°C/64°F. Keep moist and when shoots develop transfer them singly into pots of peat-based compost. Reduce the temperature slightly, keep moist and transfer to 10–13cm/4–5in-wide pots. Slowly acclimatize to outdoor temperatures and plant into baskets. Do not expose plants to low temperatures or draughts, as the buds might then drop off.

PLANTS FOR HANGING BASKETS 2

❖

THERE are many more plants to consider for planting in hanging baskets, wall baskets and mangers. Some of these form dominant centre-pieces in hanging baskets, while others are better for planting around the sides.

RAISING PLANTS

• Seed-raised Pendulous Begonias (*Begonia pendula* 'Illumination'): Sow seeds thinly on the surface of compost (do not cover) during early spring and place in 16–20°C/61–68°F. Germination takes two to four weeks. When large enough to handle, transfer the seedings into small pots and slowly acclimatize to outdoor conditions.
• Swan River Daisy (*Brachycome iberidifolia*): Sow seeds 3–6mm/⅛–¼in deep during early and mid-spring in 18°C/64°F. Germination takes about ten days. When large enough to handle, transfer the seedlings into seed-trays or small pots and plant when all risk of frost has passed.

• Slipper Flower (*Calceolaria integrifolia* 'Sunshine'): Sow seeds – just pressing them into the surface – during early spring in 15–20°C/59–68°C. Germination takes two

CAMPANULA CARPATICA *'Bellissimo'*: Height 15cm/6in, then trailing, plant about 20–23cm/8–9in apart. Masses of chalice-shaped, 5cm/2in-wide, blue or white flowers from early to late summer. Creates a massed display.

CAMPANULA ISOPHYLLA *(Star of Bethlehem)*: Height 15cm/6in, then trailing, plant 20cm/8in apart. Masses of star-shaped, 2.5cm/1in-wide, blue flowers from mid- to late summer. There is also a white form.

CONVOLVULUS TRICOLOR *'Rose Ensign'*: Height: 10–15cm/4–6in, then trailing, plant 20–25cm/8–10in apart. Masses of beautiful, rose, lemon, pink and white, trumpet-like flowers from mid- to late summer.

to three weeks. When the seedlings are large enough to handle, transfer them into small pots, slowly harden off and plant into a hanging basket.
• *Campanula carpatica* 'Bellissimo': Sow seeds – just pressing them into the compost – in late winter and early spring. When the seedlings are large enough to handle, transfer them to seed-trays or small pots and slowly acclimatize to outdoor conditions.
• Star of Bethlehem (*Campanula isophylla* 'Krystal' varieties): Sow seeds 3mm/⅛in deep in 16°C/61°F in late winter. Prick off the seedlings into seed-trays or small pots, slowly harden off and plant into containers when all risk of frost has passed. Before the introduction of 'Krystal' varieties, this species always had to be raised from cuttings.
• *Convolvulus tricolor* 'Rose Ensign': Sow seeds 3mm/⅛in deep in 15–18°C/59–64°F during early spring. When the seedlings are large enough to handle, prick out into seed-trays and slowly accustom to outdoor conditions.

BEGONIA PENDULA *'Illumination'*: Height 15–20cm/6–8in, then trailing, plant 20cm/8in apart. Masses of large, double flowers in shades of pink, many with cream centres, throughout summer.

BRACHYCOME IBERIDIFOLIA *'Splendour'* (Swan River Daisy): Height 23–30cm/9–12in, plant 15–20cm/6–8in apart. Each plant produces masses of flowers in blue to purple or white in summer.

CALCEOLARIA INTEGRIFOLIA *'Sunshine'* (Slipper Flower): Height 25–38cm/10–15in, plant as a centre-piece in a hanging basket, where it develops bright yellow, pouch-like flowers.

PLANTS FOR HANGING BASKETS 3

THERE are many more plants to consider: some are raised from seeds, others by cuttings. Plants raised from seeds are usually half-hardy annuals and are therefore discarded at the end of summer, but plants with a perennial nature, like small-leaved ivies, can be replanted in autumn into other containers.

RAISING PLANTS

• Cascade Geraniums: These are also known as Continental Geraniums and Swiss Balcon Geraniums, although botanically they are not geraniums but forms of pelargoniums. Many of the varieties are patented and are usually bought as established plants in mid to late spring, either from nurseries or through the mail from seed companies.

• Ivy-leaved Geranium *(Pelargonium peltatum)*: Increased from cuttings, 6–7.5cm/2¹/₂–3in long, during late summer. Insert them in equal parts moist peat and sharp

sand, place in a cool greenhouse and cover their leaves with newspapers for about ten days. When rooted, pot up, place in 7–10°C/45–50°F and keep barely moist. Shelter from sunlight and remove the tips of shoots to encourage bushiness. Plant into containers as soon as the risk of frost has passed. During winter, keep the compost barely moist, as soft growth must be prevented.

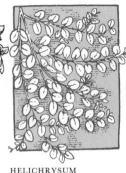

HEDERA HELIX *(Small-leaved Ivy): Height 7.5–10cm/3–4in, then trailing, plant 15–16cm/5–6in apart. Select variegated varieties for planting around a basket's edge. In autumn, plant them in windowboxes.*

HELICHRYSUM PETIOLATUM *(Licorice Plant): Height 15–20cm/6–8in, then cascading and spreading, plant 25cm/10in apart. Stiff stems peppered with roundish, white leaves covered with woolly hairs.*

IMPATIENS *(Busy Lizzie): Height 15cm/6in, then cascading, plant 15–20cm/6–8in apart. Choose cascading varieties. Masses of flowers, up to 5cm/2in across, in many colours throughout summer.*

• Variegated Ground Ivy *(Glechoma hederacea 'Variegata'/Nepeta hederacea 'Variegata')*: It is easily increased by dividing plants in early spring. Discard old, central areas and replant younger pieces from around the outside.

• Small-leaved Ivy *(Hedera helix)*: Take 6cm/2¹/₂in-long stem-and-leaf cuttings during summer and insert in equal parts moist peat and sharp sand. Place in gentle warmth and pot up when rooted.

• Licorice Plant *(Helichrysum petiolatum/H. petiolare)*: During mid- and late summer, take cuttings from sideshoots. Insert them in equal parts moist peat and sharp sand. Move rooted cuttings into small pots and overwinter in a cool greenhouse. Plant into hanging baskets during late spring.

• Busy Lizzie *(Impatiens)*: Sow seeds 3–6mm/¹/₈–¹/₄in deep during mid-spring in 15–20°C/59–68°F. Germination takes ten to fourteen days. When large enough to handle, prick out the seedlings into seed-trays, acclimatize to outdoor conditions.

CASCADE GERANIUMS *(Continental Geraniums): Height 20–30cm/8–12in, then trailing, plant 15–20cm/6–8in apart. Cascading, with masses of flowers in shades of scarlet, salmon, pink and lilac.*

PELARGONIUM PELTATUM *(Ivy-leaved Geraniums): Height 20–25cm/8–10cm, then cascading and trailing; plant one in a small hanging basket, or three in a large one. Summer flowering.*

GLECHOMA HEDERACEA 'Variegata' *(Variegated Ground Ivy): Height 7.5–10cm/3–4in, then trailing, plant 25cm/10in apart. Mid-green, kidney-shaped leaves with white marks.*

PLANTS FOR
HANGING BASKETS 4

❖

THERE are more summer-flowering plants to choose from: many of those suggested here are raised each year from seeds.

RAISING PLANTS

• <u>Trailing Lobelia</u> (*Lobelia erinus*): Sow seeds – barely covering them – from mid-winter to early spring in 15–20°C/59–68°F. Germination takes one to two weeks. When large enough to handle, prick out the seedlings into small clusters in a seed-tray. Then, slowly acclimatize the plants to outdoor temperatures.

• <u>Creeping Jenny/Moneywort</u> (*Lysimachia nummularia* 'Aurea'): It is easily increased by lifting and dividing established plants in spring. Use this yellow-leaved form instead of the normal type, as it is slightly less invasive and creates colour throughout summer. It also bears bright golden-yellow, cup-shaped flowers. It is ideal in large hanging baskets, as well as wall baskets and mangers.

• <u>Monkey Flower</u> (*Mimulus* 'Malibu Orange'): Sow seeds thinly – just pressing them into the surface of compost – during early summer in 16–20°C/61–68°F. Germination takes ten to fourteen days. When the seedlings are large enough to handle, transfer into seed-trays, then slowly accustom to outdoor conditions.

• <u>Nasturtium</u> (*Tropaeolum majus*): Sow seeds 6mm/¼in deep in 13–16°C/55–61°F in late winter and early spring. Germination takes ten to fourteen days. When the seedlings are large enough to handle, move them into small pots. Do not grow them in rich compost, as they then develop too many shoots, at the expense of flower production.

• *Nemophila maculata* '5-Spot': Sow seeds 6mm/¼in deep in 15°C/59°F in early spring. Germination

TROPAEOLUM MAJUS *'Double Gleam Mixed'* (*Nasturtiums*): Height 20–30cm/8–12in, then trailing, plant 15–20cm/6–8in apart. Semi-double, scented flowers in yellow, orange and scarlet. Also, plant the 'Whirlybird'.

NEMOPHILA MACULATA *'5-Spot'*: Height 7.5–15cm/3–6in, then trailing: plant 20cm/8in apart. Light green leaves and beautiful light blue flowers with a deep blue spot at the tip of each petal. It is ideal in light shade.

NEMOPHILA MENZIESII *'Pennie Black'*: Height 5–10cm/2–4in, then spreading to about 30cm/12in wide: plant 23cm/9in apart. Purple to black flowers, about 18mm/³⁄₄in wide with scalloped, white edges – throughout summer.

takes ten to fourteen days. When large enough to handle, transfer the seedlings into small pots and slowly acclimatize to outdoor conditions. Do not expose to frost.

• *Nemophila menziesii* 'Pennie Black': Raise new plants each year in the same way as recommended for *Nemophila maculata*, a closely related, bushy annual.

LOBELIA ERINUS (*Trailing Lobelia*): Height 10–15cm/4–5in, then trailing, plant 10cm/4in apart. Select trailing varieties, in colours including blue, white, lilac and crimson. They flower throughout summer.

LYSIMACHIA NUMMULARIA *'Aurea'* (*Moneywort/Creeping Jenny*): Height 5–7.5cm/2–3in, then trailing, plant 20–25cm/8–10in apart. Hardy, herbaceous perennial with long stems, yellow leaves and golden flowers.

MIMULUS *'Malibu Orange'* (*Monkey Flower*): Height 13–15cm/5–6in, plant 15cm/6in apart. Orange flowers during summer. Also, mixed-colour varieties – cream, golden-orange, red and burgundy – throughout summer.

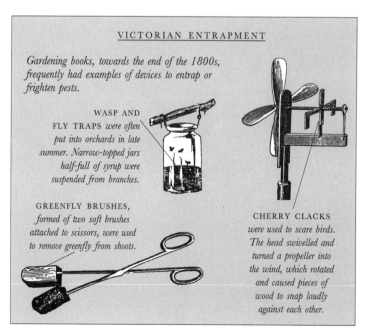

VICTORIAN ENTRAPMENT

Gardening books, towards the end of the 1800s, frequently had examples of devices to entrap or frighten pests.

WASP AND FLY TRAPS *were often put into orchards in late summer. Narrow-topped jars half-full of syrup were suspended from branches.*

GREENFLY BRUSHES, *formed of two soft brushes attached to scissors, were used to remove greenfly from shoots.*

CHERRY CLACKS *were used to scare birds. The head swivelled and turned a propeller into the wind, which rotated and caused pieces of wood to snap loudly against each other.*

PLANTS FOR
HANGING BASKETS 5
❖

THE ESSENTIAL qualities of plants for hanging baskets are that they should have a cascading or trailing nature, and create a vivid display throughout summer. Those described here will create a feast of colour.

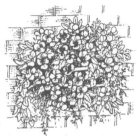

MOST *of the plants used in hanging baskets are raised from seeds sown early in the year in gentle warmth, and later transferred to pots or seed-trays.*

RAISING PLANTS
• Nierembergia 'Mont Blanc': Sow seeds 3–6mm/⅛–¼in deep in 15°C/59°F in late winter and early spring. When the seedlings are large enough to handle, transfer them into seed-trays and slowly acclimatize to outdoor conditions and temperatures.
• Pansies (viola): Sow seeds 6mm/¼in deep in 10–16°C/50–61°F in late winter and early spring. Germination takes two to

three weeks. When large enough to handle, prick out the seedlings into small pots and slowly acclimatize to outdoor conditions. Plant into containers in early summer.
• Garden Petunia (Petunia x hybrida): Sow seeds thinly on the surface of compost during winter and early spring in 15–20°C/59–68°F. Germination takes one to two weeks. When large enough to handle, move the seedlings into seed-trays and slowly acclimatize to outdoor conditions. Do not put the young plants into containers until all risk of frost has passed.
• Silene pendula 'Peach Blossom': Sow seeds 3–6mm/⅛–¼in deep in 15°C/59°F in late winter or

SILENE PENDULA
'Peach Blossom': Height 10–15cm/ 4–6in, then cascading, plant 20–25cm/ 8–10in apart. Spreading and branching, with masses of 18mm/³/₄in-wide, double flowers. Deep pink buds open to salmon and mature to white.

THUNBERGIA ALATA
(Black-eyed Susan): Height 90cm/3ft, but also trails when in hanging baskets. Thunbergia fragrans 'Angel Wings', with snow-white, lightly fragrant flowers, is also good in hanging baskets and pots. Creates a wealth of colour in summer.

VERBENA x HYBRIDA
(Vervain): Height 23cm/ 9in, then trailing, plant 15–25cm/6–10in apart. Plant three in a hanging basket. Select trailing varieties, such as 'Peaches 'n Cream', in beautiful shades of cream, apricot, orange and yellow.

early spring. When large enough to handle, transfer the seedlings into seed-trays or small pots and slowly acclimatize to outdoor conditions. Plant into containers as soon as all risk of frost has passed.
• Black-eyed Susan (Thunbergia alata): Sow seeds 6mm/¼in deep in 20°C/68°F during early and mid-spring. Germination takes about three weeks. When the seedlings are large enough to handle, transfer them to small pots. Slowly harden them off and plant into containers on patios when all risk of frost has passed.
• Vervain (Verbena x hybrida): Sow seeds 3mm/⅛in deep from late winter to early spring in 15–20°C/59–68°F. Germination takes two to three weeks. When growing strongly, transfer the seedlings into seed-trays. Harden off the plants and transfer to containers when all risk of frost has passed.

During recent years, new varieties have been developed in North America and Britain, many ideal for hanging baskets.

NIEREMBERGIA *'Mont Blanc': Height 10–15cm/ 4–6in, plant 13–15cm/ 5–6in apart. It creates a mass of 2.5cm/1in-wide, cup-shaped, white flowers throughout summer. Remove dead flowers regularly and position in full sun.*

PANSY *'Water Colours Mixed' (Viola): Height 10–15cm/4–6in, plant 10cm/4in apart. Weather-resistant variety, ideal in hanging baskets with flowers in many delicate shades in winter and spring, as well as summer.*

PETUNIA x HYBRIDA *(Garden Petunia): Height 10–15cm/4–6in, then cascading, plant 20cm/8in apart. Select cascading varieties. Some are single colours, other mixtures are blue, white, pink, blush, cerise, scarlet and violet.*

MIXING AND
MATCHING PLANTS 1

Trailing nasturiums

Dwarf marigolds

Dwarf marigolds

AS WELL as matching the colours of hanging baskets' flowers and leaves to their backgrounds, such as white, grey and red-bricked walls (page 181), colour contrasts and harmonies within each basket are desirable. Also, there needs to be a variation in the shapes and sizes of plants within each basket.

SELECTING PLANTS
Apart from the colour theme or contrasts within a basket, when selecting plants consider the following points:
• Do not select more than three different types of plants for small baskets, or four when planting larger ones. If more than these are used, creating colour contrasts become difficult. It also can be confusing to the eye – and mind – which invariably likes to analyse and separate mixtures into their component parts.

• Select trailing plants that quickly clothe the basket's sides. There are many to choose from, in a wide range of colours. Many of these plants are traditional and have been used for years, such as trailing lobelia and alyssum, but a few more recent ones such as *Nierembergia* 'Mont Blanc' are worth trying.
• Unless the basket is packed with the same plants, such as petunias, Busy Lizzies or pansies, choose a dominant plant for the centre. This will give height and create a focal point. Cascading fuchsias are frequently used in these positions and can be selected so that their colours harmonize with the trailing plants at the outside. A range of fuchsia varieties for hanging baskets is detailed on page 169.
• Foliage plants complete many trios and have the advantage of creating height and width without drenching the display in tightly packed stems, flowers and leaves.

BASKETS formed totally of flowering plants create vibrant colour displays that soon attract attention. Choose a selection of cascading, upright and bushy plants to ensure the basket becomes totally covered.

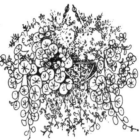

THIS basket is planted with nasturtiums, dwarf marigolds and trailing lobelia. Petunias can be substituted for the marigolds where a range of more subtle colours is desired, or to suit a different background.

PLANT hanging baskets with three or – at the most and only when the basket is large – four different types of plants. Here is a combination of flowering and foliage plants that creates interest throughout summer.

SELECT trailing forms of lobelia to cloak the basket's sides, with the attractively leaved Helichrysum petiolatum *to introduce width to the display. The Ivy-leaved Geranium creates leaf-shape contrast.*

For example, the gaps plants such as the Licorice Plant (*Helichrysum petiolatum*) create between their stems introduce light and air to a display and prevents it from appearing too solid. This is especially important in rural situations, where colour-dominant displays are less appealing than in towns. Foliage plants also help to perpetuate a display through to the frosts of autumn.

VARIEGATED TRAILERS
Several hardy variegated plants, such as ivies and Ground Ivy (*Glechoma hederacea* 'Variegata') are used to cloth the sides of baskets, but if too many are used, their colourful leaves can dominate the basket and immediately capture the eye at the expense of flowering plants. Therefore, use brightly coloured types sparingly, so that they create a framework for demure, but nevertheless attractive, flowers.

Glechoma hederacea 'Variegata' is often listed in catalogues as *Nepeta hederacea* 'Variegata'.

Ivy-leaved Geranium

Trailing lobelia

Helichrysum petiolatum

MIXING AND MATCHING PLANTS 2

❖

PLANTING schemes for flower borders in gardens are often a medley of colours, but some are formed of specific hues, such as white, grey, orange, green or blue. The same philosophy can be pursued for plants in hanging baskets, although it is best to restrict them to pastel shades, such as white and silver, and light blue. These create more relaxing ambiences on patios and terraces than if packed with vivid red flowers.

COLOUR-DEDICATED BASKETS

For white and silver baskets there are many plants to choose from, but avoid those with excessively white flowers as these will make the others look dowdy: they capture too much attention, especially when in bright sunshine. Use plenty of trailing plants, so that the display has well-covered irregular edges and appears to blend with its surroundings.

Combining them with silver-leaved or green-and-white variegated plants helps to reduce the impact of bright, white flowers.

Light blue designs have a warmer aura than white-and-silver ones and are superb when positioned against light grey, colour-washed walls. Unlike white-coloured arrangements, try to smother all the leaves with colour as green tends to dominate blue flowers, rather than complimenting them. Single-colour theme baskets bursting with light blue lobelia are especially attractive.

If there is an aged invalid in your house who is likely to sit outside during summer, use baskets planted with pastel-coloured plants, together with light green or silver-leaved foliage. Vivid reds and scarlets can soon disorientate people who are unwell, whereas restful-looking colours help to create an ambience that encourages speedy recovery.

TRAILING *fuchsias have informal outlines that harmonize with Ivy-leaved Geraniums. Select trailing lobelia with flower colours that create rich colour contrasts.*

NASTURTIUMS *are also informal, with a countrified, often lax outline. Unfortunately, they attract blackfly and therefore frequent spraying is usually essential.*

Cascading fuchsias   *Trailing nasturtiums*   *Trailing lobelia*

CASCADING *petunias are superb plants for hanging baskets, especially in large containers where they can be collared with trailing plants, and peppered with a few marigolds to add a rich yellow sparkle.*

ALTERNATIVES *to petunias could be Busy Lizzies (in a wide colour range), while trailing forms of lobelia are in white, crimson, blue and lilac, so that almost any colour harmony can be created.*

Cascading petunias   *Dwarf marigolds*   *Trailing lobelia*

VICTORIAN EXPERIMENTATION

Victorian gardeners had great vitality and a desire to explore new ways to use plants. Some of the plants they grew outdoors in suspended pots and other containers were hardy and earlier grew in borders and rock gardens.

THE *Ice Plant* (Mesembryanthemum crystallinum), *prostrate, much-branched, was grown in rock gardens. It was also ideal for planting in a suspended pot, where its stems trailed up to 60cm/2ft.*

SIEBOLD'S *Stonecrop* (Sedum sieboldii), *although half-hardy, was grown in rock gardens outdoors. When planted in a hanging pot it created a magnificent display. Today, both this and a variegated form (S. s. 'Medio-variegatum') are grown in indoor hanging baskets.*

KNOWN *widely as Mother of Thousands and Creeping Sailor,* Saxifraga stolonifera *is only half-hardy outdoors in temperate areas. When planted in ornate pots and used outdoors in summer and indoors in winter it became very popular. The thin, thread-like, wiry stems often trail for several feet.*

PLANTS FOR
LOBBIES AND PORCHES 1

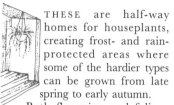

THESE are half-way homes for houseplants, creating frost- and rain-protected areas where some of the hardier types can be grown from late spring to early autumn.

Both flowering and foliage houseplants can be used, although to create interest throughout summer it is best to select those with coloured or variegated leaves. Nevertheless, Charm Chrysanthemums provide a spectacular display for several months.

PLANTING

There are two main ways of planting indoor hanging baskets for houseplants (see page 167), and the same techniques can be used for plants in lobbies and porches. These involve either removing the pots and planting the soil-balls directly into compost, or leaving the pots in place and standing them in a group in a flat-bottomed, plastic hanging basket.

OTHER HOUSEPLANTS
TO CONSIDER

In addition to the trailing and cascading plants described here and on the following pages, there are several others which are suitable for hanging baskets in lobbies and porches, including:

• *Ficus pumila* 'Sonny' (Variegated Creeping Fig): This is similar to the normal, all-green Creeping Fig (page 178) but with white edges to small, green leaves. Put three plants in a small basket.

• *Coleus pumilus* 'Trailing Queen' (Trailing Coleus): Most coleus plants are upright and bushy, but this is a trailing type and ideal in summer in a lobby or porch. They are raised from seeds sown on the surface of compost in late winter or early spring and placed in 18–24°C/64–75°F. The seeds of other trailing varieties are widely available and include 'Moulten Lava' and 'Scarlet Poncho'.

• *Callisia elegans* (Striped Inch Plant): It is related and relatively

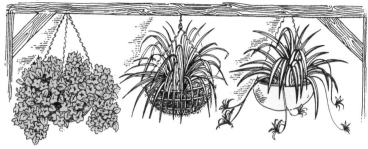

CAMPANULA ISOPHYLLA *(Star of Bethlehem/Italian Bellflower/Falling Stars): Height 15cm/6in, spread 30–45cm/12–18in. Heart-shaped, mid-green leaves and star-shaped blue flowers in mid- and late summer.*

CAREX MORROWII *'Variegata' (Japanese Sedge): Height 25–30cm/10–12in, spread 45–60cm/1¹/2–2ft. Arching, grass-like green leaves up to 30cm/12in long, with broad, creamy-white stripes. Very hardy.*

CHLOROPHYTUM COMOSUM *'Variegatum' (Spider Plant/Ribbon Plant/Spider Ivy): Height 15–25cm/5–10in, spread 60–90cm/2–3ft. Long, narrow leaves with white and green stripes. Plantlets on long stems.*

similar to the Wandering Jews (tradescantias) and develops fleshy, dull green leaves with white stripes and purple undersides. Plant it in a small pot, suspended or placed in a wall bracket.

• *Cyanotis kewensis* (Teddy Bear Vine): It is closely related to the tradescantias, but has densely hairy leaves, about 2.5cm/1in long. They are fleshy and their undersides are purple. For the best effect, display it on its own in a hanging pot.

• *Mikania ternata* (Plush Vine): A fast-growing, trailing plant for warm lobbies in summer. It makes a change from ivies, but is not as hardy and tolerant. The green, palmate leaves have an attractive purplish sheen.

• *Pellaea rotundifolia* (Button Fern/New Zealand Cliff Brake): Unusual fern, with small, button-like, leathery, dark green fronds on wiry stems. Do not mix it with other plants. Instead, plant it in a small pot and either suspend or place in a wall-bracket.

• *Peperomia scandens* 'Variegata' (Cupid Peperomia): It is often

grown in a hanging basket indoors, and is equally at home in a warm lobby. Trailing stems bear succulent, somewhat heart-shaped, green leaves with broad yellow edges and patches.

VICTORIAN
FERN LOVERS

During the Victorian era, ferns became very popular: many small ones were planted in Wardian Cases (enclosed glass cabinets evolved by Dr. Nathaniel Ward) as well as in borders and especially in damp situations. Forms of Phyllitis scolopendrium *with frilly edges were selected and formed ideal plants in cold, shaded conservatories.*

In 1866, one nursery offered eighty-two different types of this fern.

ASPARAGUS DENSIFLORUS *'Meyeri' (Plume Asparagus/Foxtail Fern): Height 30–45cm/12–18in, spread 30–38cm/12–15in. Upright, then arching, bottlebrush-like stems with mid-green leaves.*

ASPARAGUS DENSIFLORUS *'Sprengeri' (Asparagus Fern/Emerald Fern/Emerald Feather): Height 25–30cm/10–12in, spread 45–60cm/1¹/2–2ft. Arching, wiry stems bearing mid-green leaves.*

ASPLENIUM BULBIFERUM *(Mother Fern/Mother Spleenwort): Height 38–45cm/15–18in, spread 45–75cm/1¹/2–2¹/2ft. Large, finely cut fronds with small bulbils that weigh them down.*

PLANTS FOR
LOBBIES AND PORCHES 2

HERE are further houseplants that are sufficiently hardy to be displayed in lobbies and porches during summer. However, a few need warm positions, and this is indicated.

• *Cissus rhombifolia* 'Ellen Danica' (Mermaid Vine): Also known as *Rhoicissus rhomboidea* 'Ellen Danica', with leaves formed of deeply indented, dark green leaflets. Grow on its own in a pot or hanging basket, where leaves can sprawl over the edges.

• *Sedum morganianum* (Donkey's Tail/Burro's Tail/Lamb's Tail): Succulent, with long stems clothed in cylindrical, grey-green leaves. Grow it in a pot on its own and position in a wall bracket in a warm lobby. Alternatively, place it in a suspended pot.

FASHIONABLE FEAST

As well as decorating homes and gardens with beautiful, brightly coloured flowers, certain varieties of chrysanthemum in China have been grown for their edible petals, which are added to salads.

• *Selaginella uncinata* (Peacock Fern/Trailing Selaginella/Peacock Moss): Weak, trailing, straw-coloured stems bearing bluish-green leaves. Grow it on its own in a small pot and position in a wall bracket. The Mat Selaginella (*Selaginella kraussiana*) has bright green, slightly trailing stems, while 'Aurea' reveals yellow foliage.

FICUS RADICANS 'Variegata' (Trailing Fig): Height 7.5–13cm/3–5in, then trailing. Cascading, wiry stems, bearing lance-shaped, slender-pointed, mid-green leaves up to 6cm/2¹/2in long with creamy edges. Ideal in a basket on its own.

LYSIMACHIA NUMMULARIA 'Aurea' (Moneywort/Creeping Jenny): Height 5–7.5cm/2–3in, then trailing. Hardy outdoor plant with trailing stems, yellow leaves and golden flowers. Ideal for growing in cool and partly open porches.

NEPHROLEPIS EXALTATA (Ladder Fern/Sword Fern): Height 30–38cm/12–15in, spread 50–60cm/20–24in – or more. Upright and cascading, deeply-divided, sword-like fronds. N. e. 'Bostoniensis' has more arching fronds.

• *Soleirolia soleirolii* (Mind Your Own Business/Baby's Tears/Irish Moss): Earlier known as *Helxine soleirolii*, this well-known Corsican plant forms a mound of pale to mid-green leaves clustered around thin, trailing, pink stems. There are several forms, such as 'Argentea' (leaves variegated in silver) and 'Aurea' (golden-green).

• *Stenotaphrum secundatum* 'Variegatum' (Buffalo Grass/St. Augustine-grass): Long, narrow, green leaves, up to 13cm/5in long, banded in white. The stems often hang in irregular tufts.

CHRYSANTHEMUM MORIFOLIUM – Cascade Varieties: Height 10–15cm/4–6in, then trailing up to 38cm/15in or more. Masses of daisy-like flowers up to 4cm/1¹/2in across, smothering the leaves in summer. Many varieties and colours.

CORDYLINE TERMINALIS/C. fruticosa (Ti Plant/Flaming Dragon Tree): Height 38–45cm/15–18in, spread 30–38cm/12–15in. Tender and palm-like, with coloured leaves. Place in a warm lobby, with trailing plants positioned around it.

FICUS PUMILA (Creeping Fig): Height 5–7.5cm/2–3in, then trailing. It is both a climbing and trailing plant, with small, somewhat heart-shaped leaves. It is best seen against a white background, or positioned around a central plant where it can trail.

FICUS PLANTS FOR LOBBIES AND PORCHES

The Rubber Plant (Ficus elastica) is probably the best-known houseplant, but there are many related species and some are hardy enough to be grown in unheated lobbies and porches during summer.

• *The Creeping Fig (Ficus pumila) is frequently grown in hanging baskets and the ordinary, all-green type is featured opposite. There are also several variegated forms, including 'Sonny' with white edges to the slightly crinkled leaves, and 'Variegata' with leaves marbled and lined in cream and green.*

• *The Variegated Trailing Fig (Ficus radicans 'Variegata') is ideal (see above), but position it in good light to encourage the development of bright, rich colours in its spear-shaped leaves.*

Rubber plant (Ficus elastica)

PLANTS FOR
LOBBIES AND PORCHES 3

IN ADDITION to houseplants which are sufficiently hardy to be grown in porches and lobbies during summer, there are several hardy, trailing garden plants that are also ideal for these places.

INDOORS OR OUT?

The difference between a plant being hardy enough to be left outside in a garden or cosseted indoors is a matter of geography and micro-climates. Sometimes, only a matter of one hundred miles further south and a sheltered, sun-blessed position, turns a hardy houseplant into a garden type. For example, the Pig-a-back Plant (*Tolmiea menziesii*), although hardy enough to be planted outdoors in most areas, retains its foliage in better condition indoors or in a lobby.

The ordinary Creeping Jenny (*Lysimachia nummularia*) thrives well outdoors, but the yellow-leaved form 'Aurea' (page 178) retains its colour and leaves better when given protection from rain. The Star of Bethlehem (*Campanula isophylla*) is frequently grown in a hanging basket indoors, and is equally superb outdoors in summer or in a well-ventilated lobby or porch (page 177).

ANNUALS IN LOBBIES

Many of the plants suggested on pages 170 to 174, for planting in outdoor hanging baskets, can also be grown in lobbies and porches. However, unless well ventilated, lobbies can become too warm. Porches are cooler. Also, wire-framed hanging baskets will drip water over the floor. Therefore, if it is the intention to suspend them in lobbies or porches, use plastic baskets with drip trays fitted into their bases. And because of the increased temperatures they might be exposed to in lobbies, ensure water-retaining additives (see page 165) are added to the compost.

TOLMIEA MENZIESII *(Pig-a-back Plant/Youth-on-age/Thousand Mothers):* Height 15cm/5in, then spreading and trailing. Large, long-stemmed, maple-like, mid-green leaves with plantlets peppered on their surfaces.

TRADESCANTIA FLUMINENSIS *'Variegata' (Wandering Jew):* Height 5–7.5cm/2–3in, then trailing. Elliptic to oval leaves, about 5cm/2in long and striped in cream. There are many other varieties, some striped in silver.

ZEBRINA PENDULA *(Silvery Inch Plant):* Height 7.5–10cm/3–4in, then trailing. Thick stems bearing mid-green leaves with two silvery bands on their upper surfaces. Several varieties: 'Quadricolor' has green, silver, pink and red leaves.

OPLISMENUS HIRTELLUS *'Variegatus' (Basket Vine):* Height 5–7.5cm/2–3in, then trailing. Creates a mass of tumbling stems bearing white-and-pink striped leaves about 7.5cm/3in long. Ideal in a hanging pot in a lobby.

SAXIFRAGA SARMENTOSA *'Tricolor' (Mother of Thousands/ Strawberry Geranium):* Height 10–15cm/4–6in, then trailing. This variety is similar to the all-green type, but with pink and pale yellow variegations.

SEDUM SIEBOLDII *'Medio-variegatum' (Variegated Siebold's Stonecrop/Japanese Sedum):* Circular to heart-shaped, green leaves with cream blotches. Ideal in small pots in warm lobbies; position out of draughts.

MEMORIES AND MESSAGES

Memories are frequently evoked by flowers, although it is not usually necessary to garland oneself to the extent of this lady to capture thoughts of memorable moments. Bridal flowers are usually well recalled, as well as romantic strolls through gardens when often colour-rich flowers create the attraction. Some of these memories can be recaptured by planting these flowers in hanging baskets. Many flowers have messages that originated in the language of flowers, a method of communication 'without inking the fingers' that originated in Turkey in the 1600s. Each flower had a specific meaning and a few of them are relevant to plants that can be grown in hanging baskets:

- *African Marigold = vulgar-minded*
- *Chrysanthemum (red) = I love*
- *Chrysanthemum (white) = truth*
- *Chrysanthemum (yellow) = slighted love*
- *Convolvulus = bonds/uncertainty*
- *Fern = sincerity*
- *French Marigold = jealousy*
- *Geranium = gentility*
- *Heart's-ease = you occupy my thoughts*
- *Lobelia = malevolence*
- *Stonecrop = tranquillity*
- *Strawberry = perfect excellence*
- *Thyme = activity*
- *Vervain = enchantment*

ARRANGEMENTS FOR PORCHES AND LOBBIES

❖

USING porch and lobby plants in colourful and imaginative combinations is not expensive, but does need planning. Many lobby and porch plants are described on pages 177 to 179, and while some of them are ideal on their own, others are more gregarious. Together with a few others suggested here, these plants create outstanding displays.

COMBINATIONS TO CONSIDER

Several arrangements are illustrated here, but there are others to choose from, such as:

• Hanging baskets need not be packed with masses of different plants to create an interesting display. Indeed, such plant-packing techniques spoil the display. Instead, use a large fuchsia, with trailing nasturtiums around it. For a colour contrast, use a red-flowered trailing fuchsia and mixed or yellow nasturtiums.

• Flowering plants are not essential to hanging baskets. Indeed, an all-green arrangement can look exceedingly tasteful. Try a mixture of Asparagus Fern (*Asparagus densiflorus* 'Sprengeri') planted in the centre, surrounded by variegated ivies, Silvery Inch Plant (*Zebrina pendula*) and Variegated Siebold's Stonecrop (*Sedum sieboldii* 'Medio-variegatum'). This design is highlighted when positioned against a white wall.

• For a colour-packed hanging display, plant a pink-flowered *Begonia* 'Gloire de Lorraine' in the centre, with trailing, variegated ivies, cascading fuchsias and the trailing Basket Begonia (*Begonia* x *tuberhybrida* 'Pendula'). A variation on this is to substitute the silver-leaved *Helichrysum petiolatum* for the ivy. However, take care that the basket's width is not increased too much. The helichrysum has an advantage in that it is not as colour dominant as ivies.

A CENTRAL *Pouch Flower (calceolaria), trailing petunias and lobelia create a simple, inexpensive display. By using yellow and blue, the display is ideal for placing against a white wall in a cool lobby or porch.*

FOR *further interest, add a few trailing ivies, but not ones which are variegated in bright colours as they will dominate soft coloured lobelia. They could, however, be used with bright blue trailing lobelia.*

Cascading petunias

Trailing lobelia

Calceolarias

THIS *arrangement needs a warm lobby to ensure the dracaena in the centre remains healthy and grows. The Ivy-leaved Geranium and trailing lobelias introduce shape and colour contrasts.*

A VARIATION *on this hanging basket would be to use the tuberous-rooted and dominant Begonia x tuberhybrida instead of the dracaena. Select a variety with flowers that contrast with the others.*

Ivy-leaved Geranium

Dracaena

Trailing Lobelia

SINGLE-PLANT THEMES

Many of the hardier houseplants that are suitable for porches and lobbies can be grown on their own in pots suspended by wires or decorative strings. Alternatively, plant them in pots placed in wall-brackets. These plants include:

- Basket Vine (*Oplismenus hirtellus* 'Variegatus') – page 179.
- Buffalo Grass (*Stenotaphrum secundatum* 'Variegatum') – page 178.
- Button Fern (*Pellaea rotundifolia*) – page 177.
- Donkey's Tail (*Sedum morganianum*) – page 178.
- Ladder Fern (*Nephrolepis exaltata*) – page 178.
- Mind Your Own Business (*Soleirolia soleirolii*) – page 178.
- Mother Fern (*Asplenium bulbiferum*) – page 177.
- Peacock Fern (*Selaginella uncinata*) – page 178.
- Pig-a-back Plant (*Tolmiea menziesii*) – page 179.
- Plume Asparagus (*Asparagus densiflorus* 'Meyeri') – page 177.
- Plush Vine (*Mikania ternata*) – page 177.
- Silvery Inch Plant (*Zebrina pendula*) – page 179.

- Spider Plant (*Chlorophytum comosum* 'Variegatum') – page 177.
- Striped Inch Plant (*Callisia elegans*) – page 177.
- Teddy Bear Plant (*Cyanotis kewensis*) – page 177.
- Trailing Fig (*Ficus radicans* 'Variegata') – page 178.
- Variegated Creeping Fig (*Ficus pumila* 'Sonny') – page 177.

INGENIOUS VICTORIANS

Several garden tools were invented or modified by the Victorians. The Reverend Huthwaite invented the Desideratum Watering Can to enable plants on high shelves to be watered. It was formed of a 1.5m/5ft-long bamboo cane with a forked, metal top from which was suspended a watering-can. When a string was pulled the can tilted and water trickled out.

COLOUR HARMONIES AND BACKGROUNDS

LANTS in hanging baskets that colour co-ordinate with their backgrounds further enrich gardens and add a new dimension to gardening. This is especially important in small gardens, where it is essential to get the best from the space throughout the year. Here are suggested colours that harmonize with three differently coloured backgrounds – white, grey and red-brick walls. Clearly, colour is a matter of personal choice, but these suggestions offer basic guide-lines.

Many plants that are suitable for hanging baskets – such as lobelia, alyssum and petunias – have varieties in several colours. It is therefore essential to ensure the right ones are chosen. Many plants are suggested here, but they are not the only possibilities.

OTHER PLANTS FOR WHITE WALLS

• Asarina *Victoria Falls*: Cerise-purple trumpets about 5cm/2in long, borne in a tumbling mass from early summer to the frosts of autumn.
• Anagalis linifolia *Gentian Blue*: Masses of beautiful bright blue flowers from early to late summer.
• Nemophila menziesii *Pennie Black*: Deep purple to black flowers, with scalloped edges, from early to late summer.
• Geranium *Classic Scarlet*: A seed-raised geranium, with large, crimson-red flowers throughout summer. It creates a dominant display.

WHITE *walls form a bright background for plants. Plants with yellow, gold, scarlet or green flowers associate well with this backdrop, as do green leaves.*

FLOWERS *in these colours can be planted on their own or in combinations with other suitable plants. Many plants have suitable varieties that are ideal for planting in hanging baskets.*

Lobelia e:inus
(use blue varieties)

Brachycome iberidifolia
'Purple Splendour'

Impatiens
'Mega Orange'

RED-BRICK *walls form dominant backgrounds for plants. Plants with white, soft blue, silver or lemon flowers form attractive constrasts. Also, use silver-leaved plants.*

BECAUSE *the wall's colour is strong, use dominant clusters of these colours so that they are easily noticeable, rather than a mass of mixed colours that remain insipid.*

Campanula carpatica
'Bellissimo'

Alyssum maritimum
(Lobularia maritima)

Nemophila maculata *'Five-Spot'*

GREY-STONE WALLS

These create softer-coloured settings than white backgrounds and when seen from a distance are not so dominant, fusing more easily into the landscape. Harmonizing colours are deep purple, deep blue, pink and red.
• Begonia pendula 'Illumination Hybrid': Double, large flowers in shades of pink with cream centres.
• Convolvulus tricolor 'Rose Ensign': Trumpets up to 4cm/1^{1}/2in wide, combining rose, lemon, pink and white, from mid- to late summer.
• Impatiens 'Picotee Swirl': Compact plants bearing flowers with pink edges to each petal on a white to soft rose background.
• Petunia 'Celebrity Pink Morn': Beautiful pink flowers in summer.
• Silene pendula 'Peach Blossom': Cascading, with masses of frilly edged, 18mm/^{3}/4in-wide double flowers with deep pink buds changing to salmon and then white, from early to late summer.

OTHER PLANTS FOR RED-BRICK WALLS

• Brachycome iberidifolia *'White Splendour': Masses of white, daisy-like flowers from early to late summer.*
• Helichrysum petiolatum (H. petiolare): *Cascading stems bearing silvery leaves.*
• Impatiens *'Bright Eye': Large, white flowers with dark eyes. There are many other impatiens that harmonize against red walls.*
• Lobelia erinus *'White Cascade': The flowers swamp hanging baskets with masses of small flowers throughout summer. Light blue varieties also look good against red walls.*
• Petunia *'Super Cascade' (white forms): Ideal for hanging baskets, as it has a beautiful cascading nature.*

PLANTING WALL BASKETS AND MANGERS

THE TECHNIQUE of planting a wall basket or manger is similar to that used for wire-framed hanging baskets. However, it is usually easier because the basket is held firmly and often at waist height.

PREPARING AND PLANTING

It is essential to line the basket with polythene to prevent dirty, compost-soaked water running down walls and marking them. Use black polythene, as this is less conspicuous than white, although eventually it becomes clothed in trailing flowers, stems and leaves.

When piercing holes in the polythene at the basket's front, make them quite low down so that excess water can readily escape. Small wall baskets are especially susceptible to compost drying, so add moisture-retentive additives (see page 165).

Mangers and large wall baskets hold more compost and therefore have a greater reserve of moisture.

Firm the compost – but not excessively – to ensure it retains the maximum amount of moisture. After the plants have been set in position and compost firmed around their roots, the surface must be 18–25mm/³/₄–1in below the basket's rim. During the following few weeks, the surface will settle slightly. Ensure that when the compost is watered it is possible to soak it thoroughly. If only a small space is left, it is difficult to soak the compost as water runs straight off the surface.

When planting wire-framed hanging baskets it is essential to put plants into their sides, but with wall baskets and mangers this is not necessary as they are displayed lower down and plants soon smother the edges. Nevertheless, if the sides of large mangers present large, bland areas, make slits near the top and put plants in them. Any of the trailing plants recommended for outdoor hanging baskets can be used to cover the sides.

CONTAINER COMBINATIONS

If wall baskets and mangers are displayed on their own on patios, it usually leaves a space at ground level that, unless filled, looks bland and unplanned. However, when wall baskets are positioned on walls at the fronts of mews cottages, this can be as asset as the area underneath can be easily cleaned. When tubs are used in such positions, this task is difficult. However, here are a few ideas to create unified displays.

• Use a combination of a large wall basket and a tub on either side of it to create an attractive feature against a long wall. Put trailing plants with long, cascading stems – such as the Variegated Ground Ivy – at the sides of the basket so that the display appears unified. And in each tub plant a tall, bushy plant – perhaps a standard fuchsia – to extend its lines upwards.

• At the fronts of houses and where flower borders are under windows, a windowbox under the window and a wall basket on either side creates an attractive feature. It also can be colour co-ordinated with border flowers.

• Small wall baskets are ideal at the sides of front doors. For extra interest they can be positioned one above another, but beware of water dripping on to the lower one. Bright-faced Pansies look good in these positions, and do not encroach much on surrounding space.

• Wall baskets offer excellent opportunities for disabled people to garden. Try putting several baskets on walls, with large tubs positioned between them.

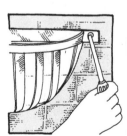

HOLD *a wall basket or manger in position and mark the positions of the securing holes. Drill the wall, insert masonry fixings and use galvanized screws to secure the basket to the wall.*

LINE *the inside with strong, black polythene, or two layers of large bin-liners. Ensure the back is covered to prevent water getting on the wall. Mould the liner to the basket's shape.*

FILL *the basket about half full with peat-based compost. Then, pierce holes in the polythene, but only at the front. This is to ensure that excess water escapes at the basket's front, not the back.*

TOP *up the basket with peat-based compost and firm it to within 7.5cm/3in of the top. If the basket is small, mix in additives such as perlite and vermiculite to assist in the water retention.*

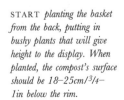

START *planting the basket from the back, putting in bushy plants that will give height to the display. When planted, the compost's surface should be 18–25cm/³/₄– 1in below the rim.*

FINALLY, *add trailing plants around the rim. Water them thoroughly to settle compost around their roots. These trailing plants will soon cloak the polythene and create a sheet of colour.*

CONTRASTS AND HARMONIES

❖

Background colours behind wall baskets dramatically affect the attractiveness of a display. Here are examples of arrangements to suit a range of differently coloured backdrops.

Some flower colours can be used against several backgrounds. This especially applies to white, which contrasts well with dark and red walls. Yellow plants also have this useful, dual role.

RED BRICK WALLS are strongly coloured and require bold splashes of soft blue, white or lemon flowers, as well as silver foliage. Above is an arrangement formed of white Marguerites (Chrysanthemum frutescens), soft blue trailing lobelia and blue stocks.

ANOTHER arrangement for a red-brick backdrop includes short-stemmed white tulips, deep blue-flowered Grape Hyacinths (Muscari armeniacum) and small-leaved, variegated ivies. This is an ideal arrangement for a spring to early summer display.

WHITE WALLS, *although bright, are uninteresting unless enriched with other colours, such as yellow, gold, scarlet or green. Above is a combination of zinnias, geraniums (pelargoniums), marigolds and the Emerald Fern (Asparagus densiflorus 'Sprengeri').*

ANOTHER *arrangement to suit a white wall is a cascading and trailing Emerald Fern (Asparagus densiflorus 'Sprengeri'), bright yellow calceolarias, several red-flowered trailing nasturtiums (Tropaeolum majus) and Iceland Poppies (Papaver nudicaule).*

DARK WALLS *can be both intimidating and dramatic. It is essential to use bright flowers as well as foliage plants with light or silver leaves. This basket is formed solely of Cinerarias.*

A MEDLEY *to suit dark backgrounds is the yellow-leaved Creeping Jenny (Lysimachia nummularia 'Aurea'), yellow caleolarias and the dominantly flowered tuberous-rooted begonias (Begonia x tuberhybida).*

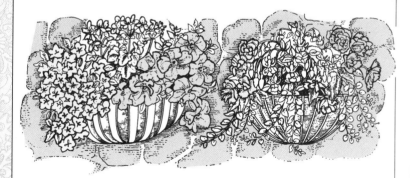

GREY STONE WALLS *present a soft, relaxing background that is ideal for pink, red, deep purple and deep blue flowers. Above is a mixture of petunias, geraniums (pelargoniums) and the blue-flowered Star of Bethlehem (Campunala isophylla), a native of northern Italy.*

A FURTHER *arrangement for grey stone walls is cascading red or pink fuchsias (see page 169 for suitable varieties), trailing begonias and an edging of silver-leaved plants such as the trailing and cascading Licorice Plant (Helichrysum petiolatum).*

(see page 169 for suitable varieties)

INFLUENCE OF LIGHT

The perception of colour continually alters throughout the day, depending on the intensity of light. For example, bright sunshine glaring down at midday highlights yellow, gold and white more then red. And with the onset of evening, light colours remain more noticeable than dark shades. At that time, red and brown become almost black. For this reason, position containers with light-coloured plants near entrances.

UNUSUAL CONTAINERS

PATIOS, as well as lobbies and porches, are soon enriched by a few unusual pots or hanging baskets. Many garden centres specialize in these containers. Also, have a look in granny's attic for old bird cages or baskets.

When using old wickerwork baskets, first line them with plastic, but instead of planting directly into them, leave the plants in their pots and stand them in plastic saucers. In this way, the plants can be changed and the basket is not ruined through being continually soaked in water.

Always use plants that harmonize with the container. For example, bright-faced flowers will compete with wall pots that depict noble Greek faces. Instead, use trailing thyme or ivies – but avoid using brightly variegated types.

In bird cages, use climbing or trailing plants, so that their sides are clothed and softened.

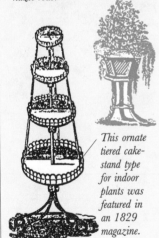

INDOOR DISPLAYS

Early Victorian plant containers could be extremely ornate. The base of this one is formed of hazel rods.

This ornate tiered cake-stand type for indoor plants was featured in an 1829 magazine.

MACRAMÉ and other string-woven pot supports are ideal in lobbies, porches and conservatories. Even ordinary wickerwork baskets, planted with summer flowers, look good when suspended from ornate brackets.

TERRACOTTA CONTAINERS *resembling faces seldom fail to attract attention when secured to walls.*

They look good when planted with ivies, the yellow-leaved Creeping Jenny (Lysimachia nummularia 'Aurea') and thyme. When choosing plants to feature in 'faced' containers (below), ensure that they harmonize with the faces and do not hide them. Ideally, position and train the plants to create an attractive frame. Sometimes they can simulate hair.

ORNATE BIRD CAGES *create dramatic homes for plants and are particularly suited for displays in large lobbies and conservatories. Wall-mounted pots enable walls to be peppered with colour, while slatted baskets have a more clinical outline than wire-mesh baskets. Novelty containers (left), where excess water appears like tears out of eyes, almost always create amusement and interest.*

KEEPING PLANTS HEALTHY

❖

WATERING and feeding are the main precautionary measures for keeping plants healthy. If these are neglected, their display is limited and may end six or so weeks earlier than it should. If you have any doubts about being able to feed the plants regularly, add slow-release fertilizers to the compost when planting the basket. Water the plants every ten days with a general plant fertilizer as well. Prepare the mixture exactly to the manufacturer's instructions, as if it is too strong it may damage plants.

CONTROLLING
PESTS AND DISEASES

Before placing hanging baskets outdoors, spray them thoroughly with a general insecticide. Then check them every week, looking both on top and under leaves.

As a precautionary measure – and especially where containers are difficult to reach and inspect – insert insecticide pins into the compost. These are like small cardboard sticks, and release an insecticide that is absorbed by the roots to protect the entire plant. Such insecticides are known as systemic, as chemicals spread within plants and kill insects that suck their sap.

Unlike most plants, even those in tubs, pots and urns, hanging baskets are free from slugs and snails, which during warm and moist summer evenings can devastate plants overnight. However, plants in wall baskets and mangers are not so fortunate and therefore it is necessary to use baits. Place them under tiles or raised pots on the ground around the basket's base. This prevents the bait becoming wet and reduces the risk of inquisitive pets and young children sampling them. Once the bait becomes wet, remove it and replace with fresh pellets. If left, it encourages the development of harmful moulds.

STORM AND WIND DAMAGE

Mid-summer storms sometimes flatten plants in hanging baskets, especially when in exposed positions. Nothing can be done during a storm – except taking them down and putting in a greenhouse or conservatory – but afterwards cut off damaged flowers and broken stems. Initially, this action may appear to be drastic, but if a tangle of stems and bruised flowers remains it encourages the presence of diseases, especially if the weather remains damp and warm. Feeding also aids quick recovery.

Should storms occur early in summer, it is better to replace damaged plants with healthy ones.

REGULARLY *pinch off dead or faded flowers from plants to induce the development of further blooms. If left on plants they encourage the presence of diseases, as well as spoiling the display's appearance.*

FEED *plants regularly throughout summer, using a fertilizer dissolved in water. Apply this every ten to fourteen days. First, however, water the compost: never apply fertilizer to dry compost – it damages roots.*

REGULARLY *nip out the growing points of young plants to encourage bushiness. Fuchsias especially need encouragement to develop sideshoots, and the tips of their shoots need to be nipped out often.*

PESTS AND DISEASES

Because the plants are packed close together, they provide concentrated meals for pests. Inspect plants regularly and as soon as pests or diseases are noticed, spray with an insecticide or fungicide. Use environmentally friendly sprays that will not harm the atmosphere.

BUYING GUIDE

Don't buy plants that are:
- *Thin and weak – they will never recover.*
- *Excessively large plants in small amounts of soil. This indicates that their roots are congested.*
- *Small plants in large amounts of soil. Such plants may have only recently been pricked out into pots and their roots not established.*
- *Infested with pests or diseases.*
- *Growing in dry compost – it shows they have been neglected.*
- *That are not labelled. If later they prove not to be the variety you want, the entire colour scheme could be ruined.*

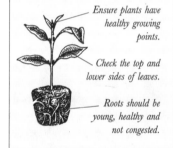

Ensure plants have healthy growing points.

Check the top and lower sides of leaves.

Roots should be young, healthy and not congested.

ITALIAN INFLUENCES

During the early part of the nineteenth century, Italian gardens were particularly noted for their romantic nature. They frequently had large, ornate pots and urns, which were a natural development from the Italian Renaissance. Many were positioned at the junctions of paths.

CONTAINER GARDENING

Growing plants in tubs, pots and urns — as well as in unusual containers such as wheelbarrows, wooden boxes and stacks of tyres — is a fascinating part of gardening. Small courtyards and patios can be brightened, flights of steps made more distinctive, unattractive architectural features hidden and focal points created in long paths and at the ends of lawns.

The range of materials from which containers are made is wide and includes wood, concrete, earthenware, plastic, fibreglass, reconstituted stone and lead. Some of these are expensive, others more widely available and reasonably priced. The range of suitable plants includes annuals, tender perennials, hardy border plants, conifers, bulbs and climbers.

Composts, watering and feeding are featured in this chapter, while raising half-hardy annuals is described in the section called Sowing Seeds in Greenhouses on page 272.

A RANGE OF
TUBS, POTS, AND URNS

PLANTS can be grown in almost any container, as long as it is strong enough to support the weight of compost and plants. However, it must also have a pleasing appearance, harmonizing with the plants and blending with its surroundings. Apart from aesthetic considerations, outdoor containers must be able to withstand frost, rain, snow and hot sunshine, to say nothing of the boisterous activities of children and large, excitable dogs.

In addition to traditional containers, growing-bags create colour when planted with a range of spring-flowering bulbs or summer-blooming plants. Patterned bags create brighter backgrounds than plain ones, but even so they are not as attractive as pots and tubs. However, trailing plants soon camouflage their edges.

Stone sinks offer the chance to grow small rock-garden plants, even on town patios where space is scarce. They also make homes

MOVEABLE SIDES

During the early eighteenth century, Charles McIntosh designed an orange tub that could be taken apart to allow roots of trees and shrubs to be inspected. It also made the task of repotting a great deal easier.

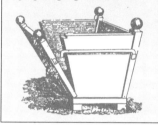

for dwarf, slow-growing conifers, miniature spring bulbs and small, evergreen shrubs.

Vegetables need not be neglected on patios; specialist containers for strawberry plants are available, as well as traditional strawberry pots with planting holes in their

ROUND, *wooden tubs form strong bases for shrubs and small trees; they are also superb for massed plantings of spring-flowering bulbs. Plant a colourful medley of different species.*

A BULB *or multiple planter – now frequently available in heavy-duty plastic – is ideal for growing small bulbs. These pots are also made in terracotta and reconstituted stone.*

CONCRETE *containers need not be heavy and dominant. Here is a small bowl set on a pedestal. Take special care not to drop one as it will smash. They become hot in summer.*

sides and tops. Alternatively, cut holes in a pensioned-off beer barrel or wine barrel.

Proprietary tubs for growing potatoes are available, with the advantage of being collapsible for storage in winter. Large plastic pots – or buckets with holes pierced in their bases – are ideal as containers for tomato plants. Runner beans are candidates for growing-bags, but ensure a supporting wire framework is available, as canes cannot normally be pushed into the bags.

Garden centres and high street shops offer a wide range of containers, especially in spring and early summer. If they are carefully used and stored in winter, when not in use, they last for many seasons. Thin plastic containers, however, are much more vulnerable to deterioration than thicker ones which, although more expensive, may prove to be a better buy.

RECTANGULAR *metal or stone containers form strong bases for climbers such as large-flowered clematis. Metal becomes hot in summer, so be prepared to water frequently.*

ORNATE *and figured terracotta pots look superb. Use lax, trailing plants such as nasturtiums to soften their rims and sides, but take care not to completely cloak them and hide attractive features.*

SQUARE, *wooden tubs have a dignity not conferred on round tubs, probably because early containers at Versailles had a similar shape. Here, one is planted with an agapanthus.*

CAR *tyres can be given a new lease of life by securing them in a stack and growing plants in a bucket placed in its top. Paint the tyres matt white to create a contrast with the plants.*

OLD *or broken wheelbarrows create eye-catching features when planted with a mixture of summer-flowering plants. Wooden barrows have a softer outline than metal types.*

LARGE, *wooden boxes are ideal for perennial plants, such as hostas. These containers, with their soft outlines, harmonize well with large-leaved and informal plants.*

MATERIALS FOR CONTAINERS

HE RANGE of materials used to make garden containers is wide and extends from traditional types, such as wood and stone, to more recent ones like plastic and fibreglass. Each material has merits and disadvantages, as well as being particularly suitable for certain types of plants and surroundings.

• Plastic has a clean, clinical appearance that especially suits formal, modern gardens. Containers include pots and planters of all sizes, as well as corner (quadrant) containers and square, Versailles-like tubs. Some are white and bright, while others are in grey, brown or black. Their durability depends on the thickness of the plastic.

• Fibreglass has many excellent qualities and can be formed into a wide range of designs and patterns. It does not decay, but is unable to withstand sharp knocks. Like plastic, fibreglass warms up rapidly, and special care is needed to ensure composts remain cool and well-watered during the heat of summer.

COADE STONE

In 1769, George and Eleanor Coade bought a factory which made terracotta-type artificial stone. Soon after, George died but Eleanor and her daughter experimented, added further ingredients and originated a weatherproof material, less easily eroded than natural stone.

They produced superbly designed figures and decorations which became much desired. The daughter died in 1821 and the factory closed in 1840. Unfortunately, the formula for the mixture was lost. The stone was also used on buildings.

CONCRETE *containers have a clinical, modern appearance and do not harmonize in informal, rustic settings. Because their sides are usually thick, the containers are almost always quite heavy.*

RECONSTITUTED *stone containers range from jardinières to urns, vases and troughs. Highly ornate surfaces and shapes are possible. They are very durable and soon assume a weathered appearance.*

EARTHENWARE *containers range widely in size and shape, the colour harmonizing with most plants. They are especially attractive in informal settings, and look good when in groups.*

• Wooden tubs and planters are superb for plants that remain outside all year: compost in them remains slightly insulated from temperature extremes. Shrubs, small trees and herbaceous perennials are especially suited to tubs.

• Clay pots have traditionally been used for plants; they are porous, decorative and offer insulation from extreme heat. Water evaporating through the pots keeps the compost and roots cool. If dropped they usually break, and are best placed under cover in winter when not in use.

• Natural stone containers are unsurpassable, but expensive and scarce. Shallow, old stone sinks are superb – if you acquire one, treasure it for life.

• Reconstituted stone is increasingly popular and used to create variously shaped containers. It is also used to form attractive statues. They are durable, and after a few years the surface colour mellows. Clean them with water and a soft brush. Do not use wire brushes, as they will damage the surface badly and could, eventually, remove decorative patterns.

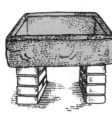

PLASTIC *is so versatile that each year its use for gardening containers widens. Simulated antique containers as well as traditional pots and planters are available, in several colours.*

WOODEN *containers have a soft, natural appearance. Most of them are formed from softwood and protected with plant-friendly wood preservatives. More expensive ones are made of hardwood.*

TRADITIONAL *jardinières were made of lead; today they are replicated in fibreglass. Aluminium is sometimes used for containers, but metal is hot in summer and cold in winter.*

FIBREGLASS *containers are varied and often given intricate patterns, sometimes to replicate wood or lead. They are light to handle, but must not be dropped, or they will break.*

SHALLOW, *old stone sinks create superb miniature gardens for alpines, miniature conifers and small evergreen shrubs. Glazed sinks can be easily given a rustic, weathered appearance.*

BRONZE *urns are sometimes available, often replicas of containers made during the mid-Georgian period. They are expensive, incomparable and desirable. Use them as special features in a garden.*

POSITIONING CONTAINERS
◆

S ELECT containers to suit your garden, rather than finding an attractive pot, tub or urn and then being unable to position it in a sympathetic setting. For example, clinically-outlined, dish-like concrete containers are ideal for placing on bright, formal patios, but not in informal woodland settings. Wooden tubs are better for rustic, rural positions.

PERSPECTIVE AND MASS
Containers on patios are invariably admired from nearby positions, but those in gardens sometimes create focal points. Others are merged in groups. Those that create focal points need positioning with care to ensure they fulfil this role, rather than obscuring other features. For example, if there is a tall hedge at the bottom of a garden, an urn festooned with summer flowers and placed on a tall pedestal in front of it will soon attract the eye. It will also create attention and be attractive if positioned two-thirds of the way down a garden, with an uncluttered

TRICKY STATUES!

Trick fountains were popular in Renaissance gardens, with balls appearing to be raised on spouts of water. Other inventive garden features were statues of naked people that were connected to a tap so that water could suddenly squirt at innocent passers-by.

background. However, it will not be attractive and a focal point if tall and placed only a small way down a garden. Small, low containers are better in this position.

SEASONAL OR PERMANENT?
Where a dominant feature is needed throughout the year, shrubs with evergreen foliage are essential, especially those with variegated leaves. Plant them in large, wooden tubs to help protect their roots from excessively cold weather. Bay trees *(Laurus nobilis)* are evergreen, and especially eye-catching when grown with clear stems up to about 1.2m/4ft high, planted in white tubs and positioned either side of an entrance. Small, evergreen, variegated shrubs, such as *Hebe franciscana* 'Variegata', are also good for providing colour in winter.

Containers such as shallow urns and those made of thin plastic are best when planted in late spring with summer-flowering bedding plants. Once the display is over, plants and compost are removed and the container cleaned and stored until the following year. If permanent plants are planted in them, their roots will soon be damaged by cold weather. Herbaceous perennials, such as hostas and agapanthus, are soon killed when planted with little soil.

Spring-flowering bulbs, which are planted in early autumn, also

suffer if the soil is too shallow and subsequently freezes. They are best planted in tubs and positioned near to a house, where they can be easily admired in spring, whatever the weather.

SMALL *courtyards are enhanced by evergreen shrubs in tubs or other large containers. Such sheltered places enable slightly tender plants to be grown.*

GROUPINGS *of pots and tubs at the tops of steps help to create focal points and to direct people to entrances. Small containers always look best when in groups.*

USE *combinations of large, dominant pots and troughs to hide unattractive features, such as drainage pipes. Alternatively, position them to act as focal points.*

A GARDEN *bench with containers formed of car tyres positioned either side helps to reduce the blandness of long hedges. The displays can be changed at the beginning of spring and summer.*

ENTRANCES *benefit from a few shrubs in large pots or tubs, highlighted by seasonal flowering plants. Small-leaved, variegated ivies enrich the scene with colour throughout the year.*

STONE *urns on pedestals create height and focal points in lawns and long, wide paths. Fill the bowl-shaped container with spreading and trailing foliage and summer-flowering plants.*

ANNUALS FOR POTS AND TUBS 1

❖

ANNUALS are plants that are raised from seeds each year, and then planted either into borders or containers on patios. When considering varieties for growing in containers, always select those with short, bushy natures. And make sure they are well developed and will soon (if not immediately) break into flower after planting.

RAISING PLANTS

• Floss Flower *(Ageratum houstonianum):* Sow seeds 3mm/⅛in deep in early spring in 10–16°C/50–61°F. Germination takes ten to fourteen days. When large enough to handle, prick off into seed-trays and later acclimatize plants to outdoor conditions. Plant outside when all risk of frost has passed.

• Sweet Alyssum *(Alyssum maritimum/Lobularia maritima):* Sow seeds 6mm/¼in deep during late winter and early spring in 10–13°C/50–55°F. Germination takes seven to ten days. Prick out the seedlings in small clusters, slowly acclimatize to outdoor temperatures and plant into a container.

• Love-lies-bleeding *(Amaranthus caudatus):* Can be sown directly into hardy annual borders, but for planting into containers sow seed 3mm/⅛in deep in late winter or early spring in 10–13°C/50–55°F. Germination takes two to three weeks. Prick out seedlings into

POT MARIGOLD

This Southern European, bushy annual has long been grown for its medicinal value: a conserve made from it was known to be a 'cureth in the trembling of the harts'. The flowers were also used to give cheese a yellow colour, while it was said that if you looked 'wyscely' on the marigold early in the morning it would preserve you from 'feveres' during the day.

AGERATUM houstonianum: *Height 13–30cm/5–12in, plant 13–20cm/5–8in apart. Clustered heads of blue, pink or white, flowers like powder-puffs, from early to late summer.*

ALYSSUM maritimum (now Lobularia maritima): *Height 7.5–15cm/3–6in, plant 15–20cm/6–8in apart. Carpeting and trailing, in white, rosy-red and deep purple throughout summer.*

AMARANTHUS caudatus *(Love-lies-bleeding): Height 38–60cm/15–24in, plant 30–45cm/12–18in apart. Trailing red, maroon or green tassels, mid- to late summer. Large tubs only.*

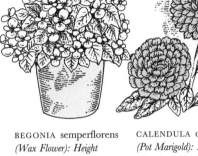

ANTIRRHINUM *(Snapdragon): Height 25–30cm/10–12in, plant 20–25cm/8–10in apart. Dragon-like heads in a wide colour range, from mid- to late summer. Choose dwarf varieties for containers.*

BEGONIA semperflorens *(Wax Flower): Height 15–23cm/6–9in, plant 15–20cm/6–8in apart. Low, bushy plants, smothered in scarlet, pink or white flowers from early to late summer.*

CALENDULA officinalis *(Pot Marigold): Height 30–45cm/12–18in, plant 23–38cm/9–15in apart. Wide colour range, mainly yellow and orange, from early to late summer. Use dwarf types.*

small pots and slowly acclimatize them to outdoor conditions.

• Snapdragon *(Antirrhinum majus):* Sow seeds 3mm/⅛in deep during late winter or early spring in 16–20°C/61–68°C. Prick off seedlings into seed-trays and later acclimatize to outdoor conditions.

• Wax Flower *(Begonia semperflorens):* Sow seeds thinly on the surface of compost (do not cover) during late winter and early spring. Water lightly with a fine-rosed can and place in 16–20°C/61–68°F. Germination takes two to four weeks. Prick off the seedlings into small clusters and slowly acclimatize them to outdoor conditions.

• Pot Marigold *(Calendula officinalis):* Mostly, it is sown directly into hardy-annual borders, but sow seeds in pots 6mm/¼in deep in 15°C/59°F during early to mid-spring. Transfer the seedlings to small pots and acclimatize to outdoor conditions.

Alternatively, sow two or three seeds in a small pot, later thinning to the strongest seedling.

MIXING AND MATCHING

Creating medleys of plants with flower colours that blend is increasingly popular. Here are a few of them to try:
• *An edging of white, trailing alyssum with a bright colour range of antirrhinums positioned in the centre.*
• *Plant rose-red trailing alyssum around the sides of containers, with Pot Marigolds in the centre. Both of these flowers create colour over a long period.*
• *Plant pink-flowering varieties of Begonia semperflorens in the centre of an urn, with blue, trailing lobelia around the edges.*
• *White-flowered forms of Begonia semperflorens with copper-colour foliage harmonize with the rich colour of earthenware pots. There are also pink, scarlet and red-flowered types, which can be used to create contrasts with other flowers in containers.*

ANNUALS FOR POTS AND TUBS 2

THE RANGE of annuals that flower beautifully in containers is extensive and includes some more unusual plants.

Many seed companies specialize in plants suitable for growing in containers and devote parts of their catalogues specifically to them. Each year, new varieties are introduced, many especially suited for planting in containers.

RAISING PLANTS

• Feverfew (*Chrysanthemum parthenium/Matricaria eximia*): Sow seeds 3mm/¹/₈in deep in late winter and early spring in 16–20°C/ 61–68°F. Germination takes ten to fourteen days. When large enough to handle, prick off the seedlings into seed-trays and slowly acclimatize them to outdoor conditions. Plant into containers when all risk of frost has passed. They are ideal for planting in containers in areas exposed to wind.

• Dusty Miller (*Cineraria maritima/Senecio bicolor*): Sow seeds 3mm/¹/₈in deep from late winter to mid-spring in 16–20°F/61–68°F. Germination takes ten to fourteen days. When large enough to handle, transfer the seedlings to seed-trays and slowly harden off.

• Tickseed (*Coreopsis tinctoria*): Sow seeds 3mm/¹/₈in deep in early spring in 16°C/61°F. Germination normally takes ten to fourteen days. When large enough to handle, move the seedlings into small pots and slowly acclimatize them to outdoor conditions.

• Kingfisher Daisy (*Felicia bergeriana*): Sow seeds 3mm/¹/₈in deep from late winter to mid-spring in 10–15°C/50–59°F. Germination takes two to three weeks – sometimes longer. When large enough to handle, prick off the seedlings into seed-trays and later acclimatize to outdoor conditions.

• Busy Lizzie (*Impatiens*): Sow seeds 3mm/¹/₈in deep during early and mid-spring in 15–20°C/ 59–68°F. Germination usually takes ten to fourteen days. When large enough to handle, prick out the seedlings into seed-trays, acclimatize to outdoor conditions and plant into suitable pots after all risk of frost has passed.

• Burning Bush/Summer Cypress (*Kochia scoparia* 'Trichophylla'): Sow seeds 3mm/¹/₈in deep during early and mid-spring in 15–20°C/59–68°F. Germination is rapid, taking only five to seven days. When large enough to handle, transfer the seedlings into seed-trays, and then plant into larger containers only after all risk of frost has passed.

COREOPSIS

These are all North American plants; some are herbaceous perennials, but Coreopsis tinctoria *is an annual. They are collectively known as tickseeds, with* Coreopsis leavenworthii *once being used by North American Indians to treat heat exhaustion.*

MIXING AND MATCHING

• *In large tubs, use* Cineraria maritima (Senecio bicolor) *as a centre plant with* Chrysanthemum parthenium *'Golden Ball' around the edges.*

• *Use* Chrysanthemum parthenium *as an edging to red pelargoniums.*

• Felicia bergeriana *looks good in a medley of other annuals in large tubs. Their bright faces are best when seen from above.*

• *Busy Lizzies* (Impatiens) *look superb in single colours and when mixed. They are ideal in tubs, troughs, windowboxes and hanging baskets.*

• *Grow* Kochia scoparia *'Trichophylla' in a large tub, with colour-contrasting trailing bedding plants around it. Alternatively, plant trailing, variegated, small-leaved ivies around the edges.*

CHRYSANTHEMUM parthenium *(Feverfew): Height 23–45cm/9–18in, plant 15–25cm/6–10in apart. Bushy plants with small, rounded flower heads, in white or golden-yellow, from early to late summer.*

CINERARIA maritima/ Senecio bicolor *(Dusty Miller): Height 45–60cm/ 1¹/₂–2ft, plant 30–38cm/ 12–15in apart. Leaves covered with white, woolly hairs. Several varieties, some with deeply cut leaves.*

COREOPSIS tinctoria *(Calliopsis): Dwarf varieties only. Height 30–38cm/ 12–15in, plant 20–25cm/ 8–10in apart. Bushy, with stiff stems bearing yellow to chestnut flowers from mid to late summer.*

FELICIA bergeriana *(Kingfisher Daisy): Height 15cm/6in, plant 10– 15cm/4–6in apart. Mat-forming and bearing grey, hairy leaves and steel-blue flowers with yellow centres from early to late summer.*

IMPATIENS *(Busy Lizzie): Choose dwarf varieties. Height 20–25cm/ 8–10in, plant 15–20cm/ 6–8in apart. Flowers in many colours (white, pink, red, scarlet and salmon) from early to late summer.*

KOCHIA scoparia *'Tricophylla' (Burning Bush): Height 60–75cm/ 2–2¹/₂ft, space 30–38cm/ 12–15in apart. Light green foliage that turns deep red in autumn. 'Childsii' is neater and more compact.*

ANNUALS FOR POTS AND TUBS 3

❖

THE RANGE of annuals that can be grown in containers continues with these summer-flowering beauties. Although the plants discussed on pages 190 to 193 are treated as half-hardy annuals, some are really half-hardy perennials. For example, Scarlet Salvia (*Salvia splendens*), petunias, the Livingstone Daisy (*Mesembryanthemum criniflorum*) and the Edging Lobelia (*Lobelia erinus*) are perennials that are only half-hardy in temperate and cool climates. In their warm, native countries, however, these plants are fully hardy.

RAISING PLANTS

• Edging Lobelia (*Lobelia erinus*): Sow seeds – barely covering them – from mid-winter to early spring in 15–20°C/59–68°F. Germination takes one to two weeks. When large enough to handle, prick out the seedlings into small clusters in seed-trays. Slowly acclimatize them to outdoor temperatures.

• *Malope trifida*: This is usually sown outdoors and grown as a hardy annual. However, to produce plants for growing in pots and tubs, sow seeds 3mm/^{1}/$_8$in deep during early spring in 16°C/61°F. Transplant young seedlings into small pots, slowly acclimatize them to outdoor conditions and later plant into containers.

NICOTIANA *x* SANDERAE *(Flowering Tobacco Plant): Height 25–50cm/10–20in, plant 15–38cm/6–15in apart. These low-growing forms (others are taller) are superb in pots and tubs.*

PETUNIA *x* HYBRIDA *(Garden Petunia): Height 15–38cm/6–15in, plant 20–30cm/8–12in apart. Trumpet-shaped flowers from early summer to the frosts of autumn. Single and double forms in many colours.*

SALVIA SPLENDENS *(Scarlet Salvia): Height 30–38cm/12–15in, plant 25–30cm/10–12in apart. Usually scarlet flowers. However, there are several other varieties, in purple, salmon and white.*

• Livingstone Daisy *(Mesembryanthemum criniflorum)*: Sow seeds 3mm/^{1}/$_8$in deep from mid-winter to mid-spring in 16–20°C/61–68°F. Germination takes two to three weeks. When large enough to handle, prick off seedlings into small pots, and acclimatize to outdoor conditions.
• Flowering Tobacco Plant *(Nicotiana x sanderae)*: Sow seeds 3mm/^{1}/$_8$in deep from late winter to mid-spring in 15–20°C/59–68°F. Germination takes ten to fourteen days. When large enough to handle, prick out the seedlings into seed-trays and acclimatize to outdoor conditions.
• Garden Petunia *(Petunia x hybrida)*: Sow seeds thinly on the surface of compost during late winter and early spring in 15–20°C/59–68°F. Germination takes one to two weeks. When large enough to handle, transfer the seedlings into seed-trays and slowly acclimatize to outdoor conditions.
• Scarlet Salvia *(Salvia splendens)*: Sow seeds 6mm/^{1}/$_4$in deep during late winter and early spring in

20°C/68°F. Germination takes two to three weeks. When large enough to handle, transfer the seedlings into seed-trays, harden off and plant into containers as soon as all risk of frost has passed.

LOBELIA ERINUS *(Edging Lobelia): Height 10–23cm/4–9in, but also trailing: plant 10cm/4in apart. Blue, white or red flowers from late spring to autumn. Trailing varieties soften container edges.*

MALOPE TRIFIDA: *Height 60–75cm/2– 2^1/$_2$ft, plant 23cm/9in apart. Bushy, hardy annuals bearing mid-green leaves and trumpet-shaped, 5–7.5cm/ 2–3in wide, rose-purple flowers, early to late summer.*

MESEMBRYANTHEMUM CRINIFLORUM *(Livingstone Daisy): Height 10–15cm/4–6in: plant 20–25cm/8–10in apart. Spreading, with daisy-like flowers about 2.5cm/1in wide, early to mid-summer.*

ANNUALS FOR POTS AND TUBS 4

THE RANGE of annuals continues with the highly floriferous, French and African Marigolds. Select only dwarf types for growing in containers – there are many to choose from.

RAISING PLANTS

• African Marigolds (*Tagetes erecta*): Sow seeds 6mm/¹/₄in deep during late winter and early spring in 18°C/64°F. Germination takes seven to ten days. When large enough to handle, transfer the seedlings into seed-trays. Slowly acclimatize the plants to outdoor conditions.

• French Marigolds (*Tagetes patula*): Sow seeds in the same way as for African Marigolds.

• Ursinia anethoides: Sow seeds 3mm/¹/₈in deep from late winter to mid-spring in 15°C/59°F. Germination takes ten to fourteen days. When large enough to handle, transfer the seedlings into

---

SPACINGS FOR PLANTS

For the plants described on pages 190 to 193, the planting distances suggested are for growing them in containers. To create a colour display quickly, plants are spaced closer than if in a garden. In gardens, increase the recommended spacings by about one-third.

---

seed-trays, then slowly acclimatize them to outdoor conditions. Plant into containers as soon as there is no risk of frost.

• Monarch of the Veldt (*Venidium fastuosum*): Sow seeds – lightly covering them – during early and mid-spring in 16°C/61°F. Germination takes two to three weeks. When large enough to handle, prick off the seedlings into small pots. Plant into containers when all risk of frost has passed.

• Vervain (*Verbena x hybrida*): Sow seeds 3mm/¹/₈in deep from late winter to early spring in 15–20°C/59–68°F. Germination takes two to three weeks. When growing strongly, prick off the seedlings into seed-trays and slowly acclimatize to outdoor conditions.

• Youth-and-old-age (*Zinnia elegans*): Sow seeds 6mm/¹/₄in deep during early and mid-spring in 15–20°C/59–68°F. Germination takes ten to fourteen days. When the seedlings are large enough to handle, transfer into seed-trays and slowly acclimatize them to outdoor conditions.

MEXICAN BEAUTY

Known in North America as the Big Marigold, the flowers of the Mexican Tagetes erecta have been used in India as a source of a yellow dye. Tagetes lucida, a native of Central America and Mexico, has flowers that have been used locally as a condiment.

MIXING AND MATCHING

• *Plant a group of orange-yellow Ursinia anethoides on their own in a large tub, then position next to it a dominantly blue-flowered container.*

• *When mixing French or African Marigolds, use fewer of them than other plants. If too many are used, they overwhelm the display.*

• *In large tubs, plant several Dusty Miller (Cineraria maritima/Senecio bicolor) surrounded by a collar of low-growing, small-flowered marigolds.*

• *Large tubs planted solely with a colour mixture of zinnias look superb, especially when in full sun. Several containers planted like this and peppered over a patio are certain to introduce vitality. However, do not cluster them together as they will then compete for attention.*

TAGETES ERECTA
(African Marigolds): Height 25–38cm/10–15in, plant 20–25cm/8–10in apart. Dark green leaves and large, daisy-like, lemon-yellow flowers from mid- to late summer. Many varieties.

TAGETES PATULA
(French Marigolds): Height 30–45cm/12–18in, plant 25–30cm/10–12in apart. Dark green leaves and yellow or mahogany-red flowers from early to late summer. Many varieties for tubs.

URSINIA ANETHOIDES:
Height 23–38cm/9–15in, plant 20–30cm/8–12in apart. Bushy plants with light green leaves and orange, daisy-like flowers with bright orange-yellow centres, from early to late summer.

VENIDIUM FASTUOSUM *(Monarch of the Veldt): Height 50–60cm/20–24in, plant 25cm/10in apart. Deeply lobed, woolly leaves and large, orange flowers with black-purple centres.*

VERBENA x HYBRIDA *(Vervain): Height 15–38cm/6–15in, plant 15–25cm/6–10in apart. Masses of 7.5cm/3in-wide flower clusters in white, pink, red, blue and lilac from early to late summer.*

ZINNIA ELEGANS *(Youth-and-old-age): Height 15–38cm/6–15in (dwarf strains), plant 15–30cm/6–12in apart. Bright-faced, daisy-like flowers in a wide colour range from mid-summer to autumn frosts.*

SPRING-FLOWERING PLANTS

SPRING displays are important in gardens; in a trice they remove winter gloom and introduce many bright, varied colours. However, unlike summer-flowering bedding plants that produce a glowing display almost from the moment they are planted, spring-flowering types are invariably biennial. This means they are raised from seed sown during the previous summer and are planted into containers in late summer or early autumn.

Bulbs are other candidates for spring colour, and those such as daffodils and tulips are planted at the same time as biennial plants.

GUIDELINES FOR SPRING COLOUR

Spring displays must be bold to create strong colour impact. Here are a few ways to achieve this:
• When planting daffodils in tubs, create dominant displays by planting bulbs in two layers, with the bases of the upper bulbs nestling in the gaps between the noses of the lower ones. This method also creates a mass of stems which are better able to resist strong winds in exposed places.
• When planting bulbs, it is better to pack one container with them than to spread out the same number in several tubs. Remember that bulbs do not spread out in the same way as bedding plants.
• Never plant bulbs that look damaged or diseased; they will not flower and subsequently leave gaps in the display.

• If you live in an exposed area, use plenty of compact bedding plants, such as daisies and pansies; they are less likely to be damaged by strong winds. They also help to create colour around the bases of tulips and daffodils.
• Large containers planted with bulbs and spring-flowering bedding plants sometimes look rather uninteresting in late autumn and winter. Therefore, use small evergreen shrubs or perhaps some variegated small-leaved ivies to provide colour throughout winter.
• Group plants that, when combined, have a long flowering period. For example, Forget-me-nots carry on an attractive display after early-flowering tulips have finished creating their display.
• Spring-flowering displays are often short-lived. Therefore, grow a few pots of other bulbs or primroses which can be transferred to the main display if bare spaces unexpectedly occur.
• In large tubs with summer-flowering shrubs, use coloured-leaved, ground-covering plants, such as *Lamium maculatum* 'Aureum' with golden leaves, to create extra colour during spring as well as throughout summer.

NAPOLEON AND VIOLETS

Napoleon was an admirer of violets and gave bouquets of them to Josephine on their wedding anniversaries. When banished to Elba he said "I will return with the violets in the spring". Immediately, violets became the symbol of the Bonapartists and he became known and 'Père Violet'. Before he was exiled to St. Helena after his defeat at Waterloo in 1811, he is said to have visited Josephine's grave and picked their favourite flower. After he died, a locket he was wearing was found to contain a small lock of her hair and a few ancient, dried violets.

POLYANTHUSES (Primula polyantha) *are superb on their own or when mixed with spring-flowering bulbs. Buy plants in early autumn or sow outdoors in seed-beds in late spring.*

WALLFLOWERS (Cheiranthus cheiri *and* Erysimum x allionii) *are suitable for tubs or large bowls. Buy plants in autumn or sow seeds outdoors in late spring or early summer.*

PANSIES (Viola x wittrockiana)*; several types, flowering through winter to spring, others in summer. Buy plants in autumn or sow seeds outdoors in early summer.*

FORGET-ME-NOTS (Myosotis alpestris) *are ideal on their own or with short tulips. Buy plants in autumn or sow seeds outdoors during early summer.*

DAFFODILS *(large-trumpeted narcissi) are the epitome of spring and look superb in tubs or troughs, on their own or with polyanthus. Plant new bulbs in late summer or early autumn.*

DAISIES (Bellis perennis) *in their double-flowered form create superb backcloths for daffodils and tulips in tubs and large bowls. Buy plants in autumn, or sow outdoors in early summer.*

TENDER PERENNIALS

ERANIUMS and fuchsias are the best known tender perennials for brightening patios and other areas around houses in summer.

A few fuchsias – the Hardy Fuchsia *(Fuchsia magellanica)* for example – are hardy enough to be left in flower borders throughout the year in temperate regions, but most are frost-tender. In any case, plants growing in pots and left outside during winter are more likely to be damaged by cold temperatures than those planted directly into flower borders, as the compost in pots is more likely to freeze, especially when excessively wet.

PELARGONIUMS

(erroneously known as geraniums) create spectacular displays in pots on patios. They are easily damaged by frost and therefore cannot be left outdoors during winter.

Instead, move them into conservatories or frost-proof greenhouses. Proper geraniums are hardy, herbaceous plants.

BUSHY, *upright fuchsias are best displayed in large pots positioned on a patio. They can also be planted in small tubs on their own, or as centre-pieces in larger ones, with other plants.*

PELARGONIUMS

The range of these plants is wide and includes both species types as well as those that have received a great deal of attention from plant breeders. For example, both regal and zonal pelargoniums are hybrids which were raised by crossing species. From these have been derived many distinctive varieties. Both of these types can be grown in pots on sheltered patios during summer.

Do not plant them outdoors until all risk of frost has passed. Regal types, which are not as hardy as zonals, are best increased from cuttings taken in late

CASCADING *fuchsias are ideal for positioning on the tops of walls, plinths or on inverted clay pots of about the same size as the one the fuchsia is growing in. The flowers must trail freely.*

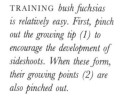

WALL-BRACKETS *are ideal for small pots planted with trailing and cascading fuchsia varieties. These can look especially good in small groups, rather than as solitary plants.*

TYPES OF FUCHSIA FLOWERS

The range of fuchsia flowers is wide and can be classified in several types: Single (with four petals); Semi-double (having five, six or seven petals); Double (with eight or more petals) and species types, such as Fuchsia magellanica.

Single-flowered   Double-flowered

Semi-double   Fuchsia magellanica (Hardy Fuschia)

summer and overwintered as rooted cuttings. Zonal types (also known as Martha Washington Geraniums) can be overwintered as growing plants in frost-proof greenhouses or conservatories.

GROWING FUCHSIAS

If you buy a tender fuchsia in early summer to plant in a pot or small tub on a patio, when considering what to do with it in late summer you have two choices: leave it until frost kills it, or take it into a frost-proof greenhouse. If the latter, gradually decrease its amount of water, and after the leaves fall, give no more until growth is restarted in spring. Then, plants are trimmed back slightly, watered and given a temperature of 10°C/50°F.

If the roots of plants are congested, repot them into slightly larger pots in early spring. Once plants are growing strongly, feed them every ten days with a weak liquid feed from early to late summer. However, ensure that the fertilizer is not strong, as otherwise it may damage the roots.

TRAINING *bush fuchsias is relatively easy. First, pinch out the growing tip (1) to encourage the development of sideshoots. When these form, their growing points (2) are also pinched out.*

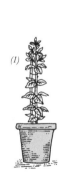

STANDARD *fuchsias are not difficult to create. Rooted cuttings grow quickly and strongly and are trained up canes (1). Remove sideshoots from all but the top three pairs of leaf joints (2).*

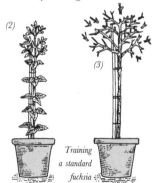

Training a standard fuchsia

REGULARLY *move plants with congested roots into larger pots. When the plant reaches the desired height, remove the growing tip and pinch out the sideshoots (3), as they develop.*

HARDY BORDER PLANTS 1

◆

THESE are plants that can be left in tubs or large pots for several years, until they are congested and need to be removed and divided. They are also grown in garden borders. Therefore, where a patio or terrace nestles alongside flower beds, similar plants can be used in tubs and pots to extend the theme and colour pattern.

LOOKING AFTER BORDER PLANTS

The main problem when growing these plants in containers is to keep the compost moist in summer, but relatively dry in winter. Compost rich in peat will help to retain moisture in summer, but should this become dry it is more difficult than soil-based compost to re-moisten. In winter, saturated soil is more likely to freeze and damage roots. Covering the surface with straw helps to keep the compost dry and prevent freezing.

SELECTING PLANTS

In addition to the border plants suggested here and on page 197, it is always worth experimenting with others. There are, however, a few guide-lines for this:
• Select relatively low-growing plants, especially if your garden is exposed to wind.
• If the leaves remain throughout winter, choose plants that are dome-headed and create little resistance to wind. Also, they are less likely to be damaged by snow.
• Choose plants that have both interesting flowers and foliage, especially if the flowering period is short. Hostas, of course, have this dual role and several are described on page 197.
• Select winter-brightening plants as well as those that reveal their beauty in summer. Winter flowers, as well as frost on large-leaved plants, such as bergenias, dramatically brighten gardens.

ANTHEMIS CUPANIANA: *Height 15–30cm/6–12in, spread 30–38cm/12–15in. Cushion-forming herbaceous perennial. Bright, white, daisy-like flowers with yellow centres during early and mid-summer.*

BERGENIA CORDIFOLIA *(Elephant's Ear): Height 30cm/12in, spread 30–38cm/12–15in. Large, rounded leaves and dominant, clustered heads of bell-shaped, slighty dropping lilac-rose flowers during early and mid-spring.*

SEDUM SPECTABILE: *Height 30–38cm/12–15in, spread 38–45cm/15–18in. Hardy, with a perennial nature and grey-green leaves. Also, clustered heads up to 13cm/5in wide, of pink flowers during late summer and autumn.*

BORDER PLANTS FOR CONTAINERS

Hardy plants feature here and on page 197.
• *Aegopodium podagraria* 'Variegata' (Variegated Ground Elder/ Variegated Goutweed): Because it is a relative of the infamous Ground Elder, this needs to be constrained in a tub. Nevertheless, it is exceptionally attractive, with light to mid-green leaves edged in white. It retains its colours even when positioned in light shade. It grows 15–25cm/6–10in high and is increased by division, but do not plant it in a border.
• *Agapanthus* 'Lilliput': A diminutive African Lily with narrow, mid-green leaves and stems topped with bright blue, trumpet-like flowers in umbrella-shaped heads during summer.
• *Dicentra* 'Snowflakes' (Bleeding Heart): Delicately and finely cut mid-green leaves surmounted by clusters of pendulous, white, bee-attracting flowers from early to late summer. It looks better in a large, round pot than in a tub, which may appear to dominate it.

AGAPANTHUS CAMPANULATUS *(African Lilies): Height 60–75cm/2–2¹/2ft, spread 38–45cm/15–18in. Herbaceous plant with strap-like leaves and crowded, umbrella-like heads of pale blue flowers in late summer.*

HELLEBORUS ORIENTALIS *(Lenten Rose): Height 45–60cm/1¹/2–2ft, spread 45–50cm/18–20in. Dark green, evergreen leaves and saucer-shaped cream flowers flecked with crimson during late winter and into early spring.*

DICENTRA SPECTABILIS *(Bleeding Heart): Height 45–60cm/ 1¹/2–2ft, spread 45cm/ 1¹/2ft. Herbaceous, with grey-green leaves and rosy-red, heart-shaped flowers on arching stems during late spring and early summer.*

CHRISTMAS ROSES

Helleborus niger, *the well-known Christmas Rose, is steeped in legend, folklore and superstition. It is said that people from Gaul – an ancient area that is now northern Italy, France and much of central and northern Europe – rubbed their arrow-heads with hellebore juice before hunting, to make the meat they killed more tender.*

In medieval times it was used to keep away evil spirits and witches, and for breaking enchantments and spells. It was also a cure for cattle that fell ill: a hole was bored through the animal's ear and a piece of hellebore root inserted for twenty-four hours. This was said to effect a cure. It was also said to cure coughs and poisoning.

HARDY
BORDER PLANTS 2
❖

THE RANGE of border plants for containers continues, with further ones to consider:

• *Hakonechloa macra* 'Albo-aurea': Although normally grown in a slightly raised bed where it can arch freely, this ornamental grass is also ideal for planting in tubs or large pots, preferably those that are quite tall so that it can cascade unhindered. The graceful, narrow leaves are vividly variegated gold and buff, with touches of bronze. It grows to about 30cm/12in high before cascading.

• *Polygonum affine* 'Dimity': Usually used to carpet borders but equally good in wide, relatively low tubs where it can smother the surface and trail over the edges. The massed, green leaves assume rich autumn shades, while from early to late summer it bears deep pink, poker-like flower heads.

• *Epimedium perralderianum* (Barrenwort/Bishop's Hat): Creeping, mat-forming evergreen plant, often used in borders as ground-cover but also good in large tubs. The bright green leaves, with bronze markings, turn coppery-red in autumn. Sprays of yellow flowers appear in late spring and early summer.

• *Alchemilla mollis* (Lady's Mantle): Beautiful plant, often positioned at the edges of borders where it softens the sides of paths. In large tubs it is just as attractive. The light green, hairy leaves are dominated from early to mid-summer by branched, wispy heads of yellowish-green flowers.

This plant is often used in floral arrangements, but when removing leaves and flowers always cut them from the rear to preserve the plant's appearance.

STACHYS OLYMPICA/
Stachys byzantina
*(Lamb's Tongue): Height
30–38cm/12–15in, spread
38–45cm/15–18in.
Spreading herbaceous
perennial with oval leaves
smothered in soft, furry
silvery hairs.*

PHORMIUM TENAX
*(New Zealand Flax): Height
90cm–1.2m/3–4ft, spread
90–1.2m/3–4ft. Masses of
tall, sword-like leaves. Many
superb varieties, some
variegated, others just one
colour. Protect crowns in
winter from excessive water.*

HEBE x ANDERSONII
*'Variegata' (Shrubby
Veronica): Height 45–
60cm/1¹/2–2ft, spread
45–60cm/1¹/2–2ft.
Shrubby, tender perennial
bearing beautiful mid-green
leaves variegated with cream.
Lavender flowers in summer.*

HOSTA CRISPULA
*(Plantain Lily): Height
38–45cm/15–18in, spread
45–50cm/18–20in. Dark
green, lance-shaped, pointed
leaves with narrow, white
edges and lilac-purple flowers
during mid-summer.*

HOSTA SIEBOLDIANA
*(Plantain Lily): Height
45–60cm/1¹/2–2ft, spread
50–60cm/20–24in. Oval,
mid-green, glossy leaves and
dull white flowers, tinged
purple, during mid-summer.
'Elegans' has lilac flowers.*

FESTUCA GLAUCA
*(Sheep's Festuca): Height
20–25cm/8–10in, spread
20–25cm/8–10in. Hardy,
perennial, ornamental grass
with bluish-grey, bristle-like
leaves that eventually form a
large tuft.*

FUNKIA OR HOSTA?

Even until quite recently, many gardeners still called hostas by their old name, funkia. Commonly, they are known as Plantain Lilies. Some of them grow 1m/3¹/2ft or more high, but it is the lower ones that make superb displays in large pots and tubs. In recent years, plant hybridists in North America, Japan and Britain have given these plants much attention, creating richer coloured leaves and a more dwarfed stance. Hostas for containers include:

• *Hosta 'Blue Moon': A superb, small-leaved hybrid with deep blue leaves and thickish clusters of greyish-mauve flowers.*
• *Hosta crispula: see left.*
• *Hosta 'Golden Prayers': Golden-yellow leaves and mauve flowers.*
• *Hosta 'Shade Fanfare': Green leaves with broad, cream edges. The green turns yellow when in sunlight.*
• *Hosta sieboldiana: see left.*
• *Hosta 'Thomas Hogg': Rich green, flat leaves with broad, white edges.*
• *Hosta 'Wide Brim': An American variety, with oval, blue-green leaves irregularly edged in cream to golden-yellow. It also bears spikes of lavender-coloured flowers.*
• *Hosta 'Zounds': Large, oval, dominant, deeply-puckered, yellow leaves.*

TREES AND SHRUBS

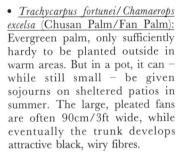

TREES, shrubs and conifers introduce permanency to patios. They can be displayed on their own or in groups. Their range of sizes and shapes is wide and there are sure to be many for you to choose from. Some develop flowers (page 199), while others have beautiful foliage (page 200). Small conifers are featured on page 201.

EXOTIC PATIOS

If your garden is warm, sunny and sheltered during summer, consider creating an exotic patio or courtyard, using slightly tender plants. Of course it is necessary to take them into a frost-free greenhouse or conservatory during winter, but their effect on a patio can be dramatic and memorable – and certainly will surprise and impress neighbours and visitors. Some of these plants, especially those in small pots, can also be put indoors in cool but bright hallways and other rooms during winter.

Popular plants include:

• *Agave americana* 'Marginata' (Variegated Century Plant): Height 45–60cm/1¹/₂–2ft. Large, thick and succulent, sword-like, grey-green leaves with yellow edges. The ordinary type just has grey-green leaves, but nevertheless is ideal in a group as a foil for variegated plants.

• *Cordyline australis/Dracaena australis* (Cabbage Palm): Eventually tall and shrubby, but in pots in homes and on patios is seldom more than 90cm/3ft high. The narrow, spiky, grey-green leaves rise from a stiff, upright, central stem. In warm, mild areas outdoors, plants more than ten years old may develop plumes of fragrant, creamy-white flowers during early and mid-summer.

• *Trachycarpus fortunei/Chamaerops excelsa* (Chusan Palm/Fan Palm): Evergreen palm, only sufficiently hardy to be planted outside in warm areas. But in a pot, it can – while still small – be given sojourns on sheltered patios in summer. The large, pleated fans are often 90cm/3ft wide, while eventually the trunk develops attractive black, wiry fibres.

• *Phoenix canariensis* (Canary Island Date Palm): In its native country it grows 4.5m/15ft or more high, but in a pot and when young is often grown as a houseplant. In warm areas, place it outdoors in summer. The slender leaves arch outwards, with stiff, mid-green leaflets attached to them.

• Yucca: Several yuccas, such as *Yucca filamentosa*, *Y. gloriosa* and *Y. recurvifolia* are relatively hardy, even in temperate zones. These look superb and exotic in tubs on patios, while some of the tender ones like *Y. elephantipes* (Spineless Yucca) and *Y. aloifolia* (Spanish Bayonet) can be placed outdoors

BUYING SHRUBS AND TREES

Buying all plants needs care, but trees and shrubs require special attention, as they will be with you for many years. Always check that the foliage is not damaged or infested with pests or diseases. Also, the compost must be slightly moist and not covered with moss or algae, which would indicate that the plant had been in the container too long and that the roots may be constricted.

during warm summer days. Take care with spiny plants not to position them where they may be a danger to children.

The variegated forms of *Yucca filamentosa* are exceptionally attractive: 'Variegata' has green leaves with creamy-yellow stripes, while 'Golden Sword' reveals upright, yellow leaves, shaped like swords and edged in green.

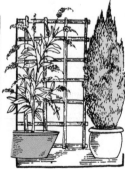

COURTYARDS *need one or two large, evergreen shrubs to form focal points and to help camouflage bland walls. If a courtyard is large, they also fill large areas and create fixed points, around which plants in small pots can be grouped.*

FLATS *and apartment blocks often have paved areas around them. These are easily brightened by shrubs and trees in large tubs. These plants can be given some protection from people by positioning them on uneven, cobbled surfaces.*

ULTRA-MODERN *patios, formed of brightly-coloured, square or hexagonal paving slabs need clinical-looking plants to compliment them. Spiky yuccas are ideal for this, especially when planted in geometric, square-edged, formal containers.*

RUSTIC *settings demand gently rounded and irregular outlines from a mixture of flowering and foliaged shrubs and trees. Create informal groups, such as shrubs in tubs and old stone sinks on brick piers, rather than using isolated plants.*

ENCLOSED *patios create wind sheltered areas, often warm and drenched in sun. These are ideal for tender, shrubby plants that elsewhere would not be successful. In such areas, daily watering is essential, especially at the height of summer.*

ROOF *gardens create exciting gardening opportunities, but too frequently are buffeted by cold winds in winter and 'fried' by strong sunlight in summer. Therefore, erect screens and windbreaks to create shelter and protection.*

FLOWERING SHRUBS

MANY flowering shrubs can be grown in containers, from dominant camellias at 1.5–1.8m/5–6ft high to tub-hugging types such as ericas. In addition to the ones illustrated on these pages, others to consider include the following:

• *Camellia* x *williamsii* (Camellia): Height 1.5–1.8m/5–6ft – in a large tub, spread 1.2–1.5m/4–5ft. Wide range of varieties, in colours from white and pale pink to rose-purple. Flowering is mainly in late winter and spring. Position out of direct, early-morning sun.

• *Genista pilosa* 'Vancouver Gold' (Broom): Height 15–30cm/6–12in, spread 90cm–1.2m/3–4ft. Compact, evergreen shrub with masses of deep golden-yellow flowers during late spring and early summer.

• *Prunus incisa* 'Kojo Nomal' (Flowering Cherry): Height 1.2–1.4m/4–5ft, spread 90cm–1.2m/3–4ft. A beautiful, deciduous flowering cherry that will delight you throughout the year: red-centred, pink flowers in spring that fade to white; colourful leaves in autumn; and twiggy, branching stems in winter.

• *Clematis florida sieboldii*: Height 1.5–1.8m, spread 75–90cm/2½–3ft. Bushy, mid-summer-flowering climber that is ideal in large pots. The large flowers, resembling those of the Passion Flower, have white petals and violet-purple petal-like stamens. Provide it with long twiggy sticks as supports.

• Roses: Several varieties within the perpetual-flowering County Series of roses grow well in containers on a patio. Those especially suited include 'Hertfordshire', with single, carmine flowers on a

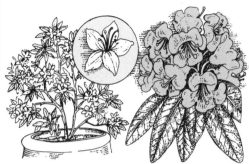

EVERGREEN AZALEAS *(Japanese Azaleas): Height 45–60cm/1½–2ft, spread 60–75cm/2–2½ft. Evergreen shrubs, some slightly tender, with flowers in massed heads during spring. Many colours.*

RHODODENDRONS: *Choose varieties no more than 1.5m/5ft high and broad. Wide range of varieties and colours, including red, pink, white, lavender and yellow. Flowers mainly in late spring.*

ROSMARINUS OFFICINALIS *(Rosemary): Normally 1.8m/6ft high, but if grown in a large tub and the growing points are pinched out several times, it can be kept to 1.2m/4ft high. Flowers all summer.*

HYPERICUM *'Hidcote': Height 90cm–1.2m/3–4ft, spread 90cm–1.2m/3–4ft. Hardy, evergreen shrub with large, dark green leaves and shallow saucer-shaped, golden-yellow flowers, up to 6cm/2½in wide, from mid to late summer.*

HYPERICUM OLYMPICUM: *Height 20–30cm/8–12in, spread 30–38cm/12–15in. Low-growing, hardy, evergreen shrub with grey-green leaves and golden-yellow flowers up to 36mm/1½in wide during mid-summer.*

LAVANDULA *'Hidcote'/L. nana atropurpurea (Lavender): Height 30–50cm/12–20in, spread 45–60cm/18–24in. Dwarf, hardy, evergreen shrub with silvery leaves and deep purple-blue flowers from mid- to late summer.*

low spreading shrub during summer. 'Suffolk' is also spreading, with bright scarlet, single flowers with golden centres.

Patio and miniature roses can also be grown in tubs and pots.

• *Convolvulus cneorum*: Height 45–60cm/1½–2ft, spread 45–60cm/1½–2ft. Compact, bushy, half-hardy evergreen shrub bearing narrow leaves covered with silky, silvery hairs. From late spring to late summer it develops pink buds that open to reveal white flowers.

• *Erica herbacea/ Erica carnea* (Snow Heather/Spring Heather): Height 10–30cm/4–12in, spread 30–45cm/1–1½ft. Wide range of varieties in various heights.

MOP-HEAD *Hydrangeas* (Hydrangea macrophylla) *are superb on patios, terraces and verandahs, where they blanket containers with large flower heads (mainly blue or pink) from mid- to late summer.*

The flowers are white and shades of pink and red from late autumn to late spring. For extra colour, choose those varieties with coloured foliage as they create colour throughout the year.

• *Mahonia* 'Charity': Height 1.5–1.8m/5–6ft, spread 90cm–1.6m/3–6ft. A tall, eye-catching shrub that eventually has to be removed from its container and planted into a woodland or wild garden setting. The large, holly-like, dark green leaflets are surmounted from late autumn to late winter by arching spires of fragrant, deep yellow flowers. Position it in sun or light shade, and away from where the sharp leaves can hurt children.

ATTRACTIVE FOLIAGE

Shrubs with attractive foliage introduce colour and vitality to patios and terraces throughout summer. Evergreen shrubs continue their display throughout winter, while the leaves of deciduous types often create a burst of exceptionally bright colour before falling in autumn. The range of attractively foliaged shrubs is wide:

• *Berberis thunbergii* 'Aurea': Height 60–75cm/2–2½ft, spread 60–75cm/2–2½ft. Deciduous shrub with masses of small, bright, soft-yellow leaves. There are several other superb forms, including 'Atropurpurea' (rich purple-red leaves), 'Atropurpurea Nana' (dwarf form with rich, purple-red leaves) and 'Helmond Pillar' (dark purple leaves).

• *Calluna vulgaris* (Heather/Ling): Height 15–30cm/6–12in (range of varieties), spread 30–38cm/12–15in. Hardy, evergreen shrub.

There are many attractively foliaged varieties, including 'Gold Haze' (bright gold), 'Golden Carpet' (golden foliage flecked with orange and red during winter), 'Beoley Gold' (golden) and 'Blazeaway' (foliage changes from gold, through orange to red).

• *Choisya ternata* 'Sundance' (Yellow-leaved Mexican Orange Blossom): Height 75–90cm/2½–3ft, spread 75–90cm/2½–3ft. Golden leaves throughout the year, with the bonus of white, scented flowers in spring.

• *Elaeagnus pungens* 'Maculata': Height 1.5–2.1m/5–7ft, spread 1.5–1.8m/5–6ft. Evergreen, spiny-stemmed shrub bearing leathery, glossy green leaves splashed with gold. Eventually it becomes too large for tubs, when it can be planted into gardens.

• *Euonymus fortunei* 'Emerald 'n Gold': Height 45–60cm/1½–2ft,

ACER PALMATUM
'Dissectum Atropurureum': Height 90cm/1.2m/3–4ft, spread 1.2–1.5m/4–5ft. Beautiful deciduous shrub with bronze-red, several-lobed leaves.

YUCCA FILAMENTOSA
'Variegata': Height 60–75cm/2–2½ft, spread 60cm/2ft. Spiky plant with stiff, mid-green leaves edged and striped in creamy yellow.

ARUNDINARIA VIRIDISTRIATA: Height 90cm–1.2m/3–4ft, spread 30–45cm/1–1½ft (clump-forming). Purplish-green canes and green leaves striped yellow.

spread 60–75cm/2–2½ft. Gloriously coloured evergreen shrub with green, gold and pink leaves. There are several other forms with colourful leaves, including 'Emerald Gaiety' (creamy-white and green leaves).

• *Hebe* x *andersonii* 'Variegata': Height 60–75cm/2–2½ft, spread 45–60cm/1½–2ft. Small, evergreen shrub with mid-green leaves variegated in cream. Additionally, from mid- to late summer it bears spikes of lavender flowers.

• *Hebe pinguifolia* 'Pagei': Height 15–23cm/6–9in, spread 38–45cm/15–18in. Low-growing, evergreen shrub with small, grey leaves. During early summer it has the bonus of small, white flowers borne in spikes up to 2.5cm/1in long.

• *Lonicera nitida* 'Baggeson's Gold': Height 1.2–1.5m/4–5ft, spread 90cm–1.2m/3–4ft (in a tub): Hardy, evergreen shrub with small, yellow leaves that turn yellowish green in autumn. It is often clipped – especially when grown

as a hedge – but in a large tub is best left with an informal outline.

• *Sambucus racemosa* 'Sutherland': Height 1.8–2.1m/6–7ft, spread 1.8–2.4m/6–8ft. Spectacular deciduous shrub with finely cut, golden-yellow leaves. Eventually it forms a handsome, much larger shrub, but when young can be grown in a big tub.

TOPIARY IN CONTAINERS

*Large tubs on patios allow an opportunity to train small-leaved evergreen shrubs, such as the Small-leaved Box (*Buxus sempervirens *'Suffruticosa'), into the shape of a small animal. Allow clusters of stems to form the head and tail – wire is usually necessary to create a framework. Pinch out the tips of shoots to ensure bushiness.*

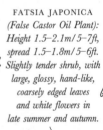

FATSIA JAPONICA
(False Castor Oil Plant): Height 1.5–2.1m/5–7ft, spread 1.5–1.8m/5–6ft. Slightly tender shrub, with large, glossy, hand-like, coarsely edged leaves and white flowers in late summer and autumn.

HEBE x FRANCISCANA
'Variegata': Height 30–45cm/12–18in, spread 30–45cm/12–18in. Dome shaped, compact shrub with glossy green leaves edged in cream, and mauve-blue flowers throughout summer.

AUCUBA JAPONICA
'Maculata' (Spotted Laurel): Height 1.5–1.8m/5–6ft, spread 1.2–1.5m/4–5ft. Dome shaped, evergreen shrub bearing glossy green leaves peppered with yellow spots. Also known as 'Variegata'.

CONFERS

D WARF and slow-growing conifers are easy to grow, as well as representing excellent value for money. They last a long time and if eventually too large for tubs and pots can be planted into a garden. In addition to the conifers illustrated here, there are many others to choose from:

• *Chamaecyparis lawsoniana* 'Aurea Densa': Compact and slow growing, with densely packed sprays of golden foliage.

• *Chamaecyparis lawsoniana* 'Minima Aurea': Dwarf, with vertical, soft golden-yellow sprays that form a conical bush.

• *Chamaecyparis pisifera* 'Boulevard': Soft, steel-blue foliage. Do not allow the soil to become dry.

• *Chamaecyparis pisifera* 'Filifera Aurea': Graceful and rounded with golden, thread-like foliage

POSITIONING CONIFERS

One of the biggest dangers to conifers – apart from letting the compost become too dry in summer or excessively wet in winter – is strong winds. Tall plants are soon knocked over and unless put upright immediately may be permanently damaged. In exposed positions, use low-growing types in tubs or heavy, reconstituted stone pots.

that eventually forms a mop-headed plant.

• *Cryptomeria japonica* 'Elegans Compacta': Slow growing and dome shaped. Tinged purple in winter.

JUNIPERUS SCOPULORUM *'Skyrocket'*/*Juniperus virginiana 'Skyrocket': Narrow, upright, slow-growing conifer, about 1.8m/6ft high after ten years. Silvery blue-green, scale-like foliage.*

JUNIPERUS SQUAMATA *'Meyeri': Irregularly shaped, with arching and ascending branches. After about ten years it forms a bush about 1.5m/5ft high. Steel-blue, needle-like leaves. If it spreads excessively, it can be pruned.*

TAXUS BACCATA *'Standishii': Narrow, columnar, slow-growing conifer, reaching only 75cm/2¹/2ft in ten years. The old-gold foliage is especially attractive in winter and forms a tight column. It is tolerant of light shade.*

• *Juniperus communis* 'Hibernica': Eventually large, but suitable for tubs when young. Narrow and column-like.

• *Juniperus x media* 'Old Gold': Spreading, eventually large but ideal for containers when young. Golden, scale-like foliage.

• *Juniperus squamata* 'Blue Star': Small, low conifer with intense steel-blue, needle-like leaves.

• *Pinus sylvestris* 'Beuvronensis': Distinctive, miniature Scots Pine creating a dome shape packed with grey-green foliage. Especially attractive in spring, when new growth is beginning.

• *Thuja occidentalis* 'Smaragd': Slow-growing, pyramidal and packed with bright, rich green foliage. It retains an attractive colour throughout winter.

• *Thuja plicata* 'Stoneham Gold': Slow growing and ideal in a small tub. The foliage is tipped in deep, golden-yellow.

JUNIPERUS COMMUNIS *'Depressa Aurea': Dwarf and slow growing with a spreading and low nature, up to 38cm/15in-high and 1–1.2m/3–4ft wide. Golden-yellow leaves, silver beneath. It is especially bright in spring.*

CHAMAECYPARIS LAWSONIANA *'Elwoodii': Slow growing and eventually 1.8m/6ft tall, but when young is ideal for pots and tubs. It is column-like and packed with dark green foliage. 'Ellwood's Golden Pillar' has golden-yellow foliage.*

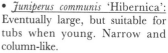

JUNIPERUS HORIZONTALIS *'Wiltonii' (Wilton Carpet Juniper): Slow growing and carpet forming (15–20cm/6–8in high) and spreading to about 1m/3¹/2ft in six years. Bright blue, dense foliage. Plant it in a large tub with space to spread.*

MINIATURE and slow-growing conifers create colour in pots, tubs and troughs throughout the year. When planted in a trough which is to be set in a central position, create a 'balanced' display. But when positioned with one end in a corner, create a slanting arrangement.

BULBS ON PATIOS

FOR AN assured display of colour in containers on a patio, few plants compare with bulbs. They are storehouses of energy and if healthy, fresh bulbs are planted at the right time (invariably in late summer or autumn for a spring display) a feast of colour is assured. In addition to the bulbs illustrated here, there are many others, including:

• *Anemone blanda* (Windflower): Height: 10–15cm/4–6in. Daisy-like flowers – mainly mid-blue, but pale blue, mauve, pink and mauve forms available – from late winter to mid-spring. Plant them 3.6–5mm/1¹/₂–2in deep in late summer. They are best when planted around shrubs in large tubs, where they can be left for several years.

• *Crocus chrysanthus*: Height 7.5cm/3in. Globe-shaped flowers in many colours, including golden-yellow, bronze, mauve-blue, white

SCENTED LILIES IN POTS

Lilies introduce dignity and history to patios – they were represented on Cretan vases about 1750 BC. There are several sweetly scented lilies that can be grown in pots, including:
• Lilium auratum *(Golden-rayed Lily of Japan): Bowl-shaped and brilliant white, with golden-yellow bands, flowering in late summer.*
• Lilium 'Empress of China': *Chalk-white, mid- to late summer.*
• Lilium hansonii: *Nodding, pale orange-yellow with brown spots during mid-summer.*
• Lilium speciosum: *Bowl-shaped, white and shaded crimson during late summer. There are also several named varieties, in white and shades of crimson.*

HYACINTHS: *Height 15–23cm/6–9in. Upright and soldier-like flowers in many colours, including white, pink and blue. Plant bulbs 13–15cm/5–6in deep and 5–7.5cm/2–3in apart in autumn. Always plant fresh, healthy bulbs.*

NARCISSUS CYCLAMINEUS: *Height 15–20cm/6–8in. A diminutive bulb, flowering in late winter and early spring with golden flowers. Plant bulbs in autumn, 2.5cm/1in apart and two to three times their own depth.*

TULIPA KAUFMANNIANA *(Waterlily Tulip): Height 20–25cm/8–10in. Large, white flowers flushed yellow and red in early and mid-spring. Plant bulbs in autumn, three times their depth and 7.5cm/3in apart.*

MUSCARI ARMENIACUM *(Grape Hyacinth): Height 15–20cm/6–8in. Spring-flowering, with clustered heads of deep blue flowers. Plant bulbs 6–7.5cm/2¹/₂–3in deep and slightly apart in autumn.*

TRUMPET DAFFODILS: *Large height range, but choose low varieties as they are less likely to be damaged by wind. Plant bulbs close together in autumn, so that they are covered by twice their depth of compost. Set them close together.*

TULIPS – *single early types: select short types. Many varieties to choose from: always buy fresh bulbs. Plant bulbs deeply, about three times their own depth and close together, in autumn. They can be mixed with hyacinths.*

and deep purple, during late winter and early spring. Plant them 5–7.5cm/2–3in deep in late summer or autumn.

• *Eranthis hyemalis* (Winter Aconite): Height 10cm/4in. Unusual flowers, with yellow bowls and pale green ruffs at their backs during late winter and early spring. Plant them 2.5cm/1in deep and 6cm/2¹/₂in apart in late summer. They look good in clumps around deciduous shrubs in large tubs.

• *Iris danfordiae:* Height 10cm/4in. Diminutive, with honey-scented, bright yellow flowers during mid- and late winter. Ideal for planting in sink gardens to create early colour. Plant 5–7.5cm/2–3in deep in autumn. They can be left in the container for several years.

• *Iris reticulata:* Height 10–15cm/4–6in. Beautiful, 6–7.5cm/2¹/₂–3in wide, deep blue, iris-like flowers with golden-yellow blazes on the insides of the lower petals. They are ideal for brightening sink gardens, pots and window-boxes in late winter and early spring. Plant them 5–7.5cm/2–3in

deep in autumn. Once these bulbs are established they can be left alone for several years.

• *Narcissus bulbocodium* (Yellow Hoop Petticoat): 10–15cm/4–6in. Diminutive, with dainty but long, yellow trumpets. They appear in late winter and early spring. Plant to twice the bulb's depth, and close together. It is ideal for planting in sink gardens.

BULBS IN GROWING-BAGS
Growing-bags that during the previous season grew tomatoes or other vegetable plants can be reused for bulbs. Just top up the bag with moist peat in autumn and set the bulbs in position. Choose short-stemmed types.

CLIMBERS IN CONTAINERS

❖

CLIMBERS introduce a new dimension to containers on a patio: some of them have a perennial nature and each year send up fresh shoots, while others are raised annually from seeds. Some of the annual types are really tender perennials that are grown as half-hardy annuals. Cathedral Bells (*Cobaea scandens*), for example, is only half-hardy in temperate climates and therefore grown as a half-hardy annual, although in greenhouses and conservatories it can be grown as a permanent, perennial climber.

ANNUAL CLIMBERS

Apart from the seed-raised climbers illustrated here, there are a few others, including:
• Chilean Glory Flower (*Eccrocarpus scaber*): Height 1.5–2.1m/5–7ft (in a container). From early summer to autumn it bears 2.5cm/1in-long, orange-scarlet, tubular flowers. Also has red and yellow

forms. Sow seeds in 55–61°C/13–16°F during early spring. Transfer the seedlings to pots, slowly acclimatize to outdoor conditions and plant into a container when all risk of frost has passed.
• Black-eyed Susan (*Thunbergia alata*): Height 1.2–1.8m/4–6ft (in a pot). From early to late summer it bears large, yellow flowers with

LATHYRUS ODORATUS *(Sweet Pea): Height 60cm–1.2m/2–4ft – low-growing varieties. Well-known climber. Sow seeds in 16°C/61°F in early spring. Flowers, in many colours, are borne throughout summer. Choose dwarf types, such as 'Bijou Mixed'.*

COBAEA SCANDENS *(Cathedral Bells): Height 1.5–1.8m/5–6ft (when grown outdoors). A tender perennial with purple, bell-shaped flowers throughout summer. Grow as a half-hardy annual outdoors. Sow seeds in 16°C/61°F during early spring.*

TROPAEOLUM CANARIENSIS *(Canary Creeper): Height 1.5–1.8m/5–6ft (in a tub). Short-lived perennial grown as an annual, with yellow flowers from mid-summer to autumn. Raise early plants by sowing seeds in 16°C/61°F during early spring.*

dark centres. Sow seeds in 16°C/61°F in early spring. Prick off the seedlings into small pots and plant into containers when all risk of frost has passed.

PERENNIAL CLIMBERS

Apart from perennial climbers such as large-flowered clematis in tubs, the herbaceous Yellow-Leaved Hop (*Humulus lupulus* 'Aureus') is worth growing. It dies down to soil level in autumn, but each spring sends up beautiful, large leaves that remain soft yellow throughout summer. In gardens it grows 2.1m/7ft or more in a season, but in a tub is more reserved. Do not allow the compost to dry out.

Wisteria is usually grown against a wall, although sometimes trained as a single stem to produce a canopy at head height. However, it can also be grown in a large tub or terracotta pot, where it creates an eye-catching display during late spring and early summer.

Clematis macropetala

CLEMATIS: *Large-flowered types. Height 1.5–1.8m/5–6ft (in tubs). Deciduous climbers with many to choose from. Flowers from early to late summer, depending on the variety. Wide colour range.*

IPOMOEA TRICOLOR/ I. violacea/I. rubro-caerulea *(Morning Glory): Height 1.5–1.8m/5–6ft (in a pot). It is grown as a half-hardy annual, with seed sown in 18°C/64°F in early spring.*

TROPAEOLUM MAJUS *(Nasturtiums): Height 38–45cm/15–18in – dwarf varieties. For planting in pots it is grown as a half-hardy annual. Sow seeds in 16°C/61°F in early spring. Flowers throughout summer.*

PLANTING GROWING-BAGS

GROWING-BAGS offer instant homes to plants. Additionally, they are unique in being both a container and compost. They are used to grow a wide range of plants, including spring-flowering bulbs and summer-flowering bedding plants. Vegetables are also candidates, but only those with fibrous or short roots are really suitable.

PLANTING A BAG

Preparing a growing-bag is detailed below. Bags can be placed directly on paving slabs or soil, but placing them on a pallet-like board enables them to be moved and makes it slightly more difficult for slugs and snails to reach the plants.

Piercing four or five holes in a bag's base is often recommended to allow excess water to escape during wet summers, especially when there is only a small amount of leafy growth on plants to use the moisture. If the bag is posi-

FLOWERS FOR VASES

Recycled growing-bags are ideal homes for bulbs such as trumpet daffodils that are being grown to produce cut flowers for decoration indoors in spring. Plant large, healthy bulbs (7.5–10cm/3–4in deep and close together) in autumn and place the bag in a sheltered position. Cut the flowers when just starting to open.

tioned on soil, holes in the base are possible. Indeed, when growing tomatoes in a bag on soil it is possible to push canes right through the bag's base, providing both drainage and support for the

FLOWERS IN GROWING-BAGS

Recycling used growing-bags saves money and is environmentally friendly. If used for bulbs, top up with peat in autumn and plant them immediately. For summer-flowering bedding plants, however, store the bag under cover during winter. In late spring, add peat and dust with a general fertilizer. Water the compost and put plants in it as soon as all risk of frost has passed. Use a combination of bushy plants in the centre and trailing ones along the edges to hide the plastic.

plants. However, if the soil is contaminated with pests and diseases, do not pierce the bag, as it could allow their entry. If the bag is on a paved surface, make the slits in its sides and support the plants with a proprietary frame.

When growing spring-flowering bulbs in these bags, make several slits to enable water to escape.

TOPS *of wide walls are ideal places for positioning reused growing-bags. Use low-growing summer-flowering types in the centre and trailers around the edges to cloak the bag's sides.*

FLAT *roofs on garages or home-extensions look bland. In summer, place growing-bags along their edges and pack with plants. In such positions, the compost dries quickly, so water frequently.*

REUSING GROWING-BAGS

As well as putting these bags on walls and flat roofs, they can be used in other ways:

• Recycled bags are especially suitable for growing bulbs, such as daffodils, hyacinths and short-stemmed tulips. Another way is to use them to create a spring hedge of bright-faced yellow daffodils along the side of a patio. Plant the bulbs close together to create a colour-packed display.

• Many herbs are suitable for growing in fresh growing-bags, but those with an invasive nature are ideal for putting in re-used types, where they can be left for several years until either divided or thrown away. Mint, for instance, eventually swamps containers with roots and stems, but in a recycled bag can be left for several seasons. Indeed, the strong roots eventually split the bags.

• At the end of a bag's recycled life, the peat can be either dug into the soil during winter or spread over the surface of borders in spring to create a thick mulch, about 7.5cm/3in deep. First, however, thoroughly water the soil.

• Early potatoes are worth trying in recycled bags: in spring, top up with peat and mix in a general fertilizer. Plant eight tubers of an early variety in each bag.

GROWING-BAGS, *when stacked in garden centres, inevitably become totally compressed. Therefore, before using one, thoroughly shake the bag to loosen the peat-based compost inside it. Shake it from both ends.*

PLACE *the bag directly on the ground or a flat, pallet-like board. Cut out the windows (along the dotted lines). Some bags have a band that can be slipped over the centre to help restrain the sides.*

SOME *people recommend piercing holes in the bag's base to allow excess water to drain during wet seasons (see above). However, it is always necessary first to moisten the peat-based compost thoroughly.*

COMPOSTS, WATERING AND FEEDING

❖

LANTS in pots, tubs and urns are the athletes of the gardening world: they are expected to perform throughout summer and to create magnificent displays. Many plants do this very well, but they must have the right diet.

WHEN *groups of pots and tubs are together, it is often difficult to water those at the back without moving them. However, by tying the end of a hose-pipe to a 1.2m/4ft-long cane it is possible to reach them. Never turn the tap on full.*

JUDGING *when plants in pots need water is difficult, but one way to find out if soil in clay pots is dry is to tap the outside with a cotton reel (bobbin) attached to a cane. If the knock creates a ringing note, the compost needs water.*

WHEN *watering plants in pots and tubs, remove the spray from the can and apply water direct from the nozzle. Water the compost gently, so that the surface is not disturbed. Each time water is applied, thoroughly moisten the compost.*

COMPOSTS

Plants in containers outdoors are mainly grown in loam-based composts, although those in shallow urns and hanging-baskets are frequently in compost predominantly formed of peat. This is to help retain more moisture in a relatively small root area. Loam, incidentally, is relatively fertile topsoil.

• Shrubs and trees are invariably grown in tubs and therefore a large amount of compost is needed. The loam-based John Innes Potting Compost No. 3 is best and will create a firm base that prevents wind knocking over plants. However, if the cost of buying compost is prohibitive, use equal parts of good garden soil, peat and sharp sand, plus fertilizers.

FEEDING PLANTS

Plants soon exhaust soil of nutrients, especially if the container is small. Once planted, bulbs do not need feeding, nor do biennials. Summer-flowering bedding plants, however, soon use up plant foods and need to be fed every fortnight from mid-summer onwards. Prepare the feed to the manufacturer's recommendation – too strong mixtures may damage or kill plants.

• Herbaceous plants are usually planted in tubs. Although they are not so long-lived as shrubs, each year they develop a vast array of stems and flowers and therefore a good supply of food is essential. Loam-based compost provides food as well as a firm base.

• Bulbs are planted in either loam- or peat-based compost. Tall bulbs, such as trumpet daffodils and tulips, need a firm base to support their stems and flowers, and this is best provided by loam-based types. When small bulbs are planted around shrubs in tubs, this invariably is also loam-based. However, low-growing types – when in sheltered places – can be grown in growing-bags which, basically, are packed with peat-based compost.

• Biennials, which are planted in autumn for spring and early summer flowers, are invariably planted in loam-based compost.

• Summer-flowering bedding plants are planted in either soil or peat-based compost. If the container has little space for compost, the peat-based type is better, as it retains more moisture.

• Rock garden plants in sink gardens need a well-drained mixture formed of loam-based compost, peat and sharp sand.

WATERING PLANTS

Knowing when to water plants and how much to give them is, perhaps, one of the most difficult gardening skills to master. If too much is given, plants wilt and eventually die; if excessively watered, compost becomes saturated, with the subsequent risk of roots being killed and plants wilting. The best general watering guide for plants in containers outdoors is to wait until the surface compost starts to dry, then thoroughly soak it. Soil-based compost, when dry, is easier to re-soak than peat types, which appear to resist water.

WHEN *filling a tub, cover the drainage holes with pieces of broken clay pots, then 6–7.5cm/2^1/2–3in of shingle or pebbles. Form a thick layer of peat, with loam-based compost on top. This creates a firm base for shrubs and trees.*

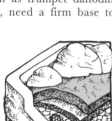

GOOD *drainage is essential in all containers. In barrels and planters, this is achieved by forming a wire-netting tube and filling with coarse drainage material. Place it securely in the container's centre, then add and firm compost around it.*

SINK *gardens need good drainage. Place pieces of broken clay pots over the plug hole, then 2.5cm/1in of pea shingle. Over this put 2.5–4cm/1–1^1/2in of moist peat, then soil-based compost with extra peat and sharp sand added to it.*

WATERING PLANTS

Watering plants in gardens and pots has always been an art, but perhaps never more so than during the mid-fifteenth century with this perforated clay pot. Once full, it continuously spouted water until exhausted.

HERBS FOR THE KITCHEN

❖

Culinary herbs have always been important, especially in earlier years when their main purpose was to suppress the incipient decay in meat. Many herbs were also used to add vitality and unusual flavours to beers and ales. Nowadays, culinary herbs are widely used to introduce unusual and attractive flavours when cooking food. Also, some are used to garnish dishes, introducing complementary flavours and adding greater eye-appeal.

The range of culinary herbs is wide and those described in this chapter, from Angelica to Thyme, include popular ones such as Parsley, Sage, Rosemary, Chives, Balm, Bay and Mint, as well as some that are less well known.

Planning a herb garden and raising herbs from seeds, by cuttings and through division, are illustrated and detailed in this chapter. Freezing and drying herbs, as well as tips for combining them with food and using them in pot-pourri are also featured.

PLANNING A HERB GARDEN

HERB gardens on a grand scale are always impressive, with dominant mounds of coloured sages perhaps overshadowed by large, umbrella-like flower heads of Angelica. But small is also beautiful and there are few gardens without space for two or three herbs, either in borders or containers on a patio or balcony.

The range of herbs is wide and includes annuals, biennials, herbaceous perennials, small shrubs and trees. Except for those with a woody nature, most die down during winter. Some, such as the well-known Parsley and Chervil, can be encouraged to grow outdoors through part or all of winter by placing cloches over them.

Herbs grow well in most soils that are freely drained and neither too acid nor too chalky. Because many herbs are native to warm climates, a sunny, wind-sheltered position is essential, especially to encourage early and late harvesting. Fertile, moisture-retentive soil encourages growth even during droughts. However, the herbs that are grown for their seeds do not need rich soil.

GAPS BETWEEN *natural stone paving create homes for low-growing herbs, such as the many thymes. More clinical settings are possible, such as formal paving slabs laid solely on a bed of sand, with gaps between them.*

BUYING HERBS

Many herbs can be raised from seeds (page 222), others by cuttings (page 223) and a few by division (page 224). Alternatively, there is always the opportunity to buy young plants. Sources for these include nurseries, garden centres, high street shops and specialist mail-order companies.

If possible, inspect plants thoroughly before buying (mail-order ones on receipt). Reject those infested with pests and diseases, roots matted and coming out of the drainage hole, moss growing on the compost, and a generally neglected appearance. Poor plants never recover to develop into healthy, eye-catching specimens. If mail-order plants are not up to standard, immediately complain and contact the company.

HERBS IN CONTAINERS

Patio containers and window-boxes make herb growing possible for everyone, even flat-dwellers with only a balcony.

While chives are handsome in pots, sages and mints in growing-bags and a medley of small herbs

in window-boxes and troughs, few are as imposing and eye-catching as a couple of Bay trees planted in large white tubs and positioned either side of a front door. They need regular clipping, but more than repay this time by their distinctive appearance.

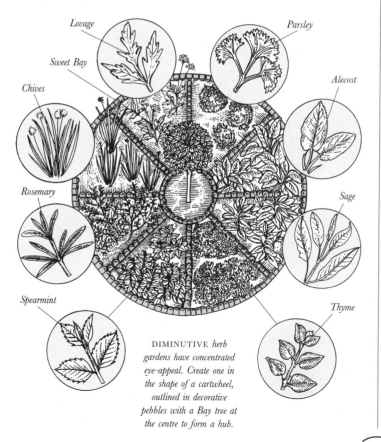

Lovage

Sweet Bay

Chives

Rosemary

Spearmint

Parsley

Alecost

Sage

Thyme

DIMINUTIVE *herb gardens have concentrated eye-appeal. Create one in the shape of a cartwheel, outlined in decorative pebbles with a Bay tree at the centre to form a hub.*

CULINARY HERBS

HERBS are some of the oldest cultivated plants we have and therefore their wide range, which includes annuals, biennials, herbaceous perennials, evergreen shrubs and trees, is not surprising. Some are grown for their leaves, which are used to flavour a wide range of dishes; others have seeds that introduce spicy flavours to foods and drinks. Roots and stems bring further flavourings.

Garnishing is another role of culinary herbs. Parsley is ideal for adding colour to sandwiches and fish, while Spearmint, as well as being added to boiled potatoes and peas, also creates interest and colour when placed on cooked food in serving dishes on tables. Dill leaves are superb when garnishing boiled potatoes, peas and beans; they have also been used in salads. Chives are a good companion to cucumber.

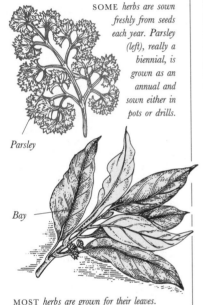

SOME herbs are sown freshly from seeds each year. Parsley (left), really a biennial, is grown as an annual and sown either in pots or drills.

Parsley

Bay

HORSERADISH *(left) is one of the few herbs grown for its long roots. When washed, crushed and prepared they create a well-known pungent, peppery condiment for use with meat, fish and salads.*

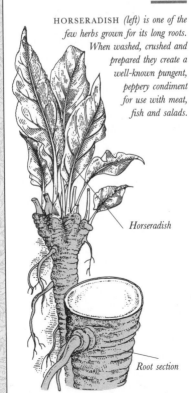

Horseradish

Root section

MOST *herbs are grown for their leaves. Some, such as the herbaceous Balm (below), have soft leaves that soon emit a pleasing bouquet when bruised, but the tree-like Bay (above) has tough leaves. Its leaves are an essential part of bouquet garni.*

Balm

CRYSTALLIZED STEMS

Angelica is widely grown for its stems, which are cut, dried and crystallized with sugar, and used to flavour and decorate cakes and confectionaries. It has been grown commercially over a wide area, from Japan to France, including England, Moravia and Bohemia.

Angelica (Angelica archangelica) severed stem

SPICY *seeds play an essential role in many dishes, introducing exciting flavours. These herbs include Anise, Caraway, Coriander and Fennel. They are easily grown and harvesting them is simple. Storage needs only a few air-tight jars. Additionally, when growing in a herb garden they create an attractive array of finely-divided leaves and flower-heads.*

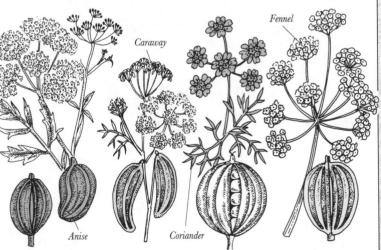

Fennel

Caraway

Anise

Coriander

FLAVOURING BEERS AND SUMMER DRINKS

Brewing barley wine was probably one of the earliest industrial arts, and is said to have been established in Egypt as early as 5000 BC. Indeed, an Egyptian papyrus records a barley-wine tax being collected in 3400 BC. The art spread to the Greeks, the Romans later acquiring it and taking it around Europe.

Later, in Northern Europe and North America, many beer-like, low-alcohol and undistilled beverages were made from plants then considered either medicinal or culinary herbs. Root beer was made from an infusion of herbs, barks and roots, including Wintergreen (*Gaultheria procumbens*) and Sarsaparilla (*Smilax*).

Beers have also been enhanced by herbs, such Alecost (*Chrysanthemum balsamita*), formerly known as Costmary. It emits a balsamic odour and is said to give ales a spicy taste.

Flavouring summer drinks is another role of herbs; Lemon Balm is frequently used, while some people use Spearmint, Peppermint or Applemint.

FREEZING AND DRYING HERBS

❖

HERBS are at their best when used fresh, but there are times during the year when this is impossible. Leaves of evergreen herbs, such as Rosemary and Bay, can be picked throughout the year, but even these are not at their best while in a semi-dormant state in winter. Also, it is possible to grow a few herbs in pots on a window sill indoors to extend their fresh season by a month or so, but to be assured of herbs throughout the year gathering and storing is an essential and interesting facet of growing culinary herbs.

Herbs can either be dried or frozen and although in these states they are not suitable as garnishes they are still superb for adding to food. Indeed, the flavour of many dried herbs is more concentrated than when fresh. Therefore only about half the amount is needed.

DRYING HERBS

There are two basic ways to dry herbs – in the air or by being placed in a gently-warm oven. The easiest and best method is by air, but both techniques are initially the same:

• Pick shoots and leaves while still young and before the plant develops flowers. Choose a warm, dry day, removing them in the morning before they feel the full sun.

• Discard aged, diseased or pest-damaged leaves.

• Tie young sprigs into small bunches. Avoid creating large clusters, as this reduces air circulation within them. Large leaves of herbs, such as sage, are best removed from their stalks and tied into small clusters.

• Frequently, blanching is recommended prior to drying and although it helps leaves to retain

FEATHERY *and small-leaved herbs such as Chervil, Fennel and Marjoram can be tied in small bunches and hung upside down in an airy place. Avoid places where the atmosphere is damp, as this encourages diseases.*

WHEN *herbs are thoroughly dry, rub them gently between your hands and store them in airtight containers with screw-top lids. Ensure hands are dry before tackling this job, as otherwise leaves tend to stick to them.*

FREEZING *is a relatively recent way to keep herbs. Instead of placing in airtight containers, put measured amounts in ice-cube trays, add water and place in a freezer compartment. To use, just drop a cube in a dish.*

colour, is not necessary. However, if you wish to do it, immerse the leaves in boiling water for a few seconds, shake to remove water and dry on clean, absorbent paper. Oven-dried herbs are usually blanched.

• Hang up the bunches in a well-ventilated, dry and fairly warm room to dry. Slow drying is better than drying rapidly in high temperatures, and usually takes five to twelve days. If the area is dusty, wrap the bunches in muslin or place in thin paper bags.

• Leaves and small sprigs are more easily dried by placing them on a tray. They then can be placed over a radiator, in an airing cupboard or even in a warming draw in an oven. Ensure they do not dry too rapidly: turn them every day. In this way, drying takes about three days.

• When oven-drying, place blanched herbs on a covered tray and put in an oven with the temperature at its lowest and the door ajar. Turn the leaves every twenty minutes – drying usually is complete within an hour. This is suitable for herbs such as sage, mint and Parsley that have been removed from their stalks.

• When leaves – whether air or oven-dried – are dry and crumbly, rub them between your hands. At the same time, remove stalks and mid-ribs. Place in airtight jars.

DRYING SEEDS

Some herbs, such as Anise, Coriander, Dill and Fennel, are grown for their seeds. These are gathered by cutting the flower-heads when fully ripe and hanging them upside down in an airy place. Either place a sheet of clean paper under them, or put in thin paper bags.

FREEZING HERBS

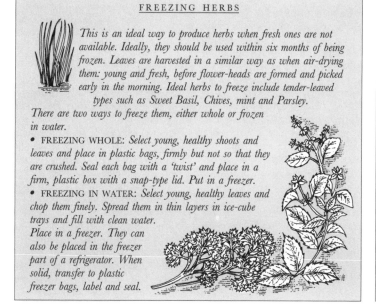

This is an ideal way to produce herbs when fresh ones are not available. Ideally, they should be used within six months of being frozen. Leaves are harvested in a similar way as when air-drying them: young and fresh, before flower-heads are formed and picked early in the morning. Ideal herbs to freeze include tender-leaved types such as Sweet Basil, Chives, mint and Parsley.

There are two ways to freeze them, either whole or frozen in water.

• *FREEZING WHOLE: Select young, healthy shoots and leaves and place in plastic bags, firmly but not so that they are crushed. Seal each bag with a 'twist' and place in a firm, plastic box with a snap-type lid. Put in a freezer.*

• *FREEZING IN WATER: Select young, healthy leaves and chop them finely. Spread them in thin layers in ice-cube trays and fill with clean water. Place in a freezer. They can also be placed in the freezer part of a refrigerator. When solid, transfer to plastic freezer bags, label and seal.*

STORING HERBS

Store dried herbs in airtight jars in cool, dark cupboards. Avoid places above ovens, as hot, dry air may cause fluctuations in temperature. Also, select cupboards away from steamy cookers. If properly dried and stored, dried herbs will keep their flavour for about a year.

ANGELICA
Angelica archangelica

NATIVE to Northern Europe, Iceland, Greenland and Central Russia, this dominant, 1.8–3m/6–10ft tall, hardy biennial is a multi-purpose plant: young stems are candied, leaves added to fish dishes and roots used to flavour gin and liqueurs.

CULTIVATION

Also known as Archangel and Wild Parsnip, by nature it is a biennial, but by removing the flowers it can be grown as a short-lived perennial.

Grow Angelica in fertile, moisture-retentive soil in full sun or light shade. Sow seeds thinly and evenly outdoors in seedbeds during late spring or early summer, in shallow drills about 30cm/12in apart. Germination takes two to three weeks and when seedlings are large enough to handle thin them 25–30cm/10–12in apart. Keep the seed-bed free from weeds and in early or mid-spring of the following year put the young plants into their permanent positions, setting them 75–90cm/2½–3ft apart.

If seeds and flower heads are not wanted, cut them off when young to encourage plants to continue for another year. If seed heads are not removed, plants die down after flowering.

HARVESTING

When stems are grown to be candied, cut them off in early and mid-summer while still tender. Also, cut off all leaf stalks. Sideshoots can also be candied and these can still be removed in late summer.

Harvest leaves for using fresh or dried before plants flower.

USES

Stems are crystallized with sugar and used to flavour and decorate cakes and other confectionaries. Roots are used with juniper berries to flavour gin, while the seeds are employed in vermouth and chartreuse, as well as some muscatel wines. Leaves and roots are sometimes cooked with apples and rhubarb to reduce acidity, while leaves, when fresh, are frequently added to fish dishes and jams. They can also be used in *pot-pourri*.

Angelica was widely employed as a preventive against evil spirits and witchcraft, and used to counter spells and enchantment.

Greenish-white flowers

Thick, fleshy roots

Hollow stem

ANISEED
Pimpinella anisum

NATIVE to Southern Europe, Near East and Egypt, where it has been grown for many centuries, as well as now naturalized in Asia and North America. As a commercial crop it has been grown from South Russia to South America, including North Africa, Spain and Malta. Earlier it was widely grown in Greece and is mentioned by the Greek physician Dioscorides and the Roman writer and politician Pliny. In Roman times it was extensively cultivated in Tuscany.

Aniseed is a hardy annual, creating a dainty plant about 45cm/18in high and developing brilliant green, finely divided and toothed leaves and umbrella-like heads bearing small, white flowers during mid- and late summer.

CULTIVATION

Aniseed, also known as Anise, needs light, fertile, slightly alkaline soil and a warm, sheltered, sunny position to grow well.

Sow seeds evenly and thinly in 6mm/¼in deep drills spaced 30cm/12in apart in mid-spring. Germination takes up to three weeks and, when seedlings are large enough to handle, thin them 20–30cm/8–12in apart.

Keep the soil weeded and well-watered during summer.

HARVESTING

Plants are ready to be harvested when the tips of the fruits have turned greyish-green. Hang plants in bundles in a warm, dry atmosphere, allow to dry, then thresh out the seeds.

White flowers

Seed

Brilliant green leaves

ANISEED *is widely used to flavour a wide range of food and drinks, but oil of Anise when mixed with oil of Sassafras, derived from the North American tree* Sassafras albidum, *and Carbolic oil has been used to repel insects. Anise oil is also a good antiseptic and when mixed with oil of Peppermint or Wintergreen (Gaultheria procumbens) used to flavour toothpaste.*

USES

Seeds have for many centuries been used to flavour food and drinks such as Anisette, an aniseed-flavoured French liqueur. They are used in soups, cakes and sweets, as well as some cough mixtures. And when crushed they are sometimes sprinkled on meat to enhance its flavour.

The Roman poet Virgil, mentions Anise being used in spiced cakes and introduced at the end of meals to prevent indigestion. Such a cake was part of a marriage feast and thought to be the origin of spiced wedding cakes.

BALM
Melissa officinalis

NATIVE to Central and Southern Europe, this bushy and branching plant has pale green, hairy, heart-shaped and nettle-like leaves that when bruised reveal a refreshing lemon bouquet. They are ideal for flavouring iced drinks and salads. During early and mid-summer, small, tubular, white flowers appear in clusters from leaf-joints.

Hairy leaves

White flowers

MEDICINALLY, leaves are infused to make Balm tea, a refreshing drink for invalids. This is made by pouring 580ml/1 pint of boiling water on 28g/1oz of fresh leaves and leaving to infuse for twenty minutes. Then allow to cool. Longevity is a claim for Balm tea: one man who lived to 116 years breakfasted for fifty years on it sweetened with honey. Carmelite water, of which Balm was an ingredient, was taken daily by Charles V, the Holy Roman Emperor from 1519–56.

CULTIVATION
Also known as Lemon Balm and Sweet Balm, this hardy herbaceous perennial grows 60–1.2m/2–4ft high and is ideal for planting in borders or herb gardens. Plant it in well-drained soil in full sun or light shade.

It is easily increased by lifting and dividing congested clumps every two or three years in autumn or spring. Replant young pieces from around the outside of the clump, setting them 38–45cm/15–18in apart. Alternatively, sow seeds outdoors in 6mm/1/4in deep drills during mid- and late spring. Germination takes two to three weeks. When the seedlings are large enough to handle, move them to their permanent positions, setting them 38cm/15in apart.

In autumn or early winter, cut back all stems to ground level. In cold, exposed areas cover them with straw as protection against very low temperatures.

HARVESTING
Pick young leaves for use fresh during summer. Leaves can also be picked and dried, but this is best done before the plant begins to develop flowers.

USES
The refreshing nature of the leaves makes them ideal for both culinary and medicinal uses, as well as in perfumery. Balm was used in making *Eau des Carmes*, now displaced by *Eau de Cologne*, a distinctively-scented toilet water.

In food, it brings a refreshing lemon flavour to iced drinks in summer, also to fruit salads. Additionally, it introduces further flavour to chicken and fish dishes. Dried leaves retain their fragrance and therefore are ingredients for many types of *pot-pourri*.

SWEET BASIL
Ocimum basilicum

NATIVE to Tropical Asia, Sweet Basil is a tender annual with four-sided stems and aromatic, shiny green leaves with purple tinged grey-green undersides. They have a strong, clove-like bouquet and are highly valued for use in kitchens, especially with Italian tomato dishes. Plants grow about 45cm/18in high, and during mid- and late summer small, white flowers develop from leaf joints. They are borne in whorls.

CULTIVATION
This is a half-hardy annual and therefore fresh plants are raised each year. Choose well-drained, light soil and a sheltered, warm position in full sun. During late spring, form 6mm/1/4in deep drills spaced 38cm/15in apart and sow seeds thinly and evenly. Germination takes two to three weeks. When large enough to handle, thin the seedlings 30–38cm/12–15in apart.

Plants can also be raised by sowing seeds 6mm/1/4in deep in seed compost in pots or seed-trays during early spring and placing in 13°C/55°F. When large enough to handle, prick off the seedlings into individual pots, slowly acclimatize to outdoor conditions and plant into herb gardens when all risk of frost has passed. Space them 30–38cm/12–15in apart. Nip out the growing tips of plants to encourage bushiness.

HARVESTING
Pick leaves to use fresh throughout summer. Leaves can also be dried or frozen.

USES
Sweet Basil is a central ingredient of Italian tomato dishes and in pesto, a herb-based Italian flavouring used with pasta. Leaves are used fresh or dried to add flavour to omelettes, salads, soups, ragoûts, fish dishes and minced meat.

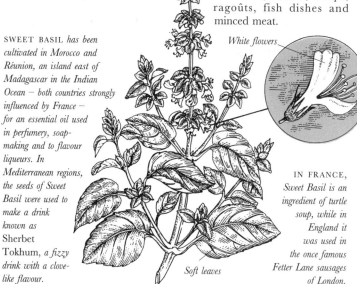

SWEET BASIL has been cultivated in Morocco and Réunion, an island east of Madagascar in the Indian Ocean – both countries strongly influenced by France – for an essential oil used in perfumery, soap-making and to flavour liqueurs. In Mediterranean regions, the seeds of Sweet Basil were used to make a drink known as Sherbet Tokhum, a fizzy drink with a clove-like flavour.

White flowers

IN FRANCE, Sweet Basil is an ingredient of turtle soup, while in England it was used in the once famous Fetter Lane sausages of London.

Soft leaves

BAY
Laurus nobilis

WELL-KNOWN evergreen shrub native to the Mediterranean region and capable of growing 4.5m/15ft high. Usually, however, it is pruned and kept to half or less of that height.

The aromatic, glossy, mid- to dark green leaves are used to flavour cooked meals. During late spring, Bay bears inconspicuous greenish-yellow flowers.

CULTIVATION

Also known as Sweet Bay and Bay Laurel, it prefers well-drained, light soil and a sheltered position in full sun or light shade. A warm position is preferable as in cold, wind-exposed areas its leaves are often damaged. Therefore, in extremely cold areas grow Bay in a tub and move into a cool entrance porch or frost-proof shed during cold periods.

Increase Bay during mid- and late summer by taking 10cm/4in long sideshoots, trimming their bases and removing lower leaves. Insert them 3.6–5cm/1½–2in deep in equal parts moist peat and sharp sand. Place in a cold greenhouse or garden frame and, when rooted, move into individual pots. When established, plant into a garden or large tub.

Regular pruning is not normally needed, but container-grown plants need trimming two or three times during summer.

HARVESTING

Pick young leaves as required. If pot-grown plants are taken into porches during winter, leaves can be used fresh, but avoid spoiling the plant's shape. When young and newly picked, leaves are slightly bitter, but become sweet as they dry. When drying them, place in the dark to ensure their rich colours are retained.

USES

Leaves are an essential ingredient of *bouquet garni* and used in many pâtés and savoury dishes, including minced meat.

Woody stems

Evergreen leaves

BAY HAS *gained many unusual common names from its wide range of uses. In France it is known as Laurier du Jambon (Ham Laurel) and in England as Fish Tree from its use in earlier days in pickling pilchards and sardines. It is suitable for planting in tubs, where invariably it is encouraged to develop a trunk up to 1.2m/4ft high. Often grown in tubs outside restaurants.*

BORAGE
Borago officinalis

THIS annual, native to Europe, has for centuries been used as a culinary and medicinal herb. Indeed, it is said that Homer – a Greek poet in the eighth century before the birth of Christ – gained relief from grief by mixing the juice of Borage with wine: it was his *nepenthes*, a potion to bring him absolute forgetfulness.

Plants grow 45–90cm/1½–3ft high, have hollow stems and somewhat oval, green leaves covered with silvery hairs. From early to late summer they bear clustered heads of five-petalled, blue flowers. There are also white and pink flowered forms.

Blue flowers

Soft, hairy leaves

CULTIVATION

Borage is a hardy annual and therefore fresh plants are raised each year. Sow seeds evenly and thinly in shallow drills 30cm/12in apart from mid-spring to mid-summer, at four- to six-week intervals. Germination takes two to three weeks. When seedlings are large enough to handle, thin them 25–38cm/10–15in apart. Plants grow rapidly and leaves are ready to use within eight weeks.

HARVESTING

Pick and use leaves while young and fresh. Young leaves can be

THE FAME *of this fresh-looking herb extends beyond the improving of food and drinks. The sixteenth-century English barber-surgeon and enthusiastic botanist John Gerard said: 'Sprigs of Borage are of known virtue to revive the hypochondriac and cheer the hard student'.*

---

dried, but it is not easy: if ventilation is poor or the temperature too high they quickly turn black.

FRENCH FACTOR

French herbalists have used the leaves of Borage to combat fevers, colds and lung complaints, such as pneumonia and bronchitis.

USES

Add young leaves to salads and fruit cups, where they introduce a fresh, cucumber-like flavour. Two or three leaves in a jug of fruit cup imparts a distinctive coolness. Indeed, one of its earlier names is Cool-tankard. The sweet-tasting flowers can be candied for sweets and cake decoration. Leaves and stems are frequently used in flower arrangements.

CARAWAY
Carum carvi

NATIVE to a wide area, from the Mediterranean to Himalayas, Caraway is extremely popular for flavouring food as well as liqueurs. It is a biennial, with seeds sown once a year to produce plants up to 75cm/2½ft high during the following season and developing flower heads that later produce the desired seeds.

CULTIVATION

Sow seeds thinly and evenly in shallow drills spaced 30–38cm/ 12–15in apart in fertile, well-drained soil during late summer. Choose a sheltered, sunny position. When the seedlings are large enough to handle, thin them first to 15cm/6in apart, later 30cm/ 12in. Because Caraway is grown entirely for its seeds, there is no need to feed it.

During the second year, Caraway grows vigorously and develops fern-like, mid-green leaves. Small, green flowers appear in umbrella-like heads during mid-summer, followed by seeds.

HARVESTING

As soon as the seeds ripen, cut down the entire plant to ground-level. Tie the flower stems into small bundles and hang upside-down in a cool, dry, airy place until the seed-heads are dry – indicated by them falling off. At this stage, it is essential either to place them in paper bags or position a large piece of paper underneath.

Gather the seeds and put them through a fine sieve to separate fine, dust-like material.

USES

Dried Caraway seeds are used to flavour buns, cakes and bread, as well as salads and cheese dishes. Meats such as lamb and pork when roasted can be given a distinctive taste by using the seeds. Cabbage dishes also benefit from them, as well as sausages.

Seeds are also used to flavour the colourless German liqueur Kümmel, while Oil of Caraway is distilled from the fruits and widely used as a flavouring agent.

Green flowers

Fern-like leaves

Seeds

SEVERAL *superstitions surround Caraway: it was said to create unity and to keep lovers together. It therefore often formed part of love potions. The seeds were also said to prevent pigeons from straying! The thick, edible roots were acclaimed by John Parkinson, a gardener and herbalist, and said to have a flavour better than parsnips.*

CHERVIL
Anthriscus cerefolium

A HARDY biennial, native to south-eastern Europe and western Asia. Additionally, it is naturalized in North America, New Zealand and Australia. Chervil reaches 30–45cm/12–18in high and is grown for its bright green, fern-like leaves that resemble those of Parsley and are used to garnish foods, introducing a delicate aniseed flavour. Its ridged stems are hollow and also aromatic.

White flowers

Bright green leaves

Bright green

Seed head

CHERVIL *has been used as a herb for several hundred years. At one time, scarcely a soup or salad did not have Chervil in it, which was frequently preferred to Parsley as a seasoner.*

HARVESTING

Use leaves when young and fresh, as these have the best flavour. Leaves can be dried or frozen, but cut them when young.

CULTIVATION

Although biennial by nature, Chervil is invariably grown as an annual and sown outdoors where it will grow and mature. It grows in most soils, preferably well drained, in full sun or light shade.

From late spring to mid-summer, sow seeds in shallow drills 30cm/12in apart. Germination takes two to three weeks and, when the seedlings are large enough to handle, thin them first to 15cm/6in apart, later 30cm/12in. Sow seeds at four-week intervals: plants develop leaves ready for cutting within eight weeks of being sown, but remember to pinch out all flower buds if seeds are not wanted. Water plants freely during dry periods to prevent flowers forming.

USES

Garnishing salads and sandwiches, as well as flavouring soups, egg and fish dishes and sauces. It is also used as *fines herbes* for omelettes. Dried leaves are frequently used in stuffings.

Sweet Cicely (Myrrhis odorata) *is often confused with Chervil as it is also known as Great Chervil, Sweet Chervil and Cow Chervil. The anise flavoured leaves of Sweet Cicely were used in salads, the stems and roots boiled as vegetables.*

It also had a medicinal use, the roots being used to counteract bites from vipers and mad dogs!

CHIVES
Allium schoenoprasum

NATIVE to a wide area in the northern hemisphere, from northern and southern Europe, through northern Asia to Japan as well as North America. This grass-like, onion-flavoured hardy perennial has been grown for many centuries to garnish and flavour food. Although mainly known as Chives, in North America it is also called Cive – a derivative of the French *civette* – and Schnittlaugh.

Plants, usually 15–25cm/ 6–10in high, are formed of tubular, mid-green leaves. During early and mid-summer, rose-pink flowers appear in dense, rounded heads at the tops of long stems.

CULTIVATION
Chives form clumps and after three or four years are best lifted, divided and young parts from around the outside replanted about 30cm/12in apart in light or moderately heavy well-drained soil in full sun or light shade.

Plants can also be raised from seeds sown in 12mm/½in deep drills spaced 30cm/12in apart in spring or early summer. Germination takes two to three weeks. When seedlings are large enough to handle, thin them to 15cm/6in apart. Later, transplant them to their permanent positions, 30cm/12in apart.

Keep plants well watered in summer and remove flower stems to encourage the development of leaves. Plants die down in autumn and develop fresh shoots in spring. Chives can also be grown in small containers and window-boxes; in autumn pots taken indoors and put on cool window sills provide leaves until mid-winter.

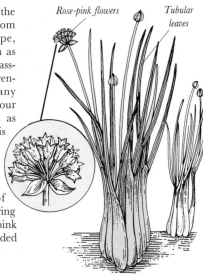

Rose-pink flowers *Tubular leaves*

CHIVES *are superb as a garnish or in soups, but have also been used in home-made sausages, croquettes and beefsteak puddings and pies. Not so flattering: chopped Chives were mixed with food and fed to newly hatched turkeys.*

HARVESTING
Cut off leaves close to their bases and use fresh. Regular cutting encourages the development of further leaves. They can also be dried or frozen.

USES
The mild onion flavour of the leaves makes them ideal for flavouring sandwiches, soups, omelettes, egg and cheese dishes. They are also used as *fines herbes* and in *sauce tartare*.

Chives can also be finely chopped and added as a garnish to mashed potatoes, as well as being boiled with fresh new ones.

CORIANDER
Coriandrum sativum

THIS native of southern Europe and Asia Minor has spread throughout many parts of the world. It has an annual nature, erect and 23–75cm/ 9–30in high, with dark green, somewhat feathery, fern-like leaves and pink-mauve flowers during mid-summer. These develop seeds which are used to flavour food. The leaves are also used as flavourings in some dishes.

CULTIVATION
It is a hardy annual and fresh plants are raised each year. Sow seeds thinly and evenly in shallow drills 30cm/12in apart during mid-spring. Germination takes two to three weeks and, when seedlings are large enough to handle, thin them to 15cm/6in apart. Plants flower in early summer and seeds ripen during mid- and late summer. It grows in most soils and is especially suitable for sowing in land well manured during the previous year. Do not sow in land where manure has been dug in during the year seeds are sown, as this encourages lush, rank growth that delays the development of flowers and seeds. A sunny, open position is essential to encourage rapid ripening.

HARVESTING
Commercially, seeds are harvested when about two-thirds of the fruits have turned from green to grey. In a home garden, however, they can be left slightly later. Stems are cut and the seed-heads dried under cover. Rub out the seeds and store them either whole or ground into a powder.

By the way, unripe green seeds, as well as the leaves, have a strange, bug-like odour, but this changes and is replaced by a pleasant, sweet, aromatic bouquet.

USES
The feathery leaves are used to add a spicy flavour to soups and meat dishes, while seeds are added crushed or whole to curries and stews. They are also introduced to some liqueurs, as well as used in perfumery and the manufacture of soap.

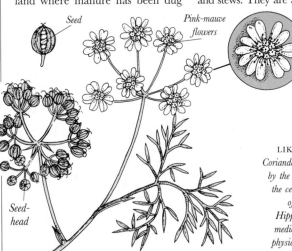

Seed *Pink-mauve flowers*

Seed-head

LIKE *many other herbs, Coriander was widely spread by the Romans, and during the century before the birth of Christ was used by Hippocrates, the father of medicine, and other Greek physicians. It was used as a stimulant and carminative.*

DILL
Anethum graveolens

NATIVE to a wide area, from southern Europe to India and naturalized in North America and the West Indies. It grows 60–90cm/2–3ft high, with upright, hollow, ridged stems and blue-green, feathery, thread-like, anise-flavoured leaves. From early to mid-summer it develops small, star-like, yellow flowers borne in umbrella-like heads up to 7.5cm/3in wide. Both the seeds and leaves have culinary uses.

Incidentally, do not grow Dill and Fennel close together as it is then difficult to identify the self-sown seedlings.

CULTIVATION

Dill is a hardy annual and grows in well-drained, fertile soil and a sunny position. Sow seeds thinly and evenly 12mm/½in deep in drills, at four-week intervals, from early spring to mid-summer. Space the drills about 30cm/12in apart. Germination takes ten to fourteen days and when seedlings are large enough to handle, thin them to 23–30cm/9–12in apart.

Keep the plants well watered to encourage rapid growth. Seeds that fall on soil soon germinate.

Yellow flowers

Seeds

Seed-head

Blue-green leaves

IN THE *Middle Ages in Europe, Dill was frequently used by magicians in spells and charms against witchcraft. In addition to its culinary value, an oil distilled from the plant is used medicinally as a stimulant and carminative to expel gases from stomachs and intestines.*

HARVESTING

Pick and use the leaves fresh, as they are rather difficult to dry: they do not retain a bright, healthy colour. Instead of using leaves in winter it is better to use seeds which have been dried and stored in airtight jars. When growing plants mainly to produce seeds, cut down stems when the seeds turn brown in late summer.

USES

Use fresh leaves to garnish and flavour salads, fish, boiled potatoes, peas, beans, soups and poultry. Seeds have a stronger anise flavour and are often added to vinegar when pickling gherkins.

NORSE WORD

The derivation of the word Dill is varied: Prior's Popular Names of English Plants *suggests it originates from the old Norse word* dilla *meaning 'to lull', referring to the plant's carminative qualities.*

FENNEL
Foeniculum vulgare

DISTINCTIVE and handsome perennial, native to Europe, growing 1.5–2.4m/5–8ft high and developing thread-like, blue-green leaves and umbrella-like heads up to 10cm/4in wide packed with golden-yellow flowers during mid- and late summer. Its leaves are used to flavour food, while the strongly anise-flavoured seeds are used in bread, cakes and soups.

CULTIVATION

Fennel needs fertile, well-drained soil and a sunny position. Sow seeds of this hardy herbaceous perennial evenly and thinly in late spring or early summer in shallow drills spaced 38–45cm/15–18in apart. If seeds are needed, it is best to sow them in early spring.

Germination is not rapid, but when the seedlings are large enough to handle, thin them to 30–38cm/12–15in apart. Alternatively, lift and divide congested plants in spring, as soon as shoots appear. Replant young pieces from around the outside, setting them 38–45cm/15–18in apart. Unless seeds are needed, pinch off all flower buds to prevent their unnecessary development.

HARVESTING

Use leaves fresh during summer. Leaves are difficult to dry satisfactorily. However, they can be gathered in early and mid-summer and frozen.

To produce seeds, do not remove the flower buds and gather the seeds in late summer or early autumn, just before they are fully ripe. Spread the seed-heads on white paper and allow to dry slowly and without artificial heat. Ensure there is a flow of fresh air over them to prevent the development of fungal growths. Turn the seed-heads daily and when all the seeds have separated store them in airtight jars in a cool cupboard.

USES

Leaves are used to flavour fish and cheese dishes, vegetables, sauces, chutneys and pickles, while the seeds bring added flavour to bread, cakes and soups.

IN MEDIEVAL *times, Fennel was frequently used, together with St. John's Wort, as a preventive against witchcraft and other evil influences. It was also mentioned in Anglo-Saxon cookery and medical recipes.*

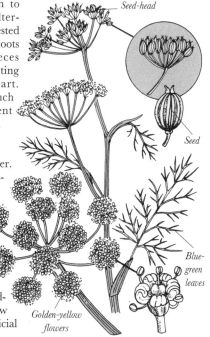

Seed-head

Seed

Blue-green leaves

Golden-yellow flowers

HORSERADISH
Armoracia rusticana

NATIVE to a wide part of Europe, western Asia and the Mediterranean region, Horseradish was widely used in the Middle Ages in Europe as a universal medicine. It has even been used mixed with vinegar to remove freckles, but since about the seventeenth century has been widely acclaimed as a condiment.

Plants reach about 60cm/2ft high and bear rough-surfaced, wavy-edged or lobed, dark green leaves about 45cm/18in long. Small, white, four-petalled flowers appear in early summer, but it is the long, yellowish-buff taproots that are the reason for growing it. They have a pungent, peppery flavour.

CULTIVATION
Horseradish is a hardy perennial. It is also known as Mountain Radish, Red Cole and Great Raifort, and earlier as *Cochlearia armoracia*.

Deeply-cultivated, fertile, well-drained soil and full sun or light shade suit it. By nature, it is a perennial and can be left in position for many years, a few roots being dug up as needed in summer. However, it can also be grown as an annual crop and roots planted each year. In early winter, dig up plants, sever main roots and cut into 15–20cm/6–8in long pieces. Store in sand or peat until shoots develop in early spring. Then, use a dibber to plant them 45cm/18in apart and with their tops 5cm/2in below the surface. Firm soil around them and water thoroughly. During late spring and summer the roots develop foliage which is cut down to soil level in early autumn.

White flowers

Yellowish-buff roots

HORSERADISH *is now mainly used as a flavouring for meals, but earlier it was recommended as a way to get rid of a persistent cough following influenza.*

HARVESTING
In autumn, dig up the roots and either use immediately or store in sand or peat.

USES
Roots are washed then crushed, grated or minced and simmered with milk, vinegar and seasoning. This peppery-flavoured condiment is used with meat, fish and salads, as well as for flavouring sauces. It is most widely used with beef.

HYSSOP
Hyssopus officinalis

THIS hardy, partially evergreen perennial is native to a wide area, from Mediterranean regions to Central Europe. It is grown for its young leaves that have a mint-like flavour, and used fresh in a wide range of foods, or dried and mixed in stuffings.

Plants grow 45–60cm/1½–2ft high, bushy and with aromatic, narrow, mid-green leaves on upright, branching stems. From mid- to late summer, plants develop purple-blue, tubular flowers.

CULTIVATION
Plant it in light, well-drained soil in full sun or light shade. It can be increased in several ways: sow seeds evenly and thinly in a seedbed during mid- and late spring in 6mm/¼in deep drills spaced 30cm/12in apart. Germination takes between two and three weeks and when seedlings are large enough to handle, thin them 15cm/6in apart. In late summer or early autumn, plant into their permanent positions, around 30cm/1ft apart.

Alternatively, take 6.5–7.5cm/2½–3in cuttings in late spring and insert in equal parts moist peat and sharp sand. Place in a cold frame or cool greenhouse and when rooted, pot up into individual pots. Plant into a herb garden in late summer.

Plants usually need replacing every three or four years.

HARVESTING
Pick the bitter, minty leaves throughout the year and use fresh. However, they are said to be at their best just before the flowers open. Leaves can also be dried, but pick when young.

USES
Fresh leaves are put in salads, as well as fresh or dried in stuffings or soups. In cooked dishes they are used to 'balance' oily fish or fatty meats. When dried they are included in *pot-pourri*.

Seed

Purple-blue flowers

Mid-green leaves

HYSSOP *is sometimes grown for the oil from its leaves which is used to flavour liqueurs. Additionally, the flowers have been used to create a medicinal tea. A recipe in an old cookery book instructs: "Infuse a quarter of an ounce of dried hyssop flowers in a pint of boiling water for ten minutes; sweeten with honey and take a wineglassful three times a day, for debility of the chest."*

S W E E T   M A R J O R A M
Origanum majorana

NATIVE to southern Europe, this bushy, small, shrubby plant with four-sided, red stems and greyish, hairy leaves grows 30–45cm/12–18in high. And from early to late summer it bears clusters of tubular, white, pink or mauve flowers from grey-green, knot-like bracts, which gives rise to one of its common names. ('Bract' is a botanical name for a modified leaf).

Apart from culinary values it has been used medicinally against rheumatism and to soothe bruises.

CULTIVATION
Sweet Marjoram, also known as Knotted Marjoram and Annual Marjoram, is shrubby in its warm, native countries, but in northerly regions is unable to survive cold winters and therefore usually grown as an annual.

Sow seeds thinly and evenly in drills 6mm/¼in deep and 23–30cm/9–12in apart during mid- and late spring. When the seedlings are large enough to handle, thin them first to 15cm/6in apart, later 30cm/12in. Alternatively, to produce leaves earlier in the year, sow seeds in late winter or early spring, 3mm/⅛in deep in pots or seed-trays and place in 13–15°C/55–59°F. Prick out the seedlings when large enough to handle into small pots and plant into a herb border in late spring.

Set the plants in well-drained soil and a warm, sunny position.

HARVESTING
Pick leaves as needed, but preferably before plants flower. Leaves can be dried or frozen – cut the shoots slightly above soil level.

USES
Young shoots and leaves are used to create a sweet, spicy flavour in meat, poultry and game, as well as fish and tomato dishes. They can also be used in salads and are frequently added to soups, stews, stuffings, omelettes and pies. Leaves have a stronger flavour when dried and are frequently used in *pot-pourri*. Also, traditionally part of bunches of mixed herbs known as *bouquet garni*.

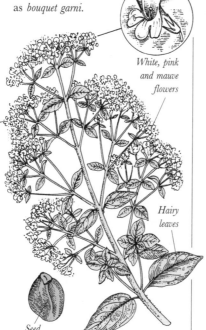

White, pink and mauve flowers

Hairy leaves

Seed

SWEET MARJORAM *is both a culinary and medicinal herb. It was said to be effective against rheumatism if boiled in water and then drunk and also to cure convulsions, cramps and toothache. Additionally, the leaves, when dried and mixed with honey, created a soothing and healing ointment for bruises and sores.*

S P E A R M I N T
Mentha spicata

NATIVE to Central Europe, this popular, aromatic, herbaceous herb has spread throughout much of the world and is famous for the sauce made from its leaves that is widely used to flavour lamb. It is most popular in English-speaking countries; infrequently used in France.

The leaves have a distinctive, spearmint-like aroma and taste which they readily transfer to sauces. Its upright shoots, which become slightly woody when old, grow 30–60cm/1–2ft high and with underground stems plants spread rapidly, becoming invasive.

CULTIVATION
It is easily grown in fertile, well-drained but moisture-retentive soil in a warm, sheltered position. Plants are easily increased by lifting and dividing congested clumps in spring and replanting young parts from around the outside. Alternatively, take 10–15cm/4–6in long cuttings of basal shoots in early summer and insert them either in equal parts sharp sand and moist peat, or directly into their growing positions if the soil is light and sandy. Plant about 30cm/12in apart and renew them every two or three years.

To prevent excessive spreading, either plant into a bottomless bucket buried to its rim in the ground, or a patio container.

HARVESTING
Pick leaves and use fresh throughout summer. Leaves can also be dried. For this, light soil produces the best plants. Leaves are rubbed through a sieve (with about twenty meshes to every 2.5cm/1in) and stored in a dry place. Leaves can also be cut off and frozen.

USES
Used to create sauces and jellies, mainly for flavouring lamb. Leaves are also put in with cooking vegetables, such as potatoes and peas. Other preparations include mint vinegar and mint punch.

Pale blue flowers

Seed

Mid-green leaves

SPEARMINT *has acquired many other common names including Common Mint, Lamb Mint, Garden Mint, Mackerel Mint, Our Lady's Mint and Sage of Bethlehem. And in addition to its culinary values, medicinally it has been used to treat stomach complaints, and commercially in the preparation of toothpaste, chewing-gum and sweets. In addition to Spearmint, there are many others, including Apple Mint with rounded leaves. It is also used to make mint sauce.*

PARSLEY
Petroselinum crispum crispum

PARSLEY has been grown as a herb for several centuries. Native of Central and southern Europe, its distinctive, mildly spicy flavour makes it invaluable in sauces, salads and garnishes. Also, it contains generous amounts of vitamins A and C, as well as being extremely rich in iron compared to any other vegetable.

Small, yellow flowers

Bright green leaves

Seed-head

THE GREEKS *held Parsley in great esteem, crowning victors of the pan-Hellenic Isthmian Games with chaplets of it. The Greeks also made wreaths of Parsley to adorn the tombs of their dead and therefore never employed its culinary virtues.*

CULTIVATION
Parsley is a hardy biennial, but invariably grown as an annual. Sow seeds 6mm/¼in deep in open ground from late winter to early summer. Choose well-drained, fertile soil and a sunny or lightly shaded position, setting the drills 20–25cm/8–10in apart. Germination is slow, but can be speeded up by watering the drill with boiling water before sowing.

When the seedlings are large enough to handle, thin them first to 7.5cm/3in apart, later 15–23cm/6–9in. Sowings can be made in greenhouses a month or so earlier, in 10–15°C/50–59°F, setting the plants 23cm/9in apart in gardens after slowly acclimatizing them to outdoor conditions.

In late summer, cut down plants and water thoroughly to encourage fresh growth. Cover young shoots with cloches.

HARVESTING
Pick leaves when plants are young to encourage the development of further leaves. For drying, gather leaves early in the day. Wash and dry rapidly in 93°C/200°F. Leaves can also be frozen.

USES
Widely used in sauces and salad dressings and as an essential ingredient of *bouquet garni*. It is also ideal for garnishing sandwiches.

PARSLEY PARADE

Its fame in kitchens is widely known, but the stems when dried and powdered have been used as a culinary colouring. While the roots have been used to create a tea, the French pounded green Parsley and snails in a mortar to form an ointment used to treat scrofula, now a rare condition but then known as King's evil.

ROSEMARY
Rosmarinus officinalis

ROSEMARY is steeped in history and has spread throughout the world from its native southern Europe and Asia Minor. It is famed for its scented flowers, while the aromatic, dark green leaves have a camphorous bouquet and, used fresh or dry, bring added flavour to food.

ROSEMARY *abounds in history and literature. It became an emblem of fidelity for lovers and was frequently used in weddings. Anne of Cleves is said to have worn a wreath entwined with Rosemary at her wedding to Henry VIII in 1540, while branches, richly gilded and tied with silken ribbons, were presented to guests as symbols of loyalty and love.*

Mauve flowers

Seed

Woody stem

Aromatic leaves

CULTIVATION
Rosemary is an evergreen shrub, widely grown in shrub and herb borders. It is easily increased from 10cm/4in long cuttings in midsummer: remove the lower leaves and insert in pots of equal parts moist peat and sharp sand. Preferably, place in a cold frame, but they root just as well in a sheltered corner on a patio. When rooted, pot up individually and plant into a border a year later.

Little pruning is needed, other than cutting out dead shoots in early spring and shortening straggly growths. Where old bushes are overgrown, cut them back by half in mid- or late spring.

HARVESTING
The leaves are used fresh or dried. When fresh, remove them from the plant as needed. When used dry, whole stems are cut and hung up, but there is a noticeable loss of flavour.

USES
In addition to its medicinal qualities – a decoction of Rosemary is said to help cure diseases of the head as well as easing aches in teeth and gums – leaves are used fresh or dried for flavouring food. It is frequently added to tomato soup, stews and, when finely chopped, to cooked peas. Additionally, the leaves are used to flavour roast meat and as an ingredient of sauces and stuffings. Use sparingly with lamb, pork, veal and chicken. Also used with fish.

Earlier, Rosemary had a reputation of strengthening the memory. Indeed, there is a saying 'Rosemary for Remembrance'.

RUE
Ruta graveolens

OFTEN known as Herb of Grace, Herb of Repentance and Herbygrass, this somewhat shrubby plant from southern Europe is widely grown both as a culinary herb and to decorate flower borders with its deeply divided, blue-green leaves. During early and mid-summer – and often into late summer – it bears clusters of 12mm/½in wide, sulphur-yellow flowers at the ends of young shoots. It is, however, the leaves, with their acrid odour and bitter flavour, that are used to add flavour to food.

CULTIVATION
Rue is a hardy, evergreen shrub, seldom more that 75cm/2½ft high. When young, it forms neat, low, rounded hummocks that are ideal alongside border edges. Using garden shears to trim plants to within a few inches of the old wood in spring helps to keep them low and neatly shaped. In autumn, cut off dead flowers.

It is easily increased by taking 7.5–10cm/3–4in-long cuttings from sideshoots during mid-summer, and inserting them in equal parts moist peat and sharp sand. Place in a cool greenhouse – or on a north-facing window sill indoors – until rooted. Then, transfer into individual pots and overwinter in a cold garden frame.

Alternatively, sow seeds 3–6mm/⅛–¼in deep in seed drills in a seed-bed outdoors during spring. When the seedlings are large enough to handle, thin them 23–30cm/9–12in apart. Later, set them 45cm/18in apart in a border in late summer or autumn. Pinch out their growing tips to encourage bushiness.

HARVESTING
Pick young leaves, for use immediately or drying. When used fresh, chop finely. For a supply in winter, pick and dry fresh leaves, then store in airtight containers.

USES
Use chopped leaves sparingly in salads, remembering that they impart a bitter flavour.

Sulphur-yellow flowers

Blue-green leaves

Seed

Woody stem

RUE WAS thought by the Greeks to have anti-magical qualities. It was used during the Middle Ages as a defence against witches. Earlier it was reported by Pliny, a Roman writer during the first century AD, that "Engravers, Carvers and Painters do ordinarily eat Rue alone to preserve their eye-sight".

SAGE
Salvia officinalis

THIS popular and widely used shrub from southern Europe has wrinkled, aromatic, grey-green and slightly bitter-tasting leaves that introduce added flavour to meals. There are purple and golden-leaved forms (see page 224), but these are mainly used decoratively.

CULTIVATION
Although hardy, sage is short-lived and usually replaced every three or four years. Also, plants tend to become straggly and with bare centres after a few years if not trimmed annually in late summer. Choose well-drained, light soil and a sunny, sheltered position. Raise plants by taking 7.5cm/3in long cuttings in late summer and inserting them in equal parts moist peat and sharp sand. Place in a cold greenhouse or frame. Pot up into individual pots when rooted and overwinter in a cold frame. Nip out the growing tips to encourage bushiness.

Sage can also be raised from seeds sown in early spring in pots of seed compost and placed in 16–18°C/61–64°F. Germination takes three to four weeks. When the seedlings are large enough to handle, transfer them to a nurserybed outdoors, setting them 15cm/6in apart. Later, when established, transplant them to about 38cm/15in apart into a herb border.

Alternatively, sow seeds 6mm/¼in deep in a seedbed outdoors in late spring. When large enough to handle, transfer the seedlings to 15cm/6in apart in a seedbed. Later in the year, plant them into their permanent positions in a herb garden.

Violet-blue flowers

Grey-green leaves

Seed

LIKE MANY other herbs, sage was well known to the Romans who spread it throughout Europe. As well as flavouring foods, it has been used to clean teeth, and infused to make tea to strengthen gums and whiten teeth. Sage tea was very popular and highly prized by the Chinese who imported it from Holland.

HARVESTING
Leaves are usually cut in bunches and used fresh or hung up and dried quickly in a warm room. Store them in airtight jars.

USES
Sage has many culinary values and is traditionally used with fatty meats such as duck, goose and pork. It is also used in stuffings as well as with cheese, veal, liver and onions. It is extensively used in Italian cooking.

SAVORY
Satureja

THERE are two types of this ancient herb: Summer Savory (*Satureja hortensis*) and Winter Savory (*Satureja montana*).

Summer Savory, native to Europe, is a bushy annual growing about 30cm/12in high and with square, hairy stems and dark green, strongly aromatic leaves. While Winter Savory, originally from Europe and Asia, is perennial with an upright but compact habit, 30cm/12in high and woody, branching stems.

Lilac or rose-purple flowers

Seed

SAVORY *is an ancient herb and thought to have been used before the East Indian spices were known. Indeed, vinegar flavoured with Savory was used by the Romans in the same way as mint is employed in England today.*

Dark green leaves

Hairy stems

CULTIVATION
Although different in nature, these two plants can be raised from seed in the same way. During mid-spring, form 6mm/¼in deep drills 23cm/9in apart where they are to grow. Choose a sunny position and fertile, well-drained soil. Germination takes two to three weeks and when large enough to handle, thin the seedlings of Summer Savory to 15–23cm/6–9in apart, and those of Winter Savory to 23–30cm/9–12in.

Seeds of Summer Savory are sown each year, while the perennial Winter Savory needs replacement every two or three years.

HARVESTING
Pick leaves throughout summer to use while fresh. At flowering time – from mid- to late summer – cut down the plants and hang up bunches to dry for winter use.

USES
The leaves and stems of Summer Savory have a strong and spicy flavour and can be added to soups as well as meat and fish dishes, stuffings and drinks. Also, they may be used in *pot-pourri*.

In France, Summer Savory is frequently used when cooking broad beans, whereas in England it is mint that is used. Winter Savory is used in a similar manner, but the flavour is coarser.

AMERICAN FACTOR

Savory must have been popular in England in the early seventeenth century as about that time it was taken by settlers to North America. An early colonist, John Josselyn, lists Savory among plants taken there, while Bernard McMahon in McMahon's American Gardener, *published in 1806, details its cultivation. Incidentally, apart from its culinary qualities, all savories give instant relief when rubbed on wasp and bee stings.*

FRENCH SORREL
Rumex scutatus

ALSO known as Garden Sorrel and Buckler-shaped Sorrel, French Sorrel is popular as a culinary herb.

CULTIVATION
French Sorrel is a slender, slightly prostrate European plant growing 30–45cm/12–18in high. Small, green to red flowers appear in clustered heads: they must be nipped out to encourage the growth of fresh leaves.

It is easily increased by lifting and dividing congested clumps in spring or late summer and replanting young, fresh pieces about 20cm/8in apart in rich, moist soil in full sun or light shade. Alternatively, sow seeds thinly and evenly 6mm/¼in deep in a seed-bed outdoors during mid-summer. When the seedlings are large enough to handle, transplant them to their permanent positions, about 20cm/8in apart.

HARVESTING
Cut off young leaves – which have a lemony flavour – when needed. Leaves are usually used fresh, but they can be dried or frozen in bags.

USES
Young leaves are added to sandwiches, salads and soups. Alternatively, older leaves can be cut and cooked like spinach. They can also be made into a purée and served with fish and rich meats.

In France they are formed into sorrel soup, as well as used to flavour sauces and omelettes.

POPULAR WITH HENRY VIII

Wild Sorrel (Rumex acetosa) is also used to flavour salads, but to many palates the leaves are too acid. Before the introduction of French Sorrel into Britain in about 1596, it was very popular and held in great repute by Henry VIII. It continued to be used, being mentioned in about 1720 by the garden writer and designer John Evelyn who wrote that it should never be omitted from salads. At one time, leaves were beaten into a mash and mixed with sugar and vinegar, creating a sauce for use with cold meat.

Reddish-green flower

FRENCH
Sorrel is a popular herb, especially in France where several forms were grown. Wild Sorrel (Rumex acetosa) is another type of sorrel and illustrated here. It has mid- to grey-green triangular leaves that form a thick clump. It is more upright than French Sorrel.

Fleshy, mid-green leaves

FRENCH TARRAGON
Artemisia dracunculus 'Sativa'

LSO known as True Tarragon, this widely-grown herb has leaves with a strong and sweet flavour, reminiscent of mint.

CULTIVATION
French Tarragon is a perennial shrub growing to about 60cm/2ft high and spreading by underground stems. The aromatic, narrow grey-green leaves cluster on upright stems. Small, white, globular flowers appear in loose clusters during mid-summer, but do not open fully in cool climates.

Tarragon thrives in light, well-drained soil and a sheltered position in full or light sun. The roots are vulnerable to severe frost: cover with straw in cold areas.

Renew plants every three or four years: in early or mid-spring, lift and divide roots, replanting young pieces 5–7.5cm/2–3in deep and 30–38cm/12–15in apart. It can also be raised from seeds, but plants raised in this way are said not to have such aromatic leaves. To encourage the development of leaves, pinch out flowering stems as soon as they appear.

HARVESTING
Use leaves fresh, picking them from early to late summer. Young shoots can also be cut and dried, although they soon lose their aroma. They can also be frozen.

USES
Apart from its use in tarragon vinegar, the leaves are a basic part of *fine herbes*, in the preparation of *sauce tartare* and in French mustard. Leaves are also employed to flavour chicken and other white meats, as well as added to sauces, salads and fish dishes.

RUSSIAN ALTERNATIVE

*Russian Tarragon (*Artemisia dracunculus *'Indora'), is also known as False Tarragon and native to Southern Europe, Asia and North America west of the Mississippi River. It is hardier than the French type but does not have such a good flavour.*

Tarragon is a corruption of the French word meaning 'little dragon', relating to the days when Tarragon was thought to be a cure for the bites of these reptiles.

White flowers

Grey-green leaves

IN NORTH AMERICA, *Tarragon is also known as Estragona, a reference to a volatile oil extracted in France from the leaves and used in perfumery. It is also recommended as a cure for toothache.*

THYME
Thymus vulgaris

HE leaves of this hardy, aromatic, sprawling, evergreen shrub have been used to flavour food for many centuries. Their slightly spicy and sweet flavour has long been in demand. Indeed, this southern European herb was well known to the Greeks who called it 'thyme', a derivative of a word meaning to fumigate and thought to allude to its use as an incense or balsamic odour. Modern medicinal uses have drawn upon its age-old antiseptic qualities.

CULTIVATION
It grows 10–20cm/4–8in high, with narrow, dark green, aromatic leaves and clusters of tubular, mauve flowers in early summer.

Plant thyme in light, well-drained soil in full sun or light shade. Lift and divide plants in spring, every three or four years, replanting young pieces 23–30cm/9–12in apart.

Thyme can also be increased by forming sideshoots into 5–7.5cm/2–3in long cuttings in early summer. Preferably, they should have small pieces of the older wood still attached to their bases – known as heel-cuttings. Remove the lower leaves, trim the heel and insert about 2.5cm/1in deep in equal parts moist peat and sharp sand. Place in a cold frame and pot up individually into small pots.

HARVESTING
Pick off shoots and leaves when needed and use immediately. For drying, cut off stems about 15cm/6in long in late summer and tie into bunches of nine to twelve shoots. Hang up to dry. Leaves can also be frozen.

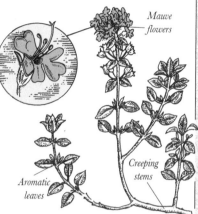

Mauve flowers

Creeping stems

Aromatic leaves

THYME *has for many centuries been used in kitchens, but it also has several medicinal qualities. In the seventeenth century the English physician and herbalist Nicholas Culpeper made an ointment from it to take away hot swellings and warts. Additionally it was used to ease sciatica, counteract dullness of sight and to take away pains.*

USES
Extensively employed in *bouquets garnis*, stuffings for rich meats, in soups and with fish, casseroles and other cooked dishes. It is often used mixed with other herbs and traditionally added to jugged hare.

LEMON THYME

*This decorative thyme (*Thymus x citriodorus*) is similar to normal thyme but with lemon-scented leaves and slightly larger flowers. It is used in a similar way to ordinary thyme, as well as included in* pot-pourri *and added to desserts.*

RAISING HERBS FROM SEEDS

THE majority of herbs are easily increased from seeds: most are sown outdoors in seedbeds, while a few are raised in greenhouses, sunrooms and conservatories to produce plants slightly earlier. Additionally, some, such as Parsley, can be grown indoors on window sills to produce leaves late in the year.

SOWING OUTDOORS

The times for sowing specific herbs is indicated on pages 210 to 221, but whatever the type there are certain requirements.

To prepare a seed-bed, from which young plants are later moved and planted into their growing positions, or where they are left after being thinned to grow, select a sheltered area away from cold winds. Additionally, the soil must be free from weeds, especially those with a pernicious perennial nature.

In winter, dig the area to about 30cm/12in deep and leave the surface rough. The action of frost, rain and wind will break down

---

ON WINDOW SILLS

Several herbs raised from seeds can be grown indoors on lightly shaded window sills. These include:
- *Parsley* (Petroselinum crispum crispum)
- *Chervil* (Anthriscus cerefolium)
- *Summer Savory* (Satureja hortensis)
- *Sweet Basil* (Ocimum basilicum)

Clearly, some of these plants are quite tall on maturity and therefore once they outgrow the home they are best discarded.

---

large lumps of soil by the time spring arrives. About a week before sowing seeds, rake the surface level, at the same time further breaking down the soil.

If, however, the soil at raking-down time is still lumpy, use a garden fork to break it down. With a slightly sloping and

---

HERBS TO *raise outdoors include Angelica, Aniseed, Balm, Borage, Caraway, Chervil, Chives, Coriander, Dill, Fennel, French Sorrel, Hyssop and Savory. Some, such as Parsley, Sweet Basil and Sweet Marjoram, can be raised in greenhouses as well as in gardens.*

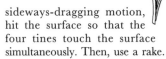

Fennel   *Caraway*

Hyssop

Angelica

sideways-dragging motion, hit the surface so that the four tines touch the surface simultaneously. Then, use a rake.

Tread over the complete surface uniformly, using a sideways shuffling motion. Do not use a roller, as this invariably consolidates one area more than another, and in any case is too heavy. Then rake the surface level.

Use a draw-hoe to form shallow drills – and either a garden line or a straight-edged board as guidance to ensure the drill is straight. Sow seeds evenly and thinly. When the drill has been sown, use the back of a rake to pull soil over the seeds. Alternatively, straddle the

row and shuffle along with your feet in a V-shape. Afterwards, walk along the row to consolidate the soil. Lightly rake along the direction of the row to level the surface. Do not rake across it, as this may disturb some seeds.

SOWING IN POTS

Herbs such as Parsley, Sweet Basil and Sweet Marjoram can be sown in greenhouses. The method for sowing these seeds is illustrated and described below, with specific details of temperatures and times on pages 210 to 221.

1. MANY *herbs can be increased from seeds. Fill a pot with loam-based or peat-based seed compost and firm it with your fingers around the edges. Fill it again, level and use the base of a small pot to firm it level.*

2. TIP *a few seeds into a piece of stiff, folded paper. Tap its edge to encourage seeds to fall evenly on the surface. Do not sow within 12mm/¹/₂in of the edges, as this is where drying often first occurs.*

3. USE *a sieve to lightly cover the seeds with finely sieved compost. Horticultural sieves are available, but as a substitute a kitchen type can be bought and reserved for this use. Avoid damp compost.*

4. WATER *the compost by standing the pot in a saucer of clean water. When moisture seeps to the surface, remove and allow to drain. Do not water the compost from above, as the seeds will then be washed about.*

WHEN *the seedlings are large enough to handle, transfer them to seed-trays or pots. Later, they are usually planted into a herb garden outdoors. Some, such as Parsley, can be moved into other pots and grown on window sills indoors.*

TAKING CUTTINGS

SEVERAL herbs are increased by taking cuttings from them. The majority of these have a permanent nature, such as Bay and Rosemary, while Pot Marjoram is a bushy, low-growing shrub with soft stems but a woody base, especially when aged.

Cuttings from soft-stemmed herbs, such as Pot Marjoram, initially need gentle warmth and cosseting, while those from Bay, which have a woody nature, are hardier and can be increased without the need of greenhouse warmth. Indeed, cuttings from Rosemary develop roots quite easily in pots containing equal parts moist peat and sharp sand, then placed on a sheltered, lightly-shaded patio. By the following spring they will have rooted and can be planted into a herb garden or tubs. Clearly, however, in extremely cold regions this is not possible and a garden frame or cold greenhouse is needed to give winter protection.

VINEGAR OF THE FOUR THIEVES

Rue has been famed since early times for warding off contagious diseases and preventing attacks from fleas and other noxious insects. But is was also an ingredient of a concoction known as the Vinegar of the Four Thieves, used by thieves in Marseilles to enter and rob homes stricken with plague. It also formed part of an ale against the plague. In the sixteenth and seventeenth centuries it was used in Law Courts to protect judges from jail-fever.

ROOT CUTTINGS

Only a few herbs are increased in this way, Horseradish being the notable one. However, the tropical spices Ginger *(Zingiber officinale)* and Turmeric *(Curcuma longa)* have rhizomes, which both provide the spices and the way to increase

SEVERAL *herbs can be increased from cuttings, including Bay, Hyssop, Spearmint, Rue, Sage and Pot Marjoram. The time to take and insert cuttings of these plants is described on pages 210 to 221. Some are softwood cuttings, such as Pot Marjoram, while others like Bay are semi-ripe heel-cuttings. They are formed during mid- to late summer.*

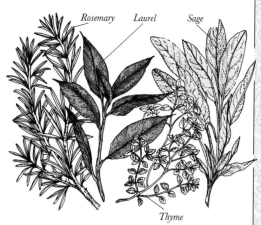

Rosemary   Laurel   Sage

Thyme

them. The fat, firm, underground stems are divided at planting time.
• Ginger is used to flavour foods in many countries, and an important flavouring in curry powder. It is also used in making ginger beer.
• Turmeric is a major ingredient of curry powders, imparting a bright yellow colour as well as a rich, spicy flavour.
• Liquorice *(Glycyrrhiza glabra)* is less tender, well-known to the ancient Greeks and grown in the British Isles since the sixteenth century. The liquorice gained

from the roots was used in Pontefract Cakes. The rhizomes and roots often reach 1.2m/4ft deep, with a similar spread. These are ground into a pulp and boiled in water, the extract then concentrated by evaporation. Division of the roots is one of the ways in which it is increased.
• Horseradish is a member of the wallflower family and said to be one of the bitter herbs eaten by Jews during the feast of the Passover. The thong-like roots form cuttings (see page 216).

1. POT MARJORAM (Origanum onites) *is easily increased from softwood cuttings. The day before severing the cuttings, thoroughly water the mother plant to ensure they will not wilt. Sever long shoots cleanly at the plant's base.*

2. TRIM *each cutting 5-7.5cm/2-3in long, severing below a leaf joint and cutting the lower leaves close to the stem. Always used a sharp knife to avoid leaving ragged ends – these delay healing and the development of roots.*

3. FILL *a pot with equal parts moist peat and sharp sand, firming it to within 12mm/1/2in of the rim. Use a dibber to form holes – about 12mm/1/2in from the pot's side – and insert a cutting in each one. Firm compost around them.*

4. GENTLY *water the cuttings to settle compost around their bases. Allow excessive water to drain, then place in a warm, lightly shaded place until they are rooted. Then, remove the cuttings and carefully transfer into larger pots.*

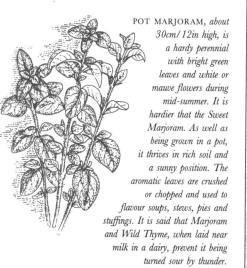

POT MARJORAM, *about 30cm/12in high, is a hardy perennial with bright green leaves and white or mauve flowers during mid-summer. It is hardier that the Sweet Marjoram. As well as being grown in a pot, it thrives in rich soil and a sunny position. The aromatic leaves are crushed or chopped and used to flavour soups, stews, pies and stuffings. It is said that Marjoram and Wild Thyme, when laid near milk in a dairy, prevent it being turned sour by thunder.*

DIVIDING HERBS

❖

F ALL the ways to increase herbs, division is the quickest method to produce established plants. Congested plants – in pots or growing in a herb garden – can be separated into smaller pieces, discarding old, central parts and retaining only the vigorous young, outer pieces.

Dividing herbs established in pots is illustrated and described below. These include Chives, which can be taken indoors and grown on kitchen window sills to produce leaves out of their normal season. Others, such as mint, are so invasive and vigorous that it is necessary to constrain them in pots on a patio or in bottomless buckets in herb borders.

DIVIDING
ESTABLISHED CLUMPS

Autumn or early spring are the best times to lift and divide congested plants. If the soil is moist there is no need to water the clump within the previous twenty-four hours. But if the season is dry, thoroughly water the plants as well as the area into which they are to be planted. However, avoid making the soil too wet and turning the area into a bog.

Use a garden fork to dig under a congested clump and place it on a large sack or piece of hessian. Do not contaminate lawns, paths or gravel chippings with soil. Usually, congested herbs can be pulled apart by hand. Discard old, central parts and retain only young pieces from around the outside. Do not divide them excessively: if too small, they do not create an attractive display within a reasonable time.

Before planting them, fork over the border and add a general fertilizer. Firm it slightly before setting the new plants in position. If space allows, always use three plants of the same type. Used singly or just in twos, they either look sparse or imbalanced. Three or five are the magical numbers for success when setting any plants in a border.

DIVISION is the most assured way to increase herbs. The types that can be increased in this way include Balm, Chives, French Sorrel, French Tarragon and Spearmint. Additionally, the many other types of mint are easily increased in the same way, as well as by cuttings. These include Peppermint (Mentha x piperita), AppleMint (Mentha rotundifolia but also known as M. suaveolens).

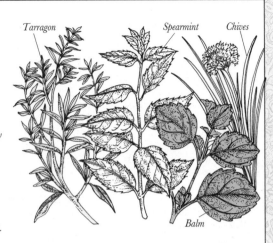

Tarragon   *Spearmint*   *Chives*

Balm

Spread out the young plants on the surface of the border. It is then possible to stand back and view the arrangement from several aspects before deciding on their exact positions. If the whole herb border is being replanted and freshly dug, replanting is often delayed: keep the roots of the plants damp during this period by wrapping them in wet newspaper or sacking. If the microscopic root-hairs become dry and badly damaged, it takes much longer for a plant to become established when planted. Indeed, if roots become very dry the plants will never recover.

Some plants naturally have 'face' sides: angles from which they are the most attractive. Ensure these aspects face the front of a border. Use a trowel to take out a hole large enough to accommodate the roots. Spread them out and cover with friable soil, firming it gently but firmly.

After planting, use an edge of a trowel to level the surface, then water the plants thoroughly but gently. Then, lightly water the compost to settle it down around the roots.

1. WATER *the clump the day before separating it. Invert the pot, place a hand under the root-ball and tap the rim on a firm surface. If the ball of roots remains in the pot, run a knife between the soil-ball and pot.*

2. GENTLY *but firmly pull the tangled roots into several pieces. Do not make these too small: it is better to have a few large clumps than many thin and weedy-looking ones. Discard old, central parts. Use only young, outer pieces.*

3. FILL *a small pot with compost and pot up the pieces individually. Repot each piece to the same depth as before, leaving about 12mm/ 1/2in between the surface and the pot's rim. Water from above.*

HERBS IN POT-POURRI

❖

FEW houses do not benefit from the fragrances of *pot-pourri*. Instead of relying on aerosols or pre-packed scented packages to refresh rooms, it is more interesting to create your own fragrances. Few dogs do not offend human noses at some time during the year with unappealing odours, while to many people cigarette smoke is even more objectionable. Sweet and penetrating scents soon suppress such smells and make homes more satisfying for residents as well as visitors.

TWO TYPES

Pot-pourri is a mixture of scented parts of plants: they can be 'moist' or 'dry' and both made at home, using garden or bought flowers. Spices and essential oils are available from specialist shops.

• Moist *pot-pourris* can be made throughout summer and usually retain their fragrance for several years. The only problem with them is their muddy-brown colour, which is not very attractive. They are therefore best covered. In earlier times, special containers were made to hold them and could be placed near a gently-warm fire to warm up the mixture to encourage the scent to escape. When the room was filled with fragrances the lid was replaced and the container moved to a cool position to be rested.

There are many recipes for moist *pot-pourri*: the one here includes ingredients detailed on the opposite side of this page.

~
• *10 cups of partially dried rose petals*
• *3 cups of coarse salt*
• *5 tablespoons powdered orris root*
• *2 tablespoons ground allspice*
• *2 tablespoons ground cinnamon*
• *2 tablespoons ground nutmeg*
• *1 tablespoon ground cloves*
• *A few drops of essential oil, such as rose oil*
~

Preparation is easy: layer the salt and petals in a large bowl and stir daily. The salt will absorb moisture from the rose petals. When intially added, they should have a limp, soft but leathery texture. If too dry they cannot be used in a moist *pot-pourri* but can be added to a dry type. It is also necessary to 'press' the mixture to ensure the layers are in close contact. About three to six weeks later, when the ingredients are dry, crumble it and add the spices and then the oil. Cover the mixture and leave for several weeks to 'cure'. It can then be used. Place a couple of dried roses on the surface for decoration.

• Dry *pot-pourri* is more attractive and therefore can be left uncovered in rooms. Because of this it tends to lose its scent rather quickly, although fragrances can be renewed by the further addition of essential oils.

There are many recipes for dry *pot-pourri* and they all can be modified to ensure that easily obtainable plants are used. Here is the basis of one recipe:

~
• *2 cups dried rose petals*
• *2 cups dried lavender flowers*
• *1 cup of cornflower petals to introduce colour*
• *1 cup lemon verbena leaves*
• *1/2 cup powdered orris root*
• *1 tablespoon ground allspice*
• *1 tablespoon ground cinnamon*
• *1 tablespoon ground cloves*
• *A few drops of essential rose oil*
~

Mix all of these together and add the essential oil until the fragrance is strong enough. Put the entire mixture in a large paper bag, shake thoroughly and leave for five to six weeks before placing in attractive containers and putting in rooms.

Essential oil

Rose for decoration

Rose petals

Cinnamon bark

Powdered Orris (Iris germanica 'Florentina')

Cloves (Eugenia caryophyllus)

Nutmeg (Myristica fragrans)

Allspice (Pimenta dioica)

THE *range of perfume-yielding plants is wide. Some are tropical or subtropical, while others such as Lavender, Larkspur and Bay grow quite easily in temperate climates. Indeed, pot-pourri need not be expensive as many ingredients are readily available in gardens. Leaves, flowers, seeds, berries as well as powdered bark and roots can create fragrant mixtures that will enhance your home.*

GROWING FRESH VEGETABLES

Few tasks in a garden bring as much satisfaction as harvesting your own vegetables. Crisp and fresh salad crops, including lettuces, spring onions and tomatoes, are not difficult to grow and can even be grown in containers on patios. Potatoes, too, can be grown in growing-bags, but like many deeply rooted vegetables are best in gardens.

A wide range of vegetables is featured alphabetically in this chapter, from artichokes (both globe and Jerusalem types) to sweetcorn and turnips. Preparing the soil, raising young plants and planting them, growing and harvesting are described in detail for each vegetable.

The yearly rotation of vegetables from one part of a plot to another is illustrated and discussed, together with the preparation of a seedbed for raising of young plants from seed. Sowing the seeds of vegetables is featured on page 275. The techniques of single and double digging are described on page 10, at the beginning of the book.

TOOLS YOU WILL NEED

STRONG tools that are easy and pleasant to use are essential for the vegetable grower. Before buying any garden tool, handle it to ensure it can be easily manipulated and is not too large or heavy. Usually, the more you pay for a tool, the better and longer lived it will be. At the top of the range are stainless-steel tools, but for normal purposes, one of lesser quality is quite adequate.

MECHANIZATION

On a garden scale, spades and forks and other hand tools are quite adequate. But for large areas, such as allotments, powered tools with revolving blades make soil cultivation easier and quicker. Often, these can be hired.

MAINTENANCE

The life expectancy of tools very much depends on the way they are used and maintained. Never strain and bend tools, especially spades and forks. After each use, wash, wipe dry and oil bright-metal parts. Wipe plastic handles and coat wooden parts in linseed oil.

HAND TROWELS *(left)* and forks *(right)* are essential for planting young plants. Choose one with a strong, comfortable handle.

LARGE DIBBERS *(left)* are invaluable for planting young cabbages. Some have metal tips. Onion hoes *(right)* enable narrow rows to be weeded.

GARDEN LINES *are* used to form straight rows. Proprietary types are easier to use than two sticks and a ball of twine.

TYPES OF HANDLE

There are three types of handle: the T-shaped, D-outline, and D-Y shape. The D-Y is popular, differing from the D-type in that the position where the handle joins the shaft is Y-shaped.

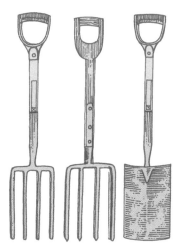

GARDEN FORKS *are often used to dig heavy, wet, clayey soil in winter. Also, they are ideal for breaking down large clods of soil in spring. Like spades, they range in size, with prongs 23cm/9in to 27cm/11in long. Potato forks (right) have wide, slightly blunt-ended tines.*

A STRONG *spade is essential. Digging types have blades about 27cm/11in deep and 19cm/7½in wide. A border type (also known as a lady's spade) is 23cm/9in deep and 14cm/5½in wide. Handle lengths range from 72cm/28in to 82cm/32in long.*

WATERING-CANS *formed of strong plastic or galvanized metal (some are also painted) are essential for watering seedlings, applying liquid feeds and when using weed-killing chemicals. (If at all possible, always use a separate watering can for this purpose.)*

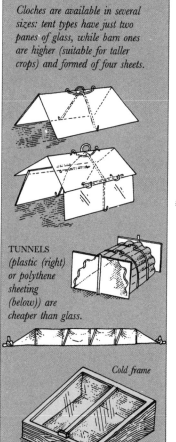

CLOCHES

Cloches are available in several sizes: tent types have just two panes of glass, while barn ones are higher (suitable for taller crops) and formed of four sheets.

TUNNELS *(plastic (right) or polythene sheeting (below)) are cheaper than glass.*

Cold frame

DUTCH HOES *(left),* and draw hoes *(right) are essential. Choose models that are easy to use and keep clean. Handle lengths vary.*

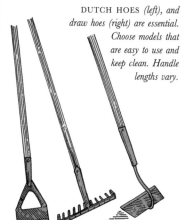

RAKES *(above, centre) are essential for levelling soil.*

THREE-PRONGED *cultivators (right) are used to scarify and aerate the soil. Most have handles 1.5–1.8m/ 5–6ft long, but some are short and ideal for infirm gardeners who operate from kneelers. They are operated by pulling, which is usually easier than pushing for elderly people. Some of these cultivators are available with clip-on heads, so that the handle length can be quickly changed. Some also have five-pronged heads.*

PREPARING A SEED-BED

❖

RAISING healthy, strong plants is essential; weak, spindly and unhealthy ones never recover. Many vegetables are raised by sowing seeds where they are to grow and mature; others are sown in seed-beds and transferred later.

In early winter, prepare a seed-bed by digging the soil. Do not break down the surface soil as rain, wind and frost will do this. If late winter and early spring are dry, thoroughly water the area with a sprinkler. When the weather is fine and the soil surface barely dry, prepare it for seed sowing, in the way indicated below.

Sow seeds evenly and thinly, and cover them by either straddling the row and shuffling along, or pulling soil over them with the back of an iron rake. Firm the soil over them and carefully label both ends of the row.

1. WHEN *planting out young plants, use a dibber or trowel. Push it about 15cm/6in into the ground. Hold the plant by several leaves and dangle its roots in the hole. Use the dibber to lever soil tightly around the plants' roots.*

2. IF PLANTS *are well rooted and have masses of roots, a trowel is better than a dibber. Form a hole large enough to take the roots, then firm soil over them. On light, sandy soils, use the heel of your shoe to ensure the soil is really firm.*

3. AFTER *planting them, thoroughly water the soil to ensure it is in close contact with the roots. Gently trickle water from a watering-can. If the surrounding soil is dry, soak it to prevent plants being immediately robbed of moisture when planted.*

PREPARING A SEED-BED

1. SINGLE DIG *the soil in early winter. In spring, shuffle sideways over the ground to evenly consolidate the soil.*

2. USE *an iron rake to level the surface and to create an evenly deep tilth into which seeds can be sown.*

3. STRETCH *a garden line across the seed-bed and use the sharp point of a stick to create drills 12–18mm/½–¾in deep.*

4. AN ALTERNATIVE *way to form a drill is with the edge of a draw hoe. Take care not to make drills excessively deep.*

TRANSPLANTING YOUNG PLANTS

If seeds have been sown too thickly it is essential to thin the seedlings as soon as they are large enough to be handled. Ensure soil is re-firmed around their roots, then water them thoroughly but gently. When young plants are large enough to be handled they can be moved to their permanent positions. A couple of days before transplanting them, thoroughly water both the seed-bed and the area into they will be transplanted. If this task is neglected, and the weather is hot and dry, the plants may die.

If possible, choose a cloudy day when transplanting them. When lifting the young plants, use a garden fork to loosen the soil; gently place them in a box lined with moist newspaper or sacking and cover them. Do not dig up more plants than can be planted within thirty minutes, especially if the weather becomes hot. A garden line is essential to ensure that the rows are neat and straight, and use either a dibber or trowel to plant them (see above).

RAISING PLANTS

Vegetables initially raised in a seed-bed include:
• *Asparagus (to form crowns)*
• *Broccoli*
• *Brussels sprouts*
• *Cabbages*
• *Calabrese*
• *Cauliflowers*
• *Kale*
• *Leeks*

Vegetables initially raised in gentle warmth in a greenhouse or garden frame include:
• *Aubergines*
• *Celery*
• *Celeriac*
• *Early onions*
• *Early leeks*
• *Sweetcorn (can also be sown outdoors, directly into its growing position, where the seedlings are subsequently thinned to leave the strongest.)*
• *Sweet Peppers*
• *Tomatoes*

CROP ROTATION

◆

THE same types of vegetables must not be grown continuously on the same piece of soil. If this happens, there is an increase in pests and diseases. Also, the soil becomes depleted of certain plant foods and growth diminishes. However, there are some crops, such as asparagus and rhubarb, which are left in one position for many years but, in general, the best crops are produced when plants are rotated annually. Additionally, do not put seed-beds (where young seedlings are raised) in the same position each year.

PLOT ONE	PLOT TWO	PLOT THREE
FIRST YEAR SOIL PREPARATION 1	SOIL PREPARATION 3	SOIL PREPARATION 2
Beetroot • Carrots Jerusalem artichokes Parsnips Potatoes Salsify Scorzonera	Aubergines • Beans Capsicums • Celery Celeriac • Leeks Lettuce • Marrows Onions • Peas • Spinach Sweetcorn • Tomatoes	Broccoli Brussels sprouts Cabbage • Cauliflowers Kale • Kohl Rabi Radishes • Swedes
SECOND YEAR SOIL PREPARATION 3	SOIL PREPARATION 2	SOIL PREPARATION 1
Aubergines • Beans Capsicums • Celery Celeriac • Leeks Lettuce • Marrows Onions • Peas • Spinach Sweetcorn • Tomatoes	Broccoli Brussels sprouts • Cabbage Cauliflowers • Kale Kohl Rabi • Radishes Swedes • Turnips	Beetroot • Carrots Jerusalem artichokes Parsnips Potatoes Salsify Scorzonera
THIRD YEAR SOIL PREPARATION 2	SOIL PREPARATION 1	SOIL PREPARATION 3
Broccoli Brussels sprouts Cabbage Cauliflowers Kale • Kohl Rabi Radishes • Swedes	Beetroot • Carrots Jerusalem artichokes Parsnips Potatoes Salsify Scorzonera	Aubergines • Beans Capsicums • Celery Celeriac • Leeks Lettuce • Marrows Onions • Peas • Spinach Sweetcorn • Tomatoes

SOIL PREPARATION 1
When preparing the soil, neither add lime nor dig in manure. Instead, rake in a general fertilizer a couple of weeks before planting or sowing.

SOIL PREPARATION 2
When preparing the soil in early winter, dig in garden compost or manure. Lime the soil in late winter and later rake in a general fertilizer prior to sowing or planting.

SOIL PREPARATION 3
When preparing the soil in early winter, dig in garden compost or manure. If the soil is acid, apply lime in late winter and rake in a general fertilizer prior to sowing or planting.

ASSESSING *soil to see if it is acid or alkaline is easy. Most lime-testing kits use chemicals that when mixed with soil produce a colour reaction which can be compared with a colour chart. More recent methods involve the use of a probe which when pushed into soil indicates the pH on a dial, ideal for gardeners who are red-green colourblind.*

THE ROTATION
Vegetables can be arranged into three different types, and it is plants within these groupings that are rotated each year.
• <u>Group one</u> (Root crops): These include beetroot, carrots, Jerusalem artichokes, parsnips, potatoes, salsify and scorzonera.
• <u>Group two</u> (Brassicas): These include broccoli, Brussels sprouts, cabbages, cauliflowers, kale, kohl rabi, radishes, swedes and turnips.
• <u>Group three</u> (Other crops): These include aubergines, beans, capsicums, celery, leeks, lettuce, marrows, onions, peas, spinach, sweetcorn and tomatoes.
  Soil preparation for each of these types of crop differs slightly and is indicated in the chart on the opposite side of the page.

CATCH CROPPING

Also known as intercropping, this is when a fast growing and rapidly maturing crop such as radishes is grown between slower growing plants. Examples include spinach between rows of leeks, and lettuces grown between rows of trench celery. The routine of growing catch crops helps to prevent the growth of weeds.

TO MAKE YOUR SOIL MORE ALKALINE

SOIL	HYDRATED LIME	GROUND LIMESTONE
Clay	610g/sq yd (18oz/sq yd)	815g/sq m (24oz/sq yd)
Loam	405g/sq m (12oz/sq yd)	545g/sq m (16oz/sq yd)
Sand	205g/sq m (6oz/sq yd)	270g/sq m (8oz/sq yd)

The lime required to decrease acidity of soil depends on the form in which it is applied and the type of soil. These amounts decrease acidity by about 1.0 pH. Aim for a pH of about 6.5.

ARTICHOKES – GLOBE

ONCE established, Globe Artichokes will continue producing large, scale-like flower-heads for four or five years. Then, it is best to plant further suckers and, after about a year, remove the old plants. The plants grow 1.2–1.5m/4–5ft high.

During the first year after being planted, a few heads will develop but they seldom mature and are therefore best cut off in autumn. In the second year, each plant will produce about ten flower-heads. Cut them, together with 5–7.5cm/ 2–3in of stem, when the globes are large and ball-like but before the scales open.

In late summer and early autumn, cut off all immature heads and later, in early winter, cut down plants to just above ground level. To protect the roots in winter, cover them with straw. In spring, remove this covering and dust a general fertilizer around the plants. Lightly hoe and water this into the soil. During summer, thoroughly water the soil.

> ### VARIETIES
>
> • 'Camus de Bretagne': Large, well-flavoured heads; best in warm regions.
> • 'Green Globe Improved': Widely grown, with large, globe-shaped, green heads.
> • 'Purple Globe': Not with the best flavour, but ideal for planting in cold areas.
> • 'Vert de Laon': One of the best and widely available.

Cardoons are grown for their fleshy, young stems which need to be blanched. Sow seeds in spring in groups of three, 45cm/18in apart. After germination, remove the weakest seedlings. Later, during late summer and early autumn, blanch stems by wrapping and tying black polythene around them. Stems are ready to lift after about five weeks.

1. GLOBE ARTICHOKES *are best raised from suckers. In spring, cut suckers (about 20cm/8in long and with roots attached) from established plants. Plant them 60cm/2ft apart in rows 75cm/2½ft apart. Thoroughly water them.*

2. DURING *summer, regularly water plants and hoe between them to remove weeds. In late summer or early autumn, cut off the immature flower-heads, and in early winter cut all the stems down to ground level. Cover plants with straw.*

3. IN THE *following spring, remove the protective straw and dust a general fertilizer around the plants. From mid- to late summer, cut off the fleshy flower-heads. In early winter, cut down stems and protect the plants with a layer of straw.*

ARTICHOKES – JERUSALEM

JERUSALEM Artichokes are completely different from Globe types: the Jerusalem ones are related to sunflowers and produce knobbly tubers which are harvested from late autumn to early spring.

Prepare the soil in autumn by digging in plenty of well-decomposed manure or garden compost. This ensures a supply of plant foods and retention of moisture.

Jerusalem Artichokes are easily grown, but do require support from stout stakes linked together with plastic-covered wires.

Plant tubers in late winter or early spring. Their main needs are watering throughout summer, especially during dry periods, and staking. Drawing up soil around their bases helps to prevent strong winds rocking plants and disturbing the roots. It also encourages the formation of young tubers near the surface. If the soil is light and impoverished, feed the plants with a liquid feed every three weeks during early and mid-summer.

Soil pests such as wireworms and slugs can be a problem; use slug baits and soil-pest chemicals.

When harvesting the tubers, retain a few for replanting during the following year. Ensure all tubers are dug up by spring; if left, they can be a nuisance when growing between other crops during the following summer.

The tubers are delicious made into soup, boiled, fried, baked, roasted or stewed.

> ### VARIETIES
>
> • 'Boston Red': Knobbly, with rosy-red skin.
> • 'Fuseau': Perhaps the best variety, growing about 1.8/6ft high and with long, white tubers.
> • 'Dwarf Sunray': Crisp and tender tubers, with plants 1.5m–2.4m/5-8ft high.
> (Note: It is also possible to plant tubers bought from greengrocers and supermarkets.)

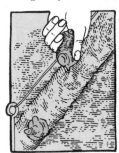
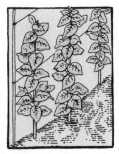

1. PLANT *tubers of Jerusalem Artichokes in early spring, 38cm/15in apart in drills 13–15cm/5–6in deep. When planting more than one row, space them 90cm/3ft apart. Water the soil thoroughly and keep it moist throughout summer.*

2. IN LATE SPRING, *after the tubers have sprouted and their positions can be seen, insert 2.4m/8ft-long canes along the row, with wire tied between them. Tie plants to these. When plants are 30cm/12in high, earth-up soil around their bases.*

3. AS SOON AS *the leaves turn brown in autumn, cut the stems about 20cm/8in above soil level. Leave the tubers in the ground, lifting them as needed between autumn and early spring. Keep back a few good tubers for replanting the next year.*

ASPARAGUS

ASPARAGUS is a long-term crop and often considered to be a luxury. But it is not difficult to grow and if there is space it is well worth establishing a bed of it. From planting one-year-old crowns in spring to being able to regularly cut asparagus spears takes two years. Once established, each plant can be expected to produce at least twenty spears each year. Asparagus beds have a life of between ten and twenty years, depending on how they are maintained: if the foliage is not cut down annually, the spears not cut and beds become blanketed in weeds, their life is very short. Additionally, asparagus beds have a longer life when in loamy to sandy soil than in clay, where the drainage is poor and plants may decay in winter. In these conditions, they are best grown in slightly raised beds.

Asparagus is an ideal crop to grow in coastal areas, in salty and light soil. However, it does need protection from cold winds.

RAISING PLANTS

Most gardeners buy one-year-old plants in spring, especially if only a few are needed. To raise your own, sow seeds outdoors in drills 12–18mm/½–¾in deep with the seeds 45cm/18in apart in early or mid-spring.

When the seedlings are established and growing strongly, thin them to 15cm/6in apart. During the following summer, pull up all weeds and ensure the soil does not become dry. In spring of the following year, plant the young crowns (see below). When planting, do not allow them to dry out: place them in a box lined with moist sacking or newspaper and keep covered.

If plants are left in a seed-bed for a further year, it is then possible to identify the female seed-bearing plants and to remove them (they are identified both by the seeds they bear and the seedlings which develop around them). The advantage in using only male plants is that, when planted in an asparagus bed,

removing unwanted seedlings is eliminated. However, one-year-old plants are much easier to establish than older ones and produce a more uniform crop than two-year-old plants which, by their nature, are variable in size. Always buy the best quality plants.

LOOKING AFTER ASPARAGUS BEDS

During summer, keep the soil free from weeds and regularly water the beds. Each year, stems bearing fern-like leaves grow to about 1.2m/4ft high. In autumn, cut these down to 7.5cm/3in above the soil's surface.

In spring, dust the bed's surface with a general fertilizer and lightly fork it into the surface. Later, in the latter part of early summer and after the last spears have been cut, again dust the surface with a general fertilizer.

HARVESTING

Always use an asparagus knife to cut the spears. Wait until they are 13–15cm/5–6in above the soil and sever them about 5cm/2in below the surface. This job is best performed early in the morning when the spears are plump and full of moisture. When cutting mature spears, take care not to damage those that are small or have not yet broken through the soil's surface. After cutting the spears, water the bed to re-settle the soil.

1. IN SPRING, *dig a trench about 25cm/10in deep and 38cm/15in wide. Dust the base of the trench with a general fertilizer and lightly fork it in. At the same time, form and firm a mound along the base.*

2. BUY *one-year-old crowns and plant them 45cm/18in apart in the base of the trench. Spread out their roots and cover the crowns with 5cm/2in of friable soil. During summer, ensure that the soil is kept moist.*

3. IN LATE SUMMER *or early autumn, use sharp secateurs to cut down the stems to 7.5cm/3in above the soil's surface. Add a further layer of soil over the crowns to help protect them during winter.*

4. IN EARLY SPRING *of the following year, pull up all weeds and lightly fork between the rows. Dust with a general fertilizer and shallowly scratch it into the surface. Keep the bed moist and free from weeds.*

5. IN AUTUMN *of the second year, cut down the stems, remove all weeds and ridge up soil over the row. It is during the following year that the young spears can be harvested. Asparagus is a long-term crop.*

6. FROM LATE SPRING *to early or mid-summer of the following year, use an asparagus knife to cut the young spears when 13–15cm/5–6in high. Sever them about 5cm/2in below the soil's surface.*

BEANS - BROAD

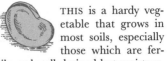

THIS is a hardy vegetable that grows in most soils, especially those which are fertile and well drained but moisture-retentive. Dig the soil in early winter and add plenty of well-decomposed manure or compost. A sunny position is desirable, especially for early crops.

Sow seeds in double rows (see below) to produce the largest crops. Germination takes between one and two weeks and from a row 3m/10ft long about 9kg/20lbs of bean seeds can be expected.

HARVESTING

Early pods, when about 7.5cm/3in long, can be picked and cooked whole. But mainly the pods are harvested when the seeds inside them start to show through. The scar on each seed should be white or green, not discoloured. Pods are best picked with a twisting and downward pull.

After the complete crop has been picked, cut down the stems to ground level. Dig the roots into the soil well.

VARIETIES

Long-pod broad beans
Narrow pods about 38cm/15in long. Hardy, with high yields.
• *'Aquadulce Claudia': White seeded and early cropping.*
• *'Hylon': New variety with long pods and white seeds.*
• *'Imperial Green Longpod': High yields and green seeds.*
• *'Imperial White Longpod': An old variety with white seeds.*
• *'Relon': Pods more than 50cm/20in long and packed with green seeds.*

Windsor broad beans
Shorter pods, each with up to seven beans. They are known for their superb flavour.
• *'Green Windsor': Heavy cropping with green seeds.*
• *'White Windsor': White seeds.*

Dwarf broad beans
Plants grow 30–45cm/12–15in high and are ideal for windy sites, small gardens and under cloches.
• *'The Sutton': White, superbly flavoured seeds.*

BEANS - FRENCH

THESE have always been popular, although not to the same extent as Runner Beans. However, they have many advantages in small or exposed gardens. There are climbing forms and varieties include 'Blue Lake' (pencil-shaped pods on plants that grow up to 1.5m/5ft high).

The seeds germinate within one to two weeks of being sown, and the normal yield for dwarf types is 3.5kg/8lb for every 3m/10ft of row. Climbing forms yield more, about 5.5kg/12lb for every 3m/10ft of the row.

LOOKING AFTER THE PLANTS

Slugs attack bean seedlings, so use baits around them. Plants are nearly self-supporting, but benefit from twiggy sticks pushed among them; this is necessary when plants are cropping heavily, and also during wet weather.

Support climbing types with string or form a wigwam of bamboo canes. Netting can also be used to support the plants.

VARIETIES

The range of dwarf French Beans is wide and includes:
• *'Masterpiece': Flat pods.*
• *'Tendergreen': Pencil podded.*
• *'The Prince': Popular and with flat pods.*
• *'Royal Burgundy': Purple, pencil-shaped pods.*

GROW EARLY *crops of dwarf French Beans by lightly forking soil in late winter and placing barn cloches over the row. In mid-spring, when the soil has warmed up, sow seeds (described below). Keep the soil moist and pick pods in early summer.*

1. IN EARLY SPRING, *form drills 7.5cm/3in deep and in pairs 30cm/12in apart. Space these pairs 60cm/2ft apart. Sow bean seeds 23cm/9in apart in each drill, cover and firm soil over them.*

2. SUPPORT *plants by inserting strong posts at each corner of the double row and tying strong string around them, 38–45cm/15–18in above the ground. For long rows, supporting sticks half-way along are needed.*

3. WHEN *plants are in full flower, pinch out the top of each shoot. This encourages the uniform development of pods on plants, as well as reducing the risk of an infestation of the black bean aphid.*

1. IN LATE SPRING or *early summer, form drills 5cm/2in deep and 45cm/18in apart. Sow the individual seeds 7.5–10cm/3–4in apart. A sunny position and fertile, moisture-retentive soil assures success.*

2. IN EARLY SUMMER, *hoe between rows to remove weeds and to break up crusty surfaces. Thoroughly water the soil and form a mulch around the plants to conserve moisture and to keep the roots cool.*

3. FROM MID-SUMMER *onwards, pick the pods when young, usually initially about 13cm/5in long. To show their freshness they should snap in half when bent. Regularly picking them encourages further beans.*

BEANS – RUNNER

RUNNER beans are one of the best known vegetables. They are easily grown and seeds can be sown in the positions where they are to grow. The essential elements for growing them are sunshine and soil that does not dry out. It is not possible to guarantee sunshine, other than positioning plants in a sunny, wind-sheltered position, but moisture in the soil can be encouraged by digging in plenty of well-decomposed garden compost or manure in late winter. Also, regularly watering the soil and forming a 7.5cm/3in mulch around plants helps in the retention of moisture. Apart from their food value, a row of beans can be used to form a peep-proof screen; it is especially attractive when in flower.

SOWING OR PLANTING

The majority of runner beans are raised by sowing their seeds in the positions in which they will grow. The precise time to sow them depends on the risk of frost, as young bean plants are soon killed by low temperatures.

An alternative way – and to produce a slightly earlier crop – is to buy established plants and to plant them as soon as all risk of frost has passed. Indeed, in cold areas, this method is especially advised. When growing beans in this way, erect the supports before setting the young plants in position. It is then easier to estimate the exact number of plants needed. It also prevents the roots of plants being disturbed by the poles.

SURVIVING GLUTS OF BEANS

Unless you have a large family with an insatiable appetite for runner beans it is almost impossible to avoid times when there are too many beans. Even in times of glut it is not wise to abandon picking for several days, as beans will become tough and old. Also, it will prevent the development of other beans. Therefore, the solution is to store or freeze them.

Storing them loose is only possible for up to about a week: pack the pods in polythene bags and place in a refrigerator. Freezing is a better solution, when they last for up to a year. Pick young, healthy beans early in the morning, when they are fresh, and wash, trim and slice them into chunks. Dip them in boiling water for two minutes and cool rapidly. Allow water to drain, then dry them and place in labelled freezer bags.

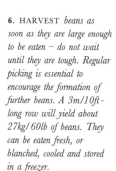

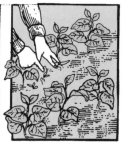

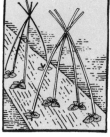

1. IN EARLY SPRING, *dig a trench about 25cm/10in deep and 75cm/2½ft wide. Fork the bottom and mix in well-decayed manure or garden compost to both feed plants and assist in the retention of moisture around their roots. Refill the trench with soil. At this stage the surface will be slightly mounded, but will settle.*

2. IN LATE SPRING *(in mild areas) or early summer (for cold regions) sow seeds. It is essential that seedlings should not be exposed to frost. Use a draw hoe to form two 5cm/2in-deep drills, 60cm/2ft apart. Sow seeds in them, 15cm/6in apart. Cover them with soil and firm it. Keep the soil moist but not waterlogged.*

3. DURING *germination, which takes up to two weeks, it is essential to keep the soil moist and free from weeds. After germination and until the plants are about 10cm/4in high the additional problem is slugs. Unless deterred by baits they can devastate a row of young bean plants overnight in warm, wet weather.*

4. WHEN *bean plants are about 10cm/4in high, erect supports 1.8–2.4m/6–8ft high. Bean poles, inserted along the outer sides of the double row, and 15–30cm/6–12in apart, are the traditional method of supporting plants. Angle the poles inwards, cross their tops and tie a horizontal pole to them securely.*

5. ALTERNATIVE *ways to support runner beans include tripods of poles (sometimes four poles are used). These are ideal where space prevents the erection of long rows of bean poles. Another way is to use strings secured by wire hooks in the ground and tied to a cross-bar at the top. It is essential that these supports are strong.*

6. HARVEST *beans as soon as they are large enough to be eaten – do not wait until they are tough. Regular picking is essential to encourage the formation of further beans. A 3m/10ft-long row will yield about 27kg/60lb of beans. They can be eaten fresh, or blanched, cooled and stored in a freezer.*

BEETROOT

BEETROOTS are sown in spring and harvested throughout summer for immediate use, or stored in boxes of dry sand or peat for eating during winter and up to early spring. Stagger sowings between spring and early summer to provide young roots throughout summer.

STORING BEETROOT

Ensure the leaves have been twisted off 5cm/2in above the crown. Also, pull off dead or decaying leaves. Then, pack dry sand or peat around them and place in a cool, vermin-proof shed or cellar.

VARIETIES

Globe beetroot
Round and quick maturing.
• *'Boltardy': Resistant to developing seed-heads when sown early. Sweet, deep red flesh with a fresh flavour.*
• *'Burpee's Golden': Superb flavour, with yellow flesh that does not bleed.*
• *'Detroit': Ideal as a main crop variety, with red flesh. Can be stored throughout winter.*
• *'Monopoly': Each seed cluster produces only one seedling, thereby eliminating thinning. Resistant to bolting. Red flesh.*

Cylindrical beetroot
Ideal for storing.
• *'Cylindra': Deep red flesh. Keeps well*

Long beetroot
Deep soil is essential.
• *'Cheltenham Green Top': Popular with exhibitors.*

1. DIG THE SOIL *in late winter but do not add manure or lime. In spring shallowly fork the soil, rake to a fine tilth and form drills 2.5cm/1in deep and 30cm/12in apart. Sow seeds in clusters of three, 10–15cm/4–6in apart.*

2. WHEN *the seedlings have formed their first leaves, other than their original seed-leaves, thin them to one seedling at each position. Re-firm soil around the remaining seedlings, then water them gently but thoroughly.*

3. IN LATE SUMMER, *use a garden fork to break the soil under each beetroot. Gently ease them from the soil without bruising the skin. Either use them immediately or carefully twist off the leaves (5cm/2in above the crown).*

BROCCOLI AND CALABRESE

THESE two vegetables are increasing in popularity. They are quite similar: purple and white broccoli varieties have small, leafy flowers on short stalks, while calabrese is often known as green sprouting broccoli. Broccoli mainly matures from mid-winter to late spring, whereas calabrese is ready for cutting in autumn.

RAISING AND LOOKING AFTER PLANTS
Both broccoli and calabrese are raised in the same way, initially in seed-beds and then transplanted when 7.5cm/3in high to their growing positions. Treat the plants against club-root when setting them in the soil.

Protect young plants from birds and keep the soil moist. For broccoli, draw up soil around their stems in late summer to support them in exposed sites.

VARIETIES

Broccoli
• *'Christmas Purple Sprouting': An ideal variety for harvesting in mid-winter.*
• *'Early Purple Sprouting': Sow in late spring for harvesting in early spring of the following year.*
• *'White Sprouting': Sow in late spring for harvesting in late spring of the following year.*

Calabrese varieties
• *'Calabrese Green Sprouting': Sow in early to late spring for harvesting the crop in late summer or autumn.*
• *'Green Comet': Sow in early spring for harvesting them from summer to autumn.*
• *'Romanesco': Sow in early to late spring for harvesting in late summer or autumn.*

1. PREPARE *a seed-bed (see page 299) in spring and sow seeds evenly and thinly in drills 12mm/½in deep and 20cm/8in apart. Keep the seed-bed well watered and free from weeds. You can also, sow seeds in early summer.*

2. IN EARLY SUMMER, *transplant early sown seedlings. For later sowings, this will be about mid-summer. Water seed-beds and planting positions the day before and space plants 45cm/1½ft apart in rows a similar distance apart.*

3. HARVEST *the central heads when mature, cutting them with a sharp knife. To assist in the development of sideshoots, water the plants with a general fertilizer. Later, the sideshoots can be harvested. when they form good-sized heads.*

BRUSSELS SPROUTS

BRUSSELS sprouts are an important and popular crop. By selecting the right varieties, sprouts can be ready for harvesting from late summer to early spring (see the opposite side of the page for suitable varieties). The main disappointment with them is 'blown' sprouts, but this can be overcome by careful soil preparation and planting (see right).

The other hazard with Brussels sprouts is cooking them for too long. Everyone has their own idea of when food has been cooked sufficiently, but sprouts are soon made soggy and unappealing by excess cooking.

RAISING PLANTS

Prepare a seed-bed in late winter. In early to mid-spring, sow seeds thinly and evenly, 12–18mm/ ^{1}/$_2$–^{3}/$_4$in deep in drills about 15–20cm/6–8in apart. Germination takes up to twelve days. Keep the seed-bed moist and when the seedlings are large enough to handle, thin them to about 7.5cm/3in apart. When the young plants are 10–13cm/4–5in high, transplant them to their growing positions (see below). Set the plants with their lowest leaves fractionally above the surface.

BLOWN SPROUTS

Occasionally, sprouts open prematurely and become leafy instead of remaining as tight buttons. This is caused by insufficient organic material such as garden compost and manure being added to the soil. If the soil is loose and has not been firmed (see below) this, too, contributes to the problem. Loose planting is another cause of this problem; to test if plants are firmly in the soil, part of a leaf when pulled should come away and not disturb the roots.

HARVESTING AND 'GLUTS'

Always start picking the buttons from the base of the stem upwards. At this stage, the sprouts should be tight and about the size of a walnut. Do not wait until the leaves surrounding them become loose. Remove sprouts from the stem by forcing them downwards with a sudden push. Alternatively, use a sharp knife. It may take several weeks before each plant has been totally cleared of sprouts.

Fresh sprouts are a culinary delight, but often – and especially when Fl hybrids are grown – too many of them are ready for harvesting at one time. Do not leave them on the plants, as they will spoil. Wash, dry and pack them in polythene bags and place in a refrigerator for up to five days.

For longer periods freezing is necessary. Wash, strip off loose outer leaves and soak them in water for about twenty minutes. Then, blanch for three minutes, cool rapidly, dry and place in freezer bags. Seal the bags, label and place in a freezer.

VARIETIES

The two main types of varieties are the standard (traditional ones) and newer F1 types.
Standard Brussels Sprouts
• *'Bedford Fillbasket': Heavy crops of large, solid sprouts from early autumn to Christmas.*
• *'Cambridge No. 5': High quality, walnut-sized sprouts from Christmas to early spring.*
FI Brussels Sprouts
These varieties produce uniform buttons, ready for harvesting all at the same time.
• *'Citadel': Tight, firm sprouts from mid-winter to mid-spring.*
• *'Icarus F1': Large crops of solid, sweet buttons. It is resistant to cold and ready for harvesting from mid-autumn to late winter.*
• *'Peer Gynt': Prolific cropping from mid-autumn to early winter.*
• *'Stabolite': Ideal in cold climates. Picking from mid-winter to early spring.*

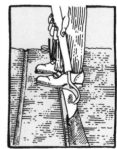

1. DIG THE SOIL *in early winter, adding manure or compost, especially if it is light and sandy. In late winter, apply lime so that the soil is slightly alkaline (see page 228). In early spring, rake and firm the soil ready for sowing seeds.*

2. AFTER *raking and treading the soil, again rake it to remove foot prints that might trap rain and cause puddles. Use a garden line and draw hoe to form drills 5cm/2in deep and 60–75cm/2–2 1/2ft apart. Plants are planted in them.*

3. DURING *late spring and early summer, transplant plants earlier raised in a seed-bed. Planting in drills conserves moisture around their roots; if the soil is moisture retentive, the V-drills are not necessary. Water each plant.*

4. DURING *mid-summer, use a draw hoe to pull up a little soil around the base of each stem. Also, remove weeds and keep the soil moist but not waterlogged, especially when the plants are young. Ensure birds do not pull off leaves.*

5. PLANTS *benefit from a foliar feed (high in potash) in the latter part of mid-summer. This rapidly stimulates growth during the late summer and into early autumn without making plants soft and susceptible to low temperatures.*

6. THE BUTTONS *can be harvested as soon as they are firm, which is usually from autumn to late winter, depending on the variety (see above). To prevent tall varieties being blown over, draw further soil up around the base of each stem.*

CABBASES

❖

THERE is a wide range of cabbages and they are ready for eating throughout the year. The main types are discussed here, together with their sowing, planting and harvesting times. It is essential to select the right type, especially for those grown during winter, when hardy varieties are particularly essential.

Cabbages are easily raised from seeds, but if only a few plants are needed, it is easier to buy them from a local nursery.

Through the centuries, cabbages have been unjustifiably maligned and the butt of schoolboy jokes. But for many years they were a staple food of country folk, and if properly cooked have a superb flavour and crispness. It is when they are boiled 'all morning' that cabbages lose their appeal and become tasteless.

As a change, both red and white cabbages can be chopped and eaten raw in salads. Stir-fried Chinese cabbage, or leaves stuffed with minced meat, are other ways to use them. Cabbages can be frozen, but as they are available throughout the year it is best to use freezer space for vegetables with a shorter harvesting season.

SPRING CABBAGES
Conical and initially provide 'spring greens', later heads.
• *Sow seeds: Mid- to late summer. Sow thinly, and pull early plants for spring greens. Leave others to mature.*
• *Planting: Autumn.*
• *Harvesting: Mid- and late spring, sometimes slightly earlier.*
• *Varieties: 'April', 'Durham Early' and 'Offenham – Flower of Spring'.*

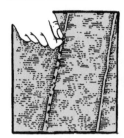

SUMMER CABBAGES
These are generally ball shaped.
• *Sow seeds: Mid-spring (or slightly earlier when sown under cloches).*
• *Planting: Late spring and early summer. Space plants 45–60cm/ 1½–2ft apart each way.*
• *Harvesting: Late summer and early autumn.*
• *Varieties: 'Greyhound', 'Hispi', 'Minicole', 'Primo' and 'Winnigstadt'.*

1. YOUNG *cabbage plants are raised in seed-beds (see page 229). The time of sowing depends on the cabbage (see below and on the opposite page). Sow seeds 12mm/½in deep, later thinning the plants to 7.5cm/3in apart.*

2. WHEN *the plants have four or five leaves, transplant them to the vegetable plot. Water the seed-bed and the garden the day before to ensure the young plants become established quickly. Use a dibber to plant them firmly in the soil.*

3. IF CLUB-ROOT *is prevalent, dip the roots in thiophanate-methyl. To check if the plants are firmly planted, pull part of a leaf. It should tear away and leave the plant's roots undisturbed. Water the plants thoroughly.*

WINTER CABBAGES
These are usually drum or ball headed and either green or white.
• *Sow seeds: Mid- and late spring.*
• *Planting: Latter part of early summer and through mid-summer. Space plants 60cm/2ft apart each way.*
• *Harvesting: Early to late winter.*
• *Varieties: 'Celtic', 'Christmas Drumhead', 'January King' and 'Jupiter'.*

SAVOY CABBAGES
These have distinctively puckered and crisp, dark green leaves.
• *Sow: Mid- and late spring.*
• *Planting: Mid-summer. Space plants 60m apart each way.*
• *Harvesting: Late autumn to late winter.*
• *Varieties: 'Best of All', 'Ormskirk Late', 'Savoy King' and 'Ormskirk Rearguard'. This last variety is especially recommended when seeking a cabbage to cut at Christmas.*

CHINESE CABBAGES
Tall and cylindrical and more like a Cos lettuce than a cabbage.
• *Sow: Mid-summer (sometimes slightly earlier for some varieties), in drills 30cm/12in apart. Space the seeds 10cm/4in apart and later thin to 30cm/12in between plants. Do not transplant Chinese cabbages. Water well during dry periods.*
• *Harvest: Early and mid-autumn.*
• *Varieties: 'Tip-top', 'Kasumi', 'Sampan' and 'Two Seasons'.*

RED CABBAGES
Distinctive, with rich, red leaves. It is widely grown for pickling, but can also be boiled and eaten in the same way as other, more ordinary cabbages.
• *Sow: Mid-spring.*
• *Planting: Later spring and early summer. Space plants 60cm/2ft each way.*
• *Harvesting: Early and mid-autumn.*
• *Varieties: 'Red Drumhead' and 'Stockley's Giant Red'.*

CAULIFLOWERS

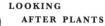

CAULIFLOWERS are popular and widely grown. There are three types – winter, summer and autumn – and between them they provide edible heads, called curds, throughout much of the year.

RAISING YOUNG PLANTS

All three types of cauliflower can be raised by sowing seeds in a seed-bed in spring, but to produce early 'summer' types it is necessary to raise plants in gentle warmth (13°C/55°F) in a greenhouse in mid-winter. Reduce the temperature after germination and prick out the seedlings into cold frames, setting them about 7.5cm/3in square. Plant them into gardens in early spring. Raising plants in seed-beds outdoors is detailed below.

Whether in the greenhouse or outdoors, sow seeds thinly.

LOOKING AFTER PLANTS

Dig the soil thoroughly during early winter and mix in garden compost or manure that is well decayed. In late winter check that the soil is slightly alkaline and, later, a couple of weeks before planting, dust and thoroughly rake in a good general-purpose fertilizer.

Regularly watering plants is essential, as growth is dramatically reduced during droughts and the curds do not subsequently develop to their full size. Always thoroughly water the soil; just dampening the surface does more harm than good.

Birds are frequently a nuisance to young plants and if they are persistent, wire-netting hoops may be needed to protect them.

On light soils, where nutrients are soon leached away, feed summer types in mid-summer. Do not feed the others, as it will make growth too soft for winter survival.

VARIETIES

Summer cauliflowers
These are ready for cutting from mid-summer to early autumn.
- 'All The Year Round': Can be sown in gentle warmth in mid-winter, or outdoors during spring.
- 'Dok-Elgon': Late-summer variety.
- 'Snowball': An ideal early variety.

Autumn cauliflowers
Ready for harvesting in autumn and early winter.
- 'Autumn Giant': Large heads in early winter.
- 'Canberra': Matures in early winter.
- 'Barrier Reef': Ideal in late autumn and early winter.

Winter cauliflowers
These are ready for cutting from early winter to late spring.
- 'Late Queen': Ideal for cutting in late spring.
- 'Snow's Winter White': Tolerant of cold weather and easily grown.

MINI-CAULIFLOWERS

These are easily grown and are increasing in popularity. They are grown by sowing seeds where the small cauliflowers are to grow. And as they are grown close together, in a space about 15cm/6in square, it means they are ideal for small gardens. Additionally, because of their size – about 7.5cm/3in across – they are easily frozen for use later.

Sow seeds thinly and evenly in mid-spring, about 12mm/½in deep and in drills 15cm/6in apart. When the seedlings are large enough to handle, thin them first to 7.5cm/3in apart, later to 15cm/6in. By making two further sowings at three-week intervals, mini-cauliflowers can be cut from mid-summer to late autumn. Suitable varieties include:
- 'Cargill Early Maturing Variety': For early sowing.
- 'Garant' (early-maturing variety): For early sowings, where the heads do not mature all at the same time.
- 'Predominant' (late-maturing variety): Ideal for later sowings and for freezing.

1. SOW SEEDS *in a seed-bed during mid- and late spring, in drills 12mm/½in deep and 15–20cm/6–8in apart. Germination takes up to twelve days. Thin the seedlings 7.5cm/3in apart.*

2. WHEN *young cauliflower plants have about five leaves they can be moved to their growing positions. Water the seed-bed and planting positions the day before moving them and lift the young plants with care.*

3. BEFORE *planting, dip their roots in a fungicide that will prevent an incidence of club-root. Plant them firmly, setting summer and autumn varieties approximately 60cm/2ft apart, and winter varieties 75cm/2½ft.*

4. WHEN *planting, firm the soil around and over the roots and leave a small depression on the surface around each plant. This then can be filled with water to ensure soil settles around the roots. Water them several times.*

5. BEND *a few leaves over summer-maturing varieties to prevent sun bleaching and drying the curds. Also, by folding leaves over winter types they can be protected from snow and frost. Wait until frost is imminent.*

6. USE *a sharp knife to harvest cauliflowers. The curds should be firm and well developed but not open. Cut summer-maturing types usually in the late morning, and winter ones as soon as frost has left them.*

CARROTS

CARROTS are a very versatile vegetable and deserve to be more widely grown. They are equally superb when grated in salads, cooked in stews or served as a hot vegetable. Long-rooted exhibition varieties need very deep, well-prepared soil. But generally, it is the shorter-rooted types that are grown for home use.

SOWING AND LOOKING AFTER PLANTS

Sowing carrots is detailed below, while the main task when growing them is removing weeds, hoeing between the rows and ensuring the soil does not become dry.

The most devastating pest is carrot root-fly (see page 341). Risk of attack can be reduced by sowing seeds thinly. To mask the smell (which carrot flies are said to be able to detect from more than a mile away) place paraffin-soaked rags between the rows, or plant onions or garlic alongside them to disguise the smell.

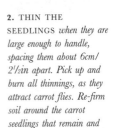

1. FROM MID-SPRING *to the latter part of early summer, sow seeds outdoors in drills 12–18mm/ 1/2–3/4in deep and 15cm/ 6in apart. Cover and firm the drills, then water thoroughly but gently. If carrots are deprived of moisture they become woody.*

2. THIN THE SEEDLINGS *when they are large enough to handle, spacing them about 6cm/ 2 1/2in apart. Pick up and burn all thinnings, as they attract carrot flies. Re-firm soil around the carrot seedlings that remain and thoroughly water the soil.*

3. AS SOON AS *young carrots are large enough to be eaten, pull them up. At this stage they will be succulent and tender. Later, when lifting roots for storage, it is necessary to use a garden fork. Twist off the foliage, just above the roots. Take care not to bruise them.*

CUCUMBERS – OUTDOOR

OUTDOOR cucumbers, also known as ridge types, are easy to grow but do need a warm, sunny, position that is wind sheltered, and plenty of water during summer.

PREPARING THE SOIL

In mid-spring, dig holes about 30cm/12in deep and 38cm/15in wide and fill them with a mixture of friable soil and decomposed garden compost or manure. Replace the rest of the soil to form a mound. Sow seeds as soon as all risk of frost has passed (detailed below). If more than one mound is formed, space them 90cm/3ft apart.

GROWING, TRAINING AND HARVESTING

Once the seeds have germinated, remove the growing tips from the shoots, spreading them out so that sideshoots can grow. If these do not develop flowers, carefully nip off the tips beyond the sixth leaf.

From the latter part of mid-summer, use a sharp knife to cut the cucumbers when 15–20cm/ 6–8in long. Do not leave them to grow further as this discourages the development of further fruits.

Harvesting stops instantaneously with the first frosts of autumn. However, if the fruits are picked while young and plants watered and fed regularly it is possible to produce a large crop.

1. PREPARE *the planting mound in mid-spring, as detailed above. In late spring in warm areas, and early summer where late frosts are likely, sow three seeds 18mm/3/4in deep and 5cm/2in apart, in a triangle. Water and cover with a large jam jar.*

2. KEEP *the soil moist, and after germination, when the seedlings have several leaves, remove the weakest seedlings to leave one strong plant on each mound. Firm soil around the remaining plant and gently water it. After about a week, carefully remove the jam jar.*

3. DURING *early and mid-summer the plant will develop sideshoots. When these have five or six leaves, pinch out their tips just beyond a leaf. Water plants regularly and feed them with a weak liquid fertilizer as soon as the first fruits start to swell.*

CELERY

◆

ELERY is grown for its blanched leaf stalks and can be used in several ways, including fresh in salads or braised as a vegetable. Fertile, moisture-retentive soil with plenty of garden compost or manure is essential to encourage strong and rapid growth. Additionally, the total exclusion of light by either earthing-up trench celery or growing self-blanching types close together is vital for producing a good crop.

EARTHING-UP

Before earthing-up trench celery, tie the tops of their stems together to prevent soil falling between them. Wrapping newspaper or corrugated cardboard around the stems keeps them clean, but may encourage pests to linger. Never completely cover the leaves at each earthing-up, and afterwards water the plants so that soil settles around the stem but never into the heart. It is better to earth-up the plants several times than to do it just once, and to damage them.

RAISING YOUNG PLANTS

Raise new plants by sowing seeds in gentle warmth (13–15°C/ 55–59°F) in early or mid-spring. After germination, reduce the temperature slightly and when the seedlings are large enough to handle, prick them out into seed-trays, setting them about 5cm/2in apart. Slowly acclimatize the plants to outdoor conditions, taking care that the compost does not become dry. In late spring or early summer plant them out.

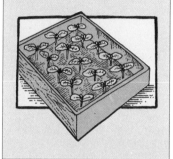

SELF-BLANCHING CELERY

This type is easier to grow than the 'trench' form, as it is not necessary to dig a trench. It is best grown in a cold frame – no glass covering is needed – so that light is excluded from the edges of the block of plants. Self-blanching celery is not so hardy as trench type, which can be left in the soil and harvested over a long period. Some varieties of trench celery can be harvested in late winter. The self-blanching type, however, is best eaten soon after it is harvested, from late summer and late autumn. Both types need copious amounts of water during summer.

DURING late winter or early spring, fork over soil in a cold frame and add garden compost or well-decomposed manure. In late spring or early summer, rake and level the surface. Mark the surface into 23cm/9in squares and put in the young plants. Thoroughly water the plants.

FROM late summer to late autumn, use a trowel or garden fork to lift the plants. Wash them and, preferably, eat immediately. After digging up a few plants, pack straw around those that remain to prevent the stems becoming tough and green.

VARIETIES

Trench celery
• *'Giant Pink': Crisp, pink sticks, ideal for use during mid- and late winter.*
• *'Giant Red': Purplish green sticks, turning shell pink when blanched.*
• *'Giant White': Well-known and widely grown white variety.*

Self-blanching celery
• *'American Queen': Widely grown, green and stringless.*
• *'Celebrity': Long sticks.*
• *'Golden Self-blanching': Early maturing, with yellow sticks.*
• *'Lathom Self-blanching': Good flavoured, yellow variety.*

1. IN EARLY SPRING, *select a well-drained piece of soil and dig a trench 38cm/15in wide and 25–30cm/10–12in deep. Place excavated soil along the sides. If there is more than one trench, space them about 1.2m/4ft apart.*

2. USE A GARDEN *fork or spade to mix plenty of well-decayed garden compost or manure into the base of the trench. Add more garden compost and mix it with further soil until within 7.5cm/3in of the surface. Then, leave the area open.*

3. A WEEK *before setting the plants in position in late spring or early summer, dust the trench's surface with a general fertilizer. Set the plants in two staggered rows 23cm/9in apart with the same distance between the individual plants.*

4. WATER *the young plants and during mid-summer, when they are 25–30cm/10–12in high, tie the stems together just below the leaves. Every three weeks, trickle some soil around the plants (earthing-up), to blanch the stems.*

5. AS PLANTS *grow and their stems lengthen, continue to mound up soil. This is best done after a shower of rain. If plants are earthed-up when the soil is dry the leaves of plants form an umbrella and never allow it to become moist.*

6. FROM *late autumn to late winter dig up trench celery, wash and eat it. Use a trowel, although if plants are deeply rooted a garden fork is needed. Cover plants with straw in winter to prevent the soil being frozen and to keep them balanced.*

LETTUCE

❖

LETTUCE is by far the most popular salad crop, with a wide range of types, sowing and harvesting times. Most are raised without the need for cloches or frames, but those that grow through winter need protection (see opposite side of page).

Growing lettuces requires three basic factors: the soil must be fertile and contain well-decomposed garden compost, both to feed the plants and assist in the retention of moisture; plants must be regularly watered; and the soil must not be acid, a pH of 6.5–7.5 being desirable (see page 228 for correcting acidity). A sunny or lightly shaded site is an advantage.

Slugs, snails and greenfly are the main pests likely to infest lettuces and unless they are controlled, crops are soon decimated (see pages 340 to 343).

BUTTERHEAD LETTUCE *is a cabbage type, with large, soft and smooth-edged leaves. Varieties include:*
• *'All the Year Round'*
• *'Arctic King'*
• *'Buttercrunch'*
• *'Dolly'* • *'Tom Thumb'*

CRISPHEAD LETTUCE *is another cabbage type, with rounded heads with curled and crisp leaves. Varieties include:*
• *'Avoncrisp'*
• *'Great Lakes'* • *'Iceberg'*
• *'Webb's Wonderful'*

COS LETTUCES *differ dramatically from cabbage types and have upright growth and oblong heads. Varieties include:*
• *'Barcarolle'* • *'Little Gem'*
• *'Lobjoit's Green'*
• *'Winter Density'*

SPRING LETTUCE

1. SOW SPRING *lettuce in mild areas in the latter part of late summer or early autumn to produce lettuces for cutting in late spring. Sow seeds 12mm/½in deep in drills 25cm/10in apart. Use a variety that is winter-hardy.*

2. 'ARCTIC KING', *'Valdor' or 'All The Year Round' are suitable varieties. When the seedlings are 18mm/¾in high (during early to mid-autumn) thin them to 5–7.5cm/2–3in apart. Then, carefully hoe between the rows.*

3. IN LATE WINTER *or early spring, again thin the seedlings, this time to 23–30cm/9–12in apart, depending on the variety, but usually 30cm/12in. At the same time, dust and hoe a general fertilizer into the surface soil.*

SUMMER LETTUCE

 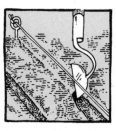 

1. SOW SUMMER *lettuce from mid-spring to the early part of late summer in drills 12mm/½in deep and 25cm/10in apart. Sow the seeds evenly and thinly, then cover with friable soil. Keep the seed-bed moist but not excessively wet.*

2. WHEN THE *seedlings are about 2.5cm/1in high, thin them first to 10cm/4in apart, later to 30cm/12in. Small varieties, however, need only be thinned to 20cm/8in apart. Regularly water the seedlings to ensure they grow steadily and rapidly.*

3. FROM THE *latter part of early summer to autumn, harvest the lettuces. Test the hearts for firmness by pressing with the back of a hand, not with fingers which may cause bruising. Use a knife to cut the stem below the lowest leaf.*

UNDER CLOCHES

By sowing seeds in mid-autumn and covering the seedlings with cloches, lettuces can be harvested in early and mid-spring.

Sow three seeds 12mm/½in deep and 7.5cm/3in apart in rows 20cm/8in apart, then place cloches over them. Ensure the cloches and their ends are very well secured.

In mid-autumn, when the seedlings are about 18mm/¾in high, thin them so that you leave just the strongest seedling in each group. Ventilate the cloches in winter, but avoid draughts. During late winter, thin the seedlings to 23cm/9in apart and keep the soil evenly moist. Dwarf varieties are thinned to 15cm/6in apart.

LOOSE-LEAF LETTUCES

These are sometimes known as loose-head types and they differ from normal lettuces in having masses of loose, wavy leaves which can be picked over several weeks. Varieties include 'Salad Bowl' and 'Red Salad Bowl'.

Sow seeds thinly and evenly 12mm/½in deep and in drills 13cm/5in apart during late spring and early summer. Do not thin the seedlings, and harvest the leaves about six weeks after sowing them. Use a sharp knife to cut off the leaves slightly above soil level. Leave the stumps to produce a further crop. Ensure that the soil is kept moist, but not waterlogged.

LEEKS

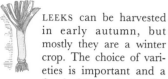

LEEKS can be harvested in early autumn, but mostly they are a winter crop. The choice of varieties is important and a range of suitable varieties for early, mid-season and late crops is shown here. Although large, fat leeks are usually grown for exhibition purposes, small ones are better suited for home use. Indeed, the flavour and tenderness usually decreases as size increases.

CULTIVATION AND HARVESTING

When planting, never fill the hole with soil; just pop in the young plant and water it thoroughly. Leeks are gross feeders, but do not feed them after late summer as it diminishes the ability of mid and late-season varieties to survive low temperatures in winter. Use a draw hoe to pull up soil around the plants several times during a season, but take care not to allow it to fall between the leaves.

Use a garden fork to dig under and to harvest the plants.

VARIETIES

Leek varieties can be arranged into three groups, according to the times they are harvested.
Early leeks
Ready for harvesting from early autumn to early winter.
• *'Early Market'.*
• *'The Lyon - Prizetaker'.*
• *'Walton Mammoth'.*
Mid-season leeks
For harvesting early to late winter.
• *'King Richard'.*
• *'Molos': For harvesting late autumn to mid-winter.*
• *'Musselburgh Improved'.*
Late season leeks
Ready for harvesting from late winter to mid-spring.
• *'Giant Winter-Royal Favourite'.*
• *'Winter Crop': Ideal in very cold and exposed areas.*
• *'Yates Empire': Does not suffer by being left in the ground.*

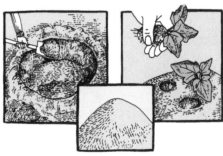

1. DURING EARLY *to mid-spring, sow seeds thinely and evenly, 12mm/½in deep and in rows 15cm/6in apart in a seed-bed. Keep the soil moist and free from weeds. Thin the seedlings to 3.6–5cm/1½–2in apart and re-firm loosened soil.*

2. WHEN PLANTS *are about 20cm/8in high, use a dibber to form holes 15cm/6in deep and 15cm/6in apart in rows 30cm/12in apart. Trim off one-third of the roots and leaves and drop a plant into each hole. Just fill the hole with water.*

3. DURING *summer, keep the soil moist and mulch the plants. Once plants are well developed, draw soil around them to create a larger blanched area. Feed leeks until late summer, and harvest them from early autumn to spring.*

MARROWS

THESE fleshy-fruited vegetables are increasingly popular, together with courgettes, which are really small marrows. Indeed, some varieties, such as the popular 'Green Bush' can be grown as both.

RAISING YOUNG PLANTS

Young plants can be raised by sowing seeds where they are to grow (see below), but seeds can also be sown in 7.5cm/3in-wide pots during mid-spring and placed in 18°C/64°F. After germination, lower the temperature and gradually acclimatize plants to outdoor conditions. Plant outdoors when all risk of frost has passed.

VARIETIES

These can be used fresh in summer or stored for winter.
• *'Early Gem': A hybrid, producing early fruits.*
• *'Green Bush': Can be cut when small as courgettes, or left until late summer to produce marrows.*
• *'Long Green Striped': Very prolific fruiting.*
• *'Long Green Trailing': Large fruits; frequently used by exhibitors.*

COURGETTES

These are like small marrows and are usually harvested when only 10cm/4in long. They are grown in the same way as marrows, but the range of varieties is different. Because they are bush varieties they do not need to be 'stopped'. Varieties include:
• 'Blondy': A hybrid with creamy-green, very sweet fruits.
• 'Gold Rush': Very prolific, with yellow fruits.
• 'Golden Zucchini': Excellently flavoured, creamy flesh.
• 'Zucchini': Prolific, with dark green fruits. Widely grown.

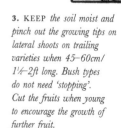

1. PREPARE *the planting positions in late spring. Choose a warm, sheltered site and dig out a hole 30cm/12in deep and 38cm/15in across. Fill the hole, forming a mound with a mixture of topsoil and decayed garden compost.*

2. IN LATE SPRING – *or early summer in cold areas – sow three seeds 18mm/¾in deep and about 7.5cm/3in apart. Placing a jam jar over the seeds hastens germination. When the young plants are 5cm/2in high, thin to the strongest.*

3. KEEP *the soil moist and pinch out the growing tips on lateral shoots on trailing varieties when 45–60cm/1½–2ft long. Bush types do not need 'stopping'. Cut the fruits when young to encourage the growth of further fruit.*

ONIONS

ONIONS are easily grown and introduce rich flavours to salads and cooked dishes. There are two main types of onion:

• 'Bulbing' types are mainly sown in spring for harvesting during late summer and autumn of the same year. It is also possible to sow hardy varieties, such as 'Reliance' and 'Autumn Queen', in late summer, to produce onions during early and mid-summer of the following year. This is rather a rarity and the information here is for spring-sown types.

• 'Spring' onions are delicious in salads and are detailed on the opposite side of the page.

HARVESTING AND USING

Part of the skill in growing bulbing onions is harvesting and ripening them. Unless care is taken about this task the bulbs have a limited storage time. Towards the end of summer – and if the leaves have not naturally toppled over – bend

---

VARIETIES

Bulbing onions

These are the onions that are grown for their large, rounded bulbs. Spring onions are detailed on the opposite side of the page.
• *'Ailsa Craig': Well-known, with large, globe-shaped bulbs. But they do not store very well.*
• *'Bedfordshire Champion': Large, globular bulbs that store quite well.*
• *'Buffalo': A hybrid with early bulbs, but they do not store well.*
• *'Noordhollandse Bloedrode': Attractive red-skinned bulbs that can be stored for a long time.*
• *'Rijnsburger': Large, globular, straw-coloured bulbs that are excellent for storing.*

---

over the stem just above the bulb to prevent growth being directed to the leaves. A few weeks later, use a garden fork to break the roots. The bulbs can then be laid on the soil's surface to ripen.

Preferably, the base of each bulb should face the sun. Turn the bulbs regularly to ensure they are evenly ripened. When they are dry, store them on trays in a dry, vermin-proof, well-aerated shed. Alternatively, tie them into onion ropes or put in net bags.

If the weather is wet, the bulbs will have to be ripened on sacking in a shed or a greenhouse. Another way is to place them in a cold frame or under cloches.

ONION SETS

Bulbing onions are sometimes grown from 'onion sets'. These are small, partly-developed onion bulbs which have been stored during winter. They are especially useful in cold regions, where the growing season is short.

Plant sets in the latter part of early spring and into mid-spring. Prepare the soil in the same way as for sowing seed. Mark out rows 25cm/10in apart and push the sets into the ground so that just the top can be seen. Space the sets about 10cm/4in apart and thoroughly water the soil. Cover with hoops of wire netting.

SPRING ONIONS

Spring onions, also known as salad onions, bunching onions and scallions, are ideal for pulling and using in salads. Sometimes, the thinnings from bulbing onions are used in salads, but there are special varieties of spring onions, including 'White Lisbon' and 'Ishikura'.

Prepare the soil in the same way as for bulbing onions and sow seeds 12mm/½in deep in drills 10–13cm/4–5in apart every two weeks from early spring to the early part of mid-summer. This produces spring onions from early summer to early autumn. Water the soil before pulling up spring onions.

Sowing seeds thinly

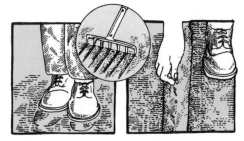

1. IN PREPARATION *for sowing seeds in spring, dig the ground in early winter and add plenty of garden compost or manure. In late winter, check the soil is slightly alkaline (see page 228). Tread the soil firm and rake level.*

2. DURING *early spring, use a draw hoe to form drills 12mm/½in deep and 23cm/9in apart. If the soil is dry, water it a few days before sowing seeds. Sow seeds thinly and evenly; carefully cover and firm friable soil over them.*

3. SEEDS *germinate within three weeks and when the seedlings have straightened up and are about 5cm/2in high they must be thinned. First, ensure the soil is moist, then thin them 5cm/2in apart. Then trim them again later to 10cm/4in.*

4. WATER THE SOIL *during dry periods and carefully hoe around the bulbs to remove weeds. By late summer or early autumn, encourage bulbs to ripen by sharply bending over the foliage immediately above each bulb's neck.*

5. A FEW WEEKS *later, use a garden fork to prise under the bulbs to break their roots and thereby stop them growing. Take care not to bruise the bulbs as this will reduce their storage ability and immediately encourage the onset of decay.*

6. A FEW DAYS *after forking under the bulbs, lift them completely, carefully rub off soil and place them on the surface to dry and ripen further. If the weather is wet they will have to be dried on sacking in a well-ventilated shed or greenhouse.*

PEAS

DRIED peas have been used in cooking for many centuries, but growing peas for eating fresh started only a few hundred years ago. By sowing seeds in the open from early spring to early summer, it is possible to harvest fresh peas from early to late summer. And by making a sowing of a variety of 'first-early' peas (such as 'Kelvedon Wonder') it is possible to extend harvesting until autumn.

SOIL PREPARATION AND SOWING

Prepare the soil in the way suggested below. When sowing seeds there are two main choices: either in flat-bottomed drills, where the seeds can be sown in three rows with about 7.5cm/3in between them, or in two V-shaped drills 20cm/8in apart. Germination takes about seven to ten days. Whichever method is used, a wide row of young pea plants is produced. The distance between the rows is dictated by the height of the variety (see right).

VARIETIES

Garden peas are classified into three groups according to the time they are harvested.

First early peas
From sowing to harvesting takes about twelve weeks.
- *'Hurst Beagle': 45cm/1½ft. Sweet and juicy.*
- *'Kelvedon Wonder': 45cm/1½ft high. Versatile variety.*
- *'Little Marvel': 45cm/1½ft high. Good flavour.*

Second early peas
From sowing to harvesting takes thirteen to fourteen weeks.
- *'Hurst Green Shaft': 75cm/2½ft high. Heavy cropping.*
- *'Onward': 75cm/2½ft high. Heavy crops of plump peas.*

Main-crop peas
From sowing to harvesting takes fourteen to sixteen weeks.
- *'Lord Chancellor': 1m/3½ft high. Heavy crops of superb peas.*
- *'Senator': 75cm/2½ft high.*
- *'Trio': 75cm/2½ft high.*

4. INSERTING *pea sticks into the ground on either side of a row of peas is the traditional way to support plants. Put the sticks in early, so that plants grow up and through the twigs, eventually covering them.*

5. AN ALTERNATIVE *method of supporting plants is to use wide-meshed wire netting, 90cm–1.2m/3–4ft high. Erect the netting when the plants are 5cm/2in high and use stout poles or canes to hold it upright.*

6. FROM *the latter part of early summer to autumn, pick the pods when young and tender. Regularly harvesting the pods encourages more pods to develop. Those at the base are ready first.*

KEYS TO SUCCESS

Garden peas are not the easiest crop to grow as they are vulnerable to pests such as birds and the notorious pea moth, which enters peas and makes them inedible. Nevertheless, with care a good crop can be grown. Here are a few hints for producing a successful crop of peas:
- Never sow seeds in cold, wet soil. Either choose a well-drained site or wait a few weeks until spring or early summer sun has dried and warmed up the soil.
- Always choose fertile soil. Add garden compost or manure when preparing the soil in early winter.
- Ensure the soil is not acid. Test the soil in late winter (see page 228).
- Choose the right variety for the time of year (see opposite).
- Protect seeds from birds by covering the rows with netting.
- Water plants if there are dry periods.
- Spray the plants with insecticides every ten days after the start of flowering.

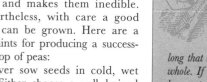
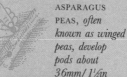

ASPARAGUS PEAS

ASPARAGUS PEAS, *often known as winged peas, develop pods about 36mm/1½in long that are cooked and eaten whole. If left to grow long, they become tough and inedible. Sow seeds in late spring (early summer in cold areas), in drills 2.5cm/1in deep and 30cm12in apart. Space the seeds 10–15cm/.4–6in apart. Keep the plants well watered once the flowers have formed; if heavily watered initially the yield is diminished. Support the plants when young by using twiggy sticks. Pick the pods regularly while they are young.*

1. IN EARLY WINTER, *dig the soil and add garden compost or manure. Test if the soil is acid; dust the surface with lime in late winter if acid. Form a flat-bottomed trench, 25cm/10in wide and 6cm/2½in deep.*

2. SOW SEEDS *7.5cm/3in apart in three staggered rows in the base of the flat-bottomed trench. Alternatively, use a draw hoe to take out a pair of V-shaped drills, 6cm/2½in deep and 20cm/8in apart.*

3. IF MORE *than one row is being grown, space them to the expected height of the variety being sown, usually 45–90cm/1½–3ft. Birds soon devastate rows of newly sown seeds; place hoops of wire netting over the rows.*

POTATOES

◆

POTATOES are native to South America and when found by Spaniards were said to resemble 'floury truffles'. They were soon introduced to Europe and have become a main part of many diets. They are easily grown but must not be planted too early in cold areas as frost soon kills young stems and leaves. In autumn their growth is curtailed by frost.

PREPARING THE 'SEEDS'

The 'seeds' are small, healthy potatoes retained from the previous year's crop. These are best bought from reputable seed companies who sell virus-free stock.

They are usually bought in late winter and must be placed in clean boxes containing about 2.5cm/1in of dry peat. Space out the 'seeds', with the rose end (sprouting end) uppermost. Put them in a light, airy place such as a cool but frost-proof greenhouse or shed.

Within five to six weeks, sturdy shoots 18–25mm/³⁄₄–1in long will have formed. Leave these shoots

IN CONTAINERS

Tubs on patios make splendid novelty homes for potatoes. Plant second-early varieties on a few inches of compost in a tub and cover with 13cm/5in of friable soil or compost, adding more as the stems grow. Growing-bags are other suitable containers.

intact, taking care not to knock them off when planting. This process of encouraging shoots to form is known as 'chitting'. It is essential for early varieties, and beneficial for main-crop types. Chitting potatoes encourages rapid growth.

PREPARING THE SOIL

Dig the soil in late summer, but do not add manure. Neither apply lime in late winter but dust the surface and rake in a general fertilizer a couple of weeks before planting is to be carried out.

VARIETIES

Potato varieties are classified according to the time they can be planted.

First-early potatoes

These are the first varieties to be ready for harvesting. The 'seed' potatoes are planted in early spring (a few weeks later in cold areas) and tubers harvested in early and mid-summer.
• *'Arran Pilot': Heavy cropping, but not suitable for cold areas.*
• *'Duke of York': Succeeds in most areas and soil.*
• *'Epicure': Ideal in cold areas.*
• *'Sutton's Foremost': High yield and good flavour.*

Second-early potatoes

These are planted in mid-spring and harvested in mid- to late summer.
• *'Estima': Heavy cropping.*
• *'Great Scot': Heavy crops and stores well. Ideal for baking.*
• *'Wilja': High, reliable yields. Good flavour.*

Main-crop potatoes

These are planted in the latter part of mid-spring and harvested in early and mid-autumn. It is also possible to lift some in late summer for immediate use.
• *'Desirée': Good flavour and resistant to drought.*
• *'Majestic': An old variety; ideal for making chips.*

HARVESTING

This is also known as 'lifting' and must be tackled with care to avoid damaging the potatoes. Do not lift early varieties before the flowers are fully open. Then, use a trowel to remove soil and to check if the tubers are about the size of a hen's egg. If possible, use a potato fork to lift them. To harvest main-crop varieties, cut off the leaves and stems once they have withered and turned brown. Clear this away and a week later dig up the tubers. Allow the tubers to dry on the soil's surface for a few hours, then place in boxes and store in a dark, frost-free shed.

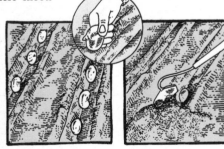

1. IN EARLY *and mid-spring, use a spade or draw hoe to form 15cm/6in deep drills. For early varieties, space the rows 60cm/2ft apart, but for main-crop types make the spacings wider at 75cm/2½ft.*

2. PLANT *'seed' potatoes in the bases of the V-drills. Space the 'seeds' of early varieties 30cm/12in apart; put main-crop types 38cm/15in apart. Position the buds (eyes) so that they face upwards.*

3. MARK THE *ends of the rows and use a draw hoe to pull soil over the 'seed' potatoes and to form a ridge 10–15cm/4–6in high. Take care not to damage the potatoes by hoeing deeply or across rows.*

4. THROUGHOUT *summer, water the soil and regularly draw up soil around the shoots. Do not completely cover the leaves. Eventually, the ridges will be 30–38cm/12–15in high. Earthing-up helps kill weeds.*

5. EARLY *varieties can be dug up during early and mid-summer. Use a potato fork (it has wide, flat tines) to carefully dig up the potatoes. Main-crop varieties are harvested from late summer onwards.*

6. REMOVE *all soil and store the tubers in boxes in a frost-free, dry, vermin-proof shed. Regularly inspect the tubers and remove those showing signs of decay. If left, the rot spreads to all the other potatoes.*

PARSNIPS

DIG soil in early winter but do not add manure or garden compost. Neither add lime in late winter, but a couple of weeks before sowing, rake in a general fertilizer. Stony soil and fresh manure soon distort and split parsnip roots.

EXHIBITION PARSNIPS

Growing exhibition parsnips is not difficult. Dig the soil deeply in early winter; do not add manure or compost. In spring, use a crow-bar to form holes about 90cm/3ft deep. Fill these with potting soil and sow seeds of an exhibition variety in the normal way.

Throughout summer, keep the soil moist to prevent roots cracking. Lift them only slightly prior to the exhibition day. Cut off any rootlets, wash off soil and wrap the roots in damp cloth to reduce the chance of them cracking.

HARVESTING

Some varieties mature early, but most parsnips are left until the foliage begins to die down in autumn. Frost soon causes the foliage to brown and die. Indeed, it is often claimed that the roots are sweeter and better after the onset of frost in autumn or winter.

VARIETIES

- *'Avonresister': Ideal in small gardens, as it takes less space than normal types. Sow spaced clusters of seeds every 7.5cm/3in, not the normal 15cm/6in.*
- *'Gladiator': A hybrid variety that is resistant to canker and is very early maturing.*
- *'Hollow Crown Improved': Long roots and often used for exhibition, as well as in kitchens.*
- *'Offenham': Broad-shouldered variety and ideal for growing on shallow soils.*
- *'Tender and True': Very long roots, resistant to canker and revealing a good flavour.*

RADISHES

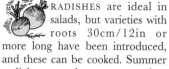

RADISHES are ideal in salads, but varieties with roots 30cm/12in or more long have been introduced, and these can be cooked. Summer radishes are the most popular, while early crops can be grown by using cloches (see below). Also, there are winter types (right).

EARLY RADISHES

Dig the soil in autumn, and in early winter break down the surface with a rake and place low cloches in a row over the soil. Placing the cloches over soil, in advance of sowing, helps it to warm up and to encourage rapid germination. Sow seeds in mid- or late winter, 12mm/½in deep in rows 10cm/4in apart. Thin the seedlings to 2.5cm/1in apart. Use a quick-maturing variety such as the popular 'Scarlet Globe' with round, bright red roots.

WINTER RADISHES

These are sown in the same way as summer types, but the rows spaced 23cm/9in apart. Thin the seedlings to about 15cm/6in apart. Re-firm soil around the roots and keep the ground moist. During late autumn, lift the roots. Store them in boxes of dry sand.

VARIETIES

Summer radishes
- *'April Cross': Roots 30–38cm/12–15in long.*
- *'Cherry Belle': Globular.*
- *'French Breakfast': Oblong.*
- *'Juliette': Globular.*
- *'Pontvil': Oblong.*
- *'Prinz Rotin': Globular.*
- *'Red Prince': Globular.*
- *'Scarlet Globe': Globular.*

Winter radishes
- *'Black Spanish Round': Large and globular.*
- *'Black Spanish Long': Roots up to 30cm/12in long.*
- *'Mino Early': Long roots, up to 30cm/12in long, and with a mild flavour.*

1. IN EARLY SPRING *sow three seeds (about 2.5cm/1in apart) in clusters 15cm/6in apart in drills 12–18mm/ ½–¾in deep. Space the drills 30cm/12in apart if more than one row of parsnips is being grown.*

2. KEEP *the soil moist and when the seedlings have germinated and produced several leaves, thin each cluster to the strongest and healthiest seedling. Re-firm the soil by gently watering the plants.*

3. HOE BETWEEN *the rows, taking care not to damage the plants. Water the soil regularly, especially during dry periods. From autumn onwards, use a garden fork to dig up and to lift the roots.*

   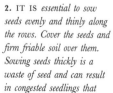

1. FROM *mid-spring to late summer, sow seeds every two weeks. Form drills 12mm/½in deep and 15cm/6in apart. Do not space the rows any closer, as it is then difficult to step between them.*

2. IT IS *essential to sow seeds evenly and thinly along the rows. Cover the seeds and firm friable soil over them. Sowing seeds thickly is a waste of seed and can result in congested seedlings that encourage diseases.*

3. GERMINATION *takes between five and seven days and when the seedlings are established and large enough to handle, thin them to 2.5cm/1in apart. Re-settle the soil around the roots by watering it.*

SHALLOTS

SHALLOTS have a milder flavour than onions and therefore are often more popular. They are planted in late winter and by the latter part of mid-summer a single bulb will have produced a cluster of eight to twelve bulbs (often known as daughter bulbs). From a row 3m/10ft long of newly planted shallot bulbs, expect to harvest about 3kg/7lb of new bulbs. They are easily grown and for gardeners new to vegetable growing can be a very satisfying crop to grow. The bulbs remain in good condition for a long time after harvesting.

VARIETIES

• *'Dutch Yellow': Popular, widely grown and frequently used in the kitchen.*
• *'Golden Gourmet': Large crops of bulbs that store well.*
• *'Hative de Niort': Deep-brown skin and widely grown by exhibitors. Well-shaped bulbs, but few in number.*

GARLIC

This bulbous-rooted plant is better known in Continental cookery than in Britain. It has a strong flavour and bouquet and must be used sparingly. Well-drained soil and a sunny position are essential. In late winter, buy a few garlic bulbs from a greengrocer and split them into cloves (segments). Plant them 2.5cm/1in deep – and with their pointed-end uppermost – 10cm/4in apart in rows with 20cm/8in between them. Looking after them is easy; just remove weeds and keep the soil moist during dry periods. In late summer the leaves turn yellow and bend over. Use a garden fork to loosen soil under them and place the bulbs on the surface to dry and ripen. Store them in a frost-free and airy shed.

SPINACH

SPINACH has its admirers and is acclaimed when combined with poached eggs. Fertile, moisture-retentive soil and regular watering are essential for this crop. In early winter, dig the soil and add plenty of well-rotted garden compost or manure. Dust the soil with lime in late winter if it is acid, and rake in a general fertilizer a couple of weeks before sowing the seeds.

VARIETIES

Summer spinach
• *'King of Denmark': An old variety, with leaves borne well above soil level and therefore not readily splashed by rain first falling on soil.*
• *'Long-standing Round': Ideal for early sowings.*
• *'Norvak': Relatively new. Prolific crops and ideal for sowing in mid-summer.*
• *'Sigmaleaf': Long cropping, and can also be used as a winter variety.*

WINTER SPINACH

By sowing seeds in late summer and early autumn it is possible to produce spinach for harvesting from mid-autumn to mid-spring.

Choose a sunny site, with well-drained but moisture-retentive soil. The soil should have been dug during the previous early winter and garden compost or manure added. In late summer, lightly fork the soil, rake level and sow seeds 18mm/¾in deep in drills 38cm/15in apart. After germination, first thin the seedlings to 7.5cm/3in apart, later 15cm/6in. Harvest the leaves when ready and from mid-autumn cover with cloches.

Varieties to choose include 'Monnopa' (good flavour), 'Sigmaleaf' (see summer varieties) and 'Broad-leaved Prickly' (dark green and fleshy leaves). In addition, the plants do not readily run to seed (bolt).

1. DIG SOIL *in early winter and add well-decayed manure or compost. In mid-winter, check that the soil is not acid. In late winter, push shallot bulbs into the soil, 15cm/6in apart in rows 20cm/8in apart.*

2. LEAVE *each bulb's top slightly above the surface and cover with a hoop of wire netting as protection against birds. Use an onion hoe to remove weeds and in mid-summer scrape soil from around each bulb.*

3. FROM *mid-summer onwards, as soon as the leaves become yellow, use a garden fork to dig up clusters of bulbs. Brush off the soil and separate them into individual bulbs. Store in a cool, dry, airy shed.*

1. SOW SEEDS *every two weeks from early spring to mid-summer. Form drills 12–18mm/½ – ¾in deep and 30cm/12in apart. Draw soil over the drills and firm it. Gently but thoroughly water the soil.*

2. KEEP *the soil moist. Germination takes up to three weeks and when the seedlings are established, thin them to 7.5cm/3in apart. Later, when the leaves touch, thin them to 15cm/6in apart.*

3. FROM *sowing to maturing takes up to thirteen weeks (slightly less for sowings in early and mid-summer). Harvest the leaves as soon as they are a reasonable size, starting with the outer ones.*

TOMATOES

OUTDOOR tomatoes are very quickly killed by frost and therefore cannot be planted outside until late spring or early summer, when the risk of cold nights has passed. Prepare the soil in early winter by digging in plenty of well-decayed garden compost or manure. In late winter, dust the soil with lime if it is acid (see page 228).

PLANTS AND PLANTING

Plants are raised from seeds sown in 13°C/55°F in a greenhouse, but if only a few plants are needed it is better to buy them. Choose sturdy plants, about 20cm/8in high and with dark green leaves. Do not buy thin and lanky plants, with long spaces between the leaf joints. These will never recover and become strong.

When planting, ensure that the top of the root-ball is only fractionally below the surface of the soil. Water the soil thoroughly after planting and use slug pellets to protect the plants, which are soon damaged by slugs.

VARIETIES

There is a wide range of tomato varieties to grow outdoors. Most are grown as cordons (upright and supported by a cane) while some are bush types, usually no more than 75cm/2½ft high, but sometimes less.

Cordon tomatoes
- *'Alicante': 60cm/2ft apart.*
- *'Moneymaker': 75cm/2½ft apart.*
- *'Outdoor Girl': 60cm/2ft apart.*
- *'Sweet 100': 75cm/2½ft apart. Masses of cherry-sized fruits.*

Bush tomatoes
- *'Florida Petit': 23–30cm/ 9–12in apart. Ideal for windowboxes.*
- *'Pixie': 45cm/1½ft apart.*
- *'Red Alert': 45cm/1½ft apart.*
- *'Sub-arctic Plenty': 45cm/ 1½ft apart. Early cropping. It is ideal for cool areas.*
- *'Tiny Tim': 30–80cm/12–15in.*

4. WHEN *a plant has formed four trusses (a flower stem which later will bear fruits) snap off the leading shoot just above the second leaf above it. Outdoor plants will not normally produce and ripen more than four trusses.*

5. PICK *the fruits when ripe. While picking them, do not squeeze. Instead, hold them in the palm of your hand and snap off the stem so that the calyx (the green, star-like growth) is attached to the fruit.*

6. IN EARLY AUTUMN *cut the tomato plants from their supports and lay them in a line on a bed of straw. Tall cloches can then be placed over them and the fruits left to ripen. Water the soil, but do not dampen the fruits.*

TOMATOES ON A PATIO

Warm, wind-sheltered patios are ideal homes for tomatoes, whether in growing-bags, pots, windowboxes or hanging baskets. It is essential, however, to select the right variety for each place. Some varieties are 'cordon' types, and therefore need to have sideshoots removed; 'bush' types do not. When planting tomatoes in window boxes, choose varieties such as 'Tiny Tim' and 'Florida Petit'.

TOMATOES IN HANGING BASKETS

Hanging baskets are unusual places for tomato plants. It is essential to choose suitable varieties and to ensure that the compost does not become dry. The variety 'Tumbler' is ideal, with sweetly-flavoured, bright red, cherry-like fruits. Do not put the plants outside until all risk of frost has passed, and select a warm, sunny and wind-sheltered position. Use a large hanging basket and line it with a thick layer of sphagnum moss to help retain moisture in the compost.

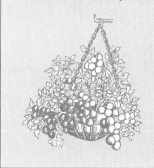

1. WHEN *all risk of frost has passed, knock in 1.5– 1.8m/5–6ft-long posts, spacing them 45cm/1½ft apart and with 75–90cm/ 2½–3ft between the rows. Position a plant on the sunny side of each post.*

2. TAKE *care not to damage the stem when setting a plant in position. Make sure that the top of the soil-ball is fractionally below the surface. Tie the stem to the cane, taking care to allow for subsequent growth.*

3. CONTINUE *to tie the stem to a supporting cane or pole, and remove shoots that develop from the leaf joints. Bend them sideways until they snap off. However, do not remove those growing on bush varieties.*

STANDARD *sized growing-bags create ideal homes for two cordon-type plants. Ensure the compost remains evenly moist and use proprietary wire frames to support the plants.*

SWEETCORN

WEETCORN must be grown in blocks, rather than in single lines, to assist with pollination. Seeds can be sown where they will grow or, for early crops and especially in cool regions, plants can be raised in gentle warmth (see details below).

Prepare the soil in early winter by digging and adding decayed garden compost or manure. In late winter, apply lime if the soil is acid. Later, in mid-spring, dust the surface with a general fertilizer and rake it into the soil.

1. WHEN *the risk of frost has passed, sow seeds 2.5cm/1in deep, in clusters of three, spaced 38cm/15in apart within rows 45cm/1½ft apart. This is usually in late spring, although in cold areas a little later.*

2. AFTER *germination and when the plants are established, remove the weakest seedlings to leave one plant in each position. Re-firm soil around them and in summer water plants during dry periods.*

3. IN LATE SUMMER, *harvest the heads when the silks (at the top of the cob) have withered and the grains, when pressed, exude a creamy liquid. Twist the cob downwards to remove it.*

RAISING EARLY PLANTS

*In mid-spring, sow seeds in a greenhouse. Use 7.5cm/3in-wide peat pots (to avoid root disturbance later) and sow two seeds, 2.5cm/1in deep, in each pot. Water and place in gentle warmth (10–13°C/50–55°F). After germination, remove the weaker seedlings, reduce the temperature slightly and slowly acclimatize plants to outdoor conditions. Plant them outdoors only when all risk of frost has passed. An alternative method is to sow seeds outdoors and to cover them with cloches. Put the cloches in place about three weeks before sowing in late spring, so the soil can warm up.*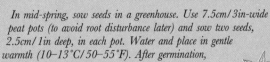

TURNIPS

TURNIPS are too frequently considered to be tough and woody vegetables eaten solely during winter. They are not; indeed, early sowings can be used in salads, while later crops are harvested in summer. Main-crop turnips are ready for lifting in autumn for eating in winter.

During early winter, dig the soil but do not add garden compost or manure. Do not add lime but a couple of weeks before sowing seeds in mid-spring, dust and rake in a general fertilizer.

 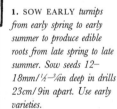 

1. SOW EARLY *turnips from early spring to early summer to produce edible roots from late spring to late summer. Sow seeds 12–18mm/½–¾in deep in drills 23cm/9in apart. Use early varieties.*

2. EARLY *sowings are usually left unthinned and the plants pulled up and eaten raw in salads. If larger roots are wanted from these early sowings, thin the seedlings so that they are 13cm/5in apart.*

3. MAIN-CROP TURNIPS *are sown during mid-summer to produce roots for lifting during early and mid-autumn. Thin these to 23cm/9in apart: these are the ones for storing and use during winter.*

TURNIP TOPS AS GREENS

Turnips tops are a popular vegetable for harvesting in early and mid-spring. Choose a main-crop variety and sow seeds in early autumn, 12–18mm/½–¾in deep in drills only 10cm/4in apart. By sowing seeds evenly and thinly the young seedlings do not need to be thinned. During early spring, when the tops are 10–15cm/4–6in high, harvest the leaves, but leave the roots to sprout again for a further crop. In mild areas, several crops can be cut from them.

LOOKING AFTER PLANTS

❖

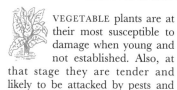VEGETABLE plants are at their most susceptible to damage when young and not established. Also, at that stage they are tender and likely to be attacked by pests and diseases (see pages 340 to 343).

Keeping the soil free from weeds and watering plants is a major task and one that takes the most time. Regularly hoe between plants, especially after applying powdered fertilizers. If hoeing is neglected there is a chance that the fertilizer will be washed into contact with young, soft stems and leaves and burn them.

Take great care when using weed-killing chemicals in vegetable plots, as there is a chance that chemicals could drift on the wind and kill plants other than weeds. And before using weed-killers always check with the label. The problem of using weed-killers is increased in small vegetable plots and especially where a wide range of plants are grown; some may be nearly mature, while others are perhaps at their seedling stage.

WEEDS *are a continual problem in vegetable gardens and must be removed before they suffocate young plants. Always dig up and burn perennial weeds; if parts are left in the soil they will continue to grow.*

PULL UP *annual weeds and place on a compost heap. Never leave them on the soil as they encourage the presence of pests and onset of diseases. Watering the soil the previous day makes them easier to pull up.*

REGULARLY *hoe between rows of seedlings and plants to eradicate weeds. Hoeing breaks up crusty soil and allows air and water to enter more freely. Additionally, a fine tilth acts as a mulch and reduces moisture loss.*

WATERING *plants is essential, especially when they are young and not fully established. Watering-cans are ideal for watering newly transplanted plants, or young seedlings when they have been recently thinned.*

ROTARY SPRAYERS *enable large areas to be watered. Gentle sprays over a long period are better than a flood of water for a few minutes, which may cause soil erosion or damage to the soil structure.*

OSCILLATING SPRAYERS *are better than rotary ones when watering rectangular areas. Several types are available; avoid those that produce large water droplets, especially if the garden is on a slope.*

ONION HOES *are ideal for hoeing around seedlings and small plants. Pick up annual weeds and place them on a compost heap. Keeping the hoe's blade sharp by using a file makes it much more efficient to use.*

BLACK PLASTIC *is ideal for forming a mulch. Remove weeds and water the soil, then roll out the plastic and insert its edges into small slit-trenches. When planting, make small slits in the plastic.*

FORMING *a 7.5cm/3in-thick layer of well-decayed garden compost around plants (but not touching) prevents weed growth and keeps the soil moist. Before applying, remove all weeds and water the soil.*

WATER TIMERS

Watering vegetable plots and other parts of gardens is far more sophisticated now than it was ten or more years ago. Nowadays, it is possible to use a battery-operated timer which turns water on and off at pre-set times. This enables water to be applied at night when the loss through evaporation is much less than during a hot day. Each timer must be fitted close to the mains water supply and all joints between it and the tap made secure. If these junctions are weak or ill-fitting they will drip water. And if the tap is left on and with the timer operating throughout a holiday, the area could become excessively wet. Always remember to check with your local water authority to find out if a special licence is required to operate a garden sprinkler.

DRIBBLE BARS *which fit on spouts of watering-cans are ideal for applying weed-killing chemicals. Keep a watering-can specially for this job and always carefully read instructions for the chemical's use.*

PROTECTION FROM BIRDS

Tunnels formed of wire netting are ideal for protecting seeds and young seedlings from the ravages of birds. Use wire hooks to secure the edges to the ground and place netting over the ends to prevent birds wandering inside the wire hoop, scratching about and totally disturbing the soil and seeds.

GREENHOUSE GARDENING

A greenhouse introduces an entirely new facet to gardening; apart from making it possible to raise many new plants from seeds and cuttings, it also creates the opportunity to grow vegetables like tomatoes and cucumbers in summer and to raise flowering plants which can later be taken indoors to decorate rooms.

This chapter gives a thorough insight into the range of greenhouses, their selection and positioning and types of glazing materials. Heating a greenhouse – as well as conserving heat – is important and a range of suitable methods is indicated. Ventilation and shading are essential to the well-being of green plants and these aspects, too, are featured, together with composts, watering and feeding. There is also information about cloches and garden frames.

Because the temperature at which a greenhouse is kept influences the types of plants that can be grown, there is detailed information about plants which suit cold, cool, and warm conditions.

RANGE OF GREENHOUSES

❖

THERE are greenhouses to suit gardens of all sizes and shapes. Mini-greenhouses are ideal in small gardens and on patios while on a grander scale, free-standing types enable a wider range of plants to be grown. Sunrooms and conservatories also introduce a new gardening dimension and are especially suitable for growing large, long-term foliage plants, such as palms.

SHAPES AND SIZES

Whatever the size of greenhouse you initially estimate to suit your needs, double it! Invariably, after gardening in a greenhouse for several months, you will wish to extend the range of plants.

The smaller the greenhouse the more rapid and extreme the tem-perature changes. Those at mid-day and during the afternoon may be excessive, while at night they fall suddenly. A greenhouse about 3.6m/12ft long and 2.4m/8ft wide is about the optimum size, having a volume of air that avoids sudden temperature changes.

There also must be provision for adequate ventilation, and this is discussed on page 257.

The range of greenhouses now available includes:

• <u>Full-span greenhouses</u>, with a ridge and two eaves, are tradition-al and widely available. Wooden and earlier types often have bricks or wooden panels up to about 75cm/2¹/2ft high. Modern, alu-minium-framed types, however, are completely glazed. Green-houses up to 2.4m/8ft wide have central paths about 60cm/2ft wide and 90cm/3ft-wide spaces on either side for staging or growing plants at ground level.

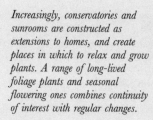

A PLACE TO RELAX

Increasingly, conservatories and sunrooms are constructed as extensions to homes, and create places in which to relax and grow plants. A range of long-lived foliage plants and seasonal flowering ones combines continuity of interest with regular changes.

• <u>Lean-to types</u> vary in length and width to suit the wall or house they are constructed against. Most have brick or wood-en walls up to 75cm/2¹/2ft high, with a framework in wood or alu-minium. Traditional types are 1.8m/6ft to 2.1m/7ft wide, but some – a compromise between mini-greenhouses and normal lean-to types – are 1.2m/4ft wide, and only large enough for a path and a few shelves.

Some lean-to greenhouses are large enough to form sunrooms and conservatories. Modern forms of these have assumed ornate Victorian styles, with double-glazing and a plastic framework. These create comfortable living areas for plants and people, but ensure they provide plenty of ven-tilation, in both the sides and roof. Too often, conservatory designers appear more concerned with heat conservation than releasing exces-sively hot air in summer, which soon kills plants and makes living in them unbearable.

FULL-SPAN *(also known as even-span) greenhouses have traditional outlines, with a ridge and two eaves. Earlier ones had brick sides up to about 75cm/2¹/2ft high, but recent types, especially when made of aluminium, have glass from ground to eaves. An alternative to bricks is wood. Most free-standing green-houses are now full-span types, although three-quarter types are sold – one side is wider than the other.*

LEAN-TO *greenhouses utilize warm, sunny walls both to economize on materials and for the warmth they retain and reflect. Many lean-to types have brick or wooden sides up to about 75cm/ 2¹/2ft high.*

HEXAGONAL *greenhouses are of a more recent design and have the advantage of absorbing the sun's rays from many angles. Some of these greenhouses have a wooden or brick framework at their bases; others are completely glazed.*

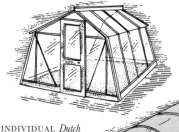

INDIVIDUAL *Dutch lights are, commercially, frequently formed into greenhouses, sometimes as temporary constructions but often as permanent features. They allow plenty of light to enter greenhouses and are ideal for plants growing directly in the soil. Lettuces and tomatoes are popular crops to grow in them, as they thrive on a large amount of light.*

PLASTIC *tunnels are made from heavy-gauge, clear or opaque plastic sheeting stretched over giant metal hoops and secured at ground level. Three or four years is usually the maximum life of the sheeting.*

MINIATURE *lean-to greenhouses are increasingly popular, especially in small gardens and on patios. They are only about 60cm/2ft deep and 1.5m/5ft to the eaves. They are stood on bricks, and for safety, firmly secured to a wall.*

FRAMING AND FLOORING

❖

ALTHOUGH some greenhouses have been made of steel (which soon corrodes) and modern conservatories are double-glazed and have decay-proof plastic-type frames, to most gardeners the choice of a greenhouse is between wood and aluminium. Plastic tunnels are used commercially, but in a garden lack permanency and the attractive visual appeal of traditional wooden greenhouses.

TIMBER CONSTRUCTIONS

The life expectancy of timber-framed greenhouses depends on the type of timber used and its maintenance. Baltic redwood, also known as yellow deal, is frequently used but needs regular painting, as well as being initially treated with a wood preservative. If neglected, extremes of temperature, both inside and outside, as well as high humidity, peel paint off the glazing bars. Additionally, the wood may eventually warp and both doors and ventilators cease to fit properly, allowing in draughts.

Western red cedar is more durable, but instead of being preserved by coats of white paint is coated in linseed oil. And rust-proof brass or galvanized nails are used in its construction.

Oak and teak have been used and are long lasting. Unfortunately, they are prohibitively expensive materials. Many early Victorian conservatories were constructed from these woods and lasted well into this century.

If the border soil is free from pests or diseases, plants such as tomatoes can be grown directly in it.

Solid-based staging is ideal for plants in summer, helping to create a humid atmosphere around them.

Slatted staging is ideal for plants in winter, helping to create a flow of air around them.

Growing-bags are ideal if the border soil is contaminated with pests or diseases.

Watering-cans with long spouts enable plants at the backs of staging to be reached.

Paths may be formed of paving slabs placed either directly on soil or on a bed of sand.

Store pots, seed-trays and boxes under staging. But ensure they are clean and not contaminated with pests or diseases.

ALUMINIUM FRAMEWORK

Most greenhouses are now made of aluminium and have the advantage of not needing any maintenance. Additionally, the supporting framework and glazing bars can be narrower than wooden ones, enabling more light to reach the plants. This is especially beneficial during autumn, winter and also in the early spring.

FLOORING

The easiest way to create a path is to lay paving-slabs either directly on the soil or on a layer of sand. If, at some later time, the layout of the greenhouse needs to be changed, they can be moved.

Conservatories, of course, need more permanent flooring and this is provided by concrete with tiles or some other surface on top.

WOODEN FRAMEWORK

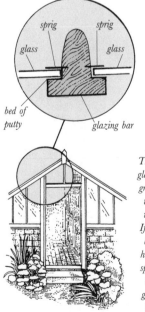

sprig *sprig*
glass *glass*
bed of putty
glazing bar

ALUMINIUM FRAMEWORK

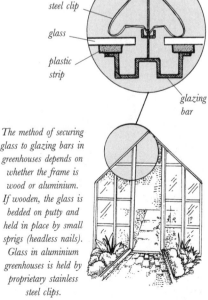

proprietary stainless steel clip
glass
plastic strip
glazing bar

The method of securing glass to glazing bars in greenhouses depends on whether the frame is wood or aluminium. If wooden, the glass is bedded on putty and held in place by small sprigs (headless nails). Glass in aluminium greenhouses is held by proprietary stainless steel clips.

RAISING THE ROOF

Positioning the roofing trusses of the glass Exhibition Building, later to be known as the Crystal Palace, demanded power and precision. The building, constructed in Hyde Park, London, was opened by Queen Victoria on May Day, 1851.

GLAZING MATERIALS

❖

ALTHOUGH initially expensive during the early 1800s, glass has proved to be the best covering for greenhouses, sunrooms and conservatories. The greatest impetus to its use in Britain was the abolition of the glass tax in the mid-1800s and the construction of the glass-clad Exhibition Hall for the Great Exhibition of 1851.

Early greenhouses had panes of glass 30cm/12in or less wide, but when glass-making techniques improved these became 45cm/1¹/₂ft wide and are now frequently 60cm/2ft across. The use of wider panes was made possible by the introduction of extruded aluminium glazing bars, which are both stronger and lighter than wooden types.

Glass used in greenhouses must be free from bubbles, with a standard weight of 7.32kg/sq cm (24oz/sq ft). The total weight of glass in a greenhouse is considerable, giving the framework rigidity as well as weight to resist winds and storms.

When clean, only 75–80% of the available light passes through, but if dirty this decreases dramatically. In summer, this reduction is not a problem, as the glass will probably be covered in a shading material, but in winter and spring all available light is needed.

THE GREENHOUSE EFFECT

Radiation from the sun contains infra-red radiation as well as visible and ultra-violet radiation. When this radiation reaches a greenhouse, the glass reflects long-wavelength infra-red radiation, but allows short-wavelength infra-red

radiation as well as visible light to pass through. These are then absorbed by the soil and plants, thereby raising the temperature. Additionally, infra-red radiation emitted by the soil and plants is of a longer wavelength and does not pass back out through the glass. Therefore it becomes trapped inside the greenhouse, causing the temperature to rise yet further.

If this continued, the temperature within a greenhouse would become unbearable. Therefore, provision must be made to open up ventilators to make the temperature suitable for the plants. Low external temperatures, and wind and rain are also resonsible for decreasing temperatures within the greenhouse and make heating the structure very expensive.

OTHER GLAZING MATERIALS

Many materials other than glass have been used to create a clear covering for greenhouses. Indeed, the Romans some two thousand years ago use thin sheets of mica in frames to cover plants.

Sheets of polycarbonate, 3mm/¹/₈in thick are amazingly strong – thick sheets are said to be bullet-proof! – and about one-third of the weight of glass. But although tough and initially allowing about 85% of light to pass through, it deteriorates after about fifteen years and eventually its structure breaks down.

Acrylic is slightly cheaper but unfortunately also has the ageing problems of polycarbonate.

SHATTERPROOF
GREENHOUSES

Shatterproof materials, such as moulded polycarbonate, have been used in glazing the upper parts of greenhouses, with lower and less vulnerable panels fitted with glass.

Hooped tunnels are covered with sheets of clear or opaque plastic, but they do not have the good warmth-retention properties of glass and after a few years discolour and perish due to the action of ultra-violet light. In commercial horticulture, these structures are very popular and create inexpensive protection for plants.

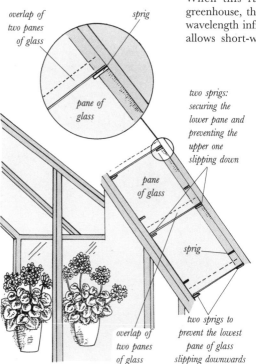

overlap of two panes of glass

sprig

pane of glass

pane of glass

sprig

overlap of two panes of glass

two sprigs: securing the lower pane and preventing the upper one slipping down

SECURING
THE GLASS

Aluminium-framed greenhouses are glazed using proprietary clips (page 252), but wooden greenhouses need a different technique. Individual panes of glass are bedded on a thin, even layer of putty, then held in place with small sprigs. Each pane is secured by four sprigs; the upper two also prevent the pane above slipping downwards. Glaze the roof from the eaves to the ridge, to enable the panes of glass to overlap.

two sprigs to prevent the lowest pane of glass slipping downwards

GLASS BLOWING

In 1845, the British glass-making industry had a swingeing tax removed and glass immediately began a revival in greenhouses and conservatories. Before this, only great estates could afford to construct glasshouses. At the end of the nineteenth century, some greenhouses at the Royal Botanic Gardens, Kew, were glazed with green glass to prevent the sun's rays scorching plants, but when plants under clear glass grew faster, it was removed.

STAGING AND SHELVING

CREATING surfaces on which plants can be displayed is important, as well as forming working areas where seed sowing, potting and other tasks can be performed at a convenient level, about hip or waist height.

In some greenhouses, the staging is a permanent feature, especially for displaying plants such as orchids where it is often tiered. Increasingly, however, flexibility of use is all important: many aluminium greenhouses have hinged shelves that can be lowered to allow plants growing at ground-level to develop.

The range of staging has widened dramatically in recent years and includes:

• Traditional staging – especially in wooden greenhouses – is formed of 5cm/2in-wide wood slats with about 2.5cm/1in between them. This creates a flow of air around plants and is especially beneficial in winter when moisture lingering on leaves readily encourages the presence of diseases. The slatted base also enables the free drainage of surplus water if plants have been excessively watered.

• Small-mesh, galvanized or plastic-covered netting nailed to a wooden framework also creates an airy base, but after several years tends to sag between the supports. Nevertheless, it is relatively inexpensive and quick to construct.

• Solid staging, where a continuous, firm base is covered with a shallow layer of pea-sized gravel chippings is ideal in summer. The chippings retain moisture and create humidity around plants. Alpine plants are frequently buried to their rims in the gravel, which also helps to keep their roots cool, while other plants are just stood on top. Other base materials include grit and expanded clay particles. All of these must be clean and free from diseases.

• Mist-propagation units – used to encourage cuttings to root quickly – need a firm, waterproof base. A wooden base and surround, covered with thick plastic sheeting, is an easy way to provide this. Access to water and electricity are essential: have the unit installed by a competent electrician and ensure all necessary safety devices are installed.

• Temporary shelving is often needed for boxes of seeds or seedlings in spring and early summer. Provide these by suspending long, narrow shelves from the glazing bars: if wooden, screw cables to the framework, but in aluminium greenhouses proprietary fittings are available. Take care when watering plants on the shelves that water does not drip on plants below. Also, remember that areas near the glass are the first to experience low-temperature falls during cold nights. It may be necessary to cover temporarily with sheets of newspaper at night. The insulating property of newspapers is high.

• Tubular metal frameworks with slatted or solid surfaces are ideal both as permanent or even as temporary fixtures.

• Tiered staging – usually permanent – is ideal for orchids, but ensure it is well constructed.

• Hinged, wire-framed staging is frequently available for fitting into aluminium houses, and has the advantage of being quickly collapsed when not required. Also, because it remains in the greenhouse there is not a storage problem. However, it does need to be thoroughly scrubbed and cleaned at the end of each growing season to ensure diseases are not present.

SOME *plants, especially alpines, benefit from their pots being partly buried in clean gravel chippings. Other plants can just be stood on the surface. Moisture around the gravel rises and creates a desirable humid atmosphere around the plants.*

FIRM, *secure surfaces are needed for mist propagation units. The base has to support and contain moist sand as well as cuttings. A wooden framework, about 10cm/4in deep and lined with plastic, creates a waterproof base.*

SLATTED *staging is ideal for supporting plants that need a flow of dry air around their leaves. In winter, this is especially beneficial, when moisture lingering around foliage quickly encourages the spread of diseases.*

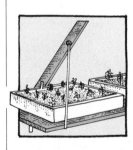

IN SPRING, *there is often a shortage of space. Narrow shelves can be suspended from wooden glazing bars, or from special brackets in aluminium constructions. When watering, take care moisture does not drip on plants below.*

MOVABLE *tubular staging is ideal where seeds of summer-flowering bedding plants are grown in spring and early summer, and the space is later needed for plants growing in pots or growing-bags at ground level in summer.*

TIERED *wooden staging both displays plants so that they can be easily seen and allows a good circulation of air around them. Orchids especially benefit from this form of staging. Ensure each tier of the staging is firmly constructed.*

HEATING

FOR tropical and subtropical plants to be grown in temperate regions it is necessary to heat greenhouses during part or all of the year. Some plants can be grown in unheated greenhouses, but usually if the temperature falls dramatically and unexpectedly they will be damaged. Heating costs can be dramatically reduced by just using a greenhouse in spring and summer, perhaps to raise summer-flowering bedding plants and to grow tomatoes.

METHODS OF HEATING

These depend on the types of plants and if the structure is a greenhouse or conservatory.

• Paraffin (kerosene) heaters are relatively cheap to buy and inexpensive to operate. Also, by increasing the length of the wick the amount of heat created can be adjusted. But excessive amounts of wick create smoke.

Single and double burners – both in a range of sizes – are available. Some have hot-water pipes attached, so that warmth is given off along the pipes and from the exhausts at the ends.

When the heater is operating, oxygen is consumed and carbon dioxide given off. Therefore, unless the heater has a flue, ventilation is essential. Additionally, burning paraffin creates moisture: for every gallon of fuel burnt, a gallon of water is produced. An open ventilator will also allow this moisture to escape.

• Bottle gas heaters are easy to use, but like paraffin heaters increase the humidity. They are more expensive to operate than paraffin types and it is impossible to finely tune the amount of heat they give off – usually high or low. Also, it is necessary to have a spare gas bottle and there is little warning when a bottle is about to

PARAFFIN *(kerosene) heaters are the simplest and cheapest way to heat greenhouses. There are several sizes and as long as wicks are properly trimmed and replaced each year they are safe and pleasant to use.*

BOTTLED *gas heaters are easy to use, but more expensive than paraffin. Also, it is necessary to have two gas bottles: one in use and the other as a spare. There is little warning when a bottle is becoming empty.*

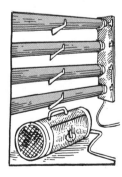

ELECTRICITY *is easily controlled, but it must be installed properly. Tubular heaters are invariably fitted against walls, but fan-heaters are best positioned on the path and opposite the door. Avoid hot blasts.*

finish. If this happens in the middle of a frosty night, the results could be disastrous.

• Electricity is ideal but expensive and therefore best installed in small greenhouses for limited periods. Temperatures can be controlled by thermostats, thereby reducing costs to a minimum. There are two types of heaters to choose from: tubular and fan.

Tubular heaters are invariably fixed to a wall and positioned about 25cm/10in above the ground. They produce a gentle flow of warm air. Ensure a 10–15cm/4–6in-wide gap is left between the back of the staging and the glass, so that heat can rise unimpeded from below.

Fan heaters create warmth and good air movement, which helps to combat fungus diseases. Do not use domestic fan heaters as they are unsafe in the high humidity of most greenhouses.

Both tubular and fan heaters produce dry heat, which may damage plants with tender leaves. Trays of water help to prevent this happening.

• Domestic heating systems can be extended to include conservatories and sunrooms. However, as the heating system is turned off at night, it may put plants at risk, especially where the construction is single-glazed. Double-glazing reduces the risk.

Clearly, the range of methods to heat greenhouses and conservatories is wide and the choice is influenced by many factors. The least expensive to install, as well as to operate, is a paraffin (kerosene) heater. It is also a flexible system as the heater can be easily moved to another greenhouse. Tubular electrical heaters, once installed are fixed, although fan types can be moved.

HEAT LOSS

The loss of warmth from a greenhouse is clearly influenced by the outside temperature. All surfaces of a greenhouse lose heat, whether glass, wood, metal or brickwork. Metal is more conductive than wood and therefore appears cooler and less cosy. Many wooden greenhouses have single-thickness brick walls at their bases, which lose warmth at about half the rate of glass. Heat loss also occurs through ill-fitting ventilators and doors, and so is avoidable in well maintained greenhouses

REDUCING HEAT LOSS

❖

Heating is a major cost factor in running a greenhouse and any way to reduce this is worth pursuing. Indeed, a wind-exposed situation or a frost-pocket could double the expense of heating a greenhouse during winter.

There are several ways to decrease the costs: correctly positioning the greenhouse, installing insulation, and carefully controlling the temperature.

POSITIONING

Orientate full-span greenhouses so that the ridge runs from east to west. This enables low, winter light to pass through the glass. Additionally, if tall plants are positioned on the side away from the sun they do not cast cooling shadows over the greenhouse.

Avoid places shaded by buildings or trees, as well as overhanging trees that might drip rain on the greenhouse.

Position the door away from prevailing winds. Most doors in metal-framed greenhouses are on runners and slide across the opening, but wooden types are hinged, if possible, so that they open away from the prevailing wind.

A hedge on the windward side helps to reduce wind speed and therefore its cooling effect. Indeed, the benefit of a hedge can be felt up to a distance of thirty times its height. For instance, a hedge 2.4m/8ft high reduces the wind's speed by 75% at a point 4.5m/15ft from it. And at a distance of 12m/40ft the reduction is still as much as 65%.

Lean-to greenhouses require warm walls, especially to encourage the development of early-maturing crops.

INSULATION

Conserving heat is essential, especially if the greenhouse is used in winter. Bubble glazing, formed of three layers of plastic with air-bubbles between them, traps warmth within the greenhouse and is especially valuable for attaching to the coldest and most exposed sides and roof. It is held in place by a range of fittings, including double-sided adhesive pads, drawing pins in wooden greenhouses and special clips in aluminium types.

Both white and green 'bubble' insulation are available: the green often makes the greenhouse too dark in winter, although if left in place in summer it creates useful shade. Other forms of insulating material include polythene sheets reinforced with wire mesh.

Large greenhouses can be made more economic to heat by partitioning them with these materials, but ensure they are firmly secured and cannot fall on top of a heater.

OPTIMUM TEMPERATURE

Clearly, the way to save money on heating is to have a 'cold house' and not provide any warmth – but this restricts the range of plants.

If the heating is limited to ensuring the temperature never falls below 7°C/45°F, this is called a 'cool house' and enables a wider range of plants to be grown.

Keeping the temperature at 16°C/61°F or more throughout the year enables tropical plants to be grown, but the cost is high.

An agreeable temperature compromise – and one that saves money – is just to heat the greenhouse in late winter and spring, when sowing seeds and raising young plants; and in summer to grow plants such as tomatoes that benefit from the protection afforded by a unheated greenhouse.

Using an electric or paraffin-heated propagator in late winter and early spring to encourage seed germination and the rooting of cuttings saves having to heat the entire greenhouse and reduces heating costs dramatically.

STOVE HOUSES

Greenhouses were first heated by stoves that were taken inside. Initially, no provision was made for hot, dangerous fumes to escape. Later, flues were installed but still plants and gardeners were at risk. Often the woodwork was set alight. However, the term 'stove' house is still used to describe very warm greenhouses.

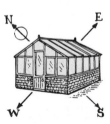

POSITION *a full-span (even span) greenhouse with its ridge from east to west. This allows maximum light to enter the structure, especially during winter. Position tall plants on the side opposite the sun, so that they do not cast shadows.*

LEAN-TO *greenhouses need warm, sun-facing walls to reduce heating costs and gain maximum light, especially in winter. Conservatories and sunrooms also need sunny situations against house walls, but sometimes this is not possible.*

AVOID *positions where trees cast shade. However, in exposed areas a windbreak or tree on the windward side helps to reduce heat loss. Position the door away from prevailing cold winds to prevent cool air rushing into the structure.*

Prevailing wind

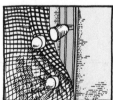

HEAT *loss can be dramatically reduced by insulating the insides of greenhouses. It is especially useful on sides exposed to cold, prevailing winds. Bubble-glazing – formed of three sheets of plastic – is especially effective.*

MANY *aluminium structures have channels in their glazing bars in which toggles can be inserted to secure insulation sheets, leaving a 2.5cm/1in gap between the material and glass. Ensure it reaches the ground and does not leave gaps.*

WARPED *ventilators and doors are a major source of heat loss. Inspect and adjust them in autumn. Avoid sealing them up in winter, as fresh air is often needed, especially when paraffin and bottle gas heaters are used to heat the structure.*

VENTILATION AND SHADING

EEPING a greenhouse, sunroom or conservatory at a temperature agreeable to plants during summer is essential. If temperatures are allowed to rise dramatically, plants soon lose moisture and eventually die. High light intensity through the glass also damages plants.

Temperatures in sunrooms and conservatories also rise quickly and, unless sufficient ventilators have been fitted, life for people as well as plants becomes unbearable.

FLOW OF AIR

Greenhouses and conservatories amply fitted with ventilators in their sides as well as roof areas have the opportunity of being well ventilated, even in summer.

On full-span greenhouses there must be ventilators on both sides, so that when cold winds are blowing only those on the lee side are opened. Cold draughts blowing on plants can cause the onset of diseases, especially in seedlings.

Preferably, roof ventilators should be fitted in every other pane of glass and in lean-to types continuously along the side. Hot air soon builds up in the roof area, and unless allowed to escape, damages plants, especially climbers with thin leaves.

Traditional wooden greenhouses with brick sides up to 75cm/2¹/₂ft high had ventilators low down that enabled an even better circulation of air.

In summer, doors can also be left open but if inquisitive birds are a problem, fit a wire-netting framework over the area. It may also be necessary to place netting over roof and side ventilators.

Automatic ventilators in both roof and side ventilators have enabled better control of summer temperatures throughout the day. Once the ventilator is installed, there is no operating cost.

Thermostatically-controlled electrically-operated extractor fans are effective and usually fitted in the gabled ends of greenhouses. Ensure louvres are fitted on the outside to prevent cold air blowing into the greenhouse.

SHADING

Strong light both damages plants and dramatically increases the temperature. The cheapest and easiest way to create shade is to paint the outside of the glass with a proprietary shading liquid. Do not paint the glazing bars and, if only light shading is needed, just coat the central two-thirds of each pane. Weather often removes the paint and during mid- to late summer fresh applications may possibly be needed.

Roller blinds, in varying widths, are better as they can be rolled up or down according to the weather. Some are made of canes, others slatted wood. Cheaper forms of roller blinds are formed from polypropylene netting, just flopped over the sunny side. Sheets of polythene can also be used.

Venetian blinds and roller blinds can be fitted to the insides of sunrooms and conservatories. Some of these are horizontal, while others are vertical and do not so easily collect dust.

VENTILATORS

Before buying a greenhouse, sunroom or conservatory, check that there are ventilators in the roof area that will enable hot air to easily escape.

On full-span greenhouses there must be roof ventilators on both sides, preferably every other pane of glass. Side ventilators are also essential. Ideally, lean-to greenhouses need continuous ventilators in the roof.

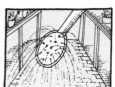

DURING *summer, light intensity – even in temperate zones – can be too strong for many plants. The easiest, quickest and cheapest way to reduce this is to paint the glass with a proprietary shading liquid.*

ROLLER *blinds are costly to install but better than using a shading paint. They can be rolled up and down as the light intensity changes. This is advantageous during periods when the weather is unpredictable.*

FINE-MESHED *sheets of weather-resistant polypropylene netting, as well as polythene sheeting, are less expensive than roller blinds and can be draped quickly and easily over the sunny side of the greenhouse.*

HUMIDITY *is essential to plants in high temperatures and strong sunlight. Regularly moisten the floor and between plants, but avoid dampening soft, hairy leaves, as well as flowers. They are soon damaged.*

AUTOMATIC *ventilators ensure temperatures within a greenhouse are constantly adjusted, even when you are not there. Both roof and side ventilators can be controlled by them and are certainly worth installing.*

EXTRACTOR *fans are often fitted into the gabled ends of the roof. Controlled by thermostats, they extract hot air from the roof area. Louvres on the outside prevent cold air blowing in on the plants.*

EQUIPMENT

EVERY year, greenhouses are increasingly full of technical innovations, from thermostats and mist-propagation units to moisture meters and new methods of feeding plants. But it does not have to be complicated and it is quite easy to start with just a greenhouse, some means of heating it, a minimum and maximum registering thermometer and a few other pieces of equipment.

BASIC EQUIPMENT
Here are the basic pieces of equipment you will need:
• Plastic propagators help to raise new plants, whether seedlings or cuttings. The majority are heated by electricity, although a few rely on paraffin (kerosene) and therefore save the high cost of having electricity cables laid and installed. Other propagators are unheated, but create a humid atmosphere that benefits cuttings and a tem-

perature – although not as uniform as in electrically-heated propagators – that is more even than in a seed-tray on its own. Also, the cover helps to prevent the compost rapidly drying.
• Sharp knives are essential when preparing cuttings: blunt ones leave ragged cuts that take longer to heal.
• Dibbers assist in transferring seedlings from the containers in which they were raised to seed-trays, where they are given more room. They are also useful when inserting cuttings into compost.
• Moisture testers are useful for assessing the amount of moisture in compost. Some have probes

that are inserted into compost; the dial then indicates if further water is needed. However, repeated insertions of the probe damages the compost and roots. An alternative method is to insert label-like 'watering signals' into the compost – they change colour when water is needed.
• Mist-sprayers are essential for creating a humid atmosphere around plants, but take care not to moisten flowers or soft, hairy leaves. If damp, they decay and encourage the presence of diseases.
• Watering-cans with long spouts are essential in greenhouses. Gardening types are usually too cumbersome and with their short spouts are unable to reach plants at the backs of benches and stag-

ing. However, garden types can be used to dampen floors. When selecting a long-spouted watering-can, choose one that is well balanced and has a long, curved handle that enables the can to be used whatever the amount of water in it. An oval watering rose is needed so that seedlings can be watered gently.
Both metal and plastic watering-cans are available.
• Thermometers of all kinds are available, but a minimum and maximum type is essential. Traditional, vertical types can be used, but more recent dial forms, where the readings are more easily reset, are clearer.
• Canes, string and metal clips are needed to support plants, firmly but not strangling them.

PARAFFIN-HEATED *propagators are available and make propagation easier, even without electricity.*

INEXPENSIVE, *unheated propagators create humid environments with relatively even temperatures.*

MIST-SPRAYERS *enable a humid atmosphere to be created around plants. Take care not to moisten flowers or soft, hairy leaves.*

SUPPORTING *plants is essential: plastic-covered metal rings that can be lightly squeezed around stems and supports are a quick method to secure stems.*

LONG-SPOUTED *watering-cans are essential to enable plants at the backs of staging to be watered without water splashing everywhere.*

SHARP *knives are essential when taking and trimming the bases of cuttings.*

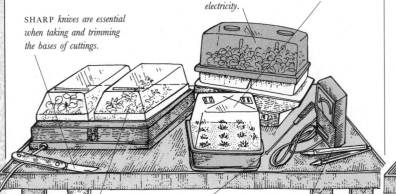
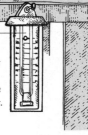

HEATED *propagators create warm, cosy environments for cuttings and seeds, encouraging rapid rooting and germination. They enable the greenhouse temperature to be lowered.*

SOIL *moisture testers take the guesswork out of assessing if compost is sufficiently moist. A probe is inserted into the compost and the amount of moisture it contains is indicated on a meter.*

DIBBERS *(like pencils) are needed to form holes in compost when seedlings are pricked out and spaced further apart.*

MINIMUM AND MAXIMUM *thermometers are essential, enabling the temperature during the previous night to be recorded and a judgement to be made about the heat required.*

TRADITIONAL *minimum and maximum thermometers have been this design for many years; a magnet is used to reposition the high and low indicators. Later designs (at left) are easier to read and reset.*

GETTING AUTOMATED

❖

REGULARLY watering plants has always been demanding, especially in summer when they may need a drink several times each day. This problem can be overcome in two ways and both are well within the abilities of most practical gardeners.

BOTTLE RESERVOIR

This system does not need a mains water supply and therefore is suitable in all greenhouses.

Invert and secure a refillable bottle of water and, using flexible piping, conduct water into a waterproof plastic tray. The neck of the bottle needs to be level with the surface of a strip of capillary matting laid in the tray's base. By adjusting the height of the reservoir, the level of water can be raised and lowered. If the reservoir has an open top, water will pass out steadily. However, if it is formed of a closed bottle, a further pipe needs to be fitted to pre-vent a vacuum forming in the bottle's top and the flow of water being stopped.

Stand pots on top of the capillary matting. Plastic pots do not have crocks (broken pieces of clay pot) placed in their bases and therefore water readily passes from the matting to the compost. Clay pots, however, are usually crocked and therefore the compost will not readily absorb water. Insert a wick into the base of each pot so that it acts as a channel for the water from the sand.

To reduce evaporation from the capillary matting, place a plastic sheet over it, with holes cut out for the pots. Alternatively, use a 12–18mm/^{1}/$_2$–^{3}/$_4$in layer of sand.

TRICKLE IRRIGATION

Once functioning, this system can be left in operation without any attention for several days. Water is usually supplied by mains water and a ballcock used to ensure the water-level remains constant. Alternatively, use a large plastic tank as a water reservoir. Unfortunately, this does not provide constant water pressure and the flow of water alters. Use tubing to direct water into the top of each pot, its flow controlled by nozzles. Initially, regular attention is needed to ensure the right amount of water is reaching each plant. Avoid waterlogging plants.

MIST-PROPAGATION UNITS

At one time, these were only available to commercial nurserymen, but now amateur types are available. They create a mist of water over cuttings, keeping them cool and reducing the need for them to absorb moisture before new roots are formed.

THERMOSTATS AND TIMERS

The range of electrical equipment is wide and includes thermostats to control temperatures. Combined with timing devices, electrical equipment can be controlled to come on and off – and to desired temperatures – at the touch of a switch.

TIMING *clocks and thermostats are invaluable for controlling temperatures and their duration. Position them where they will not be sprayed with water, as well as out of strong, direct sunlight.*

MIST-PROPAGATION *units have been used commercially for more than thirty years. There are now types for use in amateur greenhouses. They need an electrical supply, as well as mains water.*

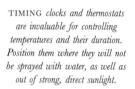

WATERING *plants demands a great deal of time, often when it is impossible to attend to them, such as during weekdays and vacations. In summer, plants in small pots dry out several times a day. Automatic watering systems, such as the above, are therefore well worth installing.*

THIS *watering system provides each plant with a regular drip of water. The amount of water each plant receives is easily controlled by nozzles. A series of small-bore, flexible pipes – known as spaghetti piping – conduct the water. The supply of water can be from the mains or a tank.*

SOLAR POWER!

In 1826, The Gardener's Magazine *revealed details of a scheme to store warm water in underground cisterns. Water was to be heated by the sun's rays warming a hollow ball. It was anticipated that the water could later be used to heat greenhouses.*

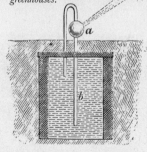

At about the same time, John Loudon, a visionary and distinguished author, outlined a way to extract heat from the earth's crust through bore holes, an idea still pursued in the late twentieth century.

POTS AND OTHER CONTAINERS

❖

CONTAINERS of all kinds are used to create homes for plants in greenhouses. Some provide temporary situations for cuttings or seeds, while others, such as pots, remain with plants until larger ones are needed.

Clay pots are the traditional homes for plants in greenhouses, but during recent decades plastic types have gained popularity. However, both types grow healthy plants, and each have advantages and disadvantages.

CLAY POTS

• Break easily when dropped.
• Heavier than plastic types and create firm bases for large plants.
• More difficult to clean than plastic types.
• If dry, they must be soaked in water for twenty-four hours before use. If not, they absorb moisture from the compost. This reduces the amount available for plants.

• Have a natural colour and harmonize with plants.
• Have a porous nature and allow damaging salts from some fertilizers to escape.
• Encourage potting composts to remain cool in summer and warm in winter.
• Are usually used in conjunction with loam-based composts.

PLASTIC POTS

• Are light and easy to handle, especially for disabled gardeners.
• Become brittle with age, especially after being stored at low temperatures.
• Are not porous and therefore do not allow damaging salts in the compost to escape.
• Are usually used in conjunction with peat-based composts.
• Available in a wide colour range and are well suited to harmonize in modern settings.
• Do not need to have broken pieces of pots in their bases, unlike clay pots.

SEED-TRAYS

Plastic seed-trays are ideal for raising seeds and for transferring seedlings into. Full-sized seed-trays measure about 35cm x 23cm x 5cm/14in x 9in x 2in; mini ones are 23cm x 18cm x 5cm/9in x 7in x 2in. There must be several drainage holes in their bases to enable excess moisture to escape.

SECTIONED SEED-TRAYS

Seed-trays are now frequently divided into sections, enabling individual cuttings or seedlings to be put in each hole. Later, when plants are transplanted, a special device is often used to force out the plants gently but firmly from their individual squares.

PEAT POTS

These are formed of sphagnum moss peat – plus fertilizers – compressed into the form of pots. Individual seedlings are grown in them and later, when the whole pot is planted into a garden, do not suffer any shock.

They range in size and shape: 36mm/1½in and 6cm/2½in square, or about 6cm/2½in round. They are sold in packs.

Because the compressed peat is exposed to the air, careful watering is needed when growing plants in them to ensure they do not become dry.

LARGE PLASTIC TRAYS

These are invaluable for housing several pots or seed-trays. Then, rather than moving them individually, they can be moved as a group. This prevents seed-trays twisting and the compost becoming disturbed and loosened.

Large trays are also useful when propagating houseplants by layering runners; a mother plant is placed in the centre and stems pregged into small pots, also on it.

A SELECTION of clean pots is essential. Most are now plastic, although clay types are still available. They are used for potting and sowing seeds.

SOME seed-trays are divided into sections so that each seedling is given the same amount of space. Later, it makes transplanting into a garden much easier.

TRADITIONAL wooden seed boxes have been replaced by plastic seed-trays, which are easily cleaned and stored. They are available in two basic sizes.

COMPOSTS

GARDEN soil is not suitable for growing plants in pots and boxes as it is variable in quality, often badly drained and may contain weed seeds, pests and diseases. Specially-prepared composts are needed and basically there are two types to choose from: loam-based and peat-based.

LOAM-BASED COMPOSTS

These are formed of sterilized loam, sharp sand and peat, with the addition of ground chalk and fertilizers. There are two types: one in which seeds are sown and the other for potting up plants. Additionally, the potting type is available in three strengths of fertilizers to suit plants throughout their lives.

They are heavier than peat-based types and therefore give more stability to large plants. Drying out is less rapid than with peat types and they have a greater reserve of plant foods.

PEAT-BASED COMPOSTS

Also known as loamless composts, these are newer. Formed basically of granulated peat, they are sold in several forms, for seed-sowing or potting. Some are multi-purpose.

They are more uniform than loam-based types, suitable for most plants and relatively light to use and carry home. Storage is easy as bags can be re-sealed and placed in a cool, dry place.

Plants growing in them need to be fed at an earlier stage than in loam-based types, and are more difficult to re-moisten if watering is neglected.

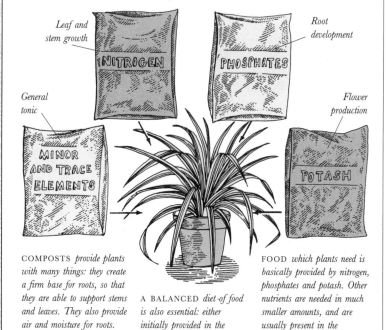

Leaf and stem growth

General tonic

NITROGEN

PHOSPHATES

Root development

Flower production

MINOR AND TRACE ELEMENTS

POTASH

COMPOSTS *provide plants with many things: they create a firm base for roots, so that they are able to support stems and leaves. They also provide air and moisture for roots.*

A BALANCED *diet of food is also essential: either initially provided in the compost or added later.*

FOOD *which plants need is basically provided by nitrogen, phosphates and potash. Other nutrients are needed in much smaller amounts, and are usually present in the compost initially.*

PLANT FOODS

THERE are many chemicals plants require for healthy growth; some are major, others only needed in small amounts and therefore known as minor or trace elements. The three major ones are nitrogen, phosphorus (phosphates) and potassium (potash).

NITROGEN

This is basically leaf-making; it encourages the growth of stems.
• Too much encourages sappy, luxuriant growth prone to attack from pests and diseases. Stems become floppy and the quality and number of flowers is reduced. Leaves also become dark green and flowering is delayed.
• Too little creates small plants, and leaves assume yellowish-green tints. Old leaves become yellow.

PHOSPHATE

Vital for the development of roots.
• Too much encourages yellowish-green leaves and young stems become mature quickly. Shoots become rigid and maturity is hastened.
• Too little creates small leaves with purple tinting on a dark green background.

POTASH

Encourages balanced growth and is vital for the development of fruits and a plant's ability to survive adverse conditions.
• Too much causes growth to harden and delays flower development.
• Too little causes stunted growth and plants susceptible to low temperature damage. Old leaves become mottled.

ALL *plants need a balanced diet of fertilizers to encourage healthy growth. Here are the results of a few deficiencies, but symptoms vary between species: the ones here relate to a tomato plant.*

YOUNG *leaves are the first to reveal iron deficiency: initially they are yellowish-green; later white.*

SMALL *leaves with purple shading on a dark green background indicate phosphate deficiency. Leaves become cupped.*

YELLOW *areas between veins on lower leaves indicate a lack of magnesium. Later, they become brown.*

PALE *green or yellowish leaves indicate a shortage of nitrogen, as does thin, leggy and weak growth.*

BROWN *leaf edges that curl upwards are symptoms of potash deficiency. It is accompanied by poor flowering and fruiting.*

PLANT *foods are mainly absorbed by roots, but it is also possible to apply some by spraying in a weak solution on leaves. This is known as foliar feeding.*

WATERING

WATER is essential to plants, but either too much or too little causes death. Plants absorb water through their roots and give it off through small, hole-like pores, known as *stoma*, mainly on the undersides of leaves. This continuous cycle of water keeps plants cool, firm and upright, as well as transporting foods from the soil to the leaves.

JUDGING WHEN WATER IS NEEDED

This is a skill not easily acquired and usually gained only after years of experience, although in recent years specialized equipment has been introduced to take the guesswork out of this task.

• The surface of compost indicates when water is needed: when dry it is pale and crumbly, but dark if wet. This is one of the best methods, as it does not disturb or compress the compost.

• Rubbing a finger or thumb on the compost is a popular method: if damp, no water is needed. However, repeated pressings eventually damage the compost.

• Tapping the side of a pot with a cotton reel (bobbin) on the end of a short cane is a traditional method, but only works on clay pots. If the knock gives a dull note, no water is needed; if a ringing tone, moisture is needed.

• Moisture-indicator strips – also known as watering signals – inserted into compost change colour when water is needed.

• Moisture-meters indicate precisely when water is needed, but repeated insertion of a probe into compost is eventually destructive.

APPLYING WATER

Most plants in pots are watered 'over the rim'. This means that a watering-can is used to fill up the gap between the compost and the rim. If water runs out quickly, water it again. The first watering expands the compost, the next thoroughly soaks it.

Soft and hairy-leaved plants are soon damaged by water on their leaves. Therefore, stand their pots in a bowl of water until moisture seeps to the surface, then remove and allow to drain.

STORE *composts and fertilizers in a cool, dry shed. Preferably, stand them on a slatted wooden framework in case the floor is damp or becomes wet.*

ENVIRONMENTALLY-FRIENDLY COMPOSTS

The continued taking of peat from peat-bogs has decimated the natural environment and destroyed the homes of many plants, birds and insects. Therefore, alternatives have been sought. Some composts – now on the market – are formed from the outer husks of coconuts and said to be as good, if not better, than peat types.

FEEDING PLANTS

ONCE plants have exhausted the food in compost, they need further nourishment. Regular feeding during a plant's growing period makes a remarkable difference. Feed both foliage and summer-flowering greenhouse plants from early spring to late summer at ten to fourteen-day intervals. Winter-flowering types, however, are fed at the same intervals during the period they remain in flower. Never feed plants when they are dormant, as they are unable to use the food.

TOPDRESSING

Large plants in greenhouses, sunrooms and conservatories are frequently too big to be repotted. Topdress them in spring instead. Allow the compost to dry slightly and then scrape away the top 2.5cm/1in. For very large plants, perhaps in tubs in a large conservatory, increase this to 36mm/1¹/₂in. Replace this with fresh potting compost, leaving a 12–18mm/¹/₂–³/₄in gap between the compost and rim to allow the plant to be properly watered.

1. MOST PLANTS *are fed by diluting a proprietary liquid fertilizer in water. Adhere to the manufacturer's instructions about the concentration.*

2. AGITATE *the solution to ensure it is thoroughly mixed and use before it has time to settle. If the mixture is too strong, it will damage the roots of the plant.*

3. DO NOT *apply the liquid to dry compost: it will either damage roots or run out of the gap between the soil-ball and pot. Thoroughly water the compost first.*

ANOTHER *way is to push pills into the compost, again about 12mm/¹/₂in from the edge. Some devices enable pills to be inserted into the compost without having to dirty your hands.*

AN ALTERNATIVE *to liquid feeding is to use feeding sticks pushed into the compost, about 12mm/¹/₂in from the pot's side. It is quick and easy and provides food over a long period.*

FERTILIZER *powders are sometimes used: they are dusted evenly on the compost's surface and watered in. They are best used on plants growing in large pots.*

PRICKING OUT SEEDLINGS

❖

AS SOON as seedlings are large enough to handle they must be transferred to wider spacings in other seed-trays. This is known as pricking out. If seedlings are left in the seed-tray they become congested, weak and spindly, a state from which they will not recover. Additionally, congested seedlings are more susceptible to diseases than those with a good air circulation around them.

PRICKING OUT

Transplanting any plant is a delicate operation, but the younger they are the more successful it is. After seeds germinate, slowly acclimatize the seedlings to lower temperatures so that they are growing sturdily. Then, as soon as they are large enough to handle move them to wider spacings.

The day before pricking out, water the seedlings in their seed-tray, so that the compost is thoroughly moist. Use a small fork (sometimes sold with dibbers) to lift out a cluster of seedlings. Place them on moist newspaper or hessian to prevent their roots drying. Push compost around the roots of disturbed seedlings in the seed-tray to prevent them becoming dry and damaged.

Fill and firm potting compost in a clean seed-tray so that its surface is 12mm/1/2in below the rim. Use a clean dibber to make holes in the compost, spacing them about 36mm/11/2in apart and no closer than 12mm/1/2in to the container's sides. This safeguards the seedlings if watering is neglected and the compost becomes dry.

Hold each seedling by a leaf and position its roots in a hole, so it is at the same depth as before. Ensure the roots are not twisted and then use the dibber to firm compost around them. Never hold a seedling by its stem as it is then soon damaged.

When the seed-tray is full, gently tap its sides to level loose compost on the surface. This prevents water later collecting in puddles on the surface. Stand the seed-tray on a level, well-drained surface, and water lightly but thoroughly from above with a fine-rosed watering-can. Allow excess water to drain before placing the seed-tray on a shelf in a greenhouse. And remember to insert a label into the compost, giving the date and also the name of the plants.

Place the seedlings in a warm and lightly-shaded position until established and growing strongly. As they develop and their leaves grow, ensure that moisture falling on them when the compost is watered has sufficient time to dry before nightfall.

If you have seedlings to spare, offer them to neighbours or friends, who might be able to make an exchange of other plants.

INDIVIDUAL HOLES

Proprietary trays in which there are individual square or round holes are an alternative to normal seed-trays. A seedling is pricked out into each hole, ensuring equal spacing. The holes or squares range from 36mm/1in wide to just under 6mm/21/2in and therefore can accommodate a wide size range of seedlings.

GREENHOUSE OR CONSERVATORY

Greenhouse and conservatory were originally synonymous terms and widely used for glass structures used to house and conserve 'greens' and 'evergreens' from warm climates. The term greenhouse was first coined during the late 1600s by John Evelyn, English garden designer, writer and translator of books.

Nowadays, a greenhouse tends to be a place where the practicalities of gardening are performed: seeds sown, cuttings rooted and plants nurtured until large enough to be taken indoors or planted into a garden. Glasshouse is a term which is mainly reserved for commercial greenhouses.

Conservatories now tend to be places as much for relaxation as growing plants, although there is no doubt plants introduce life to a structure that otherwise appears barren. Sunrooms are an American innovation and very much assume the functions of conservatories.

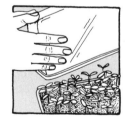

1. AS *soon as seedlings fill their seed-tray they must be given more space. This is called 'pricking out' and involves moving seedlings carefully and individually into further seed-trays containing potting compost.*

2. WATER *the seedlings thoroughly but gently, then the following day use a small fork to lift up a cluster of them. Place them on a piece of damp newspaper or hessian to prevent their roots drying.*

3. PREPARE *a seed-tray in the same manner as when sowing seeds – filling and levelling to 12mm/1/2in below the rim. Use a dibber to form holes about 36mm/11/2in apart, the outer ones 12mm/1/2in from the sides.*

4. HOLD *each seedling by a leaf and position it in a hole, at about the same depth as before and with its roots well spread out. Carefully lever compost around them, taking care not to crush the stem.*

5. WHEN *the seed-tray is full of seedlings, gently tap its edges to level loose surface compost. Water seedlings from above to settle compost around their roots. Allow excess water to drain from the seed tray.*

6. PLACE *the seed-tray in gentle warmth and light shade until the seedlings are established. Keep the compost moist, but not waterlogged, and when the plants touch each other transfer them into small pots.*

POTTING UP

❖

W HEN young plants growing in seed-trays fill their container with leaves and roots, transfer them to individual pots. If left, they become stunted, with their foliage drawn and etiolated. From this state, plants seldom recover and even if given ideal conditions, do not develop into healthy plants.

Because of the continued necessity to move plants from one container to another – to give them more space, light and air – it may appear to be easier to put them in large containers at an early stage. However, this is not so: small seedlings in large containers are surrounded by soil which remains cold and wet because of the lack of root activity in it. Additionally, it makes keeping the correct moisture content very difficult and usually it becomes excessively wet.

Another factor is the amount of space initially needed if plants are immediately put in large pots. During spring, space is usually at a premium in greenhouses and there is none to be wasted.

MOIST COMPOST

Always water plants the day before transferring them into pots. Plants with dry roots receive a check to their growth; however, they should not be swamped with water either.

Commercial nurserymen remove plants from boxes by knocking an end and side on the ground and then, with sudden movement, raising the seed-tray and tossing the plants forward so that they remain in a block. The matted roots hold the compost together. However, risking this action on cherished plants is rash and therefore the safest way for home gardeners to remove plants is to use a fork or small trowel.

Use clean, dry pots and fill the base of one with compost. Position a plant in it to ensure that when potted it will be slightly lower than before. The old soil-level can be seen on the stem. Setting the plant slightly lower than before allows for the later settlement of compost when watered.

Still holding the plant, dribble compost around and over the roots, then firming with finger tips to fractionally less than 12mm/¹/₂in below the pot's rim.

Water the compost to settle it around the roots, then place the plant in a warm, lightly shaded position. When growth resumes, decrease the temperature and give more light.

As growth progresses, space plants further apart, so that their leaves are not touching each other. Keep the compost moist but not waterlogged.

SOFT OR HARD POTTING?

Earlier, the technique of repotting plants – especially when potting greenhouse chrysanthemums into large pots – was to ram as much soil-based compost as possible into the pot. This was to ensure that the maximum amount of food was initially given to a plant, as well as to hold it secure and able to support stems up to 1.5m/5ft high. Nowadays, soft-potting is performed, where only moderate firming is necessary especially when peat-type composts are used.

POTTING TIME

The art and timing of potting up or repotting established plants in pots has been well known to gardeners for many centuries. In the early 1800s, Sir Joseph Paxton, the English gardener and architect (who designed the Crystal Palace which housed the Great Exhibition of 1851) said: "It is a standing rule with experienced horticulturalists that no plant should be allowed a larger pot till the one in which it is growing is filled with fibrous roots."

This axiom is still right and applies in all places, although in the tropics it is advantageous if plants are repotted when commencing active growth, which is usually at the beginning of the monsoon rains. Orchids are also repotted when growth begins, or otherwise when their flowering season is over.

1. WHEN *young plants that previously were pricked out into seed-trays are congested they must be transferred into small pots or planted into a garden. The day before moving them into pots (potting up) thoroughly water the compost.*

2. SHARPLY *tap the sides of the seed-tray several times to loosen the compost and prevent it adhering to the container. Then, use a fork or small trowel to lift out a plant, taking care not to damage its roots, especially the fine ones.*

3. FILL *a clean pot's base with potting compost, so that when potted the plant will be slightly lower than before. This allows for subsequent settlement of the compost when watering after potting is completed. Add compost, as needed.*

4. POSITION *the plant on the compost and gently hold its stem in the pot's centre. Trickle potting compost around the roots, taking care not to damage the stem – young plants are easily damaged and may not fully recover.*

5. USE *the tips of fingers to firm compost over and around the roots, so that its surface is about 12mm/¹/₂in below the rim. Water the compost from above to settle it around the roots. Place in gentle warmth and light shade.*

6. WHEN *growth resumes, lower the temperature and position in better light. Initially, stand the pots close together: this saves space and reduces moisture loss from the compost. As plants develop, remember to space them further apart.*

REPOTTING

WHEN plants fill their pots with roots they must be repotted to prevent growth eventually becoming stunted. It is essential that plants are progressively moved in only small stages and not given too much fresh compost at one time. If this happens, it is difficult to keep the moisture content in the compost at the correct level, especially in winter when plants are not growing rapidly.

SELECTING A POT

The size of the new pot will depend on that of the existing one. For example, the following changes are about right: move a plant in a 6cm/2½in pot into a 8cm/3½in one. Then, repot it into a 13cm/5in pot and later into a 18cm/7in one. Eventually, a change into a 25cm/10in pot might be needed for a very large plant such as a palm in a conservatory or sunroom.

WATERING SPACE

The space that remains between the compost's surface and the pot's rim is essential if the plant is to be watered properly. If too small, insufficient water is applied (or more frequent watering is necessary) and if excessively deep too much water is applied and the compost becomes very wet.

Plants in 6–13cm/2½–5in-wide pots need a 12mm/½in watering space, while those in 14–19cm/5½–7½in pots need a space of 18mm/¾in. As the sizes of pots increase, so do the spaces. Plants in 20–23cm/8–9in pots need 2.5cm/1in spaces and those in 25–30cm/10–12in ones need a gap of 36mm/1½in.

REPOTTING

Remove the plant from its existing pot by placing a hand over the soil ball, inverting the plant and knocking the rim on a hard surface. If a plant is exceptionally pot-bound (masses of roots around the sides of the root-ball) it may be necessary to run a knife between the side of the pot and the ball of roots.

If the plant is in a clay pot there might be a small piece of broken clay pot (known as a crock) in its base. This is placed over the drainage hole in the pot's base to prevent compost escaping. If the crock is present, remove it.

Exceptionally congested plants will have masses of matted roots; tease these out and remove old, dead ones.

Always choose a clean, dry pot in a suitable size. If a clay pot is being used, place a crock – concave-side downwards – over the drainage hole. Plastic pots do not require to be crocked. Fill and

REPOTTING CACTI

Many cacti have stiff, sharp spines and therefore need to be handled with respect and care. When repotting them, wrap a piece of folded newspaper around the stem to form a temporary handle.

firm compost in the base and stand the soil ball on it. Adjust its height so that the soil ball's top leaves a gap below the rim (see earlier for the right space).

Trickle compost around the soil ball and firm it gently but firmly with your fingers. Ensure that the plant is placed in the centre of the pot.

Water the compost carefully to prevent it being washed out of the pot. It may be necessary to fill the watering gap several times. Insert a plant label into the compost.

DOUBLE POTTING

To keep the roots of some tropical and subtropical plants cool, some of them are double-potted. This involves using clay pots and placing one pot inside another, with the 12–18mm/½–¾in space between them filled with damp peat. This space is then continually kept moist.

1. REPOTTING *a plant when its roots become congested is essential to prevent growth ceasing. Remove the pot by placing a hand over the soil ball, inverting it and tapping the rim on a firm surface.*

2. SELECT *a clean, slightly larger pot. Place and firm a handful of compost in its base. Stand the plant on top and adjust the compost so that the top of the soil ball is about 12mm/½in below the rim.*

3. TRICKLE *and firm fresh potting compost around the soil ball. Ensure a gap is left at the top of the pot so that the compost can be watered. Lightly tap the pot's side to level loose compost on the surface.*

AFTER repotting, place plants in attractive outer containers known as cache pots. Choose a colour and shape that enhances the plant, rather than dominating it. Here is Aspidistra elatior, widely known as Cast Iron Plant or Bar-room Plant.

PLANTS FOR COLD GREENHOUSES

COLD greenhouses have no artificial heat in winter. However, with good insulation – especially on cold and windward sides – the temperature should not fall much below freezing.

The temperature in unheated conservatories does not usually fall as quickly or as low as free-standing greenhouses: warm house walls help to prevent rapid fluctuations in temperature.

Positioning plants in the centre of a greenhouse or conservatory helps to protect them during exceptionally cold weather. Cold draughts are especially damaging, and therefore ensure doors and ventilators fit their frames tightly.

RANGE OF PLANTS

There are many ornamental plants that survive low temperatures, and while most are grown for their attractive foliage, others are famed for their flowers. Here are a few plants to consider:

• *Acorus gramineus:* the Grassy-leaved Sweet Flag grows 30–38cm/12–15in high in a pot,

CAMELLIAS *(above) are evergreen shrubs, with beautiful flowers in early spring. Aspidistras (left) are popular houseplants.*

with narrow, leathery, green leaves. The form 'Variegatus' is more attractive, with the narrow leaves being striped white.

• *Aspidistra elatior:* the Cast Iron Plant is famed for its tolerance of neglect, but when well grown is superb. There is a beautifully variegated form with cream stripes on its leaves.

• *Aucuba japonica* 'Variegata': the Spotted Laurel is an evergreen shrub that when small is ideal in cool conservatories and greenhouses. The shiny, green leaves have yellow spots.

• *Camellia japonica:* the Common Camellia is a delight in late winter and early spring, with large, waxy flowers. Avoid any sudden changes in the temperature or fluctuations of moisture in the compost.

• *Campanula isophylla:* the Star of Bethlehem is very floriferous, creating a wealth of star-like flowers during mid- and late summer. It is ideal for growing in a hanging basket as well as in a pot.

THE *Spotted Laurel (above) is ideal in unheated rooms and greenhouses. The Grassy-leaved Sweet Flag also thrives in unheated places.*

• *Chlorophytum comosum:* the Spider Plant is well-known for its narrow, white-and-green cascading leaves. Plant it in a pot where the stems can trail freely.

• *Crocus chrysanthus:* this diminutive crocus can be planted in bowls in late summer and early autumn. The bulbs must be allowed to grow naturally, with no artificial heat. They flower in late winter and early spring.

• Daffodils: These have large flowers and are distinguished from other narcissi by their trumpets which are as long as, or longer than, the petals. Bulbs are planted in late summer or early autumn for flowering from late winter to early spring.

• *Fatsia japonica:* the evergreen False Castor Oil Plant grows outdoors in sheltered areas and makes a good low-temperature plant for both greenhouses and conservatories.

• *Hedera helix:* there are many attractively variegated forms of this small-leaved ivy. They are ideal for growing up small canes or plastic trellis. They also trail.

The Star of Bethlehem (left) develops blue, star-like flowers during mid- and late summer. There is also a white form.

The well-known Spider Plant (right) eventually needs a hanging basket or pedestal to enable stems to hang freely.

Mother of Thousands (above) creates a remarkable display of trailing stems, while the False Castor Oil Plant (left) has large, hand-like leaves. It can also be grown outdoors in temperate climates.

• *Hedera canariensis* 'Variegata': also known as 'Gloire de Marengo' and the Canary Island Ivy. This ivy has large, dark green leaves merging through silvery-grey to white at the edges.

• *Hyacinthus orientalis:* hyacinths are famed for their stiff, upright, soldier-like appearance and sweetly-scented flowers, which appear from mid-winter to spring.

• *Iris danfordiae:* this dwarf, bulbous iris is well known for its honey-scented, lemon-yellow flowers that appear in mid- and late winter. Its flower stems are about 10cm/4in long, making it ideal for growing in pots and shallow pans in a cold greenhouse.

• *Iris reticulata:* another dwarf, bulbous iris, with deep bluish-purple flowers in late winter and early spring. The flower stems are about 15cm/6in long.

• *Saxifraga stolonifera:* widely known as the Mother of Thousands and Strawberry Geranium, this trailing plant never ceases to capture attention with its somewhat rounded leaves and thread-like trailing stems that bear young plants. The form 'Tricolor' has leaves variegated pink and pale yellow.

PLANTS FOR COOL GREENHOUSES

COOL greenhouses are where the temperature does not fall below 7°C/45°F in winter. This enables a much wider range of plants to be grown than in cold greenhouses. Some plants do not need warmth throughout winter, as they are raised from seeds sown in late winter or early spring.

RANGE OF PLANTS

There are many attractively flowered plants to choose from, as well as foliage types: some are permanent residents in greenhouses, while others live out their lives from spring to autumn, then die. Here are a few plants to consider:
• _Begonia semperflorens:_ the Wax Begonia is ideal for decorating greenhouses, homes and gardens with flowers – white, through pink to red – from early to late summer. Sow seeds (no need to cover) in 16–20°C/61–68°F during late winter or early spring.
• _Begonia x tuberhybrida:_ a tuberous-rooted begonia with large, rose-like flowers from early to late

THE SILVERY INCH PLANT (right) has green-and-silver bands along its glistening leaves. It is attractive throughout the year.

THE bright, small, orchid-like flowers of the Butterfly Flower (left) swamp plants from spring to early summer.

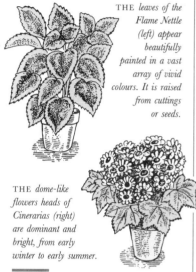

THE leaves of the Flame Nettle (left) appear beautifully painted in a vast array of vivid colours. It is raised from cuttings or seeds.

THE dome-like flowers heads of Cinerarias (right) are dominant and bright, from early winter to early summer.

summer. The tubers are packed into boxes of moist peat in early spring and started into growth. When shoots are about 5cm/2in high, move the plants into 13cm/5in wide pots.
• _Begonia x tuberhybrida_ 'Pendula':
this is the Basket Begonia, tuberous-rooted and with a trailing habit. It is ideal for growing in hanging-baskets.
• _Calceolaria x herbeohybrida:_ the Slipper Flower, with masses of pouch-like flowers in bright colours from late spring to mid-summer and used to decorate homes as well as greenhouses and conservatories. Sow seeds from early to mid-summer.
• _Senecio cruentus:_ Cinerarias are superb plants for homes and greenhouses, developing dome-like heads of flowers from early winter to early summer. Sow seeds from late spring to early summer.
• _Coleus blumei:_ Flame Nettles are ideal foliage plants for a green-

house or home. Either take 7.5cm/3in long cuttings in late summer and insert in equal parts moist peat and sharp sand, or sow seeds in mid-winter in 16°C/61°F.
• _Cyclamen persicum:_ Cyclamen flower from late summer to mid-winter. Sow seeds from mid- to late summer.
• _Primula obconica:_ the Poison Primula flowers from early winter to late spring. Sow seeds thinly in early spring.
• _Primula malacoides:_ the Fairy Primrose flowers from early winter to early spring. Sow seeds thinly in early spring.
• _Schizanthus pinnatus:_ the Butterfly Flower creates masses of flowers in greenhouses during spring and early summer. Sow seeds from mid- to late summer, 3mm/1/8in deep and in 16°C/61°F.
• _Sinningia speciosa:_ the well-known Gloxinia is superb in homes and conservatories, as well as greenhouses, and flowers from late spring to mid-summer. Sow seeds from mid-winter to early spring, just pressing them into the surface. When large enough to handle, prick out the seedlings into seed-

SLIPPER FLOWERS (right) have masses of pouch-like flowers in a rich range of colours from late spring to mid-summer.

CYCLAMEN (left) are popular flowering plants, with flowers at the tops of long stems from late summer to mid-winter.

THE Tuberous Begonia (above) creates a feast of large, rose-like flowers in many colours from early to late summer.

THE Poison Primrose (above) develops masses of flowers in shades of pink, red, lilac from early winter to late spring.

trays, later moving them into pots.
• _Tradescantia fluminensis:_ the Wandering Jew is a well-known trailing plant, ideal in pots positioned at the edges of shelves so that stems can cascade.
• _Zebrina pendula:_ the Silvery Inch Plant has leaves up to 5cm/2in long, with glistening surfaces and green-and-silver bands.

As well as being grown in cool greenhouses and conservatories, the trailing _Tradescantia fluminensis_ and _Zebrina pendula_ can be planted in hanging-baskets and displayed in cool lobbies and porches during summer.

SAVING MONEY

Use a heated propagator in winter to provide the temperature needed to germinate seedlings. This saves heating the entire greenhouse to a high temperature. Electric and paraffin heated types are available.

PLANTS FOR
WARM GREENHOUSES
❖

WARM greenhouses and conservatories are expensive to heat during winter, but the wide range of tropical and subtropical plants that can be grown is wide and includes many plants that are sure to please you. Night temperatures of about 16°C/61°F are needed, with those during the day a few degrees higher. Additionally, the atmosphere needs to be humid. Plants to consider include:

• *Acalypha hispida:* the Red-hot Cat's-tail eventually has a shrub-like stance, but when young can be grown in a pot. During summer, long tassels packed with red flowers hang from stems. A minimum night temperature about 16°C/61°F is essential, 18–24°C/64–75° during the day. Mist spray the leaves frequently to create a humid atmosphere.

• *Anthurium andreanum:* the Painter's Palette is very distinctive, with shiny-green, heart-shaped leaves and flowers that resemble a painter's palette. These are red,

CROTONS *(below) are well known plants with leaves that display a wealth of colours. Also known as Joseph's Coat.*

THE PEACOCK PLANT *(above) has gloriously coloured, paper-thin leaves. Earlier, it was known as Maranta makoyana.*

with a straight, central spire about 5cm/2in long. Do not let the temperature fall below 16°C/61°F in winter. Mist spray plants regularly.

• *Anthurium crystallinum:* the Crystal Anthurium has gloriously coloured, large, velvety, dark green leaves with veins lined in ivory. Keep the night temperature in winter at 16°C/61°F or above.

• *Caladium x hortulanum:* the Angel's Wings has arrow-shaped, paper-thin leaves up to 30cm/12in long, in many bright colours. There are several named varieties. High temperatures are essential, never below 16°C/61°F and preferably about 21°C/70°F. Plants die down in late summer and the tubers are replanted in early spring. At this time, moist compost and a temperature about 24°C/75°F is needed. Mist spray plants regularly.

• *Calathea makoyana:* the Peacock Plant is one of the prettiest of all

foliage plants, with paper-thin leaves beautifully patterned silvery green and edged in mid-green. From below there are zones of purple or red. Temperatures of at least 16°C/61°F are needed, and avoid rapid fluctuations.

• *Calathea zebrina:* the Zebra Plant has narrowly oblong, soft emerald-green leaves banded in dark green. These bands appear as purple on the undersides. It is slightly easier to grow than the Peacock Plant, but nevertheless needs a minimum temperature of about 16°C/61°F.

• *Codiaeum variegatum:* the well-known Croton is also called Joseph's Coat, which very much describes the richness and varied nature of the thick leaves. The shapes of the leaves vary widely and there are many named varieties. A minimum temperature not less than 16°C/61°F is needed in winter, together with regular mist spraying.

• *Philodendron melanochrysum:* the Black Gold Philodendron was earlier known as *P. andreanum.* It has

COPPER LEAF *(below right) creates a wealth of leaves mottled in many bright colours. Angel's Wings (below) has large, arrow-shaped, paper-thin leaves in many colours – and borne on long stems.*

RED-HOT CAT'S-TAIL *(below) develops long, tassel-like stems packed with bright red flowers. Its other name is Chenille Plant.*

THE *Painter's Palette (above) has large, heart-like leaves and shiny red, waxy 'palettes' with straight, central tails. A close relative, the Flamingo Flower, has curly tails.*

large, dark green leaves with a coppery sheen and veins lined in ivory. Mature leaves are up to 60cm/2ft long. When young, however, the plant has juvenile leaves, heart-shaped and velvety dark green. It needs a minimum winter temperature in the region of 18°C/64°F.

• *Sonerila margaritacea:* the Frosted Sonerila has coppery green leaves with silvery spots. A minimum winter temperature of 18°C/64°F is needed to enable plants to survive in good condition.

• *Syngonium podophyllum:* the Goose Foot Plant, also known as Arrowhead Vine and Nephthytis, has a climbing nature and needs a minimum winter temperature of 16°C/61°F. It has juvenile and adult leaves. When young, they are arrow shaped, but with age develop ears and lobes. There are several named forms, some attractively variegated. Occasionally, these plants are sold under the name *Nephthytis podophyllum.*

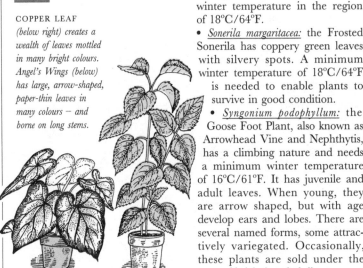

THE FROSTED SONERILA *(above) reveals coppery green leaves with silvery spots, while mature Black Gold Philodendrons have large, dark green leaves with a coppery sheen and ivory veins.*

CLOCHES AND GARDEN FRAMES

LOCHES are versatile, enabling crops to be protected during their early stages as well as later when maturing. As well, they are used in late winter and early spring to warm up strips of land in preparation for sowing seeds.

The range of cloches has increased dramatically in recent years. In addition to glass, rigid plastic types are widely available, as well as those covered with polythene sheeting.

• Tent cloches are formed of two pieces of glass held together at their tops with wires that also form handles. In most tent cloches glass is used, but plastic is also available. Also, rigid netting is sometimes secured under the plastic, to protect plants from birds when glass is removed.

Because tent cloches are relatively low they are only suitable for warming soil, initial sowing and raising plants, and for low, salad-type crops. Ensure the ends of the row are blocked to prevent it becoming a wind-tunnel.

• Barn cloches are higher than tent types and formed of four sheets of glass held together with wires that also form handles. Crops are ventilated by opening one of the roof panes. These cloches function in the same way as tent types, but with the benefit of covering taller crops. Blocking off the ends of the row is important, as they are less stable than tent types.

• Corrugated PVC plastic cloches are strong and light, but they must be well secured to the ground to prevent them blowing away. Their uses are the same as tent types. Ventilation is created by removing every other cloche during the day. Storing them is not a problem as they are soon dismantled and stored flat.

• Polythene tunnels create inexpensive protection for seeds while germinating, young plants and low salad crops. They are bought as kits and easily assembled by stretching a sheet of polythene over wire hoops anchored in the

POLYTHENE TUNNELS *are inexpensive and increasingly popular, although the polythene has to be replaced fairly frequently. It is secured over metal hoops, then held down by thin wires.*

OLD, PLASTIC UMBRELLAS, *as well as clear bottles with their bases cut out, make cheap covers for plants during spring. They do, however, need to be well secured by pegs or wire hooks into the soil.*

DUTCH LIGHTS, *mounted on a wooden base, create ideal places in which to acclimatize summer-bedding plants to outdoor life. Lettuces and other low-growing salad crops can be grown in them.*

ground. Thin wires are put over the top to secure the polythene.

It is an excellent way to provide protection on rows 6m/20ft or more long. The life of polythene is variable, but usually not more than two years: it deteriorates in sunlight and is soon ripped. If in good condition at the end of the year, wash and allow to dry before storing. Ventilation is provided by rolling up the side away from the prevailing wind.

• Recycled clear plastic umbrellas make excellent temporary protections for plants, but they must be anchored securely into the soil. Plastic bottles and containers – with their bases cut out – are other possibilities and worth using in an effort to conserve natural resources.

• Dutch lights, about 1.5m/5ft long and 75cm/2¹⁄₂ft wide, are ideal for forming garden frames in which plants can be acclimatized to outdoor conditions after being raised in greenhouses. Salad crops, such as lettuces, can also be grown in them. Each frame is

formed of a single sheet of glass secured in a wooden frame. These are placed on a south-facing, sloping, wood or brick base: 20cm/8in at the front and 30cm/12in at the back.

TENT CLOCHES *are made of two panes of glass secured with wires. New types have netting secured under a plastic cover: with the covering removed the netting gives protection in summer against birds.*

BARN CLOCHES *are formed from four sheets of glass, supported by a thick wire frame. One side of the roof can be opened to increase the amount of ventilation. There is a wire handle at each cloche's top.*

CORRUGATED PVC *combines strength with lightness. Because of their light weight they are folded around half-moon metal frames with spikes on their lower ends. These are pushed into the soil.*

BELL-SHAPED CLOCHES

Bell-shaped glass cloches with a knob on the top for handling were used in the early seventeenth century. The term 'cloche' is derived from the French and means a bell or dish-cover.

Earthenware jars have also been used to cover plants, especially in winter and to encourage blanching.

RAISING NEW PLANTS

Raising new plants is a central desire of most gardeners, not just from seeds but from cuttings, layers or, perhaps, by budding and grafting. Many plants can be raised from seeds and these are detailed in sections on sowing seeds in greenhouses (page 272), sowing hardy annuals, biennials and herbaceous perennials (pages 273 and 274) and sowing vegetables (page 275).

Taking cuttings is another popular method of propagation and involves both indoor and outdoor plants. Some cuttings are formed of mature wood, others from soft shoots, while others are created from roots or whole or parts of leaves. Division is an easy and popular way to increase plants with fibrous roots, including herbaceous perennials grown outdoors and some houseplants.

Unusual ways to propagate plants that are also described include air-layering, when roots are encouraged to form on bare stems of such plants as Rubber Plants, and rooting plantlets which form on leaves.

The information in this chapter also relates to plants featured in other parts of this book.

SIMPLE PROPAGATION

◆

THE range of plants that can be easily propagated is wide and includes annuals and biennials, vegetables, herbaceous perennials, cacti and other succulents, ornamental shrubs, houseplants and fruit bushes.

SIMPLE EQUIPMENT

The majority of plants can be increased without the need of specialized equipment. Some benefit from heated propagation cases in greenhouses or sunrooms, but often seeds germinate and cuttings develop roots quite easily in boxes and pots on window sills indoors.

Most vegetables, as well as annuals and biennials, are raised from seeds. Herbaceous perennials, although sometimes increased from seeds, are more frequently propagated by dividing established clumps in autumn or spring.

Ornamental shrubs are increased in many ways, including layering and cuttings. Most soft fruits, such as gooseberries, red currants and blackcurrants, are raised from cuttings.

A few plants grown as houseplants in temperate regions are increased in unusual and distinctive ways, such as by runners and plantlets, often to the amusement of children.

Fruit trees are increased by budding or grafting – a means of uniting a good fruiting variety with hardy roots. No special equipment is needed, other than a knife, raffia and grafting wax.

Mother-in-Law's Tongue

Peace Lily

English Ivy

Spider Plant

African Violet

MANY *houseplants are easily increased indoors on lightly shaded window sills, by division, cuttings, layering or plantlets.*

EQUIPMENT AND COMPOSTS

◆

CLEAN equipment and composts are essential. If pots, seed-trays or boxes are dirty they may contain disease spores from the previous year, while contaminated compost soon decimates seedlings and cuttings.

Wash all equipment in disinfectant, rinse, allow to dry and let fumes disperse before using.

COMPOSTS *are either soil- or peat-based. Soil-based types are a mixture of loam, sharp sand and peat, while peat ones are mainly granulated peat.*

POTS *are needed in a range of sizes for potting up established seedlings and cuttings.*

UNHEATED SEED-TRAYS *with plastic lids are an inexpensive way to retain warmth for cuttings and seed germination.*

PLASTIC SEED-TRAY *are ideal for seeds and cuttings, as well as for pricking out seedlings.*

HEATED PROPAGATION *cases enable seeds to be sown early in the year, as well as being a more assured way to root soft-stemmed cuttings.*

SHARP KNIVES *are essential when preparing cuttings, as well as for budding and grafting.*

SHARP SECATEURS *are useful when preparing hardwood cuttings.*

SOWING SEEDS IN GREENHOUSES

HALF-HARDY annuals are sown in gentle warmth in greenhouses or sunrooms in late winter or spring. They are planted outdoors in the garden after all risk of frost has passed, then flower throughout summer. A few houseplants are also raised from seeds.

An advantage of increasing plants from seeds is that large numbers of them can be raised at one time.

REQUIREMENTS FOR GERMINATION

Whatever the type of plant, the seeds need three basic conditions to encourage germination: moisture, warmth and air. Most seeds germinate in darkness, but a few, such as the Wax Flower (*Begonia semperflorens*), need light.

Moisture is provided by sowing seeds in moisture-retentive peat- or loam-based compost. Soil from a garden is not suitable as it is likely to contain pests, diseases and weed seeds. Also, it usually has insufficient fertilizers and the wrong proportions of loam, peat and sand.

AFTER SOWING TREATMENT

The temperature and moisture in a compost are the main influences on germination. Air is also necessary, but if an open, well-drained compost has been used enough oxygen will reach the seeds.

Warmth is provided by placing a domed plastic lid or sheet of glass over the seed-tray. Electrically-heated propagation frames are another possibility, enabling seeds to be sown earlier in the year without having to warm up the entire greenhouse.

The precise temperature needed to initiate germination varies from one species to another. Check the instructions on the seed packet – usually between 16– 21°C/ 61–70°F. Most seeds germinate in darkness. Therefore, cover the plastic dome or sheet of glass with newspaper until seedlings appear; then allow light in.

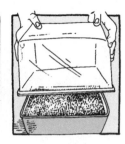

4. TAKE *care not to sow seeds within 12mm/½ in of the tray's sides. Most seeds germinate in darkness, so use a sieve to sprinkle compost over the surface.*

5. WATER *the compost by placing the seed-tray in a bowl of clean water until moisture seeps to the surface. Then, remove and allow excess water to drain.*

6. PLACE *a transparent lid over the seed-tray to help conserve warmth and to prevent the compost's surface drying out, harming the seeds and preventing germination.*

HELPING GERMINATION

Most seeds germinate within a few weeks, but some need help:
• Hard-coated seeds such as Sweet Peas and Morning Glory *(ipomoea)* resist the entry of moisture and air. Either gently rub the seed on sandpaper or carefully nick the coat with a sharp knife.
• Fluctuating temperatures help to break dormancy in seeds such as some lilies, tree paeonies and daphnes. Cold periods, followed by warm spells and then another cold period are often needed. Others need high night temperatures and low day ones. Specific instructions are usually detailed on seed packets.
• Cold periods initiate germination for seeds of trees and shrubs. Initially, place seeds on moist blotting paper for a few days, then put in a sealed container in a refrigerator for a few months. At the end of this period, seeds behave as though spring has arrived.
• Growth-inhibitor chemicals, present in some seeds, prevent rapid germination. Soaking in water leaches out chemicals, as well as softening them, and is ideal for cyclamen, *cytisus* (Broom), *caragana* (Pea Tree) and *clianthus* (Parrot's Bill).

1. FILL *a clean seed-tray with seed compost and firm it, especially around the edges as these are the areas that inevitably dry out first if watering is neglected.*

2. ADD *further compost and use a straight-edged piece of wood to level it with the sides. Then, use a presser to firm the surface about 12mm/½ in below the rim.*

3. TIP *seeds into a piece of stiff paper folded into a V-shape. Sprinkle a few seeds into it and sow them evenly and thinly by tapping the edge of the paper.*

F.1 HYBRIDS

These are produced by crossing two pure bred, closely related varieties. They are known as F.1 hybrids, which is short for 'first filial' generation. There are both vegetable and flowering F.1 varieties and most seed companies offer them in their catalogues.

Plants produced in this way are:
• *Larger and stronger than normal varieties.*
• *Uniform plants, creating a formal and unvarying appearance. This is ideal for summer-flowering bedding plants in formal arrangements, but does not create a cottage-garden display unless plants are placed at irregular intervals throughout a border.*
• *Uniformity in vegetable varieties has advantages and disadvantages. Plants are larger, but those raised from the same sowing tend to mature at the same time.*
Freezers help to utilize gluts; alternatively, make several sowings.

SOWING HARDY ANNUALS

❧

HARDY annuals are traditional residents of gardens, sometimes in borders totally devoted to them or as fillers in herbaceous borders. Occasionally they are planted in mixed borders, where a wide spectrum of plant types are used to create variety.

Hardy annuals are nature's pace-setters: in one season they germinate from seeds sown outdoors, they develop stems and leaves and then they bear flowers that produce seeds before the onset of winter.

Half-hardy annuals, incidentally, are not so hardy and are sown in gentle warmth earlier in the year and planted into a border when all risk of frost has passed. They are also known as summer-flowering bedding plants.

CHOOSING THE SITE
If you have a large garden, there is a possibility of choosing a warm, weed-free, wind-sheltered place where the soil is fertile, well-drained but moisture retentive.

Often, however, it is more a matter of filling empty borders with colour. Nevertheless, digging the soil in winter, ensuring it is well drained and adding plenty of decomposed compost or manure is part of the recipe for success.

WHEN TO SOW
Sow hardy annuals from early to late spring, depending on the weather pattern in your area. In warm regions where frost is seldom experienced, seeds can be sown in early spring, but in other areas late spring or early summer are better. If you are new to an area, talk to knowledgeable neighbours – most gardeners are keen to air their knowledge about plants and the weather!

Birds and cats are often a nuisance: creating a network of black cotton 10-15cm/4-6in above the surface acts as a deterrent, although birds sometimes get underneath. Alternatively, place twiggy sticks over the sown area. Remove them when the seedlings

are established and growing strongly. In dry weather, water the total area thoroughly but gently.

THINNING THE SEEDLINGS
When the seedlings are large enough to handle, thin them out, removing weak, sickly or damaged ones and leaving the others spaced apart equally. These spacings vary: whereas Love-lies-Bleeding (*Amaranthus caudatus*) seedlings are left about 38cm/15in apart, those of Love-in-a-Mist (*Nigella damascena*) need only be 15–23cm/6–9in. Check spacings on the seed packet. Thin the seedlings carefully and refirm those that remain, followed by a thorough but light watering. Seedlings left loosely in the ground soon become dry, and may die.

STAKING AND SUPPORTING
Immediately after thinning, insert twiggy sticks around plants so that they grow up and through them. Insert these sticks firmly in the ground and to a height slightly lower than each plant's predicted height – see seed packet.

CHILDREN IN THE GARDEN

From toddler to gardening enthusiast can be rapid and dramatic. When the novelty of repeated mud pies loses its fascination, children look for other gardening experiences and these often are sowing seeds.

The result of sowing seeds, however, has to be rapid and spectacular to retain their attention. Few annuals are better for this than Sunflowers, often the size of dinner plates, on plants 1.8m/6ft high and in rich, vibrant colours. Sown in their flowering positions in mid-to late spring, they burst into flower in mid-summer.

Snapdragons are other fun plants and provide endless amusement for 'nipping' noses, while Foxgloves make tiny gloves for dolls and Nasturtium leaves form dolls' hats.

1. DIG *the soil in winter, leaving the surface rough but level so that by spring, frost, rain and wind will have reduced it to a fine tilth. In spring, use a large rake to break down lumps; level the surface and remove big stones.*

2. FIRM *the soil by systematically shuffling over the surface. This is the best way to consolidate soil evenly. Do not use a roller as invariably it is too heavy and if stopped, consolidates one area more than another.*

3. SKETCH *the border on graph paper and indicate the sowing areas. Then, transfer the plan to a border, using a pointed stick.*

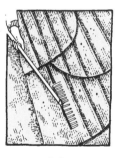

4. FORM *shallow drills 15–20cm/6–8in apart with the back of a garden rake. With experience, drills can be formed without using a straight-edged board or garden line. Draw hoes can also be used.*

5. SOW *seeds evenly and thinly. Do not sow them during windy weather or if the soil is very wet or dry. Do not feel obliged to sow the complete packet of seeds, as congested seedlings are susceptible to diseases.*

6. COVER *the seeds by shallowly using a garden rake. Do not disturb the seeds and avoid raking them out of the drill, as this makes weed identification difficult. Firm along the drill, using the rake's head.*

BIENNIALS AND HARDY HERBACEOUS PERENNIALS

ALTHOUGH they are different types of plants, biennials and hardy herbaceous perennials are both raised in seed-beds outdoors and later transplanted to their growing and flowering positions.

Biennials and hardy herbaceous perennials are sown in shallow drills in spring and early summer. When large enough to handle, thin the seedlings: these spacings vary according to a plant's stature and vigour.

The Daisy (*Bellis perennis*), a hardy perennial grown as a biennial, reaches only 10–15cm/4–6in high and is thinned 7.5–10cm/3–4in apart. Whereas Yarrow (*Achillea filipendula*), which grows up to 1.2m/4ft, is thinned to 30cm/12in. The hardy perennial Columbine (*Aquilegia*), growing 45–60cm/1½–2ft high, is thinned 15–20cm/6–8in apart.

The distances to which individual biennials and herbaceous perennials are thinned are usually indicated on seed packets.

TRANSPLANTING

In autumn of the same year, transplant young plants into their flowering positions, setting them slightly wider apart than when thinned out. Ensure that plants are firmly planted; in spring, re-firm those lifted by frost.

In extremely cold areas transplanting is sometimes left until early spring of the following year.

RAISING VEGETABLES IN SEED-BEDS

Several vegetables, such as cabbages, Brussels sprouts, cauliflowers and broccoli are initially raised in seed-beds and later transplanted to their growing positions. Asparagus seedlings and leeks are also raised in seed-beds. Established young plants, ready for transplanting, are frequently sold by garden centres and nurseries.

NATURAL INCLINATIONS

Some plants grown from seeds are raised in a different way from their natural inclinations.

ANNUALS *An annual is a plant that grows from seed, flowers and produces seeds within the same year. However, a few plants that are not strictly annuals are treated as such. For instance, Lobelia (Lobelia erinus) is a half-hardy perennial invariably grown as a half-hardy annual. Marvel of Peru (Mirabilis jalapa) is a perennial grown as a half-hardy annual, while Busy Lizzie (Impatiens walleriana) is a greenhouse perennial treated as a half-hardy annual.*

BIENNIALS *A biennial makes its initial growth one year and flowers the following one, then dying. However, several plants not strictly biennial are treated as such. For example, the Daisy (Bellis perennis) is a hardy perennial invariably grown as a biennial. Sweet William (Dianthus barbatus) is another perennial cultivated as a biennial.*

BIENNIALS RAISED FROM SEEDS

These include many plants that bring colour to borders in spring and early summer, such as:

- Canterbury Bell (*Campanula medium*)
- Foxglove (*Digitalis purpurea*)
- Hollyhock (*Alcea rosea/Althaea rosea*)
- Honesty (*Lunaria annua*)
- Sweet William (*Dianthus barbatus*)
- Wallflower (*Cheiranthus cheiri*)

HERBACEOUS PERENNIALS RAISED FROM SEEDS

- Anchusa (*Anchusa azurea*)
- Bee Balm (*Monarda didyma*)
- Columbine (*Aquilegia vulgaris*)
- Cupid's Dart (*Catananche caerulea*)
- Fleabane (*Erigeron speciosus*)
- Incarvillea (*Incarvillea delavayi*)
- Sea Holly (*Eryngium maritimum*)
- Shasta Daisy/Max Daisy (*Chrysanthemum maximum*)
- Valerian (*Centranthus ruber*)
- Yarrow (*Achillea filipendula*)

1. PREPARE *the soil in winter, digging the seed-bed, removing perennial weeds and mixing in decomposed compost and manure. In spring, use a large rake to level the surface, breaking it down to a fine tilth.*

2. FIRM *the surface by systematically shuffling over it. As well as consolidating the soil, shuffling helps to break down large lumps. Do not use a garden roller: it always makes the surface uneven.*

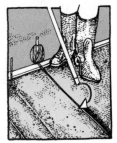

3. RAKE *the surface again and use a draw hoe to form shallow drills. A garden line or straight-edged board helps to create straight drills spaced 15-20cm/6-8in apart. Remove the garden line or board before sowing seeds.*

4. SOW *seeds evenly and thinly in shallow drills, taking care not to drop them in clusters. Congested seedlings are susceptible to diseases, as well as creating unnecessary competition for water, air and nutrients.*

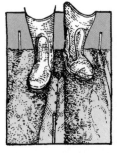

5. COVER *the seeds by straddling the row and shuffling along, directing soil over them. Alternatively, use a garden rake. Afterwards, firm soil over the seeds either with your feet or the top of a garden rake.*

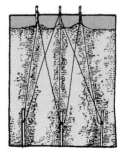

6. RAKE *lightly over the surface – in the direction of the drills – to remove feet marks and depressions. This prevents rain water resting in puddles on the surface. If birds are a nuisance, cover with wire netting or sticks.*

SOWING VEGETABLES

M̲OST vegetables are raised from seeds sown in V-shaped drills or, in a few cases, in flat-bottomed trenches.

V-SHAPED DRILLS

Use a draw hoe to form these drills. Their depths, of course, need to be related to the seeds and their sizes. The depths of drills for a range of vegetables are:
- 12mm/½in: Chicory, Endive, Leeks, Lettuce, Onions, Salsify.
- 12–18mm/½–¾in: Asparagus, Carrots, Kohlrabi, Marrows, Parsnips, Radishes, Spinach, Squashes, Swedes, Turnips.
- 18–25mm/¾–1in: Broccoli, Brussels sprouts, Cabbages, Cauliflowers, Kale.
- 25mm/1in: Asparagus peas, Beetroot, Sweet corn.
- 5cm/2in: Garden Peas, Beans – French, Runner, Haricot, Soya.
- 7.5cm/3in: Broad beans
- 15cm/6in: Jerusalem artichokes and Potatoes.

IN TRENCHES

A few vegetables, such as peas, are sown in flat-bottomed trenches. They can also be sown in V-shaped drills, but to produce more peas from a similar sized area they they are best sown in 20–23cm/8–9in wide and 5–6.5cm/2–2½in deep, flat-based trenches.

Sow seeds in three rows, 7.5cm/3in apart and the seeds similarly spaced within the rows. Stagger the seeds in the centre row so that they have the maximum amount of space. Spacing out seeds in this way helps to reduce the amount of seed needed, as well as eliminating the need to thin out seedlings later.

CONTINUOUS LINES

Most vegetable seeds are sown thinly and evenly in continuous lines in drills. After germination and when large enough to handle, the seedlings are thinned out to the desired spacings. It is therefore a waste of seed and money to sow seeds thickly.

IN CLUSTERS

Instead of sowing seeds in continuous trickles in drills, vegetables such as parsnips are sown in groups of three or four seeds spaced 10–15cm/4–6in apart. After germination and when the seedlings are large enough to handle, they are thinned to leave the strongest at each position.

THINNING SEEDLINGS

When seedlings are large enough to handle they can be thinned. Leaving this task too long results in thin, leggy and weak seedlings.

Unless the soil is already moist, lightly but thoroughly water the soil during the previous day.

Usually, seedlings are thinned in two stages; first to half the ultimate distance, later to the full spacing. This ensures that should a seedling die after the first thinning, the maximum gap left between them will only be one-and-a-half times the full spacing, not twice the distance.

Carefully pull up unwanted seedlings, taking care to re-firm those that have been loosened. Afterwards, lightly but thoroughly water the seedlings.

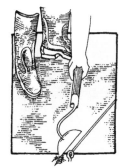

FORM *V-shaped drills by using a draw hoe. Use a garden line to ensure the row is straight and walk backwards using the hoe. If the row is long, stand on the line to prevent it being moved sideways.*

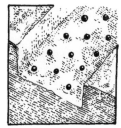

FLAT-BOTTOMED *trenches are formed either with a draw hoe or spade: 20–23cm/8–9in wide and 5–6.5cm/2–2½in deep. Sow peas in three rows, 7.5cm/3in apart and a similar distance in rows.*

SOW SEEDS *evenly and thinly in a single line along the base of a V-drill. Ensure seeds are spaced out, as if they are congested it encourages unnecessary competition for light, air, moisture and nutrients.*

SOW *some seeds, such as parsnips, in small groups. After germination, remove the weakest seedlings, leaving only the strongest. This ensures that the remaining seedlings are at the desired and optimum spacings.*

THIN *seedlings as soon as they are large enough to handle. Re-firm the remaining seedlings and thoroughly but lightly water them. Pick up unwanted seedlings; leaving them on the soil encourages pests and diseases.*

FLUID SOWING *is when seeds are mixed with a fluid gel such as wallpaper paste and squeezed out into the base of a drill. It helps to retain moisture around seeds and encourages rapid and even germination.*

SOFT-WOOD CUTTINGS

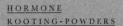

ROOTING soft-wood cuttings is a popular and easy way to increase soft-stemmed plants. These include many plants grown as houseplants in temperate climates, as well as dahlias and chrysanthemums that are raised in greenhouses early in the year and planted outdoors as soon as all risk of frost has passed.

CHRYSANTHEMUMS AND DAHLIAS

These popular plants frequently grow more than 1.2m/4ft high and have stems that harden and become slightly woody as the season progresses. In late winter and spring, however, they can be increased from soft-wood cuttings.

Roots (known as stools) are dug up in autumn, stems cut down to about 15cm/6in high and packed in boxes with clean soil around them. In late winter or spring – after being watered and placed in gentle warmth – the stems will produce soft shoots that when 10–15cm/4–6in long can be formed into 6–7.5cm/2½–3in long cuttings.

These are prepared by cutting beneath a leaf joint and removing the lower leaves. Then, insert them about 2.5cm/1in deep in equal parts moist peat and sharp sand. Water gently to settle compost around their bases.

PLASTIC BAGS

Cuttings are encouraged to root by placing them in plastic bags or propagation units.

Some units are unheated, while others are warmed by electricity. However, a popular and inexpensive way to create a warm, humid atmosphere is to place a plastic bag over them. It should not touch the leaves or stems: therefore first insert four or five thin canes in the compost. Draw a plastic bag over them and secure to the pot with an elastic band.

Regularly check the cuttings to ensure they are not touching the bag. Pot up when rooted.

MIST-PROPAGATION

Until recently, only commercial mist-propagation units were available, but ones for enthusiastic amateurs are now widely sold.

Mist propagation units are electrically operated and designed to automatically maintain a thin film of water droplets over the cuttings. This keeps them cool and prevents leaves wilting while the bases of their stems are forming roots.

The compost in which the cuttings are inserted is warmed by electricity cables and this further encourages the rapid development of roots.

ROOTING CUTTINGS IN WATER

Encouraging soft-stemmed cuttings to root by suspending their stems in water delights children as well as producing new plants.

Busy Lizzie (Impatiens walleriana) *readily develops roots: prepare each cutting by severing the stem just below a leaf joint and removing the lower leaves. Fill a glass or milk bottle to within 2.5cm/1in of the top with clean water. Place a piece of card over the container's top and pierce a hole in it so that the stem passes through but is held firmly. The lower 2.5cm/1in of stem should be in the water.*

Position the glass or bottle on a warm, lightly shaded window sill. Take care not to let the water-level fall as it then allows roots that have formed to dry out. When rooted, pot up and place in light shade until established.

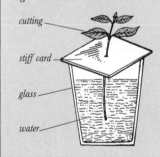

cutting

stiff card

glass

water

1. MANY *houseplants, such as the Swedish Ivy, are increased from soft-wood cuttings. Use a sharp knife to sever a stem (above), just above a leaf joint. Do not leave unsightly spurs that will decay and encourage the entry of diseases.*

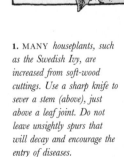

2. REMOVE *the lower leaves and trim each cutting (left) just below a leaf-joint. Insert and firm the cutting (above) 18–25mm/³⁄₄–1in deep in equal parts moist peat and sharp sand. This holds the cuttings firm and provides moisture and air.*

The white-edged Swedish Ivy (Plectranthus coleoides 'Marginatus') is an easily grown houseplant. It creates colour and interest throughout the year.

HALF-RIPE CUTTINGS

THESE are also known as semi-mature and semi-hardwood cuttings, and are formed of shoots more mature than soft-wood types but not as old and tough as hardwood ones.

Half-ripe cuttings are taken from 10–13cm/4–5in long shoots during mid-summer and into the early part of late summer.

PREPARING CUTTINGS

Shoots with 'heels' have their lower leaves removed and the heel slightly trimmed, removing whisker-like pieces from their edges. Normal half-ripe cuttings also have their lower leaves removed, but their bases are cut to just below a leaf joint.

Heathers are increased from cuttings only 6–7.5cm/2¹⁄₂–3in long, usually with heels of older wood attached to their bases.

INSERTING CUTTINGS

Insert the cuttings – three in a 7.5cm/3in-wide pot or five in a 13cm/5in one – to about one-third of their length in equal parts moist peat and sharp sand, after having dipped their bases in a hormone rooting-powder.

Place in a cool, sun-sheltered garden frame or under a cloche. Alternatively, they often develop roots when placed against a warm but sunless wall – but this is not recommended for cold areas.

Rooting is not rapid and usually it is not until spring of the following year that plants can be planted into a nurserybed in a sheltered, lightly shaded corner of your garden. Ensure that their roots do not dry out. Later they are moved to their permanent positions. Do not set them in a border until they are well established.

HARDWOOD CUTTINGS

THESE are taken mainly from early to late autumn from mature shoots of the current season's growth. In theory, hardwood cuttings can be taken from autumn to early spring, whenever plants are dormant, but usually it is an autumnal task.

Some hardwood cuttings are taken with 'heels', but by far the majority are not. These cuttings are variable in length, from 15–38cm/6–15in but the vast majority are 23–30cm/9–12in.

PREPARING HARDWOOD CUTTINGS

Use sharp secateurs to cut their bases slightly below a bud. If the top of a cutting is green and immature, cut it back to just above a healthy, mature bud.

Most hardwood cuttings are taken from deciduous plants and therefore by the time shoots are formed into cuttings they are bare of leaves. If, however, semi-evergreen plants are increased in this way, remove the lower leaves.

INSERTING HARDWOOD CUTTINGS

In a sheltered, out-of-the-way and well-drained part of a garden, form a 15–20cm/6–8in deep drill with one vertical side. Place sharp sand in its base and position the cuttings along the vertical side. Firm soil around them.

In spring, re-firm the soil, as it is likely to have been loosened by winter frost. Use the heel of your shoe to do this job.

These cuttings take about a year to develop roots. Then they are moved to wider spacings in a nurserybed until large enough to be given permanent positions.

1. TAKE *half-ripe cuttings during mid-summer when shoots are firmer than for soft-wood types. Remove 10–13cm/4–5in long shoots, preferably with a piece of older wood still attached to their bases.*

2. REMOVE *the lower leaves and trim the cutting's base, cutting off whisker-like growths from around the heel. These heels – formed of older wood – are not essential, but they encourage rapid rooting.*

3. DIP *the base of each cutting in hormone rooting-powder and insert 3.6–5cm/1¹⁄₂–2in deep in equal parts moist peat and sharp sand. Firm compost around the cuttings. Then, water the compost thoroughly.*

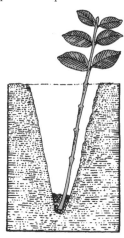

1. SELECT *healthy, mature, pest- and disease-free shoots produced during the current season. Their lengths vary according to the species, but usually they are 23–30cm/9–12in.*

2. REMOVE *lower leaves and trim beneath a leaf joint. Most plants increased by hardwood cuttings are deciduous, but some, like the Privet shown here, are partially evergreen.*

3. FORM *a trench with one vertical side and place a handful of sharp sand in its base. Insert cuttings to about half their lengths and firm soil around them, using your shoe to ensure firmness.*

ROOT CUTTINGS

◆

SOME plants can be increased by cutting up their roots and encouraging these to develop roots. It enables many new plants to be raised from a single parent.

Root cuttings are used to increase many herbaceous perennials, as well as a few shrubs with fleshy roots. Some shrubs, however, that are candidates for being increased by root cuttings, also develop sucker-like growths and frequently it is easier to increase them by that method. The Staghorn Sumach (*Rhus typhina*), frequently grown for its coloured leaves in autumn, is an example of this dual role.

The thickness of roots varies from one species to another: those about 12mm/¹/₂in thick are inserted vertically, while thinner ones are laid horizontally on to moisture-retentive compost.

All of the roots must be free from diseases and pest damage.

Do not take root cuttings from the roots of budded or grafted plants, as they will not produce replicas of the varietal part.

PLANTS INCREASED FROM THIN-ROOT CUTTINGS
- Drumstick Primrose (*Primula denticulata*)
- Perennial Phlox (*Phlox paniculata*)

PLANTS INCREASED FROM THICK-ROOT CUTTINGS
- Anchusa (*Anchusa azurea*)
- Californian Tree Poppy (*Romneya coulteri*)
- Cupid's Dart (*Catananche caerulea*)
- Mullien (*Verbascum*)
- Oriental Poppy (*Papaver orientale*)
- Sea Holly/Eryngo (*Eryngium*)
- Staghorn Sumach (*Rhus typhina*)

THIN-ROOT CUTTINGS

1. LIFT *plants during their dormant periods, in autumn and winter. An alternative to lifting an entire plant is to expose a few roots and to sever them. Wash the roots to remove soil and to make preparing them easier.*

2. CUT *thin roots into pieces 3.6–7.5cm/1¹/₂–3in long and lay them on the surface of equal parts moist peat and sharp sand to which has been added a dusting of more sand to increase aeration and drainage.*

3. COVER *the roots with a 12mm/¹/₂in layer of equal parts sharp sand and peat. The surface of the compost should be12–25mm/¹/₂–1in below the seed-tray's top. Lightly but thoroughly water the compost to settle it around the roots.*

THICK-ROOT CUTTINGS

1. LIFT *or expose (above) the roots of plants with thick roots in the same way as for thin types. Sever the roots into pieces 6–7.5cm/2¹/₂–3in long. Make a flat cut at the end nearest the plant's centre, and a slope at the other end.*

2. INSERT *the cuttings, slant-side downwards, in equal parts moist peat and sharp sand. Press the top flush with the compost and add a 12mm/¹/₂in layer of equal parts sharp sand and peat. Lightly but thoroughly water the compost to settle it around the roots.*

AFTERCARE
After root cuttings have developed roots they are best planted into a nurserybed until large enough to be transferred to their permanent positions in a garden.

However, if they are small, instead of planting them directly into a nurserybed, first pot them up into loam-based compost in small pots. Keep the compost moist and place in a cool position.

AERIAL ROOTS IN TROPICS
In warm, humid regions, some trees produce aerial roots that grow downwards, fix themselves in the soil and develop roots. They then either support the parent tree, prolonging its life, or are severed and encouraged to become independent plants.

On a smaller scale, several houseplants native to warm regions develop aerial roots. These include philodendrons and monsteras. They, too, have roots that sprawl and frequently trail around the plant's base.

MAN'S INFLUENCE
In Sri Lanka (former Ceylon), aerial roots of certain rubber plants were encouraged to reach the ground and develop roots. Long canes of a giant bamboo, with stems up to 15m/50ft high and more than 13cm/5in in diameter, were split lengthways and the inner part removed.

The two parts were then placed around an aerial root and tied together in several places.

The lower end was securely fixed in the ground, while the upper one had moss tightly packed around the stem to prevent vermin such as rats and squirrels entering the bamboo tunnel and damaging the root.

After the aerial root had developed normal roots, it was severed from the parent and transplanted to its permanent growing position.

In recent years, with the introduction of propagation frames with controlled warmth and humidity, many of these traditional and tropical ways to increase plants have ceased. However easy and clinical modern methods are, they do not have the mystique and country-craft fascination of techniques used in earlier years.

LEAF-STEM CUTTINGS

THIS is an excellent way to increase plants with long stems that are packed with small leaves. It is frequently used to reproduce climbing and trailing houseplants grown for their attractive foliage, such as the many attractively variegated ivies.

Increasing plants by leaf-stem cuttings has the benefit of enabling one long stem to produce many cuttings. Specimen plants are therefore not decimated and their appearance spoiled, especially if only a single stem is cut from the plant's back.

PLANTS INCREASED FROM LEAF-STEM CUTTINGS
• Canary Island Ivy (*Hedera canariensis* 'Gloire de Marengo': also known as 'Variegata')
• English Ivy (*Hedera helix* – including the many varieties with attractive leaves, such as 'Glacier', 'Jubilee', 'White Kolibri', 'New Sicilia', 'Pittsburgh', 'Chicago', 'Gold Child', 'Little Diamond', 'Sagittaefolia', 'Eva' and 'Anne Marie')
• German Ivy (*Senecio mikanioides*)
• Wax Ivy/Cape Ivy (*Senecio macroglossus* 'Variegatus')

1. CUT *a long, young, healthy stem from a parent plant, severing it either at the plant's base or close to a leaf joint. Do not leave unsightly spurs.*

2. USE *a sharp knife to cut the shoot into several cuttings. Cut slightly above each leaf joint, leaving a handle-like piece of stem 36mm/1½in long.*

3. USE *a small dibber to form a hole 18–30mm/ ¾–1¼in deep in equal parts moist peat and sharp sand. Firm the compost around each cutting.*

4. WATER *the cuttings. Insert split canes at the edges, draw a plastic bag over them and secure it with an elastic band.*

5. PLACE *in light shade and gentle warmth. When young shoots appear at the leaf joints, remove the bag and give them fresh air.*

6. POT UP *rooted cuttings. Put one, three or five cuttings in each pot – a high number creates an attractively bushy plant quickly.*

LEAF-PETIOLE CUTTINGS

THIS is a novel but practical way to increase plants, and frequently used to propagate African Violets *(Saintpaulia ionantha)*. It enables a single mother plant to create many new ones. Petiole is the botanical term for leaf stem.

CREATING LEAF-PETIOLE CUTTINGS
These can be taken throughout the year, but spring and early summer are the best times.

Their preparation is easy and involves trimming the stem to about 36mm/1½in long. It is then inserted in equal parts moist peat and sharp sand, leaving the leaf blade resting slightly above the surface. The leaves of African violets are soft and hairy, and must not become wet.

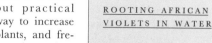

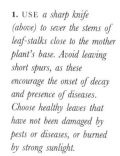

1. USE *a sharp knife (above) to sever the stems of leaf-stalks close to the mother plant's base. Avoid leaving short spurs, as these encourage the onset of decay and presence of diseases. Choose healthy leaves that have not been damaged by pests or diseases, or burned by strong sunlight.*

2. TRIM *stems to 36mm/1½in long (left). Dip ends in hormone rooting-powder using a small dibber, insert and firm each stem 2.5cm/1in deep (above). Gently water. Insert split canes into the compost and cover with a plastic bag.*

WHOLE-LEAF CUTTINGS

Several large-leaved plants grown in greenhouses and homes can be increased by placing a leaf flat on damp compost to encourage the formation of roots and new, healthy plants.

Use only leaves that are healthy and representative of the species. Do not use those that are old, or through neglect have dried and withered edges – they never produce vigorous, attractive plants.

When severing leaves from a mother plant, take them from several sides so that the plant's shape does not become imbalanced.

MOTHER PLANT
The day before cutting the leaves, water the mother plant thoroughly to ensure that its leaves are full of moisture. Wilting leaves do not create good cuttings and seldom root satisfactorily.

Leaves can be encouraged to form new plants throughout the year, but spring and summer are the best times as mother plants are usually healthier. Also, leaves root more quickly when the light is strong and plentiful.

Take care not to place the leaves in high temperatures or strong, direct sunlight. A north-facing window sill indoors, or a shaded greenhouse bench, is much better than scorching heat – a constant day temperature of 15–18°C/59–64°F is desirable. High temperatures dry the compost and desiccate leaves.

PLACING ON DAMP COMPOST
Leaves are selected, stalks removed, veins severed and the whole leaf laid flat on damp compost formed of equal parts moist peat and sharp sand. Secure them to the compost with U-shaped pieces of wire or small pebbles. Cover with a transparent lid and place out of direct sunlight. Check the compost regularly and if dry, stand the seed-tray in a bowl shallowly filled with water, until moisture seeps to the surface. Remove and allow excess water to drain.

4. ALTERNATIVELY, *place small stones on top of the leaf and around its edges. The disadvantage of this method is that shoots, as they grow, may be obstructed. However, if the leaf is regularly checked they can be quickly removed.*

5. PLACE *the seed-tray in a bowl shallowly filled with water. Remove it when the surface is damp, and allow excess water to drain away. Cover the seed-tray with a transparent lid. Regularly wipe off condensation from the inside of the lid.*

6. WHEN *young plants develop on the leaf's surface, carefully remove them and pot up into individual pots of potting compost. Water the compost and place the plant in gentle warmth and light shade until established. Avoid strong sunlight.*

POTTING UP
When roots have formed and shoots developed from the leaf's surface, carefully detach each young plant and pot up individually in a potting compost. Water and keep shaded until established.

Take care when potting up young plants: they should not be put in too large pots. When small plants are in large pots it is difficult to keep the moisture content in the compost just right. It usually becomes too wet and subsequently too cold. Under these conditions, plants soon decay.

PLANTS INCREASED FROM WHOLE-LEAF CUTTINGS
Iron Cross Begonia (*Begonia masoniana*) is a distinctive large-leaved begonia, ideal as a centre-piece on a coffee or dining room table. The lop-sided, somewhat heart-shaped, crinkled-surfaced, mid-green leaves have four or five deep bronze bars radiating from their centres.
Rex Begonia (*Begonia rex*), also known as King Begonia and

Painted-leaf Begonia, dislays colourful, variedly patterned leaves and is ideal for decorating tables. In winter, place on a north-facing window sill, but in summer avoid direct sunlight.
Cape Primrose (*Streptocarpus x hybridus*) has long, spoon-like, corrugated, mid-green leaves and a wealth of trumpet-shaped flowers on long stems from late spring to late summer. These flowers include shades of red and purple, as well as white. It is ideal for decorating cool, lightly shaded rooms in summer.

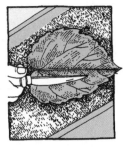

1. USE *a sharp knife to sever the stem of a leaf close to the plant's base. Do not leave short spurs at the base as they look unsightly. Try not to spoil the plant's shape: select leaves from around the complete plant.*

2. TURN *the leaf upside down and sever the stalk. Then, make several cuts, 18–25mm/³⁄₄–1in apart, through the main and secondary veins. Try not to cut through the whole leaf, as it then might fall apart.*

3. PLACE *the leaf – vein-side downwards – on equal parts moist peat and sharp sand. Use small pieces of bent wire to secure the leaf to the compost. It must be in close contact with the soil.*

The Rex Begonia (Begonia rex) is a superb houseplant, creating a dominant feature throughout the year. Placing it in a white cache pot highlights the attractive leaves.

LEAF SQUARES
AND LEAF TRIANGLES

THESE are both ways to increase large-leaved begonias, and from one healthy leaf it is possible to produce eight or more new plants.

Healthy, relatively young leaves, free from pests and diseases, create the best cuttings. And ensure the compost is moist before severing them from the parent plant. Indeed, it is best to thoroughly water the compost several times during the preceding week, and to position it out of direct sunlight.

Dry, shrivelled leaves never produce strong, fast-rooting cuttings. A reserve of moisture within each cutting is essential.

CREATING CUTTINGS

From spring to mid-summer is the best time to take and root these cuttings. Use a sharp knife to sever the stalk close to the leaf. Turn the leaf over so that it is the right way up, and with a sharp knife form triangles. The apex of each cutting must be towards the centre, where the stalk originated. Always use a sharp knife as ragged cuts take longer to heal and produce roots.

INSERTING CUTTINGS

Fill a seed-tray with equal parts moist peat and sharp sand, and firm it to within about 12mm/½in of the top.

LEAF SQUARES

These are used similarly to leaf triangles – but are square. Earlier, the squares were more popular than triangles, but now are not so fashionable. This is because:
• It is easier to insert triangles into the compost and to get them to stand upright.
• There is less chance of triangles falling over when initially watered.
• Leaf squares are smaller than the triangles and therefore do not contain such as large reserve of food and moisture.
• It is easier to ensure that the cuttings are inserted the right way up.

Use a knife or thin spatula to form holes 18–25mm/¾–1in deep in rows in the compost. Insert each cutting point down: hold its top, place in a hole and firm compost around its base. After insertion, the cuttings should not touch each other.

Lightly water the compost to settle it around the cuttings. However, take care not to water them excessively as this may disturb them from the best rooting position.

Insert a label in the seed-tray, indicating the date of planting and the plant's name.

Place a translucent plastic lid over the seed-tray, and position it in gentle warmth and a lightly shaded position. Avoid high temperatures and direct sunlight, as this soon dries the compost and shrivels the cuttings. Indeed, successful rooting is more likely on a cooler east or north-facing window sill than a southerly one in strong sunlight.

Periodically, wipe away condensation from the inside of the

Iron Cross Begonia (Begonia masoniana) is ideal for decorating tabletops in cool rooms.

translucent lid. If left, it drips on the cuttings and causes the onset of decay.

Regularly check the compost to ensure it is moist. Water by standing the the entire seed-tray in a bowl shallowly filled with water. When moisture percolates to the surface, remove the seed-tray and allow excess water to drain.

Do not water leaf cuttings from above, as moisture then remains on their surfaces and encourages them to decay. Leaves are usually at more risk than stems from decay caused by moisture.

POTTING UP

Rooting is indicated when shoots appear from the bases of the cuttings. Pot them up individually – the small leaf still intact – in small pots of potting compost. The leaf will eventually decay and fall off.

After potting, water gently and place in light shade until established and the young plant is growing strongly.

1. USE *a sharp knife to cut a leaf-stalk close to the plant's base. Do not leave short, unsightly pieces of stem on the mother plant as these decay and encourage the presence of diseases.*

2. TURN *the leaf upside down and cut off the leaf-stalk close to the blade. The leaf must be healthy and turgid: if dry and shrivelled it will not readily produce healthy roots.*

3. PLACE *the leaf – the top side uppermost – on a flat board and use a sharp knife to form triangles. The tip of the triangle must always be in the leaf's centre, from where the stem originates.*

4. INSERT *the cuttings, pointed ends downward and to about half their lengths, in equal parts moist peat and sharp sand. Firm compost around them, then carefully and lightly water.*

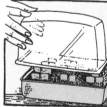

5. COVER *with a translucent lid. Periodically, check compost; if dry, stand the tray in water until the surface is damp. Avoid wetting the leaves as they may decay.*

6. WHEN *rooted, pot up into a small pot of potting compost; water and place in gentle warmth.*

CROSS-SECTIONS OF LEAVES

SOME plants are reproduced by cutting their leaves crosswise into strips about 5cm/2in deep. They are then inserted in moisture-retentive but well-drained compost, watered and placed in gentle warmth.

PREPARING CUTTINGS

Water the plants several times during the few days before taking the cuttings. Dry leaves never root quickly and soon die.

Choose healthy and relatively young leaves that are good examples of the species.

Use a sharp knife to sever them at their bases. Do not leave small stubs of leaves as they are unsightly and eventually will decay.

Place the leaves on a clean board and use a sharp knife or scalpel to cut them into 5cm/2in-wide strips. Take care not to mix up the pieces as it is essential that the side nearest to the leaf stalk is inserted into the compost.

When inserting leaves of Mother-in-Law's Tongue, allow their surfaces to dry for a day before insertion – it encourages more rapid rooting.

INSERTING CUTTINGS

Fill a seed-tray or pot with equal parts moist peat and sharp sand. Sprinkling sharp sand on the surface encourages greater aeration around the cuttings and induces faster rooting.

Use a knife or spatula to form slits in the compost into which the cuttings can be inserted 18mm/³⁄₄in deep. Firm compost around their bases.

Lightly water the compost to settle it around the cuttings, taking care not to disturb them. Avoid watering them too heavily.

After all moisture has dried from the leaves, either cover with a translucent plastic dome or place in a propagation frame.

Gentle warmth encourages root development, but do not expose them to high temperatures. Indeed, a gently warm but shaded, north or east-facing window sill is better than a southerly one in full sun. Cuttings soon become brittle and dry in strong sunlight and high temperatures.

Periodically, remove the cover and wipe away condensation. Also, check the compost and if dry, stand the pot or seed-tray in a shallow bowl of water until moisture rises to the surface. Then, remove and allow to drain.

When young shoots develop, pot up the cuttings into individual pots. Water the compost and place in gentle warmth and shade until established. Then, reduce the temperature and place the young plants in light shade.

Mother-in-Law's Tongue (Sansevieria trifasciata) is an eye-catching plant with upright, sword-like, dark green leaves displaying transverse bands mottled light grey.

1. SELECT *a healthy, relatively young leaf and cut it off close to its base. Take care not to spoil the plant's shape by removing too many leaves at one time or by taking them from the same position. The leaves are tough and therefore the knife must be sharp.*

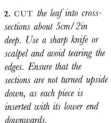

2. CUT *the leaf into cross-sections about 5cm/2in deep. Use a sharp knife or scalpel and avoid tearing the edges. Ensure that the sections are not turned upside down, as each piece is inserted with its lower end downwards.*

3. FILL *and firm a pot with equal parts moist peat and sharp sand. Spread a thin layer of sharp sand over the surface. Use a knife to make slits in the compost to insert them 18mm/³⁄₄in deep. Firm compost around each cutting. Lightly but thoroughly water the compost from above.*

Cape Primrose (Streptocarpus hybridus) creates red, purple or white, foxglove-like flowers from late spring.

1. SELECT *a healthy, young leaf and cut into 5cm/2in-wide sections. Leaves taken from dry plants do not readily develop roots, so water the compost during the previous day.*

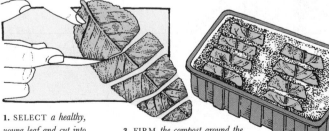

2. FILL *and firm a seed-tray with equal parts moist peat and sharp sand. Use a knife to form slits and insert the cuttings 18mm/³⁄₄in deep. Ensure they are upright.*

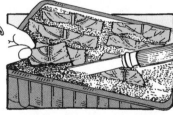

3. FIRM *the compost around the cuttings. Water lightly but thoroughly to settle compost around their bases. Place in a propagation frame or cover with a translucent lid. Avoid moistening the leaves as this encourages decay.*

CANE CUTTINGS

CANE cuttings are formed from stems and resemble thick cuttings. They are frequently created from the stems of plants that have lost their lower leaves.

Cutting up a main stem clearly destroys a plant, however tatty it may appear through the loss of its lower leaves. However, each stem can be used to create several new plants, so the original plant is not entirely wasted.

Spring and summer are the best times to form cane cuttings, as once rooted they have time to establish themselves before the onset of cold winter weather.

There are two types of cane cuttings: those laid flat on moist compost, and the ones that are inserted vertically. Horizontal cuttings usually root more quickly than tougher vertical ones.

VERTICAL CANE CUTTINGS

After a few years, yuccas invariably lose their lower leaves and although these plants have a distinctive and 'architectural' appearance they eventually outgrow available space indoors.

Chop up the stems into 7.5–10cm/3–4in long pieces – but

1. INCREASE *yuccas by forming vertical cane cuttings. Cut or scrape away wax (if present) from the lower end, but leave it on the top part.*

3. PLACE *the pot in a plastic bag and position in gentle warmth. Inspect the compost every ten days to ensure it is moist. Water as necessary. When shoots appear, remove the bag and slowly acclimatize the plant to a lower temperature.*

Placing the plant in a plastic bag both increases the temperature and humidity, but the compost must remain moist at all times.

2. FILL *a pot with equal parts moist peat and sharp sand and insert the lower 36–50mm/1½–2in of the cutting. Firm the compost, water and allow excess to drain.*

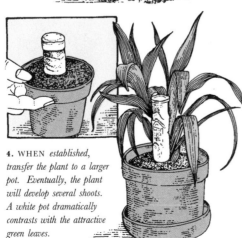

4. WHEN *established, transfer the plant to a larger pot. Eventually, the plant will develop several shoots. A white pot dramatically contrasts with the attractive green leaves.*

 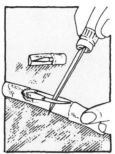 

1. DUMB *canes are increased from cane cuttings during spring and early summer. Use a sharp knife to sever healthy stems at their bases, but try not to spoil the plant's shape.*

2. USE *a sharp knife to cut a stem into 5–7.5cm/2–3in lengths, each piece having at least one strong and healthy bud. These buds grow from the old leaf joints.*

3. FILL *a pot with equal parts moist peat and sharp sand. Position the stems, bud-side upwards, and secure with bent wires. Cover with a plastic bag and place in gentle warmth.*

take care to remember which are the tops and bottoms of the canes. These are then inserted 36–50mm/1½–2in deep in equal parts moist peat and sharp sand.

Place in an opaque bag and position in gentle warmth. Regularly check the compost to ensure it is moist. Remove the bag when shoots appear and slowly acclimatize the rooted cutting to a lower temperature and less humidity. Later, it can be transferred to a larger pot.

HORIZONTAL CANE CUTTINGS

Dumb Canes, dracaenas and cordylines are increased from cane cuttings laid flat on damp compost. Sever a strong and healthy stem from a mother plant and cut it into 5–7.5cm/2–3in long pieces, each with at least one bud.

Push each cutting into a mixture of equal parts moist peat and sharp sand. Secure the cuttings in the compost with bent wires.

Water lightly, allow surplus to drain and cover with a plastic dome. Alternatively, insert four or five small split canes in the com-

post, and close to the pot's edge, then draw a transparent plastic bag over and secure around the pot with an elastic band. Place in gentle warmth, and when rooted remove the covering and decrease the temperature. When established, transfer to a larger pot.

PLANTS INCREASED FROM CANE CUTTINGS
• Cordylines
• Dracaenas
• Dumb Cane (*Dieffenbachia*)
• Yuccas

HOLIDAY GIFTS

Frequently, when holidaying in warm countries, Ti-log cuttings are sold as gifts to take home. Cuttings from Brazil are sold as Lucky Plants and usually have their ends sealed with paraffin wax to prevent desiccation.

The top of each cane is indicated by a specific colour. This ensures the cuttings are inserted into the compost the right way up.

CACTI AND OTHER SUCCULENTS

AS WELL as being grown from seed, many cacti and other succulents can be propagated from cuttings taken during spring and summer.

Cacti with clusters of small stems are easily increased by severing them at their bases. Water the plant during the previous day and use a sharp knife to sever stems. Ensure short, unsightly stubs are not left on the mother plant. Wear gloves to prevent spines damaging your hands.

Allow the cut surfaces to dry for a couple of days before inserting them about 12mm/$\frac{1}{2}$in deep in equal parts moist peat and sharp grit, with a surface covering of sharp sand.

Water lightly but thoroughly to settle compost around the cuttings and place them in gentle warmth. Make sure they are away from direct sunlight.

INCREASING SUCCULENTS

Many succulents are easily increased from cuttings. The Jade Plant (*Crassula argentea*) has fleshy leaves that can be inserted vertically into well-drained and aerated compost, while the October Plant (*Sedum sieboldii*) has flat, coin-like leaves that are laid flat on the surface of compost.

Like cacti cuttings, they must be taken from well-watered plants and the cut surfaces allowed to dry for several days before insertion in compost.

When inserting cuttings, do not place them within 12mm/$\frac{1}{2}$in of the container's sides as this is where the compost first becomes dry if watering is neglected.

Place the cuttings in gentle warmth and light shade. Check the compost regularly to ensure it is moist – stand the pot in a tray of water if necessary.

CACTI OR SUCCULENT?

There is often confusion about these widely used terms:

• Both cacti and succulents are succulent plants because of their ability to store water, but not all succulents are cacti.

• Cacti belong exclusively to the Cactaceae family and are distinguished by having areoles (resembling small pincushions) from which spines or long and woolly hairs grow. Flowers and stems also develop from the areoles.

• All cacti, with the exception of Pereskias – a group native to the New World and known as Leaf Cactus – do not bear leaves.

• Cacti are divided into two general groups: desert types whose natural environment is warm, semi-desert regions in the American continent, while forest types come from tropical America. Forest cacti are recognised by their trailing habit. They include the Christmas Cactus (*Schlumbergera truncata*, also known as the Crab or Claw Cactus), and *Schlumbergera russelliana*.

CIRCULAR LEAVES

*Succulent plants such as the October Plant (*Sedum sieboldii*) are increased by pulling off mature leaves, allowing the surfaces to dry for a couple of days and then pressing them flat on well-drained and aerated compost, such as equal parts moist peat and sharp sand with a thin surface layer of sand. Lightly water and place in gentle warmth in light shade.*

*The variegated form (*Sedum sieboldii 'Medio-variegatum'*), with cream and bluish-green leaves, is increased in the same way, and is a much more attractive form for growing indoors.*

1. CACTI *with small stems can be increased in spring and summer. Select a young, healthy plant and with a sharp knife cut stems at their bases. Stems taken from around the outside of a clump root faster than old ones at the plant's centre.*

2. LEAVE *the cuttings exposed to the air for a few days. This encourages them to root faster than if inserted immediately after being severed. Take care not to remove the cuttings from just one part of the mother plant.*

3. FILL *and firm a small pot with equal parts moist peat and sharp grit, then add a sprinkling of sharp sand over the surface. Use a small dibber to form a 12mm/$\frac{1}{2}$in deep hole and insert and firm the cutting.*

1. SUCCULENTS *such as some crassulas and echeverias can be increased from entire leaves. Select a well-watered plant and gently pull off mature, fleshy leaves, close to the stem. Do not leave short spurs on the mother plant.*

2. ALLOW *the cut surfaces to dry for a couple of days before inserting them in well-drained and aerated potting compost, formed of equal parts moist peat and grit, with a surface layer of sharp sand.*

3. WATER *the compost to settle it around the cuttings, and place in gentle warmth but away from direct sunlight. When shoots appear from their bases, gently pot them individually into sandy potting compost.*

DIVIDING HERBACEOUS PERENNIALS

HERBACEOUS plants survive in cold regions because during autumn and early winter they die down to ground level and are perpetuated in the soil as dormant roots. In spring, they develop shoots and stems that later in the season produce flowers. In autumn, plants again die down.

AUTUMN OR SPRING?

Divide herbaceous plants any time between early autumn and mid-spring, whenever the weather and soil are suitable. Usually, this means in autumn where the weather is mild, but in areas where cold winters are regularly experienced.

First, cut all stems to within a few inches of the ground. Clear away all debris, including weeds, and use a garden fork to dig up the clump.

If the clump is removed from the border and put on a lawn or path, first place sacking underneath. To divide small clumps, either lever the pieces apart with two hand forks placed back-to-back and their handles pulled together, or just with your hands. Large, woody and matted clumps are separated with two garden forks inserted back to back and levered together.

Discard old, central parts and retain only young pieces from around the outside. If roots are extremely matted, wash them in water and use a label or small, pointed stick to comb them out.

Replant the new pieces before their roots become dry. If this is impossible, wrap them in moist sacking and place in a cool shed. But plant them as soon as possible before their roots suffer.

Preferably, water the soil a few days before setting new plants in the ground: if planted in dry soil they will immediately lose moisture and may die.

If the divided plants are extremely small, they are best planted into a nurserybed for one or two years before setting them in a border. Also, if they are slightly tender, plant them in pots and place in a cold frame until large enough to be set in their permanent places in a garden.

1. FIBROUS *rooted herbaceous perennials when congested are easily increased. Use a garden fork to lift a matted clump. Place on sacking to prevent soil making paths or grass dirty.*

2. GENTLY *pull the clump into small but good-sized pieces. Discard central, old and woody parts and retain only those from around the outside. Pieces from around the edges are the youngest.*

3. MATTED *roots are sometimes so entangled that a knife is needed to separate them. However, usually they can be pulled apart by hand. Replant the pieces as soon as possible. Firm the soil.*

TYPES OF HERBACEOUS PLANTS

There are several types of herbaceous plants, their growth and roots influencing the ways in which they are increased:

<u>Plants with fibrous</u>, spreading roots are easily increased by lifting whole plants and gently dividing them (see base of previous page). Suitable plants include:
- Artemisias
- Asters (including the autumn-flowering Michaelmas Daisy as well as summer-flowering types)
- Bee Balm *(Monarda didyma)*
- Coneflower *(Rudbeckia fulgida)*
- Golden Rod *(Solidago)*
- Herbaceous campanulas
- Herbaceous geraniums
- Herbaceous phloxes
- Loosestrife *(Lysimachia punctata)*
- Masterwort *(Astrantia)*
- Meadowsweet *(Filipendula)*
- Pearl Everlasting *(Anaphalis)*
- Perennial Spiraea *(Astilbe)*
- Perennial Sunflowers *(Helianthus decapetalus)*
- Purple Loosestrife *(Lythrum)*
- Shasta or Max Daisy *(Chrysanthemum maximum)*
- Sneezewort *(Helenium)*
- Tickseed *(Coreopsis)*
- Yarrow *(Achillea)*

<u>Plants with fleshy roots</u> and woody crowns are increased by lifting the plant and using a sharp knife to separate the crowns. Plants include:
- Delphiniums
- Lupins *(Lupinus polyphyllus)*

<u>Plants with rhizomatous roots</u> are frequently grown in herbaceous borders. Their division is detailed on page 286.
- London Flag or Fleur-d-Lis *(Iris germanica)*
- Orris Root *(Iris florentine)*

detailed on page 286.

DIVIDING LARGE, TOUGH CLUMPS

Neglected borders frequently have large clumps of herbaceous plants that have matted roots and masses of stems. Their centres are frequently very woody.

INSERT *two garden forks back to back (above) in a large clump and lever their handles together (right). This pulls them apart and disentangles their roots. This technique may need to be carried out several times before a clump is in small pieces. Do not use a spade as this invariably damages the roots, as well as the shoots.*

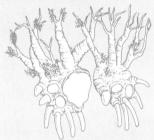

USE *a sharp knife to separate woody crowns of herbaceous plants such as delphiniums and lupins. Ensure that each new piece has strong roots and several growth buds.*

DIVIDING RHIZOMES AND TUBERS

◆

PLANTS with rhizomes or tubers are readily propagated by dividing. These food storage organs enable them to survive winter, live from one season to another and develops flowers quickly.

There are several types of irises: some bulbous and diminutive and including *Iris reticulata* and the honey-scented *Iris danfordiae*, both flowering in late winter and early spring. Other irises are bigger, more dominant and develop rhizomatous roots that securely anchor them in the ground.

The Fleur-de-lis or London Flag Iris (*Iris germanica*) is a rhizomatous type, with fleshy, tough and thick, concertina-like roots that often protrude above the surface. Such plants are easily increased after their flowers fade in early summer, or alternatively in late summer.

Clumps soon become congested, and lifting and dividing them every three years ensures that the flower quality does not diminish.

FLEUR-DE-LIS

Stories abound about this famous iris. In the twelfth century, Louis VII of France in his crusade against the Saracens adopted irises into his heraldry. Initially they were known as Fleur de Louis, corrupted into Fleur de Luce and later to Fleur de Lys and Fleur de Lis.

Lily-of-the-Valley (*Convallaria majalis*) has slender rhizomes. Lift plants with a garden fork at any time from late autumn to early spring and divide them.

Gently pull them apart and replant individual crowns just below the surface with about 10cm/4in between them.

These highly-scented, late spring and early summer-flowering plants are frequently planted

1. SOME *irises have thick, fleshy root-stems known as rhizomes – slightly buried or, with age, partly on the surface. After flowering, dig up the plants gently.*

2. DIVIDE *clumps, carefully selecting young pieces from the outside. Discard old, central parts. A sharp knife is essential. Each piece must have one or two fans of leaves.*

3. REPLANT *the rhizomes, either in a nursery bed or directly into a flower border. Tops of young rhizomes should be just level with the soil's surface.*

1. DAHLIAS *develop swollen roots known as tubers. In autumn, dig them up, cut off the stems and store in a cool, dry shed. In mid- to late spring, use a sharp knife to divide the tubers – each new plant must contain a stem because dahlia tubers do not contain buds.*

2. PLANTS *that have grown vigorously during the previous year often have congested tubers but only a few stems. Such plants can have their stems cut vertically with a sharp knife, but ensure that each new stem segment has at least one healthy bud.*

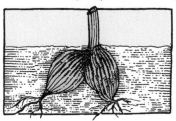

3. AFTER *division, dust cut surfaces with a fungicide to prevent the entry of diseases. Plant the new plants about 15cm/6in deep. If practical, insert strong stakes first. If stakes are inserted later there is the possibility of them piercing tubers.*

alongside house walls – but take care as when congested they disturb brickwork.

DIVIDING DAHLIAS

Bedding dahlias are usually raised from seeds, but border types are increased from cuttings or division of the tubers.

Division is the easiest and simplest method and does not need specialized equipment. It is essential, however, that tubers are lifted in late summer or early autumn and stored in a frost-proof shed during winter.

DAZZLING DAHLIAS

The first European to describe the dazzling Mexican dahlias and their medicinal qualities was Francisco Hernandez, the sixteenth-century physician and botanist to Philip II of Spain.

In 1789, Vincent Cervantes of the Botanic Gardens in Mexico City sent dahlia seeds to the Royal Gardens in Madrid, where they germinated and developed a rich medley of flowers.

At this stage, by the way, it was thought that the tubers were edible, like those of the potato, another American plant.

Dahlias spread to France and the Empress Josephine grew them in her world-famous garden at Malmaison, near Paris. Dahlias sent from Spain to England in the 1790s failed to establish themselves and it was plants from Malmaison that eventually introduced dahlias to England.

Dahlias also became popular in Germany, where they became known as *Georgine*, after the Russian botanist Georgi of St Petersburg.

DIVIDING HOUSEPLANTS

THIS is the easiest and quickest way to create new houseplants. And as long as mother plants are not divided into too small pieces, the new plants immediately look attractive.

Any plant with masses of stems is suitable for division. Often, houseplants such as ivies, Peace Lilies and Mind-your-own-Business are grown and sold with several small plants in the same pot. This enables nurserymen to produce marketable plants earlier than if only one plant was put in each pot. This invariably produces a plant that when congested with foliage can be divided into several separate plants.

The day before dividing a plant, thoroughly water the compost. Remove the pot by inverting the plant, placing a hand under the root-ball and tapping the pot's rim on a firm surface. If the roots are very matted and congested, pass a knife between the soil-ball and the inside of the pot.

Gently pull the roots apart to produce several good-sized and attractive plants, each with as much root as possible. Do not break the plant into a lot of pieces that do not look attractive.

REPOTTING

Select a clean pot that size-wise is in balance with the plant to be set in it. Apart from small plants in large pots appearing imbalanced, it is difficult to keep the moisture content of the compost right when a plant's roots do not fill at least half of it. The compost often then becomes too wet and cold to encourage root development.

Fill the base of a pot with compost and position the plant to check its depth. Set the plant fractionally lower than before – to allow for subsequent settlement of the compost – and ensure a space about 12mm/½in is left between the compost's surface and rim. This enables the plant to be watered. If a small space is left, the plants are not properly watered.

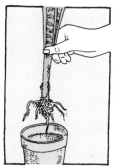

1. DIVIDE *plants with a few stems, such as Mother-in-Law's Tongue by removing the pot and gently pulling the root-ball into several pieces. Do not divide it into too small pieces which may look unattractive.*

2. SELECT *a clean pot, add a small amount of compost, place a plant on top and adjust its height so that its level is the same as before. Ensure the roots are well spread out and not congested in one place.*

3. FILL *the pot with compost and firm it around the roots, leaving 12mm/ ½in between the compost and pot's rim. Water the compost and place in gentle warmth and light shade until established.*

Spread out the roots, then trickle and firm compost around them. Carefully water the compost to settle it around the roots. Use a rose on the end of a watering-can to avoid compost being unduly disturbed around the roots.

Place the plant in a warm, slightly shaded position until established and growing strongly.

As well as being increased by leaf-petiole cuttings, African Violets can be propagated by dividing congested plants. Old specimens are often formed of several small plants. In spring or summer, remove the plant from the pot and gently separate into several pieces. Discard old pieces and pot up the youngest.

1. DIVIDE *congested plants with masses of stems, such as Peace Lilies, by first removing the pot. Invert the pot, place one hand under it and tap the edge on a firm surface. The soil-ball will separate from the pot.*

2. GENTLY *pull the roots and stems into several pieces, each formed of several shoots. Do not try and create a large number of plants: it is better to form two or three good-sized plants than five or more sparsely-leaved ones.*

3. POT *up each new plant. Place potting compost in the pot's base and hold the plant in the centre. Trickle compost around its roots, ensuring the plant's depth is slightly lower than before. Firm compost to 12mm/¹/₂in below the top.*

HOUSEPLANTS INCREASED BY DIVISION

- African Violet (*Saintpaulia ionantha*)
- Aspidistra/Bar-room Plant (*Aspidistra elatior*)
- Bead Plant (*Nertera depressa*)
- Buffalo Grass (*Stenotaphrum secundatum* 'Variegatum')
- Common Ivy (*Hedera helix* – and its many varieties)
- Ferns – many can be divided
- Japanese Sedge (*Carex morrowii* 'Variegata')

- Mind-your-own-Business (*Soleirolia soleirolii*)
- Never Never Plant (*Ctenanthe oppenheimiana tricolor*)
- Palms – some can be divided
- Peace Lily (*Spathiphyllum wallisii*)
- Peacock Plant (*Calathea makoyana*)
- Prayer Plant (*Maranta leuconeura*)
- Selaginellas
- Spider Plant (*Chlorophytum comosum*)
- Sweet Flag (*Acorus gramineus*)

LAYERING PLANTS OUTDOORS

L AYERING is an easy way to increase garden plants and does not need specialized equipment. Shoots and stems are left attached to parent plants and severed after roots form. They are then transferred to a nursery bed or a border.

LAYERING SHRUBS

Shrubs with low-growing stems – as well as trees with pendulous branches – are easily increased by layers. It can be performed at any time throughout the year but late summer to early autumn, as well as spring, are best. Essentially, shoots must be pliable so that they can be lowered to the ground.

LAYERING HEATHERS

Heathers, ericas and daboecias, when old, spread and often develop bare areas at their centres. Instead of using young shoots from them as cuttings and then digging up and throwing these plants away, they can be layered and encouraged to form new sets of roots.

In autumn or spring, form a mound of friable soil in their centres. Work this between the stems. Later, when roots have formed, dig up the complete plant and cut off rooted parts. If small, plant them in a nursery bed until established.

This is not a quick way to produce new plants, often taking up to two years, but is easily done:

- Select a healthy, vigorous, low-growing stem or branch, one or two years old. Lower it to soil level and form a sloping trench, 7.5–15cm/3–6in deep at its lowest point and 23–45cm/9–18in from the shoot's tip.
- Lower the shoot into the depression and bend its tip upright. Either make a tongued cut at the point of the bend, or cut half-way around the stem and remove part of the bark.
- Use a wooden peg or piece of bent wire to hold the stem in the soil. Cover and firm with soil, then water.
- Tie the end of the stem to an upright cane.
- When young shoots develop from the shoot's tip, sever the stem and plant into either a nursery bed or a border.

INCREASE *Holly by pegging down a branch in a trench in winter, but not immediately burying it. In spring, when shoots develop, regularly earth them up. Sever and pot up in autumn.*

LAYERING RIGID STEMS

Most stems are layered at ground-level. However, rigid stems that cannot be lowered to form roots are encouraged to form roots by wrapping sphagnum moss or peat around a purposely damaged part and enveloping it in polythene.

An earlier form of this method was used in China and India and known as Gootee-layering or Marcottage, but another way was to layer a shoot in the top of a large bamboo cane. A wide bamboo cane, about 1.5m/5ft long, was fixed in the ground. At its top, a 13cm/5in deep, 12–18mm/ $^1\!/_2$–$^3\!/_4$in-wide slit was cut on one side and a 5cm/3in deep one on the other, to form an aerial pot.

Fine soil was packed in the bamboo's top, and the stem partly cut and inserted into the cane, with soil packed around it. Keeping the compost moist was essential to encourage roots.

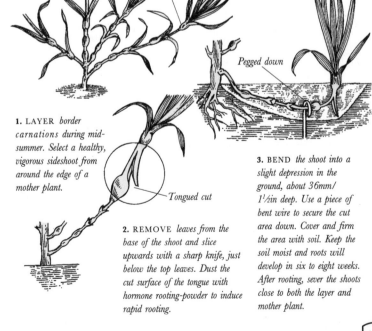

Young, low-growing stem

Pegged down

1. LAYER *border carnations during mid-summer. Select a healthy, vigorous sideshoot from around the edge of a mother plant.*

Tongued cut

2. REMOVE *leaves from the base of the shoot and slice upwards with a sharp knife, just below the top leaves. Dust the cut surface of the tongue with hormone rooting-powder to induce rapid rooting.*

3. BEND *the shoot into a slight depression in the ground, about 36mm/ 1$^1\!/_2$in deep. Use a piece of bent wire to secure the cut area down. Cover and firm the area with soil. Keep the soil moist and roots will develop in six to eight weeks. After rooting, sever the shoots close to both the layer and mother plant.*

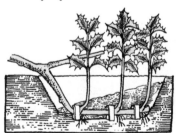

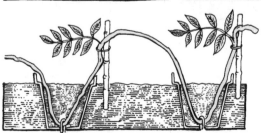

TIP *layer blackberry and loganberry shoots in late summer. Peg down the tips with a large stone or U-shape wire. Cover and firm with soil. Shoots develop roots by late spring and can be severed. To make transplanting easier, peg shoots in pots of compost.*

SERPENTINE *layering produces several plants from one shoot and is ideal for increasing clematis and wisteria. Peg down a shoot at regular intervals into pots of well-drained compost.*

LAYERING HOUSEPLANTS

LAYERING long shoots of houseplants grown for their attractive foliage and climbing or trailing nature is an exceptionally easy way to increase these plants.

Layering is a slow way to increase plants, but it is easy and does not need expensive or specialized equipment.

When taking leaf-stem cuttings, many new plants can be created from a single stem, whereas a layered shoot will produce only one new plant. However, several long shoots from one mother plant can be layered at the same time.

Layering performed indoors creates a focus of interest for several months, and although a slow way of increasing plants it is a more certain method than by cuttings.

Late spring and early summer are the best times to layer houseplants, when they are growing strongly. Rooted layers produced from them are then able to become fully established before the onset of winter and relatively poor light conditions.

EQUIPMENT REQUIRED

All that is needed is a few 7.5cm/3in-wide pots, a mixture of equal parts moist peat and sharp sand, bent pieces of wire, scissors or a sharp knife.

It is also useful to have a large plastic tray in which the mother plant and pots of layered shoots can be stood while forming roots. This makes moving them easier than if they are all separate.

The day before forming the layers, water the mother plant several times to ensure its stems are fully charged with water. Dry shoots are difficult to bend without breaking and they do not readily develop roots.

Select a healthy shoot and bend it 10–15cm/4–6in from its tip. This constricts the flow of sap and thereby encourages the development of new roots.

Fill and firm a pot with equal parts of moist peat and sharp sand to within 12mm/$^{1}/_{2}$in of its rim. Position the pot near the bend and pin it into the compost with a piece of bent wire. Firm compost over and around it, then water.

If the end of the shoot flops over and tends to loosen the layer in the compost, use a thin, short split-cane to hold it up.

AFTERCARE

Until roots develop, keep the mother plant well watered, as well as the compost in the small pots containing the layers.

Place the mother plant and layers in good light and gentle warmth. Unlike cuttings, which are formed from severed pieces of plants and therefore cannot normally be exposed to high temperatures, layered shoots can be given their normal temperatures and occupy the same positions.

After several weeks, new shoots develop from the tips of shoots. This is a clue to the formation of roots. Remove the bent wire and gently tug the stem. If it resists being pulled up, this is an indication that roots have formed.

Sever the stem close to the new plant's base. Also, tidy up the stem by cutting it back to the mother plant's base.

ESTABLISHED PLANTS

After newly-rooted houseplants have been severed from their parents, they can be displayed indoors. Unfortunately, as each plant has only one stem, its initial display, when compared with established plants raised from cuttings and where several are put into the same pot, is not so eye-catching. However, when used to trail from wall-brackets or the tops of high shelves or bookcases they are equally as attractive.

LAYERING A SWEETHEART PLANT

ALSO *known as Heart-leaf,* Philodendron scandens *develops heart-shaped leaves on trailing or climbing stems. Pin a stem into a pot of moist peat and sharp sand.*

When young shoots grow from the shoot's tip, sever the stem close to the new plant. Also, tidy up the mother plant by cutting the stem close to its base.

HOUSEPLANTS RAISED FROM LAYERED SHOOTS
- Canary Island Ivy (*Hedera canariensis* 'Gloire de Marengo')
- English Ivy (*Hedera helix* – and its wide range of varieties)
- Grape Ivy (*Cissus rhombifolia*)
- Kangaroo Vine (*Cissus antarctica*)
- Swedish Ivy (*Plectranthus coleoides* 'Marginatus')
- Sweetheart Plant/Heart-leaf (*Philodendron scandens*)
- Wax Ivy/Cape Ivy (*Senecio macroglossus* 'Variegatus')

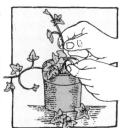

1. SELECT *a healthy, relatively young ivy shoot – still attached to the parent plant – and bend it near to a leaf joint, 10–15cm/ 4–6in from its tip. This constricts the flow of sap and encourages the rapid development of roots.*

2. USE *a U-shaped wire to secure the bent part in a small pot of equal parts moist peat and sharp sand firmed to 12mm/$^{1}/_{2}$in of the rim. Water to settle compost around the stem. Place the mother plant and layer in a plastic tray.*

3. KEEP *the compost moist and when young growths start to appear from the shoot's tip, sever the layer from the mother plant. Use sharp scissors and cut close to the new plant. Also cut the stem near to the mother plant's base.*

AIR LAYERING

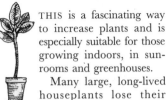

THIS is a fascinating way to increase plants and is especially suitable for those growing indoors, in sun-rooms and greenhouses.

Many large, long-lived houseplants lose their lower leaves, and although still attractive towards their tops, appear bare and disfigured at their bases. Instead of having to throw them away, they can be air layered, lowered and given a new span of life.

Candidates for air layering must be healthy and with at least 45cm/1½ft of stem at their tops packed with leaves. Although this technique can be performed throughout the year, it is more successful from spring to late summer when growth is strong.

TECHNIQUE OF AIR LAYERING

Using a sharp knife, make an upward-slanting cut about two-thirds through the stem and 7.5–10cm/3–4in below the lowest leaf. At this stage, take care that the upper part does not snap off.

Wedge open the cut, using a matchstick, and dust the cut surfaces with hormone rooting-powder. Push it well inside the cut.

Wind a piece of polythene around the stem and secure it 5cm/2in below the cut. Pack moist peat or sphagnum moss into it and tie a similar distance above the injury.

AFTERCARE

Keep the compost moist and the plant in gentle warmth. Within six to eight weeks, roots develop from the cut and can be seen through the polythene.

Sever the stem below the peat and pot up into a clean pot. Until established, support with a cane.

Cut the old, leafless plant down to 15–23cm/6–9in high and just above a bud. Keep the compost moist and young shoots will soon develop. If a bushy plant is desired, leave all shoots intact, but to produce a single stem remove all but one shoot.

PLANTS INCREASED BY AIR LAYERING
- Dracaena
- Dumb Cane (*Dieffenbachia*)
- Rubber Plant (*Ficus elastica* – and its many varieties)
- Swiss Cheese Plant (*Monstera deliciosa*)

GOOTEE-LAYERING

Also known as Marcottage, this form of encouraging stems to develop roots was practised in China and India in early times.

It was originated to propagate trees too difficult to increase by cuttings but which could be raised from layers. Normally, layers are encouraged to root in soil at ground level, but with Gootee-layering a stem is cut immediately under a leaf-bud or node with a slanting cut upwards and a stone or small piece of stick placed in it.

Around this was packed a ball of sticky soil, then covered with coir fibre or moss. Because Gootee-layering was used before polythene was available to retain moisture around the stem, a source of dampness was provided by a bamboo bucket suspended above it and a wick employed to transfer water.

1. AIR *layer a Rubber Plant by using a sharp knife to make an upward-slanting cut, two-thirds through the stem and 7.5-10cm/3-4in below the lowest leaf.*

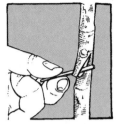

2. USE *a matchstick to keep the cut open. At this stage, latex (sticky, white sap) will exude from the cut: wipe this away with a damp cloth.*

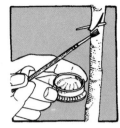

3. DUST *the cut surfaces with a hormone rooting-powder. Use a small brush and push powder well inside the cut. Cut off the ends of very long matchsticks.*

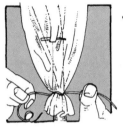

4. WIND *a piece of strong, clear polythene film – about 30cm/12in long by 25cm/10in wide – around the stem. Tie it about 5cm/2in below the cut.*

5. FILL *the tube formed by the polythene with moist peat or sphagnum moss. It is essential to pack it firmly around the stem and to about 5cm/2in above the cut.*

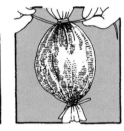

6. TIE *the polythene around the stem, firmly but not so tight that it restricts growth. If excessive polythene is left above and below the string, this can be trimmed back.*

7. KEEP *the potting compost in the mother plant's pot moist, and within six to eight weeks roots will appear inside the polythene. Use sharp secateurs or a knife to carefully sever the stem below the peat.*

8. REMOVE *the polythene. Pot up the plant immediately, retaining as much peat or sphagnum moss as possible, before the roots dry out. Until established, support the plant with a stake.*

Rubber Plant (Ficus elastica)

RUNNERS

ENCOURAGING runners to grow roots is an easy and assured way to increase the sort of plants that develop plantlets at the ends of long stems.

In nature, plantlets on the ends of runners normally rest on the soil, and eventually roots develop from them to form new plants.

A few plants that are grown as houseplants also produce runners, and are easily increased by pegging them in small pots of equal parts moist peat and sharp sand. It can be done at any time of the year, but spring and summer are the best as the plants are then growing strongly.

Spider Plants are dramatic and eye-catching, especially when displayed in indoor hanging-baskets or on pedestals.

WATER THOROUGHLY
Water the mother plant the day before pinning down the plantlets.

Place several small pots around the mother plant and use small pieces of U-shaped wire to secure each plantlet.

Place the mother plant and small pots in a large plastic tray: this enables all the plants to be moved at the same time without any risk of plantlets being dislodged. It also ensures that when they are watered, excess moisture does not create problems. At this stage, each plantlet is still attached to the mother plant.

Rooting is indicated when plantlets develop fresh shoots and leaves. Use sharp scissors to cut the runner, close to the plantlet as well as at the mother plant's base.

Place the young plants in gentle warmth and light shade until established and growing strongly.

Spider Plants are easily increased by pinning down young plantlets that develop at the ends of long, white, arching stems into compost in small pots. Several new plants can be raised at one time from a single mother plant. Stand all the plants in a plastic tray – it makes handling them much easier.

1. POSITION *small pots containing equal parts moist peat and sharp sand around a mother plant, so that plantlets can be easily pinned into them.*

2. USE *bent pieces of wire to secure each plantlet in a small pot. Firm compost around the plantlets. Water the compost lightly but thoroughly.*

3. WHEN *the plantlets develop roots and fresh shoots, sever each stem close to its plantlet. Also, cut it off right at the base of the mother plant.*

INCREASING STRAWBERRIES
Plants of this popular fruit are easily increased by pegging down runners in small pots.

During early and mid-summer, select runners on one-year-old, healthy, disease-free plants and use pieces of U-shaped wire to peg them down in 7.5cm/3in-wide pots of compost. Bury these small pots to their rims in soil around the mother plant.

Do not layer more than five runners from any plant; remove all others.

Keep the compost moist and remove all flowers.

When the runners have developed roots – six to eight weeks later – sever the stems and plant into a fruit garden.

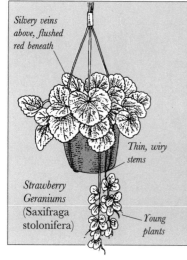

Silvery veins above, flushed red beneath

Thin, wiry stems

Strawberry Geraniums (Saxifraga stolonifera)

Young plants

STRAWBERRY GERANIUMS

Few trailing houseplants are as popular and widely grown as this stunningly attractive East Asian plant. In warm regions it is also placed outdoors during summer.

Also known as Mother-of-Thousands, it has roundish, somewhat heart-shaped leaves. Runners, often 90cm/3ft or more long, bear young plants that can be encouraged to form roots. The form 'Tricolor', widely known as Magic Carpet, has leaves variegated in pink and pale yellow.

STRAWBERRY RUNNERS IN TUBS

Strawberry plants are ideal for planting in a large barrel, where they fruit ten to fourteen days before those at ground-level.
- *Drill drainage holes in the tub's base. Stand it on bricks.*
- *Drill 6–7.5cm/2½–3in holes, 15–20cm/6–8in apart, in its sides.*
- *Insert a 15cm/6in wide, wire-netting tube in the barrel's centre. Fill with clean rubble.*
- *Fill around the drainage tube with compost, at the same time setting a plant in in each hole.*
- *Set several plants at the top and lightly water.*

PLANTLETS

A FEW plants develop plantlets on their leaves and thereby provide a fascinating way to increase them – one with special appeal to children.

Few ways of increasing plants are as easy as rooting plantlets. Some plants, such as the Chandelier Plant and Devil's Backbone, have plantlets that can be removed and pressed on moist compost. Others, like the Hen-and-Chicken Plant and Pig-a-Back Plant, have leaves with plantlets on their upper surfaces. These are laid flat on moist compost and pegged in position.

Early and mid-summer are the best times to propagate these amusing and fascinating plants.

PLANTS INCREASED FROM PLANTLETS

- Chandelier Plant (*Kalanchoe tubiflora/Bryophyllum tubiflorum*)
- Devil's Backbone (*Kalanchoe daigremontiana/Bryophyllum daigremontianum*)
- Hen-and-chicken Plant (*Asplenium bulbiferum*)
- Pig-a-back Plant (*Tolmiea menziesii*)

HEN-AND-CHICKEN PLANT

Also known as Mother Fern, the Australian and New Zealand *Asplenium bulbiferum* has finely-cut, mid-green, feathery fronds that when mature develop small plantlets known as bulbils on their upper surfaces.

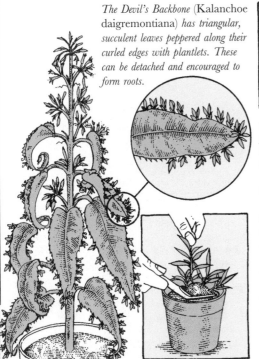

The Devil's Backbone (Kalanchoe daigremontiana) *has triangular, succulent leaves peppered along their curled edges with plantlets. These can be detached and encouraged to form roots.*

1. DETACH *mature plantlets and press (above) on the surface of equal parts moist peat and sharp sand. Water lightly to settle the compost around them.*

2. PLACE *in light shade and gentle warmth and keep the compost lightly moist. When rooted and about 2.5cm/1in high (left), transfer the plantlets into small, individual pots. Use a small dibber to form a hole, hold the rooted plantlet in it and lever compost around the roots to hold them firmly.*

The Chandelier Plant (Kalanchoe tubiflora) *grows to about 90cm/3ft high and produces groups of plantlets at the ends of succulent, cylindrical leaves.*

The plantlets naturally fall off plants and when sprinkled on moist compost soon develop roots. They root rapidly and when about 2.5cm/1in long are potted up, setting three in a 7.5cm/3in-wide pot. Each stem is then able to offer slight support to its neighbour.

In spring, plants develop a crown of small orange, bell-like flowers.

In nature, these bulbils gradually weigh down fronds, and on reaching the ground develop roots and create more plants. The bulbils, however, can be removed, pressed into moist compost and encouraged to form roots.

Fill a large tray or box with equal parts moist peat and sharp sand. Detach a mature leaf and press it on the compost. Either place small stones on the frond, or secure with pieces of bent wire.

Keep the compost moist, place in gentle warmth and light shade. The bulbils develop roots and are potted up individually.

PIG-A-BACK PLANT

Variously known as Young-on-Age, Pickaback, Piggyback Plant and Thousand Mothers, *Tolmiea menziesii* is native to and grows wild in the western states of North America. It develops small plantlets on the upper surfaces of its maple-like, 10cm/4in-wide, dull green leaves.

It is easy to grow and survives in cool rooms and low light.

Detach leaves with plantlets and place on moist compost in a seed-tray. Use U-shaped pieces of wire to secure the leaf. Place in gentle warmth and light shade.

The plantlets soon develop roots and when established are potted up into 7.5cm/3in pots. Later, transfer into a larger pot.

TROPICAL PROPAGATION PITS

In tropical regions, high temperatures and strong sunlight are a problem and likely to desiccate cuttings before they have a chance to develop roots.

Earlier, propagation pits were an answer to this problem, creating cool and shaded areas. Pits about 90cm/3ft deep were dug in sheltered places and covered with palm leaves. A layer of sand in the pit's base created a cool and well-drained base for pots of cuttings, although it needed to be kept damp.

At high elevations in India, permanent pits were dug and given glass-covered roofs. If warmth at the bases of cuttings was required, the bottom of the pit was filled with fermenting horse dung and then covered with a layer of fine soil.

In some areas, protection from wind and rain was also needed and often provided by a thatched roof, 1.2m/4ft at its back and 1.8m/6ft at the front, and facing the morning sun.

GRAFTING TO
CREATE NEW PLANTS

 WHEN grafts are made to create new plants, there are always two distinct parts: the root section and the variety.

WHIP AND
TONGUE GRAFTING

Widely used to create new fruit trees such as apples and pears, this method appears complex because of the tongue, but is actually easy to prepare.

Grafting is performed at the end of the dormant season. Cut down the root part (stock) to 7.5–10cm/3–4in above the ground. Use a sharp knife to create a 36mm/1½in-long sloping cut. Half-way down the slant, make a cut in a downward direction. This forms one of the tongues.

Prepare the varietal (scion) part from a healthy, one-year-old shoot. Cut the top slightly above a healthy bud and the base fractionally under the third or fourth bud below it. On the side opposite the lowest bud, form a slanting cut 36mm/1½in long. Half way along the slope, make an upward cut. This forms the other tongue.

Gently push the tongue on the scion into the tongue of the stock. Do not force them: it may be necessary to increase one cut.

When the scion and stock are the same diameter they usually fit together easily. However, if the scion is much smaller, ensure that instead of being positioned in the centre, the edges are aligned on one side. This is to ensure that the cambium (inner bark) layers unite.

Tie raffia around the graft and cover with grafting wax. Additionally, put a blob of wax on the top of the scion. Remove the wax and raffia as soon as growth commences.

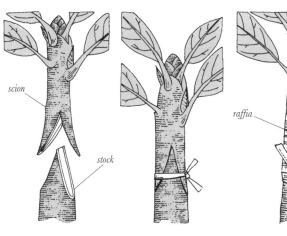

scion

stock

raffia

1. SADDLE *grafting is frequently used to propagate named varieties of rhododendrons. It is usually performed in gentle warmth in a greenhouse, in late winter or early spring.*

2. CUT *the root part (stock) 5–7.5cm/2–3in high and use a sharp knife to create an inverted V-shape. Cut the scion to fit and position on top of the stock. Tie quickly with one piece of raffia.*

3. USE *raffia to secure the stock and scion. It is not necessary to cover the grafted area with wax, as the plant is left in a greenhouse and moisture can be kept off the grafted area.*

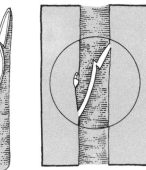
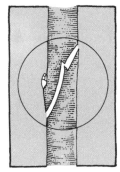
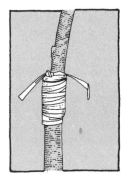

1. WHIP *and tongue grafting is widely used to produce fruit and ornamental trees. The varietal part (scion) is formed of a shoot three or four buds. Form a slanting cut, 36mm/1½in long, on the side opposite the lowest bud.*

2. CUT *the root part (stock) 7.5–10cm/3–4in above the ground and make a 36mm/1½in long slanting cut. Use a sharp knife to cut a 'tongue' in the stock and scion, so that they will lock together and hold the scion part secure.*

3. BIND *raffia around the graft and cover with grafting wax to make it waterproof. The edges of the stock and scion should be in contact, as this is where they initially unite. Place a small piece of wax on the top of the scion to seal it.*

SADDLE GRAFTING

As its name indicates, this graft resembles a saddle-like stock, with the varietal part sitting on top.

Unlike whip and tongue grafts, it does not have a special device to keep the scion fixed to the stock. This is because saddle grafting is mainly performed in a greenhouse and special care can be taken to ensure the two parts are not knocked and separated.

Saddle grafting is performed in late winter or early spring. It is mainly used to propagate rhododendrons.

The first stage is to cut the root part 5–7.5cm/2–3in high and to create an inverted V-shape. Cut the scion to fit and position on top of the stock. Use raffia to secure them together. It is not necessary to cover the grafted area with wax, as moisture can be kept off the area in a greenhouse.

If the scion is smaller than the stock, ensure they unite on one of the sides. Preferably, the size of the scion should match the width of the root-stock. Do not leave the saddle in the middle of the stock. To reduce the amount of moisture needed to keep the scion part healthy, cut about a third off the ends of large leaves.

APPROACH GRAFTING
was popular in the nineteenth century to increase fruit trees.

The root-stock was grown in a pot and positioned near the desired variety, grafted and later severed.

REJUVENATING OLD FRUIT TREES

◆

IN EARLIER years it was common to see apple trees 6m/20ft or more high, crowned in late summer with fruits too high to be picked. If such trees are inherited in a garden the choice is either to dig them out or to rejuvenate them by grafting new varieties on the branches.

TOPWORKING

This is when the branch system is cut off 60–90cm/2–3ft above the crotch and a completely new branch system formed.

There are several grafts used in topworking, but the easiest one to master is rind grafting, also known as crown or cleft grafting, and illustrated below.

Cut off the main branches any time during winter. In mid-spring, when the sap is starting to flow, prepare the varietal parts (scions), cutting slightly above a bud and just above the fourth or fifth bud below it. Then, at its lower end, make a sloping cut about 36mm/1½in long on the side opposite the lowest bud.

Prepare the tree by cutting the branches back slightly and smoothing the wood. Use a sharp knife to make two or three cuts vertically and 2.5–5cm/1–2in long down the sides of each branch. If the rind does not lift easily, use a thin spatula to start it. Then, insert a scion into each slit.

Bind the branch with soft string or raffia and cover with grafting

TOPWORKING

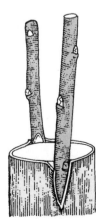

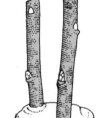

2. CUT *the main branches to within 60–90cm/2–3ft of the crotch. Make two or three, 2.5–5cm/1–2in-long cuts down the stub's side and push a varietal part firmly into each one.*

1. RIND *grafting is a way to rejuvenate old apple trees. Prepare the varietal part by cutting above a bud at its top, and just above the forth or fifth bud below it, making a slanting cut.*

3. TIGHTLY *wrap raffia or soft string around the branch, to secure the scions (varietal parts) and cover with grafting wax. Additionally, cover the cut tops of the scions with wax.*

FRAMEWORK GROWTH

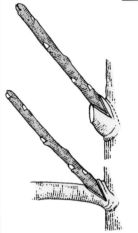

STUB GRAFTING *involves partly severing a shoot and inserting a scion. The branch is then cut off and tension secures the scion in the slit (top).*

SIDE GRAFTING *involves cutting a branch, inserting a scion and positioning it at the cut's side. The tension of the cut holds the scions in place.*

INVERTED-L GRAFTING *is when an L-shaped cut is made in the rind and a scion inserted in it. Secure with a small nail and cover with wax.*

wax. In summer, when the scions start to grow, cut the binding to prevent it constricting growth.

FRAMEWORK GRAFTING

This is less radical than topworking, and involves leaving the tree's main branches in place and replacing the side branches. Framework grafting takes longer than topworking, but there is less risk of diseases entering large cuts and the tree is returned to cropping much quicker.

The range of framework grafts is wide and interesting: stub, side and inverted-L grafting are three of many. Each of these types of graft is illustrated above.

• Stub grafting uses the tension in a shoot to hold the graft secure. A cut is made close to a branch, a scion inserted and the shoot severed. Cover the bare surfaces with grafting wax.

• Side grafting is performed on a main branch to produce a sideshoot. Make a shallow cut and insert a scion at an angle, so that it aligns with one of the cut's sides. Cover with wax.

• Inverted-L grafts also create sideshoots. Secure the graft with a small nail and cover with wax.

GRAFTING IN TUDOR TIMES

Gardeners during the fifteenth and sixteenth centuries knew about grafting trees and frequently used a technique we now know as cleft grafting.

A vertical slit was cut in the bark and the scion (varietal part) inserted in it.

The scions were bound and covered with a paste, created from mud, straw, dung and water, to prevent drying out.

BUDDING

THE technique of budding very much resembles grafting, but involves uniting only one bud with each rootstock. It is also a quicker method and, commercially, is much more economic as fewer buds are needed.

The vast majority of roses are raised by budding. This is when a bud of the varietal part is united with the rootstock.

Budding is also used to increase many ornamental trees and shrubs, including crab apples, but its main value is to raise new rose bushes each year.

BUDDING ROSES

Bush roses are budded 36–50mm/ 1¹/₂–2in above the ground.

Successful budding depends on the rind lifting easily from the wood and therefore mid-summer is the best time. Prepare the varietal part in the way shown below.

For bush roses, initially scrape away soil from the rootstock's base. In hot areas, make the T-cut on the side most protected from strong sunlight; in others, the side towards the prevailing wind is best as the bud is not then easily blown off. Insert the bud as indicated right, severing the raffia later.

The technique of budding standard roses is exactly the same as for bush types. The only difference is that three buds are used and inserted well above the ground: 75–90cm/ 2¹/₂–3ft for half-standards and 1.2–1.3m/ 4–4¹/₂ft for full standards. Root-stocks are prepared by allowing a single stem to grow well above the desired height and supporting it with a stake.

In late autumn or early winter, sever it about 15cm/6in above the desired height and in spring allow three shoots to develop from the head. Rub off buds lower down.

In mid-summer, insert three buds into the shoots, on their upper surfaces and close to the main stem. Later, cut off the stems about 2.5cm/1in beyond the buds, as well as cutting the main stem slightly above the uppermost shoot.

The above applies when using briar roses (*Rosa canina*), whereas with rugosa (*Rosa rugosa*) types the buds are inserted directly into the plant's main stem.

Until the buds develop and produce shoots, sucker-like growths are frequently a problem on the stems of standard roses. If seen early, they can be easily removed by just rubbing them sideways. If left, they attempt to dominate the plant and their removal often initiates the development of further suckers on the main stem. Also, remove suckers from the roots.

1. BUDDING *is the main way to raise roses. Select a shoot with young, plump buds and cut off the leaves, leaving stalks 12mm/¹/₂in long. Insert a sharp knife 18mm/³/₄in above the bud and, passing under it, emerge 12mm/¹/₂in below it so that the bud is cut off.*

2. SCRAPE *away loose soil from around the root-stock and 36–50mm/ 1¹/₂–2in above the ground, make a T-shaped cut. The vertical cut is about 36mm/ 1¹/₂in long and the horizontal one 12–18mm/¹/₂–³/₄in. Use the spatula end of a budding knife to lift the rind.*

3. HOLD *the bud by its leaf-stalk and insert into the T-cut. It may be necessary again to use the spatula end of a budding knife to open the flaps. When it is securely in the T-cut, use a sharp knife to carefully cut off any woody part that may be protruding above it.*

4. SECURE *the bud firmly in position either with raffia or a proprietary budding tie. When using raffia, first make it pliable by immersing in water for a few minutes. Ensure that the bud is not covered and that the leaf stalk is not knocked or damaged in any way.*

5. SUCCESSFUL *budding becomes apparent three to four weeks later: the bud will appear plump and the leaf stalk drops off. At this stage, use a sharp knife to cut the raffia on the side opposite the bud. If left, it constricts growth by cutting off sap flow.*

6. USE *sharp secateurs to cut off the part of the root-stock 12mm/¹/₂in above the budded position in early or mid-spring of the following year. At the same time, cut off, as close as possible to their point of origin, any sucker shoots growing from the root-stock.*

THE ART OF PRUNING

Pruning has, for many gardeners, gained an unnecessary mystique, yet it is only the removal of stems and shoots, usually from woody plants such as trees and shrubs, to encourage the development of a better shape or the regular production of flowers or fruits. The areas of confusion and complexity in pruning usually lie in its timing, the positions of cuts and the amount of wood to be removed.

This chapter describes the pruning of hedges – deciduous types and evergreens – and shrubs and trees grown in borders for their flowers or coloured stems. Bush roses, as well as climbing and rambling types, are featured, together with apples, pears, peaches and nectarines, and soft fruits such as raspberries, gooseberries and blackcurrants.

Outdoor grapevines and figs are also featured, together with pruning climbers and creating romantic arbours.

PHILOSOPHY OF PRUNING

FEW gardening skills are cloaked in as much mystique as pruning. It is performed mainly on woody plants, such as ornamental and fruiting trees, shrubs, hedges and roses, and mainly involves the removal of stems and branches. This directs a plant's activities in several ways, including shaping, regeneration of shoots, larger and more attractive flowers and regular production of fruits. It also keeps plants healthy and encourages a long life-span.

In warm climates, the objectives of pruning also include the development of straight, clean stems, essential in rubber cultivation; twisted or bent stems for use in furniture construction; and the development of wide-spreading trees that create shade. Additionally, nipping out growing tips from tea plants encourages an abundance of fresh, young shoots.

TIMING

The time of the year when plants are pruned is important. Basically, pruning is a task solely dictated by the type of growth a plant has and when it is dormant. Invariably, this inactive period is influenced by the weather and in particular by winter. In tropical and sub-tropical regions, droughts frequently enforce periods of dormancy, but for gardeners in temperate regions the dictating factor is cold weather.

MANY *flowering shrubs are pruned each year to encourage the development of flowers. Forsythias flower in spring and are pruned as soon as their flowers fade. However,* Hibiscus syriacus, *flowering from mid-summer to early autumn, needs no more pruning than to cut off straggly shoots. The Common Broom* (Cytisus scoparius), *which bursts into colour during late spring and early summer, needs pruning after flowering.*

Woody plants, such as ornamental and fruiting trees, are invariably pruned during their dormant period. However, peaches, nectarines, apricots, cherries, plums and gages are susceptible to silver leaf disease and to reduce the risk of spores entering cut surfaces they are pruned in spring when growth is beginning. Conversely, trees with sappy wood, such as birches, Horse Chestnuts, conifers and some maples are likely to bleed profusely if cut during summer when their sap is flowing strongly. Therefore, prune them in late autumn or early winter.

BROKEN, *diseased and misplaced branches must be removed. Cut off branches, pare surfaces smooth and coat with fungicidal paint.*

INFLUENCING FLOWERING

If cold winter weather was not an influencing factor, pruning could be performed immediately an ornamental shrub finished flowering, leaving the maximum amount of time for the development of fresh shoots before its blooming period during the following year. In warm regions this is possible, but where frosts and low temperatures are experienced, any pruning performed late in summer is likely to encourage soft shoots that would be damaged later.

For this reason, in temperate regions, deciduous flowering shrubs are divided into three main groups:
• <u>Flowering in winter</u>: pruned immediately flowering ceases. Little pruning is usually needed.
• <u>Developing flowers from spring to early and mid-summer</u>: prune

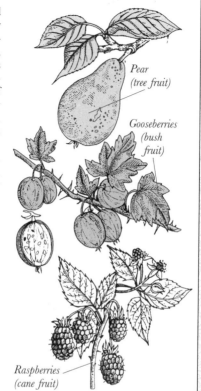

Pear
(tree fruit)

Gooseberries
(bush fruit)

Raspberries
(cane fruit)

ALL *fruiting plants need yearly attention, whether growing as trees, bushes or canes. If this is neglected, yields decline and individual fruits are small and poor in quality. Pruning fruit trees, bushes and canes is detailed on pages 314-321.*

directly the flowers fade, so that ensuing growth has time to ripen before the onset of winter.
• <u>Flowering in late summer</u>: prune in early to mid-spring of the following year.

These are the general rules, but shrubs grown for their attractive stems, such as the dogwoods, are exceptions. These are severely pruned in mid-spring, cutting stems just above the ground.

Golden Bells
(Forsythia)

Shrubby Hibiscus/Shrubby Althaea (Hibiscus syriacus)

Common Broom/Scotch Broom (Cytisus scoparius)

EQUIPMENT YOU WILL NEED

THE range and quality of pruning and hedging tools has improved dramatically during recent years. High-quality steel gives knives and secateurs keen cutting edges, plastic handles reduce maintenance and introduce longevity, while power tools make gardening even more of a pleasurable pursuit.

SECATEURS

There are two types of secateur: 'bypass' (earlier known as parrot models) is where the cutting action is created by one blade overlapping the other. The other is 'anvil', when a sharp blade cuts against a base known as an anvil.

Each of these types has its devotees; the anvil type is often preferred by professionals because replacement parts are available.

The bypass type has a more surgical cut than the anvil model, which, if the cutting blade is blunt, may bruise stems.

Both types are available in a range of sizes, most cutting 15mm/⅝in stems, while heavy-duty types cut up to 25mm/1in.

Most secateurs are sold to suit right-handed people, but left-handed types are available.

LOPPERS

These are like large secateurs and have similar cutting actions – bypass or anvil. Loppers with handles 38–45cm/15–18in long cut shoots up to 36mm/1½in thick, but heavy-duty types, with handles 75cm/2½ft long, sever 5cm/2in wood.

Some anvil types have a compound cutting action, enabling thick shoots to be easily cut.

HEDGES

Hedging shears

Cordless hedge trimmer

Electric hedge trimmer

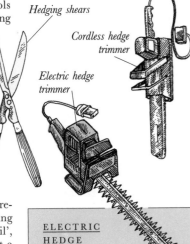

ELECTRIC HEDGE TRIMMERS

For cutting large hedges without becoming unduly tired, an electrically powered trimmer is essential. But ensure there is a power-breaker (also known as a circuit-breaker) fitted into the circuit so that if the cable is severed the power is immediately cut off.

CUTTING *blades range in length from 33–75cm/13–30in. A few have cutting knives on one side only; others cut on both, making them user-friendly for both left- and right-handed people. Some trimmers have dual reciprocating blades.*

STORING AND LOOKING AFTER TOOLS

The life expectancy of all garden tools depends on the way they are used and stored.

- *Don't force secateurs to cut branches too thick for them – the blades soon buckle.*
- *After use, wipe away all residue, especially sap.*
- *Wipe bright-metal parts with an oily rag.*
- *At the end of the pruning season, clean and wipe wooden handles. Smear with linseed oil.*
- *Most handles, nowadays, are plastic and only need to be occasionally wiped clean.*
- *Hang up tools in a damp-proof, airy, shed or garage. Peg boards are ideal places.*
- *Regularly check cables for damage and have all electrical equipment inspected every year by a competent electrician.*
- *Keep sharp-edged tools out of reach of children.*

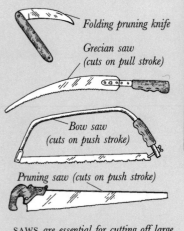

Folding pruning knife

Grecian saw (cuts on pull stroke)

Bow saw (cuts on push stroke)

Pruning saw (cuts on push stroke)

SAWS *are essential for cutting off large limbs. Easily-accessible branches are best cut with a bow saw, but in confined areas a Grecian type is easier to use.*

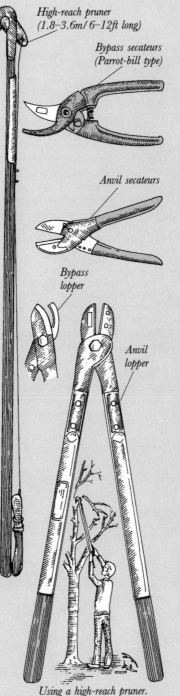

High-reach pruner (1.8–3.6m/6–12ft long)

Bypass secateurs (Parrot-bill type)

Anvil secateurs

Bypass lopper

Anvil lopper

Using a high-reach pruner.

PRUNING CUTS

❖

SECATEURS, loppers, knives and saws are the best tools with which to remove shoots, stems and branches. However, in addition to the 'when and how' of pruning individual plants, it is essential that cuts are made in the right positions relative to buds and other shoots.

TOO HIGH OR TOO LOW

Each pruning cut must be slightly above a bud – not so high that a small stub of the shoot remains above it, nor so low that the cut leaves the bud perched high above it. A range of pruning cuts is shown in the illustrations below.

As well as each cut being positioned slightly above a bud, to encourage a shrub or tree to develop outwards, the bud that remains must point in the desired direction. If buds point inwards they eventually create a congested central part of the plant. Air circulation is reduced and the presence of diseases encouraged.

WEEPING NATURE

On plants with a cascading nature, it is essential that cuts are made to leave buds on the upper sides of stems. This helps to create a better weeping appearance than if they are cut to leave downward-pointing buds.

THE ROSE FACTOR

In recent years, different ways to prune roses have been tested by the English magazine *Gardening Which?* in conjunction with the Royal National Rose Society. Three different methods of pruning roses are being tested:
• using secateurs in a careful and traditional manner
• using secateurs but in a rough way – not just above buds
• using a hedge trimmer.
The results have amazed many gardeners: floribundas (now called cluster-flowered roses) produced better-quality and more flowers when pruned roughly with secateurs or hedge trimmers than traditionally and carefully with secateurs. Hybrid teas (now known as large-flowered roses) were as good

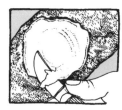

1. CUT *off a large branch by initially cutting it about 30cm/12in from the trunk. First, make a cut on the lower side, then complete the cut from above. Cut back apple and pear trees in winter when dormant.*

2. USE *a saw to cut off the short stub. Saw from above and hold the stub to prevent it falling and damaging the bark. Use a sharp saw – more accidents occur from blunt tools than sharp ones that cut wood easily.*

3. USE *a sharp knife to smooth the cut area, especially at its edges.*

4. PAINT *the cut area with fungicidal paint to help it heal and to prevent the entry of diseases. Use an old brush for this job.*

GUILLOTINE ACTION

Barrow's Patent Pruner was introduced in an age of great ingenuity, towards the end of the nineteenth century. It had a guillotine-like action.

with the rough technique and hedge trimmer as when carefully pruned with secateurs.

The long-term effects of pruning with hedge trimmers are yet to be known, as well as evaluating the wisdom of not cutting to outward-pointing buds.

POLLARDING

To most gardeners, pollarding is just another term for butchering trees! It is invariably performed on trees that have grown too large for the area in which they were originally planted.

It is a technique of cutting all branches back to the tree's crotch. This results in a mass of vigorous stems growing straight up from the trunk. Invariably, after several years, the tree has to be pollarded again often making it unsightly.

Sometimes, pollarding is necessary where roads have been widened or buildings constructed too close to them. However, the moral of this is to select trees with shapes and sizes that suit the areas in which they will grow.

LIFE, LIMBS AND EYES

Powered hedge trimmers as well as chain-saws have changed gardening out of all recognition during the last twenty years, but there is a price to be paid:
• *Don't use them during wet weather or on wet hedges.*
• *Ensure children and domestic pets are indoors.*
• *Always use a power-breaker.*
• *Wear goggles to prevent dust or splinters going in your eyes.*
• *If you are right-handed, move from left to right while using a hedging trimmer: vice versa for left-handed gardeners.*
• *Either use a cable harness, or loop the power lead over your shoulder to keep it safe.*
• *Wear stout gloves and a thick coat while using a chain-saw – do not wear a scarf or tie.*

PRUNING CUTS
All pruning cuts should be made at a slight angle and just above a bud. Only the cut on the right is correct: the others are too high or low.

PRUNING AND CLIPPING HEDGES

❖

HEDGES have several functions in gardens: creating perimeters and forming internal barriers that provide shelter and privacy. Some are evergreen, others deciduous. A few develop flowers but most are grown for their foliage.

Once planted, hedges last for many years and if they are to remain attractive they must be pruned regularly and properly throughout their lives. Early pruning is essential.

Basically, there are three types of hedge: formal and deciduous, coniferous, and informal.

FORMAL
DECIDUOUS HEDGES
These must be pruned immediately they are planted. If left to grow naturally, their bases become bare of shoots and leaves. Directly after being planted, cut all shoots back by a half to two-thirds.

If bare-rooted plants have been used, this will be at any time from late autumn to early spring. Hedges formed from container-grown plants – which can be planted at any time whenever the soil is not frozen or waterlogged – are pruned immediately after they are planted.

As well as encouraging shoot-packed bases, shortening a plant's growth reduces the risk of strong winds rocking plants and loosening their roots in early years.

During the second year, again use secateurs to cut back all new shoots by half to two-thirds. Although continually cutting back hedges in this manner may appear drastic, if neglected the hedge will be ruined. Sometimes, pruned hedges initially look unsightly.

During the third year, use hedging shears or electric hedge trimmers to cut the new stems back by

SHAPING *a hedge so that it has a uniform outline is easily achieved by forming a wooden template. It is an ideal guide when cutting back hedges that have become neglected.*

one-third. In subsequent years, regular clipping is essential – at least three or four times a year.

KNOT GARDENS
An early description of knot gardens comes from Venice in about 1499, where the background to knot-like figures was filled with herbs and flowers. Nearly a century later, the English gardener Thomas Hill in *The Gardener's Labyrinth* mentions knot gardens set in thyme and hyssop.

In Tudor times, from about 1485 to 1605, knot gardens were usually rectangular beds with intricate patterns outlined in Edging Box, Rosemary or even Thrift.

INFORMAL HEDGES
Like formal hedges, these too must be cut back after planting to encourage the development of bushy shoots from ground level. This is especially important, as many informal hedges are grown for their flowers and if initial pruning is neglected the base will be bare of flowers.

Neglected flowering hedges are easily identified by their bare bases and flowers borne high up.

During subsequent years, leave informal hedges to develop naturally. However, if it is not making much side growth, cut back the top shoots in spring by removing half of the growth made during the previous year.

Many informal hedges have large leaves, so therefore only use secateurs or long-handled loppers. If hedging shears are used, they chop up leaves and create an unsightly hedge.

Always cut just above a leaf-joint, and the best time is in spring or autumn, when excessive growth is most apparent.

Cutting back old, neglected hedges that are full of dust is a dirty job. As well as wearing old clothing, take care to use protective goggles to prevent dust getting into eyes, and also to prevent shoots poking in eyes.

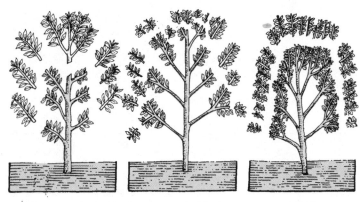

1. PRUNING *newly planted deciduous and formal hedges is essential. If plants are neglected at this stage, their bases become bare of shoots and look unsightly. Cut all shoots back by half to two-thirds to ensure bushiness.*

2. DURING *the following year, cut back all new shoots by half to two-thirds. Although cutting back plants in this manner may appear drastic, eventually it creates a fully clothed hedge, from its top to the base.*

3. IN THE *third year, cut the new stems back by one-third and during subsequent years by about the same amount. Regular clipping – three or four times a year – is essential if the hedge is to remain attractive.*

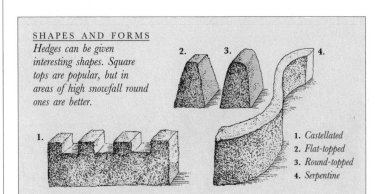

SHAPES AND FORMS
Hedges can be given interesting shapes. Square tops are popular, but in areas of high snowfall round ones are better.

1. *Castellated*
2. *Flat-topped*
3. *Round-topped*
4. *Serpentine*

CONIFEROUS HEDGES

ALTHOUGH not all conifers are evergreen, those used to create hedges are. They include many attractive forms of *Chamaecyparis lawsoniana*, *Thuja plicata* and *Thuja occidentalis*, as well as the exceedingly fast-growing X *Cupressocyparis leylandii*.

Coniferous hedges should not be pruned when planted. They naturally develop shoots from their bases, although long shoots can be trimmed back in spring.

DESIRED HEIGHT

When the hedge reaches the desired height, cut 15–30cm/ 6–12in off the leading shoots. During the following year, the hedge will thicken and hedging shears or electric hedge trimmers should be used to trim the sides.

When planting conifers – or any other boundary plant – remember that with age a hedge thickens dramatically.

RENOVATING OLD HEDGES

Eventually, hedges can become too large, usually because of excessive vigour or neglect.
• If the hedge is too wide and high, correct this over two or three years. In early spring of the first year, use long-handled lopping shears to cut back top growth. The following year, cut back one or both of the sides.
• Not all hedging plants can be severely cut back, but those that can include: aucuba, beech, Box, elaeagnus, forsythia, Gorse, hawthorns, Hornbeam, Privet, pyracantha, rhododendrons, Sweet Bay and Yew.
• Large, straggly hedges of Rosemary and lavender are best pulled out and replaced.
• Conifers, with the exception of Yew, should not be cut hard back. Instead, pull out and replace them. However, the tops of conifers can be cut out, but the result is not always attractive.

WHEN *the leading shoots on conifers rise 15–30cm/ 6–12in above the desired height, cut them off. Stretch a garden line between the hedge's ends to ensure it is cut at a uniform height. Use secateurs or loppers.*

WHEN *pruning large-leaved evergreen hedges, use secateurs (left) rather than hedging shears that shred large leaves and make them unsightly. Cut out dead shoots (right) close to the bases of hedges. Also, pull away and remove all dead leaves.*

CREATING ROMANTIC ARBOURS

LEAFY arbours packed with scented plants and climbers usually evoke thoughts of a romantic and perhaps mystical age long passed. Indeed, William Shakespeare, at the end of the sixteenth century, wrote:
Love-thoughts lie rich when canopied with bowers.

A bower, by the way, is a shaded, leafy recess, although it is possible that Shakespeare partly used its poetic meaning – a private chamber or boudoir.

CONSTRUCTING AN ARBOUR

These need not be large or expensive: a few brick or wooden columns and a roof create an attractive framework. They can be soon covered by climbers such as wisteria or Mountain Clematis. The pruning of these is described on page 303; roses are other candidates and their pruning is detailed on page 313.

TRAINING *plants to create unusual features has been a continual pursuit of Man. Here is a seventeenth-century engraving of an arbour where friends could be entertained.*

LEAFY *bowers, packed with scented flowers and colourful leaves, create secluded, restful and contemplative places in which to relax.*

SCENTED CLIMBERS FOR ARBOURS
• Japanese Wisteria (*Wisteria floribunda*). Pendulous, violet-blue, vanilla-scented flowers.
• Mountain Clematis (*Clematis montana*). Pure-white, sweetly-scented flowers.
• Fragrant Virgin's Bower (*Clematis flammula*). Small, white, hawthorn-scented flowers.
• Common White Jasmine (*Jasminum officinale*). White and jasmine scented.
• Orange-peel Clematis (*Clematis orientalis*). Yellow, bell-shaped, nodding, slightly sweet flowers.
• Honeysuckle (*Lonicera japonica*). White to pale yellow, sweetly-scented flowers.

TOPIARY

CLIPPING and shaping plants dates back to the Romans and Pliny the Elder, in the first century AD. It became so popular then that even the name of the topiarist was often depicted in clipped Box.

After the decline of the Roman Empire, topiary also ceased, although in the Middle Ages plants were trained and clipped, often upon frames formed of thin, flexible stems, such as osier (Willow).

RENAISSANCE REVIVAL

A revival took place in Renaissance Italy in the second half of the fifteenth century, with plants formed into geometric shapes, human figures and animals.

The gardens at Hampton Court Palace in England were also decorated at the end of the sixteenth century with topiary, which gained such popularity that even Rosemary was trained and clipped.

In about 1629, the gardener and herbalist John Parkinson recommend Privet for topiary, adding that Thrift, lavenders, Germander and thyme were also widely used.

1. CREATE *a topiary squirrel by selecting a young, bushy Box plant with several pliable stems. It is possible to begin with a rooted cutting, but takes several years longer.*

2. BEND *two pieces of galvanized-wire to form the head and tail. Tie them to the plant's main stems. Clip central shoots to encourage bushiness, but allow others to develop.*

3. TIE *in body and tail shoots to the wire, at the same time regularly but lightly clipping back the young growths to encourage the development of a dense covering of leaves.*

THE FRENCH CONNECTION

During the seventeenth century, the fashionable French-inspired parterre gardens were created: plants performed the role of embroidery against a background of coloured earth or bands of turf. This gave fresh impetus to topiary and evergreen plants such as Yew, holly, laurel and Bay that were widely used to create pyramids, balls and other figures.

Large-leaved evergreens became especially fashionable and desirable because large topiary figures could be created from them.

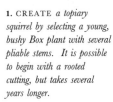

UNFASHIONABLE

During the latter part of the eighteenth century, the passion for topiary declined and was considered to be old-fashioned. But in the early part of the following century it was partly revived during the construction of gardens that wished to re-capture the atmosphere of earlier years.

Although gardening on the grand scale ceased to use topiary, it nevertheless survived in cottage gardens, frequently depicting animals.

Yew, Box and the Shrubby Honeysuckle (*Lonicera nitida*), are now mainly used for topiary, mostly when creating animals.

TOPIARY *never fails to attract attention, whether neat and symmetrical in the form of balls, pyramids, cones or spirals, or when depicting peacocks or other animals. It is an age-old craft, frequently creating a cottage-garden aura.*

FORMATION TRAINING

There are several secrets to success with topiary:

• Select sturdy plants, well clothed with leaves and stems. If a plant's base is bare at this stage, it will always appear unsightly.

• Start the training as soon as plants are large enough.

• Encourage the development of strong, vigorous growth during the early years.

• Above all, be patient. It may take four or more years to produce simple box outline when using Shrubby Honeysuckle (*Lonicera nitida*) or Dwarf Box (*Buxus sempervirens* 'Elegantissima'), also known as Edging Box. Creating the same feature in yew (*Taxus baccata*) could take twice that time.

GETTING STARTED

As a novice, do not be over ambitious; it is far better to produce a pyramid or rabbit successfully than to make a mess of a giraffe!

To create a simple shape – such as a pyramid, cone, sphere or cube – begin with a single, bushy plant with healthy, strong stems and allow them to grow unchecked until 20–30cm/8–12in high. Shrubs such as the Shrubby Honeysuckle and Privet will achieve this by mid-summer during their first year of growth after being planted. Cut these shoots back by half.

As sideshoots develop, clip these shoots back by half. Repeatedly clip the vertical shoots by a third to half when the new growth is 15–20cm/6–8in long.

Continue to trim the plant in this way, to broaden and thicken it as well as to create strong, upright growth.

After about five trimmings, the plant will be bushy and ready to be cut into the desired shape. Use sharp shears.

TOPIARY *has been taken up all around the world. There is a topiary elephant at Ayutthaya in Thailand.*

PRUNING CLIMBERS

MOST climbers need to be pruned at some time, either to restrain their growth or encourage the development of flowers.

Deciduous climbers grown for their handsome foliage need little pruning, other than occasionally restricting their size.

Evergreen climbers such as ivies also need little attention. Flowering climbers, however, are the ones that need regular pruning to encourage the development of flowers. Flowering wall shrubs also need regular attention.

A TO Z OF PRUNING CLIMBERS AND WALL SHRUBS

• *Actindia chinensis* (Chinese Gooseberry): Thin out and restrict growth in late winter.
• *Actinidia kolomikta* (Kolomikta Vine): Restrict growth during late winter.
• *Akebia:* Thin out and shorten straggly shoots in late winter.
• *Berberidopsis corallina* (Coral Plant): Thin out overcrowded shrubs in late winter.

• *Clematia macropetala:* In spring, cut out dead and thin shoots.
• *Clematis montana* (Mountain Clematis): Cut out old flowering stems in mid-summer.
• *Clematis flammula:* In late winter to early spring, cut back all shoots that flowered during the previous year to healthy buds near their bases. Also, cut out all weak and dead shoots.
• *Clematis orientalis* (Orange Peel Clematis): As for *C. flammula*.
• *Clematis tangutica:* As for *C. flammula*.
• *Clematis* (Large-flowered): For pruning, these can be divided into two main groups.
Lanuginosa and Patens types: cut back old flowering shoots after the flowers fade. Old, neglected plants can be pruned severely in late winter, but the first crop of flowers will be lost. Examples of these includes 'Nelly Moser', 'Lasurstern', 'The President' and 'Vyvyan Pennell'.
Jackmanii and Viticella types: cut plants severely, to within 30cm/12in of the ground, in early

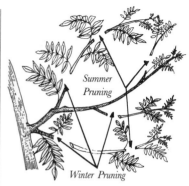

PRUNE *wisterias in late winter, cutting back sideshoots to just beyond the second leaf. Additionally, to control the growth of large, vigorous specimens, cut sideshoots back to three or four leaves during the latter part of mid-summer.*

spring. Examples of these includes 'Ernest Markham', 'Mrs Cholmondely' and 'Ville de Lyon'.
• *Eccremocarpus scaber* (Chilean Glory Flower): Cut out any frost-damaged shoots in late spring.
• *Hedera* (ivies): If necessary, prune in spring to restrain growth.
• *Humulus lupulus* 'Aureus' (Yellow-leaved Hop): Cut down and remove old shoots in autumn.
• *Hydrangea petiolaris* (Climbing Hydrangea): No regular pruning needed, other than cutting out dead shoots in spring.
• *Jasminum nudiflorum* (Winter-flowering Jasmine): After flowering, cut back flowered shoots to 5–7.5cm/2–3in of their bases. Also, remove old and weak shoots.
• *Jasminum officinale* (Common White Jasmine): After the flowers fade, thin out shoots to their bases.
• *Lonicera* (Honeysuckle): No regular pruning needed, other than occasionally thinning out old shoots after the flowers fade.

• *Parthenocissus:* No regular pruning needed, other than cutting out dead or overcrowded shoots in spring to tidy them up.
• *Passiflora caerulea* (Passion Flower): In late winter, cut out tangled shoots to soil level or their bases. At the same time, cut back sideshoots to about 15cm/6in of the main stems.
• *Polygonum baldschuanicum* (Russian Vine/Bukhara Fleece Flower): Trim back large plants in spring.
• *Solanum crispum* (Chilean Potato Tree): Prune back the previous season's growth in mid-spring to 15cm/6in long. Also, cut out weak and frost-damaged shoots.
• *Vitis coignetiae* (Crimson Glory Vine): No regular pruning needed.
• *Wisteria:* See above left. Prune in winter and in summer.

HERBACEOUS *climbers are not common but an eye-catching one is the Yellow-leaved Hop (Humulus lupulus 'Aureus'). Pruning is simple: just clear away all old stems down to ground level in autumn.*

FLOWERING *climbers are ideal for clothing arches and pergolas with rich colours throughout summer. This includes the large-flowered clematis (above). Wisteria, honeysuckle and jasmine provide more subtle colour.*

CLIMBERS *with evergreen, variegated leaves – such as some small and large-leafed ivies – create colour through-out the year. Other climbers have richly coloured leaves in autumn and early winter which brighten the garden.*

EARLY-FLOWERNG
DECIDUOUS SHRUBS

❖

DECIDUOUS shrubs flowering in spring and early to mid-summer are some of the most richly coloured of all woody garden plants. The spring-flowering ones bloom as soon as winter disappears, with early summer-flowering types soon after them and many lasting into mid-summer.

PHILOSOPHY OF PRUNING

The time of the year when shrubs are pruned is dictated solely by the weather and the time of year when a shrub flowers.

In areas where frosts are unknown, clearly the weather is not an influence and plants can be pruned immediately they finish flowering. In other places, low temperatures have a strong influence, and a sufficiently long period must be left for fresh shoots that inevitably develop after a shrub is pruned to grow and ripen before the onset of cold weather. If insufficient time is left, tender shoots are killed in winter.

In areas where the time of pruning is dictated by the weather, shrubs are grouped into three main flowering periods:

• Spring to mid-summer flowering deciduous shrubs that flower on stems produced during the previous season. These are pruned immediately flowering ends.

• Late summer- and early autumn-flowering deciduous shrubs that flower on stems produced earlier in the same season. These are pruned during spring or early summer of the following year (see pages 305).

• Winter-flowering deciduous shrubs. These require little pruning, other than cutting out unrequired stems in spring (see page 306).

PREVIOUS SEASON'S WOOD

Spring-flowering shrubs, as well as those that produce their display in the early part of summer, develop flowers on stems and shoots that developed during the previous

year. The precise times when they flower is strongly influenced by the local climate and duration of winter. Indeed, flowering may vary by four weeks or even more in latitudes only five hundred miles apart.

These shrubs are pruned immediately their flowers fade, cutting back flowered shoots to fresh young growths. During the remaining part of summer and early autumn these will develop into shoots that bear flowers during the following year.

If pruning is neglected, plants soon become congested. Also, new shoots remain thin and spindly and the quality of flowers dramatically decreases.

LIGHT AND AIR

At the same time as cutting out shoots that have just borne flowers, remove:

• Thin and spindly shoots: if left, they are an eyesore and never bear satisfactory flowers.

• Shoots that cross the shrub's centre: these restrict the flow of air through the shrub and encourage the presence of diseases. They also reduce the amount of light, which prevents stems ripening properly before the onset of cold winter weather.

• Damaged shoots: if left, these encourage the presence of pests and diseases.

• Pest-ridden and diseased shoots: if left, they spread infection.

BALANCED GROWTH

As well as encouraging a shrub to develop a good display of flowers, pruning also ensures

that it is growing evenly and not lop-sided. Inevitably, after a few years a shrub develops a thick base and it may be necessary to cut out old stems. When this is done it often results in imbalanced growth. Therefore, take this into consideration and remove stems from the other side of the shrub as well.

SHRUBS PRUNED
IN THIS WAY
INCLUDE:
• Golden Bells (*Forsythia*)
• Mock Orange (*Philadelphus*)
• Flowering Currant (*Ribes*)

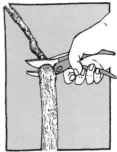

1. USE *sharp secateurs to cut slightly above a healthy, outward-pointing bud. This helps to create a shrub with an open centre where light and air can penetrate to ripen young shoots.*

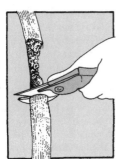

2. CUT *out dead or damaged shoots, severing them just above a bud. Shoots die from many reasons, including frost, pest and diseases. Immature stems are easily killed.*

3. CUT *out diseased stems, cutting slightly above a bud. These are likely to occur when shrubs have centres congested with stems. If left, they encourage the spread of disease to all parts.*

BILLHOOKS *have been used for centuries, either for harvesting plants or crudely pruning them. Here is an industrious harvester from a German calendar, in 1487.*

LATE SUMMER-FLOWERING SHRUBS

❖

These are richly flowered shrubs that brighten borders in late summer and frequently into early autumn. Their growth is curtailed by the onset of cold weather during early winter.

Unlike shrubs that flower early in the year, late summer-flowering ones develop their flowers on shoots produced earlier in the same year. They are therefore pruned in spring as soon as all risk of cold weather damaging young shoots has passed.

The time when the risk of frost has passed depends on the locality and latitude. Some places may seldom have frosts, while others still experience them in late spring and early summer. It is, therefore, essential to be guided by the weather pattern in your area, rather than by a fixed date that cannot, in all cases, be right.

SEVERE PRUNING

Many late summer-flowering shrubs respond to being cut back severely to fresh, young shoots near their bases. Because these shrubs develop vigorous shoots within a few months they must be grown in fertile soil.

Crossing and twiggy shoots must be cut out, in the same way as when pruning spring and early summer-flowering types.

SHRUBS PRUNED IN THIS WAY INCLUDE:
• Butterfly Bush *(Buddleia davidii)*
• Californian Lilacs (deciduous types, such as *Ceanothus* 'Gloire de Versailles' and *Ceanothus* 'Topaz')
• Tamarix/Tamarisk *(Tamarix pentandra)*

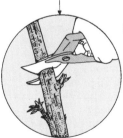

1. CUT *flowered stems back to outward-pointing buds to ensure plants grow outwards and develop open centres, through which air can penetrate and light enter to ripen shoots.*

2. EVERY *year, cut out a few old shoots to their bases, to encourage the development of others. This is essential to ensure shrubs eventually do not become full of old stems at their bases.*

3. CUT *out twiggy stems close to their bases. If left, they congest the centres of plants, reducing air circulation and encouraging the avoidable presence of pests and diseases.*

QUEST FOR PLANTS

Early in man's development, plants were mainly prized for their food or medicinal value. Later, spices and herbs became desirable as ways to cloak the incipient decay in an increasingly wide range of food. Indeed, in Europe it was the denial of essential spices from the spice islands in eastern Indonesia that triggered the westward search and Christopher Columbus's chancing on the shores of North America.

The Romans spread food and herb plants throughout Europe, but they also appreciated plants solely for their beauty. Indeed, Cleopatra, in about 50 BC, is said to have seduced Mark Antony on a bed of rose petals. At the same time, the Romans imported roses from Alexandria in North Africa.

EARLY HERBALS

Plants were recorded and discussed by Roman botanists, but it was not until the invention of movable type in Germany in 1440 that there began a wider interest in herbals and plants.

By 1600, plant nurseries were established and in 1601 and 1609 the French nurseryman Jean Robin issued catalogues of plants, some from North America. In England, in 1605, James I granted a Royal Charter to the Company of Gardeners which banned the sale of poor-quality plants.

With an increased demand for new plants, there was a tremendous impetus in many countries for nurseries and botanic gardens to send botanists and gardeners abroad to bring back new plants.

Spain, France, Holland, Sweden and England were prominent in creating botanic gardens and sending out botanists and plant hunters. Trading institutions such

as the East India Company and Dutch East India Company also helped in plant exploration.

The first crossing of North America in search of plants was made by Captains Merriweather Lewis and William Clark in 1804. They started from St. Louis and reached the Columbia River, on the borders of what are now the states of Washington and Oregon. One of the areas rich in plants was China, but its borders remained closed to foreigners, even in the mid-eighteenth century. North America, however, was freely open and many shrubs and trees from there have been spread throughout the world.

WINTER-FLOWERING SHRUBS

THESE are the easiest of all deciduous shrubs to prune. They appear to burst into flower each winter, regardless of what is done to them, but there are several basic pruning techniques that will prolong their lives for many years. Deciduous winter-flowering shrubs usually flower on short, leafless spurs that arise from the main branches. These increase slightly in size each year, but not noticeably and the shrub therefore appears to remain the same size for many years. In reality this, of course, is wrong as a young witch hazel planted when 90cm/3ft high will, after about twenty years, be three or more times that height. Nevertheless, unlike late summer-flowering shrubs, where growth is dominant and a large part of the shrub removed each spring, the winter-flowering types have a less vigorous nature.

REGULAR PRUNING

Like all other shrubs, winter-flowering types are equally likely to have damaged shoots, either physically or from diseases.

Exceptionally cold winters sometimes injure unripened shoot tips, while those that rub against each other create damaged areas susceptible to diseases. Such areas may also occur as a result of insect and bird damage during summer.

CUTTING OUT IN SPRING

Damaged areas must be cut out in spring, but not before all risk of severe frosts has passed. Always cut stems back to healthy buds; this is usually possible when trimming damaged shoot tips, but if a diseased area occurs on an old shoot this may not be possible.

Thin, twiggy shoots growing towards the plant's centre must be cut out before they develop into large branches. An open centre to the shrub encourages air to circulate freely, as well as light to enter

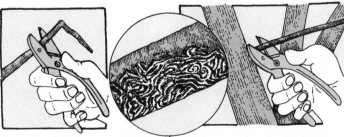

1. IN *spring, cut back damaged shoot tips (above) to healthy, outward-growing buds. This is usually only necessary in exceptionally cold areas, and even then it only generally occurs on unripened, young, immature shoots.*

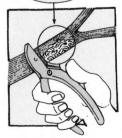

2. CUT *out (left) diseased areas. If left, they eventually girdle the stem and cause it to die. Insect pests, as well as birds, cause injuries that encourage the presence of diseases. Also, cut out all twiggy and crossing shoots (above).*

WITCH HAZELS

These are superb deciduous shrubs for brightening winter. The Chinese Witch Hazel (Hamamelis mollis), *pictured here, has sweetly scented, deep-yellow, strap-like petals. It is, however, the bark of the North American* Hamamelis virginiana *that produces the well-known, medicinal witch hazel. It flowers earlier than other witch hazels and is variously known as the Common Witch Hazel, Spotted Alder and Winter Bloom. Its bark provides an astringent liquid frequently employed as an antiseptic and skin cleanser. It has also been used as a tonic and sedative and is most valuable in checking internal and external haemorrhages. Long before Christopher Columbus chanced upon the New World the Indians used its inner bark for external applications to treat sore eyes, tumours and inflammations.*

---

to ripen young wood in summer. Also, branches that are allowed to develop in the plant's centre may eventually rub on other shoots and cause damage.

RESTRICTING SIZE

All shrubs ought to be selected to suit a particular position in a garden, so that drastic, size-diminishing pruning is not eventually needed. In the real world, however, this sometimes does not always happen and shrubs eventually need quite extensive and severe pruning.

Fortunately, it is easier to restrain the size – within reason – of winter-flowering shrubs than any others. This is because each year they put on less growth than most types.

When restricting its size, do not imbalance the shape and create a lop-sided specimen. This is not only quite

THE *Winter Sweet* (Chimonanthus praecox *'Grandiflorus'*) *has spicy-scented flowers from mid to late winter. It is ideal for planting alongside paths, where it creates a wonderful aroma.*

unpleasant to the eye, but puts extra strain on the main stem and increases the chance of wind loosening the plant.

Always cut stems back to other shoots: leaving stubs is unsightly and encourages the presence of diseases. If cuts are large, pare them smooth with a sharp knife and cover with a fungicidal tree paint to stop infection.

SHRUBS PRUNED IN THIS WAY INCLUDE:

- Chinese Witch Hazel (*Hamamelis mollis*)
- Cornelian Cherry (*Cornus mas*)
- Japanese Witch Hazel (*Hamamelis japonica*)
- Ozark Witch Hazel (*Hamamelis vernalis*)
- Winter-flowering Viburnums (*Viburnum farreri/fragrans, V. grandiflorum, V. x bodnantense* 'Dawn' and *V. x bodnantense* 'Deben')

DECIDUOUS TREES

ECIDUOUS trees need very little pruning, but as they are long-lived it is essential to create an evenly-shaped, attractive outline when young.

Part of the initial training and pruning is to ensure the trunk is upright and this is achieved by regularly checking the stake and tie securing it. The top of the stake should be just below the crotch, with the tree secured to it by two proprietary tree ties. For standard trees with long trunks, use three tree ties. These need to be checked every few months in summer to ensure the trunk is not constricted. Proprietary, plastic types are easily adjusted as the trunk ages and broadens.

WELL-SPACED STEMS

There should be three or four well-spaced stems growing from the top of the trunk – eventually they will form the main branches. Cut off shoots growing inwards from these main stems to ensure that the tree's centre is open.

If the ends of shoots are damaged, cut back to healthy, upward pointing buds.

PRUNE WHEN DORMANT

Most pruning of deciduous trees is performed in winter, when dormant. But flowering cherries and other members of the Prunus family are best pruned in late spring or early summer when the sap begins to rise. This is because disease spores are less likely to enter cuts when the tree's sap is rising.

If pruning in late spring or early summer means cutting off a large amount of blossom, prune in late summer instead.

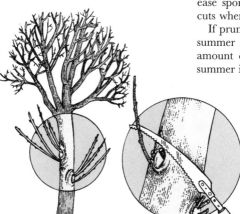

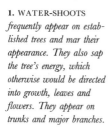

1. WATER-SHOOTS *frequently appear on established trees and mar their appearance. They also sap the tree's energy, which otherwise would be directed into growth, leaves and flowers. They appear on trunks and major branches.*

2. USE *a sharp saw to cut the shoots close to the trunk or branch. Normal saws are often impossible to use between congested shoots. A curved Grecian saw that cuts on the pull stroke is the best type to use in constricted places on trunks.*

3. USE *a sharp knife to smooth the cut ends, level with the trunk. Do not make the area larger than necessary as this may encourage the development of further water-shoots. Cover large areas with a fungicidal paint.*

TREE DOCTORING

Trees are part of our heritage and occasionally some need help to see them through to old age. From infancy, many branches naturally droop, the weight of the branch itself and foliage forever bearing downwards. Also, the weight of snow can be a problem in some areas.

Branches are easily supported by fixing stout, metal or wooden props under them. This has the advantage of being independent of the rest of the tree. Alternatively, hooks are bolted into the branch, which is then suspended from a branch higher up and towards the tree's centre. Whatever the method, it must not constrict the branch.

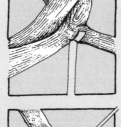

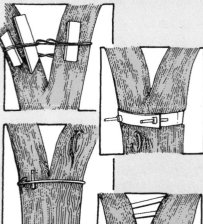

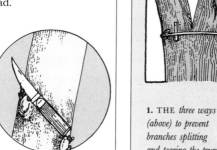

SUPPORT *large branches (above) with either metal or wooden props, positioned on a firm base, or by a large hook drilled into the branch and secured by nuts and washers. A cable secured to a higher branch can then be used to hold it in position.*

1. THE *three ways (above) to prevent branches splitting and tearing the trunk are initially effective, but after a few years cut into the bark and constrict growth. Even placing wood to form a pad between the wire and tree restricts growth after a few years of active growth.*

2. BRACE *split trunks with threaded rods inserted through drilled holes and secured at their ends with large washers and nuts. Ensure that the washers are large, so that they are not forced into the bark when the nuts are tightened at the ends of the rods.*

FILLING CAVITIES *Large, old trees often have cavities that if left untreated cause the entire trunk to decay.*
* *Remove dead and diseased wood. Scrape the area back to sound, healthy and firm timber.*
* *Paint the area with a wood preservative. Allow to dry and cover with a thick coating of a bituminous compound.*
* *Create a drainage channel by boring a hole from the lowest point to the outside.*
* *Fill up the whole area with cement – level with the inner bark.*

EVERGREEN SHRUBS

EVERGREEN shrubs, unlike deciduous types, are clothed in leaves all year round, although they regularly drop them throughout the year. Most leaves live for at least one full year before falling.

Once established, evergreen shrubs usually need no more attention than to shape them and cut out weak, diseased and straggly shoots in spring. In cold areas, leave this job until early summer.

AVOID WINTER PRUNING

It is essential not to prune evergreens in winter, as any young shoots that develop after pruning will be killed and may mean that pruning has to be carried out again to remove unsightly shoots and to encourage the development of further ones.

DELAY UNTIL AFTER FLOWERING

If the evergreen shrub blooms in spring, delay pruning until the flowers have completely died. Examples of this are Darwin's Berberis (Berberis darwinii) and Berberis x stenophylla.

ROOM DECORATION

Evergreen shrubs with variegated leaves are ideal for including in floral arrangements indoors – especially in winter when there is a dearth of colourful flowers available. The Spotted Laurel (Aucuba japonica 'Variegata') is popular with flower arrangers.

Always cut shoots from the back of a shrub and in several different places, rather than from one position. Also, sever each stem just above a leaf joint.

MAJOR SURGERY

Sometimes, major surgery is needed when evergeens become too large and spreading. This is best tackled as soon as growth begins in spring so as to allow as long a period as possible for young growths to develop before the onset of cold winter weather.

Occasionally, when evergreens are cut back dramatically, the flowers that would have developed during the season following pruning have to be sacrificed.

Remember that the further back into old wood evergreens are cut, the more difficult it is for them to develop fresh shoots.

If a neglected shrub is exceptionally old and tough, cut only a few of the old shoots back during the first season. If these produce shoots, cut back the other ones in the following season. If not successful, cut them less far into the older wood.

WHEN *pruning large-leaved evergreens, do not be tempted to use garden shears or electric trimmers, as they shred leaves. Instead, use sharp secateurs for thin stems and loppers for thick ones.*

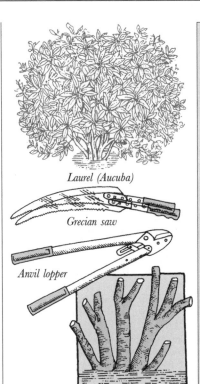

Laurel (Aucuba)

Grecian saw

Anvil lopper

MANY *large, neglected, evergreen shrubs eventually dominate gardens. They can, however, be given a new lease of life by cutting them back to their bases in spring.*

PRUNING EVERGREEN CONIFERS

A few conifers, such as larches and the Maidenhair Tree (Ginkgo biloba), are deciduous, but most are evergreen and create attractive screens and features throughout the year. Conifers – as well as other trees with sappy wood, such as birch, Horse Chestnut and some maples – bleed profusely when pruned in spring and summer. These are therefore best cut in late autumn or early winter when there is not an active flow of sap. It gives cuts ample time to heal before spring.

PICKING TEA LEAVES

Few people have not drunk tea, which is prepared from Camellia thea, *a relative of the much desired* Camellia japonica *that adorns gardens in late winter and spring.*

Tea was grown in China as early as 2700 BC and there is a Japanese legend that China is its home, although it has never been found in a wild state in that country. It has, however, been discovered growing wild in the forests of Assam in eastern India and it is conceivable that Chinese traders travelled there to obtain seeds of the precious plant.

For a long time, India remained unaware of the treasure bestowed by nature on her doorstep and started cultivating tea by importing seeds from China. Records indicate that Assam Tea was introduced into Ceylon (now Sri Lanka) in 1839, and from China in 1824.

Picking – or plucking as it is widely termed – both provides the source of tea and prunes the bushes so that they develop further sideshoots. The best tea is obtained by 'fine plucking', when the leading shoot and two leaves are removed. 'Coarse plucking' yields lower-quality tea and is when the leading shoots and four leaves are removed.

When the bushes stop producing leaves (known as flushing) they are pruned back severely. In warm, low lands this is performed every sixteen to twenty months, but at higher elevations it is carried out every three years.

SHRUBS WITH COLOURED STEMS

SEVERAL shrubs are grown for their coloured stems, which look especially attractive in winter. When planted around a pond they reflect in the pool's surface.

To encourage these suckering shrubs to develop attractive, stems, cut the complete plant down to within about 7.5cm/3in of the ground in mid-spring. This drastic pruning encourages the development of fresh shoots.

Repeated hard pruning eventually creates plants with masses of stubby shoots at their bases. This need not be a problem, as fresh shoots soon grow.

Because each year these shrubs develop a complete new array of stems and leaves, they need to be planted in rich, moisture-retentive soil. In poor, dry soils they do not create a good display.

SHRUBS WITH COLOURED STEMS INCLUDE:
• *Cornus alba* (Red-barked Dogwood). Red stems.
• *Cornus alba* 'Kesselringii'. Purplish-black stems.
• *Cornus alba* 'Sibirica' (Westonbirt Dogwood). Bright crimson stems.
• *Cornus stolonifera* 'Flaviramea'. Young shoots yellow to olive-green in winter.

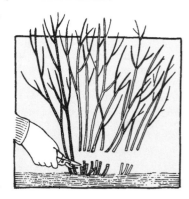

Cut stems of dogwoods to within 7.5cm/3in of the ground in mid-spring to encourage fresh ones.

DEAD-HEADING RHODODEDRONS

Large-flowered rhododendrons benefit from having their dead flowers removed. This encourages development of further shoots, rather than seeds.

After the flowers fade, snap the stem just below the old flower head, while holding the stem firmly.

PRUNE *Mop-headed Hydrangeas (left) every year. Cut off dead flower heads immediately after flowering in late summer. Alternatively, leave the flower heads on the plants until spring – they look attractive in winter when covered with frost. In spring, cut out thin, weak and damaged shoots, as well as a few two- or three-year-old stems to encourage the development of fresh, strong, young ones. Do not shorten young, vigorous shoots as they may have dormant flower-buds.*

HEATHERS AND HEATHS

CALLUNAS, ericas and daboecias are kept tidy and with a neat outline by lightly trimming them with hedging shears. Do not use secateurs, as these do not allow contoured outlines to be created.

CALLUNAS AND SUMMER-FLOWERING ERICAS

Trim callunas and summer-flowering ericas in spring. Use hedging shears to trim off dead flowers and to create a neat, undulating outline. Ensure this job is tackled before growth starts in spring, as otherwise young shoots that would bear flowers later in the season are clipped off.

Plants pruned in this way:
• Bell Heather/Twisted Heather *(Erica cinerea)*
• Cornish Heath *(Erica vagans)*
• Corsican Heath *(Erica terminalis)*
• Cross-leaved Heath *(Erica tetralix)*
• Heather/Scotch Heather/Ling *(Calluna vulgaris)*

WINTER AND SPRING-FLOWERING TYPES

These are trimmed after they finish flowering, again lightly cutting off dead flower heads and creating a pleasing outline.

Do not leave the trimmings on the plants: brush them off with a soft broom.

Plants pruned in this way:
• Heather *(Erica x darleyensis)*
• Mediterranean Heather *(Erica mediterranea/ E. hibernica)*
• Spring Heather/Snow Heather *(Erica herbacea/ E. carnea)*

DABOECIAS

Use hedging shears to trim off old flower heads and the loose ends of shoots in late autumn, after flowering has finished. In cold areas,

Heathers and heaths are best clipped with hedging shears, removing old flower heads and creating a neat, attractive, undulating outline.

leave this job until early spring.
Plants pruned in this way:
• St. Dabeoc's Heath/Irish Heath *(Daboecia cantabrica)*

TREE HEATHS

These need little pruning, other than shortening long ends of straggly shoots in late spring after the flowers fade. Also, remove straggly shoots to maintain an even and attractive shape.

Plants pruned in this way:
• Tree Heath *(Erica arborea)*
• Spanish Heath/Portugal Heath *(Erica lusitanica)*

BRIAR PIPES

The roots of the Tree Heath (Erica arborea) *were widely used in southern France and the Iberian Peninsula to make pipes for smoking tobacco. Briar is in fact a corruption of the French word 'bruyère'.*

PRUNING ROSES

REGULARLY and systematically pruning roses is relatively new and dates back only to the middle of the nineteenth century. It did not develop into a technique until the introduction of hybrid teas in 1867, although the hybrid perpetuals that reached the peak of their development slightly earlier were also regularly pruned. Before then, roses were not highly considered as shrubs for borders and the only treatment they were given was thinning: cutting out dead or overcrowded shoots.

Nowadays, the purpose of pruning is to encourage the yearly production of healthy, well-sized flowers on plants that have a long lifespan. It is an essential part of growing roses, but regrettably too often steeped in mysticism.

MYSTIQUE REMOVED

If one considers that hybrid tea and floribunda roses – by far the most popular of all bush roses – are just vigorous, deciduous shrubs that flower mainly on new shoots developed earlier in the same year, then the mystique is removed. The other important factor is winter, as this influences the time of year when pruning is performed.

**AUTUMN OR
SPRING PRUNING?**

Although pruning can be done at any time during a plant's dormant period, in exceptionally cold areas it is best left until early spring. There are, however, advantages of both times where temperatures are not too low.

TRADITIONALLY, roses have been planted as 'bare-rooted' plants. Before planting bush roses, cut back stems of hybrid teas to about 15cm/6in long, and floribundas to 20–23cm/8–9in. Additionally, cut out weak, twiggy and inward-growing shoots. Shorten long roots to about 30cm/12in, and cut out damaged ones. Before planting, immerse the roots in water overnight. Plants with dry roots take longer to become established.

Pruning in autumn makes both diseased shoots and other shoots from the plant's base easier to see and remove. Also, because diseased shoots are removed early there is less chance of spores being carried over to another year.

Pruning in autumn removes much of a plant's top growth and thereby reduces the area that can be battered by strong winter winds that may loosen roots in the soil. However, even if pruning is left until spring, long shoots can be cut off in autumn and the risk of root disturbance diminished.

If roses are pruned in autumn there is a chance that young, newly-formed shoots may be damaged by cold winter weather: pruning in spring reduces this risk. Also, by leaving pruning until spring, it is possible to enjoy the attractive fruits (hips or heps) of some rose species when there is a dearth of interest in a garden.

REMOVING SUCKER SHOOTS

Because most roses are budded and therefore do not grow on their own roots, sucker shoots often develop from ground level. Remove them as soon as they are seen, but do not cut them off as this encourages even more shoots. Instead, dig down around the sucker and pull it off. Wear strong gloves when tackling this job.

If removing suckers is neglected, they eventually dominate the plant. Shoots also appear on the stems of standard and half-standard roses. Rub them off as soon as seen.

PRUNING CUTS

Traditionally, roses have been pruned with secateurs and cut slightly above outward-pointing buds. Cuts too close or too near a bud, or with blunt secateurs, were avoided. For the moment, these rulings are still the best for home gardeners, but other techniques are now being tried (see page 299).

SLIGHTLY *sloping cut bud facing outwards*

WRONG CUTS

TOO *high above the bud*

BLUNT *secateurs*

TOO *close to the bud*

THE *range of roses is wide and includes hybrid teas (now large-flowered roses), floribundas (now cluster-flowered roses), climbers, ramblers, miniatures and shrub types. All need slightly different pruning.*

DEAD-HEADING

Cutting off dead flowers from hybrid tea and floribunda roses encourages further blooms. Cut slightly above the second or third leaf below the dead flower head.

DISBUDDING

Performed on hybrid tea roses to produce larger blooms.

HYBRID TEA AND FLORIBUNDA ROSES

IF YOU ask twelve rose experts how to prune a bush rose you would probably get a dozen different answers. As well as considering the basic technique they would take thought about the soil, vigour of the variety and weather pattern in their locality. Here, however, we first present the basic philosophy, later highlighting a few other considerations.

FROM LIGHT TO HARD

There are three basic methods of pruning: 'Light' (in some areas known as Low Pruning), 'Moderate' (also known and Medium Pruning) and 'Hard' (frequently referred to as High or Long Pruning).

All of these terms refer to the amount of wood pruned out of a plant, whether when young or established. And although hard pruning is recommended for both hybrid tea and floribunda roses when young, for most it is not the best way to prune established bushes. Then, most rose bushes are moderately pruned; while a few exceptionally vigorous types, as well as those on light, sandy and impoverished soils that dry out in summer, are lightly cut.

FINE TUNING

Rose varieties vary widely in their vigour: those with a weak nature are pruned harder than vigorous types. This is because the harder a shrub is pruned, the more growth it makes. Rose catalogues frequently indicate a plant's vigour. Where soils are light, exceptionally well-drained and impoverished, light pruning is recommended. However, continued light pruning over several years produces tall, spindly bushes that bear poor quality flowers.

Hybrid tea roses with flowers in shades of yellow frequently respond well to light pruning.

EXHIBITION BLOOMS

Varieties of hybrid teas grown primarily to produce exhibition

WEEPING STANDARDS

With their pendulous growth, weeping standards have grace and elegance. Varieties with a slender, pendulous habit are budded on root-stocks 1.3–1.5m/ 4½–5ft high. A wire umbrella is secured to the top of a stout stake and the weeping stems are trained over them.

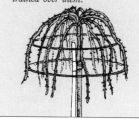

blooms with long, straight stems are frequently hard pruned, although many rose experts consider this too dramatic for long-term health of the bush.

CLOSELY PLANTED BUSHES

Where hybrid tea roses are planted close together in beds, hard pruning is often practised and consists of cutting all shoots to within 20cm/8in of the ground. It encourages strong growth.

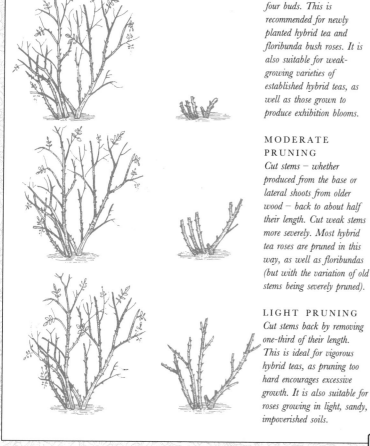

BEFORE	AFTER	TYPE

HARD PRUNING
Cut stems back to three or four buds. This is recommended for newly planted hybrid tea and floribunda bush roses. It is also suitable for weak-growing varieties of established hybrid teas, as well as those grown to produce exhibition blooms.

MODERATE PRUNING
Cut stems – whether produced from the base or lateral shoots from older wood – back to about half their length. Cut weak stems more severely. Most hybrid tea roses are pruned in this way, as well as floribundas (but with the variation of old stems being severely pruned).

LIGHT PRUNING
Cut stems back by removing one-third of their length. This is ideal for vigorous hybrid teas, as pruning too hard encourages excessive growth. It is also suitable for roses growing in light, sandy, impoverished soils.

Before pruning

After pruning

HALF- and full-standards are superb for bringing height to borders. Half-standards are budded on a root-stock at about 75cm/2½ft above the ground, and at 1m/3½ft high for full standards. They are pruned less severely than bush types. It is essential to build up a well-balanced head. Remove dead, twiggy and congested shoots from the standard's centre.

SHRUB ROSES

PRUNING shrub roses is important and best tackled in late winter, although any time up to the end of early spring is all right. Unlike hybrid tea and floribunda roses, which need to be pruned hard during their first year, shrub roses can be left without being pruned for the first two years after being set in the ground.

PRUNING OBJECTIVES

During their early years, allow shrub roses to build up their growth and to form strong stems. Thereafter, prune them every year, including the following:

• Cut away dead and diseased shoots. Carefully inspect around the shrub's base, where stems are often congested.

• Prune out, close to their bases, very weak and twiggy shoots.

• With age, shrub roses usually become crowded with stems: cut away to their bases very old stems so that space is left for young ones. Severely cutting back aged stems also has the advantage in encouraging the production of young shoots. The aim should be to continually initiate the formation of fresh shoots.

• Once all the old, dead and twiggy shoots are removed, there is a decision to be made about the severity of pruning the remainder of the shrub. Cutting back shoots dramatically, perhaps by a half, encourages large, high quality flowers. However, if you want masses of flowers, just lightly cut off the tips of shoots. Usually, it is better to aim for something between these two extremes.

• Roses that are true species – as well as those with a similar nature – need no pruning except the removal of dead, twiggy and diseased shoots, and an occasional thinning of old shoots.

• Often, shrub roses are allowed to scramble and sprawl into other plants. In such cases, little pruning is needed other than to remove old, dead and diseased shoots.

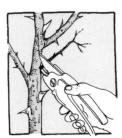

1. FROM *late winter to early spring, cut out thin, weak, twiggy and diseased shoots. This aspect of pruning is common to most roses, as well as other shrubs, but is no less important for the health and vigour of shrub roses.*

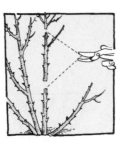

2. THE *degree of hard or light pruning dictates the amount of growth during the following year: for large, high quality flowers cut shoots back severely, perhaps by a half. Light pruning, however, creates more but smaller flowers.*

3. SHRUB *roses can even be lightly pruned so that existing stems and branches remain and fill a specified area. Nevertheless, regularly remove a few old stems from the base of the shrub to encourage the development of others and continuing beauty.*

ENGLISH ROSES

The main criticism of 'old roses' is that they usually only have one flush of flowers and that their colour range is rather limited. With this in mind, English roses have been developed. They are recurrent flowering, which means that after their first flush they continue to produce blooms, although perhaps intermittently. Also, they have a wider colour range. Their growth is usually bushy and most have a pleasing fragrance.

Because of the improved characteristics – and especially the repeat flowering – they need slightly different pruning.

The aim must be to build up a bushy plant. If you are buying from a nursery specializing in English roses, they probably will have been initially pruned before despatch and therefore no further pruning is needed during the first year. However, always cut out thin, decayed and damaged growths. During following years:

• Cut out weak, and twiggy growth, as well as dead and diseased shoots.

• With age – and when the bush is well established – each year cut out a few of the older shoots to make way for younger ones.

• Then cut back the remaining branches to half of their length. This will encourage the development of fresh shoots.

Another pruning method is to treat them in the same way as hybrid tea roses, and is especially suited for the shorter, bushier varieties. This method has the advantage of encouraging the development of finer flowers, but the plant's stance will not be so attractive. Nevertheless, it is an ideal method for the small, less vigorous varieties.

RAMBLER ROSES

RAMBLER and climbing roses are frequently thought to be the same, but they differ dramatically and the methods of pruning them are also different.

Ramblers develop long, pliable shoots during one year, which in the following season produce clusters of flowers, mainly during mid-summer.

PRUNING TECHNIQUE

• In autumn, cut out all dead and diseased wood.

• Also, sever at the plant's base all shoots that produced flowers during the current year. This will encourage the development of fresh shoots. Tie in young shoots to replace them.

• If there are insufficient young shoots (produced during the same season) to replace those that are cut out at the plant's base, leave a few of the old ones and and cut their lateral shoots back two or three buds from their bases. During the following season, cut these very old shoots out at the plant's base.

• A few varieties need only light pruning: besides cutting out their dead wood, tip back lateral shoots that have flowered. Examples of these types of varieties include 'Emily Gray' and 'Félicité et Perpétue'.

• Prune neglected ramblers by cutting out all old wood to the plant's base, even if this means that most of the shoots are removed. During the following season, it then will be easier to differentiate between old and current shoots.

ROSES IN POTS

Growing and exhibiting roses in pots became highly fashionable during the latter half of the nineteenth century. Increasingly, rose shows were held, both in Europe and North America, and many new societies came into existence.

RAMBLERS *are usually vigorous, producing long stems each year and therefore well able to cover arches and trellises. 'Albertine' is a well-known climber, as well as 'Sanders' White' which is a Wichuraiana type with small, semi-double, deliciously fragrant flowers.*

'Veilchenblau'

'Albertine'   'Sanders' White'

CLIMBING ROSES

THESE are the traditional roses that clothe walls and create a galaxy of flowers in large clusters during the latter part of early summer and into mid-summer. Many varieties also have small flushes of flowers in autumn.

These climbers are derived from several sources: some are natural climbers, a few sports of bush hybrid tea or floribunda varieties, while others have more complex ancestry.

PRUNING TECHNIQUE

• In late winter or early spring, cut out all dead, thin, weak, twiggy and diseased shoots.

• Most climbers flower on shoots produced during that same year. Therefore, build up a permanent framework of branches of well-spaced branches that will be able to clothe the wall.

• Cut back short laterals which produced flowers during the previous year to two or three buds.

• If vigorous young shoots appear

'Kiftsgate'

'Sympathie'   'Morning Jewel'

The range of climbers is wide and includes varieties developed from naturally climbing rose species such as 'Kiftsgate', a variety of Rosa filipes, a true climber. Others include climbing forms of Floribundas, like 'Morning Jewel', while 'Sympathie' is a Kordessi climber and raised by the German Wilhelm Kordes in 1964.

high up on the plant, leave them to extend the plant's framework. In autumn tie them to the supports, and in spring secure them properly and cut off only damaged or soft tips.

 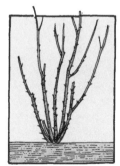

1. CLIMBING *roses have stiffer stems than ramblers, as well as a more permanent framework of branches. For this reason, build up a strong framework of well-spaced branches that clothe the wall.*

2. PRUNE *out twiggy, weak, dead, crossing and diseased wood in late winter or early spring. Also, cut back short laterals which produced flowers during the previous year.*

3. DURING *the previous year, strong growths will have developed. In autumn, temporarily tie them to the supporting framework. In spring, secure them properly and cut off damaged tips.*

RED AND WHITE CURRANTS

◆

BOTH of these two soft fruits are grown on 'legs': that is, they have short stems that connect the branches to the ground. Gooseberry bushes are also grown on a leg. This is a significant difference from blackcurrants, which have a bushy base with many stems arising from the soil.

INITIAL TRAINING

When a young red or white currant bush is bought, it will have been raised from a cutting about 30cm/12in long and where all but the top three or four buds were removed. The lower 10cm/4in of the cutting would have been inserted in the ground, thereby producing a plant with a clear stem about 10cm/4in long. Thereafter, it is essential that this leg remains clear of shoots.

When bought as a young, bare-rooted plant, it will have been set in the ground at any time from late autumn to late winter. Pruning does not begin until the winter of the following year, when it has formed several branches and its roots are established.

• During the first winter after being planted, cut each shoot back by half, pruning to an outward-pointed bud. At the same time, cut out, at their bases, all crossing, weak and dead stems.

• In the winter of the second year, cut back all shoots made during the previous summer by about 20cm/8in. Also, cut all lateral shoots (those growing from the main stems) to within two buds of their bases. Additionally, remove crossing shoots so that light and air can enter the bush.

• During the third winter, cut back shoots made during the previous summer by 10–15cm/4–6in. Also, cut back all laterals to within two buds of their bases. Check that the plant's shape is even and

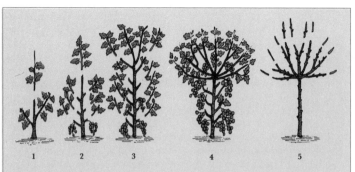

CREATING A STANDARD RED CURRANT

Standard red currants take several years to develop. They are normal red currant bushes, but on stems 75–90cm/2½–3ft high. The development of the stem, although time consuming, is easy and the only problem is to maintain growth before the head is formed.

1. DURING *the plant's first year, secure the main stem to a stout cane. Allow the main stem to grow unhindered, but cut back the lower shoots in summer to form fruiting spurs. Eventually, these will be removed.*

2. IN *the second year, allow the central stem to grow, but cut back the sideshoots to 7.5cm/3in long in summer.*

3. DURING *the third year – when the stem is about 90cm/3ft high – allow four or five shoots to develop at its top to form the head. Cut these shoots back by half in winter and prune lateral shoots to two buds long.*

4. IN *the fourth year, allow the shoots at the head to develop, cutting them back by about 15cm/6in in winter. Cut lateral shoots in the head back to within two buds of their bases. By now, the head will be well developed.*

5. DURING *the following winter, lightly trim shoots at the plant's head, cut back lateral shoots and those growing from the stem.*

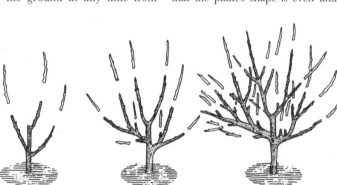

1. RED *and white currant bushes are winter pruned in the same way. During their first year after being planted, cut all shoots back by half, pruning to an outward-pointed bud. Also, completely cut out crossing, weak and dead stems.*

2. DURING *the following winter, cut back all shoots made during the previous summer by about 20cm/8in, and lateral ones (those growing from the main stems) to within two buds of their bases. Also, cut out crossing shoots.*

3. IN *the third winter, cut back all shoots made during the previous summer by 10–15cm/4–6in. Also, cut back all laterals to within two buds of their bases. Check that the plant's shape is even and not lop-sided, and remove crossing shoots.*

not lop-sided, and remove crossing shoots that cross the plant's centre.

• In subsequent years, red and white currants produce fruit buds in clusters at the bases of one-year-old shoots and on short spurs on the older wood. A permanent framework of shoots is therefore needed, with fresh spurs being created by cutting back sideshoots.

As stems grow old, they need replacement and this is achieved by cutting a few out each year.

RED currants are principally used for cooking, although sometimes eaten as a dessert. White currants are invariably eaten as a dessert.

SUMMER PRUNING

As well as pruning the bushes in winter, prune them at the end of early summer. Shorten lateral shoots to about five leaves, but do not cut the leading stems. This helps to encourage the development of fruiting spurs without producing vegetative growth.

As with all highly trained fruit bushes and trees, summer pruning is essential to encourage fruit-bud development.

BLACKCURRANTS

UNLIKE red and white currant bushes that grow on short legs, blackcurrants create a mass of stems from ground level. Therefore, they must be pruned to encourage new shoots from their bases.

Because blackcurrants develop many new shoots each year, as well as being pruned they must be planted in fertile soil, fed copiously and mulched in early summer. Use well-decomposed compost or manure to support the amount of growth the plant has to make.

BLACKCURRANTS *are superb in pies, tarts, jams and jellies.*

Immediately after planting, cut the entire plant to less than 5cm/2in above the soil's surface.

No attempt must be made to let bushes develop fruit in their first year. Their sole energy must be devoted to developing strong, new shoots and a large root-system. During the first autumn after being planted, cut down the weakest shoots that formed during summer. Further growths will develop during the following season and will become fruiting shoots.

INITIAL TRAINING
During its dormant period, from late autumn to early spring, select a well-rooted bush and plant it fractionally deeper than before to allow for settlement of loose soil around the roots. The soil-mark on the stem indicates the earlier depth at which it was planted.

SECOND AND SUBSEQUENT YEARS
In autumn, after fruits have been picked, cut back to their bases all shoots that produced fruits during the previous summer. This will leave the fresh, new shoots that formed during summer to bear fruits in the following year.

1. PLANT *bare-rooted blackcurrant bushes from late autumn to early spring. Dig out a hole large enough to accommodate the roots. Set the plant slightly deeper than before to allow for settlement of the soil.*

2. SPREAD *out the roots and work fine soil around them, covering and firming it in layers rather than all at one time. Lightly rake the surface to remove depressions and foot prints in which rain would settle.*

3. IMMEDIATELY *after planting, cut down all stems to within 5cm/2in of the soil's surface. This is essential, as no attempt should be made to produce fruit during the first season after planting.*

GOOSEBERRIES

LIKE red and white currants, gooseberry bushes are grown on short stems, descriptively known as 'legs'.

Plant young, bare-rooted gooseberry bushes in winter. During summer they develop shoots which in the following winter are pruned back by half to two-thirds. Sever them just above an upward-pointing bud.

GOOSEBERRIES *are ideal for eating fresh, stewing and making into pies.*

Additionally, cut lateral shoots 5–7.5cm/2–3in long. Completely remove crossing and damaged shoots to ensure both light and air penetrates to the centre.

FOLLOWING YEAR
In winter cut back, by one-third to a half, all shoots produced during the previous summer. Also, cut back laterals and completely remove crossing shoots.

In later years, cut back by a third all shoots produced during the previous summer and continue to cut back laterals. Occasionally, it is necessary to cut out whole shoots if the plant's centre becomes congested.

As well as pruning in winter, at the end of early summer shorten all lateral shoots to about five leaves to encourage the formation of fruit buds. Pruning at this time does not encourage masses of growth. If shoots appear on the plant's stem, remove them immediately as it must be kept clear. Cut them off with secateurs close to their bases – do not leave short, unsightly snags.

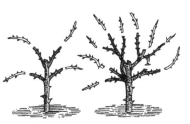

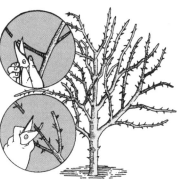

YOUNG, *newly planted gooseberry bushes (top) are initially pruned severely in winter by cutting back shoots by half to two-thirds. Later, winter pruning is less severe. Established bushes (above) have their main shoots cut by a third. Additionally, cut back laterals to 5–7.5cm/2–3in.*

EXHIBITION GOOSEBERRIES

Produce large gooseberries by:
- *Regularly syringing the bushes throughout summer.*
- *Mulching the soil in summer to prevent moisture loss, keep the soil cool and to feed the plants.*
- *Feed copiously in summer.*
- *Thinning out to leave the shapliest and best berries.*

RASPBERRIES

◆

FEW summer fruits are as succulent and tasty as newly picked raspberries. They are borne on long stems known as canes that develop from soil-level and, collectively with blackberries and hybrid berries, are known as cane fruits.

Most raspberries bear fruits in midsummer on canes produced during the previous year, and these are known as summer-fruiting types. There are also varieties that develop fruits from late summer into autumn. These are widely known as autumn-fruiting raspberries and bear fruits on shoots developed during the same year. Therefore, there is a distinct difference in the way and time autumn-fruiting types are pruned – detailed opposite.

RASPBERRIES *are a popular summer fruit, usually eaten fresh although some are made into jam.*

PLANTING

Both summer- and autumn-fruiting raspberries are best planted in late autumn or early winter, although in cold areas this can continue to early spring. Prepare the soil by adding generous amounts of compost and manure, then dig out a deep trench for the roots.

Space the canes 38–45cm/15–18in apart in rows with about 1.5m/5ft between them. Orient the canes north to south to ensure even growth on both sides of the row. Immediately after pruning, cut the canes of both varieties to 30cm/12in high.

If planted in winter, summer-fruiting types will bear fruits eighteen months later; autumn types in late summer and autumn of the same year.

  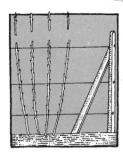

1. PRUNE *established summer-fruiting raspberries in autumn. Cut out at their bases all old stems that produced fruit during summer. Leave the young shoots unpruned.*

2. AS *the young stems grow, space them out and tie to the supporting wires. Secure them individually or with a long piece of string looped around the canes and then the wires.*

3. IN *late winter, cut back the tips of the canes to just above the top supporting wire. This concentrates growth on the lower buds and subsequently improves the quality of fruits.*

ESTABLISHED PLANTS

Prune established summer-fruiting varieties in autumn. Because these develop canes one year that bear fruits during the following one, regularly cut out to their bases all canes that have produced fruits. Young canes are then spaced out, tied to their supports and allowed to develop.

These young canes are usually tied individually to the supporting wires. Alternatively, loop a long piece of string along the row, taking it around the canes and then the supporting wire. The latter method holds the canes securely, without slipping, but by tying them individually late-developing canes can be easily accomodated and secured.

In late winter, cut off the tips of the canes to just above the top supporting wire. This encourages the development of buds and improves fruit quality.

VARIETIES TO LOOK FOR
Summer-fruiting:
• 'Delight' – heavy crops of large fruits. Ideal for freezing.
• 'Glen Cova' – early fruiting,

with flavoursome fruits.
• 'Malling Jewel' – well-known, virus resistant variety.
Autumn-fruiting:
• 'Heritage' – ideal in mild areas, with plenty of medium-sized fruits.
• 'Fallgold' – late, yellow-fruiting variety, which has sweet, medium-sized fruits.

 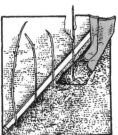 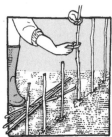

1. PLANT *young raspberry canes in autumn or early winter, although it can be undertaken up to early spring. Dig out a trench, deep and wide enough to accommodate the roots. If possible, orient the rows north to south.*

2. PLANT *the canes 38–45cm/15–18in apart in rows with about 1.5m/5ft between them. Ensure that the roots are well spread out and planted slightly deeper than before. The old soil-mark can usually be seen on the cane.*

3. FIRM *soil around the roots and cut the canes of both summer- and autumn-fruiting varieties to 30cm/12in above the surface. This prevents them fruiting too soon and encourages the development of strong root-systems.*

> ### AUTUMN-FRUITING RASPBERRIES
>
> *These develop fruits on shoots formed during the current season. Therefore, they are easier to prune than summer-fruiting varieties. During late winter, cut all canes to within 5cm/2in of the ground. This encourages the development of fresh canes that will bear fruits during the following late summer and autumn.*

APPLE AND PEAR BUSHES

REGULAR pruning is essential, initially to form a framework of branches and the desired shape; later to ensure a balance between fruit production and new growth. The initial pruning is performed in winter, when trees are in a dormant state.

APPLES *and pears are the most popular tree fruits in temperate climates.*

Most apple trees are bought either as bare-rooted trees during winter, or established and growing in containers.

Bare-rooted types are planted during winter, whenever the weather and soil allows, while container-grown types can be set in the ground at any time of year when it is not frozen or waterlogged, but avoid periods when the soil is very dry or the weather excessively hot.

YOUNG TREES

After planting a maiden tree (one that is one year old and has not produced sideshoots) cut back to about half its height during late winter.

Cut just above a bud. This causes the maiden tree to extend its growth upwards during the following summer, as well as to develop sideshoots.

During the following winter, reduce the lengths of all shoots by half, at the same time removing dead, crossing and damaged shoots. Ensure the tree's centre is open and free from branches.

In the following winter, prune the shoots less severely: cut main shoots by one-third. Weak, less-vigorous shoots are pruned by half to encourage stronger growth.

1. MOST *apple trees are bought as established bushes with several shoots forming the tree's framework. However, when planting a maiden tree, cut it to about half its height in winter, severing the stem just above a strong, healthy bud.*

2. DURING *the following summer shoots develop, and in winter are reduced by about half their lengths. Cut to outward-pointing buds. At the same time, remove dead, crossing and damage shoots, close to their bases. Always use sharp secateurs.*

3. BY *the following winter, the tree will have developed a strong framework. Cut back vigorous shoots by one-third; weak ones by a half. Select the best positioned shoots to form the permanent framework. Inspect the tree from several angles.*

PRUNING PEARS

Pears need similar pruning to apples but can, if necessary and when established, be pruned slightly more severely.

Most pears bear fruits on spurs. With these, shorten new growth formed by leading shoots by about a third and cut back laterals to three or four buds. Also, cut out overcrowded spurs and ensure the plant's centre is kept open. A few varieties – 'Josephine de Malines' and 'Fargonelle' – are tip-bearing and need only the longest laterals cut to four buds long.

SOME *apple varieties, such as Cox's Orange Pippin, bear fruits on spurs arising from their branches. Prune them to encourage the development of fresh, young spurs (see above).*

OTHER *varieties, such as Worcester Pearmain, bear fruits towards the tips of shoots. Therefore, instead of cutting back shoots to encourage the development of spurs, most are left to encourage fruits to develop towards their tips (see above).*

Always make pruning cuts slightly above a bud that faces outwards.

ESTABLISHED BUSHES

Pruning established bushes uses one of two different methods, depending on the variety. Some apple varieties bear fruits on two-year-old shoots and short shoots known as spurs growing on older wood. Other varieties develop fruits on the tips of shoots formed during the previous year. A few varieties combine these two methods of fruiting.

SPUR-BEARING

During a tree's formative years, continue to cut back the tips of leading branches by about a quarter. Also, cut back young laterals that are growing too close to the leading shoots.

On older trees – apart from removing dead, overcrowded and crossing shoots – encourage the development of spurs on shoots away from the branch leaders by cutting them to about six buds long. In the following year, other shoots further up the branch can be pruned in the same way. Additionally, new shoots growing from cut-back ones are pruned to three buds each.

TIP-BEARING

These varieties bear fruits towards the tips of shoots. Prune established bushes in winter, removing crowded branches and cutting out crossing and crowded ones. At the same time prune the branch leaders: cut back the growth made during the previous year by about a third.

At the same time, leave all but the most vigorous lateral shoots unpruned. However, to encourage the development of more shoots, cut back by half those that are more than 25cm/10in long.

ESPALIER APPLES AND PEARS

TRAINED fruit trees, such as espaliers and cordons, are frequently much easier to fit into small gardens than bush types. They can be planted and trained against warm walls or alongside tiered wires tensioned between posts. Espaliers can even be formed into arches covering paths.

GETTING STARTED

Novice fruit growers may wish to start training an espalier by planting a partly-trained tree, perhaps with two or three tiers of branches. A less expensive beginning is to plant a one-year-old specimen.

The first task is to erect tiers of 10-gauge galvanized wires, the lowest one 38cm/15in above the soil and then spaced 25–30cm/10–12in apart. Allow for five or six tiers of wires.

Plant a young, bare-rooted tree in winter and cut it slightly above a bud, 5cm/2in above the lowest wire. During summer, when growth begins, rub out all buds except the top one and a couple on either side that will form two arms. Select buds that face the intended direction of growth. Insert a cane to support the leading shoot. Also, use two 1.2m/4ft canes to support the two 'arms'. Initially, train them at 45 degree angles: if one grows faster, raise the angle of the other one to encourage more rapid growth and to make them even.

This is based on the fact that vertical shoots always grow faster than horizontal ones, although the latter will produce fruits earlier than those that are upright. Towards the end of the growing season, lower the canes and tie them to the horizontal wires.

In the second winter, the central stem will have grown above the next wire. Again, cut it off 5cm/2in above the wire and remove all buds, except the top three, that are between the first and second wire.

During the second summer, train the top two shoots in the same way as in the previous year. Also, cut back to the third leaf all sideshoots growing on the bottom tier. Additionally, lightly cut back their ends to leave a short piece of new wood. It is essential not to cut into the older wood.

In the following season, repeat these treatments. When the central stem reaches the desired height, cut it off slightly above the top supporting wire.

PARTLY TRAINED ESPALIERS

These save two or three years of work, but because they are larger it takes longer for them to become established. They are also more expensive to buy.

Before planting, measure the distances between the tiers of branches and then erect supporting wires to suit them. If wrongly spaced, the branches cannot be supported properly

CORDONS

Cordon apples and pears can be grown in rows alongside paths and trained between 35 and 45 degree angles up wires tensioned between posts. Instead of tying cordon stems directly to the wires, first secure them to strong bamboo canes. In mid to late summer, cut back lateral shoots (right) to the third leaf above the basal cluster. Also, cut back the end of the main shoot (left) to leave a short length of new wood.

Plant bare-rooted plants during their dormant period in winter and when the soil is not frozen or waterlogged. Container-grown trees are planted at any time, whenever the weather and soil allows – but not during droughts when the soil is very dry.

Spread out the roots and firm soil in layers around them. At this stage, only loosely tie the main stem and tiers to the wires. It is possible that the soil will settle slightly, and unless the branches are intially tied loosely they may be put under unnecessary tension.

After a couple of months, check the tree and secure the ties properly. Also, check the ties regularly to ensure they have not perished and are too loose.

PRUNE a maiden tree to a bud 5cm/2in above the bottom wire (right). In summer it will form side branches and further growth at its top (far right). During the following winters, cut the leading shoot above the next wire until five or six tiers have been formed (below and below right).

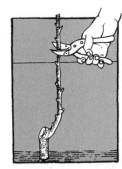

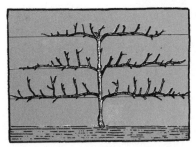

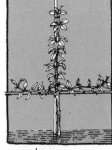

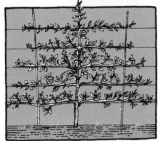

APPLE and pear trees are occasionally trained to create arches 1.8–2.4m/6–8ft high and 2.4–3m/8–10ft wide, and are especially attractive when forming a canopy over gravel paths. They are like espaliers, with lateral stems trained on wires.

PLUMS AND GAGES

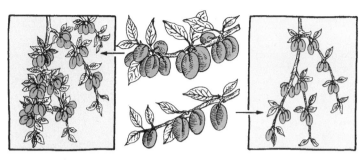

STONE fruits, such as plums and gages, are succulent and juicy. Dessert varieties need a sunnier and more sheltered position than cooking varieties, which tolerate greater exposure to low temperatures. They are sometimes grown as fan-trained trees against warm walls, but are usually planted as half-standards, with an eventual trunk length of 1–1.2m/3½–4ft. Alternatively, they are grown as bushes, with a 60–75cm/2–2½ft clear stem that forms a trunk.

PLUMS and gages are succulent fruits, eaten fresh, bottled or made into jam.

HALF-STANDARDS

Plums and gages are susceptible to silver leaf disease if they are pruned in autumn or winter when dormant. Therefore, always prune them in spring when growth is beginning and wounds will heal over quickly.

Training and pruning a one-year-old (maiden) tree as a half-standard is not difficult, although it takes four or five years before the tree's main framework is formed. Buying a partly-trained tree clearly reduces this period.

Plant a bare-rooted maiden tree in winter. At this stage it will be about 1.5m/5ft high with thin shoots growing from its stem.

Support the tree, either by inserting a vertical stake while the tree is being planted, or by an H-shaped one afterwards. Inserting a vertical one after planting may damage the roots. The top bar of the H-stake should be 1–1.2m/3½–4ft high. In spring, cut the top of the plant's stem to 1.3m/4½ft high, about 15–20cm/6–8in above the stake. Also, cut back all sideshoots to 10cm/4in long. These are later removed, but initially are left to assist the main stem to thicken.

During the following summer, shoots develop from its top. In spring, cut these back by half. Also, cut out all crossing, rubbing, thin and dead shoots. At this stage, try to form a framework of evenly spaced branches.

In the following summer, further shoots will develop, and in spring are cut back by half, at the same time removing crossing and thin shoots. Also, cut off the twiggy shoots growing from the stem.

Repeat this process during the following spring, by which time the tree will be four years old and have a good framework of branches. In subsequent years, cut the shoots less severely, removing only one-third of their new growth and removing congested and crossing shoots.

THINNING is essential when plum trees are carrying a heavy crop of fruits. If unthinned (left), the fruits remain small, flavourless and poorly coloured. Also, branches bearing excessive amounts of fruit may break off the tree. Thinning fruits is carried out in two stages: first, when the fruits are the size of hazelnuts and when the stones have formed, usually in early summer. The second thinning is when fruits are about twice that size, leaving 5cm/2in between them.

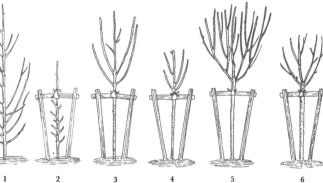

PLANT *a bare-rooted, maiden plum tree in winter* (**1**). *Support the stem with a vertical stake or H-formation* (**2**). *Cut back the main stem to 1.3m/4½ft, about 15–20cm/6–8in above the stake. Cut back side-shoots to 10cm/4in long.*

A TWO-*year-old plum tree during the following winter* (**3**). *It will have developed long shoots from its top. Prune these just before growth begins in spring, cutting them back by half* (**4**). *These will form the main branches later.*

DURING *the following summer the head will develop further stems, which are cut back by half in spring. By the following winter, these will have formed a large head* (**5**), *and in spring are again reduced by half* (**6**).

PEACHES AND NECTARINES

MOST peaches and nectarines are grown on fan-trained trees against warm, sunny walls. The aim is to train the tree to fill the wall with branches that radiate from near the main stem's base. They will then receive the maximum amount of light and air, as well as benefiting from warmth radiated by the wall. Growing and training peaches and nectarines in this way is not quick and it will take several years to form the fan. Plum and gage trees are also often grown as fans, in the same way.

PEACHES and nectarines are delicious, juicy fruits. Peaches have a fuzzy covering, whereas nectarines are smooth skinned.

MAIDEN TREE

Plant a bare-rooted, one-year-old (maiden) tree in winter, about 15cm/6in from the base of a warm, sunny wall. In spring, cut the main stem to about 60cm/2ft high and just above a bud.

Remove side-shoots, or buds – all but the top five. Although only three good buds are needed (the top one to produce vertical growth and the two laterals) leave a couple more in case the others are damaged. They can be removed later.

During the following summer, the bud at the top will continue growth upwards, while two shoots – one at each side – are encouraged to form the branches. When it can be seen that they are growing strongly, remove the others.

Insert canes to enable the vertical and lateral shoots to be supported. In spring, sever the vertical shoot fractionally above the two sideshoots, and cut back the side branches to buds on their upper sides and 38–45cm/15–18in from the main stem.

During the following summer, encourage shoots to develop from

PRUNING ESTABLISHED FAN-SHAPED TREES

1. PRUNE *established fan trees in spring and summer. In spring, prune one-year-old shoots. Leave a replacement shoot at the base of each one, but reduce other growths to a single leaf.*

2. BRANCHES *that have been trained and tied in as extensions to the main framework are also pruned in spring. Shoots growing from it are carefully thinned to about 15cm/6in apart, preventing congestion later.*

3. AFTER *the fruits have been picked, prune lateral shoots that carried the crop back to the replacement shoots that were left at their bases. These are the ones that appeared in the first illustration.*

these two arms. On each side, allow two buds on the upper side and one on the lower side to produce shoots. Tie these to canes and then to a framework of wires.

By the following spring they will have developed into long shoots. Cut each shoot back to a triple bud so that 45–60cm/1½–2ft of ripened wood remains on each fan. In the following year, allow further shoots on the insides of the inner branches to develop.

FOLLOWING SUMMER

During the following summer, allow each of the eight branches to grow, tying new shoots first on to canes and then on the wires. Also, rub out all buds growing directly towards or away from the wall to keep the shape flatter.

Allow shoots to develop every 15cm/6in apart on the tops and bottoms of the branches. Carefully rub out those shoots that are not wanted as the fan develops.

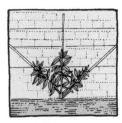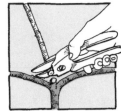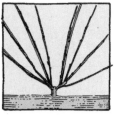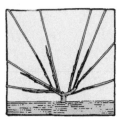

1. IT IS *possible to start with a one-year-old fan-trained tree, but to save time, two- or three-year-old ones can be bought. The two-year-old plant shown above has developed two strong sideshoots, as well as terminal growth.*

2. IN SPRING, *when new growth begins, cut off the terminal stem to just above the sideshoots, taking care not to damage them. This pruning directs growth into shoots that subsequently will develop into the lowest branches on the fan.*

3. AS WELL *as severing the leading shoot, also cut sideshoots to buds on their upper sides, 38–45cm/15–18in from the main stem. In summer, allow them to grow, and select two young shoots on the upper side and one the under side to develop.*

4. IN THE *following summer, shoots will develop from the lowest branches and start to fill in the fan's centre. Each shoot is tied to a strong cane, which is then secured to a tiered framework or wires spaced 20–25cm/8–10in apart.*

5. IN WINTER, *ensure the canes – together with the shoots tied to them – are spaced equally apart, but leaving the centre of the fan open for the development of further shoots. The centre is always the last part of the fan to fill with shoots.*

6. DURING *spring, cut back each branch to a triple bud so that 45–60cm/ 1½–2ft of ripened wood remains on each fan. In the following summer, shoots on the inner sides of the two central branches are allowed to develop.*

OUTDOOR GRAPES AND FIGS

GRAPES are frequently grown in greenhouses in cool climates, but in warm countries are cultivated outdoors. Even in temperate climates, outdoor grapes are increasingly possible to grow through the introduction of hardier varieties.

The method of pruning greenhouse and outdoor grape-vines is basically the same, and the objective is to grow a single rod (plant stem) and to encourage the development of sideshoots which eventually will develop into strong branches and bear fruits. To ensure the branches are spaced out, train them on alternative sides of the rod.

Incidentally, pruning commercially grown outdoor grapes is more complicated than the method suggested here, which is best suited to home gardeners.

OUTDOOR GRAPES

Tiers of horizontal, 10-gauge galvanized wires spaced 30cm/12in apart and 13–15cm/5–6in from a wall are essential. Position the bottom wire about 45cm/1½ft above the ground and choose a sheltered, warm and sunny wall.

Plant bare-rooted and container-grown vines in spring, then shorten the main shoot (rod) to about 60cm/2ft high. Cut off all other shoots to a single bud, and tie the rod first to a cane and then to the horizontal wires.

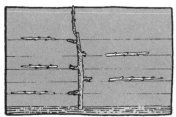

1. DURING *the first summer, prune the lateral shoots. Pinch out – or use scissors – their ends just beyond the fifth leaf. Also, remove flowers before they develop into fruits.*

2. IN AUTUMN, *cut back the rod to half of the growth it made during the current season. Also, cut back all lateral shoots to form stubs, each with only two buds.*

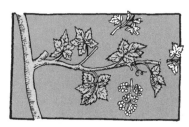

3. DURING *the following summer, cut back lateral shoots to just beyond the fifth leaf. Also, cut back sub-laterals to one leaf and remove all flowers before they develop fruits.*

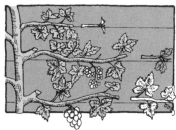

4. IN AUTUMN, *cut back laterals to leave two buds at their bases. In summer (above) allow two or three bunches to develop and prune to two leaves beyond them.*

PRUNING SEQUENCE

Pruning begins in the first summer after being planted. Either pinch back or use sharp scissors to cut lateral shoots to just beyond the fifth leaf. Also, cut off all flower trusses. If young vines are allowed to flower and then develop fruits this will weaken and delay their development.

• In the following autumn, cut back the rod to half of the growth it made during the current season. The purpose is to remove soft, unripened wood. Cut to just above a bud. Additionally, cut all lateral shoots back to leave two buds at their bases.

Vines are vigorous plants and every year they are pruned in this manner. Each spring, new shoots develop that will bear fruits.

• In the following summer, again cut back laterals to just beyond the fifth leaf. Also, sever the sub-laterals to just beyond a single leaf and remove all flowers.

• During the following autumn, again cut back the vertical, leading shoot by half, as well as cutting back the laterals to leave two firm, healthy buds.

• In early summer, when growth begins from the bases of laterals, allow only the strongest to develop. Allow two or three bunches of grapes to develop from them and prune these to two leaves beyond the young fruits.

• In autumn, again cut the rod to half of the wood made during the previous summer, as well as carefully trimming back lateral growths to two buds.

• In summer, again select the strongest shoot for each lateral. This summer, allow further laterals to develop fruits – this is a continuing process.

• When the top of the rod reaches the top wire, cut it off just above the topmost lateral.

THINNING GRAPES

This is essential to ensure individual grapes are a good size. As soon as the berries start to swell, use scissors with long-pointed blades to gradually cut out the smallest berries, especially those from the bunch's centre.

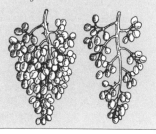

PRUNING FIGS

Figs are best grown as fans against a warm, sunny wall. Buy a two-year-old container-grown plant and specify the need for a fan-trained type. Plant it in early spring, about 15cm/6in from a wall. Install tiered wires, 15cm/6in apart, the lowest one 45cm/1½ft above the ground and the top one 2.4m/8ft high.

In spring, cut back both branches to a bud about 45cm/1½ft from their bases. In summer, allow each branch to develop two shoots on its upper side, one on the lower side and a further one at the growing tip. As shoots develop from these, tie them first to canes, then to wires.

Once fans have been formed, trim young shoots back to five leaves in early summer.

FIGS *are succulent fruits but need a sunny and sheltered wall, and a warm climate.*

GARDEN PROJECTS

❖

Creating an attractive patio or courtyard and laying functional and aesthetically pleasing paths throughout a garden are important to gardeners. Walls and fences are essential, to define the extent of a garden, or to subdivide it into separate areas, and to provide features against which plants can be grown. Also, in some situations drainage may be needed to create a successful garden.

Within this chapter there is a wide range of garden projects and features that can be easily achieved, from levelling ground and installing drains to making steps and constructing carports and trellises.

Tackling the construction of garden features yourself can save a large amount of money, as well as generating a great deal of personal satisfaction.

LEVELLING AND SHAPING THE GROUND

CREATING the desired levels in a new plot of land is fundamental to its design, and unless these are right you will never be completely satisfied with the garden. It does, however, often involve moving soil from one area to another, which is heavy, labour-intensive work. Therefore, once an area immediately around a house is levelled or terraced, allow the rest of the garden to assume its natural contour.

TO ENSURE *an area is level in all directions, knock in 23cm/9in-long pegs about 1.5m/5ft apart. First, however, mark each peg, 10cm/4in from its top. Use a spirit-level to ensure they are at the same height, then rake the soil level with the marks.*

PRECIOUS TOPSOIL

There is always the risk, when levelling soil, of mixing topsoil with the subsoil, or totally inverting them so that the surface is covered with sticky clay. Therefore, first remove the surface soil. This may appear tedious, but annuals, herbaceous perennials and alpine plants especially will not thrive in thick clay. Many shrubs and trees are more tolerant of such conditions, but even they will not perform well there. If the area is totally formed of clay, buy in clean, fresh topsoil.

ASSESSING LEVELS

This needs 23cm/9in-long, flat-topped pegs, a builder's spirit-level, a straight, uniformly thick plank about 1.8m/6ft long to rest it on, and a club hammer for knocking in the pegs. Levelling nearly flat areas is relatively easy, and is shown above.

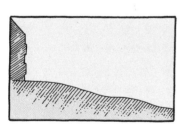

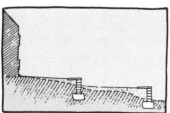

IF GROUND *slopes around a house, it is usually more convenient to form several terraces than to leave a steep bank. It is essential that the level of the top terrace is below the damp course on the house.*

THE ART *in making a terrace is not to move more soil than is necessary. Immediately around a house this may not be possible, as it is desirable to have only one or two steps' difference between each level.*

SUBSEQUENT *levels, however, are formed by taking soil from the upper half to fill the lower part. Remove the topsoil, so that good soil is not buried. This is vital where plants are to be grown.*

CREATE *a uniform slope by knocking pegs into the ground, 1.5m/5ft apart. Place a spirit-level across the top two pegs; knock in the lower peg until the required slope is formed. Mark the bubble's position on the spirit-level. Repeat this down the slope, each time leaving the bubble in the same place.*

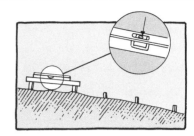

AN ALTERNATIVE *way to produce an even slope is to place a piece of wood under the lower end of the spirit-level to represent the amount of slope between any two pegs. When using the spirit-level, the bubble must be in the centre. Repeat this process with the next two pegs.*

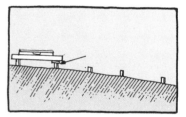

A FURTHER *way to create an even slope is to knock pegs into the soil at equal distances apart. Use a spirit-level to ensure they are all at the same height. Then, mark progressively increasing distances from their tops. The soil can then be sloped by making the surface touch these marks.*

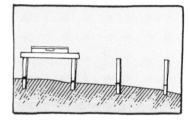

CONTOURING LAND

An alternative to levelling large areas is to form dells or slightly sloping banks. Unless grassed, avoid creating banks with angles of more than 30 degrees, as the soil may be too easily eroded. If grassed, consider how the bank will be cut – hover-type mowers are ideal for this.

When forming sunken gardens, always ensure the drainage is adequate, especially if a pond is planned in its base. Should it overflow through rain or water draining into it, the fish will be washed out. In such areas, it is better to consider a 'bog' garden, perhaps planted with moisture-loving primulas.

Take advantage of natural hollows and mounds within a garden, as these introduce character, and the opportunity to create features not possible in totally flat areas.

USING HOSE-PIPES

Assessing differences in levels over long distances is difficult without specialized equipment. However, home gardeners can use hose-pipes. Secure the top of each end to a peg at the upper level, then fill with water until both ends of the pipe are full. Measure the height of the water to give the difference in level. Putting a piece of plastic tubing in each end makes it easier to see the levels.

DRAINING LAND

❖

IDEALLY, soil should be free-draining, yet retain moisture. If it is totally saturated with water, this prevents air penetration and stops roots and soil organisms breathing. If this happens, drains need to be installed.

ASSESSING GARDENS
Large puddles of water remaining on the surface clearly indicate the need for drains. So, too, do the presence of rushes and sedges. If these are not readily apparent, but you wish to check the level of water in the soil (water-table), dig a 1.2m/4ft deep hole in autumn and see how much water remains in it during winter. If water stays in it and within 23cm/9in of the top for long periods, the installation of drains is essential.

RANGE OF DRAINS
There are several ways to drain land. On a large scale, it is possible to install 'mole' drains by mechanically (usually using a special tractor) drawing a metal, bullet-headed spike through the

polythene

RUBBLE *drains are cheaper than tile types. Prepare trenches in the same way and fill to within 30cm/12in of the surface with rubble. Then, cover with double-thickness polythene.*

clean, coarse rubble

——

ground, 45–75cm/1¹/₂–2¹/₂ft below the surface. In suburban gardens this is not practical, and drainage relies on clay pipes, rubble drains or a continuous plastic type of drain.

• Pipe drains involve digging a main trench that leads to a sump or ditch. At intervals, side drains join it and gather water from a larger area. The spacings between the side drains depend on the soil's nature: 3.6–4.5m/12–15ft for clay soil, to 12m/40ft on light sandy types. Dig the trenches 60–75cm/2–2¹/₂ft deep and 30–45cm/1–1¹/₂ft wide, with a minimum slope of 1 in 90 towards

DIG *out a trench to the depth and width of a spade when laying the relatively new, rectangular, plastic-type drains. They are formed of a continuous plastic core which is surrounded by a porous fibre.*

ON MODERATELY *heavy soil the plastic can be laid directly on the trench's base and covered with soil. On heavy land, however, mix sharp sand or gravel with soil immediately around the tube to aid water flow.*

FILL THE *trench with soil and firm it with a foot. Leave the soil slightly proud of the surface to allow for slight soil settlement. Direct the end of the pipe into a ditch or sump, where water can drain freely.*

the outlet. Place a spirit-level on top of the pipes to check that they slope in the right direction. Laying pipe drains is illustrated on the opposite side of the page.

Main drains are formed of unglazed clay pipes, about 30cm/12in long and 13cm/5in wide, while the side, feeder ones are the same length but only 10cm/4in wide.

• Rubble drains are cheaper than pipe types, and ideal where builders have left a great deal of broken bricks and other clean rubble on the site. Prepare the trenches in exactly the same way as for pipe drains. Their life expectancy is less than with pipe drains, as eventually soil seeps among the rubble and clogs up spaces through which water could drain. However, even pipe drains have a limited life if trees such as willows are nearby: their roots soon can cause blockages.

For both pipe and rubble drains, the widths of the trench may vary: machines can dig deeper and narrower than a man using a spade and shovel.

• Plastic drains are formed of a continuous core surrounded by porous fabric. They are bought in lengths several metres long and easily laid in the base of a narrow trench. Only on heavy, clay soils do they need to be laid with gravel surrounding them. The technique of installing them is described at the top of this page.

SUMP OR DITCH?

Some gardens have ditches into which excess water can drain, but most do not. It is illegal to drain surplus soil water into domestic drainage systems, and therefore a sump is needed. At the lowest point, dig a hole about 1.2m/4ft square, making its base about 30cm/12in below the pipe that takes water into it. Fill the sump to about half its depth with clean, coarse rubble, then with gravel to about 30cm/12in below the surface. Cover with double-thickness polythene, then with topsoil and, finally, turf.

INSTALL *pipe drains by digging trenches with a slight slope. Form a 7.5–10cm/ 3–4in-thick layer of gravel and place the pipes on top. Link in the side drains and cover joints with double-thickness polythene.*

COVER *the joints and pipes with gravel. Alternatively, cover them with broken pieces of tile. Then, spread gravel over the pipes and tiles. This prevents soil seeping into the pipes and eventually blocking them.*

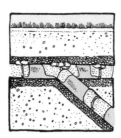

THE *life expectancy of pipe drains depends on the thoroughness with which they are installed. Fill the trench with topsoil and firm it level with the surface. It may settle, so be prepared to add further soil later.*

MAKING A CONCRETE DRIVE

❖

CONCRETE is an adaptable material, flexible before it is set, and so able to be formed into a wide range of shapes. When dry, it creates a strong, hard-wearing surface. Its strength is derived as much from the thorough preparation of the foundations as from its thickness and ratio of Portland cement to sharp sand and aggregates.

PREPARING THE SITE

Careful preparation of the site is essential.
• Remove all plants and rubbish.
• Dig out the topsoil, placing it in an out-of-the-way position.
• Concrete can be laid directly on most well-compacted ground, but if the soil is mainly formed of clay a 10cm/4in-thick layer of compacted, broken bricks or stones is needed. Ensure this layer is free from rubbish: spread 15cm/6in wider than the area to be concreted.

ROMAN INFLUENCE

Mortar was created as early as two thousand years ago by the Romans. But instead of using Portland cement – first introduced in the nineteenth century – they employed lime.

• Construct a framework of strong, straight-topped wood around the area, so that a space is left to create a slab of concrete 6–7.5cm/2½–3in thick. Support the framework with strong pegs knocked into the ground on the outside. Their tops must be below the framework, and securely nailed to it.
• If the drive is long, it is necessary to split it up to prevent cracking later when it expands as a result of high temperatures. As a guide, no area should be longer than 3m/10ft. The wood used to separate the area should join the outer framework at right-angles.

SURFACE TEXTURES

These are made before the concrete has set, using wooden floats, trowels and shovels.

1. Using a soft brush
2. Soft brush plus water
3. The back of a shovel
4. Wooden float
5. Steel trowel

1. Soft lines

2. Gritty surface

3. Rustic and circled

4. Sandpaper texture

5. Smooth and flat

LAYING CONCRETE

Never lay concrete if the weather is frosty, extremely hot or if it is likely to rain before setting.
• If the base area is dry, water it before laying the concrete.
• First, place concrete around dividing strips of wood.
• Start laying concrete at the end furthest from the mixer or supply, and follow the information below.
• Use a mixture (by volume) of:
~1 part Portland cement
~1½ parts sharp sand
~2½ parts 20mm aggregate
(Alternatively, use a mixture of 3½ parts combined aggregate to one of Portland cement)

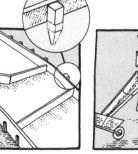

1. CONCRETE *forms a strong base, but it can look bland and unexciting unless given an attractive finish. First, form a strong framework around the sides, with pegs holding it secure. Divide large areas into several parts to allow for expansion.*

2. BUYING *ready-mixed concrete in bulk is an easy and quick way to create a base. However, ensure there is a team of at least five people to help: three to barrow the concrete and two to level and lay it. Buy 10% more than you need.*

3. HAND-MIXING *is the cheapest way to mix concrete, but can be heavy work if the area is large. To create a strong surface it must be laid continuously, so ensure that one mix of concrete does not become dry before the next one is added.*

4. ELECTRICALLY OPERATED *mixers can be hired: choose one with a capacity of about 100 litres. Machine mixing removes much of the hard work but does need a team of at least three people if the cost of hiring is to be economic.*

5. SPREAD *the concrete, packing it well around the edges, then level but leave it slightly higher than the wooden surround. Use a tamping beam to compact and level the surface. This is a two-man job and involves pushing and pulling.*

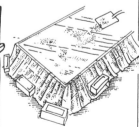

6. WHEN *the concrete has hardened slightly, cover it with polythene sheeting to prevent rapid drying. Secure the sheeting at the sides with bricks, as well as lightly sprinkling sand on the surface to prevent it 'ballooning'.*

PATIO SURFACES

IN RECENT years, the range of materials for forming patios, terraces and the surrounds to houses has become much wider and more decorative.

The Romans constructed ornate, mosaic pathways, while in the late 1800s wood blocks cut from the Australian Jarrah Tree (*Eucalyptus marginata*) were used in London to form roads and other surfaces. In the early and mid-1900s, the choice of surfacing materials included natural paving, plainly coloured pre-cast slabs, or bricks or rafts of concrete; but in recent years the range has widened dramatically and now there are surfacing materials in textures, shapes and sizes to suit everyone's taste.

PAVING SLABS

Pre-cast paving slabs are man-made and have a uniform outline: square, rectangular, hexagonal or round. They can be laid on their own or in combination with bricks or cobbles. Indeed, although paving slabs may not initially appear to be an inspiring choice, when used in combination with other materials and attractive edgings they can be given plenty of eye-appeal.

Slabs with raised, patterned surfaces create added interest and can, if spaces are left between them for plants, be given an informal appearance at a fraction of the cost of using natural stone.

NATURAL STONE

Stone is expensive to buy and, because of its uneven thickness, difficult to lay. Nevertheless, when laid it has an attractive quality that is unsurpassed in natural and informal settings.

Part of the beauty of this material is its characteristic non-uniform outlines and surfaces, but some slabs, such as sawn sandstone, are available in a clinically-cut form; while for a slightly less rigid outline they are sold 'dressed'. When the stone has an irregular outline it is called 'random'.

PAVERS

House-type bricks have been used to create paths in cottage gardens for several centuries, but in regions where winters are wet and extremely cold they soon disintegrate. Nowadays, weather-resistant bricks are available. (Some are interlocking; others just butted together.) They do not have to be laid on a concrete base or with mortar; instead, they are bedded on an evenly compacted layer of sharp sand. This creates an attractive, stable surface, but it is essential that the area is surrounded by a brick or wood framework that restrains the bed of sand. Indeed, if strong edgings are omitted, the sand will spread at the edges and the pavers collapse.

GRANITE SETTS

These are grey quarried stone, extremely hard, either brick-shaped or square, and about the size of a half-brick. Take care not to use too many of them as they have a dominant appearance. Rather, employ them as a decorative contrast with other materials. They are laid on a mortar base.

PAVING MATERIALS

Paving slabs and bricks, with formal or informal outlines, are widely used to create attractive surfaces. Most patios are totally formed of one type, while others are attractive combinations of two or three.

 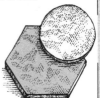

CONCRETE *slabs with raised patterns. Several attractive colours.*

HEXAGONAL *and round slabs with smooth surfaces. Several colours.*

SQUARE, *brick-coloured slabs marked in brick-like and square patterns.*

IRREGULARLY *shaped, natural stone slabs create informal patios.*

GRANITE *setts create hard-wearing surfaces for informal areas.*

COBBLES *are eye-catching but are best combined with other surfaces.*

INTERLOCKING *pavers create a strong, hard-wearing surface.*

BRICK *pavers are hard-wearing and laid on bed of evenly compacted sand.*

COTTAGE *gardens need informal patios, preferably formed from natural, irregularly shaped stone paving. Gaps can be left between them in which small, prostrate plants can be set, such as thyme.*

MODERN *houses harmonize with square or rectangular paving slabs, in a range of bright colours. Choose symmetrically shaped, plastic, glass-fibre or concrete containers to complete the somewhat formal scene.*

WEATHERED, *square or rectangular flag-stones create semi-informal patios. Lay them irregularly, so that there is no clear pattern. Wooden troughs and ornate pots harmonize in this informal and rustic setting.*

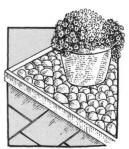

LARGE *cobble-stones create ornamental areas that are difficult to walk on, but ideal as positions for plants in tubs. It safeguards them from passers-by knocking and damaging the flowers or foliage.*

LAYING PAVING SLABS

❖

Store slabs by standing them on wooden slats and leaning against a firm surface.

PRE-CAST paving slabs create firm patio surfaces, either on their own or when combined with materials such as bricks. They range in thickness from 42–50mm/ 1³/₄–2in; and the most common size is 45cm/1¹/₂ft square – as well as quarter and half sizes so that patterns can be formed. Plain slabs 60cm/2ft square and 75cm/2¹/₂ft by 60cm/2ft are available, but are difficult to handle.

DAMP COURSES

Where patios adjoin buildings, they must be at least 15cm/6in below the damp course. If this is impossible, leave a 10cm/4in gap between the slabs and the wall, to a depth of 15cm/6in below the damp course. Fill this area with 6mm/¹/₄in pea-shingle. If this is omitted, there is a risk of damp passing into the building.

CREATING A FIRM BASE

Where paving slabs are being laid as a path that will not have people continuously walking – and, with children, jumping – on it, laying them on a bed of mortar is not essential. Just lay them on a 5cm/2in-thick layer of sharp sand. However, if the area is around a house and expected to be in use throughout the year, form a sharp-sand base and bed the slabs on a mixture of:

~

*1 part Portland cement
3 parts soft sand*

~

The technique of laying them is described below.

Where slabs are to be laid on clay soil, first form a 10cm/4in-thick, well-compacted hardcore base. Over this, form a 5cm/2in-thick layer of evenly consolidated sharp sand, then lay the slabs on the above mortar mix. If the area is large and will be in continual use, form a 6–7.5cm/2–2¹/₂in-thick concrete base over the hardcore, using a mixture of:

~

*1 part Portland cement
2¹/₂ parts sharp sand
3¹/₂ parts 20mm aggregate*

~

Lay the slabs on top using the 'blob' or 'box' method (below, left).

MIXING AND MATCHING

Patios should be as visually exciting as the rest of the garden. Indeed, as they are permanent features, careful planning and a great deal of thought is needed to ensure they both harmonize with the house, and have distinctive features. Here are a few simple ways to create a unique patio:

• If the area is large, leave out a few slabs at random and fill the area with cobbles or gravel. Use these gaps to direct people to steps and other features, rather than blocking their paths.

• Between every large paving slab (or four smaller ones) build in weather-resistant bricks, either revealing their backs or sides. Continue this brick theme into a surrounding wall.

• Omit a slab and cement a central pillar of a circular table into its middle. Then, fill the remaining part of the area with cobbles.

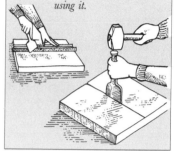

CUTTING SLABS

To cut a slab, first score across both faces. Then, using a bolster chisel and club-hammer, progressively chip away at the surface. Alternatively, use a powered tool called a disc-cutter. Wear gloves and goggles while using it.

• Leave out four or six slabs and construct a raised garden pond. This could be in the centre of the patio, or merged at one side of the area into a small wall.

• Omit two or three slabs and form a raised flower bed. This is ideal for people in wheelchairs.

• Position a statue towards one side of the patio and introduce lights to create a focal point.

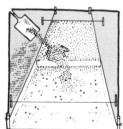

1. REMOVE *plants and rubbish from the site. To ensure the patio's surface will be right, it may be necessary to excavate some soil. Mark out the area and spread a 5cm/2in-thick layer of sharp sand.*

2. FIRM *the sand and rake level. First, lay slabs along the longest, highest side (there should be a gentle slope). One way to lay a slab is to form a 36–50mm/ 1¹/₂– 2in ridge of mortar in a box-like formation.*

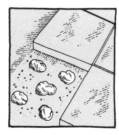

3. ALTERNATIVELY, *use the five-blob method, setting one 36–50mm/ 1¹/₂–2in high mound in the centre and four others, at each corner. This is a quicker method than the box formation and uses less mortar.*

4. GENTLY *set the slab in position. Slabs 45cm/1¹/₂ft square are easily lifted by one person, but ones 60cm/ 2ft square – or larger – require two pairs of hands if they are to be set down evenly on the mortar.*

5. USE A *builder's spirit-level to ensure there is a slight slope in one direction. If slight adjustment is needed, tap with the handle of a club-hammer. If a radical change is needed, it is easier to remove the slab.*

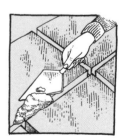

6. AFTER *the mortar holding the slabs is set, fill the gaps with a stiff, dry, weak, mortar mixture, well rammed into the joints until fractionally below the slabs. Use a damp sponge to clean the edges of the slabs.*

LAYING PAVERS

THESE are relatively new and increasingly popular. They are also known as concrete paving blocks and are widely used for paths, drives and patio areas. There are several different patterns in which they can be laid, illustrated below. Where they are being used for drives and hard-wearing surfaces, the herringbone pattern is best, but for small areas on terraces and patios the parquet design (sometimes known as basket weave) is less baffling to the eye. If a running-bond pattern (see below) is used for drives, it must run across the main line of traffic.

PREPARING THE SITE

Laying pavers does not involve the use of Portland cement or mortar: instead, the blocks are laid on a bed of sharp sand. It is therefore essential that the sand is restrained to prevent it escaping and the surface collapsing, especially at its edges. Sometimes there is a wall that can be used on one side, but usually either wooden, brick or concrete edges have to be constructed to restrain the sand.

Ensure vegetation and rubbish is removed, as well as the topsoil. If the area is to be a drive, a 10cm/4in-thick base formed of evenly consolidated hardcore is essential to help spread and support the load. Clay soils need the same treatment. When laying pavers it is essential to hire a mechanical plate vibrator to settle them into position: this can also be used to consolidate hardcore.

The pavers are about the size of house bricks and available in several thicknesses: 60mm/2½in or 65mm/2¾in is suitable for patios and lightly trafficked areas, whereas ones 80mm/3½in thick are essential where lorries pass over the surface.

Construct the restrainer around the site so that it is 10cm/4in above the hardcore. Sharp sand is then spread and levelled (without consolidating it) by using a scraping

1. REMOVE *plants, rubbish and topsoil. If the area is clay or for cars, form and consolidate a 10cm/4in hardcore base between side restraining boards.*

2. SPREAD *sharp sand over the first metre/yard of the site. Strike this 45mm below the edge if using 60mm thick blocks, 50mm if laying 65mm pavers.*

3. DO NOT *stand on the sand, then start laying the pavers from the end nearest the supply. Stand on a wooden plank to prevent unnecessary disturbance.*

4. DEPENDING *on the pattern in which the pavers are laid, cutting is necessary. The easiest way is to hire a stone-splitter.*

5. USE *a plate vibrator (available from tool-hire shops) to bed the pavers into the sand. Two or three passes are needed – keep the vibrator moving.*

6. BRUSH *a thin layer of sharp sand over the pavers, making two or three further passes with the vibrator. Later, brush the surface, and lightly water.*

board (see illustration two). If 60mm/2½in-thick pavers are used, leave the sand's surface 45mm/1¾in below the restraining board's top. When using 65mm/2¾in-thick pavers, leave it 50mm/2in below the edges. These measurements allow for later consolidation of the pavers. Do not lay the sand more than a metre/yard or so in front of paver-laying area.

LAYING PAVERS

Start at the end where the pavers are stacked. Decide on the pattern to be used and begin at one corner. Position the bricks one at a time, just gently resting them on the sharp sand. Use a plank to spread your weight and systematically work down the area. When about 2.4m/8ft has been laid, use the vibrator to compact them, passing over the surface two or three times. Keep the machine moving except when switched off.

Use an hydraulic stone-splitter to cut the bricks – essential with the herringbone pattern.

When the area is complete and the bricks bedded into the sand by the vibrator, spread a thin layer of sharp sand over the surface and make two or three passes of the vibrator. Finish off by spreading sharp sand with a broom and then lightly watering the surface through a fine-rosed watering-can. The surface can then be used.

PAVERS *can be laid in many attractive patterns that help to give surfaces added interest. This is a herring-bone pattern and is especially suitable for hard-wearing, informal and irregularly-shaped areas.*

THE *running-bond pattern is fairly easy to lay but is not really suitable for hard-wearing areas. If used for paths or drives, lay the pavers across the area and not lengthwise. Always stagger the joints.*

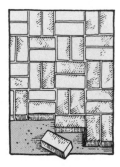

THE *parquet pattern is easy to lay if the area is square or rectangular and kept in multiples of 20cm/8in (the length of a brick). However, it is not a strong bond and may shift if used on a drive. It is ideal as a path.*

CREATING PATHS

FIRM, all-weather surfaces are essential in gardens, enabling access to sheds, greenhouses, fuel stores and garages throughout the year and in all weathers. Also, there needs to be a good path around a house to enable regular maintenance.

At one time, domestic pressure ensured that new gardens were instantly designed: washing lines were immediately needed and therefore two poles were installed with a line and path between them, away from walls, fences and overhanging trees. The path and washing line then dominated the garden for generations. Nowadays, clothes driers have changed all of this and garden design is much more flexible. New trends and materials have also encouraged the introduction of more attractive and interestingly shaped paths.

INNOVATIVE PATHS

Concrete gives superb all-weather paths but there are other choices, to be used alone or together. Here are a few to consider:

• Stepping stones in lawns have traditionally been formed from irregularly shaped, broken paving slabs. But slices of tree trunks also make paths: not through lawns but across areas covered with pea-shingle and with pots and tubs displayed on them.

• Ordinary concrete paving slabs, about 60cm/2ft square, can be made into an attractive path by spacing them 10cm/4in apart, forming wooden or concrete sides 30cm/12in on either side and filling the areas between them with gravel or small pebbles.

• Gravel paths with logs along their edges are especially attractive in informal settings. The path, however, has to be relatively flat to prevent the gravel gradually moving downhill.

• Grass paths are attractive, either straight and totally formed of grass, or combined with a log edging and used in informal settings. Strimmers have made edging grass close to logs very easy and have

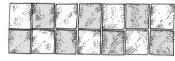
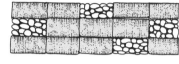

removed the earlier impracticalities of this design.

• Unedged gravel paths have a soft, unassuming texture that harmonizes with plants that spill over their edges. Constructing them is not difficult: dig out and remove the surface soil to about 7.5cm/3in deep. Then, fork over the top, 15cm/6in deep, and generously add cement powder. Mix it with the surface soil. Walk over the area, ram down the soil and then water it generously. Finally, cover with 5cm/2in of gravel.

• Narrow, crazy-paving paths are often bewildering to the eye, but if made slightly wider and with

CONCRETE *forms functional paths, ideal in vegetable gardens but not sufficiently attractive for most ornamental areas. Existing paths that are in good condition can be improved by creating attractive surfaces on top of them.*

bays for plants in tubs and other containers staggered along their sides, they assume a better dimension. Crazy paving is an adaptable material and can be used to fill oddly shaped corners in a way square or rectangular paving slabs do not allow. But it needs a firm base to create a strong surface.

1. REMOVE *plants, rubbish and topsoil. Mark the area with strings and add an even layer of clean rubble or stones. Compact it with a roller. Alternatively, ram it with the end of a heavy, vertical plank.*

2. USE *strong, 2.5cm/1in-thick timber to construct frameworks on either side of the path. Use a spirit-level to check they are level and allow for a 6–7.5cm/ 2½–3in-thick layer of concrete to be created.*

3. MIXING *concrete by hand is best if the path is short; if long, hire a cement-mixer. Spread cement, working it against the sides of the framework and initially leaving it about 2.5cm/1in higher.*

4. USE *a straight-edged board to level the surface. Draw it along the frameworks, at the same time tamping to ensure the concrete is compacted. Occasionally, draw the wood forward to remove excess.*

5. FOR *paths, use a mixture of 1 part Portland cement, 1½ parts sharp sand, and 2½ parts aggregate. Do not lay concrete during frosty weather (it might freeze) or when very hot (it dries too quickly).*

6. IMPROVE *the surface's appearance by using a stiff broom. Wait until it is nearly set, then brush vigorously to create a rough-textured surface. There are also some other surfaces (see page 325).*

MAKING STEPS

❖

WELL-PROPORTIONED steps can be a major feature in a garden, acting as a link between two levels and having a unifying influence. They must, at the same time, harmonize with the nature of the garden.

The proportions of steps is important and in general the riser (vertical distance) should be 15cm/6in high and the tread about 38cm/15in, with an overhang at the front of the step of about 5–7.5cm/2–3in.

Most steps are constructed from pre-fabricated slabs and bricks, but unique ones can be created from a wide range of materials:
• Log steps are popular in rustic and informal gardens, especially in naturalized and wild areas. Use logs 10–15cm/4–6in thick and cut to the width of the path. Excavate a shallow trench so that the log is buried about 5cm/2in to stabilize it. Additionally, use stout pegs to secure them into position. As well as the logs providing a rise in height, the path between them can rise or fall.

SLOPES

As well as steps, slopes are important if someone in your family is wheelchair bound or needs to use a walking stick. Consider a gently curved slope that unites all levels. Avoid forming slopes greater than one in twelve.

• Cross-sections of tree trunks – about 45cm/18in across and 10–15cm/4–6in thick – look superb when slightly overlapped and used to form a flight of steps. Pack soil around them to secure their positions. Take care when using them in wet weather, as they can be slippery.
• Railway sleepers create excellent steps. Cut them to the required width, bury slightly and use pegs to secure them and prevent movement. Avoid making the complete treads of wood, as they will then be very slippery, especially if covered with moss.

1. SOMETIMES, *retaining walls that separate one level from another are too long and steps are needed. First, mark out the area with strings, excavate the soil and use bricks to build the first riser.*

2. MEASURE *from the front, and build the second riser 38cm/15in from the front. By using 45cm/18in-wide slabs, this allows for a 38cm/18in tread and an overlap at the front of about 7.5cm/3in.*

3. COMPLETE *the top riser and then put the slabs in place. Use a mixture of 1 part Portland cement and 3 of soft sand. It may be necessary to cut or replace the ornamental stones along the top of the wall.*

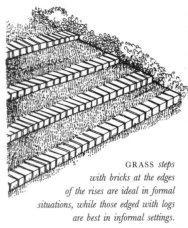

GRASS *steps with bricks at the edges of the rises are ideal in formal situations, while those edged with logs are best in informal settings.*

• Grass terraces and steps were widely used on a grand scale in the late 1800s to create dramatic effects. On a smaller scale, however, they also attract attention. Bricks or logs are used to form the risers and to prevent erosion during wet seasons. In formal situations, regular grass cutting is essential to create a uniform outline. In informal situations, however, where logs are used as the risers to steps, the grass can be left slightly longer. Strimmers help to keep the steps tidy.

• Clinical steps – where treads do not overhang the risers – harmonize well with modern architecture. Such steps can be made by setting a series of bricks on their sides and forming them into flights.
• Large rock gardens – or even a series of narrow, waterfall cascades – can be more effective with a series of random steps alongside them. Use the same type of stone as used in the rock garden, perhaps with areas of shingle between them.
• Old, spiral, metal staircases are decorative and can be used in basement gardens and are superb when covered with ivy – even if they do not go anywhere!

LOG *steps are ideal in informal, naturalized gardens. Secure the rises with stout pegs.*

1. PAVING *slabs and bricks enable steps to be quickly constructed. At the base of the slope, lay a couple of slabs on compacted sand and mortar. Then, cement in place one layer of bricks to form the riser.*

2. USE *a spade to excavate the next step, forming a layer of sand and cementing the next slab in place. This is called the tread and should be about 38cm/15in long. Ensure each slab is firm and level.*

3. FORM *the next row of bricks that create the riser and repeat the laying of another slab to produce the tread. Continue like this until the flight of steps is complete. Place a further row of slabs at the top.*

BRICK WALLS

❖

BRICKS are the units from which most houses are constructed, and they are also excellent for building garden walls. They are adaptable and can be formed into walls one or two bricks thick and up to about 1.8m/6ft high.

The life expectancy of a brick wall depends on several factors: the depth of the footings; quality of bricks; thickness and type of bond used; care taken during construction; and the installation of a water-proof capping at its top.

FOUNDATIONS

The depth of the foundations depends on the type of soil and the load they are to carry. Walls built on soils such as clay with a high water content clearly need deeper foundations than those on well-drained, gravelly soils. In most cases, however, trenches excavated 45–60cm/1¹⁄₂–2ft deep, initially filled with 10cm/4in of compacted hardcore, and then with a mixture of 1 part Portland cement, 2¹⁄₂ parts sharp sand and 3¹⁄₂ parts of 20mm aggregate to at least 15cm/6in thick, are suitable. The foundation's width must be at least three times the wall's thickness. Damp courses are essential to prevent ground moisture rising through the bricks.

RANGE OF BRICKS

There are three types of brick suitable for use in walls:
• Common bricks are general-purpose building types and used where appearance is not vital. They have no special facing side and are best when rendered or painted. Do not use them to support heavy loads or where they are subjected to stress. They are the cheapest type of brick.
• Facing bricks produce an attractive finish and are made in several colours and finishes, including rough and smooth. Mostly, these are either hand finished or have wire-cut, weather-resistant finishes on the sides and ends only.
• Engineering bricks are dense, smooth and impervious to water, making them ideal for use where a wall is partly buried or exposed to damp conditions.

RANGE OF BONDS

These are varied and complex and can create exceptionally attractive walls. For novice brick layers, however, the choice is between the 'running bond' when building a wall one-brick thick, or 'English bond' for a double one. With the 'running bond', after laying one course the next one starts half-a-brick in from the end, so that the vertical joints are staggered. For the 'English bond', every other row is laid across the wall, the other one along it, two bricks side by side. In all cases, lay bricks with the frog (side with the depression) downwards.

CONSTRUCTIONAL CARE

Ensuring the courses of bricks are level and upright encourages long life. Once the wall starts to lean, collapse soon follows. To ensure water does not penetrate through the mortar, point the joints. This involves waiting until the mortar has slightly stiffened, then using a small trowel to create a slope so that its lower side is level with the top of the lower brick but the upper side is partly recessed. Alternatively, run the end of a plastic hosepipe along the mortar.

WALLS *need not be plain and unappealing. Creating patterns with differently coloured and textured bricks introduces eye-appeal.*

NATURAL *stones create walls that often harmonize with local buildings. Use large blocks at the corners to create rigidity.*

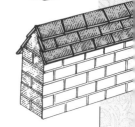

DOUBLE-BRICK *walls are strong and long-lasting. Make them even more attractive by covering with unusual cappings.*

CAPPING

To prevent rainwater seeping down into the wall, either use facing bricks, shaped concrete slabs or attractively shaped tiles. These often help to create an attractive, distinctive wall.

LAYING *bricks is an age-old craft. It is based on the fact that mortar – a mixture of soft sand and cement or lime, or a combination – bonds one brick to another. Use a mixture of 1 part cement to 3 of soft sand.*

A LONG, *builder's spirit-level is essential to ensure courses of bricks are level and the structure upright. Keep the level clean, do not drop it and regularly check newly-laid bricks while the mortar is soft.*

LAY *bricks at both ends of the course, then tightly stretch a line between them to ensure the wall is not constructed with a bulge. Lay bricks so that they are staggered and vertical joints not continued from one course to another.*

AS WELL *as using a builder's spirit-level to ensure courses are level and upright, use it at an angle across the face of the wall to check for bulges. A long, straight-edged board can also be used for this purpose.*

HALF-BRICKS *are needed to fill gaps. First, lightly score around them with a bolster chisel. Place the brick on a bed of sand before using the chisel and club-hammer: angle the chisel towards the waste part.*

USE *a gauge rod (made from a piece of straight wood marked in brick-plus-mortar increments) to check that courses are rising consistently along its full length. Regularly check levels and vertical lines.*

SCREEN-BLOCK WALLS

◆

LARGE, pre-cast concrete, open-screen walling blocks are excellent for creating ornamental walls without totally blocking off light. They are 30cm/12in square and 10cm/4in thick, with either square or rounded designs within them. Some of these contain a single design, while other designs are revealed when four or more blocks are put together. Blocks cannot be cut, and there are neither half nor quarter sizes.

DESIGN FACTORS
Because these blocks are stack bonded (one immediately on top of another) walls constructed from them do not have great strength. Strong piers are needed at either end, and walls over 3m/10ft long need additional supports. As well as creating walls solely formed of them, they can also be set into solid brick walls, perhaps at eye-height to enable views to distant parts of a garden.

Unlike solid walls and fences, screen-block walling allows a flow of air which during summer can be especially welcome. However, avoid creating vast walls from them as they can look rather boring on their own. Climbers, as well as wall shrubs, can eliminate this problem.

The clinical nature of this walling enables it to blend well with patios formed of pre-cast square or rectangular paving, as well as cobbles. Indeed, any material with a bright, concrete surface harmonizes with them.

In addition to creating walls 1.8m/6ft high, low ones around the perimeter of a front garden are effective. Lay two or three courses of bricks and then one row of screen-block walling with concrete coping blocks on top. Around patios, increase this to two courses of screening blocks: ensure that the foundations are firm and strong.

They are also versatile enough to form surrounds for dustbins and sides of carports.

WALLING IDEAS
Walls should be more than dividers between parts of a garden, or just around a garden's perimeter. Here are a few ideas:
• If your house is pebble-dashed and painted white, use breeze- or concrete blocks to create a wall quickly. Foundations are needed, the same as used for brick walls. After construction and when the mortar has set, skim a thin layer of cement and sharp sand over the surface. When dry, apply another layer, at the same time adding 6mm/¼in shingle. Add a coping and paint white.
• Old, second-hand bricks create superb ornamental walls, and to make them cover a large area, they do not have to be made into a solid wall. Create strong foundations, then lay the first course, leaving about a 7.5cm/3in gap between each brick. In the centre of each gap lay half-bricks, then a full one on top. Then use full bricks to join these up, but again leaving about 7.5cm/3in between them. Continue to build up the wall to the desired height.
• Logs about 1.2m/4ft long and 15–20cm/6–8in wide create novel

LOW, DOUBLE WALLS

These are ideal for separating areas of the garden and to enable low, cascading plants to be grown. Ensure water can escape from the compost (insert pipes low down in the wall), but add plenty of moisture-retentive materials, such as peat, to the soil to prevent rapid drying in summer. Indeed, hot and dry summers can soon kill plants in raised walls: water the plants regularly.

'walls' for children's play areas. Bury their ends about 30cm/12in in soil and ram it tightly around their bases. Young children like to think of this as a fortress – and when the youngsters grow up the logs can be formed into log steps. They can also be used to enclose large areas of sand.

Concrete   Compacted hardcore   Reinforcing rod

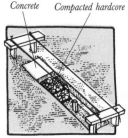 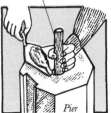    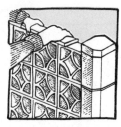

Pier

1. CREATE *foundations by digging a trench 30cm/1ft deep and 38cm/15in wide. Knock pegs into the base every 60cm/2ft to indicate the top of the concrete. Check that their tops are level. Fill the base with consolidated hardcore, then concrete.*

2. USE *specially-bought pier units as the ends. These enable blocks to be slotted into them. Use mortar to secure them to the foundations as well as to each other. Also, reinforce tall piers with metal rods and mortar.*

3. START *laying the blocks along the base, ensuring mortar does not get on the face side. Place mortar evenly over the ends and systematically butt one block against another. Regularly check that the bricks are being laid level and upright.*

4. ENSURE *the ends fit snugly into the piers, so that they support each other. As an alternative to these piers, build brick ones about 23cm/9in square. They help screen-block walling to harmonize with other, nearby brickwork.*

5. BUILD *up the tiers of blocks, checking each one is level and vertical, as well as not bulging sideways. To produce a regular pattern, ensure the blocks are perfectly aligned vertically as well as horizontally. If the pattern is askew, they look a mess.*

6. FINISH *by cementing copings into place along the top of the wall. Also, cement coping on the piers. These both create a professional appearance and prevent deterioration from rain penetrating the joints and blocks, then freezing.*

DRY-STONE WALLS

WHEN watching a craftsman constructing a dry-stone wall, the technique looks easy, but it requires skill and observation to select a suitable stone for a particular position. Both free-standing and retaining walls can be created: those used to retain soil have a slope (batter) while ordinary walling types are given an equal slope on both sides. Do not make them more than 1.2m/4ft high.

Stones can be obtained from garden centres, builders' yards, stone merchants and quarries. Many types can be used, granite or basalt being the hardest and most durable. It can be bought irregularly shaped or with regular, flat edges. Whatever the type of stone,

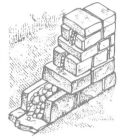

THE key to success with dry-stone walls is firm foundations and to ensure water does not remain in the structure. Build up the sides, but allow some stones to cross the centre. These walls create wonderful opportunities to grow rock garden plants, especially if you do not have space for a rock garden.

ensure its colour and texture harmonizes with the rest of your garden. About one tonne/2205lbs of rock is needed for every cubic metre of wall, and when buying it ensure the delivery charge is included in the price of the stone. A sound base is essential: dig out a trench, about twice the width of the expected top and 45cm/1½ft deep. Fill with rubble and thoroughly ram it into place. Lay several rows along the outside and fill between them with small stones. As the wall is built up, place large stones across the complete wall to tie the two sides together. Towards the top, use sandy soil in the centre to form pockets for plants. Finish by laying a coping of large, flat stones, with a slight tilt to one side.

1. DRY-STONE *walls are superb in rural areas. They can also be used in gardens to create retaining walls: to withstand the pressure of soil they are 'battered' or sloped. Mark out the wall's shape with a frame and strings .*

2. BUILD *up the wall from a firm base (see above). Lay a few courses of large stones and fill between them with small stones. Use extra large ones to cross the wall. Finish off at the top with coping stones.*

3. FILL *in behind the wall with coarse stones to ensure excess water rapidly drains away. Towards the top, use a layer of sandy topsoil to enable either grass to be sown or plants to be grown in the wall.*

RETAINING WALLS

THESE create the opportunity to attractively and practically separate one level in a garden from another. Additionally, gardens on severe slopes can be made easier to maintain by building a series of retaining walls, producing terraces.

These walls – especially informal types – create the chance to grow plants. Select the type of wall to harmonize with the rest of your garden (examples of each are shown below).

The most destructive force to retaining walls is water, not soil mounded against them. It is therefore essential that provision is made to enable water to escape, either through open gaps left between stones in informal walls, and holes between the brickwork in formal types. Pipes can also be fitted into the structure.

CONSTRUCTING WALLS

When using bricks to construct formal retaining walls, choose water-resistant, engineering types and use a mortar mix of one part cement to three of soft sand. About every 90cm/3ft, leave gaps to allow water to escape.

The wall can be given a longer life by putting a waterproof membrane (such as polythene sheeting, although proprietary ones are available) between the wall and drainage material placed against it. But take care not to block the drainage holes.

Natural stone is not cemented together and therefore water can seep out. Even so, narrow pipe drains installed across the wall's base encourage rapid drainage.

Trailing plants help to soften the edges of the wall, as well as hold the bricks together.

FORMAL

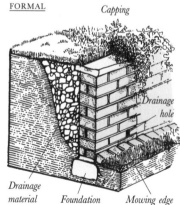

Capping

Drainage hole

Drainage material　*Foundation*　*Mowing edge*

FORMAL, *vertical retaining walls must be kept relatively low (75cm/2½ft) if they are to withstand the pressure of water as well as soil. Gaps in the wall's base are essential to enable water to escape.*

INFORMAL

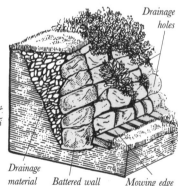

Drainage holes

Drainage material　*Battered wall*　*Mowing edge*

INFORMAL, *battered (leaning and angled backwards) retaining walls are stronger than vertical ones, but even these need a strong base and gaps to allow water to drain. Fill the back of the wall with clean rubble.*

FENCES

❖

FENCES should be pleasing to look at as well as functional. Their heights must suit their position and if needed to create a screen, they should be solid. In towns and cities, rigidly outlined types such as close-boarded and overlapped types are suitable, whereas in rural areas woven or wattle-hurdles are more sympathetic and have softer tones. Picket fencing also has rural characteristics and is easy to construct.

The range of fencing is wide, and in addition to those illustrated here a more recent type is ranch fencing: often seen in suburban gardens, painted white and with gaps left between the horizontal rails. A variation on this is to nail rails to both sides of posts, each overlapping the opposite one by about 12mm/1/2in.

In height, fences range from 90cm/3ft to 1.8m/6ft, but often 1.5m/5ft is a better choice. Most local planning regulations state that fences at the fronts of houses must not be more than 90cm/3ft, whereas in back gardens 1.8m/6ft is the limit.

CLOSE-BOARDED *fences are constructed on site by first erecting posts, then arris rails.*

OVERLAPPING *boards nailed to framework create strong fences. Usually sold in panels.*

WOVEN *wood fences are sold in panels and later secured to strong posts.*

WATTLE *hurdling is inexpensive, sold in panels and has a soft, rustic nature.*

PICKET *fences have a country nature. Usually painted white, they have pointed or rounded tops.*

CONSTRUCTION AND MAINTENANCE

Whatever the type of fencing, it must be firmly secured to posts that have a long life-span. Here are a few ways to ensure fences remain in good condition:

• Check that posts are upright and secured in concrete. At the top of the concrete, smooth and angle it so that water runs off.

• Buy pressure-treated posts that have been impregnated with rot-resistance chemicals. For extra decay prevention, stand the bases overnight in cans filled with wood preservative.

• Do not allow the bases of panels to rest on the soil. Close-boarded fences should have an additional rail (gravel board) at their bases to fill the gap between the bases of vertical boards and soil. These are quickly replaced should they rot.

• Use only galvanized nails to secure fencing panels to posts. If nails rust, the whole panel might collapse and smash.

• Nail wooden caps to the tops of posts. Most are wooden, but some are formed of zinc. Alternatively, slant the tops of posts so that water runs off quickly.

REPAIRING BROKEN POSTS

If a fence post breaks, through old age or as a result of a storm, a new one can be easily fitted by using a special metal post base. These are hammered directly into the ground, but first place a wooden cap on top to prevent its top being damaged. Remove the cap, insert the post and secure its base. If not exposed to strong winds, low fences can be completely erected by using these spiked, metal bases.

• Regularly paint plain-wood fences with wood preservative. Coat both sides and ensure the paint reaches right into overlapping joints. Also, cover white picket and ranch-type fences with good quality paint.

• Regularly clear away soil and plants from the bases of fences as they encourage dampness and wood decay.

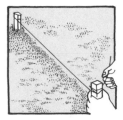

1. USE *string and pegs to mark the line of the fence. Ensure it is in the correct position and does not encroach on a neighbour's property. Allow for the width of posts when assessing its position.*

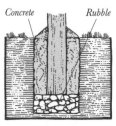

Concrete   Rubble

2. DIG *the first hole, 60cm/2ft deep and 30cm/12in square. Fill the base with 5cm/2in of rubble. Stand a post in it and check its top is 36mm/1½in above a panel placed on a brick.*

3. PLACE *a panel on the ground and mark the next hole's position. Allow for space around the post when digging the hole. Check its height and concrete into position. Check that the post is upright.*

4. BEFORE *securing each panel to the posts, check that its base is about 5cm/2in above the soil – about the thickness of a brick. The bases of panels left resting on the ground soon deteriorate and rot away.*

5. SECURE *each panel firmly to posts by using 5cm/2in-long galvanized nails. For a 60cm/5ft high fence, four or five nails are needed at each end of a panel – the top and bottom – and then two in between.*

6. TO PREVENT *a post decaying through water entering its top, use two 36mm/1½in-long galvanized nails to secure a capping to each post. These are readily available from suppliers of fences.*

CONSTRUCTING A BOARDED FENCE

❖

UNLIKE panelled fencing that arrives in prefabricated lengths, usually 1.8m/6ft, and is then secured between posts, boarded fencing is constructed on site. First, holes are dug about 3m/10ft apart, posts positioned in them and arris rails inserted into slots in their sides. The posts are propped upright and held in position with supports while concrete is poured around them. When dry, the props are removed and erection of the feathered boards can begin. However, if the arris rails and posts need coating in wood preservative, now is the time to do it, when they can be readily reached with a brush.

GRAVEL BOARDS

The first part to be fitted is the gravel board. This is about 3m/10ft long, 15cm/6in deep and 18–25mm/¾–1in thick, and secured at the bases of fences to fill the gap between the feathered boards and soil. Its prime function is to prevent the main part of the fence rotting. Cleats (pieces of wood 2.5cm/1in square and the depth of the gravel board) are nailed to the sides of the posts and then the gravel board to them.

The main part of the fence is formed of feathered boards – these are tapered to one side. Cut them to the desired length, about 5cm/2in below the tops of the posts. These are then nailed to the arris rails. Use a notched gauge to ensure each feathered board overlaps its neighbour evenly, and use one nail at the top and another on the lower arris rail. Towards the end of each 3m/10ft section, adjust the overlapping spacings to ensure the boards fit evenly. Either fit protective caps to the tops of posts or cut their tops at an angle, so that water rapidly drains off.

Immediately after completion, coat the fence with a wood preservative. Repeat the coatings every year, forcing the preservative well into the wood. After a few years – and especially during dry, hot summers – the boards twist. Nail them back into position.

WIRE-MESH FENCING

This fencing is also erected on site and the traditional form is the chain-link type, with bent wires that link with others and form a mesh. It is commonly sold in rolls – 10m/33ft, 25m/82ft and 50m/164ft long, and in heights from about 75cm/2½ft to 1.8m/6ft. As well, there is a range of mesh sizes, 36–50cm/1½–2in being about right for most gardens. Initially, this type of fencing appears cheaper than panel types of the same height, but it can be more expensive to install. This is because strong, firmly secured end posts are essential, so that wires can be strained between them. The mesh is then secured to the tensioned wires.

In addition to chain-link fencing there is the traditional chicken wire. This has been greatly improved for home gardens by a plastic coating. There are other plastic-coated wires in attractive patterns, in heights from 30cm/1ft to 1.2m/4ft – or more.

As well as forming fences, wire-mesh netting, when coiled into small, circular columns, supports climbing plants.

CONSTRUCTING A HA-HA

Also known as a haw-haw and sunken fence, this is a ditch that acts as a hidden fence, allowing uninterrupted views. The side towards the house usually has a slight slope, while the other one is vertical and lined in old stone walling to prevent crumbling.

It is said to have been used by French landscape designers in the seventeenth century and to have gained its name from people who came upon them suddenly and said Ah! Ah! It was introduced to Britain by Charles Bridgeman in the early eighteenth century to replace the 'unnaturalness' of walls. Lancelot 'Capability' Brown made the ha-ha popular.

1. ARRIS *rails (horizontal bars on which vertical boards are nailed) often rot at their ends and fall out of their sockets. If this happens, use proprietary, rust-resistant brackets to replace them.*

2. SECURE *gravel boards to the bases of posts. These are essential to ensure vertical boards do not touch the soil, become damp and decay. It also improves the fence's appearance.*

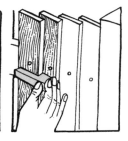

3. NAIL *the feathered-edged boards to the arris rails. To ensure a uniform overlay, use a notched gauge to measure each board, top and bottom. Only one galvanized nail is needed at the top.*

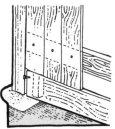

4. AT THE *base, rest each feathered-board on the gravel board and use one nail to secure it to the lower arris rail. Progress along the fence, but near to the next post adjust the spacings.*

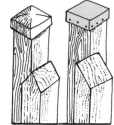

5. POSTS *used for boarded fences are usually given sloping tops to enable rain to run off quickly. Alternatively, use wooden caps or pieces of zinc folded over the top and nailed to it.*

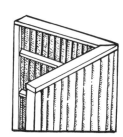

6. AS AN *added refinement, secure a strip of wood about 6cm/2½in wide and 18–25mm/¾–1in thick along the top of the fence. This protects the end grain on the feathered boards.*

GATES

❖

WELL-PROPORTIONED gates that harmonize with a garden and house enhance a property. Most gates are chosen for a combination of aesthetic and practical reasons, including keeping out wandering dogs, restraining your own pets and keeping children safe. Sometimes, their role is solely functional, perhaps to screen off a side entrance or to create a security barrier. Whatever the reason, there are many styles to choose from, and a nearly infinite range of sizes. The basic materials are metal and wood.

WOODEN GATES

Wood is a very adaptable material and can be formed into many styles, from solid-screen types to those with an open nature. Most are painted – usually white – but some are constructed in hardwoods that require only oiling or varnishing. Here are a few types of gate to consider:

• Picket fencing-type gates harmonize with similar style fencing

as well as between two brick posts that mark the ends of a neat, relatively low hedge.

• Country gates, in softwood painted white or hardwood with a natural colour, are ideal for drives. Narrow ones for paths are also available. They look superb when used with post-and-rail fencing.

• Solid boarded gates – especially tall ones – must be firmly constructed and secured to strong hinges and posts as they are likely to be buffeted by wind. They have

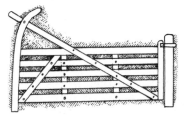

arched or flat tops and are available in planed softwood or hardwood.

• Ranch-style gates are essential for fences with a similar design. Occasionally, instead of constructing them with horizonal rails, these are put in vertically to create a contrast.

METAL GATES

Weather-resistant, wrought-iron gates have been used for many decades. These are made in single and double-gate forms and in a range of sizes. Most modern types are fitted with adjustable hinges to make fitting them easier.

There are many gates to choose from and, clearly, the more ornate their design the costlier they are. Ensure that the design harmonizes with its surrounds: avoid using highly ornate gates in relatively plain gardens.

• Tall gates with rounded tops are ideal for fitting into arches. Manufacturers produce these gates in many sizes, filling gaps from 75cm/2½ft to 1.2m/4ft, but allow space around them for hinges and latches.

• Both single and double gates look superb when combined with brick walls. Their appearance can be complemented by fitting matching railings into the wall.

THE range of gates is wide, in both metal and wood. They are sold in a wide range of sizes to fill practically all positions. Most have a 'see-through' nature, but completely boarded types are available.

WOODEN gates are popular but soon decay if not maintained properly. Long metal hinges are essential to ensure the gate is well secured. When fitting, first attach the hinge to the gate, then to the post.

THE stress points on wooden gates are the hinges, latches and where the wood is jointed. Rain, sun and freezing temperatures soon destroy a gate that is not well maintained – and prevent children swinging on it.

SELF-CLOSING latches are essential, especially if you have young children or a dog. Special springs – about 20cm/8in long – can be fitted to the hinge side to ensure that the gate closes and is secured by its latch.

TRELLISES

TRELLISES are essential to create support for climbers that twine naturally or have tendrils or leaf stalks that need something to which they can cling. These include flowering climbers such as clematis, Passion Flower and Sweet Peas, as well as the yellow coloured Golden-leaved Hop. Climbers that lean, such as roses and the Winter-flowering Jasmine, also need support.

TYPES OF TRELLIS

Trellises are traditionally made of wood, but plastic types are now widely available.

• Wooden trellises are formed of either square or diamond-shaped holes. The square-hole type is sold in sizes 1.8m/6ft high and widths such as 30cm/1ft, 60cm/2ft, 90cm/3ft, 1.2m/4ft and 1.8m/6ft. Each has an outer wooden framework, making it ideal for both fixing to walls and as a free-standing unit within a garden. This type is also available in fan-style units, about 1.8m/6ft high by 60cm/2ft at their widest point.

The diamond-shaped type is sold in a collapsed form and later expanded to cover areas 1.8m/6ft high and widths including 30cm/1ft, 45cm/1¹/₂ft, 60cm/2ft, 90cm/3ft and 1.2m/4ft. Because it is expandable, it does not have a firm surround and therefore needs to be nailed to a framework or directly on to a fence or wall.

• Rolls of plastic mesh are widely available, in many shapes and several colours. This does not have a rigid shape and must therefore be secured to a fence or other framework. It is relatively cheap to buy and can be adapted to fit most positions.

• Tubular, plastic-covered metal frameworks to form arches are sold in kit form.

JOINTED TRELLIS

Prefabricated, square-hole trellis-work invariably has cross-members nailed on top of vertical timbers. However, when making a trellis at home, the timbers can be let into one another by using cross-halving joints and creating trellises ideal as free-standing

FREE-STANDING TRELLIS

Prefabricated, square-hole units can be formed into a free-standing trellis. But ensure they have a firm frame. Secure posts into the ground (see page 334) and nail the trellis between them. This is an ideal way to separate one part of the garden from another. Use climbers to cover the trellis units.

units. Be careful not to use them against walls as they do not allow space for shoots to clamber behind them unless wooden spacers are used.

Use 2.5cm/1in square timber slats and cut half of them to the desired width of the trellis, the others to the depth. If the trellis is square, place all the timbers together, side by side, and secure them with adhesive tape. Use sufficient timber to create 18–23cm/7–9in squares. Use a long ruler to mark the wood 2.5cm/1in from both ends, then at equal spacings between, remembering to allow for the width of the timber at each position. Use a saw to cut

half-way through, then separate them and use a chisel to cut out the sawn areas. Then, slot the slats together, using a waterproof glue and 2.5cm/1in-long galvanized nails to secure the trellis.

SCREEN-COVERING CLEMATIS

• Clematis flammula:
Sweetly-scented, small, white flowers during mid- and late summer.
• Clematis macropetala:
Light and dark blue, bell-shaped flowers during early summer.

1. POSITION *the trellis on a wall so that its base is 23–30cm/9–12in above the ground. Use a spirit-level to ensure it is straight. Do not position the base of the trellis on the soil as it soon rots.*

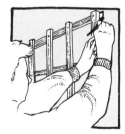

2. MARK *the exact position of the trellis on the wall to ensure it can be relocated in the same place later. While doing this, support the base on a box to ensure its position is constant.*

3. MARK *on the trellis the positions where it is to be drilled. Most trellises need to be secured to a wall in at least six places. At the same time, check that the brickwork is sound.*

4. PLACE *the trellis on several pieces of wood and use a drill to form holes in the wood. Do not force the drill through the timber. Rather, let it pass gently through the wood.*

5. RELOCATE *the trellis on the wall, place a long, thick nail in each hole and knock with a hammer. This will mark the surface of the wall so that the drilling positions are clearly marked.*

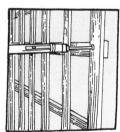

6. REMOVE *the trellis and use a masonry drill to make holes in the wall. Insert wall-fixing plugs, relocate the trellis and initially only partly tighten the screws. Later, tighten them fully*

CARPORTS

❦

THESE are relatively new in concept and a reflection of man's passion for motoring and protecting his car. Garages are a natural and logical transition from coach-houses, but carports are more a mid-century, inexpensive expediency to protect cars from the rain – and therefore rust.

Most are attached to house walls, with both ends directly accessible and the fourth side partially screened, perhaps by brickwork, wood or screen-block walling. However, instead of aligning it alongside a house or existing garage, position it at a right-angle and use one side – perhaps bricked – to form a courtyard.

Firm, all-weather surfaces are essential for cars and these are described earlier, but an alternative includes laying large paving slabs for the car's wheels to run upon, and creating a gravel surface between them. The advantage of gravel is that if a car drips oil, the contaminated area can be removed and quickly replaced with fresh chippings.

PLANNING

Do not ignore the planning stage and apply for – should it be necessary – permission from local authorities. Planning officers are very helpful and a visit or phone call could save you money and time. If permission is needed, part of this depends on your house's building line.

CONSTRUCTION

Methods vary widely, with supports formed of brick pillars, wood or tubular metal. Roofing is frequently made of corrugated, transparent sheeting, overlapping several corrugations and directing water into guttering to drain it into a water-barrel or a sump dug in a garden. Eventually, sunlight deteriorates the roofing material.

Some carports have a secondary and more ornate roof secured to the lower sides of the roofing bars, helping to create a structure more harmonious with its surroundings. Before deciding on your carport's construction, inspect as many as you can and talk to the owners

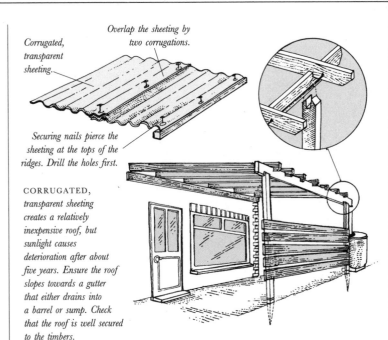

Corrugated, transparent sheeting.

Overlap the sheeting by two corrugations.

Securing nails pierce the sheeting at the tops of the ridges. Drill the holes first.

CORRUGATED, *transparent sheeting creates a relatively inexpensive roof, but sunlight causes deterioration after about five years. Ensure the roof slopes towards a gutter that either drains into a barrel or sump. Check that the roof is well secured to the timbers.*

about construction as well as as the ease of maintenance.

Screen-block walling – perhaps combined with a brick wall – offers an easy way to create extra protection and to prevent rain lashing on the sides of cars.

BLENDING

Use shrubs, climbers and wall-shrubs to soften the construction's outline and to harmonize it with the garden. Positioning yellow-leaved, narrow conifers on either side of the entrance is useful when negotiating it at night. Avoid setting climbing or rambling roses up the supports as their thorns are certain to tear clothing. More importantly, however, long stems on rambling roses may blow into your face. Large-leaved ivies – such as the variegated Persian Ivy, *Hedera colchica* 'Dentata Variegata' – soon soften the lines of supports and the fronts of roofs.

ENSURE *the design and constructional materials harmonize with the house. Make it appear part of a garden's overall design, not something added later. Walls along parts of the sides provide extra protection, but ensure they do not create a wind-tunnel. Also, make sure the structure complies with local building regulations.*

CARPORTS *made of wood have a softer outline and texture than those of brick and soon become part of the garden. If constructed as part of a shed or existing garage, use the same materials and a similar design. Ensure there is provision for water drainage from the roof. Use water-butts, but ensure they are covered to prevent leaves entering.*

CAMOUFLAGING GARAGES

If when moving house you inherit an unattractive garage do not despair as it can quite easily be camouflaged. Self-clinging climbers such as ivies – large and small-leaved types – can be trained to cover unsightly walls and roofs. But another way is to plant an evergreen hedge next to it. Wall shrubs, such as Firethorn (pyracantha) can be trained to clothe entire walls, while the evergreen Californian Lilac (Ceanothus thrysiflorus) creates a screen of blue flowers during late spring and early summer. For year-through brightness the beautifully yellow-leaved evergreen Lonicera nitida 'Baggesen's Gold' has few rivals.

TIMBER AND BRICK PERGOLAS

❖

TIMBER is a very adaptable and versatile material: when planed it has a formality that especially harmonizes with modern architecture, while if roughly sawn and painted with a dark preservative it blends with old, white-painted cottages.

Pergolas were known in antiquity, in Egypt, and later in Italy. Initially they simply supported plants, but later became architectural features. During the Italian Renaissance they started to spread throughout Europe.

Nowadays, formal types are formed with brick or wood supports, but invariably the cross-members are timber. Clearly, those made from wood are cheaper and quicker to erect than ones created with brick or stone pillars. Foundations for both brick and stone pillars must be sound, especially on clay soil, and involve digging footings 60cm/2ft deep.

Indeed, the life expectancy of brick pillars depends on the footings and the accuracy in subsequent construction. Securing cross timbers to them is a matter of cementing bolts or threaded rods to the tops or, with tall, narrow columns, a reinforcing rod that extends from the foundations to the top and is secured by a nut.

Cross-halving joints are used to join and hold timbers together. This involves measuring the width of the area to be cut and using a set-square to inscribe around the timber. Mark the depth of the cut. Hold the timber firm and use a tenon saw to cut the sides. Also, make several cuts to the same depth in the centre, depending on the area to be removed. Turn the timber on its side and use a chisel to cut out the piece that will enable another timber to be let into it. Ensure it fits comfortably, but not too tightly, as, if the wood swells, the timber may split.

BRICK PILLARS

Pillars constructed of bricks or stone create distinctive and elegant pergolas. Columns, about 35cm/14in or 45cm/18in square, are needed, their thickness and proportions depending on the beams and the pergola's extent. The beams are secured to the tops of pillars either by masonry bolts or threaded metal rods secured with concrete in the columns and held with nuts.

35cm/14in square

3m/10ft

Screw nut

Concrete filling

Reinforcing bar

2.4m/8ft

Ground level

Concrete foundations

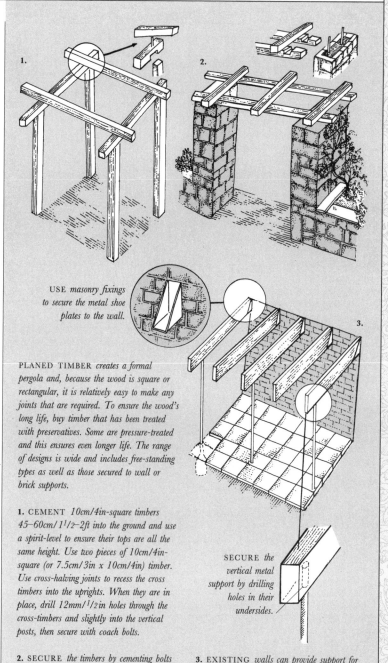

USE *masonry fixings to secure the metal shoe plates to the wall.*

PLANED TIMBER *creates a formal pergola and, because the wood is square or rectangular, it is relatively easy to make any joints that are required. To ensure the wood's long life, buy timber that has been treated with preservatives. Some are pressure-treated and this ensures even longer life. The range of designs is wide and includes free-standing types as well as those secured to wall or brick supports.*

1. CEMENT *10cm/4in-square timbers 45–60cm/1¹/₂–2ft into the ground and use a spirit-level to ensure their tops are all the same height. Use two pieces of 10cm/4in-square (or 7.5cm/3in x 10cm/4in) timber. Use cross-halving joints to recess the cross timbers into the uprights. When they are in place, drill 12mm/¹/₂in holes through the cross-timbers and slightly into the vertical posts, then secure with coach bolts.*

2. SECURE *the timbers by cementing bolts or threaded rods to the tops of the brickwork. When all the timbers have been jointed, drill holes in them, place on top and secure with washers and nuts.*

SECURE *the vertical metal support by drilling holes in their undersides.*

3. EXISTING *walls can provide support for one side of a pergola. Use metal wall shoes to hold them, with tubular, metal supports at the other side. Fix them firmly in concrete blocks in the ground.*

PESTS AND DISEASES

❖

Whenever plants are grown in groups in gardens, pests and diseases soon appear. They are especially attracted to groupings of similar plants, such as cabbages and beans, and large plantings of soft-leaved ornamental border plants, including dahlias. Insects have only two aims in life – reproducing themselves and eating. And when given a suitable climate and an unlimited diet of succulent plants they breed rapidly and soon devastate crops.

WHY USE INSECTICIDES AND FUNGICIDES?

If the control of insects and prevention of diseases is neglected, cultivated plants become unsightly and yields of vegetables, fruit trees and soft fruits radically diminish. As well as chewing and sucking plants, many insects, such as caterpillars and aphids (greenfly), excrete on leaves and cause further damage. And with aphids, the honeydew they deposit on stems and leaves encourages the presence of ants.

In addition to using chemicals to control pests and diseases there are several cultural ways to reduce their presence. Certain varieties of vegetables reveal resistance to some diseases. Also, creating a good circulation of air around plants reduces the incidence of several diseases.

Eradicating weeds, which compete with crops for nutrients, light and water, helps further. Also, weeds harbour pests and enable them to persist from one season to another. Feeding plants regularly with a balanced diet contributes to their resistance to pests and diseases, while removing dead flowers from ornamental plants reduces the risk of diseases damaging healthy ones. Nipping out the young tips of broad beans diminishes the incidence of blackflies.

USING INSECTICIDES

Insecticides kill insects in several different ways:
* *By coming into direct contact with them.*
* *By leaving a deposit on the plant which, later, an insect eats.*
* *By being absorbed into the sap of plants and later taken in by insects which suck sap. This type is known as a systemic insecticide.*

APPLYING INSECTICIDES

There are several ways to apply insecticides:
* *Spraying plants with a chemical dissolved in clean water is the most common method, especially in gardens and when controlling pests on ornamental plants, vegetables, fruit bushes and trees.*
* *Aerosols and dusts are convenient and ready for immediate use. They are available for gardens and greenhouses, as well as indoors on houseplants.*
* *Smokes are effective but only in greenhouses and conservatories.*
* *Some soil insecticides are available in granular form.*

APPLYING FUNGICIDES

These are best applied before an attack, rather than afterwards. They act when in contact with the disease, by coating leaves or penetrating the tissue and passing into the sap. In this second form they control current diseases as well as creating protection from further attack for up to two weeks, regardless of the subsequent weather.

RANGE OF PESTS AND DISEASES

The range of pests and diseases which attack garden plants is wide and may appear formidable. Fortunately, with vigilance and regular spraying it is possible to garden and not to encounter vast numbers of them. The following pages feature a wide range of pests and diseases.

SAFETY–FIRST WITH CHEMICALS

All garden chemicals must be handled carefully. Pesticides are deadly to insects and if used negligently can be just as dangerous to gardeners. Here are a few ways to ensure their safe use:
* *Before selecting a chemical, check it is suitable for killing the pest or controlling the disease.*
* *Check that the chemical will not harm the plant. Ferns, palms and cacti are easily damaged by some chemicals.*
* *Do not mix two different chemicals, unless recommended.*
* *Do not use bottles or packages of chemicals that have lost their labels.*
* *Always follow the manufacturer's instructions. Using chemicals at higher than recommended concentrations will not improve their effectiveness and may damage some plants.*
* *Keep all chemicals away from children and pets. Also, do not transfer chemicals into bottles children might believe to hold a refreshing drink.*
* *Store chemicals in a locked cupboard, above the reach of young children.*
* *Do not store chemicals in greenhouses or conservatories, as the temperature may rise dramatically. Also, keep them out of direct sunlight.*
* *Before spraying vegetables, check the time recommended between spraying and harvesting the crop.*
* *When spraying plants indoors, use only those recommended for houseplants. Also, remove fruit and take care not to spray wallpaper and curtains.*
* *Do not use chemicals indoors when caged birds, fish and other pets are present.*
* *Do not allow pets to lick or chew plants that have been newly sprayed. Many chemicals have a residual effect for several weeks.*
* *Do not use the same equipment for garden chemicals and weedkillers.*
* *Thoroughly wash all spraying equipment after use.*
* *Wash hands after using garden chemicals and, when recommended, use protective clothing such as gloves and face-masks.*
* *If a chemical burns your skin or splashes into your eyes, consult a doctor and take the packaging and container along with you.*

SAFE DISPOSAL OF UNWANTED GARDEN CHEMICALS

After several years of gardening, unwanted bottles and packages of chemicals accumulate and need to be disposed of. Do not just tip them down a drain or bury them in your garden. Instead, consult your local waste disposal authority for advice, especially when the packaging indicates the chemical is either harmful, oxidizing or an irritant. If the packaging is missing, assume the chemical is one of these classifications.

WILDLIFE AND PET SAFETY

When pesticides are used according to the recommendations on the packaging, and unwanted chemicals properly disposed of, there is little risk to wildlife and pets. However, here are a few extra precautions.
* *When chemicals are being mixed or used, and equipment cleaned, keep pets indoors.*
* *Do not allow plant-eating animals such as guinea pigs and rabbits to chew plants recently sprayed. Additionally, where lawns have been treated with weedkillers, do not place cages with runs on them until the grass has been cut.*
* *Do not use chemicals near garden ponds or bird baths, neither allow chemicals to drain into ditches and streams.*
* *Use sprays late in the day when few beneficial insects are flying and bees are not active. Avoid spraying open flowers, as these especially attract beneficial insects.*
* *Do not spray around wildlife ponds, as toads and frogs may be present; these eat garden pests and are very sensitive to garden chemicals.*
* *Slug pellets often attract pets and wildlife, especially when in heaps. Therefore, scatter them in bands between crops. As an extra precaution, place them under a slate to prevent hedgehogs eating them. This also keeps the pellets dry and more effective.*

ANTS *are sometimes a problem, especially in rock gardens; they cluster in soil around plants, loosening it and disturbing roots. Their presence is encouraged by aphids. Use an ant killer.*

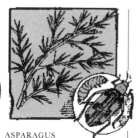

APHIDS *(greenfly) are the main pest of plants. They suck sap, causing mottling and distortion of shoots, leaves and flowers. Spray with a proprietary insecticide regularly throughout summer.*

ASPARAGUS BEETLES *(square orange markings on a black body) soon strip stems of leaves. Spray with an insecticide as soon as they are seen. Also, pick off and destroy beetles.*

CATERPILLARS *chew leaves and flowers, eventually completely destroying plants. Pick off and remove these pests. Alternatively, use an insecticide. Pull up and burn seriously infected plants.*

CATS *like digging up light, well-drained soil. Dusting soil with pepper is often recommended. A 2.5cm/1in mulch of pea-shingle in a rock garden helps to protect the roots.*

CELERY FLIES *have larvae which tunnel into leaves, causing them to shrivel and die. Spray with insecticides at the first sign of infestation. Also, pull off infected leaflets.*

BIRDS *often disturb newly sown seeds, and tear young shoots and leaves. Place twiggy sticks over the surface, or stretch black cotton between sticks. Remove this protection later.*

BLACK LEG *is a disease of cuttings, especially pelargoniums. Stem bases become soft and black. It is encouraged by cold, wet, compacted and airless compost. Destroy.*

BLACK SPOT *is a fungal disease that causes black spots on leaves of roses. Spray with a fungicide several times. Remove and burn fallen, infected leaves to prevent infection spreading.*

CHOCOLATE SPOT *forms small, brown spots on the leaves of broad beans. Dig up and destroy infected plants and spray the remaining ones with a fungicide. Avoid soils rich in nitrogen.*

CLUB-ROOT *is a notorious disease of the cabbage family. Roots distort and plants die. Acid soil encourages the disease. Treat seedlings, when they are being planted, with a proprietary fungicide.*

COCKCHAFER GRUBS *live in garden soil and graze on roots. Later they pupate and beetles appear. Pick up and destroy the grubs; dig borders deeply in winter; use insecticide.*

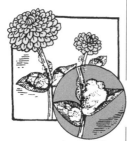

BOTRYTIS *(grey mould) forms a fluffy mould on leaves, stems and flowers, especially where damp, cool, airless conditions prevail. Avoid congestion and spray with a fungicide if necessary.*

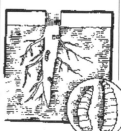

CABBAGE ROOTFLIES *soon kill young plants by tunnelling into roots. Infested plants grow slowly and have blue-tinged leaves. Use an insecticide before setting plants in position.*

CARROT FLIES *have small, creamy maggots which devastate parsnips, celery and carrots. Rake in suitable insecticides before sowing seeds. Also, remove and burn thinnings.*

CUCKOO-SPIT, *a white and frothy spittle enclosing Froghoppers (see page 342). Leaves may wilt and be distorted. Spray with water to dislodge, remove by hand or use an insecticide.*

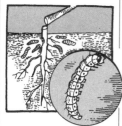

CUTWORMS *are the larvae of certain moths. They live in the topsoil and chew the stems of seedlings, causing them to collapse. Dust the soil with an insecticide and remove all weeds.*

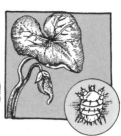

CYCLAMEN MITES *are dust-like spiders that infest plants. Leaves curl and wrinkle, plants are stunted. Remove and burn seriously infected plants. Spray with malathion or insectidal soap.*

DAMPING OFF *causes seedlings in seed-trays to collapse and die, due to overcrowding, high temperatures and excessively moist compost. Attacks can be prevented by using a proprietary fungicide.*

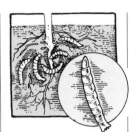

DIE-BACK, *a disease that causes tips of shoots progressively to die downwards, has several causes: frost, canker, waterlogging and diseases. Cut out and burn infected parts.*

EARWIGS *chew flowers, soft leaves and stems, especially at night. Pick off and destroy these pests or trap them in pots of straw inverted on canes. Alternatively, dust with a proprietary insecticide.*

MICE *in search of food often dig down in winter to feed on bulbs and corms, especially during severe weather. The best protection is to cover bulbs with wire netting, pegged on the surface.*

MILLIPEDES *chew stems and roots and are especially troublesome in damp soil to which organic material has been added. Dust the soil with an insecticide and dig it deeply in winter.*

MINT RUST *is not common, but is difficult to eradicate. Orange pustules appear on the undersides of leaves. Spray plants regularly especially if it is a problem in your area.*

FLEA BEETLES *eat holes in the leaves of brassica seedlings, sometimes killing young plants, especially during dry seasons. Keep seedlings watered and treat seeds with an insecticide.*

FROGHOPPERS *create masses of froth, widely known as cuckoo-spit, usually in leaf joints. They pierce soft stems and leaves and suck sap, causing distortion. Spray them with an insecticide.*

LEAF-ROLLING SAWFLY *causes leaves to roll, enclosing a greyish-green grub. Leaves later shrivel and die. Pick off and burn small infestations, or prevent damage with an insecticide.*

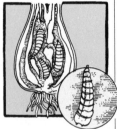

MOLES *are often a problem in rock gardens as plants cannot easily be moved out of the way of their tunnels. Block up runs with slate. Do not use metal traps, as they are cruel.*

ONION FLIES *have small, white maggots that burrow into bulbs. Leaves turn yellow and wilt. Pull up and burn infected plants and rake insecticides into the soil before sowing.*

PEA MOTHS *infest pea pods and cause maggoty peas, making them unusable. Early and late crops sometimes escape attack. Use insecticides about seven days after flowers appear.*

LEAFHOPPERS *create pale, mottled areas on leaves. Growth is checked, leaves become distorted and may fall off if the attack is severe. Spray with a systemic insecticide.*

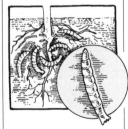

LEATHERJACKETS *are the larvae of craneflies and live in soil, chewing roots and causing plants to wilt. They are a particular problem in newly dug grassland. Dust soil with an insecticide.*

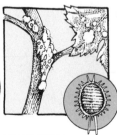

MEALY BUGS *resemble white, waxy woodlice. They suck sap, causing distortion and yellowing. Wipe off small colonies with cotton swabs dipped in methylated spirits.*

PEA AND BEAN WEEVILS *chew notches from the edges of pea and broad bean leaves. Regularly hoeing around plants helps to prevent attack; when first seen, use insecticides.*

POTATO SCAB *creates raised, distorted, scabby areas on the skins of potatoes. Only the skin is affected and the tubers can still be cooked and eaten. Do not add lime to the soil.*

POWDERY MILDEW *forms a white, powdery coating on leaves, stems and flowers. It is encouraged by congestion, lack of air circulation, and dry soil. Use a fungicide to combat it.*

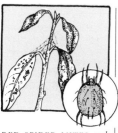

RED SPIDER MITES *suck sap, causing mottling and, eventually, webs. Leaves drop prematurely. Syringe plants regularly and spray with an acaricide or insecticidal soap.*

ROOT APHIDS *are pests in warm areas; they graze on roots, causing wilting and discoloration. The only solution is to drench the soil thoroughly with a proprietary insecticide.*

ROOT ROTS *are encouraged by wet, cold soil. Rock garden plants are often susceptible to excessive soil moisture. Ensure the soil is well-drained: add sharp sand to the planting pockets.*

SOOTY MOULD *is a fungus that lives on honey-dew excreted by aphids. It blackens stems and leaves. Spray regularly to kill the aphids. Pull off and destroy badly affected leaves.*

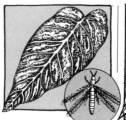

THRIPS *are tiny flies that jump or fly from leaf to leaf, causing silvery streaks on leaves. Flowers become distorted. Spray with an insecticide. Worse when compost is dry.*

TORTRIX MOTHS *chew irregular holes in leaves, then spin fine threads to hold the edges together. Pick off and destroy the larvae if the infestation is light, or spray with an insecticide.*

ROSE SCALE *is most often seen on old and neglected rose bushes. Scurfy scales cluster on stems. Wipe off colonies with methylated spirits (rubbing alcohol) and use a systemic insecticide.*

ROSE SLUGWORM *creates skeletonized leaves by eating soft parts between veins. Plants are soon disfigured. Greenish-yellow grubs can often be seen on the surface. Spray with an insecticide.*

RUST *is especially a problem with Hollyhocks and Mallows (Lavatera). Rusts are difficult to control and therefore it is best to pull up and burn severely infected plants.*

VINE WEEVILS *are small, white beetle grubs. They chew roots, causing plants to wilt and die. If a plant in a pot wilts unexpectedly, check the compost. If they are present, drench with an insecticide.*

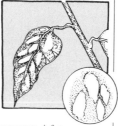

VIRUSES *infect many plants and although they seldom kill, their host's vigour is reduced. Aphids and other sap-sucking pests spread them. Therefore, eradicate all pests.*

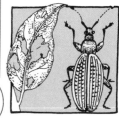

WEEVILS *are beetle-like and often have long, divided snouts. Their larvae are legless grubs. Both adults and larvae feed on roots, stems and leaves. Regularly dust or spray with insecticide.*

SCALE INSECTS *create waxy-brown discs under which young ones are produced. They suck sap, causing speckling. Destroy badly infected plants or treat as for mealy bugs.*

SLUGS *are especially troublesome during wet and warm weather, when they chew all parts of plants. They feed at night and therefore are not always seen. Use slug baits.*

SNAILS *are, like slugs, pests of the night and especially damaging during warm, wet weather. They chew and tear leaves and stems. Pick off and destroy as soon as they are seen. Also, use baits.*

WHITEFLIES *are small, moth-like pests, primarily of houseplants. They suck sap, causing yellowing and leaves to fall off. When disturbed they flutter about. Use an insecticide.*

WIREWORMS *are the larvae of clickbeetles. They inhabit soil, chewing roots and causing the death of plants. They are troublesome on newly dug grassland. Use an insecticide.*

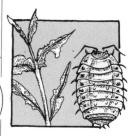

WOODLICE *are hard-coated pests living in damp, dark places. They come out at night and feed on stems, roots and leaves. Dust with an insecticide and keep the area free from rubbish.*

USEFUL GARDENING TERMS

❖

ACARICIDE: *A chemical used to kill parasitic spider mites, such as red-spider mites.*

ACID: *Used to describe potting compost or garden soil with a pH below 7.0.*

AERATION: *The loosening of soil to enable air to enter. Digging the ground in late autumn or winter breaks up the top spit (about 25cm/10in), while hoeing soil at any time of year disturbs the crust. Breaking up a crusty surface also enables water readily to enter the ground.*

AERIAL ROOTS: *Roots that arise from a stem above soil-level, such as with the popular and widely grown houseplant Swiss Cheese Plant (Monstera deliciosa), ivies and some orchids. Their prime task is to gain support for the stems.*

AIR LAYERING: *A method of propagating plants by encouraging roots to form on stems. The Rubber Plant (Ficus elastica), a well-known houseplant in temperate countries, is often increased in this way.*

ALKALINE: *Used to describe soil or potting compost with a pH above 7.0.*

ALPINE: *A plant native to mountainous zones classified as being above the upper limit of trees but below the permanent snow line. Alpine plants can be grown in rock gardens, scree beds and shallow stone sinks. Additionally, alpine plants with leaves that are easily damaged by winter rain can be grown in an alpine house.*

ALPINE HOUSE: *A greenhouse used to protect delicate alpine plants from excessive dampness and rain, especially during winter. Usually it is unheated and well ventilated.*

ALPINE LAWN: *Instead of using grass to form a lawn, such plants as Thyme (Thymus serpyllum) are used. Alpine lawns are more for decoration and to form a background for other plants than to create a hard-wearing walking or play area.*

ANNUAL: *A plant that completes its life-cycle within a year: seeds germinate, the plant grows, bears flowers and produces seeds within one growing season. However, many plants grown in this way are not true annuals. For example, the well-known Busy Lizzie (Impatiens walleriana) is a tender perennial invariably raised as a half-hardy annual when grown in temperate regions.*

APHIDS: *Another term for Greenfly.*

AQUATIC: *A plant that lives totally or partly submerged in water.*

AXIL: *The junction between a stem and leaf, from which sideshoots or flowers may develop.*

BALLED: *Young shrubs - usually evergreens – that have been dug up from a nursery bed and their roots wrapped in hessian prior to being sold. This method of selling plants was especially popular before the introduction of container-grown plants.*

BALLING: *A physiological disorder of roses, when the outside petals of a flower cling together, fail to open and turn brown. Varieties with large, thin-petalled blooms are most susceptible.*

BARE-ROOTED PLANT: *A deciduous tree or shrub which has been dug up during its dormant period (late autumn to late winter) and sold for replanting into a border or container. The plant has little soil around its roots and is bare of leaves. It must be planted into its growing position as soon as possible, so that the roots do not become dry.*

BASE DRESSING: *An application of fertilizer just before seeds are sown or a crop planted. The fertilizer is lightly raked into the soil's surface.*

BEDDING PLANTS: *Plants that create seasonal colour in gardens or containers. Spring-flowering bedding plants are usually biennials, which were raised during the previous summer and planted into their flowering positions mainly in autumn, although in cold and exposed areas this is sometimes left until late winter or early spring. Summer-flowering bedding plants are mainly half-hardy annuals which after being raised in gentle warmth in late winter or early spring are planted into borders as soon as the risk of frost has passed.*

BIENNIAL: *A plant which takes two seasons to grow from seed and to produce flowers. Many spring-flowering plants are grown as biennials, such as wallflowers and daisies.*

BIENNIAL BEARING: *The tendency of some apple varieties to bear more fruit one year than another. This uneven production of fruit can be partly counteracted when pruning trees or bushes.*

BLACKFLY: *A type of aphid that especially infests crops of beans. They congregate around soft stem tips, suck sap and cause debilitation. They also spread viruses.*

BLEEDING: *The loss of sap from a plant after being damaged or, usually, pruned at the wrong time.*

BLOOM: *Means either a flower or a powdery coating on flowers, stems or leaves.*

BLOWN: *When a flower is fully open and the petals fade or fall off.*

BOG GARDEN: *A moist area – usually natural but may be constructed – around a garden pond. Usually the soil is slightly acid.*

BOG GARDEN PLANTS: *Plants, also known as waterside plants, moisture-loving plants and poolside plants, that grow in soil that remains moist throughout the year.*

BOLTING: *Premature flowering and production of seeds, usually caused by a check to growth through drought or because the soil is poor. Vegetable crops such as lettuce and beetroot are especially likely to bolt.*

BONSAI: *A technique used to enable shrubs and trees to remain small and to be grown in shallow containers. Traditional bonsai is essentially an outdoor technique, with specimens being moved indoors for only a day or so at one time. However, a variation known as Chinese or indoor bonsai is now used to dwarf tropical and sub-tropical shrubs that can be grown indoors throughout the year. Dwarfing is achieved by pruning roots, leaves and stems.*

BROADCAST: *Applies to sowing seeds or distributing fertilizers by spreading them evenly over the surface of soil, rather than by forming them into straight lines.*

BUDDING: *A method of increasing plants, whereby a bud (the varietal part) is united with a rootstock of known vigour. Hybrid Tea roses (now known as Large-flowered Roses) and Floribunda roses (Cluster-flowered Roses) are invariably raised in this way.*

BULB: *A food storage organ with a bud-like structure. It is formed of fleshy scales attached at their base to a flattened stem called a basal plate. Examples of bulbs include hyacinths, daffodils and tulips.*

BULBIL: *A miniature and immature bulb, usually arising at the base of another bulb. Additionally, some plants, such as the Mother Fern (Asplenium bulbiferum), develop plantlets on their leaves which are also known as bulbils. These can be detached and by pushing them into compost encouraged to form roots.*

CALCICOLE: *A plant that likes lime in the compost or soil in which it is growing.*

CALCIFUGE: *Means lime-hating and refers to plants that cannot be grown in chalky or limey soil.*

CALLUS: *Hard, raised, protective surface that forms over a wound.*

CAPILLARY ACTION: *The passage of water upwards through potting compost or soil. The finer the soil particles, the higher the rise of moisture through it. This principle is used in some self-watering systems for plants grown in pots in greenhouses and conservatories, as well as indoors.*

CATCH CROP: *Sowing and growing quickly maturing crops, such as radishes and lettuces, between vegetables that take a long time to grow and mature, such as leeks.*

CHLOROSIS: *The mottling and yellowing of leaves due to lack of chlorophyll (the green colouring material in plants). Sometimes this is caused by viruses transmitted by sucking pests such as greenfly. Mineral deficiencies can also be the cause.*

CLONE: *Each of a group of identical plants, all of which have been raised vegetatively – from cuttings, layers or division – from a single parent.*

COIR-BASED COMPOST: *A type of environmentally friendly compost, formed of coir (fibre from the husk of a coconut). Such composts do not use peat and therefore do not contribute to the destruction of the environment. Both seed- and potting-type coir-based composts are available.*

COMPOST: *This has two meanings. The first refers to a mixture of vegetable material when formed into a heap (a compost heap) to decay. When decayed, the material is either dug into the soil during winter or spread over the surface as a mulch. The other meaning is the medium in which plants grow when in pots or other containers. There are two basic types of these composts; 'potting* compost' is the type in which plants are grown and into which they are repotted, while 'seed compost' is the formulation in which seeds are sown. These composts are either loam-based (a mixture of loam, peat, sharp sand and fertilizers), peat-based (peat and fertilizers) or environmentally friendly and formed from materials such as coir or mixtures of bark, wood-fibre or coir, manure and straw.

COMPOST ADDITIVES: Moisture-retentive materials such as Vermiculite and Perlite added to compost used in hanging baskets. They help to reduce the frequency of watering during summer.

COMPOUND FERTILIZER: One formed of the three main plant foods – nitrogen, phosphorus (phosphates) and potassium (potash).

CONTAINER-GROWN PLANT: A plant grown and offered for sale in a container. Such plants can be planted into a garden whenever the soil is not frozen or excessively wet.

CORDON: A fruit tree (apple or pear) or soft fruit (red or white currant) that is planted, trained and pruned to form one, two, three or four stems. Mostly they are grown at a 45-degree angle, although some are upright.

CORM: A swollen and thickened stem-base, usually covered with a papery skin. At a corm's top there is a bud which produces a further shoot, as well as roots.

CROCK: A piece of broken clay pot put hollow-side downwards into the base of a clay pot to prevent compost blocking the drainage hole.

CROP ROTATION: The yearly rotation of individual vegetables from one part of a vegetable garden to another. When the same type of crop is grown in the same position year after year, it encourages the build-up of pests and diseases, as well as exhausting the soil of the same nutrients.

CULTIVAR: A variety raised in cultivation by selective breeding.

CUTTING: A vegetative method of increasing plants, whereby a severed piece of plant is encouraged to develop roots.

DAMPING DOWN: Increasing the humidity in a greenhouse or conservatory by using a fine-rosed watering-can or hosepipe to spray water on the floor and around plants. It is best carried out early in the day, so that excess moisture dries before nightfall. Excessive moisture at night encourages the presence of diseases.

DAMPING OFF: A fungal disease that causes seedlings to collapse at soil-level. It usually attacks congested seedlings in seed trays when the compost is kept excessively wet and the temperature too high.

DEAD-HEADING: The removal of dead or faded flowers to prevent the formation of seeds and to encourage the development of further flowers. It also helps to prevent diseases infecting decaying flowers and spreading to healthy ones.

DECIDUOUS: A plant, usually a tree or shrub, that loses its leaves in autumn and develops fresh ones in spring.

DIBBER: A rounded, blunt-pointed tool for making planting holes outdoors as well as in compost in pots and boxes in greenhouses. Large

dibbers (often made from broken spade or fork handles) are used for planting cabbages and other brassicas, while pencil-like ones are ideal for pricking-off seedlings and inserting cuttings in compost.

DIE-BACK: When a shoot decays backwards from its tip. On fruit trees this is often the result of frost damage, faulty pruning and, sometimes, pest and disease damage.

DIVISION: A vegetative method of propagation involving the division of the roots of plants. Fibrous-rooted herbaceous perennials are often increased in this way.

DORMANT: A resting period, usually during autumn and winter, when a plant makes no noticeable growth.

DOUBLE DIGGING: When soil is dug to the depth of two spade blades. While doing this, soil from the upper level is not mixed with that from the lower part.

DRAWN: Thin and spindly shoots or plants after having been grown in crowded or dark places.

DRILL: A shallow – V-shaped or flat-bottomed depression in soil into which seeds are sown. In the open ground and when sowing vegetables, mostly V-shaped drills 6–12mm/^{1}/$_4$–^{1}/$_2$in deep are used. Flat-bottomed drills, in which peas are sometimes sown, are about 5cm/2in deep and 20–25cm/8–10in wide.

DRY-STONE WALL: A wall formed of natural stone and without the benefit of mortar to hold the stones together.

DUTCH LIGHT: A large, single sheet of glass – about 1.5m/5ft long by 75cm/

2^1/$_2$ft wide – secured in a wood frame and placed on a low-walled structure formed of bricks or stout wood. It is mainly used to harden-off plants in spring or to grow low-growing salad crops, such as lettuces.

EARTHING-UP: Drawing up soil around plants to exclude light and thereby to whiten stems. Vegetables such as leeks, trench celery and chicory are treated in this way.

EPIPHYTE: A plant that grows above ground-level, either on another plant or, occasionally, on mossy rocks. Unlike parasites, which live and feed on their host, epiphytes only gain support. They live on, and take nourishment from, debris that collects on branches and rocks.

ETIOLATED: Blanched and spindly and usually the result of being grown in poor light.

EVERGREEN: A shrub or tree that appears to retain its foliage throughout the year. However, leaves are constantly falling, to be replaced by fresh ones.

EYE: An immature or undeveloped growth bud. This term is especially applied to grapevines and roses.

FASCIATION: A freak condition, when stems or flowers are misshapen and fused or flattened. These parts are best cut out.

FLAT: A North American term for a seed-tray.

FLEXIBLE LINER: Also known as a pool liner, this is a waterproof material formed of either polythene, PVC or butyl (synthetic rubber) and frequently used to create a garden pond.

FLOATERS: Also known as floating plants, they float freely in a pond, with their leaves and stems on or just below the water's surface. As well as creating an attractive feature, they provide shelter for fish.

FLORE-PLENO: Flowers with more than the normal number of petals.

FLORIBUNDA ROSES: A type of rose now correctly known as Cluster-flowered Roses. However, they are still widely listed under their earlier name.

FLUID SOWING: A method of sowing seeds (mainly vegetables) outdoors. Seeds are mixed with a fluid gel (often wallpaper paste), placed in a polythene bag with a small hole in its corner and squeezed into a drill. The gel helps to retain moisture around the seeds, thereby encouraging rapid and even germination.

FOLIAR FEEDING: Spraying foliage with fertilizers mixed in water as a way to apply nutrients. Plants respond rapidly to this treatment, but not all can be fed in this way.

FRIABLE: Applies to soil which is crumbly and can be raked to form a fine tilth.

FROST-TENDER: Plants that are killed or seriously damaged by exposure to frost. Such plants include tender perennials and half-hardy summer-flowering annuals.

FULL-SPAN GREENHOUSE: A greenhouse with equal areas of glass on both sides of the central ridge bar.

FUNGICIDE: A chemical used to eradicate or deter fungal diseases.

GARDEN COMPOST: Formed of vegetable waste such as cabbage leaves and potato peelings from kitchens, and soft-tissued plants from gardens, including grass-cuttings. It is formed into a heap about 1.2m/4ft square and allowed to decompose. When fully decayed it is either dug into soil or used as a mulch.

GERMINATION: The process that occurs within a seed when given moisture, warmth and air. However, to most gardeners germination is when shoots appear through the surface of potting compost or soil.

GRAFTING: A method of propagation in which a piece of wood of the varietal part is united with a rootstock of known vigour.

GRANDIFLORA: A North American term for a vigorous Floribunda rose (Cluster-flowered Rose) with Hybrid Tea (Large-flowered Rose) type flowers.

GREENFLY: Also known as aphis and aphids, these sap-sucking pests are the most frequently encountered garden pest. While sucking sap and causing debilitation, they spread viruses from one plant to another.

GROUND COVER: When low-growing, usually evergreen plants, are planted so that they cover the soil with leaves. They prevent the growth of weeds, create an attractive backdrop for taller plants, camouflage unsightly features, and help to reduce the risk of soil erosion.

GROWING-BAG: A large polythene bag filled with peat-based compost. Originally introduced to enable tomatoes to be grown on disease-infected soil in greenhouses, growing-bags are now also widely used as homes for flowering and food plants on patios. Bulbs can also be grown in them.

HALF-HARDY ANNUAL: An annual which is raised in gentle warmth in late winter or early spring and, after being hardened off, planted into a garden or container.

HARDENING OFF: Acclimatizing plants which have been raised in gentle warmth in a greenhouse or conservatory to outdoor conditions. This usually applies to half-hardy annuals in spring; first the greenhouse temperature is progressively lowered, then plants are placed in a cold frame and given increasing ventilation.

HARDWOOD CUTTING: A cutting formed of mature, ripe wood. The cuttings are taken from autumn to late winter and plants increased in this way include bush fruits such as blackcurrants, gooseberries and red and white currants. Many shrubs are also propagated in this way.

HARDY ANNUAL: An annual that can be sown outdoors in spring or early summer and which develops flowers and seeds during the same season.

HAULM: The aerial part of a vegetable crop and specifically used to refer to the stems and leaves of potato plants.

HEEL CUTTING: A cutting, usually a semi-hardwood type, with a small part of the shoot to which is was attached left at its base. This small piece of old wood is lightly trimmed and known as a heel.

HEELING-IN: Covering the roots of deciduous, bare-rooted trees and shrubs with soil while they are waiting to be planted. Occasionally bare-rooted shrubs and trees arrive from nurseries when the ground is frozen or too wet to enable them to be planted. Such plants are best unpacked and their roots placed in a shallow trench in a sheltered corner of a garden and covered with soil.

HEP: Also known as hip and refers to the fruit of a rose.

HERBACEOUS PERENNIALS: Plants that persist from one year to another, but in autumn all stems die back and fresh ones develop in spring or early summer.

HUMUS: Derived from the decomposition of organic material such as vegetable waste, leaves and manure. It is essential to the well-being of soil and growth of plants.

HYBRID: A plant that results from a cross between two distinct and unrelated parents. Some hybrids are crosses between two varieties, others between two species within the same genus, while a few are crosses between two different genera.

HYBRID TEA ROSE: A type of rose now correctly known as Large-flowered Roses.

INFLORESCENCE: The part of a plant that bears flowers.

INSECTICIDE: A chemical used to kill insects.

INTERNODAL: Referring to the part of a stem or shoot between two leaf-joints (nodes).

JOHN INNES COMPOSTS: Loam-based compost, originated during the 1930s at the John Innes Horticultural Institute, England. There are standardized composts for sowing seeds and potting and repotting plants.

LAYERING: A vegetative way to increase plants, involving lowering stems and shallowly burying them in soil or compost while still attached to a parent plant. After the formation of roots, the new plant is severed from its parent and replanted.

LEAN-TO GREENHOUSE: A greenhouse constructed against a wall, preferably a south- or west-facing one.

LEGGY: Refers to a plant that becomes tall and spindly, often through being kept in a dark place or positioned too close together.

LOAM: Fertile, well-drained, good-quality top soil. It neither has a high clay content, nor is excessively sandy.

LOAM-BASED COMPOST: Compost formed of a mixture of loam (good quality topsoil), peat and sharp sand. These composts do not retain as much moisture as peat-based types, but have a greater reserve of nutrients.

MINIMUM- AND MAXIMUM-THERMOMETER: A thermometer that indicates the lowest and highest temperature since it was last read and reset.

MINI-GREENHOUSE: A small greenhouse, usually lean-to and with a depth of no more than 60cm/2ft and height about 1.5m/5ft.

MIST PROPAGATION: An electrically-initiated, mechanical device that sprays the leaves of cuttings with fine water droplets. This keeps cuttings cool, as well as reducing their need to absorb moisture before they have developed roots.

MIST SPRAYER: Used to create a humid atmosphere around plants.

MOISTURE-INDICATOR STRIPS: Inserted permanently in compost in a pot to indicate if a plant needs further water.

MULCH: The formation of a layer (about 10cm/4in thick) of decayed organic material on the soil's surface. It reduces the evaporation of moisture from the soil's surface, prevents the growth of weeds, contributes to fertility and keeps the ground cool in summer. Black polythene can also be used.

NEUTRAL: Used to describe soil that is neither acid nor alkaline, with a pH of 7.0.

NIPPING OUT: The removal of the tip of a shoot to encourage the growth of sideshoots.

NODE: A leaf-joint or the position where a shoot grows from a stem.

NURSERY BED: A sheltered and warm area in a garden in which seeds can be sown and young plants transplanted before being planted into a garden.

OVER-POTTING: Repotting a plant into a pot which is too large for it. When this happens, it is initially difficult to keep the compost evenly moist and not too wet.

OVER THE RIM WATERING: Watering a plant in a pot by filling the gap between the compost and the pot's rim with water.

PAN: A hardy, usually impervious layer beneath the soil's surface that prevents the drainage of water and growth of roots. Digging soil in winter helps to break it up.

PEAT: Partly decomposed vegetable material, usually with an acid nature. Because of its ability to retain water it is used in seed and potting composts. However, its continued removal from peat-beds is destructive and causes the natural habitat of birds, animals and insects to be destroyed.

PEAT-BASED COMPOSTS: Compost formed of peat, with the addition of plant foods. Some composts are formulated for the sowing of seeds and rooting of cuttings, while others are suitable for potting. A few have a dual role.

PERENNIAL: Usually used when referring to herbaceous perennials, but also applied to any plant that lives for several years, such as shrubs and trees.

PERLITE: A moisture-retentive material often added to compost in hanging baskets.

PETIOLE: A leaf-stalk.

PH: A measure of the alkalinity or acidity of soil. It is assessed on a logarithmic scale which ranges from 0 to 14, with 7.0 as neutral. Most plants grow best in soil with a pH between 6.5 and 7.0.

PHOTOSYNTHESIS: The growth-building process in plants: chlorophyll in leaves is activated by sunlight and together with moisture and nutrients absorbed by roots, and carbon dioxide absorbed by leaves, creates growth. During this process, oxygen is given off.

PLANTLET: An offset produced on a plant's leaves or stem.

PLASTIC TUNNEL: Metal hoops over which plastic sheeting is tightly drawn to create a protected area in which plants can be grown.

PLEACHING: Training and pruning a line of trees planted close together to form a 'hedge' at their top. The base of each tree is free from shoots and leaves.

POLLINATION: The transfer of pollen from anthers (male part of a flower) to the stigma (female part). Fertilization does not necessarily follow pollination.

POT BOUND: When a plant fills its pot with roots and needs to be transferred to a larger pot.

POTTING-ON: Transferring an established plant from one pot to a larger one.

POTTING-UP: When a plant is initially moved into a pot.

PRICKING OFF: Transferring seedlings from the seed-tray in which they were sown into pots or other seed-trays and given wider spacing.

PRICKING OUT: This has the same meaning as pricking off.

PRUNING: The controlled removal of stems and shoots, usually from woody plants such as trees and shrubs, to encourage the development of a better shape or the production of fruits or flowers.

RCD: *Means a residual current device, an essential part of all outdoor and greenhouse electrical systems. Should a fault occur in an appliance, or a cable be damaged, the supply of electricity is immediately cut off.*

RESPIRATION: *A continuous process in plants, when oxygen is taken in through holes in the leaves and carbon dioxide given off.*

ROOT-PRUNING: *Severing roots on a tree to reduce its vigour and to encourage the development of fruits.*

ROOTSTOCK: *The part of a plant on which varieties are budded or grafted.*

RUBBLE DRAINS: *Land drains formed of trenches partly filled with clean rubble. They are dug in a herringbone-fashion and drained into a ditch or sump.*

SCREE BED: *A well-drained area, usually positioned at the base of a rock-garden, where alpine and other rock garden plants can be grown, including miniature conifers and small bulbs.*

SEED LEAF/LEAVES: *The first leaf (or leaves) developed by a germinating seed.*

SEED-TRAY: *Known in North America as a flat. Flat-based tray in which seeds are sown and seedlings pricked off.*

SEMI-HARDWOOD CUTTING: *A cutting that is more mature than a softwood type, but less than a hardwood form. Such cuttings are usually taken during the latter part of summer.*

SEMI-EVERGREEN: *A shrub or tree that may wholly or partly lose some of its leaves during winter, depending on its severity. For example, in most areas the Common Privet retains its leaves, but during cold winters may lose some or all or its foliage.*

SHADING: *Reducing the amount of light entering a greenhouse to prevent the temperature rising and to stop plants being burned by strong sunlight.*

SHRUB: *A woody plant with several stems arising directly from ground-level.*

SINGLE DIGGING: *When land is dug to the depth of a spade's blade.*

SINK GARDENS: *A way to grow alpine plants, miniature conifers and small bulbs in confined areas. Shallow stone sinks are best, but glazed types can be used.*

SOFTWOOD CUTTING: *A cutting formed from a non-woody shoot.*

SPECIES: *A group of related plants within the same genus.*

SPHAGNUM MOSS: *A type of moss, earlier and widely used to line wire-framed hanging-baskets to assist in the retention of moisture in compost. It also assists in the retention of compost in the basket. Nowadays, it has been almost totally replaced by the use of black plastic.*

SPIT: *The depth of a spade's blade. This ranges from 25cm/10in to 30cm/12in.*

SPORT: *The natural deviation of part of a plant from its normal state. The flower colour may change, or parts such as leaves and flowers be bigger or smaller.*

SPRING-FLOWERING BEDDING PLANTS: *These are usually biennials which are planted into borders and containers in late summer or early autumn for flowering in spring and early summer of the following year.*

SPUR: *A short, lateral branch which bears flowers and fruit buds.*

STANDARD: *A plant with a single stem between its roots and lowest branches. Many fruit trees and roses are grown in this way, as well as semi-hardy plants such as fuchsias.*

STONE SINKS: *Old sinks, usually shallow, frequently used to create miniature gardens for alpine plants, miniature conifers and small bulbs.*

STOOLING: *Cutting down deciduous shrubs and trees to just above soil-level to encourage the development of young shoots. Some willows and Dogwoods are regularly treated in this way to induce the yearly production of coloured stems.*

STOVE HOUSE: *An old term for a greenhouse that is kept at a high temperature.*

STRAIN: *Seed-raised plants from a common ancestor.*

SUBMERSIBLE PUMP: *A type of water pump designed to operate under water. It can be used to pump water to fountains and waterfalls.*

SUCCULENT: *A plant with thick, fleshy stems or leaves that enable it to survive dry conditions. All cacti are succulents, but not all succulents are cacti.*

SUCKER: *A shoot that arises from the rootstock of budded or grafted plants. Bush roses especially suffer from suckers growing from their roots, while standards, half-standards and weeping standards sometimes have suckers on their stems, but below the position where they were budded.*

SUMMER-FLOWERING BEDDING PLANTS: *Plants raised mainly from seeds sown in gentle warmth in late winter or early spring, slowly acclimatized to outdoor conditions and planted into borders and containers when all risk of frost has passed in late spring or early summer. In late summer or autumn they are dug up and discarded.*

SURFACE PUMP: *A type of water pump designed to operate in a dry chamber above the water's surface. It is more powerful than a submersible type and used where a large volume of water needs to be moved, or where water has to be pumped to a great height.*

TERRACOTTA (ALSO TERRA-COTTA): *A hardy, brownish-red material formed of clay, fine sand and, occasionally, pulverized pottery waste. This is used to make containers – usually unglazed – for plants.*

THINNING: *The process of removing surplus seedlings so that the remaining ones have more space in which to develop.*

THREE–QUARTER SPAN: *A greenhouse in which the glass area on one side of the ridge bar is greater than on the other.*

TILTH: *A layer of fine, surface soil into which seeds can be sown. It is created by digging soil in winter and later by hoeing and raking. A tilth also helps to reduce the loss of water from the ground.*

TOPDRESSING: *The removal of soil from the surface of plants in large pots or other containers and replacing it with fresh potting compost. Plants are topdressed when they are too large to be repotted into fresh compost in a larger pot.*

TRANSPIRATION: *The continual loss of moisture through small holes (stomata) in the surface of leaves. This helps to keep plants cool, as well as transporting minerals and water from the roots to the leaves.*

TREE: *A woody-stemmed plant with a clear stem (trunk) between the roots and the lowest branches.*

TRUNK: *The main stem of a tree.*

TRUSS: *A term used to describe clusters of flowers (on roses) or fruits (tomatoes).*

TUBER: *Either a fleshy underground stem (potato) or a fleshy root (dahlia). Both are storage organs and enable a plant to perpetuate itself from one season to another.*

UNDERPLANTING: *Planting bulbs or small, low-growing plants under trees and shrubs to provide additional colour.*

VARIETY: *A naturally occurring variation within a species. The term is commonly used to include both true varieties and variations which have occurred through the endeavours of Man and now correctly termed cultivars.*

VERMICULITE: *A moisture-retentive material often added to compost in hanging baskets.*

WATER-TABLE: *The level of water in ground. This rises and falls throughout the year, according to the weather and season. The height of water in the soil can be determined by digging a hole about 75cm/2½ft square and 1m/3½ft deep. If the water level regularly remains within 30cm/12in of the top, drains are needed.*

WATERSHOOTS: *Thin, willowy shoots which grow on the trunks of trees, often from where stems and branches were earlier removed.*

WEEPING HOLES: *Holes left in the lower parts of retaining walls to enable water to escape from the soil. If these are omitted, the pressure of water eventually pushes over the wall.*

WHIP-AND-TONGUE GRAFTING: *A method of propagating fruit trees, mainly apples.*

WILD GARDEN: *An area where plants – including trees, shrubs, herbaceous perennials and bulbs – are grown in a controlled, semi-wild condition.*

WILDLIFE POND: *An informal pond, usually positioned towards the far end of a garden, which encourages the presence of wildlife such as frogs, birds, insects and small mammals.*

WIND ROCK: *The buffeting of a plant by wind, thereby loosening its roots in the soil. It can be prevented by staking a plant securely and refirming soil over roots during the first few seasons after being planted.*

WOUND PAINT: *A special paint, usually combined with a fungicide, used to coat pruning cuts to encourage healing and to prevent the entry of diseases.*

INDEX

The Concise Gardening Encyclopedia

Designed and created by

THE BRIDGEWATER BOOK COMPANY LTD

Art Director: Peter Bridgewater

Designer: Terry Jeavons

Editor: Margot Richardson

Illustrated by Vana Haggerty FLS

CLB 4136

This edition published in 1996 by Leopard, a division of
Random House UK Ltd, Random House
20 Vauxhall Bridge Road, London SW1V 2SA

Copyright © 1995 CLB International, Godalming, Surrey

ISBN 1 85170 563 5

Printed and bound in Singapore